# CASE STUDIES ON HUMAN RIGHTS AND FUNDAMENTAL FREEDOMS

# CASE STUDIES ON HUMAN RIGHTS AND FUNDAMENTAL FREEDOMS

## *A World Survey*

VOLUME FIVE

WILLEM A. VEENHOVEN

*editor-in-chief*

WINIFRED CRUM EWING

*assistant to the editor-in-chief*

CLEMENS AMELUNXEN, JAN PRINS
KURT GLASER, NIC RHOODIE
STEFAN POSSONY, JIRO SUZUKI
L. P. VIDYARTHI

*associate editors*

PUBLISHED FOR THE FOUNDATION FOR THE STUDY OF PLURAL SOCIETIES

BY

MARTINUS NIJHOFF / THE HAGUE
1976

ISBN 90 247 1779 5
90 247 1957 7 (*vol. V*)



PRINTED IN THE NETHERLANDS

# Table of Contents

# Discrimination and Conflict in Northern Ireland

DAVID E. SCHMITT

David E. Schmitt is an Associate Professor in the Department of Political Science, Northeastern University, Boston, Massachusetts. He obtained his B.A. from Miami University in 1961 and his Ph.D. from the University of Texas in 1971. His teaching experience covers many aspects of Public Administration and Comparative Politics, including Latin American Politics, Politics of the Developing Nations and Politics of the United Kingdom.

He has been invited by a number of scholarly associations to deliver papers at conferences, particularly relating to Northern Ireland and South America, and some of these papers have been published as monographs or as a chapter in a book compiled by the conference sponsors.

David Schmitt's other publications include articles and books: *The Irony of Irish Democracy: The Impact of Political Culture on Administrative and Democratic Political Development in Ireland*, Boston: D. C. Heath, 1973; *Dynamics of the Third World: Political and Social Change* (editor- and co-author), Cambridge, Mass.: Winthrop, 1974; *Public Bureaucracy Values and Perspectives* (with James A. Medeiros, Duxbury Press, forthcoming); and a major study: *Violence in Northern Ireland: Ethnic Conflict and Radicalization in an International Setting*, Morristown, N.J.: General Learning Press, 1974.

# Discrimination and Conflict in Northern Ireland

DAVID E. SCHMITT

The Catholic and Protestant communities of Northern Ireland have evolved through a long and conflict-ridden history. Catholics trace their heritage to the Gaelic society that developed throughout Ireland following the invasion of the island by the Celts in the fourth century B.C. Gaelic culture was distinctive and rich in language, music, law, and social customs. Politically decentralized, Gaelic Ireland proved remarkably resistant to domination by outside powers. Scandinavian invasions and military adventures from 800 to 1014 A.D. failed to destroy Irish (Gaelic) society, though certain facets of the Scandinavian culture were assimilated. Of far greater significance to contemporary conditions in Northern Ireland was the Anglo-Norman invasion that began in the twelfth century when a deposed Irish king sought assistance from Anglo-Normans across the Irish Sea.

The Anglo-Norman conquest failed to achieve full control of Ireland, and efforts by the English to subdue the Irish were to continue up to the twentieth century. Efforts to plant loyal English settlers in southern Ireland failed. In fact, the colonizing people from Britain were typically assimilated into the Irish culture. Efforts to conquer Ireland reached a climax in 1603, when the Irish earls of Ulster, the northern province of Ireland, were defeated in battle by English forces. At this point Ulster was one of the most backward areas of Ireland. It had no system of towns, and its people followed a traditional Gaelic and pastoral existence.

Following the departure of the Irish leaders from Ulster, the English government initiated a policy of plantation. Lands reputedly belonging to the former Irish rulers were confiscated and made available to settlers from Scotland and England. Though partly of economic motivation, a principal goal of the plantation was the creation of a politically loyal population. Unlike the earlier settlements in southern

Ireland, the plantation of Ulster succeeded in establishing a sizeable population that retained many of its British roots. Moreover, in the eastern Ulster counties of Antrim and Down, which were not a part of the plantation, a large influx of predominantly Scottish settlers occurred in which land was taken from the native Irish by fair means and foul.

The colonization of Ulster by settlers from England and Scotland was a complex process that produced a sizeable alien population in the North. By the end of the seventeenth century, Ulster had become an area of two principal cultures. One was Gaelic in origin, Irish in language, and followed a clannish mode of existence thought to be barbaric by the colonizers. According to one Gaelic custom, for example, a father's son could be reared in another family's house – a practice that strengthened social and political bonds. Because the Reformation had failed to convert the Irish masses, it also happened that the natives were of the Catholic faith.

The remainder of the population was Protestant. Of course the Scottish and English had important differences from one another, and membership in different Protestant sects constituted a significant source of potential conflict among the settlers. But a common fear of retaliation or domination by the native Irish population eventually produced a culture overwhelmingly united in its opposition to the Catholics of Ulster. The plantation and settlement of Ulster by Scottish and English Protestants had failed to produce a politically loyal population because large numbers of the native Irish remained. Moreover, the indigenous population, relegated to positions as menial labourers or tenants on poorer lands bitterly resented the seizure of their lands.

The seventeenth century helped establish a tradition of violence between the Catholics and Protestants of Ulster. In 1641, for example, a rising by the native Irish, joined by some of the older Catholic English in Ireland, produced the Catholic Army and a military campaign in which many Ulster settlers were killed. The English Civil War spilled over into Ireland, and Oliver Cromwell's armies mercilessly avenged the Protestant deaths and losses of 1641. The advent of King James II in England, a Catholic, resulted in further insecurities for Protestants. Fleeing from England, James II proceeded to Ireland, where he hoped to establish a base for regaining power in England. In attempting to gain control of Ulster, the forces of King James further solidified Protestant communal identity. The defeat of James by the armies of William of Orange, a Protestant, at the Battle of the Boyne in 1690 produced a decisive victory that resulted in virtually complete control by Protestants. The warfare of the seventeenth century together with the agrarian violence and abortive rebellions in the following two centuries served to heighten the intensity of hostility and fear between Ulster Catholics and Protestants.[1]

## I. Early Discrimination against the Catholics

In addition to having their lands seized and being relegated to the more lowly labouring tasks, the Catholic population of Ulster (and Ireland) was subjected to a variety of repressive measures. It should be noted that penal legislation against Catholics had been even more repressive in England than in Ireland. However, in Ireland Catholics constituted a majority of the population. Moreoever, by the 1690's the Irish Parliament, a Protestant-dominated body under the jurisdiction of the English government, began the imposition of the infamous Penal Code.

The conflicts of the seventeenth century had destroyed the Catholic aristocracy and the bulk of desirable lands had been transferred to Protestant owners. The Penal Laws further condemned most Catholics to the lower social ranks. With few exceptions Catholics could not educate their children in continental Europe, operate public schools, or bear arms. They were restricted in the inheritance and purchase of land, and they could not own horses valued at more than five pounds. They were also severely restricted in the practice of law, and could not join the army. Of an especially pernicious character were the statutes attacking the Roman Catholic Church. The Catholic bishops, for example, were banished, with those few remaining living in personal danger. Although the Mass was allowed, it could be conducted legally only by priests who took an oath of allegiance. The effort, however, was not to destroy Catholicism but to secure the country to Protestant economic and political control. In general the laws against the practice of the Catholic faith were neither complete nor totally enforced. Far from being destroyed, Catholicism contined to maintain a strong hold on the majority of Ireland's inhabitants.[2]

Ulster dissenters, e.g. the Presbyterians of Scottish origin in Ulster, also received discriminatory treatment, though of a far less serious nature. For example, they could practice the trades and the professions and could purchase and inherit land, but their ministers were not granted legal recognition and were for a period excluded from official positions in government. Yet revolutionary activities never successfully united Catholics and Protestant dissenters. Economic competition, cultural bias, and historical hatreds proved to be an unbridgeable gap between the two groups.

## II. The Struggle for Irish Independence

Agrarian hostilities between the Catholic and Protestant masses of Northern Ireland in the eighteenth century were sparked partly by competition for land. Generally more destitute and desperate than their Protestant neighbours the Irish Catholic population could be induced to pay higher rents. Indeed, Protestant tenants were sometimes expelled by Protestant landlords seeking higher rents. As Belfast industrialized during the nineteenth century the fear of competition for jobs also contributed to Protestant fears.[3]

Abortive insurrections of 1798, which began as a movement potentially linking Protestants dissenters and Catholics against the Anglican establishment, concluded with the populations more divided than ever into Protestant and Catholic communities. Stories of atrocities by one group against the other coupled with institutional developments made hope for the emergence of an integrated society more bleak than ever. The Protestant Orange Order, for example, had emerged after a skirmish between Catholics and Protestants in 1795, in which as many as forty Catholics may have been killed. This organization is dedicated to preserving Protestant supremacy. Even after the Union of 1801, when the English government established a United Kingdom of Britain and Ireland, sectarian skirmishes continued.

The Catholic Emancipation of 1829 spawned by the political activities of Catholic leaders led eventually to the removal of various discriminatory restrictions. Politically, Ireland by 1884 acquired a degree of adult suffrage comparable to that of England. Moreover, local government reforms replaced unrepresentative and often corrupt local government bodies with more representative elected bodies. Even the repressive land system of tenant farming underwent substantial reforms. The 1903 Land Act, for example, provided opportunity for farmers to purchase their lands.

Yet even with representation in the British parliament, Ireland in practice continued to be governed largely as a colonial dependency by

British officials in Ireland. Moreover, ineffective British policies to relieve the mass starvation and death of the Great Famine in the 1840's coupled with evictions of farmers helped encourage the re-emergence of vociferous nationalist sentiment, identified for the most part with Catholic leaders. Peaceful demands for a Home Rule parliament and the Agrarian violence of the Fenian Movement in the 1860's reflected essentially Catholic Irish dissatisfaction with British political control and the economic power of the Protestant Ascendency in Ireland.[4]

The Protestants of Ulster, however, had little sympathy for Irish nationalism. Ulster was more economically advanced than the rest of Ireland. The processes of nineteenth-century industrialization also made northern industrial leaders identify with British industrial needs and oppose a local parliament for Ireland. For the Protestant masses of Ulster the old fear of domination by Catholics welded them solidly against Home Rule. Catholics would have outnumbered heavily the Protestants in an all-Ireland parliament. Their privileged economic position as well as political and cultural security would have been threatened.

Home Rule bills, which would have granted only limited powers to an Irish parliament while maintaining Ireland as part of the United Kingdom, sparked rioting between Catholic and Protestant mobs in the Falls Road area of Belfast in 1886 and 1893. After defeat of the first Home Rule Bill, Catholics set their chimneys on fire causing black smoke to spew into the sky. In celebration, Protestants of the Shankill Road area of Belfast lit tar-barrel fires. Scores were injured and sometimes killed as a result of riots and police efforts to quell the disturbances.[5]

In 1912 another Home Rule bill produced demonstrations by Ulster Protestants and motivated approximately 500,000 of them to promise to employ "... all means which may be found necessary to defeat the present conspiracy to set up a Home Rule parliament in Ireland...." A Protestant paramilitary organization called the Ulster Volunteers was so determined to remain under direct British rule that it was even prepared to fight British troops to maintain the status quo.[6]

Although a Home Rule Bill finally passed in 1914, its implementation was delayed by the outbreak of the First World War. The Irish nationalist movement, comprised and led predominantly by Catholics, became increasingly frustrated and militant. It also acquired a distinct cultural emphasis that stressed Gaelic heritage. Demanding complete independence, Irish nationalists initiated an abortive rising in Dublin in 1916. Captured leaders were executed by British authorities and quickly became heroes to the Catholic masses, who at first had been apathetic and critical of the rising. Later efforts by the British to conscript Irish men for service in the First World War alienated not only Catholic popular sentiment but even the usually conservative Catholic Church hierarchy. Eventually the Anglo-Irish War of 1919–1921 produced a British decision to extricate themselves.

Ulster's Protestant leaders, who at first had resisted suggestions that Ireland be partitioned, conceded three of Ulster's nine counties in order that Protestants would comprise a secure majority in the new Northern Irish political system. In 1920 the Government of Ireland Act of the United Kingdom Parliament carved out six counties of Ulster, to be given its own local parliament while remaining a part of the United Kingdom. A treaty between nationalist leaders and the British government was signed in 1921 and provided for an independent Irish nation with Commonwealth status for the remainder of the island.[7]

As the above account indicates, Ireland's history is extremely important in understanding the problems of discrimination in Northern Ireland. Animosities between Catholics and Protestants have roots centuries old. Grievances were partly economic: Catholics had been dispossessed of their land and under the penal laws had suffered numerous penalties such as exclusion from the professions. Later during the nineteenth century, discrimination against Catholics in Northern Ireland's growing industries was perpetrated informally by Protestant owners. Through both legal and informal channels, then, Catholics had little chance for economic equality.

Politically, Catholics were excluded from participation until the repeal of the Penal restrictions in the nineteenth century, and only in the latter nineteenth and early twentieth centuries did Catholic representation help contribute to meaningful political and economic reform. Political expression by both Catholics and Protestants found frequent release through violence. The warfare of the seventeenth century as well as recurring agrarian unrest, mob violence in Belfast, and the Anglo-Irish war all left a legacy of bitterness and hatred that would make future understanding and tolerance virtually impossible.

Cultural differences contributed to Protestant hostility toward Catholics. The Celtic language, patterns of social interaction, religion, and cultural norms distinguished Catholics from Protestants and provided an additional rationale for Protestant distrust and animosity.

Their Celtic heritage gave Catholics social mores and norms as well as language patterns that limited their capacity to manipulate the symbols of an essentially Protestant and British economic and social order. Even without formal mechanisms of discrimination, the Catholics of Ulster probably would have had difficulty in a society dominated by a culture that to them was essentially alien.

Finally, unlike the rest of Ireland, the historical development of Ulster resulted in a large Protestant population comprised not only of the wealthy, but of working and lower-farming classes as well. Discrimination against Northern Ireland's Catholic population was virtually assured when northern Protestants were protected through a partitioning of the island that gave them a majority of numbers and nearly complete control of internal affairs.

## III. Discrimination under the Stormont Government

Constitutionally, the state of Northern Ireland was a creation of the United Kingdom Parliament. Such matters as foreign affairs, defence, major taxation (income, sales, corporate, etc.) remained under control of the United Kingdom. Yet the Northern Ireland government had nearly a free hand in the internal administration of Ulster.[8] The British Government of Ireland Act provided for a local parliament at Stormont, on the outskirts of Belfast, fashioned after the Westminster parliamentary model. Power resided in the House of Commons, with the upper chamber having little influence. The prime minister and his cabinet were members of Parliament. A system of party responsibility meant that they ordinarily could be assured that their measures would be supported by the majority of house members. There was no autonomous supreme court with power to review acts passed by Stormont. Additionally, Stormont had ultimate control of local government bodies. In sum, the Northern Ireland system of government concentrated great power in the hands of the Stormont leadership.

Comprising approximately two-thirds of the population of Northern Ireland, Protestants were in a position to dominate the political system – provided they voted together as a community. The border between Northern and Southern Ireland provided the major basis of that cohesion. When the political system of Northern Ireland was created in 1920 most of Ulster's Catholics identified with the nationalist cause and favoured an all-Ireland nation independent from Britain. Protestants, of course, favoured the link with the United Kingdom with many viewing themselves as British. Moreover, the treaty between nationalist and British leaders providing for the partitioning of Ireland did not mean that all southern nationalists had permanently abandoned Northern Ireland. Northern Protestants, therefore, were faced with a neighbouring political system many of whose inhabitants and leaders harboured aspirations of reunification. Even worse from the northern Protestant viewpoint was the existence in their midst of a sizeable minority of Catholics who were also in favour of a united Ireland. Thus, Northern Ireland's Protestants voted overwhelmingly for parties favouring retention of the border. In practice, the Unionist Party commanded the support of most Protestants and had as its primary goal the preservation of Northern Ireland and the connection with the United Kingdom.

Despite the fact that institutional arrangements and communal voting patterns gave Protestants control of the political system, their power was further consolidated by various discriminatory practices. For local elections voting restrictions and manipulation of electoral district boundaries significantly weakened Catholic political influence. To illustrate, more than sixty percent of the population of Derry in 1961 was Catholic, yet Protestants controlled sixty percent of the seats on the local council.[9] Voting restrictions such as the exclusion of subtenants, servants, lodgers and adult children living with parents, penalized Catholic voters more than generally wealthier Protestants. Electoral abuses for Stormont elections were less serious but generated some resentment as in the refusal to maintain a system of proportional representation and in the drawing of electoral boundaries.

The lower courts in Northern Ireland came under Stormont's jurisdiction, while the Supreme Court was in practice manned by Unionists or Unionist sympathizers. The Royal Ulster Constabulary handled regular police duties. Comprised mostly of Protestants, the force was regarded by many Catholics as an unfriendly arm of an alien government. Particularly hated was the Special Constabulary (B-Specials) comprised entirely of Protestants, which performed support functions such as guarding installations and manning road checkpoints. Training at the Orange Order lodges, this reserve force often displayed blatantly anti-Catholic sentiments.

The Civil Authorities (Special Powers) Act provided that persons guilty or suspected of crimes against the state could be interned without trial and without being formally charged. Police could enter dwellings without search warrants and forcibly gain access if they deemed it necessary. The Act was employed primarily against those suspected of ties with the Irish Republican Army, a secret nationalist organization dedicated to unification of Northern and Southern Ireland and willing to employ force.[10] In effect, the Special Powers Act meant that the police, at their option, could suspend basic democratic safeguards in their dealings with the minority.[11]

Among the most important aspects of the Northern Ireland government were its informal links with the Protestant community. The Orange Order, committed to maintaining Protestant supremacy, was a primary instrument of political control as well as ethnic solidarity among Protestants. Nomination for political office by a local Unionist Party organization required that the candidate be a member of the Orange Order. Stormont MP's, including the Prime Minister and Cabinet members, belonged to the organization. Both formal and informal linkages between the government and the Orange Order reinforced Protestant political dominance. Though some of these relationships may have been covert, Unionist politicians made no secret of their ties to the Orange Order. Lord Craigavon, the first Prime Minister, said in 1934: "... I am an Orangeman first and a politician and member of this parliament afterwards. ..."[12] More openly still, he maintained that theirs was "a Protestant Parliament and a Protestant state."[13]

Economically, the Catholic minority was greatly disadvantaged. Protestants were typically given preference in government jobs, a fact of great importance in a society with chronic problems of unemployment. During the 1920's the unemployed numbered over twenty percent and reached over thirty percent during the depression. After the Second World War, Northern Ireland maintained the highest rate of unemployment of the principal United Kingdom regions. Most local government jobs were controlled by Unionist councils and were regularly awarded to Protestants. Catholics were given preference by Catholic-controlled local governments, but these were in a small minority. The system of favouritism worked heavily to the disadvantage of Catholics. In the predominantly Catholic city of Londonderry, Catholics held only thirty percent of clerical, technical and administrative jobs.[14] Discrimination in the assignment of public housing also constituted a serious problem, especially since unemployment rates were significantly higher among Catholics. The 1968 Civil Rights demonstrations were in fact sparked by the assignment of a house to an unmarried Protestant secretary, when a large Catholic family had been unable to obtain a decent place to live.

High level political and professional jobs in the Northern Ireland government bureaucracy rarely went to Catholics. Though not excluded by law on the basis of religion, discriminatory hiring and promotion practices helped produce the same results. To be sure, some Catholics undoubtedly refused to seek employment in a system they regarded as hostile to their community. Also, because of the historic discrimination against the minority, Catholics were not educationally in a competitive position in seeking higher paying government or private jobs. In any event, with comparatively few jobs available in the private sector, voluntary refusal to accept government jobs does not adequately explain the small percentage of Catholics. Especially since many middle-class Catholics favoured retaining the link with Britain, it is obvious that favouritism toward Protestants contributed to their predominance in the public service.

There is also some merit to the argument that economic discrimination against Catholics had a geographical component. Areas west of the Bann River, including the city of Londonderry, are predominantly Catholic, while Protestants are concentrated in the eastern part of Ulster, including the city of Belfast. Not surprisingly the Northern Ireland government focused on eastern regions in its economic development plans. Though the Unionist government claimed that it made economic sense to develop the more industrialized areas because of easier communications and more facilities, they undoubtedly preferred to stimulate the development of their own Protestant areas rather than those of Catholics.

In the private economic sector, discrimination against Catholics was also rampant. Ulster businesses typically employ people of the same religion, but Catholics suffered more because Protestants control most of the locally owned commercial and industrial wealth. Though job applicants sometimes have been asked their religion outright, more subtle techniques usually have been employed. Catholics usually attend schools operated by the Catholic Church, so required information on educational background usually discloses the applicant's religion. A person's home address may also be a useful guide since many working-class areas are exclusively Catholic or Protestant. Additionally, Protestant workers have sometimes helped exclude

Catholics from jobs. A Catholic employee might experience various forms of harassment including physical violence.

In summation, control of the political system and a primary voice in the economic sector gave Protestants the opportunity to discriminate in both government as well as private business. One of Northern Ireland's largest employers, the Harland and Wolff shipyards in Belfast, employed only about five percent Catholics. Organizations such as the Ulster Protestant League were created with the main goal of reserving jobs for Protestants. The Northern Protestant mentality toward the employment of Catholics is dramatically illustrated by a comment made by the Minister for Agriculture in the 1930's: "... I recommend those people who are loyalists not to employ Roman Catholics, ninety-nine percent of whom are disloyal. ..."[15]

Discrimination also occurred in the area of symbolic and cultural matters. Catholics tend to hold a less puritanical notion of Sundays than do Protestants. Yet they were sometimes subjected to Protestant morality through Unionist political control. Belfast playgrounds, for example, were closed on Sundays because of the religious views of local government leaders. Catholics were also required to take oaths of allegiance for government jobs, even those of a completely manual character. Similarly, Catholics were prevented from displaying the flag of Ireland.

Discrimination against Catholics in the political, economic, and social areas undoubtedly contributed to their unwillingness to identify with the Northern Ireland political system. Whatever chance there may have been for eliciting greater support from the Catholic community was seriously weakened by the failure of Protestant leaders to attempt legitimizing the political system to all of Northern Ireland's inhabitants. No component of successful government is so important as the development and maintenance of popular support. Of course, the Protestant community, frightened by the thought of unification and hostile because of centuries of conflict, would have replaced excessively liberal leaders through the electoral process. Yet some conciliatory gestures might have been made by leaders concerned not only with justice but also with the long-term survival of Northern Ireland. The United Kingdom government bears a particular responsibility for discrimination under Stormont. At the least, British leaders could have attempted to prevent the more blatant forms of official discrimination perpetrated or sanctioned by Unionist politicians.

## IV. Continuing Cultural Separation under Stormont

Many facets of culture are common to both Catholics and Protestants of Northern Ireland. Both communities speak the English language, both follow essentially British forms of etiquette, and both hold many customs in common such as meal patterns and the celebration of common holidays such as Christmas and Easter. Yet given the history of Ulster, the remaining differences and even some of the similarities provide an important basis for continuing prejudice and alienation. Some nationalists, for example, blame the British and their Irish Protestant sympathizers for the destruction of the Irish language.

In the Northern Ireland context, many of the remaining differences are significant. Protestants tend to resent Catholic social clubs and organizations that seek to encourage Celtic music as well as the Irish language. There are also subtle differences in dress, pronunciation, and possibly demeanour that distinguish the two groups from one another. Some people in Northern Ireland even claim that they can identify Protestants and Catholics by physical or racial characteristics. There may indeed sometimes be minor differentiation such as a tendency toward certain facial shapes. But the physical similarities are so great and the overlapping of physical traits between the two groups so common that differences are neither a source of group self-identity nor a reliable guide to the identity of others.

The social life of Catholics and Protestants tends to separate the two groups. Catholics often prefer Irish sports such as hurling and Gaelic football, while Protestants identify more with sports popular in Britain such as rugby. Of course, association football and other sports common to both communities have sometimes sparked clashes between players and spectators when teams of the two communities have met. Social functions such as dances also have been sponsored by groups distinct to each community. Both Protestant and Catholic churches or other organizations such as Orange lodges hold various social events.

Largely following the wishes of the Catholic Church hierarchy, there exists a system of education in which most Protestant children attend public schools, while Catholic children typically attend those controlled by the Catholic Church. Among the differences fostered by separate education are different perceptions of history. Protestants, for instance, tend to learn history from a British viewpoint. Catholic schools, on the other hand, tend to emphasize Irish history. Nor has there been much intermarriage in Northern Ireland. Mixed couples in working-class areas have frequently suffered much harassment and abuse.

With few successful integrating mechanisms to provide opportunity for the gradual erosion of hostile stereotypes, each side has a rather distorted view of the other. Attitudes of Protestants toward Catholics seem to be particularly uncharitable. They tend to see Catholics as poorer and disadvantaged not because of discrimination but because they regard Catholics as lazy and irresponsible. One hears frequent reference to Catholics in Northern Ireland as dirty and undisciplined. While attitudes among Northern Ireland's middle classes of both religions are more moderate, one still finds prejudice. A spokesman for the Unionist party once explained to the writer that apparent conditions of poverty in Catholic ghettos resulted from the untidy nature of Catholics. Graffiti in working-class Protestant neighbourhoods includes signs such as "Kick the Pope" and "Remember 1690," when the Protestant King William of Orange defeated James II at the Battle of the Boyne.

While Catholics seem a bit more charitable in their view of individual Protestants, they nevertheless are inclined to view them as aloof and cold, with an excessively materialistic view of life. Some also view Protestants as holding weaker moral standards. In Catholic working-class neighbourhoods one finds such graffiti as "Up the IRA" and "Long Live the Republic." The symbolism of both sides thus emphasizes national identity.[16]

Since 1920, the overriding issue for Protestants has been the maintenance of the border and the threat of being subsumed in a Catholic nation where they would be outnumbered more than three to one. To Protestants the Catholic minority has constituted a genuine threat since many supported the idea of a united Ireland. Those Catholics were seen as disloyal since they favoured the destruction of the political system of Northern Ireland.[17]

An important secondary issue for Protestants has been privilege. Particularly given the depressed Northern Ireland economy, Protestants had a great concern for reserving jobs for themselves. Their economic livelihood as well as opportunities for upward mobility were increased by discriminating against one-third of the population. For wealthy Protestants communal conflict provided the convenient result that Northern Ireland's working classes remained divided. However immoral, undemocratic, and unfair may have been the treatment of Catholics, Protestant fears of a united Ireland as well as their concern for economic supremacy had an element of plausibility – a fact which helps explain the intensity of their resistance to change and the ferocity with which some were willing to repress the struggle for civil rights in the 1960's.

Yet Protestant fears were only partly based upon fact. Most Protestants know little about the government of the Republic of Ireland, yet many assume it to be a priest-dominated society in which the population is instructed how to vote by local parish priests, who may be under directives from the Catholic bishops of Ireland or even the Pope in Rome.

In reality, the influence of the Church hierarchy in Southern Ireland on government is substantially less than the Protestant stereotype portrays it to be. It has on occasion successfully opposed legislation such as a mother and child health care bill, yet on most government business it has neither the resources nor interest to attempt to run a theocratic state.[18] More important has been the impact of a quite conservative Catholic political culture that makes politicians sensitive to the anticipated reactions of citizens as well as church officials. Censorship of literary materials as well as the regulation of family and sexual matters have followed Catholic morality. The sale of contraceptive devices, for example, were banned and only recently have efforts been made to liberalize their sale. Similarly, divorce is prohibited by the Constitution of the Republic. Until 1972 the Constitution posited a "special position" for the Catholic faith while guaranteeing religious freedom for all others. Perhaps most provocative from the northern Protestant point of view was the constitutional provision claiming that the national territory included the entire island.[19]

Finally, cultural hostilities have been reinforced by continuing violence. From the Protestant perspective, several small and abortive campaigns by the IRA against Northern Ireland military and economic targets reinforced their fears of unification and their distrust of Catholics. It should be added that most northern Catholics did not support these violent efforts against the political system. From 1920–22 over five hundred people were killed in sectarian riots and fighting between nationalist Catholics and government forces. In sectarian violence in 1935 twelve people died and many had their homes destroyed. Catholics suffered the highest losses in both instances. Considering that the major symbols of each group are often different and in opposition – e.g., Irish nationalism versus a fierce rejection of reunification – it is remarkable that there were not more serious assaults by the minority on the repressive political and social system of Northern Ireland. Partly this can be explained by economic motivation. Salaries and social welfare benefits, for instance, have been until quite recently significantly higher in the United Kingdom than in Southern Ireland.

Also, the degree of repression and discrimination should not be overstated. Equating the Stormont government with a fascist "totalitarian" regime is an exaggeration and misses an important component of discrimination. There was substantial, though imperfect, freedom of the press and freedom of expression. Militant and violent organizations such as the IRA were not allowed, but northern Catholics could criticize the government and read material of their choice. The Nationalist Party, supported by most Catholics, could contest elections and its members hold office. Catholics could also maintain separate schools and were free to practice their religion. Furthermore, Northern Ireland remained a part of the democratic nation of the United Kingdom and elected twelve representatives to its parliament. Of course, this provided little protection to the minority, and the United Kingdom government maintained a hands-off policy with respect to Northern Ireland. Nevertheless, it seems obvious that the United Kingdom government would not have tolerated certain actions such as Hitler-style genocide.

The significance of not exaggerating the degree of repression under the Stormont regime is that it allows consideration of the crucial nature of majoritarian democratic structures in providing a *de facto* disenfranchising of the minority. Given the absence of pluralistic voting coalitions or autonomous regions in Northern Ireland, as well as the absence of competing government structures such as a powerful upper house or an independent supreme court, democratic processes helped guarantee permanent control of the political system to Protestants. They also served to deceive those in the majority as well as outsiders such as the British authorities, who wanted to believe that the system was essentially democratic.

Discrimination for decades further solidified and expanded Protestant control of Northern Ireland. Yet in the long run it stimulated a civil rights movement and ignited a conflict that led to the destruction of the Stormont government and Protestant control of the political system.

## V. The Struggle for Equality

In the 1960's moderate middle-class Catholics, supported by some liberal Protestants, began to challenge the injustices of discrimination in Northern Ireland. In 1964 a physician and his wife established the Campaign for Social Justice, an organization that investigated and published findings concerning cases of discrimination against Catholics. The founding of the Northern Ireland Civil Rights Association in 1967 marked a further step in the quest for equality for Catholics. The movement constituted no immediate threat to Protestant fears of a united Ireland. Though there appears to have been some limited infiltration by a few IRA activists, the civil rights movement was lead primarily by people who sought reforms within the context of the Northern Ireland state.[20] It sought the eradication of discrimination in housing and employment, the termination of the Special Powers Act and the B-Specials, and an end to unfair electoral practices and regulations.

Furthermore, the activities of the civil rights movement were non-violent. One of its main goals was to prod the British government into requiring the Stormont government to reform. Unfortunately the British government had for so long detached itself from the internal affairs of Northern Ireland that it had little understanding of the subtleties of Northern Ireland politics. Having conveniently ignored the injustices for decades, it also had little inclination at this point to become involved.

The civil rights struggle, however, began to provoke increasing violence by the police and by Protestant activists. As early as 1966, for example, the Reverend Ian Paisley organized a march of rabidly anti-Catholic supporters through a Catholic section of Belfast and touched off a riot. A peaceful civil rights demonstration in 1968, held despite a government ban, resulted in police attacking the civil rights group, which numbered about two thousand. An ensuing riot produced injuries to eighty-eight demonstrators and policemen. This march reflected a trend toward disobedient but non-violent protest, in answer to government inaction and police over-reaction.

A frequent response of both the Northern Ireland police and Protestant opposition groups was hostility, repression and, sometimes, brutality. In January 1969 Protestant extremists, apparently including off-duty members of the B-Specials, viciously attacked students and other activists with iron bars, stones and other weapons. Government police did little to protect the marchers. In fact, venting their hostility toward the civil rights movement and believing there to be republican or IRA involvement in disturbances, police raided the Catholic Bogside community of Londonderry.

An investigating commission found that "... a number of policemen were guilty of misconduct which involved assault and battery, malicious damage to property ... and the use of provocative sectarian and political slogans."[21] A typical account was related by a department store employee: "The doors burst open, and about twenty policemen came in. They just started batoning all the customers. They took runs at people and smashed the glass of the counters. They struck a boy to the ground, and kept on hitting everyone unmercifully with their batons. I saw them beat a man who was carrying his groceries."[22]

The Northern Ireland Prime Minister, Terence O'Neill, had made superficial attempts to reassure the Catholic community and to be outwardly conciliatory. On television he called upon all citizens to work together toward a better Northern Ireland and argued that greater equality of treatment would reduce the threat of republicanism (the quest for a united Ireland) by the minority. He had even met in 1965 with the Prime Minister of the Republic of Ireland, which to most Unionists was heresy. Yet nothing O'Neill did significantly altered the structure of power in Northern Ireland nor provided economic or social equality for Catholics. Even so, he came under increasing attack by Protestant leaders for capitulating to the demands of people they believed to be republican and IRA supporters.

In response to mounting conflict, however, the British government began to place increasing pressure on Stormont to reform. Under British influence Unionist leaders did manage to force certain reforms on the Unionist politicians of Stormont. Some reforms, such as proposals for a commissioner to investigate citizen complaints concerning the Stormont bureaucracy and later a commissioner for complaints involving local authorities, produced little reduction in discrimination. In individual cases discrimination can sometimes be easily masked in part because administrators can usually find objective, though invalid, reasons for their actions. Such strategies, moreover, place emphasis after the fact and focus on individuals, not communities. Also, in the case of Northern Ireland, resistance among the Protestant community made certain reforms unworkable. For example, efforts to eradicate discrimination in housing through a points qualifying system ultimately broke down because of intimidation by para-military organizations.

There was also a statement of intent to reform local elections according to the "one man one vote" principle. This reform, however, could not be implemented immediately because not until 1973 were province-wide local elections to be held again. Similarly, the promise to abolish provisions of the Special Powers Act also was not implemented by the Northern Ireland government on the basis that the level of violence prevented such action. The B-Specials, however, were disbanded. Moreover, a Development Commission replaced the Unionist-controlled local government in Londonderry and gave fairer representation to Catholics. But overall control of the province remained in the Unionist hands.[23]

The promise of reform may have had a negative impact on the conflict. On the one hand Catholics were promised meaningful reforms and equal opportunity, yet the system as a whole remained discriminatory and Protestant dominated, producing disillusionment. On the other hand, Protestants viewed the promise of reform as a capitulation to republican forces that were trying to destroy the political system and to bring about a forced unification of the political system. They were therefore unwilling to support moderate leaders.[24]

Levels of violence increased dramatically during 1969. The Protestant parades of July 12, 1969 sparked riots in Londonderry and elsewhere. Interestingly, the Unionist government still permitted a parade by the Apprentice Boys, a Protestant organization, in Londonderry on August 12, 1969. While some Unionist politicians opposed it, the government permitted the parade with the argument that the police could not stop it. Whatever the merits of the decision, it illustrates one of the central characteristics of the emerging conflict – a transfer of power from government leaders to the increasingly radicalized masses and to politicians less willing to compromise.

The August 12th parade provoked Catholics of Bogside to throw rocks and bottles as the marchers passed them. Barricades were erected when the police tried to enter the Catholic community. With the use of gasoline bombs, Catholics forced the police to retreat and proclaimed the establishment of "Free Derry." In the town of Armagh, the B-Specials, enlisted to maintain control, fired on demonstrators after a civil rights meeting. British troops entered Derry on August 14, 1969 in an attempt to restore order, demonstrating the Stormont government's inability to cope adequately with the crisis.

The escalation of the conflict continued in Belfast where an ominous new element emerged – direct confrontation and violence between Protestant and Catholic mobs of adjacent communities. Catholics are greatly outnumbered in Belfast, and the working classes tend to live in enclaves surrounded by Protestants. Rioting erupted on August 14, 1969. Rows of Catholic houses were burned down by Protestant mobs. Police, possibly under the belief that they were under fire, shot indiscriminantly with machine guns at a block of Catholic housing and killed a boy of nine. British troops were also sent into Belfast, where they were at first welcomed by outnumbered Catholics as a means of protection against Protestant mobs. During the August turbulence some of the RUC police activity seems to have been aimed genuinely at the restoration of order and the protection of citizens. Yet documented instances of excessive use of force, as in the machine gunning of Catholic flats, were evident. Where employed during 1969, the B-Specials seldom showed restraint. As the Scarman Commission suggested, moreover, the Catholics and civil rights activists saw the police as always facing or charging the minority population and never Protestants.[25]

Increasingly the Catholic community came to view the police as oppressors. Up to this point the IRA was not a large or popularly backed organization among the minority. Yet its size and activities mushroomed. From 1969 to 1970 its role was essentially defensive, and it had probably even tried to quell violence on several occasions believing the Catholic population to be greatly outnumbered and incapable of self-defence. But confrontation between security forces and the Catholic community gradually turned it into an offensive force dedicated to the goal of driving the British out of Ireland and the achievement of unification between North and South. Efforts to develop the IRA in Northern Ireland included support from the Republic. The 1970 arms trial in Dublin, for example, involved a cabinet member of the southern government. Though he was acquitted, it seems apparent that several key officials in the Republic did in fact support the Provisionals.[26] By early 1973 the Provisional IRA had become a large, relatively well-equipped force that was responsible for the major part of over 3,00 bomb explosions and over two hundred fatalities among the army and police.[27]

The development of the Provisionals and the smaller, less militant Official Branch of the IRA was not primarily the result of a conspiracy perpetrated by a handful of Southern politicians or proponents of violence in the North. Rather, the IRA's growth was a response to the violence levied against the Catholic working-class areas by the security forces, including the British army. The organization could not have survived had not the Catholic community sympathized with it and been so hostile to the security forces.

Discriminatory treatment by the British government and its army forces in Northern Ireland against Catholics was not by design. British politicians generally hold liberal-democratic values and had no desire to alienate large sectors of the population. Nevertheless, through ignorance, through excessive deference to Unionist politicians, and through unenlightened policy decisions, Britain's treatment of the Catholic community was often repressive and typically counter-productive. The use of CS gas against demonstrators in Catholic areas affected more than just rioters. Though non-poisonous, CS gas was an indiscriminate weapon that could drift into windows and sometimes harm children and the ill. A curfew was imposed on a Catholic section of Belfast in July 1970 following a riot provoked by British army searches for weapons. As with the CS gas, the innocent suffered along with the activists. Catholics noted that such strict enforcement measures were seldom employed on Protestant demonstrators, and they increasingly viewed the British forces as consistently backing the Stormont regime at the expense of the minority.

A principal difficulty with British policy in Northern Ireland was their dependence upon Stormont politicians for advice. Further, the British government correctly perceived that Unionist leaders were under great pressure from the Protestant masses not to grant major concessions and to crack down hard on Catholic demonstrators and, of course, the IRA. British leaders also feared a confrontation with Protestant para-military organizations which could present an important military threat and place the army militarily between two communities. In the 1960's, for example, the Ulster Volunteer Force had emerged as a secret organization of Protestant extremists willing to employ bombings and murder to achieve its goals. Other Protestant para-military organizations acquired an increasing legitimacy among the Protestant community of Northern Ireland, who viewed them as a means of insuring their survival against republicanism.

Additionally, British soldiers, who had little interest in the affairs of Northern Ireland, began to view Catholics with hostility as they came under attack from the IRA. They became increasing rough and abusive in their handling of the minority population. As one British officer explained to the writer in 1973: "We don't kick pregnant women in the stomach, but we don't try to be kind or gentle. Our men are being killed." But the principal impact of force employed by the United Kingdom was to stimulate greater violence from the IRA and engender greater hostility from the Catholic community.

Perhaps the greatest single British miscalculation of the entire conflict was internment. In August 1971, on recommendation of the Unionist leaders, the army swooped into Catholic communities in an attempt to capture members and leaders of the IRA. They sometimes mistakenly arrested completely innocent men and terrorized the men, women and children. The Special Powers Act provided the legal basis for detaining men in internment camps without formal charges and without trial. Prisoners were grossly mishandled and sometimes subjected to modern forms of torture. Some were hooded, subjected to loud noises, and denied sleep. Though the British government denied that this was torture, they eventually promised to cease such practices.[28] Numerous accounts of prisoner beatings and other government violence throughout the conflict suggest the intensity of feeling by the security forces.[29] Though some Protestants were to be interned, the Catholic population, including the middle classes, perceived internment to be an assault upon the entire Catholic community. In recognition of the great alienation this practice caused, the British belatedly terminated internment in 1975.

In addition to employing force, the British also continued to require reforms designed to eliminate grievances of the Catholic community. Not only did British leaders demand reforms because of pressure from the Catholics of Northern Ireland, they also had to confront increasing external pressure. At a time when Britain was attempting to enter the Common Market the conflict was an embarrassment. United States Congressmen and Senators with Irish constituents also protested. The Republic of Ireland took the matter of discrimination and ill-treatment of Northern Ireland Citizens to the European Commission on Human Rights, which agreed to look into certain aspects of the situation.[30] After admission into the Common Market, the United Kingdom government had as a fellow member the Southern government which thus had further leverage. Perhaps the greatest source of external pressure upon the British, however, was their dependence upon the Republic of Ireland to assist in law enforcement. Without the help of the Republic, the IRA would have a completely safe haven in Southern Ireland.

## VI. Direct Rule and the Quest for a Solution

After British paratroopers fired on a crowd of civil rights demonstrators in 1972 killing thirteen people, it became apparent to English politicians, who had listened to Unionist demands for firm law enforcement measures, that the Stormont system of government could not possibly provide the basis of satisfactory accord between the two communities. Reaction among Catholics to this "Bloody Sunday" was particularly hostile. None of the victims was proven guilty of firing on the paratroopers and most were clearly innocent.[31] In March 1972 Stormont was suspended.

The suspension of Stormont was followed by direct rule. A British cabinet member and a few assistants replaced the Unionist cabinet and prime minister and took direct control of the Stormont bureaucracy. The objective of British officials was the achievement of a stable settlement and the extrication of the British government and military from direct involvement in Northern Ireland affairs. Throughout the crisis they genuinely hoped to encourage Catholic support as a means of achieving stability. They had little love for the Northern Irish of either community. Even the Conservative party of the United Kingdom, which had been allied with the Unionist party in the United Kingdom Parliament, had little desire to continue to prop up a Protestant regime illegitimate in the eyes of the minority. Northern Ireland, with a population of only about one and one half million, had less than three percent of the United Kingdom's population. It had no crucial political or strategic importance in the atomic age. It certainly did not constitute a source of colonial wealth. Northern Ireland's poorer economic base as well as payments resulting from the violence meant that the British had to provide significant amounts of financial aid amounting to hundreds of millions of pounds in recent years.

British strategy after direct rule included continued application of force against para-military organizations and groups employing violence. Aware that such measures resulted in lost support, the security forces from their perspective attempted to employ it in minimum levels. For example, they used rubber bullets in riot control. These bullets, however, sometimes blinded or maimed innocent bystanders. By 1973 they also began to use stronger measures against Protestant extremists including those who had begun to use random assassination. Units of the IRA began responding to this form of sectarian terror by similar killings. Increasingly bombs were exploded in Britain. The Provisional leadership seemed to have decreasing control over their organization's activities. The number of casualties continued to mount, and by the end of 1975 over thirteen hundred people had died from the violence.

Another major strategy toward resolving the conflict has been economic development. The British correctly perceived unemployment and lack of economic viability to be one of the sources of trouble in Ulster. With fewer jobs available, Protestant demands for economic discrimination and militancy against Catholics were more plausible. Similarly, the unemployed had a smaller stake in maintaining stability and less to lose in employing violence. Greater unemployment among Catholics also provided further evidence to Catholics of the discriminatory nature of the system. Pockets of unemployment in Catholic ghettos were often severe. For instance, one author reported the results of a survey conducted in 1972 showing the unemployment rate to be thirty-eight percent in the Turf Lodge section of Belfast.[32] Hence, one of the British government's strategies has been a campaign, thus far only marginally successful, to develop the Ulster economy.

Through a variety of programmes and laws, British leaders have also continued to seek reforms aimed at fair housing, equal employment opportunities, more equitable criminal justice, and elections held under fairer electoral arrangements. However, control of the political system had passed in large measure to extremist and para-military organizations, which had the support of large numbers of the populace. Catholics continued to be driven from their homes by intimidation as Northern Ireland became increasingly ghettoized into warring communities. Efforts to terminate discrimination in jobs thus far have had little impact where Catholic workers were driven off by the threat and sometimes the actuality of violence that sometimes included murder.[33]

The principal effort of the British government, however, has been the development of political institutions that would involve meaningful participation by both communities. In a white paper the government stated that "... the Executive itself can no longer be solely based on any single party, if that party draws its support and its elected representation virtually entirely from only one section of a divided community."[34]

The electorate was polled in March 1973 on the question of whether or not it favoured retaining the border between North and South. Designed to reassure Protestants, the great majority of the electorate naturally voted in the affirmative. The United Kingdom government has acknowledged repeatedly that it would not support re-unification unless the majority of voters in the North desired it. Catholics boycotted the poll in large numbers.

The British government then published a white paper that provided for the development of the plural executive (cabinet). Elections to a new assembly were to be held on the basis of proportional representation and thus help prevent dominance by any single party. Certain powers such as law enforcement were to be retained by the British Secretary of State, with the idea that the evolution of fair political structures and procedures could enable the return of authority in such matters to Northern Ireland. The British acknowledged an Irish dimension in providing for the possible establishment of a Council of Ireland by the new Northern Ireland government and government of the Republic.

In June 1973 elections for the new assembly returned a majority of assembly members committed to considering the idea of power-sharing arrangements. The Unionist party platform had even included a provision that up to half of strengthened parliamentary committees were to be chaired by opposition party members. The Social Democratic and Labour party (a more militant but non-violent replacement of the Nationalist party) won most of the Catholic votes.[35]

Although Loyalist members (those opposed to power sharing) refused to take part in efforts to form an executive, agreement by the majority of Assembly representatives on a power-sharing executive was reached in November, 1973. There followed the Sunningdale Conference in December, at which representatives of the Assembly (excluding loyalists) as well as the United Kingdom and Republic of Ireland governments took part. Among the outcomes of this conference was the announcement that the Council of Ireland would be comprised of equal representation from the two political divisions of Ireland. This council was intended to deal with problems of mutual concern, though its exact details were not yet worked out. It was not presented at the Sunningdale Conference as having major political powers or as being a prelude to unification. The Irish government promised to respect the wishes of the majority in Northern Ireland. The United Kingdom government also pledged to support the majority, even if it favoured unification.[36]

On December 31, 1973 the new Executive was appointed to office. The Sunningdale Conference, however, had generated intense debate in Northern Ireland. In particular, loyalist leaders backed by Protestant masses rejected the Council of Ireland as a subversive threat to the Northern Ireland political system. Their fears were reinforced by indiscreet exaggerations by some SDLP and Southern leaders. An increasingly radicalized Protestant population displayed its lack of support for the Protestant Assembly leaders in the February 28, 1974 general elections of the United Kingdom. Loyalist candidates won eleven of the twelve Northern Ireland seats, polling over fifty percent of the vote. Following some parliamentary manœuvering in the Assembly and a general strike organized by the Ulster Workers' Council, Unionist members of the Executive resigned. On May 29, 1974 the United Kingdom government terminated the Executive and the Assembly.

The next British attempt to develop a viable Northern Ireland political system offered greater opportunity for Northern Ireland leaders themselves to develop institutional arrangements. Elections were held in May 1975 for the purpose of choosing delegates to a constitutional convention, where delegates were "... to consider what provisions for the government of Northern Ireland would be likely to command the most widespread acceptance throughout the community there.[37] The election produced a landslide victory for loyalist party candidates of the United Ulster Unionist Coalition, who captured forty-seven of the seventy-eight convention seats with approximately five-sixths of the Protestant vote. The more moderate Faulkner Unionists won only five seats, while the SDLP won seventeen. The Alliance and Northern Ireland Labour parties between them took nine seats. As might have been expected given its composition, the Convention failed to produce power-sharing arrangements acceptable to the United Kingdom government. With direct rule still in force, there is at present no permanent resolution of the conflict in sight.

## VII. Conclusion

Discrimination against Catholics under the Stormont government had significantly increased Protestant domination of the political and economic systems of Northern Ireland. Yet in the long run, discrimination produced a civil rights movement that led to the destruction of the Stormont parliamentary system and terminated many of the formal discriminatory structures and procedures. The B-Specials, for example, were abolished, and voting requirements were modified according to the one-man-one-vote guideline. Despite efforts by the United Kingdom government, however, viable power-sharing political structures have not yet been devised, nor has the informal discrimination in such areas as employment and housing been eliminated. Especially through its law enforcement strategies, the British have in fact contributed to the unequal treatment of Northern Ireland's Catholics.

The violence perpetrated by both government and non-government forces after 1968 left the Protestant and Catholic communities of Northern Ireland more divided than ever. Protestants have turned to loyalist politicians and para-military groups, while many Catholic working-class areas have provided support to the Irish Republican Army. Mixed housing areas in working-class communities are rare, and the violence has made both Catholics and Protestants turn increasingly to churches and non-integrated organizations for entertainment and social activities. In the present climate of fear, resentment, and hostility the likelihood of an integrated, democratic society emerging in the near future is problematic at best.

Nationalist sentiment looks toward a British withdrawal and the unification of Ireland as a solution. The chances of unification occurring, however, must be regarded as nil for many years to come. Any serious effort to unite Ireland would motivate the well-armed Protestant community to unrestrained resistance. It might be noted that members of Protestant para-military organizations almost certainly outnumber the 13,000-man army of the Republic of Ireland. The occasional related suggestion by nationalists that the Protestants of Northern Ireland be driven off the island seems even more unrealistic.

The development of power-sharing political institutions within the present confines of Northern Ireland also presents quite formidable difficulties given the polarization of the Catholic and Protestant communities. While this strategy may seemingly present the most logical means to an integrated or at least democratic and non-discriminatory society, power-sharing institutions might very well break down even if they could be established initially. Dealing with law enforcement and security would be a particularly difficult problem. It is argued by some in Northern Ireland that independence from Britain would enable the leaders of the two communities to reach agreement. But the potential for violence and political breakdown would be enormous even if such an accord could be reached. Of course, many

Protestants consider independence to be desirable because it would give them the opportunity to re-establish Protestant control.

In the event of a full-scale civil war in Northern Ireland sparked by a British withdrawal or other causes, a likely outcome would be the repartitioning of Ireland as Catholics in Belfast and the northeast sections of Ulster fled to predominantly Catholic areas. In Catholic sections, e.g., West of the Bann River, Catholics would undoubtedly gain control, perhaps with the support of the army of the Republic of Ireland. Repartition might also occur through planning and with the agreement of interested parties. Such problems as relocation would make this solution difficult to achieve, but it would have the advantage of permanently separating most members of the two hostile communities and removing the threat of sectarian discrimination for most inhabitants of the island.[38]

Finally, the struggle for a solution under the direction of the United Kingdom government could continue indefinitely, perhaps with intermittent violence gradually tapering off and with some of the worst aspects of discrimination gradually being overcome. Yet so long as violence continues and so long as government lacks the support of the people, achievement of an equitable, just, and democratic society will not be possible.

## Notes

1. For a useful discussion of this period see Edmund Curtis, *A History of Ireland*, 6th ed., Methuen & Co., London, 1950.
2. *Ibid.*, chapter xi.
3. See Liam de Paor, *Divided Ulster*, Middlesex, Penguin Books, England, 1970.
4. For a useful, brief history of this period consult Oliver MacDonagh, *Ireland*, Prentice-Hall, Englewood Cliffs, N.J., 1968.
5. Andrew Boyd, *Holy War in Belfast: A History of the Trouble in Northern Ireland*, Grove Press, New York, 1969, p. 127.
6. A. T. Q. Stewart, *The Ulster Crisis*, Faber and Faber, London, 1967.
7. For further information see F. S. L. Lyons, *Ireland Since the Famine*, Scribner, New York, 1971.
8. The term "Ulster" will henceforth refer to the six counties of the original province of Ulster that now comprise Northern Ireland.
9. Northern Ireland, *Disturbances in Northern Ireland*, Cmd. 532 Stationary Office, Belfast, 1969, p. 59.
10. The IRA, outlawed on both sides of the border, is a militantly nationalistic organization committed to the re-unification of Ireland. For a discussion of its development see J. B. Boyer Bell, *The Secret Army*, Blond, London, 1970.
11. After the imposition of direct rule, provisions of the Special Powers Act were modified by such measures as the Detention of Terrorists (Northern Ireland) Order, 1972. For a discussion of problems of law enforcement in dealing with

terrorism see United Kingdom, *Report of a Committee to Consider, in the Context of Civil Liberties and Human Rights, Measures to Deal with Terrorism in Northern Ireland*, London, Stationery Office, 1975.

12. Quoted in de Paor, *op. cit.*, p. 114.
13. Northern Ireland, House of Commons, *Parliamentary Debates*, Vol. 16, 1095.
14. *Disturbances in Northern Ireland, op. cit.*, p. 60.
15. Quoted in de Paor. *op. cit.*, p. 115.
16. For a further discussion of cultural differences consult Denis P. Barritt and Charles F. Carter, *The Northern Ireland Problem: A Study in Group Relations*, 2nd ed., Oxford University Press, London; 1972.
17. For data on attitudes regarding national identity as well as related issues see Richard Rose, *Governing Without Consensus: An Irish Perspective*, Beacon Press, Boston, 1971.
18. John H. Whyte, *Church and State in Modern Ireland, 1923–1970*, Gill and Macmillan, Dublin, 1971.
19. Further discussion is contained in David E. Schmitt, "Catholicism and Democratic Political Development in Ireland," *Eire-Ireland: A Journal of Irish Studies*, Vol. 9, Spring, 1974, 59–72.
20. Vincent E. Feeney, "The Civil Rights Movement in Northern Ireland," *Eire-Ireland: A Journal of Irish Studies*, Vol. 9, Summer, 1974, 30–40.
21. *Disturbances in Northern Ireland, op. cit.*, p. 73.
22. Bowes Egan and Vincent McCormack, *Burntollet*, L.R.S. Publishers, London, 1969, p. 58.
23. Northern Ireland, *A Record of Constructive Change*, Cmd. 558 Stationery Office, Belfast, 1972. See also Northern Ireland, *The Future Development of the Parliament and Government of Northern Ireland*, Cmd. 560, Stationery Office, Belfast, 1971.
24. Henry Kelly, *How Stormont Fell*, Gill and Macmillan, Dublin, 1972.
25. Northern Ireland, *Violence and Civil Disturbances in Ireland in 1969*, Cmd. 566, Stationery Office, Belfast, 1972, pp. 11, 15, and *passim*.
26. For a discussion see *Sunday Times* (London) Insight Team, *Northern Ireland: A Report on the Conflict*, Vintage, New York, 1972, chapter xi.
27. The Provisional's programme was outlined in Sinn Fein (Provisional), *Eire Nua: The Social and Economic Program of Sinn Fein*, Sinn Fein (Kevin Street), Dublin, 1971. The Provisional Sinn Fein party is the political wing of the Provisional IRA.
28. United Kingdom, *Report of the Enquiry into Allegations Against the Security Forces of Physical Brutality in Northern Ireland Arising Out of Events on the 9th of August, 1971*, Cmd. 4823, Stationery Office, London, 1971. See also United Kingdom, *Report of the Committee of Privy Councillors Appointed to Consider Authorized Procedures for the Interrogation of Persons Suspected of Terrorism*, Cmd. 4901, Stationery Office, London, 1972.
29. For example, see Fr. Denis Faul and Fr. Raymond Murphy, *British Army and Special Branch RUC Brutalities, December, 1971–February, 1972*, Abbey Printers, Cavan, Ireland, 1972.
30. The 1976 *Report of the European Commission on Human Rights* concerning this matter has not at this writing been made public, although copies have been presented to the British and Irish governments. According to government sources as well as journalistic accounts, the Report criticizes the British government for partially violating the Convention of Human Rights concerning its internment and interrogation of prisoners. Though most objectionable practices probably have been stopped, the inquiry may have contributed to more humane treatment of prisoners. See "The European Dimension," *Fortnight*, Northern Ireland, February 20, 1976, p. 4.

31. United Kingdom, *Report of the Tribunal Appointed to Inquire into The Events on Sunday, 30th January 1972, Which Led to Loss of Life in Connection With the Procession in Londonderry on that Day*, Stationery Office, London, 1972.
32. Niall Duff, "Community Self-Surveys," *Community Forum*, Vol. 3, 1973, pp. 19–21.
33. The well-intended Fair Employment Act of 1976, for example, may be rendered partially ineffective because of intimidation. Also, the provisions of the Act stress current and future employment practices; they do not emphasize quotas or other strong techniques for rectifying past patterns of discrimination (which might, of course, help incite violence by Protestants). Thus, The Fair Employment Act will not quickly alter previous injustices. Although it could produce symbolic support for the British, it might also breed alienation among disillusioned Catholics as well as resentment among Protestants. For discussion see David Lowry, "The Fair Employment Act," *Fortnight*, Northern Ireland, April 2, 1976, pp. 6–8.
34. United Kingdom, *Northern Ireland Constitutional Proposals*, Cmnd. 5259, Stationery Office, London, 1973, p. 13.
35. In the May, 1973 local council elections under the reformed electoral procedures, a similar pattern emerged. In the Assembly elections of June, the seventy-eight seats were filled as follows: Official Unionists 22, SDLP 19, Alliance and Northern Ireland Labour (both nonsectarian) 9, Loyalists (Protestants against power sharing) 17, and 11 for Unionists not committed to giving reforms a chance.
36. The Council of Ireland was to be comprised of a fourteen member Council of Ministers with the chair rotating between North and South. A Consultative Assembly was to be established on the basis of sixty members made up of thirty members each of the Irish parliaments. Among other important matters discussed at Sunningdale was the establishment of a joint Commission on Law Enforcement. Many Northern Ireland Protestants believe that the Republic of Ireland failed to keep its promises in providing enforcement against IRA activities.
37. United Kingdom, *The Northern Ireland Constitution*, Cmd. 5675, Stationery Office, London, 1974, p. 17.
38. For further discussion of the repartition option see my article "Ethnic Conflict in Northern Ireland: International Aspects of Conflict Management," in Milton Esman, ed., *Ethnic Conflict in the Western World*, Cornell University Press, Ithaca, N.Y., forthcoming.

# Human Rights in Northern Ireland

## WINIFRED CRUM EWING

Winifred Crum Ewing, a native of Great Britain, is a professional journalist, scriptwriter and novelist. She has travelled extensively, both before and after World War II, acquiring familiarity with political and social problems in many parts of the world. Elected to the governing body of the Association of Cinematograph and Television Technicians, she plays an active part in the Trade Union movement, specialising in industrial relations. For several years Mrs. Crum Ewing was the Administrator of the Women's Press Club of London, and she is the British member of the Board of the World Association of Women Journalists and Writers (AMMPE).

Mrs. Crum Ewing was for a number of years associated with the Conservative Central Office, first as organiser of the youth groups, and later as the party's film and television producer. After leaving the Conservative Central Office in 1959 she formed her own production company, Mandson Films Ltd., which specialises in documentary films. Among those she has written and directed are a television obituary of Winston Churchill and films on conservation and national defence.

# Human Rights in Northern Ireland

WINIFRED CRUM EWING

Some citizens in Northern Ireland have been deprived of some human rights as defined by the United Nations Universal Declaration of Human Rights and by the Council of Europe's Convention for the Protection of Human Rights and Fundamental Freedoms.

The questions to be answered are:

1. Which citizens?
2. What rights?
3. Why has this happened?

The simple answers which might be accepted as common knowledge are that the deprived citizens are Roman Catholic, particularly those who are poor; the discrimination they suffer mainly concerns political and legal rights, employment and housing; the reason is that a single Protestant Party has been in power for the fifty years that the six counties of Ulster have had a separate existence from the twenty-six counties under the control of the Dublin Government.

The real answers are not simple, but are deeply complex. Millions of words have been written by dedicated and honest people seeking to record the truth about Northern Ireland as they understand it after weeks, months, years of intensive research. Probably no subject has been more fully documented. To distil the essence from such wealth of evidence is a daunting task, yet such is the purpose of this paper.

As compared with other parts of the world where different groups are in conflict over human rights and discrimination, Ulster enjoys many advantages which should make solutions easier to find.

1. The area is very small, only 5,242 square miles.

2. The mother tongue of the 1,500,000 inhabitants is English. A few will also speak the Irish form of Gaelic.

3. Television, radio and newspapers are readily available, making simultaneous communication possible.

4. Roads give quick and easy access to all parts.

5. Ethnic differences are not apparent, even though some Irish would claim to be instantly aware of the ancestry of others as being English or Scottish rather than Irish. This must be insignificant when compared with tribal and racial differences in other continents.

6. The people are accustomed to living in a Parliamentary democracy.

There are, therefore, no extenuating circumstances to excuse failure, such as the difficulty in communicating in wild mountainous country, or in jungle or tropical forests, where many different languages are spoken. The failure is the failure of society as a whole, and as such, in all humility, it must be recognised. As Professor Richard Rose writes in the introduction to his book, *Governing Without Concensus*:[1]

> Because Northern Ireland politics differ so much from the Anglo-American ideal, it may provide better insights into the worldwide problems of authority than does a study of England, America or New Zealand. Most Afro-Asian regimes were founded, like Northern Ireland, in less than ideal circumstances. Their peoples often lack the internal unity, except that experience of Imperial rule has given them a common desire to seize authority for themselves, as Irish Nationalists and Ulster Unionists did half a century ago. The leaders of these regimes, like the men in Stormont Castle outside Belfast, rest uncertainly in authority today. These parallels do not mean that the experience of Northern Ireland can easily be transferred to the far corners of the earth. They do suggest that viewing the non-Western world through orange-and-green spectacles is, *prima facie*, at least as sensible as viewing it through lenses tinted red, white and blue. Moreover, until Western social scientists can encompass such hard cases as Northern Ireland in their theories of politics, only modest claims should be made on behalf of putative general theories.

## I. Flash Point 1968

It is an ancient Irish custom to stage marches to commemorate historical events, and to demonstrate loyalty to a chosen cause. In Ulster the Stormont Parliament ruled that, in the interest of public order, the route such marches propose to take must be approved by the authorities to avoid provoking counter-action by those with different loyalties.

The trouble in Londonderry on 5th October, 1968 was that the march organised by the Civil Rights movement proposed a route part of which was commonly used by "Protestant" and "Loyalist" marches. The Civil Rights movement did not regard itself as partisan, but accepted support from any group or individuals who subscribed to its purpose to establish civil rights without discrimination. Such objectivity was not accepted as genuine by many in Northern Ireland. Classic obstruction tactics to prevent the march from taking place were initiated by the Committee of the Apprentice Boys of Derry. (The purpose of this Committee is to ensure that the stand of the Apprentice Boys of Derry in 1690 in support of the protestant King, William of Orange against the deposed Catholic King, James II should not be forgotten.) The Committee gave notice to the authorities on the 1st October that they would hold their "Annual Initiation Ceremony" on 5th October, and would march on the same route at the same time as the Civil Rights supporters. Incidently, there was no evidence to support the *annual* nature of this ceremony.[2]

On 3rd October the Minister of Home Affairs, realising that if both processions took place violent trouble would be likely, exercised his right to ban both processions within the City walls and in the disputed ward outside. The Civil Rights organisers decided to defy the ban. The police were instructed to ensure that the ban was enforced. The violent tactics of the police caused uproar in Britain.

Those are the simple facts which brought to an end "peace" in Northern Ireland. From that day violence has escalated, with more than fourteen hundred dead, and fifteen thousand injured.[3]

The Stormont Prime Minister, Terence O'Neill, called on the Governor of Northern Ireland, Lord Grey of Naunton, to appoint three Commissioners under the Chairmanship of Lord Cameron, a distinguished Scottish judge,

> to hold an enquiry into and to report upon the course of events leading to, and the immediate causes and nature of the violence and civil disturbances in Northern Ireland on and since 5th October, 1968; and to assess the composition, conduct and aims of those bodies involved in the current agitation and in any incidents arising out of it.

The Commissioners were authorised to call any witnesses whom they wished to examine, and they were given access to all books, documents, registers and records.[4]

Their report was presented to the United Kingdom Parliament in September, 1969. The clarity with which they present their evidence and conclusions defines precisely the nature and extent of discrimination in Northern Ireland. Before going through this in detail, and with cross references to many other studies, it may help to sketch briefly the historical background.

## II. Historical Background

The peoples of Ireland have never been united under one ruler. It would seem that the island was first inhabited by people from Britain and Scandinavia around 6000 BC. The Celts arrived about 4,000 years later and developed about 150 small kingdoms, loosely linked by payment of tribute, but frequently quarrelling with each other. Small pockets of invaders added to the ethnic mix, particularly the seafaring Norsemen.

The system of "plantation," that is the gift of land to citizens likely to uphold the authority of those who possess the power of patronage, was customary even before the English in the Twelfth Century began using it as a method to check the use of Ireland to attack England. The Anglo-Norman invasion of Ireland in 1169 was the start of 800 years of English endeavour to maintain authority in Ireland.[5] It is interesting to note that Papal authority played an important part in initiating this campaign.

In the Sixteenth Century at the time of the Reformation, when Henry VIII asserted the English right to independence from Rome, he met the stiffest and most effective resistence in Ireland. Christianity had come to Ireland in the Fifth Century, and for the next thousand years Irish monks had played a great part in the missionary field for Rome. When the English King, therefore, tried to convert Irish Catholics into becoming loyal members of the Church of Ireland, subject to the English Crown, he linked in the minds of the Irish hatred of England with the love of the Roman Catholic faith.

Those who would destroy England have always regarded Ireland as a useful base, both because of its geography and because of the political passions available for exploitation. Queen Elizabeth I, challenged by her Catholic brother-in-law, Philip II of Spain, had to defend her realm against his ambitions. When her sister Mary had been Queen she and Philip II had used the plantation system extensively by giving their supporters land in mid-Ireland in the shires of Leix and Offaly. These shires were re-named King's County and Queen's County with royal fortresses at Philipstown and Maryborough.[6]

Queen Elizabeth decided that Ulster should be settled by men who could be trusted to convict rebels and traitors. So on through history, the enemies of Britain have used Ireland, thereby forcing the British to take some counteraction. The French in the Seventeenth, Eighteenth and Nineteenth Centuries were followed by the Germans in the Twentieth Century. Some Irish were openly working for a German victory in both World Wars, while thousands of others enlisted as volunteers in the British forces, and served with distinction in every rank.

In the Nineteenth and early part of the Twentieth Century Irish Home Rule was a burning political issue. Many Protestants regarded the issue as "Rome Rule," and as most of them lived in Ulster there was naturally passionate resistence to any device which would make them a threatened minority under an Irish Parliament based in Dublin. The Irish Home Rule Bill went through the United Kingdom Parliament in the summer of 1914, but because of the outbreak of war it was not implemented. The Easter Rebellion of 1916, coming at a time when the fortunes of war seemed to be favouring the Germans and their allies, powerfully strengthened the fears of all the Irish who wished to remain part of Britain. The divide was not really between Protestant and Catholic but between pro-British and anti-British. Very few Protestants could be found on the anti-British side, but certainly there were many Catholics on the pro-British side. The troubles and violence which followed the end of the war were finally resolved by setting up two Irish Parliaments, one in Dublin covering the twenty-six counties, known as "the South," even though it included the most northerly county of Donegal, and one in Belfast, covering six of the nine counties which had comprised Ulster. It was a compromise designed to meet the minority rights of Irish Protestants, and as such it was not accepted by the Irish majority who were Catholic.

When the Irish, or any other people for that matter, do not accept a political decision they may take the option of refusing to participate. "Boycott" is a word given to the English language by the Irish, being the name of a man who was so disagreeable that no one would have anything to do with him. So it was when the Government of Ireland Act, 1920, came into force a number of Irish decided to operate a boycott. The main provisions of the Act were:

1. It provided for the establishment in Belfast of a bicameral Parliament, consisting of a 52 member House of Commons elected by Proportional Representation, and a Senate of 26 members, 24 elected members by the members of the Northern Ireland House of Commons and two (the Lord Mayor of Belfast and the Mayor of Londonderry) sitting *ex officio*.

2. This Parliament was given a general power to make laws for

"peace, order and good government" of Northern Ireland, subject to certain specific reservations, conditions and safeguards. In particular:

(a) The Act specifically reserved to the Parliament of the United Kingdom certain powers principally relating to the Armed Forces, the Crown and international matters.

(b) The fiscal powers of the Northern Ireland Parliament were severely restricted by the reservation to the Parliament of the United Kingdom of power to levy income tax and customs and excise duty.

(c) The Northern Ireland Parliament was specifically prohibited from making laws, and the Northern Ireland Governments from taking administrative action other than on a basis of religious equality.

(d) Section 75 of the Act provided that: "the supreme authority of the Parliament of the United Kingdom shall remain unaffected and undiminished over all persons, matters and things in Northern Ireland and every part thereof."

3. The Governor of Northern Ireland, in whom the executive powers of the Northern Ireland Parliament were vested, was "aided and advised" by the executive committee of the Privy Council, or the Cabinet consisting of the Ministers of Northern Ireland.

4. Northern Ireland was to be represented in the Parliament of the United Kingdom by 12 members for territorial constituencies, and one for the Queens University of Belfast.

5. Northern Ireland was to make towards "Imperial liabilities and expenditure" a 'just' contribution having regard to the taxable capacities of Northern Ireland and the United Kingdom as a whole.[7]

In the belief that the Border would not last it appeared right to the Catholics in Ulster to do nothing at all to help the new regime to get going. They did not volunteer for the civil service or the police. They did not participate in local government, except to a very minor degree. The logical result of this inaction was Protestant domination of these services. After forty years when two new generations had grown up the disadvantages of non-participation began to be recognised. This historical fact had considerable bearing on the Civil Rights movement in the 1960s. There was both Catholic and Protestant support for reform, but, as always, the enemies of Britain in the form of international Marxists saw their opportunity to exploit a situation for their own ends. Their appearance on the scene inflamed the worst fears of many Ulster Unionists, so that necessary reforms to prohibit discrimination became equated in their minds with the extreme Left desire to end the "capitalist system," and prepare the ground for a Communist take-over.

In search of the truth Lord Cameron and his two fellow Commissioners set to work to unravel the complex story, without fear or favour.

## III. Discrimination in Political Rights

The Cameron Commission of Enquiry decided that with the exception of one meeting in Belfast they would hold their sessions in private, as being the best way to elucidate the truth. This, they believed, gave greater freedom to witnesses to speak with complete sincerity, and avoided the risk of the Enquiry being used as a platform for propaganda purposes. Although the Commission had the right to invite any individual or body to give evidence, they had no power to compel or to examine under oath. For the greater protection of witnesses the Attorney General gave the assurance that no statement, whether given orally or in writing, would be used as a basis of a prosecution. Through public advertisement individuals and organisations were invited to submit evidence, either orally or in writing. There was a wide response, and nearly every individual specially invited to do so co-operated with the Enquiry, with a few notable exceptions. These included Mr. William Craig, the Minister for Home Affairs who banned the marches on 5th October, the Rev. Dr. Ian Paisley, Chairman of the Ulster Constitution Defence Committee, which controlled the Ulster Protestant Volunteers (the UPV), and Major Bunting, the Commandant of the UPV.

The Cameron Report states:

It is plain from what we have heard, read and observed that the train of events and incidents which began in Londonderry on 5th October 1968 has had as its background, on the one hand a widespread sense of political and social grievance for long unadmitted and therefore unredressed by successive Governments of Northern Ireland, and on the other sentiments of fear and apprehension sincerely and tenaciously felt and believed, of risks to the integrity and indeed the continued existence of the state. These opposing sentiments had by that time built up tensions and pressures within the community of such a kind that incidents comparatively small in themselves could readily lead to explosions of violence of a dangerous and serious character. We have also no doubt whatever that the sentiments of grievance expressed in the representations and evidence placed before us were passionately and sincerely held, and supported by a formidable catalogue of supporting facts .... At the same time ... it very soon became plain to us that in such a situation as we have described, politically subversive and mischievous elements could and in the event did, for their own purposes deliberately inflame passions on all sides and either irresponsibly or deliberately invoke violent incidents to their own assumed advantage. And we were not without ample evidence and information which have led us to conclude that such elements were and are present and are ready to foment and exploit for their own ends genuine grievances or complaints.[8]

Confining themselves to the local authority areas in which major disturbances had taken place, the Commission investigated the charge of gerrymandering and manipulation of electoral boundaries to achieve and maintain Unionist control of local government. The following table indicates the extent of imbalance.[9]

| Local Authority Area | Population Census 1961 | | Council Representation as at 30.9.68 | |
|---|---|---|---|---|
| | Adult R.C. | Adult others | Non-Unionists | Unionists |
| Armagh U.D.C. | 3,139 | 2,798 | 8 | 12 |
| Dungannon U.D.C. | 1,845 | 2,041 | 7 | 14 |
| Dungannon R.D.C. | 7,329 | 7,476 | 6 | 13+3 co-opted |
| Fermanagh County Council | 15,884 | 15,222 | 17 | 33+2 co-opted |
| Londonderry Co. Borough | 18,432 | 11,340 | 8 | 12 |
| Newry U.D.C. | 5,843 | 1,364 | 12 | 6 |
| Omagh U.D.C. | 2,605 | 1,949 | 9 | 12 |

The breakdown of the figures for Londonderry County Borough illustrate the situation in 1968. When the Commission asked the Unionists to explain this imbalance.

They did not contest the general basis of the figures, but argued that the original arrangement of ward boundaries and local government had been based on rateable values as well as population, that population changes had upset arrangements which were originally fair.[10]

The assessment of the Commission was:

Accordingly it is our view that the arguments used to justify the existing arrangements when they were introduced, mainly rationalised a determination to achieve and maintain Unionist electoral control. The Government's dissolution of the Londonderry Corporation, and its replacement by a nominated Commission, was thus the most tangible victory of the Civil Rights Campaign.[11]

In considering political discrimination in Northern Ireland it is necessary to draw particular attention to the difference between elections for local and national government. The local government franchise (changed in 1969) was available only to occupiers of dwelling houses and their spouses. This excluded sub-tenants, lodgers, servants and children over the age of 21 living at home. This franchise arose from the principle that those who pay rates on their property elect those who administer the funds derived from rates, the local government services. At the time this system was introduced after the Government of Ireland Act 1920 local government impinged much less on the lives of ordinary families. With the growth of the welfare services and publicly owned housing the situation has changed extensively.

Commenting on the effect of the limited franchise in local Government the Commission says,

> Whilst this exclusion affected all sections of the population, it was felt to operate mainly against poorer elements and in particular against Catholics.[12]

The franchise to elect the Parliaments at Stormont and Westminster is based on universal suffrage. There is no discrimination. The result is that the electoral roll for local government is only about 75% of the roll for national government.

The results of Parliamentary elections are such that no fair minded observer could conclude that any group of Northern Ireland citizens is deprived of their human rights to express their political opinions, to endeavour to get others to agree with them, and to vote for the candidate of their choice. Take the UK 1970 election, among the 12 Members elected for Ulster were Dr. Ian Paisley, the extreme Protestant Unionist, Bernadette Devlin, the extreme Marxist revolutionary calling herself Independent Unity, Robert Chichester-Clark, moderate Unionist and brother of the reforming Prime Minister at Stormont, and Gerry Fitt, now the Leader of the Social Democratic Labour Party, himself a Catholic though the S.D.L.P. has a few Protestant members.

As a test of electorial fairness and the right of voters to be free effectively to exercise their own judgment, the constituency which

Gerry Fitt still represents, West Belfast, has an interesting record. The electorate is predominantly working class with some very strong Catholic wards.

In 1951 the seat was won by the Northern Ireland Labour Party with a slender majority of 25 over the Unionist Candidate. In 1955 the Unionist Candidate was Mrs. Patricia McLoughlin. She campaigned on Conservative policies, refusing to use sectarian arguments, and not permitting Dr. Ian Paisley to speak for her. The result was:

| | | |
|---|---|---|
| Patricia McLoughlin | Ulster Unionist | 34,191 |
| J. Beatie | Irish Labour Party (HQ Dublin) | 16,050 |
| E. Boyce | Sinn Fein | 8,447 |
| | Unionist majority | 18,141 |

Eamon Boyce, a labourer from Dublin, was not able to campaign personally as he was in prison, sentenced for 12 years for his part in the raid for arms on the military barracks in Omagh.

1959 result:

| | | |
|---|---|---|
| Patricia McLoughlin | Ulster Unionist | 28,899 |
| J. Brennan | Independent Labour | 20,898 |
| T. A. Heenan | Sinn Fein | 4,416 |
| | Unionist majority | 8,001 |

In 1964 Patricia McLoughlin was prevented from standing through illness. The Unionist Candidate was less firm in resisting a sectarian line. The result:

| | | |
|---|---|---|
| J. A. Kilfedder | Ulster Unionist | 21,337 |
| H. Diamond | Republican Labour | 14,678 |
| W. R. Boyd | N. Ireland Labour | 12,579 |
| L. McMillan | Republican | 3,256 |
| | Unionist majority | 6,659 |

1966 result:

| | | |
|---|---|---|
| Gerry Fitt | Republican Labour | 26,292 |
| J. A. Kilfedder | Unionist | 24,281 |
| | Republican Lab. | 2,011 |

1970 result:

| | | |
|---|---|---|
| Gerry Fitt | Republican Labour | 30,649 |
| B. Roberts | Unionist | 27,451 |
| | Republican Lab. | 3,198 |

1974 (February) result:

| | | |
|---|---|---|
| Gerry Fitt | Social Democratic Labour Party | 19,554 |
| J. McQuade | United Ulster Unionist Coalition | 17,374 |
| A. Price | Independent Republican | 5,662 |
| J. Brady | Republican Clubs | 3,088 |
| W. Boyd | N. Ireland Labour Party | 1,989 |
| | S.D.L.P. majority | 2,180 |

1974 (October) result:

| | | |
|---|---|---|
| Gerry Fitt | S.D.L.P. | 21,821 |
| J. McQuade | U.U.U.C. | 16,265 |
| Kitty O'Kane | Republican Clubs | 3,547 |
| S. M. Gibson | Volunteer Political Party | 2,690 |
| P. Kerens | Marxist Leninist | 203 |
| | S.D.L.P. majority | 5,556 |

Both the voting figures and the names of the Parties are revealing. Over the past 20 years the non-sectarion Unionist achieved the highest personal vote and the largest majority over her next opponent. The Republican who became a Social Democrat has held the seat longer than any other Member. "Republican" in any form signifies the wish to abolish the Border, overthrow the Constitution and sever the British connection. The S.D.L.P. would like a united Ireland, but only with the consent of the majority of Ulster citizens. They are fully aware that at present the vast majority of both Protestants and Catholics do not want to lose British nationality. The S.D.L.P. is firmly against force and violence. The Volunteer Political Party was formed after the strike in May 1974, called by the Ulster Workers Council in order to end the power sharing Executive. Although the Ulster Volunteer Force is regarded as extreme Unionist anti-Catholic and anti-reform, the Volunteer Political Party campaigned on a class, not a religious basis. They opposed both the Unionist and S.D.L.P. Candidates.

West Belfast provides the proof that there is real political freedom in Northern Ireland, at least that is the intention of the law and constitution. Nevertheless, there is sinister and serious political discrimination operating outside the law, and daily brought to the attention of the public through the media. There are those who say in effect, "Accept my politics, or risk death or mutilation for yourself or your family." Is this discriminatory force organised and co-ordinated, or is it merely generated by fear and the inevitability of "backlash"?

The Cameron Commission, seeking the truthful answers to these questions, examined very carefully the organisation, finances, constitution and declared aims of the Civil Rights Association and all the organisations involved in the disturbances. They concluded:

There was early infiltration of the Civil Rights Association both centrally and locally by subversive left wing and revolutionary elements which were prepared to use the Civil Rights movement to further their own purposes, and were ready to exploit grievances in order to provoke and foment, and did provoke and foment, disorder and violence in the guise of supporting a non-violent movement.

This infiltration was assisted by the declared insistence of the Civil Rights Association that it was non-sectarian and non-political, and its consequent refusal to reject support from whatever quarter it came provided that support was given and limited to the published aims of the Association.

What was originally a Belfast students' protest against police action in Londonderry on 5th October and support for the Civil Rights movement was transformed into the People's Democracy – itself an unnecessary adjunct to the already existing and operative Civil Rights Association. People's Democracy provided a means by which politically extreme and militant elements could and did invite and incite civil disorder, with the consequence of polarising and hardening opposition to Civil Rights claims.

On the other side the deliberate and organised interventions by followers of Major Bunting and the Rev. Dr. Paisley, especially in Armagh, Burntollet and Londonderry, substantially increased the risk of violent disorder on occasions when Civil Rights demonstrations or marches were to take place, were a material contributory cause of the outbreaks of violence which occurred after 5th October, and seriously hampered the police in their task of maintaining law and order, and protecting members of the public in the exercise of their undoubted legal rights and upon their lawful occasions.[13]

Following the Report of the Cameron Commission another independent Tribunal was set up under Mr. Justice Scarman to take the investigations a stage further. Commenting on serious disturbances on 14th August, 1969 the Northern Ireland Prime Minister, Mr. James Chichester-Clark had said, "There was a conspiracy of forces seeking to overthrow a Government democratically elected by a large majority." Answering this point the Scarman report stated,

In our judgement there was no plot to overthrow the Government or to mount an armed insurrection....

But although there was no conspiracy in the sense in which that term is normally used, yet it would be the height of naivity to deny that the teenage hooligans who almost invariably threw the first stones were manipulated and encouraged by persons seeking to discredit the Government. While accepting that the major riots that occurred in Londonderry, Belfast, Armagh and Dungannon were not deliberately planned, we are satisfied that, once the disturbances started, they were continued by an element that also found expression in bodies more or less loosely organised, such as the People's Democracy and various local Defence Associations, and in associating themselves with bodies such as the Northern Ireland Civil Rights Association, and several Action Committees. The public impact of the activities of this element was tremendously enhanced by the coverage given by the mass media of communication....

Neither the I.R.A. nor any Protestant organisation nor anybody else planned a campaign of riots. They were the communal disturbances arising from a complex political, social and economic situation. More often than not they arose from slight beginnings, but the communal tensions were such that, once begun, they could not be controlled. Young men threw a few stones at some policemen or at an Orange Procession; there followed a confrontation between police and stone throwers now backed by a sympathetic crowd. On one side people saw themselves, never the others, charged by a police force which they regarded as partisan. On the other side, police and people saw a violent challenge to the authority of the State. These attitudes were the creature of recent events. Their own interpretation of the events of 1968 and early 1969 had encouraged the belief among the minority that demonstrations did secure concessions, and that the police were their enemy, and the main obstacle to a continuing programme of demonstrations, while the same events had convinced a large number of Protestants that a determined attempt, already gaining a measure of success, was being made to undermine the constitutional position of Northern Ireland within the United Kingdom. In so tense a situation it needed very little to set going a major disturbance.[14]

Mr. William Whitelaw, Secretary of State for Northern Ireland, in presenting the Report to Parliament, said, "Mr. Justice Scarman and his colleagues had provided the definitive historical account of these tragic and traumatic events." To analyse tensions and attitudes accurately may be a major contribution towards relaxation and correction but responsibility for action to restore the rule of law under which human rights can be defended rests on the police, supported by the army, and the legal system.

## IV. Discrimination in Legal Rights

Professor Richard Rose draws attention to the difference between political rights and justifiable rights:

A basic paradox of democratic government is that political decisions presuppose rule by the majority, whereas judicial decisions presuppose the rule of law. In a representative assembly, the majority wins; the minority always loses. In the courts, by contrast, judges do not count heads but weigh arguments. The decisions of the courts, like those of representative assemblies, create losers as well as winners. The losers in court cases are not identified by their relative fewness, but by the weakness of their arguments and evidence.

The acceptance of two arenas of decision-making – one of which is governed by the doctrine of majority rule and the other by the rule of law – implies that citizens in a democracy have more than one kind of rights. A majority of elected representatives has the right to decide what the government of the day will do, according to agreed procedures. But everyone has certain rights, by virtue of their citizenschip, that cannot be denied by any government acting on behalf of a majority.[15]

The Civil Authority (Special Powers) Act, 1922 has been frequently condemned as a clear case of Government denying the rights of the citizen. It is beyond dispute that the "Special Powers" were in conflict with the European Convention on Human Rights and Fundamental Freedoms and also the United Nations Universal Declaration of Human Rights, in particular Article 10 (against arbitary arrest), Article 12 (the right to be presumed innocent until proven guilty), and Article 13 (against subjection to interference with personal privacy, home or correspondence).

The Act was passed in 1922 to cope with the emergency situation following the division of Ireland when the whole community suffered from the raging campaigns of mutual murder and reprisal, initiated by the Irish Republican Army and countered by equally determined groups of Unionists. To impose the rule of law the Royal Ulster Constabulary and the Ulster Special Constabulary (to become known as the 'B' Specials) were authorised to take action beyond what is permissable under British common law. The "Special Powers" Act would have been terminated long ago had Stormont deemed that the threat from the IRA to destroy the state no longer existed. At no time in fifty years did the IRA provided such evidence.

The 1956 example of the IRA campaign code named "Operation Harvest" is a reality which has to be taken into account. The Army Council of the IRA had declared that the campaign plans to disrupt the Ulster administration by cutting all forms of communication was the "decisive stage in the struggle against British rule in occupied Ireland." Mobile IRA columns demonstrated their power in numerous acts of destruction. "Operation Harvest" was contained and finally suppressed by 2,800 R.U.C., supplemented by 1,000 full time and 11,600 part time members of the 'B' Specials. There was no active participation of the Army.[16]

The number of the official and independent enquiries during the early 1970s into the operation of the Special Powers bears witness to the widespread concern. The published reports studied side by side, even though approached from different angles, produce remarkably corroborative evidence. Their differences are more of emphasis and definition than of substance. The subject matter of these reports can be divided to cover the action of the police and security forces and the operation of the legal system after arrest.

### A. *The Citizen and the Police*

The Cameron Commission summarised their findings:

The police handling of the demonstration in Londonderry on 5th October 1968 was in certain material respects ill co-ordinated and inept. There was use of unnecessary and ill controlled force in the dispersal of the demonstrators, only a minority of whom acted in a disorderly and violent manner. The wide publicity given by press, radio and television to particular episodes inflamed and exacerbated feelings of resentment against the police which had been already aroused by their enforcement of the ministerial ban.

Available police forces did not provide adequate protection to People's Democracy marchers at Burntollet Bridge and in or near Irish Street, Londonderry on 4th January. There were instances of police indiscipline and violence towards persons unassociated with rioting or disorder.... and these provoked serious hostility to the police, particularly among the Catholic population of Londonderry, and an increasing disbelief in their impartiality towards non-Unionists.[17]

The Scarman Tribunal had also to report about the attitude of the R.U.C. in certain incidents. The R.U.C. clearly felt that their duty was to protect Protestants from assault by Catholic demonstrators. While they were endeavouring to control a riot in one place, they failed to arrest Protestants who at the same time were assaulting Catholics and burning their homes. The R.U.C. was seriously under strength, working very long hours under great strain. It was far from true that on all occasions they turned a blind eye to Protestant law breakers, as this paragraph shows:

There was serious rioting by Protestants on the Shankill Road near Unity Flats in the early days of August. In the course of three riots the Protestant mobs made a determined attempt to invade Unity Flats, and also appeared in force in Crumlin Road. They were successfully resisted by the sustained efforts of the police, who incurred the anger of some sections of Protestant opinion by their baton charges up the Shankill Road. It is significant that during these Protestant riots of early August two senior policemen, the Commissioner and Deputy Commissioner for Belfast, concluded that the police were unable any longer to control serious disturbances in the City of Belfast. . . . The time had come to call the Army to aid the civil power.

Mr. Justice Scarman declared that their enquiry was "in a very real sense an investigation of police conduct." Their conclusion was:

Undoubtedly mistakes were made and certain individual officers acted wrongly on occasions. But the general case of a partisan force co-operating with Protestant mobs to attack Catholic people is devoid of substance and we reject it utterly.[18]

Whilst it is not denied that some Catholics did suffer discrimination against them at the hands of the police, to arrive at a true balance it is necessary to look closely at the whole complex picture. The painstaking official reports ring true, all the more so because impartial individuals have covered much the same ground with dedicated sincerity. Professor Richard Rose adds his comment:

At the most elemental level of equal protection of life, person and property, substantial departures from justice have existed for decades in Northern Ireland, yet few persons are ever tried or convicted for causing deaths in political disorder. The same is true of individuals causing bodily injury, whether demonstrators or policemen. It is even more true that individuals engaged in burning houses and intimidating inhabitants from their homes. From October 1968 until Easter 1970, Catholics were a disproportionate number of those killed, injured or intimidated from their homes. There is little solace for Protestants in noting that in the subsequent nine months there was a move towards greater equality, as more Protestants became the victim of attacks of organised and unorganised Republican and Catholic action groups in Belfast. . . .

Immediately after the British Army became established in Belfast, the situation changed abruptly. Catholics still were unequally protected, but in the autumn, 1969, they were the favoured group. The R.U.C. was 'expelled' from the Bogside of Londonderry and the Falls Road area of West Belfast. Barricades were established to keep police – especially police in armoured cars – from entering the areas. The British Army stood sentry near Catholic baracades. Their efforts were supplemented with vigilante groups, with armed Republicans available for defence in the last resort. The establishment of this 'No go' land for the police became the subject of a steady stream of complaints from Protestants who viewed it as an unpunished rebellion against the regime. Complaints increased when it became evident that arms were being stored in the 'No go' areas. In spring, 1970, the Army and the R.U.C. began to co-operate closely in covering the two areas. The Army-RUC arms raid and curfew in the Lower Falls in July, 1970, demonstrated that these Catholic areas were no longer provileged. Later in the month the Prime Minister announced that policemen would be returning to 'Free' Belfast and 'Free' Derry in increasing numbers till normality was restored. By September, 1970, the Falls Road Citizens' Defence Committee was complaining that the security forces were engaged in 'one-sided' search for arms in Catholic districts. It asked for an 'equality of searching' in Protestant and Catholic districts. It did not specify whether it wished the security forces to search an equal number of Protestant and Catholic homes, or search until they found an equal or proportionate amount of arms on each side. By February, 1971, some Catholics in Belfast felt the hand of Republican 'courts', established by IRA groups to mete out summary punishment in areas where civil authorities were not welcome. Sentences ranged from tarring and feathering to death.[19]

The Minority Rights Group is a specialised research and information unit registered in Britain as an educational trust. The first of its principle aims is "To seek to bring about an improvement in the position of persecuted or disadvantaged minorities, or majorities, by investigating their situation and publicising the facts widely in the international press and other media of mass communication." They commissioned a journalist, Harold Jackson, to write a comprehensive report on Ireland which they published in January 1971. Commenting on the burning of homes, Harold Jackson wrote:

> There have been few more shattering experiences in twenty years of reporting than to arrive among the smouldering remnants of Conway Street and Norfolk Street in the Catholic Falls area of Belfast. In a few hours at the height of the rioting in August 1969 ninety houses were methodically burned out by the Protestants from the nearby Shankill district.... I walked among the ruins with a middle-aged man who could only repeat time and again "They were decent working-class folk. What had they ever done?"
>
> But the Protestant men from Second Street and Third Street, who were said to have been responsible, were also decent working-class folk as became evident when one talked to them later. Between the two groups lay a miasma of suspicion and misunderstanding which had far transcended any normal moral instinct.[20]

Many steps have been taken to meet legitimate grievances and improve the organisation and impartiality of the police. Space does not permit detailed description of action taken by Stormont and by Conservative and Labour Governments at Westminster, but the signifiicance of any action can hardly penetrate minds so confused as described above. From the point of view of the ordinary citizen, of whatever political or religious persuasion, the conclusion of the Hunt Committee on the Police, reporting in 1969, holds good:

We cannot stress too strongly the catastrophe which must befall any society which ceases to respect the rule of law and takes the law into its own hands.[21]

## B. *The Citizen and the Legal System*

The European Convention for the Protection of Human Rights and Fundamental Freedoms lays down standards for the legal system to provide protection for the citizen without discrimination. Both nationally and internationally concern has been expressed that the Special Powers Act contravenes this Convention. The accusation, which comes from many quarters, is that although Britain has signed the Convention yet in Northern Ireland, a part of Britain, citizens suffer legal discrimination.

So serious an accusation has not been taken lightly. Lord Cameron, Sir Edmund Compton,[22] Lord Parker,[23]. Lord Scarman, Lord Diplock[24] and Lord Gardiner[25] have all chaired Commissions examining related aspects of the way the legal system operates in Northern Ireland. Their collective reports, incisively and lucidly written, run to some 300,000 words. Added to this documentation Amnesty International commissioned an enquiry by a Norwegian lawyer, a Swedish journalist, a Dutch doctor and the Secretary a New Zealander, a researcher employed by Amnesty International. Their report added another 20,000 words.[26]

An important aspect of human rights is illuminated when all this evidence is examined, namely, the human rights of those employed by the people to ensure that their rights are defended, and required by the people to wear uniform while on duty to identify themselves to the public. Members of the police and the armed forces also have their right to life and to a fair trial if they are accused of indiscipline or crimes.

When a para-military organisation assumes the right to kill a man without trial and without identification apart from the clothes he is wearing, all members of the security forces are deprived of their basic human rights. Comparison between the working methods of the Commissions of Enquiry set up by the Government and by Amnesty International illustrate the point. Consider the terms of reference:

*Compton Committee*: To investigate allegations by those arrested on 9th August under the Civil Authorities (Special Powers) Act (Northern Ireland) 1922 of physical brutality while in the custody of the Security Forces prior to either the subsequent release, the preferring of a criminal charge, or their being lodged in a place specified in a detention order.

*Parker Committee*: To investigate whether, and if so in what respects, the procedures currently authorised for the interrogation of persons suspected of terrorism and for their custody while subject to interrogation require amendment.

*Amnesty International*: To examine the allegations of ill-treatment of prisoners and internees detained under the Special Powers Act, as well as conditions of imprisonment and internment.

Because government has responsibility for the life and safety of public servants the Committees were asked to adopt procedures designed to protect the lives of those who had conducted the arrests and interrogation. This meant, of course, that evidence had to be taken in private, and individual charges of indiscipline or crime investigated by the security forces themselves. Any procedure which would have made known the names and ranks of the security forces involved, whether they had acted correctly or incorrectly, would have amounted to publishing a death list for revenge killings.

Amnesty International on the other hand had no special responsibility for the security forces. Their purpose was to discover whether the State itself was depriving individuals of their human rights through the operation or distortion of the legal system. In particular they were concerned with Article 5 of the Universal Declaration of Human Rights, that "No one shall be subjected to torture or to cruel, inhuman or degrading treatment or punishment."

All Commissions invited the public to come forward to give evidence, particularly those who felt aggrieved. Complainants flocked to the Amnesty hearings, but only one gave evidence to Compton as well. Amnesty invited the U.K. authorities to participate or at least send an observer to their sessions. This offer could not be accepted. Any official representative would have been put in an impossible position of having to remain silent, whatever allegations were made, or else answer and thereby publish the names to go on the "death list." Amnesty admitted,

> As the Commission received no co-operation from the authorities, its sources of information were necessarily one-sided, except for those cases.... investigated by the Compton Committee. Evaluation of such information can only be based on a subjective impression of the complainant and his account, viewed in the light of any corroborative or contradictory evidence that might be available.[27]

Amnesty's final advice to the Parker Committee was:

...no physical or mental torture, nor any form of coercion, should be inflicted on prisoners to secure from them information of any kind whatever; prisoners who refuse to answer should not be threatened, insulted or exposed to any unpleasant or disadvantageous treatment of any kind.[28]

The result of all this diligent investigation was that there was much argument about the meaning of words, nevertheless the laws and interrogation procedures were changed. Yet the answer still has to be found to the genuine conflict in human rights. When an individual is suspected of terrorist activities, because those who know will not or dare not give evidence, has he the right to his freedom to carry on his activities? What about the human rights of his selected or indiscriminate victims?

The Diplock Committee examined this dilemna in respect of Article 6 of the European Convention. The essential clauses of that Article are:

... everyone is entitled to a fair and public hearing within a reasonable time by an independent and impartial tribunal established by law....

Everyone charged with a criminal offence shall be presumed innocent until proved guilty....

... to be informed promptly... of the nature and cause of the accusation against him....

... to examine or have examined witnesses against him.

The Diplock report states:

The minimum requirements are based upon the assumption that witnesses to a crime will be able to give evidence in a court of law without risk to their lives, their families or their property. Unless the State can ensure their safety, then it would be unreasonable to expect them to testify voluntarily and morally wrong to try to compel them to do so.

This assumption, basic to the very functioning of the courts of law, cannot be made today in Northern Ireland as respects most of those who would be able, if they dared, to give evidence in court on the trial of offences committed by members of terrorist organisations....

The fear of revenge upon "informers" is omnipresent. It is not limited to urban areas. It extends to those who live in relative isolation in the country exposed to terrorist raids from across the border. It extends to all classes of society. It is not an idle or irrational fear. It is justified in fact by many well authenticated instances of intimidation, and not least by the example, familiar to all other potential witnesses, of a witness who was shot dead in his home in front of his infant child the day before he was due to give evidence on the prosecution of terrorists.[29]

Article 15 of the European Convention does permit derogation from minimum requirements in time of public emergency threatening the life of the nation. An example of why Article 15 is appropriate to the Northern Ireland situation concerns the right of the citizen to be promptly informed about the cause of the accusation against him. Under British law arrests are normally made by trained policemen who will know the identity of the person he is arresting, or will have seen the criminal act committed. The Diplock report comments:

Here it is not practicable in present conditions for the initial arrest of a suspected terrorist to be made by a police officer. It can only be made by soldiers either when in the course of an armed patrol they believe they recognise a wanted man in the street or in a passing vehicle or when, as a result of information received, they conduct a surprise search of premises on which terrorists are thought to be present..... There are often a number of people on the premises whose identity is not known to members of the search party... Arrest is liable to be hindered by crowds of sympathisers, including women and children, hurling stones and other missiles and possibly carried out under fire of snipers.

It is, we think, preposterous to expect a young soldier making an arrest under these conditions to be able to identify a person whom he has arrested as being a man whom he knows to be wanted for a particular offence so as to be able to inform him accurately of the grounds on which he is arresting him.[30]

The report goes on to give a number of graphic examples to show why the normal processes of law cannot operate and they make a list of recommendations. Careful study by Parliament of all the evidence in this report, and in all the others, resulted in the replacement of the Special Powers Act by the Northern Ireland (Emergency Provisions) Act, 1973. This introduced trial by a judge without a jury and procedures for admitting written statements as evidence for scheduled offences. This measure protected both witnesses and jury from exposing themselves to punishment and intimidation. Juries were not abolished for crimes not scheduled as terrorist. The Act defined powers of arrest, detention, search and seizure, consistent with the actualities of the Ulster situation. An important point to note is that detention orders are issued for *crimes*, not for political *opinions*. There are no political prisoners in Northern Ireland, though a number of terrorists convicted for crimes of violence claim they should be classified as political prisoners.

The 1973 Act has to come up for review every year and can only be extended for one more year by a vote in Parliament. The 1975 review was preceded by a Committee appointed by the Secretary of State for Northern Ireland, Mr. Merlyn Rees,

> to consider what provisions and powers, consistent to the maximum extent practicable in the circumstances with the preservation of civil liberties and human rights, are required to deal with terrorism and subversion in Northern Ireland, including provisions for the administration of justice, and to examine the working of the Northern Ireland (Emergency Provisions) Act 1973; and to make recommendations.[31]

The Chairman, Lord Gardiner, with his very distinguished and impartial team examined every clause of the Act with legal thoroughness. They summarised their conclusions and recommendations under forty-seven headings. They criticised the inadequate prison accommodation, organisation and staffing, and declared the introduction of "special category" for convicted prisoners was a mistake. Apart from that, ten of their recommendations advised adding something to an existing clause, three advised repeal of a clause and three suggested minor amendments. The rest of the recommendations broadly supported continuation of the Act for another year.

This report could reasonably be regarded as a means to measure the Ulster citizens' rights within the legal system today. It produces evidence to show that the United Kingdom is no longer in breach of the European Convention, having repealed the Special Powers Act, and having given due notice of derogation necessary to deal with terrorism.

The report shows acute awareness that detention is permissible only in the short term. Acting on this Mr. Merlyn Rees decided to phase out detention by Christmas 1975. Whether or not this action has added to the protection or hazards of Ulster citizens only time will tell.[32]

The nature of the dilemna of defending human rights in a tense communal situation is summed up by Lord Gardiner and his colleagues:

> We have been set a difficult task of maintaining a double perspective; for, while there are policies which contribute to the maintenance of order at the expense of individual freedom, the maintenance without restriction of that freedom may involve a heavy toll in death and destruction. Some of those who have given evidence to us have argued that such features of the present emergency provisions as the use of the Army in aid of the civil power, detention without trial, arrest on suspicion and trial without jury are so inherently objectionable that they must be abolished on the grounds that they constitute a basic violation of human rights. We are unable to accept this argument.[32]

## V. Discrimination in Employment

The Minister of State in Northern Ireland, Mr. William van Straubenzee took the chair for a Working Party set up by his predecessor in August 1972:

To consider what steps, whether in regard to law or practice, should be taken to counter religious discrimination where it may exist in the private sector of employment in Northern Ireland.[33]

Two members of this Working Party were nominated by the Confederation of British Industry, two by the Northern Ireland Chamber of Commerce and Industry, and four by the Northern Ireland Committee of the Irish Congress of Trade Unions. All served in an individual capacity, not as representatives authorised to speak on behalf of their nominating organisations.

The Working Party agreed that discrimination existed and ought to be dealt with in the interest of justice and human dignity. They had invited Dr. John Benn to join their discussions as he also held the recently created posts of Parliamentary Commissioner for Administration and Commissioner for Complaints for Northern Ireland. Their extensive studies of methods operating in other countries to avoid discrimination in employment, and the basic options which were open to meet the particular problems of Northern Ireland led them to the conclusion that:

... the Government should invite representative organisations of employers and Trade Unions to sign, and to recommend their members to sign, a Declaration of intent to observe the principles of full equality of employment opportunity.... It is our view that voluntary measures of this nature have an important role to play in countering religious discrimination.

We also propose that the Fair Employment Agency should maintain a register of signatories to the Declaration who would be entitled upon registration to style themselves "equal opportunity employers." A subsequent finding of discriminatory practice would involve removal from the register.[35]

They expanded their ideas about the way these measures might work. In doing so they came up against the inevitable difficulties where voluntary action rather than statutory power to compel is recognised as the more likely means to achieve the desired end.

In assessing the impact on the individuals who *feel* that the reason for their misfortune in being unable to obtain work or promotion lies in discrimination against them on grounds of religion, declarations of intent are far from satisfactory. Whatever procedures are laid down for fair employment policies it is all too easy, when there are several applicants for one job, to observe the letter of the policy while privately ensuring that favoured candidates come at the top of the list. As Harold Jackson in the Minority Rights Group report comments:

A major change might come if Ulster suddenly found itself with full employment and the modest affluence which most of the rest of the United Kingdom enjoys. But that is a hope on the far horizon and we shall have to wait a long time to see an end of this major aspect of insecurity which accounts for some of the most primitive instincts in Ulster.

One of the effects of the recurrent upheavals has been to frighten away the industrialists most needed to help lower the tensions caused by too many people chasing too few jobs. Factories burned, production lost: no ordinary businessman will face that possibility. So the creation of new jobs falls behind target and the downward trend of economic and social forces quickens.[36]

The origin of discrimination in employment lies primarily in the lack of available jobs, though as in all other subjects in Northern Ireland, there are complex contributing causes. Back in the early 1930s when massive unemployment was the greatest social evil afflicting the United Kingdom – as well as other countries – the Ulster Protestant League against the employment of Catholics was formed. The argument followed the centuries old train of thought – if the country is threatened with disaster it is essential to rely on the Protestants to save the day.

As a leading Unionist said at that time,

Catholics are out to destroy Ulster with all their might and power. They want to nullify the Protestant vote, take all they can out of Ulster and then see it go to hell.[37]

Today, when the most urgent need is to find work for the unemployed, the use of bombs to destroy buildings where people work can be seen as contributing not only to greater unemployment, but also to the bitter fears of many that the purpose of those who claim responsibility for such acts is to destroy the state itself. Such a fear may be woven into current attitudes as moral justification for discrimination.

Discrimination in employment is not all one way. It is only natural where serious tensions exist that people like to work alongside their friends and neighbours in a community, and so avoid social situations which are embarrassing and humiliating, such as when a friend at work may not be treated as a friend at home because of what the neighbours would think. Catholic firms prefer to employ Catholics just as Protestant firms prefer to employ Protestants.

Human rights in employment, therefore, have some direct bearing on where the workers live, and the whole question of housing. This sequence of reasoning was clearly expressed in the recommendations of the Gardiner Committee in 1975:

A number of developments are desirable: the implementation of the recommendations of the van Staubenzee Report on Discrimination in the Private Sector of Employment; further improvements in housing; and a new and more positive approach to community relations.[38]

## VI. Discrimination in Housing

In a situation where there is a shortage of housing which the state is endeavouring to remedy by building publicly owned homes, let at subsidised rents, there has to be a method of allocation of these homes according to need, uninfluenced by discrimination on grounds of religion or politics. There is plenty of evidence that considerations other than need came into the allocation of housing in Northern Ireland when the responsibility rested on elected councillors. As the Cameron Report comments:

A situation in which individual councillors effectively control the allocation of houses is objectionable in many ways, but in the context of our enquiry it is its political bias which is relevant....

It is in a sense understandable that, given the political history of Northern Ireland, in certain areas in particular, local Unionist groups should seek to preserve themselves in power by ensuring that local authority housing is developed and allocated in ways which will not disturb their electoral supremacy. It is however equally natural that most Catholics and many Protestants should feel that the basis of public administration in such areas is radically unfair.[39]

Professor Richard Rose took immense trouble to cross check the actual discrimination in housing which took place under the system. He placed a comprehensive questionnaire in the hands of trained interviewers to enable them to obtain both Catholic and Protestant views and official figures in many areas of Ulster. In his book, *Governing Without Consensus*, he analyses the result:

The figures show that *in aggregate* Catholics are more likely than Protestants be living in council houses. Aggregate figures do not necessarily evidence the absence of any discrimination. Protestant-dominated councils could discriminate on behalf of Protestants, and Catholic-dominated councils discriminate in the opposite direction. To test for this possibility, patterns of tenancy were analysed by the political pattern of control. As it is most unusual for the party governing a local authority to change, there has been ample time for discrimination to become cumulatively effective. Here again the survey found no evidence of systematic discrimination against Catholics. The greatest bias seems to favour Catholics in that small part of the population living in local authorities controlled by Catholic councillors. Systematic discrimination cannot be found when patterns are examined in each of the six counties and two county boroughs, all controlled by Unionists. In five of the eight instances, a larger proportion of Catholics than Protestants were living as subsidised tenants.[40]

He applied many other tests, such as income of tenants, size of family, etc. While some obvious cases of discrimination could be found, and these were mostly taken up by the Civil Rights Movement, this research did not reveal consistent bias against the Catholics.

Nevertheless positive action was expedient to check abuse. The Stormont government, in line with the recommendations of the Cameron Report, put into operation what might be termed the "simple solution": to take housing development and allocation away from elected councillors and place such responsibility in the hands of a central housing authority. The Housing Executive was given powers to cover the whole field of housing, not merely the management of publicly owned property. Its duty was to assess housing need, to study the entire housing stock with a view to preventing neglect and decay, and to produce a programme for new building and rehabilitation and improvement, so that in due course good housing would be available to all.

The complex part of the "simple solution" lay in the fact of civil unrest. At the outset of their work the Housing Executive stated:

This is not an easy period in which to effect transitions, and one should not minimise the difficulties with which the Executive is faced. Housing cannot be isolated from the general political disturbances. The building programme has been affected by vandalism, squatting and other by-products of the troubles. Rent strikes, intimidation, robberies, and bomb damage have disrupted normal housing management services..... Those engaged on housing duties have had to cope with these additional pressures during a period of uncertainty as reorganisation is taking place.[41]

The question to which this paper seeks an answer is, "who suffers discrimination in housing now?" The second Annual Report of the

Housing Executive (1st April 1972 – 31st March 1973) states:

We believe that we achieved some successes during the period under review, but we have had our disappointments and frustrations. In a year which saw 1,334 explosions in the province, 464 people killed in explosions and shooting incidents, and 174 assassinated, our efforts have often seemed non-productive and occasionally even irrelevant.[42]

The Minority Rights Group report throws further light on the complexity of the human problems which the Housing Executive was called upon to solve. Harold Jackson writes:

The gerrymandering cannot be defended. But it could not have been achieved so easily had it not been for the insistence of the Catholics in grouping together. The tradition goes back so far that there is no hope of eradicating it for generations; it is being perpetuated even now. The slum clearance schemes being carried out all over the province are achieved district by district. As new housing estates are completed, so the slum families are moved out to them to allow their former houses to be demolished. This means that the ghettoes are merely being transferred wholesale to another place and the problem revitalised for another eighty years or so.

The pressure to preserve things as they are often comes from the families themselves. Their disinclination to live in a mixed area has been heightened by the latest riots. As each outbreak has occurred families of one religion, isolated in a neighbourhood predominantly of the opposite persuasion, have received threats that they will be attacked unless they move out. These threats are often condemned by their neighbours but that gives little reassurance. The family packs its belongings and seeks the security of living among its own kind, where there is both group and territorial protection.[43]

The question relating to human rights which arises from this situation is again one of conflicting rights. Should the state compel families to live in one place when they would choose to live in another?

It is easy to diagnose that segregation of communities encourages the growth of tensions, therefore of discrimination, therefore of the diminution of human rights. Forced de-segregation also involves serious infringement of human rights.

In this dilemna the emotive word "ghetto" is given a new and false meaning. Historically a ghetto is a Jewish quarter where Jews were strictly confined. They were not *permitted* to live elsewhere. Under British law no one is compelled to live in a set place. There can be many reasons, mostly economic, why certain groups congregate in certain areas, but there is no control to force them to do so. In Northern Ireland economic reasons are not the most important. A far more fundamental human right is at stake.

## VII. Discrimination in Education

Any infringement of the rights of individuals to exercise the freedom of religious belief would be deeply resented. This right includes the right of parents to bring up their children in the faith and according to the teaching of their church. This freedom was enshrined in the Government of Ireland Act 1920.

Catholic parents, therefore, are absolutely free to choose whether they send their children to the state school, with non-denominational religious instruction (as in England) or to Catholic schools where they will be taught by Catholics and educated in the faith. In 1968 the Unionist Government increased the grant in respect of capital costs to all denominational schools, mostly Catholic, from 65% to 80%. The complaint that more public money is given to state schools than to Catholic ones is answered by the fact that there are more children in the state schools. Because of the obedience of the Catholics to the instructions of their church, very few of their children attend state schools, thereby causing these schools to be for Protestants.

At university and technical college level Protestants and Catholics are no longer segregated.

It is, of course, customary when a youngster starts earning a living, or later on when he changes his job, for the potential employer to ask about educational experience and qualifications. Then education in a Catholic school marks the applicant as a Catholic and removes any necessity to ask "unfair" questions about religion. This opens the door to the possibility of private discrimination which is impossible to check. Suspicion generates fear and a sense of grievance.

It is not surprising, therefore, that many researchers into the problems of Northern Ireland diagnose the root cause of communal tensions to be the educational system. A great many Catholics and Protestants agree that until there is an integrated school system misunderstandings and blind prejudice will continue to bedevil Ulster affairs in every field. This is a very difficult thought for the Catholic hierarchy in this or any other country. Their profound belief that children must be brought up in the faith, be guarded from the corruption of secular values, is absolute. Arising from this, other changes which many think desirable are quietly blocked. It is convenient for the parish priest to have his flock living close to each other, to the church and to the school. It is also convenient for families with many children to have both the school and the church close by. To scatter the flock would add to the burden of both priest and parents. For the state, or more particularly for the Unionist Party to insist that the flock must be scattered so as to become integrated would be hailed as the grossest example of discrimination, arousing the passionate sympathy of every Catholic community in the world.

As every aspect of discrimination in Northern Ireland is examined the trail always leads back to the starting point. Seen from outside as an academic problem, a reasonable solution should be simple. Seen from the inside as a human problem solutions are infinitely complex. Those who do not live in Northern Ireland but believe that they can influence events by condemning one group and sympathising with another, contribute only to the prolongation of violence and the consequent destruction of human rights. It is the Irish themselves who have to work out the means of living – or dying – with each other. The rest of the British people with great patience, and at a high price, can only help by striving to provide time to allow wise and humane councils to prevail.

## VIII. The Irish Dimension

All political parties in Britain agree that there is an "Irish Dimension." The people of Ulster are Irish as well as being British, and so the special relationship they have with the Republic must be taken into account. Ulster is the only part of the United Kingdom which has a land frontier with another state. It is an open frontier. Irish citizens have the privilege of dual nationality. They can work without restriction either side of the border. They can legally own two passports, and, given residence, there is nothing to stop them from voting in either country, or even in both if they time their residential status correctly.

If this free movement across the border exposes the North to republican penetration, it also exposes the South to the influence of successful terrorism and contempt for the rule of law. The Official IRA and the Provisional IRA are recognised as a threat to the authority of government in Dublin as well as in Belfast. Although the Constitution of the Republic lays claim to all the 32 counties in Ireland, no government of the Republic has ever tried to make good this claim. The words, however, have been regarded by the Republicans in the North as giving them constitutional right to do anything which lies within their power to abolish the border.

This situation has made it difficult and embarrassing for politicians in the Republic to offer co-operation to the British authorities to bring the disturbances in the North to an end, much though they would like to see peace restored. Disturbances are very bad for their tourist trade. While solutions to the Ulster problems seem as far away as ever, there has been a significant change in the statistics of violence, and this change alters in some degree the balance of interest in the Republic. As a result of the long drawn out struggle and escalating violence, plus the counter-measures of extensive reform, political initiatives and strengthened security, there has been much fragmentation among the passionate and extreme factions on both sides. A breakaway group needs substantial funds to take action in defiance of the parent group. Bank raids and the protection racket provide a quick and easy way to fill the coffers.

Any nimble witted criminal whose only ideals are to get as much money and power for himself as he can will recognise the opportunities that there are for him to take advantage of such a situation. The political para-military groups will also recognise that they cannot afford to allow the criminal element to cash in on their preserves, and at the same time discredit their cause. So a system of summary punishment by death or mutilation is set up, both to discipline their own group and eliminate rivals. What is often described as a sectarian killing has little to do with religion but much with power.

Extortion with menaces is a crime calculated to destroy the fundamental freedoms of members of any community. When intimidation makes it inexpedient to apply to the police or courts for protection it amounts to a grave deprivation of human rights. A small operator can knock on doors in a humble street and ask the family to put something in his collecting box for "the boys behind the bars." It is not wise to argue or ask questions, better to pay up so that the family is not marked as "unsympathetic" or ripe for "persuasion." The big operators work on a much larger scale, demanding protection money from hotels, factories, contractors, stores, etc. Such racketeers have no respect for borders on a map, and the Dublin government is fully aware of this. It may be speculation to attribute changed attitudes in Dublin politicians to this awareness, but it is a fact that attitudes have changed.

The Prime Minister of the Republic, Mr. Liam Cosgrave, did not mince his words when warning the Americans not to contribute funds which would be used to buy arms to murder Irish men, women and children. It is estimated that more than £2,000,000 has been collected in America, ostensibly to relieve suffering, but actually to purchase guns, ammunition, explosives and Russian rockets. It is not only the kind hearts of the Americans that have been touched by a well told story, as the Gardiner Report stresses:

> The presence of influential communities of Irish descent in many parts of the English-speaking world means that a number of Britain's allies and Commonwealth partners have a keen interest in the stability of communal relations in Northern Ireland. Yet some of these same Irish communities have themselves helped to sustain violence there by their support for the para-military organisations.[44]

The wise development of the "Irish Dimension" could contribute much to ending the lawlessness in Northern Ireland. There are many meeting grounds for co-operation where Ulster already identifies with Ireland rather than with Britain, such as the Irish Council of Trade Unions, the Irish Banks Standing Committee, the Irish Rugby Football Union, the Gaelic Athletic Association. The "special relationship exists on many levels, so too does the common interest.

## IX. The Complex Answer

The three simple questions which set the confines of this paper must inevitably have a complex answer.

Which citizens in Northern Ireland are deprived of human rights? All of them in varying degree.

What rights? First, the right to life, to be free from sudden death in the home, at work or on the street. Then the right to a fair trial before any punishment of any sort may be inflicted. The right to be protected from extortion and intimidation.

Why has this deprivation happened in Northern Ireland? The readers must find the answer to that by their own interpretation of the evidence.

There are grounds for saying that religious conflict between Protestants and Catholics is the cause of all the trouble. As an Ulsterman said with a sigh, "If only the Protestants and Catholics were both heathens they could live together in Christian charity!"

There are grounds for saying that religious differences, though contributing to the tensions, are not the primary cause. Harold Jackson's analysis is:

The twin pillars of the Ulster problem are group loyalty and territorial integrity. If either or both of these elements come under attack the response is total, unreasoning and devastating. The Stormont government has frequently claimed that much of the trouble stems from the work of professional agitators from the Irish Republican Army or from the equally extreme Ulster Volunteer Force. This is plainly true but to a great degree irrelevant. Neither faction could make much headway if it did not have readily explosive material to work on and the reason for this volatility is a fine-crocheted network of interdependent tensions. These will only be unstitched over a long period of gradual reasurrance for which no pace can be determined. It can only happen by consent: and consent in turn depends on the pace at which it happens. It is as simple but as complex as that.[45]

## NOTES

1. Richard Rose, *Governing Without Consensus*, Faber and Faber, London, 1971, Beacon Paperback, Boston, 1972, p. 19.
2. *Disturbances in Northern Ireland*, Report of the Commission presented to Parliament, September 1969, Cmd 532, Her Majesty's Stationery Office, Belfast, (Chairman of the Commission The Honourable Lord Cameron, D.S.C., Professor Sir John Biggart, C.B.E., Mr. James Joseph Campbell, M.A.) p. 26.
3. Statistics of Security, Northern Ireland Office, Belfast.
4. Cameron Report, *op. cit.*, p. 3.
5. John Biggs-Davison, M.P., *The Hand is Red*, Johnson Publications, London, 1973, p. 16.
6. *Ibid.*, p. 35.
7. *The Future of Northern Ireland*, Her Majesty's Stationery Office, (HMSO) London, 1972.
8. Cameron Report, *op. cit.*, p. 11.
9. *Ibid.*, p. 57.
10. *Ibid.*, p. 59.
11. *Ibid.*, p. 60.
12. *Ibid.*, p. 92.
13. *Ibid.*, p. 92.
14. *Report on Violence and Civil Disturbance in Northern Ireland in 1969*, Chairman of Tribunal Mr. Justice Scarman; commissioned by the Northern Ireland Government August 27, 1969, presented to United Kingdom Parliament April 1972. HMSO Belfast, Cmd 566. 2 Vols. (Other members of the Tribunal were Mr. G. K. G. Lavery and Mr. William Marshall).
15. Professor Richard Rose, "The Priorities of Citizenship," University of Strathclyde, Glasgow, 1975. A portion of the research for this article was undertaken while the author was a Fellow of the Woodrow Wilson International Centre, Washington D.C. Full version of the study to be published in *Journal of Politics* during 1976.
16. John Biggs-Davison, *op. cit.*, p. 134–5.
17. Cameron Report, *op. cit.*, p. 92–3.
18. Scarman Report.
19. Richard Rose, *Governing Without Consensus*, *op. cit.*, p. 438–9.
20. Harold Jackson, *The Two Irelands: a dual study of inter-group tensions*, Report No. 2, Minority Rights Group, 36, Craven Street, London, WC2N 5NG, 1971.

21. Lord Hunt, the conqueror of Mount Everest, with two leading British policemen, was appointed by Stormont to look into and advise on the Royal Ulster Constabulary and the B. Specials following serious criticism of riot control. They reported in October 1969, and their recommendations led to the disarming of the R.U.C. and the disbanding of the B. Specials, with the duty of armed patrols being taken over by the Army and guard duties taken over by the newly formed Ulster Defence Regiment.
22. *Report of the enquiry into allegations against the Security Forces of physical brutality in Northern Ireland arising out of events on 9th August, 1971.* Chairman, Sir Edmund Compton, GCB, KBE; presented to Parliament November 1971. HMSO, Cmd 4823.
23. *Report of the Committee of Privy Councillors appointed to consider authorised procedures for the interrogation of persons suspected of terrorism.* Chairman: Lord Parker, members: Mr. J. A. Boyd Carpenter and Lord Gardiner; presented to Parliament March 1972. HMSO London, Cmd 4901.
24. *Report of the Commission to consider legal procedures to deal with terrorist activities in Northern Ireland.* Chairman: Lord Diplock, members: Professor A. R. N. Cross, FBA, The Right Hon. George Woodcock, CBE and The Rt.Hon. Sir Kenneth Younger; presented to Parliament December, 1972, HMSO London, Cmd 5185.
25. *Report of a Committee to consider, in the context of civil liberties and human rights, measures to deal with terrorism in Northern Ireland.* Chairman: The Rt.Hon. the Lord Gardiner, PC, members: Professor Alastair Buchan (OBE, Judge J. P. Higgins, Professor Kathleen Jones, The Rt.Hon. the Lord MacDermott, MC, Mr. Michael Morland QC, Dr. J. H. Whyte; presented to Parliament January 1975, HMSO London, Cmd 5847.
26. *Report of an enquiry into allegations of ill-treatment in Northern Ireland,* Amnesty International, 53, Theobald's Road, London WC1X 8SP. Members of Commission: Mr. Gunnar Lind, Mr. Thomas Hammarberg, Dr. Herman van Geuns. March 1972.
27. *Ibid.*, p. 3.
28. *Ibid.*, p. 46.
29. Diplock Report *op. cit.*, p. 9.
30. *Ibid.*, p. 20.
31. Gardiner Report *op. cit.*, p. 1.
32. The Faulkner Government (Stormont) introduced internment without trial on 9th August 1971. When direct rule started the basic rules for internment were modified by the Northern Ireland (Emergency Provisions) Act 1973. This made detention a quasi-judical system whereby the Secretary of State had to be satisfied that the person had committed a crime, but because of intimidation it would be difficult to present the case in court. At least six reports from security forces were needed by the Secretary of State before he signed the detention order. The system of detention was further amended in 1975 by the Northern Ireland (Emergency Provisions) (Amendment) Act 1975 whereby the quasi-judicial system of detention was abolished and a number of advisers were appointed to advise the Secretary of State concerning the detention and release of terrorists.
33. Gardiner Report, *op. cit.*, p. 6.
34. *Report and Recommendations of the Working Party on Discrimination in the Private Sector of Employment.* Chairman: Mr. William van Straubenzee, MP. The Working Party was appointed on 3rd August, 1972 with Mr. Paul Channon, MP as Chairman. He moved to another office in November 1972. The Report

was submitted to the Secretary of State, The Rt.Hon. William Whitelaw MP on 23rd May, 1973.

35. *Ibid.*, p. 34–5.
36. Harold Jackson, Minority Rights Group, *op. cit.*, p. 15.
37. Quoted by Richard Rose, *Governing Without Consensus* p. 95.
38. Gardiner Report, *op. cit.*, p. 50.
39. Cameron Report, *op. cit.*, p. 61.
40. Richard Rose, *Governing Without Consensus*, p. 293.
41. *The Work of the Housing Executive*, 1, College Square East, Belfast BT1 6BQ, December 1972, p. 5.
42. Second Annual Report, Housing Executive, March 1973, presented to Mr. David Howell, MP, Minister of State for Development.
43. Harold Jackson, Minority Rights Group, p. 11.
44. Gardiner Report, *op. cit.*, p. 5.
45. Harold Jackson, Minority Rights Group, *op. cit.*, p. 9–10.

# The Case of the Jews from Arab Countries: A Neglected Issue

MAURICE M. ROUMANI

MAURICE M. ROUMANI is Research Associate, Institute for the Study of Ethnic and Religious Groups, Bar-Ilan University, Ramat Gan: Head of the Research Division of the Department of Sephardic Communities of the World Zionist Organisation, Jerusalem. He was formally Research Associate of the Truman Peace Institute of the Hebrew University, Jerusalem, and the Center for Middle East Studies, Harvard University, United States.

He is the editor of *Forces of Change in the Middle East,* (Worcester State College, Massachusetts, U.S.A.). Other publications: "Jews and Arabs in Libya: Myths and Realities," paper prepared for the Israel Academic Committee on the Middle East in co-operation with the Columbia Unit Alumni Association, March 19, 1975; and "Some Aspects of Socialisation in the Israeli Army: The Integration of the Oriental Jew" in Poll, Solomon and Krausz, Ernest (Eds), *Ethnic and Religious Diversity in Israel,* Ramat Gan: Bar-Ilan University, 1975.

# The Case of the Jews from Arab Countries: A Neglected Issue

MAURICE M. ROUMANI

## I. The Dispersion of Jews from Arab Countries

In 1948 there were over 850,000 Jews living in the Arab and Muslim countries of Asia and North Africa. By 1974 this population dwindled to a mere few thousands. Hundreds of communities, extending from the Atlantic seaboard to the mountains of Kurdistan, originating over two thousand years ago, disappeared almost entirely.

Where flourishing centres of Jewish communal life existed since Biblical times, only a few Jews remain today. In urban capitals that at one time were dominated by the commercial influence of prosperous Jews, the Jewish communities no longer exist. Not unlike the disappearance of European Jewish communities as a result of Nazi atrocities during World War II, the Jewish communities of the Arab World were forced to undergo a similar fate. Although the magnitude of destruction in Europe was greater than in Asia and North Africa, the fate of Arab Jewry must also be recognized as a case of destruction, engineered through forced emigration and prompted by intensified anti-Semitism.

### *A. Conditions for Jews become Unbearable*

Life for Jews in Arab countries was always circumscribed by anti-Jewish sentiment. Therefore, the position of Jews in these countries, throughout their two thousand years of settlement there, was always insecure and unstable. The inferiority of Jews was not only enforced by

---

This paper consists of extracts from a Report written by Maurice M. Roumani in collaboration with Deborah Goldman and Helene Korn, published by The World Organisation of Jews from Arab Countries (WOJAC), Jerusalem, 1975.

degrading civil codes, it was also legitimized by religious writings which officially decreed Jews as 'infidels'.

By the 20th century, anti-Jewish sentiment was dramatically translated into actions and legislation which made life for Jews in these countries increasingly unbearable. The rise of Arab nationalism, the founding of the Arab League and the subsequent resentment expressed in the light of the establishment of the State of Israel, were significant factors which intensified anti-Jewish persecutions.

On December 1, 1947, riots broke out in numerous Jewish communities throughout the Arab world, in protest against the recent UN resolution on the partition of Palestine. Conforming to the known Arab tradition of anti-Jewish practices over the past 1,300 years, Jewish shops, homes, and synagogues were burned and looted; hundreds of Jews were murdered in the streets, thousands were imprisoned in the following months as criminals and suspicious people. Movement was restricted, immigration to Israel banned and many Jews were deprived of their citizenship. Jews who at one time were influential in commerce, suddenly lost their holdings; bank accounts belonging to Jews were frozen, and property valued at millions of dollars was gradually confiscated. As in previous centuries, Jews were further removed from government agencies and their admission to public office was severly restricted. Jews lost their means of survival; they became hostages in their own countries of origin. Consequently, they could no longer remain in these countries. One time flourishing communities suddenly disintegrated as more and more Jews were compelled to leave.

TABLE 1. *Jewish Population in Arab Countries, 1948 and 1974*

| | *1948* | *1974* |
|---|---|---|
| Morocco | 265,000 | 25,000 |
| Algeria | 140,000 | 500 |
| Tunisia | 105,000 | 2,000 |
| Libya | 38,000 | 20 |
| Egypt | 75,000 | 350 |
| Iraq | 135,000 | 400 |
| Syria | 30,000 | 4,350 |
| Lebanon | 5,000 | 1,800 |
| Yemen | 55,000 | 1,000 |
| Aden | 8,000 | 0 |
| TOTAL | 856,000 | 35,420 |

Entire communities disappeared. Between 1948 and 1951, the Jews of Yemen and Iraq were air lifted *en mass* to Israel, a natural haven from their sufferings. Similarly, the Jewish community of Libya was almost entirely relocated to Israel. The table opposite summarizes the dramatic disappearance of Jewish communities in the Arab world between 1948 and the present time.[1]

### *B. The Exodus*

The majority of Jews forced to emigrate from Arab countries found refuge in Israel. To this day, a total of 586,268 arrived in Israel[2] with at least another 200,000 emigrating to France, England and the Americas. Including their offspring, the total number of Jews who were displaced from their homes in Arab countries and who live in Israel today is 1,136,436, about 41% of the total population.[3] At least another 500,000 currently reside in France, Canada and the United States.

The high influx of Jews from Arab countries into Israel shortly after its establishment as a state, had a significant influence on the demographic makeup of its population. In 1931, only 1 out of every 4 Jews living in the Land of Israel came from Asia and Africa. By 1948 there were still only 70,000 of the latter in Israel as compared to 253,661 Israeli born Jews and 393,013 Europeans and Americans, out of a total population of 716,678 Jews.[4]

In the early 50's the picture changed dramatically. By 1951 Jews from Arab countries made up nearly 30% of the entire population. This unusually rapid change in the demographic makeup of the population was due to the thousands of Jews that were pouring into Israel as a result of persecutions throughout the world including that of Arab and Muslim countries. During the years 1948 to 1951, nearly 50% of all immigrants, totalling 387,000, came from Asia and Africa compared to a similar number emigrating at the time from Europe and America. During the 2 year period, from 1955 to 1957, the percentage of Jews from Arab lands arriving in Israel rose to 69% and in 1955 alone this group represented 92% of all immigrants. This high proportion is not surprising in view of the approximately 100,000 that came during those years from Morocco, Algeria and Tunisia alone.[5]

The majority of Jewish refugees from Arab lands arrived in Israel during the first three years of statehood. Of the total *586,268* that

TABLE 2. *Immigration of Jews from Arab Lands to Israel from 15/5/48–22/5/72*

| *Country* | *number* |
|---|---|
| Morocco, Tunisia, Algeria * | 330,833 |
| Libya | 35,666 |
| Egypt | 29,325 |
| Syria, Lebanon * | 10,402 |
| Yemen, Aden * | 50,552 |
| Iraq | 129,292 |
| TOTAL | 586,070 |

* Invidual statistics for these countries were not recorded before 1950; therefore, we find it more accurate to list them together.

arrived to date, nearly 400,000 entered the country between 1948 and 1951.[6] The effects of this mass immigration in such a short period of time can also be observed in the total population increase for those years. Before May 15, 1948, there were little more than 700,000 Jews living in Israel. By 1951 the population figure doubled to 1,404,400.

The table above shows the number of Jews that emigrated from Arab countries between 1948 and 1972:[7]

Immigration of Jews from Arab countries to Israel was not an entirely new phenomenon in 1948. Jews had arrived in Israel from Arab countries as early as 1881 when a group of more than 2,000 Yemenite Jews succeeded in completing the long trek to Palestine a year before the first Eastern European settlers (*Bilu*) arrived. By 1948, over 45,000 Jews from Arab countries had immigrated to the Land of Israel. The motivation of these early settlers was primarily spiritual. Prompted by a messianic hope, they were determined to make the long journey to the land of their ancestors.

Jews arriving in Israel after 1948 were similarly inspired by the ideal of returning to their homeland. However, for the most part, these people were refugees, forced to flee from their homes and to abandon centuries of established culture and tradition as a result of persecutions which made life for Jews in Arab countries increasingly unbearable at that time.

### *C. Dwindling Jewish Communities: A Survey*

*Morocco*

The Jewish community of Morocco dates back to the destruction of the First Temple in the year 586 B.C. By 1948, this ancient community, the largest in North Africa, numbered 265,000. Composed primarily of money changers, artisans, and traders, the Jewish population was 73% urban and constituted 9% of the total urban population of Morocco. In 1947 a large Jewish community existed in Casablanca with over 86,000 inhabitants. Other cities which had large Jewish populations were Marrakesh, Fez, Meknes and Rabat, each comprising a population of more than 15,000 Jews in 1947.[8]

Immigration to Israel started upon the initiative of small groups who arrived at the time of Israel's independence. However, the mass immigrations which brought a total of more than 250,000 Moroccan Jews to Israel, were prompted by anti-Jewish measures carried out in response to the establishment of the State of Israel. On June 4, 1948, riots broke out in northern Morocco killing and injuring dozens of Jews. Shortly afterwards, the Jews began to leave *en masse.*

During the two year period between 1955 and 1957 alone, over 70,000 Moroccan Jews arrived in Israel. In 1956 immigration to Israel was banned and by 1959 Zionism became illegal in Morocco. During these years more than 30,000 Jews left for France and the Americas. In 1963, the ban on immigration to Israel was lifted bringing another 100,000 to her shores.

Today, the Jewish community of Morocco has dwindled to less than 10% of its original size. Of the 25,000 Jews that remain two-thirds live in Casablanca. Since 1964, 30 Jewish courts have been closed down, including the High Rabbinic Court. Jewish schools still exist but many are under Muslim administration. There has been no Jewish press in Morocco since 1966.[9]

Generally speaking, the Jews who remain in Morocco have a reasonably stable existence; however, occasional outbursts of anti-Israel sentiments make daily life for Jews increasingly insecure.

*Algeria*

In 1948, there were 140,000 Jews in Algeria. Before 1962, there were 60 Jewish communities in Algeria, each maintaining at least one synagogue, one Rabbi, and its own educational services. During the

3 months between May and July of 1962, almost all the Jews of Algeria left the country following the Avian Agreement which granted independence to Algeria.[10] Today, the community consists of a mere 500 people.

As early as 1940, Jews were deprived of their citizenship in Algeria. Subsequently, during the struggle for independence, pressure was placed upon Jews to endorse the nationalist cause. A spokesman for the Liberation Party indicated in 1960: "Jews will endure the consequences of their hesitant attitude when Algeria will come into being." In addition, they were also harassed by the existing government. Consequently, 14,000 Jews immigrated to Israel and another 125,000 to France leaving behind only a tiny fraction of what used to be one of North Africa's largest Jewish communities.[11]

Today, the Jews that remain in Algeria no longer maintain any independent form of communal organization. They are under the supervision of the French Secretariat of the World Jewish Congress. In Algiers, a community that numbered 30,000 in 1960 had 12 synagogues, now only one synagogue remains.

*Tunisia*

Similar to the conditions for Jews in Algeria, the rise of Tunisian nationalism influenced anti-Jewish legislation and caused Jews to leave in great numbers starting in 1961. In 1948, the Tunisian Jewish community numbered 105,000 of which 65,000 lived in Tunis alone. By 1961, the population declined to 70,000 and in 1968 there were only 12,000 Jews left in Tunisia. Heightened anti-Jewish persecutions during the Six-Day War influenced even more to leave. In that year 7,000 immigrated to France.[12]

The Jews of Tunisia constituted a wealthy, prestigious community including, at one time, a Member of Parliament. The change that occurred in government policy generated fear and insecurity for the Jews which eventually caused most of them to flee. Over 50,000 immigrated to Israel. In 1958, the Jewish Community Council was abolished. Today only 2,000 Jews remain in Tunisia.

*Libya*

The Libyan Jewish community, which numbered 38,000 in 1948, is an example of a Jewish community which disappeared entirely as a result of anti-Jewish pressures. Intensified persecution of Jews began as early as 1942 when Italy, involved in World War II anti-Jewish measures, deported 3,000 Jews to the Giado concentration camp.[13] With the outbreak of anti-Jewish riots in 1945 and in 1948, the Jewish community witnessed a wave of pogroms resulting in the loss of life and property. In 1951, upon Libya's independence and membership in the Arab League, conditions worsened.

Jews were thus forced to leave *en masse*. The overwhelming majority, 35,612, immigrated to Israel, of which as many as 30,000 arrived by 1951. Illegal immigration to Italy started in 1949 which enabled 2,107 Libyan Jews eventually to find refuge in Israel. Entire communities were forced to uproot themselves. The whole community of Zliten numbering 604 arrived in Israel in July of 1949. Similarly, entire communities from the province of Tripolitana, including the ancient cities of Garian-Tigrina and Jefren (approximately 15,000 people) arrived in Israel during 1950.[14]

In the 60's only a few hundred Jews remained in Libya. With the increased hostilities resulting from the Six-Day War, they too were forced to flee, leaving behind all their possessions. Today, a mere 20 Libyan Jews remain in the country.

*Egypt*

In 1948, the number of Jews living in Egypt was 75,000. By 1956, this figure declined to 40,000. Ten years later, the number dwindled even further to 2,500 and today there remain only 350.

The exodus of Jews from Egypt in the latter part of the 20th century was prompted by a history of continuous anti-Jewish measures. In 1947, Jewish employment and economic opportunities were curtailed. In 1948, Jewish property was confiscated and hundreds of Jews were arrested.

Consequently, Jews were forced to flee, leaving behind all their property. By 1957, 25,000 Jews from Egypt arrived in Israel. Another 10.000 fled to England and France. Small communities still remain in Cairo and Alexandria. However, Jewish welfare institutions, schools and synagogues have in most cases been closed down.[15]

*Iraq*

The Jewish community in Iraq, one of the oldest and largest in the Arab world, numbered 135,000 in 1948. Over 77,000 lived in Baghdad alone, comprising a fourth of the capital's population. The community was wealthy and prestigious. Before World War II, Jews held a dominant place in the import trade and occupied high government positions.[16]

Today, only 400 Jews remain in Iraq. The overwhelming majority of the population was relocated to Israel, as a result of intensified anti-Jewish actions which started with the UN resolution on the partition of Palestine in 1947 and extended till after the cease fire with Israel in 1949. Hundreds were killed and imprisoned during anti-Jewish riots. Zionism became a capital crime and Jewish property was confiscated.

Jews were thus forced to flee, and to leave all of their belonging behind. Between 1949 and 1952, 123,371 Iraqi Jews were airlifted directly to Israel in what came to be known as "Operation Erza and Nehemia."

Few Jews remain in Iraq today and those who do are continuously threatened by the harassment of local officials.

*Syria*

In 1943 the Jewish community of Syria had 30,000 members. This population was mainly distributed between Aleppo, where 17,000 Jews lived, and Damascus which had a Jewish population of 11,000.

Anti-Jewish riots which broke out as early as 1945 and 1947, prompted the denial of basic civil rights to Jews. By 1945, the government restricted immigration to Israel. Jewish property was burned and looted. In 1949, banks were instructed to freeze the accounts of Jews.

This situation caused 15,000 Jews to leave Syria by 1948. 10,000 immigrated to the U.S.A. and another 5,000 to Israel. Today, 4,350 Jews remain in Syria, 3,000 live in Damascus, another 1,000 in Haleb and 350 in Kamishli. The remaining Jews in Syria are denied free movement or contact with the outside world. Those who have family in Israel are always in danger of violent attacks by local officials.

*Lebanon*

The emigration of Jews from Lebanon followed a somewhat different pattern as compared to the Jews of other Arab countries, primarily as a result of the Christian-Arab rule which characterized the political structure of this country and which extended a policy of relative tolerance towards its Jewish population.

Despite the basically positive circumstances enjoyed by Lebanese Jews, they too decided to emigrate. The majority left for France, Italy, England and South America and some immigrated to Israel in 1967.

Today, 1,800 Jews remain in Lebanon, the majority concentrated in Beirut.

*Yemen*

"Operation Magic Carpet," the dramatic airlift which brought 48,818 Yemenite Jews to Israel in 430 flights during 1949 and 1950, is another example of the displacement of an entire Jewish community from its ancient origins in the Arab world.

55,000 Jews lived in two main cities and in 150 rural and desert localities in 1948. Today only a few hundred remain.

Immigration from Yemen to Israel started as early as 1881 when over 2,000 arrived in Palestine. Another 15,000 came between 1919 and 1948 mainly for Zionist and religious reasons. Their followers of the 1950's, however, were forced to flee persecutions and increasingly difficult social conditions.

*Aden*

The history of modern anti-Zionist persecutions in Aden is a bitter and long one. On December 2, 1947, the Arabs proclaimed a solidarity strike in protest of the UN resolution on the partition of Palestine. 100 Jews were murdered, the great synagogue was burned, Jewish property was rampaged looted and destroyed. Riots of the same magnitude destroyed Jewish property again in 1958, 1965 and 1967.

The Jewish community of Aden, numbering 8,000 in 1948, was forced to flee. By 1959 over 3,000 arrived in Israel. Many fled to the U.S.A. and England. Today there are no Jews left in Aden.

## *D. Conclusion*

Despite the unstable and insecure life which Jews led in these countries, they were compelled to remain for generations. They believed they had little choice of improving their conditions by emigration. In addition, many did not have the necessary means to leave. Most important, was their deep rooted affinity with the culture and organic attachment to the environment which precluded them from seeking refuge elsewhere.

It was not until the establishment of the State of Israel that these Jews were finally given a dual opportunity to save their communities from extinction and to fulfill their centuries long messianic aspiration to return to Zion.

## II. Transfer to Israel: Hardships of Displacement

Out of 856,000 Jews living in Arab Countries in 1948, the overwhelming majority found refuge from Arab persecution in Israel. The remaining were dispersed throughout the world. In the various countries that they inhabited previously, many were wealthy and prestigious members of their local Jewish communities. However, confronted with a political and social climate of intensified and unbearable hostility, they were compelled to uproot themselves leaving behind all of their possessions and the value of their property. Consequently, the majority arrived in Israel without any means of their own.

They came from countries in which they were repeatedly denied the opportunity of equal citizenship. At various times, different Arab countries imposed limitations on the Jews in the fields of education, professional life, and economic enterprise. When these circumstances compelled them to leave, the Arab states did not hesitate to proclaim appropriate decrees designed to strip the Jews of their own possessions.

Thus, upon their arrival in Israel, these Jews had no means with which to sustain themselves and, therefore, became dependent on the new State, which, at that time, was struggling for its survival. The young country, poor and lacking in natural resources, was continuously being attacked by hostile neighbours and plagued by economic difficulties. Immigrants were pouring into the country by the hundreds of thousands, many of them the exhausted survivors of concentration and displaced persons' camps. In 1949 alone, 240,000 immigrants were absorbed in Israel.[17] *Between 1948 and 1951, a total of 687,739 immigrants arrived in the country, a figure virtually identical to the total population of the new state in 1948, and almost half the number that arrived in the 24 year period from the establishment of the State until 1972.*[18]

Under normal circumstances, it would be impossible for a country to deal with so many immigrants at a time. Yet, the period was critical. Jews were being snatched from pits of destruction and Israel absorbed them.

In effect, during her early history, Israel was a country of refugees. Unlike her Arab neighbours, who were also faced with the influx of refugees and who entrusted their fate and rehabilitation into the hands of the UN, Israel with the help of world Jewry, did everything possible to offer her Jewish refugees equal opportunity and the basic resources necessary for settlement and absorption. However, due to the difficult circumstances, the process was one of great suffering and struggle. The immigrants arrived with nothing and needed everything. They came in great numbers at a time when housing facilities were not readily available for so many people.

The *ma'abarah* (transit camp – familiar to the Arabs as "refugee camp") was the most common form of temporary settlement. Thousands of people were often crammed into a small space where shelter consisted of tin huts, tents, shacks made of cardboard or whatever materials were at hand. Often groups of immigrants were directed to open fields where they were instructed to build their own shelters because labour and materials were not available. Immigrants with families of 7, 8 and even 10 children were forced to huddle together under cramped conditions, and with little to eat. Disease and illness were thus common in those early years of distress.

The following account describes only certain aspects of the suffering encountered by Jews from Arab countries upon their immigration to Israel:[19]

The great majority of them (immigrants from Arab countries) were housed in tents which were drenched from above and flooded from below during the heavy rains of the winter of 1949–50. The original plan called for a sojourn of a few weeks only in the immigrants' camps, after which each immigrant was to be sent to a permanent place of settlement. Actually, however, in view of the large number of immigrants, the rate of evacuation from the camps lagged constantly behind the rate at which the new immigrants were brought into Israel, and the period of sojourn in the camps was prolonged from three months to four months to six months to eight months . . .

One of the main immigrant's reception camps was that of Rosh Ha'ayin, in which, at the height of its occupancy in 1950, there were some 15,000 Yemenite Jewish immigrants. They were all lodged in tents, fifteen of them in each tent. The few buildings in the camp were used to house the hospital and the clinics, the babies' homes, the kitchen and dining room, and the school. When the immigrants arrived, many of them were very weak. Mortality was high, and as many as 20 deaths occurred daily. In this respect a definite improvement was noticeable, very soon, mortality decreased and generally the strength of the people increased. Practically all the immigrants (98% to be exact) suffered from trachoma when they arrived at Rosh Ha'ayin. After a four month's sojourn in the camp, and constant medical treatment – often administered against the wishes of the patients – this percentage sank to 20%. The health of the children was also in very bad shape. Many adults as well as children suffered from venereal diseases.

By 1951, 256,000 immigrants were still living in temporary settlements.[20] Compared to the 1,400,000 inhabitants of Israel at the time, this group composed no less than 1/5 of the total population.

## III. The Persecution of the Jews in Arab Lands

Arab spokesmen have claimed that it was Zionism which disrupted the warm and amicable relations between Arabs and Jews, that, in short, the Jews "never had it so good" as under Muslim rule, till the State of Israel brought to a sudden end the centuries-long "interfaith utopia."[21] As Ahmad Shukeiry describes it:

Since God decreed their dispersion in the countries of the world, we have never heard that they were saved from harm and found a good life and security for themselves and their property anywhere except in the Islamic countries ... In every Muslim country, they enjoyed the protection of Islam and lived under its wing, safe, peaceful, free to trade, enjoying equality in all civil rights and not suffering from any oppression whatsoever.[22]

This may be a very inspiring picture – but history proves it false.[23] It is true that the lot of Jews under Medieval Muslim rule compares favorably with their condition in Christian countries. It is true that they enjoyed periods of great prosperity and cultural development. It is true that they were legally considered "protected subjects" of the Muslim rulers – but it was a "protection" honoured as often as not in the breach:

As the distinguished Arabist von Grunebaum writes:

While it would not be difficult to catalogue a significant quota of Jewish subjects who rose to a high rank in Islamic lands in places of power, in financial influence and in impressive and recognized intellectual achievements ..., it will be just as easy to cite a long inventory of persecutions, arbitrary confiscations, attempts at forcible conversion and pogroms.[24]

Indeed, not only have Jews suffered oppression – including discrimination and pogroms which bring to mind the worst of medieval Christian Europe – their entire existence in lands under Muslim rule was based on sufferance, *not* rights, this despite the fact that Jews had lived in those lands long before the Islamic conquest. The Jews under Islam were a tolerated minority – and tolerance does not mean equality.[25] From the days of Muhammad on, the Quran and Islamic law emphasized and prescribed a status of inferiority for the Jews; their humiliation, in fact, was a condition of their retaining "protected" status and remaining alive in these lands.

What then are the roots of anti-Jewish discrimination in traditional Islam? We must begin with the Founder of Islam, with Muhammad. The historical circumstances confronting Muhammad as he began to preach his new faith and to seek supporters moulded his attitude toward the Jews – and that of his followers. By the 7th century C.E., many influential and long-established Jewish tribes dwelt throughout Arabia.[26] Muhammad's admiration for the 'People of the Book' who had received divine revelation in the Scriptures – expressed in his adoption of many Jewish traditions and practices – turned to active hostility when the Jews of Medina refused to accept the new faith. Between 625 and 627, Muhammad and his followers eradicated the Jewish tribes' opposition by completely exterminating the Banu Quraiza and driving out the Banu Nadhir and Banu Qainuqa.[27] This and other victories contributed to the growing power and prestige of Muhammad, who began to give the inherited Jewish and Christian customs a more Arabian flavour or to drop them entirely. "What emerged was thus an ambiguous attitude towards Jewry – the recognition of the adherents ... as People of the Book and, at the same time, ... hostile contempt towards (them) as unbelievers."[28]

In 628, the Muslims attacked the Jewish oasis of Khaibar. There the precedent was set for relations between Muslim authority and a conquered non-Muslim people: the Jews of Khaibar were allowed to retain their land but had to pay a 50% tribute. The Quranic expression of this is found in the injunction (Sura IX, 29): "Make war upon those who have received Scripture ... until they pay tribute, being brought low," i.e., in a state of humiliation. As von Grunebaum stated, "Their personal safety and personal property are guaranteed them at the price of permanent inequality."[29] The tribute they paid as a mark of their subordination developed into a yearly poll tax obligatory on all males over age 15, usually collected from a representative of the whole community (who received a slap in the face to remind him – and his brethren – of their inferior status) and a kind of property tax. The poll tax "could be crushing and the property tax could amount to expropriation. To this the ruler could always add supplementary taxes for the support of his army not to speak of goodwill gifts that the weak paid to those in power."[30]

The Jews' inferior position was reinforced by subsequent legislation, enacted as early as the eighth century, codified in the 11th century and known as the Covenant of 'Umar. It comprised a series of regulations designed to separate Muslims from non-Muslims and guard the superiority of the former through the humiliation of the latter. Observance of these regulations was the price paid by the non-Muslim, 'people of the Covenant' called '*dhimmis*', for living under Muslim rule. What did these regulations demand?

On pain of death, Jews, as *dhimmis*, were forbidden to revile the Quran, Islam or Muhammad, to marry Muslim women, to proselytize among Muslims, to injure Muslims in life or property, to assist the enemy or to harbour spies. They were, in addition – and with slightly less grievous penalties attached – forbidden to build houses higher than Muslims, to ride horses (and later mules, too), to drink wine in public and to pray, mourn or bury their dead with loud voices or in a way which might be offensive to Muslims; and they had to wear distinctive clothing or distinguishing coloured patches. Their public behaviour, their outer appearance, the very structure of their homes were to reflect their inferiority and reinforce it.[31] Moreover, the *dhimmis* were forbidden to bear arms; their oath was invalidated by a Muslim's and not accepted in a Muslim Court; and the blood price demanded for the death of a *dhimmi* was almost always less than that of a Muslim.[32]

Islam, is thus the first religion from its inception, to legalize and systematize such discrimination for other peoples and religions.[33]

The Covenant of 'Umar reflected as well as determined actual practice. We know from a contemporary document that Jews in 7th century Egypt were already forced to wear special signs on their clothing.[34]

Moreover, once the Covenant of 'Umar's discriminatory requirements became law – they were only a precedent for further elaboration. "The severity of the laws against the *dhimmis* depended on the degree and manner in which they were enforced. When the Muslim ruler was liberal minded and understanding, the laws were bearable; when the ruler was tyrannical and cruel, the condition of the *dhimmi* was that of a virtual slave."[35] Clothing restrictions, for example, were not uniform, the heights of ludicrousness – and humiliation for the wearer – to which, these laws reached, were dependent only on the whim and cruelty of the Muslim ruler. El-Mutawakkil (847–861) ordered Jews to wear yellow clothing, ropes instead of a belt (the latter considered a mark of honor), put colored buttons on their turbans and then (850) to wear yellow patches on the front and back of their outer garments centuries before this custom was introduced in Europe.[36] El-Hakim

(1004) compelled the Jews to wear first, a wooden image of the Golden Calf, then wooden balls, then six-pound blocks around their necks in the streets and baths of Cairo.[37] Fatimid Khalif al-Mustansir (1086) ordered Jews to wear black belts with yellow fringes;[38] Mamluk rulers decreed that they wear yellow turbans only (1301)[39] and (in 1363) different color shoes.[40] In the same century, Moroccan Jews had to put black slippers on,[41] in the 19th century they were forbidden to wear shoes at all when leaving the Jewish quarter.[42] In 20th century Yemen, the "most Arabic of the Arab countries,"[43] Jews were forbidden (1905) to wear bright colored garments or to use stockings;[44] Yemenite Jewish women were already wearing one white and one black shoe.[45]

What was the practical outcome of these decrees – their toll in human life, dignity and property – through the countries and centuries of Muslim rule?

Despite the alleged 'protection' Islam afforded 'its' Jews, it will not be hard to list instances of Muslim massacres or murders of Jews, though actual numbers of casualties have not always been preserved in sources. In Morocco alone in the 8th century for example whole communities were wiped out by Idris I,[46] in the 11th century 6,000 Jews of Fez were massacred (1033) by a ruler who declared persecution of the Jews legal;[47] when Fez was again the scene of mass murder of Jews in the 15th century, only 11 Jews were left alive;[48] between the years 1864 and 1880, in Marrakesh, more than 300 Jews were murdered.[49] In 1776, Basra Jews were despoiled and slaughtered.[50] The Jews of Algiers were massacred in 1805, 1815 and 1830;[51] the Jews of Mostaganem in 1897.[52] The 12th century tide of terror spread throughout North Africa by the Almohads, a fanatical Muslim sect that gave 'infidels' the choice between Islam and death, and led to the destruction of Fez and Tlemcen Jewry; many other communities – like Meknes, Ceuta, Fraa Sijilmassa – were decimated or forcibly converted. Later legislation forced the new converts to wear humiliating garb and undermined the economic basis of the remaining Jews.[53] Through the centuries, "the Jews were easy prey for a population embroiled in inter-tribal and inter-dynastic warfare. Usually unarmed, they were at the mercy of the mob eager for rape and pillage. Every change of regime, every famine or epidemic, every incident, no matter how small, was likely to mark an outburst of gory uprisings against the Jews."[54] Muslim religious holidays were also occasionally used as an opportunity for attacking the Jews. In late 18th century Egypt a German traveller notes that the holiday of Ramadan was marked by delirious fanaticism and considered incomplete unless at least one non-Muslim was killed. In Iraq, till 1950, Jews were forbidden to smoke in the streets during Ramadan. The fall – by intrigue or assassination – of a Jew in high office[55] usually meant anywhere from a few days to a few months of murder and pillaging of his unhappy co-religionists (as in Morocco, 1465 and in Algiers, 1805).[56]

Destruction and seizure by Muslim of Jewish property (homes and shops, synagogues and revered tombs) were even more common than murder and physical attacks. Decrees ordering the destruction of synagogues were frequently promulgated in Egypt and Syria (as in 1014, 1293–4, 1301–2),[57] Iraq (as in 854–859, 1344)[58] and Yemen (1676).[59] A law prohibiting the construction of new synagogues or the repair of old ones could always be used as a pretext and precedent for such action... Heavy taxes were often imposed specifically on the Jews (Iraq 809,[61] Morrocco 1790)[62] and the *jizya* (poll tax) doubled (Iraq 859),[63] While Ali Bey effected the complete financial ruin of Cairo Jewry within three years (1768–1771) by extorting over 255,000 tallars from them.[64] A predecessor, Qaid Bey (1468–1495) had extorted 75,000 pieces of gold from Egypt's Jews.[65] It would be hard to say that the Jews, even when they "kept their place" were always granted the protection of Islam. In 1801, the Quaid of Boghni promised his soldiers "eight times their pay, white bread and the right to sack the Jews for 4 days."[66] A description of the situation of the Jews in the remote mountainous areas of North Africa is also revealing. "Every Jew ... belongs, body and assets, to his lord, his *sid* ... The *sid* protects his Jews against strangers in the same way as everybody defends what he owns ... He takes them to the market himself, puts them up for auction and sells them ... The Jews are robbed, their homes are destroyed, they are chased away with their families. Villages can be seen with an entire deserted quarter in them, and the surprised passerby learns that there was a *mellah* here and that the *sids* by common consent turned against their Jews one day and drove them out. Nothing in the world can protect an Israelite against his lord, he is at his mercy."[67] In the cities, the Jews were not better off. A 19th century traveller writes: "the Israelite merchants are endlessly subjected to a most ruinous system of plunder. Customs tariffs are arbitrarily doubled, tripled or even multiplied tenfold, without any hope of obtaining justice from higher authority."[68]

And since the testimony of a Jew was inadmissable in a Muslim court and his oath invalidated by a Muslim's[69] – the Jew could scarcely hope for redress for the attacks and accusations he suffered. A constant threat and source of particular insecurity for Jews under Muslim rule was the accusation that a Jew had blasphemed Islam or Muhammad – a crime punishable by death. Even under the enlightened rule of Muhammad Bey, an innocent Tunisian Jew, Batto Sfez, was executed on the basis of just such an accusation (1857). The first instance *ever* in Syria of a Muslim executed for the murder of a Jew occurred once in 1869 and, writes the English consular agent in Damascus, "the Muslims, considering themselves much degraded by being placed on an equal footing even, as they say, with the Jews, . . . have betrayed a feeling of repressed rage."[70]

How did the centuries of arbitrary treatment and reinforced second-class status – institutionalized degradation – affect the Jews?

"The humiliations that accompanied the status of *dhimmi* were accepted by the Jews as inescapable realities of life – . . . the customary degradations, the blows administered in passing, the deliberate jostling, the swallowed insults."[71] Arminius Vambèry is even more unambiguous: "I do not know of any more miserable, helpless and pitiful individual on God's earth than the Yahudi in those countries . . . The poor Jew is despised, belaboured, and tortured by Muslims, Christians and Brahmins alike, he is the poorest of the poor."[72]

That the Jews in Muslim lands were often able, despite their precarious and humiliating status, to develop and maintain a lively culture and contribute to their environment is a tribute to their tenaciousness and unquenchable spirit and to occasional periods of less stringent application of the Covenant of 'Umar and its variations under moderate Muslim rulers; but the myth of that golden "interfaith Utopia" is just a myth.

*Arab oppression of Jews is* not, *therefore, a post-1948 phenomenon. It is rooted in Islam and has been an inescapable characteristic of the relations between Muslims and Jews since Muhammad's time, 20th century Arab persecution of Jews is only a continuation and intensification of this centuries-long tradition, in which the socially and religiously inferior Jew bore the brunt of the Muslim masses' contempt and the Muslim governments' arbitrary policies and financial troubles.*

There is a difference, however, in the Arabs' attitude toward the Jews in Muslim-Arab countries – as elsewhere – since the Balfour Declaration recognized the rights of Jews to a national home in their ancestral land, which has led to ever more systematic and vicious persecution. "Zionism, and especially the creation of a modern Jewish state within this area, was the last but probably most powerful lever for anti-Jewish animosity."[73] Before the rise of Zionism and the growth of the Yishuv in Palestine, the Arabs had generally recognized the right of Jews living under their rule to life, livelihood and the practice of religion – though only under the conditions and restrictions the Arabs imposed.[74] Their attitude was one of derision, at worst contempt, the attitude of masters toward their slaves.[75] The modern Muslim Arab regimes – notably Syria, Iraq, Egypt and Libya – have systematically undermined the Jews' means of earning a livelihood by restricting the types of jobs they can work at or train for and by instituting boycotts of Jewish establishments and professional people; they have practically destroyed Jewish religious and communal life by restricting its organizational activities and demolishing or confiscating its buildings – schools, synagogues, communal institutions; and they have again – especially in Syria and Iraq – engaged in the taking of Jewish lives, whether by public execution on trumped-up charges or by condoning murder, torture and rape of Jews in streets, homes and jails. All of this is accompanied by virulent anti-Jewish hate campaigns in the often government-controlled press and mass media.[76]

This did not all happen at once. How did it begin? And how did it finally assume such proportions that 95% of "Arab Jews" were forced to leave these lands where their ancestors had lived for over 2500 years, often at the risk of their lives and in forfeiture of all their material possessions?

The Government of Iraq began to take specifically anti-Jewish steps practically from the moment of its independence; in 1934 the teaching of Hebrew was prohibited and Jews began to be dismissed from certain government positions and their entry into high schools and universities restricted. Physical attacks on Jews in Baghdad – including murders – became frequent from 1936 on; anti-Jewish propaganda was spread by an openly pro-Nazi and anti-Zionist regime. The tension and "shadowy persecution" erupted into violence in other cities too, where local Muslim leaders used the opportunity to extort money from the Jews. During the 1–2 June 1941, on the Jewish holiday of Pentecost, armed and incited mobs with full government knowledge attacked Jews and Jewish property throughout Baghdad. 170–180 Jews were butchered to death, hundreds were wounded; 14,500 sustained material losses. Police and army joined the rioters and looters.[77]

From 1936 to 1939. Syria served as the headquarters of the Palestine

Arab High Command and its anti-Jewish propaganda centre; this was intensified after a 1937 visit of Nazi officers. Anti-Jewish demonstrations and attacks, including fatal stabbings of Jews in the streets of Damascus, became more and more frequent from 1938 on; the Jewish quarter was twice attacked by mobs in 1944.[78]

In Egypt, certain nationalist parties began to lobby for a boycott against the Jews in 1938; in July 1939, bombs were discovered in three Cairo synagogues (before they exploded) wrapped with warnings to the Jews not to support their co-religionists in Palestine.[79]

"From 1933 onwards, the spread of anti-Jewish propaganda among the Arabs was no longer left to chance or to private enterprise. Nazi Germany made a truly immense effort in the Arab countries and won many converts. This work was continued by Nazi emigres after the war."[80] In 1934 Nazi-inspired anti-Semitic incitement led directly to the pogrom in Constantine, Algeria, which left 25 dead, scores injured and homes, shops and property pillaged.[81]

Between the end of World War II – during which the ever-vulnerable Jews had suffered from Vichy legislation in Morocco, Tunisia, Algeria and Syria and from Axis occupations of Tunisia and Libya – and 1948, the situation of Jews in Arab lands dramatically worsened. In 1945, the year that saw the founding of the Arab League, in Egypt (on 2 Nov.) and in Lybia (on 4–7 Nov.) there were mass anti-Jewish riots, accompanied by plundering of Jewish homes, shops, synagogues and communal buildings. In Tripoli at least 120 Jews were slaughtered and hundreds wounded; the riots spread to other towns as well. In Syria, where the campaign of terror against the Jews was gaining momentum, Muslim religious leaders telegraphed Allied leaders threatening a Holy War against the Jews if immigration to Palestine were not stopped.[82] The Alliance school assistant headmaster in Damascus was murdered in June,[83] a mob broke into the Great Synagogue in Aleppo (18 Nov.).

When, in 1947, the Iraqi Foreign Minister, Muhammad Fadhil Bey al-Jamali, told the UN Committee on Palestine that the fate of the Jews in Muslim countries was dependent on developments in Palestine, he was only stating what was already accepted in practice. The Egyptian delegate to the UN, Haykhal Pasha, declared (on 24 Nov. 1947) that Arab governments would do their best to protect the Jews, but, he added ominously, "We are all aware that mob fury is often stronger than the police."[84] On 25 Nov. 1947, the *N.Y. Times* reported him as saying, "The United States which has not been able altogether to suppress outbursts of racial passion in the form of lynching – will appreciate that with the best will in the world the Near Eastern governments might not be able to control the infuriated Muslims." The Syrian delegate, Faris al-Khuri, was more direct: "Unless the Palestine problem is settled, we shall have difficulty in protecting and safeguarding the Jews in the Arab world" (*N.Y. Times*, 19 Feb. 1947).

"With the entire Arabic press fulminating against the perfidy of Zionism and with Arab politicians rousing their underfed and enervated masses to a dangerous pitch of hysteria, the threats were certainly not empty."[85] In December of the same year, in Aleppo, an unknown number of Jews was butchered to death by mobs that burned four big synagogues, 14 smaller ones and destroyed 150 homes. Damage was estimated at $2.5 million.[86] Prior to this, the death penalty was imposed for emigration to Palestine, the Jewish community was forced to proclaim its opposition to Zionism and Jews were arrested and tortured by police for no apparent reason. "All this was accompanied by governmental restrictions on the movement of Jews, denial of governments jobs, withholding of licences, making virtually impossible admission to schools, prohibiting acquisition of land or the opening of commercial establishments, engaging in any trade or disposing of property."[87] The Jews of Syria were completely paralyzed, isolated and terrified by the close of the year.

This process was the beginning of the end of Jewish communities in Muslim lands – not only in Syria. In December 1947, in Aden, a bloody pogrom left 82 dead, more wounded, and the remaining Jews with only the remnants of a community – two Jewish schools, 4 synagogues, 220 homes, 110 (out of 170 )shops had been looted and burned. The community was in shock – their means of livelihood wiped out within three days.[88]

In 1948, with the proclamation of the State of Israel and the Arab armies' invasion of the new State, arrests of Jews (Egypt: 14–15.V.48; Iraq, Syria), interrogations, beatings (Egypt, Iraq, Syria) sequestration of property (Egypt 30.V.48), forced contributions to the Arab war funds (Cairo Jewry: £E. 40,000; Alexandria: £E. 60,000; Damascus: £S. 10,000; Baghdad: 500,000 dinars), restrictions on movement of Jews (especially emigration) (Egypt: 25.V.48, 26.VII.48; Iraq: 15.V.48; Syria: mid-1947) and anti-Jewish outbreaks characterized almost all Muslim countries. Despite government warnings and precautions, bloody riots broke out against the Jews in Oujda and Djerada, Morocco, in June, 1948. In Oujda, within three hours, five had been killed, 30 seriously injured, shops and homes sacked. In Djerada the

Jewish population of 100 suffered 39 deaths and 30 severely wounded, the remainder less seriously.[89] An unofficial popular economic boycott against Morocco's Jews was begun. A few days later, the Jewish quarter, the *hara*, in Tripoli was attacked; "Muslim gangs poured through, ... killing young and old, women and children hacking to pieces the bodies of their victims."[90] On June 20, the Jewish quarter of Cairo was shaken by explosions which left 34 dead and 60 injured; four blocks of Jewish-occupied tenements lay in rubble. From then on, bomb outrages occurred in July, September, October and November, leaving at least 38 dead, 137 injured and much Jewish property destroyed, including large department stores. Attacks and rape of Jews in the streets went on for a week while Egyptian security forces did nothing; only repeated foreign protests and threats compelled the government to bring the rioting to an end.[91] In Iraq, aside from dismissing Jews from all Government departments and prohibiting Jewish banks to transact with foreign countries, the government left the anti-Jewish campaign to the police and the military, who took full advantage of their opportunities for blackmail. Many Jews arrested for "Zionist activities" (including the possession of a map of the Holy Land in a Bible) or "economic crimes" were used by the government to finance its war effort – all fines were to be paid to the Ministry of Defence. The execution of a Jewish millionaire by courtmartial sentence enriched the Government by £5,000,000.[92] When Iraq Jews were suddenly allowed one year to register for emigration if they forefeited their citizenship (Law No. 1,3.III.1950), the termination of this period was the beginning of government measures to speed up seizure of property of the denationalized Jews (Law No. 5, 10.III.51 and 22.III.51).[93]

As the North African Muslim countries began to receive their independence, the Jews – who had suffered in the often bloody struggles which preceded it – began to be squeezed out of the economy, replaced and boycotted by the Muslims.[94] The new governments' ties with the Arab League and their policies of Islamization and nationalization left no place for ethnically distinct and economically active Jewish communities.[95] Rabbinical tribunals and community councils were dissolved in the name of "national unity" (Iraq, 1958; Syria, December 1949; Egypt, 1960; Tunisia, July 1958; Libya, 1958); ancient synagogues, cemeteries and quarters were destroyed for urban renewal (Tunisia 1958). Libya forced its Jews to cut their ties with Israel and Jewish organizations abroad in 1951 when it became independent; in 1964, their right to vote was rescinded, postal ties with Israel cut and they were forbidden to hold public office.[96]

The Six-Day War marked another turning point in the deteriorating situation of the Jews in Muslim countries. The War itself set off anti-Jewish riots in Tunisia, Algeria, Libya (where they were especially bloody) and Aden;[97] these and the growing hatred for the Jews in Morocco caused many to flee to Israel, Europe and the Americas. In Egypt there were mass arrests of Jews, including the sick and the elderly, some of whom were not released until 1970, after three years of torture and degradation. Some were released directly from jail to the airport, given 30 minutes to bid farewell to their families, made to sign a renunciation of all property and of their citizenship and expelled, taking only their meagre personal belongings with them.[98] In Syria and in Iraq, the War also meant mass arrests, torture, growing insecurity and virulent governmental anti-Jewish campaigns, praising the murder and persecution of the Jews, taking out on their helpless Jewish hostages their anger at being defeated. Muslim religious leaders also gave legitimization to the extermination of Jews in Arab countries in the name of Islam. At the World Islamic Congress (Amman, Jordan, 22 September 1967) it was resolved:

> *Jews in Arab Countries*: The Congress is certain that the Jewish communities living in Islamic countries do not appreciate the Moslems' good treatment and protection over the centuries. ... The Congress declares that the Jews residing in Arab countries who contact the Zionist circles or the State of Israel do not deserve the protection and care which Islam provides for the free non-Moslem subjects living in Islamic countries. Moslem Islamic Governments should treat them as aggressive combatants. Similarly, the Islamic peoples, individually and collectively, should boycott them and treat them as deadly enemies.[99]

As early as 1950, Ismat, an Arab author, had warned, "Let no one advice us to exonerate from Zionism the Jews in the Arab countries who pretend to be innocent, no matter how wretched and degraded they appear to be, for they are Zionists like the rest of the Jews of the world ... If they conceal their Zionism for a while, they will reveal it at a suitable opportunity ... They are nothing but a fifth column in every country."[100] This theme of Jews as a fifth column was picked up by governments and media [101] after the Six-Day War and used to legitimize the dismissals, persecutions, arrests and executions of the Jews remaining in Arab countries such as the hangings in Iraq in January and August 1969.

Since 1967, even more stringent restrictions have been in force, especially in Syria and Iraq. In Syria the impoverished community is not allowed to own telephones, radios, send or receive mail from the outside world, move more than 3 kilometers from their homes. Palestinian terrorists and secret police have been moved into the Jewish quarter where they harass, attack and rape the Jews with impunity. In Aleppo, an Arab whose brother had fallen in the '73 war entered the home of a Jew and shot him to death before his family the murderer, who is well-known, has not been arrested. A government boycott of Jewish merchants is in effect since 1967; Jewish doctors and tradesmen are allowed to deal only with Jews. Jews are allowed only an elementary education in schools run and staffed by Muslims; there is no future for the youth.[102]

In Iraq, too, the Jewish community is also economically paralyzed, unable to withdraw more than a small sum each month, under constant surveillance – politically, physically and mentally crippled. An Iraqi Jew (who escaped) writes in his diary on February 1970 – "Ulcers, heart attacks and breakdowns are increasingly prevalent among the Jews ... The dehumanization of the Jewish personality resulting from continuous humiliation and torment ... have dragged us down to the lowest level of our physical and mental facilities, and deprived us of the power to recover."[103] Recently, the government decided to allow Jews over 65 or under 15 years to emigrate – on payment of an exit tax of £1,500 a person; few can afford this. Cases of murder of Jews have been reported. As in Syria, the Jews are allowed no contact with the outside world.[104]

In June 1967, the UN Security Council passed Resolution 237, which empowered the Secretary-General to send a special Representative to the Middle East with the task of inquiring into the welfare of civilians in the wake of the war. U Thant informed the Representative, Dr. Nils Gussing of Sweden, that this included investigation of treatment of Jewish minorities in Arab countries as well as Arabs in Israeli-occupied territory. Egypt, Syria and Iraq *refused* to allow that first mission – or a second one in April 1968 – to include their countries in the investigation.[105]

## IV. Conclusion

Even though the Jews of the Middle East belong to the area as much as the Muslims themselves, the domination of the latter has never allowed them to exist in conditions of anything better than toleration within the framework of discrimination.[106]

Relations between Muslims and Jews could be friendly and cordial. Partnerships were formed and business transacted – indeed, in some areas, the two groups were mutually dependent. The Jews often played an important role in the various countries' economies and in some cases in the political life. Food and dress, customs and beliefs were also shared to a great extent – even certain revered saints' tombs were sometimes venerated in common. Muslims rulers and religious leaders – who were the source of the humilating decrees and the instigators of anti-Jewish violence or destruction of property – sometimes went to great lengths to protect "their" Jews. But the legacy and legal framework of discrimination were there. The Covenant of 'Umar regulations which inspired all successive Muslim legislation down to modern times "aimed to convince every Muslim that the Jew was part of some unimportant sub-species that it was necessary to accept and respect to a certain degree in order to remain faithful to the teaching of the Prophet."[107]

During the twelve centuries of Muslim domination, the Jews of North Africa and the middle East suffered massacres, forced conversions, arbitrary confiscations and taxation, attacks, accusations, humilating legislation and the contempt of the Muslim masses as a result of their inferior and precarious status; yet they did not disappear. "The position of the Jews . . . under traditional Muslim rule certainly fell a long way short of the interfaith utopia imagined by modern romanticists and apologists, but it was one which enabled them to survive and at times to flourish."[108] Recent Arab persecutions of the Jews, however, finding legitimization in Islam, fired by xenophobic nationalism, and nourished by intensive and eclectic anti-Semitic propaganda,[109] have made it impossible for Jews to survive – much less flourish – in most Muslim countries. ". . . The old tolerance has gone, the new equality has proved a fraud."[110] In certain countries the regimes were directly responsible for the dissemination of inflammatory propaganda and for the deterioration of the political, economic and social position of the Jews, who found themselves the object of increasing restrictions and vilification and suffered from frequent and vicious attacks by the incited mobs.

Even in those few countries where the government was sympathetic, it could not guarantee the Jews complete security from mob attacks or from nationalization and economic reforms which left little place for the Jews. The Jews also saw what was happening to other non-Muslim, non-Arab minority groups in the independent Arab states. "The very first year of Iraq's full sovereignty was marked by a massacre of the Assyrians (1933) ... This was followed by expeditions against the Kurds and the persecution of the small Yezedi people who for centuries had lived in the mountains of northern Iraq."[111] The half-million Kurds in Syria have been stripped of their citizenship since 1962 and suffered many disabilities in consequence.

European settlers had been the object of anti-foreigner riots in Egypt as early as the 19th century. Even native Arab Christians could write that: "they have no future in a country which is becoming all the time more socialistic and totalitarian. Their children are indoctrinated in the schools, where the syllabus is devoted more and more to Islam and their faith is in danger. Debarred increasingly from public office ... robbed of the property of their parents and unable to engage in profitable business ... how can they survive?"[112]

Since 1959 between 500,000 and 600,000 non-Muslim Negroes of the Southern Sudan have been slaughtered by the Muslim Arabs of the North (with the help of Egypt) in a "colonialist" attempt, as Arnold Toynbee said, "to impose themselves, their religion, language and culture on a non-Arab African people that wants to be itself and does not want to be dominated."[113] All minorities in the Muslim Arab countries are in danger – or at best – in a difficult position.

For the Jews, however, the intensification of Arab persecution and developing Arab nationalism coincided with the re-establishment of Jewish autonomy in the Jewish people's ancient homeland. The Jews in Muslim countries, knowing full well that "no Muslim state, however 'liberal' it would like to be, ... could so depart from the line of conduct followed in the past and ... pursued at present, as to allow its Jews anything but a status of 'protection' forever ... and in no way a status of integration ..."[114] these Jews in some cases faced with expulsion or economic, social, political – and physical – extinction, finally had somewhere they could escape to; uprooted from the lands of their birth, they could return to the land of their forefathers. Within a generation, these 2,500-year-old communities have all but disappeared, the handful of Jews left in Syria. Egypt, Iraq and Libya suffering a slow death-in-life, as hostages of the governments, and scapegoats for the inequalities of the regimes and the ire of the incited masses.

## REFERENCES

Alon, Dafna. *Arab Racialism*. Jerusalem: Publishing House, 1969.
Ashtor, E. *Toledof Hayehudim B'mitzrayim uv-Suria* (Heb) (History of the Jews in Egypt & Syria). Jerusalem: Mossad Harav Kook, Vol. I, 1947: Vol. II, 1950; Vol. III, 1970.
Ben Yaakov, Avraham, *K'varim K'doshim B'bavel* (Heb.). (Revered Tombs in Babylonia). Jerusalem: Mossad Harav Kook, 1973.
—. *Kitzur Toledot Yehudei Bavel* (Heb.). (Abridged Version of the History of Babylonia). Jerusalem: Reuben Mass, 1971.
—. *Yehudei Bavel* (Heb.). (The Jews of Babylonia). Jerusalem: Ben Zvi Institute, Hebrew University, Kiryat Sefer, 1965.
Berger, Monroe. *The Arab World Today*. Garden City, N.Y.: Doubleday & Co., 1962.
Chouraqui, Andre. *Marche vers l'occident – Les Juifs d'Afrique du Nord*, Paris: Presses Universitaires de France, 1952.
Cohen, Hayim J. *Hayehudim B'artzot Hamizrah Harikhon B'Yamenu*. (Hebrew). (The Jews in the Middle East in our Days). Jerusalem: Institute of Contemporary Jewry, Hebrew University, 1973.
Fischel, Walter. *Jews in the Economic & Political Life of Medieval Islam*, New York: Ktav Publishing House, Inc., 1969.
—. *Unknown Jews in Unknown Lands, The Travels of Rabbi David d'Beth Hillel* 1823–1832. New York: Ktav Publishing House, 1973.
Gilbert, Martin, *The Arab-Israeli Conflict: Its History in Maps*. London: Weidenfeld & Nicolson, 1974.
—. *Jewish History Atlas*. London, Weidenfeld & Nicolson, 1973.
Goitein, S. D. *Jews and Arabs; Their Contacts through the Ages*. New York: Schocken Books, 1964.
—. *Studies in Islamic History & Institutions*. Leiden: E. J. Brill, 1968.
Grunebaum, G. E. von. *Classical Islam: A History 600 AD-1258 AD*. Chicago: Aldine Publishing Company, 1970.
—. *Medieval Islam*. Chicago, University of Chicago Press, 1945.
Harkabi, Y. *Arab Attitudes Toward Israel*. Jerusalem: Israel Universities Press.
—. *Ha-amana Hapalestinait U'mashmauta* (Heb.). (The Palestinian Covenant and its Significance). Jerusalem: Ministry of Education, 1971.
—. *Kaitzad Husbera Ha'emda Ha'aravit Negred Yisrael Batzava Hamitzri* (Heb.). (How the Arab Case against Israel was Explained in the Egyptian Army). Israel Defense Ministry, 1967.
Hirschberg, H. Z. (Ed.) *Mimizrah U'mima'arav* (Heb.). (From East and West). Ramat-Gan: Bar-Ilan University, 1974.
—. *Toledot Hayehudim B'afrika Hatzefonit* (Heb.). (The History of Jews in North Africa). Jerusalem: Mossad Bialik, 1965.
—. *Yisrael B'arav* (Heb.). (Israel in Arabia). Tel-Aviv: Mossad Bialik and Massada, 1946.
Landshut, *S. Jewish Communities in the Muslim Countries of the Middle East; a survey*. London: The Jewish Chronicle, 1950.

Lane-Poole, Stanley. *A History of Egypt in the Middle Ages*. London: Methuen & Co., 1936.
Lestchinsky, Jacob. *Jewish Migration for the Past Hundred Years*. New York: YIVO Institute, 1944.
Lewis, Bernard. *Islam in History*. New York: Library Press, 1973.
—. *Race and Color in Islam*. New York: Harper & Row, 1971.
—. *The Arabs in History*. New York: 1966. Harper & Row.
Parkes, James. *Antisemitism; a concise world history*. Chicago: Quadrangle Books, 1963.
—. *A History of Palestine from 135 AD to Modern Times*. New York: Oxford University Press, 1949.
Robinson, Nehemiah. *The Arab Countries of the Near East and their Jewish Communities*. New York: Institute of Jewish Affairs, 1951.
—. *Convention Relating to the Status of Refugees; its history, significance and contents*. New York: Institute of Jewish Affairs, World Jewish Congress.
Sawdayee, Max. *All Waiting to Be Hanged: Iraq Post-Six Day War Diary*. Tel Aviv: 1974.
Schechtman, Joseph B. *Population Transfers in Asia*. New York: Hallsby Press, 1949.
—. *On Wings of Eagles: The Plight, Exodus and Homecoming of Oriental Jewry*. New York: Thomas Yoseloff, 1961.
—. *The Refugee in the World: Displacement and Integration*. New York: Thomas Yoseloff, Ltd., 1963.
Yahudiya Masriya. *Les Juifs en Egypte*. Geneva: Editions de l'Avenir, 1971.

*Articles*

Friedman, Saul S. "The Myth of Arab Toleration," *Midstream*, January, 1970.

*Yearbooks*

*American Jewish Year Book*. New York: American Jewish Committee.
*Encyclopedia Judaica*
*Jewish Year Book*. London: Jewish Chronicle Publications.
*United Nations Demographic Yearbook*.

*Newspapers*

*Al Huda*, June 6, 1951.
*Al-Tahrir*, March 25, 1953.
*Beirut Telegraph*. Interview with Mr. Emile Ghoury. Sept. 6, 1948.
*Cairo Daily Akhbar*.
*Neue Zuercher Zeitung*. "Conservations with Palestine Refugees." Sept. 19, 1958.
*Utah Herald*. "Comments on Mideast Issues." May 4, 1975.

## Notes

1. Based on: official census of each country; yearbooks of the Jewish communities: The Jewish Case Before The Anglo-American Inquiry; Hayyim Cohen, 1952 and 1973; David Sitton, 1974; Andre Chouraqui, 1952; Joseph B. Shechtman, 1961; David Littman, 1975.
2. Government of Israel. Central Bureau of Statistics, 1975. This figures does not, of course, include Jews from the non-Arab countries of Islam, e.g. Iran, Turkey or those from Kurdistan.
3. *Ibid.*
4. Government of Israel, *Statistical Abstract*, 1974 (Jerusalem: Central Bureau of Statistics, 1974).
5. Government of Israel, *Immigration to Israel*, 1948–1972 (Jerusalem: Central Bureau of Statistics, 1974).
6. *Statistical Abstract*, 1974, *op. cit.*
7. Central Bureau of Statistics, 1974.
8. Joseph B. Schechtman, *On Wings of Eagles*, p. 273.
9. American Jewish Congress, *Jewish Communities in the World*, p. 48 (Heb.).
10. *Ibid.*, p. 12–13.
11. *Ibid.*, p. 13.
12. *Ibid.*, p. 74.
13. Schechtman, *op. cit.*, p. 132.
14. *Ibid.*, p. 143.
15. American Jewish Congress, *op. cit.*, p. 47.
16. Schechtman, *op. cit.*, p. 104.
17. Government of Israel, *Immigration to Israel 1948–1972* (Jerusalem: Central Bureau of Statistics, 1974), p. 4.
18. *Ibid.*, p. 2.
19. Raphael Patai, *Between East and West*, p. 207–208.
20. Jewish Agency, *Report of the Executive Submitted to the 24th Zionist Congress 1951–1955* (Jerusalem: Zionist Organization, 1955), p. 147.
21. Lewis, Bernard. *Islam in History*, p. 143.
22. Quoted in Harkabi, Y. *Arab Attitudes Israel*, p. 218.
23. Parkes, James. *A History of Palestine*, p. 253: "It might indeed be said of the Turkish authorities that they exhibited the toleration of indifference when suitably paid to do so. But, apart from this, the legend of good treatment of the (Christian and) Jewish minorities has no support in the Muslim history of the last thousand years ..."
24. Von Grunebaum, G. E. "Eastern Jewry under Islam – Reflections on Medieval Anti-Judaism," *Viator*, vol. 2. 1971 quoted in Littman, D. "Jews and Arabs – Myths and Realities," p. 4.
25. Berger, Morroe. *The Arab World*, p. 251.
26. Lewis, Bernard. *The Arabs in History*, p. 31–32. *Encyclopedia Judaica*, vol. II p. 235.
27. Landshut, Siegfried. *Jewish Communities in the Muslim Countries of the Middle East*, p. 4.
28. Landshut, *op. cit.*, p. 5.
29. Von Grunebaum, *Medieval Islam*, p. 178.
30. Chouraqui, *Between East and West*, p. 47.
31. Landshut. *op. cit.*, p. 6. Robinson, Nehemiah, *The Arab Countries of the Near East and their Jewish Communities*, p. 50–51.

32. Chouraqui. *op. cit.*, p. 47.
33. Landshut, *op. cit.*, p. 5.
34. Mann. J. *The Jews in Egypt and Palestine*, p. 13–14 quoted in Yahudiya Masriya, *Les Juifs en Egypte*, p. 14.
35. Chouraqui, *op. cit.*, p. 46–47.
36. Yahudiya Masriya, *op. cit.*, p. 15. Ben-Yaakov, *Kitzur Toldot Yehudai Bavel*, p. 59–60.
37. Yahudiya Masriya, *op. cit.*, p. 19. *Ency. Jud.*, vol. XV, p. 640.
38. *Ibid.*, p. 19. Friedman, Saul. "The Myth of Arab Tolerance" in *Midstream*, January 1970, p. 58.
39. Lane-Poole. *History of Egypt* in the Middle Ages, p. 301.
40. Ashtor, E. *Toldot Hayehudim be'Mizraim u'v'Suria*, vol. I, p. 321.
41. World Jewish Congress, *The Jews of French Morocco and Tunisia*, p. 7.
42. Chouraqui, *Between East and West*, p. 119.
43. Goitein, *Jews and Arabs*, p. 74.
44. Cohen, Hayyim J. *The Jews of the Middle East* (Heb.), p. 63–64.
45. Friedman, *op. cit.*, p. 58.
46. Israel Museum, *Hayei Haychudim B'Morocco*, p. 8. Harari, *Toldot Yehudai Al-Maghreb*, pp. 35–36.
47. Israel Museum, *Hayei Hayehudim B'Morocco*, p. 9–10.
48. Hirschberg, *A History of the Jews of North Africa* (Heb.), vol. I, p. 291.
49. Martin Gilbert, *The Jews under Arab and Muslim Rule*, map of Morocco.
50. Ben-Yaakov, *op. cit.*, p. 85.
51. *Ency. Jud.*, vol. II, p. 615.
52. Information Briefing No. 19, Foreign Ministry.
53. Chouraqui, *Between East and West*, p. 51–2. *Ency. Jud.* vol. II, p. 612.
54. Chouraqui, *op. cit.*, p. 51.
55. Fischel, Walter. *Jews in the Economic and Political Life of Medieval Islam*, p. XV.
56. *Ency. Jud.* vol. II, p. 615 and *Hayei Hayehudim B'Morocco*, p. 10.
57. *Ency. Jud.* vol. XV, p. 640. Yahudiya Masriya, *op. cit.*, p. 23; Ashtor, *op. cit.*, vol. I, pp. 258–259.
58. Ben-Yaakov, *op. cit.*, p. 59–60 and p. 81.
59. *Ency. Jud.*, vol. XVI, p. 743.
60. Robinson, *op. cit.*, p. 50. Yahudiya Masriya, *op. cit.*, p. 26.
61. Ben Yaakov, *op. cit.*, p. 58.
62. *Hayei Hayehudim B'Morocco*, p. 11.
63. Ben Yaakov, *op. cit.*, p. 60.
64. *Yahudiya Masriya*, p. 28.
65. *Ibid.*, p. 26.
66. Chouraqui, *op. cit.*, p. 115.
67. *Ibid.*, p. 118.
68. Joseph Halevy, quoted in Schwarzfuchs, S. "Persecution of Jews in the Lands of Islam" (from *L'Arche*, Deventer 1973), p. 9.
69. Robinson, *op. cit.*, p. 50. Goitein, *Jews and Arabs*, p. 72.
70. C. Wood to Elliot, F-O. 195/927 No. 16, Damascus Oct. 1, 1869 in Ma'oz, *Mekorot Letoldot Yehudai Suria v Eretz Israel Bameah Ha*-19, pp. 46–50.
71. Chouraqui, *op. cit.*, p. 50.
72. *The Story of My Struggles*, p. 395 quoted in Lewis, *Islam in History*, p. 3.
73. Robinson, *op. cit.*, p. 53.
74. Lewis, *op. cit.*, p. 164.
75. H.E.W. Young. British Vice Counsul in Mosul (1909). *Middle Eastern Studies*, vol. VII, (1971) p. 232. "The attitude of the Moslems towards the Christians and Jews is that of a master towards slaves whom he treats with a certain

lordly tolerance so long as they keep their place. Any sign of pretension to equality is promptly repressed."

76. "The sharpening of the conflict since 1948 has been accompanied by an increase in manifestations of anti-Semitism in literature and press" (Harkabi, *op. cit.*, p. 229). "Since the creation of the State of Israel, anti-Semitic propaganda has not needed to be imported from Europe" (Berger, *The Arab World*, p. 262).
77. Cohen, Hayyim J. *The Jews of the Middle East* (Heb.), p. 33–35.
79. *Ibid.*, p. 49–50.
79. *Ibid.*, p. 52.
80. Lewis, *Islam in History*, p. 144.
81. Chouraqui, *op. cit.*, p. 153.
82. *Ibid.*, p. 58.
83. Landshut, *op. cit.*, p. 58.
84. *Ibid.*, p. 26.
85. *Ibid.*, p. 26.
86. Robinson, *op. cit.*, p. 77.
87. *Ibid.*, p. 77–78.
88. Landshut, *op. cit.*, p. 13. The locally-raised police force took part in the looting and rioting.
89. Chouraqui, *op. cit.*, p. 181–182.
90. *Ibid.*, p. 182.
91. Landshut, *op. cit.*, p. 34–38.
92. *Ibid.*, p. 48–51.
93. Robinson, *op. cit.*, p. 61–67.
94. Schechtman, J. *On Wings of Eagles*, p. 316–317.
95. Chouraqui, *op. cit.*, p. 281–284.
96. Ma'ariv and W.J.C., *Hakehillot Hayehudiot Ba-'Olam*, p. 44.
97. *Ibid.*, pp. 74, 12, 44, 54.
98. Alon, Dafna. *Arab Racialism*, p. 76; *International Conference for the Deliverance of Jews in the Middle East*, pp. 32, 67, 79.
99. Students' Committee for Human Rights in the Middle East, *Persecution of Jews in Arab Lands*, p. 11.
100. 'Ismat, 'Abd al-Rahman Sami, *al-Sahyuniyya wa-alMasuniyya* (Arabic), (*Zionism and Freemasonry*), pp. 49–59.
101. Students' Committee for Human Rights in the Middle East, *op. cit.*, pp. 11–12.
102. Ministry of Education and Culture, *Metzukat Hayehudim B'Artzot Arav*, p. 11.
103. Sawdayee, Max. *All Waiting to Be Hanged*, p. 115.
104. Ma'ariv and W.J.C., *op. cit.*, p. 56.
105. Students' Committee for Human Rights in the Middle East. *op. cit.*, p. 5–6.
106. Landshut, *op. cit.*, p. 23.
107. Chouraqui, *op. cit.*, p. 47.
108. Lewis, *Islam in History*, p. 165.
109. "During the last twenty years a vast anti-Jewish – not merely anti-Zionist or anti-Israeli – literature has appeared in the Arab countries, in which racial theological and demonological themes, as well as political arguments are used." ... Lewis, *Ibid.*, p. 317. "Religious motives are exploited to strengthen and deepen the hatred of Israel and the Jews ..." Harkabi, *op. cit.*, p. 263.
110. Lewis, *op. cit.*, p. 145.
111. Schechtman, *op. cit.*, p. 91.
112. Lewis, *op. cit.*, p. 15.
113. Israel Government Ministry for Foreign Affairs, Information Brief no. 213, 19.9.75. p. 2.
114. Vajdia, Georges. Quoted in Littman, *op. cit.*, p. 8–9.

# Malaysia's Forgotten People: Education, Cultural Identity and Socio-Economic Mobility among South Indian Plantation Workers

N. J. COLLETTA

NAT COLLETTA earned his Ph.D. from Michigan State University in sociology and comparative education. While at Michigan State he worked in the Institute for International Studies in Education. His experiences in education range from working with migrant farm workers' children in the early sixties to teaching in the inner city schools of Buffalo to two years of service in the Peace Corps in Micronesia. Later he returned to Micronesia to do field research among the Ponapeans of the Eastern Caroline Islands. He has lectured at the University of Missouri and the Science University of Malaysia, where he recently spent one year as a Visiting Fulbright Hayes Lecturer in Education and Society. While in Malaysia, he also conducted fieldwork on the education of plantation workers' children. He is currently lecturing in the area of comparative education at the State University of New College at Buffalo.

# Malaysia's Forgotten People: Education, Cultural Identity and Socio-Economic Mobility among South Indian Plantation Workers

N. J. COLLETTA

Throughout the last century two raw materials, rubber and tin, have dominated Malaysia's economy. As early as 1916 rubber exports began to surpass tin, and have continued increasingly to reign as the central commodity underpinning the Malaysian economy. In 1962, Pan-Malayan rubber output reached a level of 752,000 tons as compared with 547,000 tons in 1940, while in the tinindustry, the output dropped from 83,000 tons in 1940 to 59,000 tons in 1962 (Lim 1967).

Although the scientific and economic aspects of rubber production have been exhaustively studied from a managerial perspective, little attention has been given to the labour force which contributes to the prosperity of Malaysia's rubber economy in the modern world. While rubber products are highly visible in the urban centres of Malaysia and throughout the world, the hands that so diligently tap thousands of trees daily remain hidden from the public eye in isolated pockets of rural poverty scattered throughout Malaysia's interior.

It is the aim of this paper to shed light on the conditions of the Indian estate labour force with particular reference to the complex inter-relationship of education, cultural identity, and social mobility. Education is the focus of this paper because of the author's belief that schooling has become the principal mechanism for either insuring socialization into the estate class structure, or for providing social mobility from that environment into the larger Malaysian society.

The primary data from which this paper is written emanate from the work of a seven-member, multi-racial Malaysian research team.[1] Their efforts were directed at exploring the problems of educating

---

Originally published in *Contributions to Asian Studies* (Gen. Ed. K. Ishwara), Vol. 7: *Pluralism in Malaysia: Myth and Reality. A symposium on Singapore and Malaysia*, edited by Judith A. Nagata. (Brill, Leiden, 1975).

plantation workers' children through an in depth case analysis of one rubber estate in Kedah, West Malaysia. Pulau Estate was chosen primarily on the basis of its representativeness of the broader population of estates throughout Malaysia, and secondarily because of the management's willingness and cooperation in undertaking the project on the estate premises.[2]

The methodological emphasis was on a qualitative research model which encouraged the estate population under study to construct and relate their own definition of estate reality, with special reference to estate education. Supportive quantitative data in the form of socio-economic and demographic information were also collected. The traditional social anthropological techniques of intensive interviewing, participant observation ,and the maintenance of diary accounts were utilized over a period of six months (from December 1972 to June 1973) with one intensive three week period of living in the labourer line-sites.[3]

## I. Background

Although the Indians have a long history of crossing the Bay of Bengal from the Coromandel coast of South India first as traders, and later as learned and holy men to sit in the Sultanic courts of Kedah (Ryan 1962), massive Indian immigration to Malaysia was not initiated until the late 1800's under the pressure of British economic exploitation of her colonies' raw materials for transport and conversion into marketable goods in England. These later migrants were not traders, nor learned and holy men, but rather predominantly poor, indentured labourers.

When the British expanded their overseas plantation economy from India and Ceylon into the neighbouring colonies of Burma and Malaysia, they again found a need for a cheap, readily controllable source of labour to work the new plantations. But finding the indigenous Malaysians tied to their lands, the Chinese involved in tin and commerce, Europeans and Blacks distant, unavailable, and unwilling, and the Javanese both difficult and expensive to acquire, the surplus labour of South India became the key to the extension of the British plantation economy in Malaysia (Sandhu 1969). The prevailing British attitude in these early stages of Indian migration was succinctly stated by the late South African statesman, Sir Thomas Hyslop: "We want Indians as indentured labourers but not as free men" (Gordon 1970).

Although the conditions of immigration have changed substantially over the years from indentured, through assisted, to non-assisted independent labour immigration, the working and living conditions on the estates remain sub-standard. As Gordon (1970) observed:

There are 238,070 plantation workers in Malaysia of whom 188,772 with their dependants of 347,974 totalling more than half a million people, work, live, and die, within a fetid, unending, plantation environment, effectively removed from the wider society.

In the 1957 census, of the three hundred thousand gainfully employed Indians in Malaysia, 59.5% were engaged in the primary sector of the Malaysian economy, and 83% of those were employed in the rubber industry (Enloe 1970). This depressed labouring class, along with smallholders, produces 40% of the total export earnings of the nation (P.K.R. 1971). But what percent of those earnings do they share? More central to this paper, what percent can their children hope to share?

With independence has come an increased emphasis on education as a means to realizing the stated objective of a 'just society'. The culturally plural composition of Malaysian society (which in 1970 was 55.5% Malays and aboriginals, 34.1% Chinese, 9.0% Indian and 1.4% other) coupled with the growing evidence of a multi-national political-economic elite[4] replacing the former British colonial hegemony, has made this goal easier to verbalize than to actuate. The emotive nature of this culturally plural setting has further tended to blur the underlying injustices rooted in social class differences by stressing communal disparities.

Although the Razak Report (1956) among others, has sought to redress equal opportunity among the Malaysian masses through educational reform, the fact still remains that rural children, especially those of the plantation environment, regardless of race, have yet to derive maximum benefit from such reforms. They are still underachievers, early leavers, and acquire jobs of low socio-economic status (Murad 1973). Furthermore, in discussing estate Indian children, Ponniah (1970) has contended that, "They possess low levels of aspiration and motivation, low self-esteem and feelings of frustration in the face of environmental insults." The recent National Dropout Study (Murad 1973) tends to verify many of these observations.

As Thompson (1955) found, "There have been few channels of advancement in Malaysia by which Indian labourers could rise into the local middle class. Doctors, lawyers, teachers, and clerks, they claimed, came from the middle class of South India or, with few exceptions, were recruited from descendants of that class in Malaysia." Ampalavanar (1972) supports this in her study of class, caste and ethnicity among Indians in Malaysia, noting that, "The labouring class is generally constituted of the lower castes originating from Madras and Andhra provinces." The more general frustration of the Indian labouring classes comes not simply from the perceived discriminatory practices of the British colonial past and present Malaysian government policy, but rather is a suffering derived from a feeling of what the American welfare scholar, Daniel Moynihan termed 'benign neglect'. In Malaysia, this takes the form of managerial patronage on the estate and general indifference on the part of the government.

Lim's (1967) work on economic development in modern Malaysia has emphasized the impact of the rubber industry on ethnic differentiation while ignoring the effect of that same industry on social class formation. However, in light of the major concerns of this study, it is essential to raise three central questions: First, is socio-economic status in Malaysian society ethnic-specific, or is social class derived from a strict adherence to a particular mode of subsistence? Secondly, are ethnicity and occupation so inextricably linked in present day Malaysia that social class is established through ethnically dominated modes of subsistence? Finally, what is the relationship of education to both social class formation and the preservation of ethnic identity, with particular reference to the children of South Indian plantation labourers?

A review of the data obtained in our intensive enquiry into the institutional process and outcome of vernacular schooling on one multi-cultural rubber plantation, Pulau Estate, will hopefully provide some degree of insight into the above concerns, however presumptuous it might be to attempt to answer these questions fully. In addition to an analysis of the school process, of special relevance to this discussion will be the relationship of Indian estate vernacular schooling to such matters as the preservation of cultural identity (pluralism) and social class formation in Pulau Estate and in the wider Malaysian society. Any comparative analysis will have to await a later comprehensive treatment of each of the estate's communal populations. Before proceeding to a discussion of the Indian community and vernacular education on Pulau Estate, some further historical background of estate structure is in order.

## II. A Brief History of Pulau Estate with Emphasis on the Indian Community and School

Without historical perspective, it is almost impossible to comprehend the complexities of the plantation environment and the relative position of any one group in that environment. In some respects, studying an estate is like putting the whole of Malaysia under a microscope. For the dynamics of estate life partly reflect in miniature those of the larger society.

Pulau Estate came into being in 1939 when Malaysian Securities Ltd., a European owned company, purchased 4,000 acres of land in the state of Kedah, Northern Malaysia. The early efforts of clearing and planting developed into what today is a segment of the 6,000 plus acres of the present site. Although the Labour Code of 1923 stipulated that a school be established on every estate with ten or more children of school age (Wong and Ee 1971), this was not an immediate concern on Pulau Estate.

In 1941, war broke out, the estate was occupied by invading Japanese forces, and all rubber production came to an abrupt halt. During this period until 1945, the estate labour force was put to the task of growing vegetables and fruits to feed both themselves and the occupying Japanese army, large numbers of the rubber trees being laid waste in the process. Many of the Indian males were taken off the estate, never to return, as they were compelled to work on the 'Death Railway' in Thailand. When the war terminated in late 1945, the Japanese were repatriated and Malaysian Securities returned to begin anew the attempts to grow rubber.

The early period of estate history indicates that the labour force consisted almost totally of South Indians, with Chinese being brought in on a contractual basis for periodic tasks such as large-scale land clearing operations. At this period in Malaysian history the Chinese were still preoccupied with tin mining and urban commercial enterprises, the North Indians were emerging as urban professionals, merchants, and money lenders, while the Malays remained attached to small rice plots, fishing, and the government service.

The postwar demand for rubber to replenish depleted military stocks, as well as to meet the growing needs of the automobile industry throughout the western world, meant a thriving business for the Malaysian rubber industry. This prosperity was little felt by the field labourer as profits were quickly siphoned off to England and elsewhere, rarely being reinvested in the labour force. If reinvested in the estate at all, the profits typically went into technological advancements at the neglect of the labourer's human condition. This neglect was to trigger reaction in the form of a vigorous trade union movement of the late 1940's. The National Union of Plantation Workers (NUPW) was quick to decry estate injustices, making canvassing for membership among the labourers a relatively easy chore. On Pulau Estate, as elsewhere, strikes were organized and violence ensued, with several incidents of staff being assaulted by angry workers. The management finally brought the police in to restore order. Several months of hard bargaining between management and union leaders followed, leading to a series of concessions and promises by the management for among other things, an increase in wages, better housing, a proper Indian school and a creche. Previously, the only schooling had consisted of haphazard sessions in the temple with few students attending. The Indian school was in fact established at this time, but other concessions were soon forgotten when in the spring of 1948 a state of emergency was declared throughout Malaysia because of the growing Communist menace.[5]

As a result of the prewar associations of the Malaysian Communist Party with incidents such as the Klang strike of Indian Rubber tappers (Thompson 1955), the Indian plantation trade union movement was readily labelled, 'Communist inspired'. Several leaders were arrested and held in 'unlimited detention', while others were immediately deported to India as 'undesirables'. Thus, at the very moment that the conditions of estate labourers had emerged into the public view, the emergency entered to serve as a handy tool for management to regain its original leverage over the work force. During the remainder of the emergency, union activities were confined to a weak recruitment effort crippled by the stigma of being connected with the Communist cause. Although the Communist propaganda was effective in convincing young Indian tappers to join the terrorist movement of the management's injustices, the "officially admitted" number of Indians participating in terrorist activities in 1949 was less than 1% (Konadapi 1947). Devoid of leadership and labelled Communist sympathizers, the union movement as the lone voice of the plantation labouring masses, became virtually extinct.

To insure control over the local estate populace, a plan of centralized resettlement was initiated within the extent of the estate, as barrack-like housing was erected and scattered homesteads were demolished. The rather graphic term 'line site' was applied to these new quarters which have remained the common estate housing pattern for labourers up to the present. Throughout this period a makeshift Indian school, inaugurated in 1948, was barely functioning with unqualified teachers, multiple grades to one instructor, and sporadic attendance. Through centralized line-site housing, human variability of behaviour was reduced, communication lines were shortened, and the more subtle bureaucratic symptom of dehumanization through standardized treatment ensued. Through this structural change in the labourer's ecological patterning, centralized authority and control were much easier to exercise. In 1948, the owners constructed a factory near the line-site. With the addition of the factory the Pulau Estate labour force began to look even more like an alienated, dispossessed proletariat. Had they not now become part of the faceless mass living in line 1, block 45, cubicle c?

As rubber prices continued to increase during the 1960's and profits began to swell the estate treasury, another 2,000 acres of land was purchased and an extensive replanting scheme was embarked upon. The estate factory plus the new plantings led to a rise in the overall demand for labour. This demand, coupled with the immigration law of 1953 restricting alien labour and the decline of the tin industry, led to more and more Chinese and Malays enlisting in the estate labour force. Soon a town sprang up amidst the rubber, and Pulau Estate began to take shape as a microcosm of the entire culturally plural nation. In essence, a miniature closed society within a greater nation state had evolved. Pulau Estate was even self-sufficient in such fundamental areas as electricity, water, a hospital, and a police force.

In the realm of education, while the Indian community had the only official school, the Malays were now conducting religious classes in a newly constructed *madrasah*. The Chinese estate population, which emigrated chiefly from the mines of Ipoh, brought with them their long tradition of vernacular schooling and soon began holding classes in a portion of the school originally constructed solely for the Indian labourers' children. In short, the roots of Malaysia's plural school system quickly took shape on the plantation as the growth of estate institutions began clearly to reflect the more culturally diverse estate membership.

By 1960, the emergency had faded, but the structural changes on the estate remained. Now, the management not only had the advantage of a highly centralized control system around line-site housing and factory assembly line production, but also the added benefit of a culturally plural labour force which, in the words of one early planter:

> You could then always play one against the other . . . and in case of a strike, you will never be left without labour, for the coolies of one nationality, will think twice before they make terms if they know that you are in a position that you can do without them (Jackson 1964).

The 1960's were not without their dramatic moments in Pulau Estate history. With rubber production stabilizing and the estate population increasing in number and changing in cultural composition, conflict over economic interests was inevitable. In 1969, racial riots in Kuala Lumpur as a result of the national elections[6] led to many Chinese families leaving the estate in fear of living surrounded by Malay villages (*kampongs*). Rumours of rapings of young Chinese tappers by neighbouring Malay *kampong* dwellers became numerous, thus increasing the fear and departure of approximately 100 Chinese labourers from the estate between 1967 and 1970.

In early 1970, when many red identity card holders (non-Malaysian citizens) were given an ultimatum to either stay and wait for Malaysian citizenship or leave the country immediately, an exodus of both Chinese and Indians began. Because of the difficulty of obtaining Malaysian citizenship, many Indians opted to return to their homeland. Strangely, in the case of the Indians, their passage back was partially subsidized by the South Indian Labour Fund, the very same colonial institution which brought their forefathers to Malaysia's plantation frontier in earlier decades.

This period of emigration temporarily relieved the emerging problem of unemployment created by a growing imbalance between estate labour supply and demand. But the Pulau Estate postwar population explosion in conjunction with a stabilizing of the world demand for raw rubber has made estate unemployment a definite problem for the seventies. Ironically, the management has contributed to the growing problem of unemployment, albeit unconsciously, through the creation of an elaborate paternalistic welfare system on the estate. In effect, it is profitable to produce children, at least in the short run, as birth is subsidized not only by an initial M$ 90 allotment, but also by free medical care and maternity leave, followed by another payment of M$ 90. Thus, the estate welfare system has enacted a well hidden incentive system for reproduction and the related problems of unemployment, crime, and racial hostility, an inter-relationship we will touch upon throughout the paper.

As a result of recent government quotas on hiring (with preferential treatment for Malay applicants) many Indian and Chinese youth have found the plantation jobs they thought rightfully theirs by birth in the estate, increasingly being filled by 'outsiders'. This situation has frequently manifested itself in estate inter-racial violence. Questions of territoriality and the right to plantation work are claimed by both cultural groups, particularly those reared in the estate environment, the Indians.

During the past two decades (1950–1970), the history of Indian education on the estate has undergone little 'real' change. Although the National Education Committee produced a major report on education under the assistance of an Oxford consultant (1948), recommending a bilingual Malay-English national language policy for all schools, the recommendations were never implemented. Both the Chinese community through the Fenn-Wu (1951) rebuttal of the report, and the Indian community via the Malaysian Indian Congress (1951) study, presented staunch cultural opposition. Conditions remained stable until the post independence national education reports of Razak (1956) and Talib (1960) which advocated primary schools in each of the vernaculars with the introduction of a common syllabus as a first step toward the utilization of the schools for the establishment of a national identity. But both the transformation of Indian curriculum materials from their former allegiance to India and the limited training of qualified Indian teachers has inhibited the full application of this policy to estate vernacular primary schools.

Since 1970, racial stirrings on Pulau Estate have developed due to the expanding problem of unemployed youth. Although the Chinese and Malay youth also find themselves unemployed in great numbers, in a random sample of fourteen Indian households, it was recorded that for every member employed there were at least four, typically in their teens or early twenties, unemployed.

Two new government vernacular schools, one Indian and one Malay, have recently been constructed adjacent to one another on three acres of purchased estate land. During the course of this research project the activity on the field between the two schools appeared more like that of a demilitarized zone than a primary school playground. It would seem that the function or disfunction of this growing estate vernacular school system is somehow related to the issues of rising unemployment, racial animosity, and the general alienation of youth with "nowhere to go" and "nothing to do".

In this context it is upon the relationship of the Indian vernacular school to the Pulau Estate social structure, with particular reference to problems of cultural identity and social mobility in the larger Malaysian society, that the remainder of this paper will endeavour to focus. But properly to undertake this charge, it is first necessary to survey briefly the present socio-economic structure of Pulau Estate.

## III. The Pulau Estate Socio-Economic Structure

The three dominant cultural groups on the estate comprise respectively: Indians (65%); Malays (20%); and Chinese (15%).[7] At present, according to data on estate immigration, emigration, and birth-death rates, the Malays are increasing at a greater rate than either the Chinese or the Indian estate populations. The average estate nuclear family consists of approximately six members, although any given household may include a transient group of extended relatives, often swelling the household dependants to ten members or more. Sixty-five percent of the estate population is under 21 years of age. This demographic picture further illustrates some of the trends and problems pointed to in the preceding section on estate history, e.g., rising estate unemployment linked to a general population explosion.

Furnivall (1956) stated that in a culturally plural society:

> The community lacks a common social will except perhaps in time of necessity and in issues which effect livelihood ... they mix but do not combine. Each group holds by its own religion its own culture and language, its own ideas and ways. As individuals they meet, but only in the market place, in buying and selling.

It might be further mentioned, that in the case of Pulau Estate, segregated social activities, housing patterns, schools, and work assignments support isolation by ethnic group, social class (as established through estate mode of subsistence) and caste, and all categories from that of the superordinate European manager.[8] Thus, fragmented by ethnic differences, social class, and caste, the estate communal groups find the economic process of rubber production the major source of estate systemic integration.

This pattern of communal division, caste, and systemic economic integration is intertwined within a system of social class stratification directly related to the estate hierarchical economic enterprise. There are at least three distinctly identifiable classes: managerial, staff, and labourer (tappers and weeders).[9] The staff constitute a class slightly above that of the labourers. They receive better housing, higher salaries and other fringe benefits. There is little social interaction between these groups outside exchanges in the market place or on matters related to these divisions, as the children of labourers tend to go to vernacular schools on the estate, drop out early, and replace their fathers in the occupational structure, while children of staff and the management attend English medium schools in the large towns and frequently proceed to gainful employment outside the estate, though some return to replace their fathers at the higher levels.[10] Thus, these class divisions readily solidify into closed strata as the continuity of mode of subsistence between father and son, especially for the labourer, is maintained. It should be further noted that the Indians as a communal group are also delineated into sub-ethnic, (e.g., Tamil, Telugu) and caste, (e.g., Kandu, Pariah) groupings, with the Tamils stressing the transference of caste patterns from the motherland in estate social interactions. As one lower caste informant verified:

To the Indians here caste is important. A person who is of low caste is treated badly on this estate. For example, after a temple feast we give much money like the other people, but we are not served food or treated in the same manner as the others. Many fights arise out of caste differences . . . the lower caste cannot serve food to the higher caste. At a festival if a lower caste person serves food the higher caste will leave. Also when we go to work we keep our food in one place. When we break, the tendal asks one person to go and get the food. If it happens to be a low caste person the people would shout and torment him, saying, 'How dare you touch our food. They will not come and even take a drink from our house.

Another added, "On the way to work in the lorry if one pariah were to accidently touch a Tamil, the Tamil might become very wild and start a fight."

The discrepancy between the European manager's life style (large house on the hill, car), that of the staff (small bungalows, scooter), and that of the labourers (barrack-like line-sites, bicycles) graphically illustrates their socio-economic differentiation and rank in the estate authority structure. It is difficult to locate the Indian teachers in this class hierarchy because although they may have the income and life style of the staff, they come from the labouring class and are perceived as having a social status akin to the labourers.

Although the Indians and Chinese are prominent among the managerial class, and the Chinese who make up the bulk of the artisans, further combine with the Indian office and hospital staff to dominate the second-class level, the labouring class are multi-ethnic as is the sub-class of unemployed youth. The lack of Malays in either the staff or managerial ranks can be explained by their relatively late arrival on the plantation frontier, although more recently one may find Malays in such jobs as watchmen or drivers, which are parallel in status to the staff.

In examining social clique formation, it was found that various communal groups do not interact within social classes, nor do they (with the exception of the Malays) mix with similar communal groups across classes. For example, the Chinese staff will socialize with Chinese storekeepers or Malays before mixing with Indian staff, Chinese labourers, or management. Likewise, the Indian staff prefer to interact with fellow Indian staff rather than Indian labourers, Chinese staff or the management. Yet the Malay watchmen and drivers will freely socialize with Malay tappers and weeders. If one could draw any line in the Malay community it would be between neighbouring *kampong* Malays and estate Malays as each group has separate mosques and political party branches.

Thus, Pulau Estate exhibits a unique blend of cultural pluralism, class stratification, and caste separation. It is the author's contention that these divisions reflect a unique combination of historical development, mode of subsistence, and educational attainment.

The following chart of Pulau Estate's economic organization clearly depicts the foregoing social class formation.

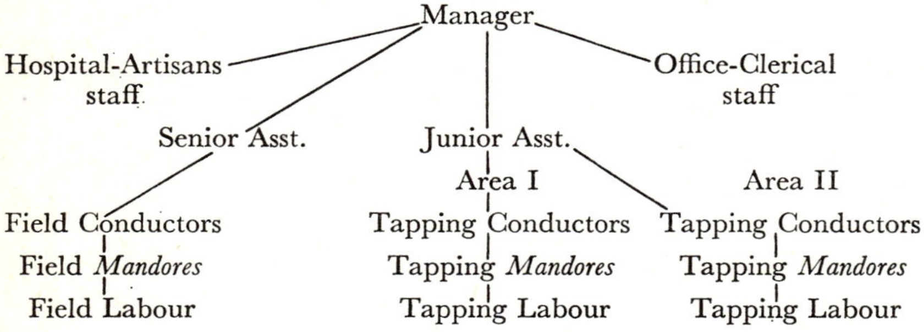


FIGURE 1. Pulau Estate Economic Organisation.

The manager and his two assistants triangularly form the top crust of the estate system's social strata. The hospital attendants, artisans, and office clerks are in a staff relation to the managerial level and form the second layer in the socio-economic hierarchy. The conductors, *mandores* (overseers), and laborers can be placed together in the lower reaches of socio-economic strata. The conductors and *mandores* could be further slightly differentiated from the field labourers as an upper level of the lower class, while the tappers and weeders (labourers) compose a middle and bottom sector of the lower class. The formal and informal power of the conductors and *mandores* over the tappers and weeders in terms of tree allocation, rubber weighings, and work evaluation make them powerful men in the labouring class. A great deal of estate corruption revolves around the uses and abuses of power by these men, as well as the semi-autonomous transactions of hospital and clerical staff.

The estate dresser (medical assistant) has a focal role in the estate social system in that he has numerous transactions with all levels of the system from labourer to manager. In an unofficial capacity he therefore acts as transmitter of messages and arbitrator of disputes between the diverse elements, factions, and social classes of the estate hierarchy. In short, he commands fear from the workers, response from the management and has great informal power throughout the system.

The workers represent the most depressed and exploited sector of the estate community. For the majority of them, the South Indians in particular, the estate is a 'total institution'[11] with limited physical and psychological mobility. As Jain (1970) acknowledged, "The Indian labourers not only produce rubber for export but also grow up, marry, save and consume, quarrel and cooperate, and die on the estate." Social, spatial, and occupational boundary maintenance revolves around the informal organization of communal groups and the formal structure of the economic enterprise of rubber production. Barring emigration, the only significant hope for social mobility among the labourers is education.

It is a central thesis of this paper that even the prospect of social mobility through schooling has turned against the labourer, as the estate vernacular school system has traditionally served as an agent of control and socialization into depths of this "total institution." As Thompson (1943) observed when discussing plantation education in the Americas, "The schools have been tolerated and maintained by being brought into line with the class and racial traditions of the plantation system." Moreover, as Beckford (1972) stated, "Vernacular education has to be limited in nature, for reading and writing in the master's language would surely not increase production among labourers, and might even put ideas of insurrection in their heads." The estate dresser, among others, confirmed in an interview, "Some children in standard six of the Indian school cannot even write their names nonetheless (sic) read."

In sum, the isolated estate Indian vernacular primary school has insured both the physical containment and psychological indoctrination of labourers' children in the lower strata of estate and Malaysian society. In the case of estate education, the informal aspects of formal schooling have been most effective. While the schools formally transmit a dysfunctional literacy in terms of the larger Malaysian economy, they informally develop efficient and prompt behaviour, an unquestioning attitude toward authority, and other characteristics highly regarded in a productive labourer. It is this latent function of estate vernacular schooling that insures the management a continuing source of exploitable labour.

Of all the Asian aliens in Malaysia, Thompson (1955) noted that the Indians were culturally, politically, and economically the most attached to their mother country. On countless occasions Malaysian Indian leaders such as Dr. Rama Subbiah stressed the need for vernacular education to uphold the culture:

> For the well being and prosperity of any race or country it must protect its language. There is a saying 'to eradicate a race first destroy its language.' (Vadiveloo 1972).

Paradoxically, this call for Indian vernacular education in an endeavour to insure cultural identity has simultaneously served as a barrier to social mobility for the Indian estate labouring class. In fact, the very citadel of worker liberation, the labour union, in its relentless bargaining of the 1960's won what appeared to be the only concession the management honoured in full, the Indian vernacular schools, which in the long run became the very chains that bound their children to the estate economic process.

It is within the context of this conflict between cultural identity and social mobility that we will now investigate the present education of South Indian labourers' children on Pulau Estate.

## IV. The Indian Vernacular School

The attempt to transplant Tamil Nad to Malaysia has meant a limited and deprived education that has only allowed Tamil children to join the Tamil language sector of the economy: To tap and weed, to build roads, to live on the rails, to clean cars, and to clear the malarious jungle.

(P.K. R. 1971)

The new Indian primary school is located in a quiet area about 500 yards from the estate town of Malau and away from the line-sites. It is situated in a compound directly across a playing field from the new Malay school. Although the physical plant is new, it would be deceptive to imply that the facilities are good in terms of books and teaching aids. There is not one library or reading room in the entire school. Teachers keep a handful of texts in their classroom cupboards to be drawn upon and shared, but even these books are outdated and insufficient in number. As far as could be observed, although there existed the above mentioned Tamil texts, there was barely one book per classroom in either English or Malay. Sometimes in standard six the children are asked to share in the purchase of magazines or comic books to increase the reading selection. The students are not permitted to take even the few books that do exist from the building for fear of soiling, theft, or destruction. As one researcher recorded when reviewing the use of teaching aids:

When I arrived at the school a number of teachers were busily preparing charts and other aids. They definitely intended to impress me with the exhibition of all kinds of teaching aids on the walls. Through a student, I later discovered that only that very week had they been put up on the walls.

Although the school had a facility earmarked for a student canteen, it was closed due to the lack of a tender. When asked as to why it was not functioning, one teacher remarked, "What's the point of running the canteen when one can barely get $M .50 a day from the poverty stricken students." Thus, most students go hungry or bring snacks of leftover breakfast to last them till the late evening meal. Needless to say, this has great physiological impact on their attention level, a matter we will return to in a later section of this paper.

Turning to the structure and organization of the school, we find some interesting anomalies. First, the school is a National Type Primarily School, which means that instruction is in the Indian vernacular, with the syllabus having a national orientation with both Malay and English languages as compulsory subjects. But in the case of Pulau Estate, the Indian vernacular school mirrors the mixture of Tamil and Telugu Indian subcultures in that there are two mediums of instruction within the same building, a Tamil stream and a Telugu stream, with separate teaching staffs and texts, except in the instruction in English and Malay. The total school enrollment is 235 students, 183 Tamil and 52 Telugu. The staff composition is roughly 7 Tamil, 4 Telugu, 1 Chinese (for English instruction), and a Tamil Headmaster. Although in the Tamil stream there is a separate class for every standard (grade) and one teacher per standard, the Telugu stream has multiple or mixed standards, typically two per one teacher. It is not surprising that a Telugu teacher moving from one class to the next in the same room experiences great disciplinary problems, not to mention the impact of the noise level on the students' learning ability. The school classrooms are further organized in rows according to academic ability determined by teacher observation and testing. Thus, in the first row are seated the 'smartest' 'A' students, second row, 'B' students and so on. The teachers rationalize this seating arrangement by ability grouping by arguing that it allows them to deal with each row separately so that all will benefit. But in fact the following classroom observation typified how such 'best laid plans' can go astray:

> Accordingly, only the first two rows pay attention when the teacher is teaching. The rest will be engaged in some mischievous activity such as jumping from desk to desk, hiding or talking.
>
> (Observation, April, 1973)

Beyond the organizational format of Tamil and Telugu streams, single and multiple classes, and ability grouping by seating the school is further structured into split sessions to accommodate the large population of estate Indian children. In the morning session standards one, four, five, and six attend, while in the afternoon session standards two and three attend. In view of this organizational structure it is a wonder how much, and what kind of learning transpires.

In observing the teaching-learning dynamics of the Indian classroom, be it Tamil or Telugu, it appears that what is learned, is learned in a 'rote' fashion, in an authoritarian manner, and often wiped out through the lack of secondary reinforcement in the home environment. Also, a great deal of the time there is little academic learning at all as a result of the strong subversion of the teachers' efforts. The school itself then becomes a daily battleground between the teachers expanding energy to 'keep order' and the students devising entertainment to pass time until they take their places in the plantation economy. That the students are united against the staff and headmaster is demonstrated in the many nicknames they have created to deal with their perceived adversaries. Unfortunately, even the community shares these names for the headmaster and some teachers, making the school-community relationship just as tenuous as that of the teacher-student. But before describing the staff, their attitudes, qualifications, and relationship to the community, a few more comments on other school activities are warranted.

The school has little or no organized sports or play. There has not been a single recorded sports day since the school's inception in 1948. As alluded to earlier, the common playing field between the Indian school and the adjacent Malay school is analogous to a demilitarized zone. If the Indian boys play on the field, their ball is subject to being taken by the Malay students, leading to quarrels and fights. So teachers discourage the use of the field and risk of ethnic conflict that they might ultimately be held responsible for. Segregation and racial prejudices are socialized early on the school playground and reinforced in the home environment. Children can even be seen walking to and from schools in groups according to ethnicity, only later to transact their adult lives in a fear laden, segregated pattern.

From this discussion of the student interaction patterns, we now turn to the school staff. The headmaster and staff have a generally negative image in the community. And although this image is shared by the students in regards to the Headmaster, it is not so for all the teachers. Virtually all parents viewed the headmaster as being outdated, bumbling, and corrupt.[12] Common estate rumour has it that he confiscated a government grant of $M 2,000 originally meant for a library and recreational equipment, and has also been known to purchase textbooks with government grant money at wholesale prices and sell them to the students at retail prices. Some believe that the reason he has not stimulated a parent-teacher organization at the school is his fear of being confronted with these matters. Both students and parents have all sorts of names for him, from 'Kalithai' or donkey, to 'the teachers' sleeping master'. Although the students sometimes pointed to staff as being physically abusive, they unanimously accused the headmaster of being callous in treatment. It is repeatedly claimed that because of his apathetic leadership, labouring parents neither understand nor take an interest in school affairs. It is not surprising that the plantation management and staff send their children to Kulim schools, and that even some labourers go to the extent of sending their children to schools on nearby estates rather than to the Pulau Estate Indian School. Moreover, the headmaster's daughter and his assistant's children attend primary school in Kulim. In fact, it was reported in one teacher interview that most of the estate staff were curious as to what the researchers were doing at the school and what was going on there as they themselves had never even visited the place.

A large number of the teachers grew up in the estate environment as labourers' children, and although they have risen in income, they presently have little status in the parents' eyes. As one parent stated, "Teachers are tappers' children, their wives are tappers, they are one of us, so why respect them?" The teachers also serve as scapegoats for parents jealous of their higher income. They are highly visible and easily blamed for the poor quality of education on the estate. It is frequently suggested that since the estate teachers grew up in the closed world of the estate, they have narrow vision and limited perspective, therefore little to offer the children.

The fact does remain that the staff of Pulau Estate Indian Vernacular School have poor qualifications and inadequate training. A number of the teachers are former estate clerks and office hands who were initially employed as temporary teachers after receiving some training on holidays and weekends. Of the twelve teachers at the Indian school only two, the headmaster and assistant headmaster, have a School Certificate. Three of the other teachers are temporary and four are still undergoing training. As one reseacher expressed it, "The school seems to be an experimental field for testing out teachers under training or those who have temporary or insufficient qualifications." As historically noted in the Aziz report (1971) on the teaching services of West Malaysia with respect to Tamil/Telugu teacher certification:

> The minimum entry qualification for such training was initially a pass in the Government Standard five (grade 5) exam but this was subsequently raised to standard six and finally (until 1960) to a pass in the standard seven Preparatory Examination for Tamil/Telugu teachers. On successful completion of their training the teachers were termed "Certified Teachers" Those who failed to complete their training were termed "Uncertified Teachers."

Thus, one need not necessarily be fully "certified" to continue teaching in a vernacular school. The poor qualification of Indian teachers is not confined to Pulau Estate for as Arasaratnam (1970) stated in his history of Indians in Malaysia and Singapore:

> Very few estates would undergo the expenditure of employing teachers. Clerks, *kanganys,* and even literate labourers would function as part-time teachers.

In terms of the perceived worth of Indian vernacular education in both economic and cultural situations, the teachers were quick to point out that vernacular education was irrelevant to the economic realities of the estate. Unless one wanted to become a tapper or Indian teacher, they saw vernacular schooling as useless. In fact, many pointed to the barrier it presented in terms of going on to secondary schooling in either Malay or English (there is no Indian vernacular secondary education in Malysia). As one teacher submitted:

Those who are in Tamil school are at a disadvantage when they go to secondary school with regard to language. They have to spend a year in remove class just to make up and then they still are at the bottom in their examinations and throughout their future education.

However, the entire school staff saw Indian vernacular education as essential for preserving the culture through the preservation of the language. They felt that the family was too busy merely trying to survive, therefore the school had to undertake this crucial function. As one teacher summarized:

Traditional customs and language should be preserved. It is part and parcel of the way of life of the Indians. If we don't preserve traditional customs then it will affect the lives of the Indians because they will find themselves 'nowhere'!

As another staff member added, "If language goes then the race will be gone."

The possible conflict between the functioning of education for economic mobility and for cultural transmission was a troublesome matter often left to the individual or family to decide. In the words of one staff member:

It depends on the individual whether his aim is economic or cultural. If one's sole aim is economic, then it will be in conflict with his culture because by indulging in western ways he would soon forget his culture.

It is this dilemma which lies at the heart of Indian education, that is, the relationship of vernacular schooling to cultural identity and social mobility in the Malaysian context.

## V. General Problems of Indian Education on Pulau Estate

Unlike the Chinese and Malay communities, there is a blatant lack of Indian community support for, or dialogue with, the school. There is no parent-teacher association nor monthly collection to support school programming. As Thompson (1955) noted, in the greater Malaysian society:

> Because of the instability of the local Indian population, Indian schools have lacked the wealthy patronage that in Malaya has been a great boon to the Chinese education ... Basically it was the varying prosperity of the Indian community that determined the quality of education received.

One might add that the transference of the divisive caste system into the estate environment has not helped matters of Indian communal cooperation. Therefore, lacking either wealthy Chinese patronage or Malay communal unity, the estate Indian school remains desperately in need of community commitment.

Basic to the problem of Indian education on the estate is the demand of growing population versus fixed financial resources. This problem is compounded by the growth of managerial, labour force, and union paternalism.[13] As mentioned earlier in this paper, the role of the estate managerial patronage as exhibited in the elaborate internal welfare system, has served to chain the labourer in a dependent fashion to the estate environment. Part of this welfare package, that is, maternity leave, allotments and free medical care, incidentally provide a well hidden incentive for labourer reproduction, increased dependence on credit (debt) and a parasitic tie to the estate economic and welfare system.

While holding dreams of a future plot in distant India and being faced daily with the reality of survival from dusk to dawn in Malaysia, the estate labourer increasingly uses managerial benefits which act to strengthen his dependency on the estate economic process and cement his place at the bottom of the estate and Malaysian social class hierarchy. This conspicuous lack of self-reliance, abetted by a patronizing estate managerial class, has kept the labourer locked into a vicious cycle of poverty, unconsciously increasing his bonds with the acceptance (and often demand) of every handout.[14] One wonders whether the unions, in their fight for increased benefits, have not in effect unwittingly tightened the managerial grip on the lives of the labouring class. Vernacular schools were instituted in the estates as a part of a labour welfare package manifestly functioning to appease the labourers' demands for education, specifically geared to cultural transmission and preservation, while latently functioning to ensure a future source of cheap and controllable estate labour, limited in opportunity and perspective, and locked into the lower social echelons.

## VI. Education, Cultural Identity, and Social Mobility: Emerging Issues on the Plantation Frontier

It has been the contention of this paper that the Indian estate vernacular school in its endeavour to transmit South Indian culture has acted as a major barrier to social mobility among the Indian labouring class. Furnivall (1956) made the crucial distinction between English and vernacular education in colonial areas of South-east Asia. Simply stated, the English medium education functions to teach people 'how to make a living' (in the modern economic context), while vernacular education teaches people 'how to live' (in the traditional cultural context). While Malaysia's plural school system has manifestly served to ensure cultural pluralism through the transmission of varying cultural heritages, it has latently functioned to deprive segments of some communal groups access to an emerging Western economy. This has been the case on Pulau Estate in particular, and the Malaysian rural plantation frontier in general. Data from the Murad report (1973) clearly demonstrate a strong relationship between type of schooling (vernacular) and socio-economic class formation. Quoting from the report with reference to the Indian community:

> However, for the Indian youths, the findings of this study show that they have, on the average, the lowest socio-economic status of the three communities and have lower motivation than the Malays.

Further reference is made relating poverty to vernacular schooling in the following report (1973):

> Analysis supports the earlier statement that it is the poor who send their children to the vernacular schools, while the favourably placed parents send their children to the English medium schools, the highest concentration of the poor is in the Malay medium primary schools ... While all of the vernacular schools are impoverished when compared to the English medium schools ... The Tamil medium schools are the smallest and the poorest.

Thus, the relationship of low socio-economic status and vernacular schooling reinforce one another in a vicious circle with little hope of escape in sight for the isolated estate child. Subramaniam (1970) discussed this dilemma in calling for revolutionary change in estate education:

The usefulness and role of Tamil schools must be called into question. These schools cut away from the mainstream of education and almost exclusively catering for working class backgrounds, are educational lagoons or backwaters.

While institutions such as schools have historically emerged in heterogeneous environments to serve an acculturating, political function (Thompson 1943) the Malaysian plantation environment has uniquely endeavoured throughout the decades to maintain separate ethnic schools akin to homogeneous groupings where enculturation is the dominant educative function. In the instance of Pulau Estate, political control was guaranteed through a colonial paternalistic policy stressing cultural transmission instead of socio-economic parity. Moreover, while the formal aspects of vernacular education acted to transmit the local culture and heritage of a specific communal group, the informal aspects of doing this in the non-traditional technological setting of a school served to structurally socialize the children of estate labourers into prerequisite value and attitude sets necessary for a docile, efficient labouring role.

The hidden curriculum of the Pulau Estate Indian school teaches an unquestioning respect for authority. The emphasis on segmented time frames and a fragmented view of reality through the compartmentalization of the school into curricular subject areas prepares the child to adapt readily to his father's daily routine as a prompt, efficient, alienated labourer. The arrangement of physical space suggests an acceptance of the social concept of power in the superordinate relationship of teacher to student, and the ensuing demand for docile obedience and compliance. Learning to appease the teacher in the authoritarian climate of the school readily transfers into learning to appease the management and staff in the similar hierarchical ordering of the estate production process. Independent thought is discouraged as rote learning prepares the child amiably to exchange his books for a tapper's pail and his grades for wages, in the process justifying his plight as his *karma* (fate). Learning school rules, regulations, and 'appropriate' behaviour make adjustments to estate rules, regulations, and 'desirable' behaviour an unconscious transformation. Thus, demanded by the labouring class for primarily cultural reasons estate Indian education reaches no higher a level than the needs of the estate economic process requires.

The key point to remember is that in performing this function at the expense of opening a window to the world outside the estate environment, the Indian vernacular school has become an instrument of labourer control in the hands of the planters, ensuring a flow of future labourers, while fulfilling an emotive need for preserving cultural identity. Instead of improving or reconstructing the plantation environment, education has become a mechanism for initiating the labouring class's children into the estate class structure and encompassing cycle of poverty.

The introduction of the technology of vernacular schooling into the isolated estate context has been instrumental in maintaining this cycle of poverty and attendant structured inequality. As Murad (1973) summarized:

The segregation of the disadvantaged youth creates an encapsulated society with a distinctive sub-culture. They are a community by themselves. In many respects their members are similar to one another. They are disadvantaged financially in their prospects, in their perception of the value of education, in their developed verbal and intellectual skills, in their outlook and interests. They talk, play and quarrel with members of their own kind. They often emulate and reinforce each others' values rather than challenge ... they are segregated and living in an encapsulated world of their own, totally divorced from other influences.

In directing the report findings specifically to the school setting and learning, Murad (1973) continues:

... we have commented on the effects of grouping and isolation of socially and culturally homogeneous groups. We have pointed out that a child's verbal development and reasoning skills are enhanced through active interaction with others in a diversified socio-cultural setting than in one that is homogeneous ... In a diversified socio-cultural setting like a heterogeneous urban school, a child relates himself with other children who bring along with them a variety of skills (e.g., verbal and reasoning skills) which they have acquired and developed from their differing home backgrounds.

... In a homogeneous socio-cultural setting, where members of the groups do not differ very much from each other in social status, values, etc., a child is confronted with a climate which is totally different from what has been described above. At home the children do not learn much that would contribute to the development of their verbal and reasoning skills. At school they interact with children who face similar circumstances as they do.

One reseacher's account of the structural impact on Pulau Estate was as follows:

On Palau Estate the workers remain separate from the staff and interact only with their own stock. There is little one can learn from another. Every one is in the same boat, that is, all are tappers. If there were interaction between people of different social status as sometimes happens in the urban area, then it might contribute to a change in attitude. Information is freely flowing in the urban area. The people are well informed of educational opportunities and also the benefits derived from education. This is almost non-existent on the estate. The worker sees his children and those of others going to school and finally ending up doing the same job as the others do. So he does not give his whole-hearted support to his child's education.

Without reference groups to which labourers can aspire, convinced that they can never rise to the class of staff or management, the labourers in effect become 'status assenters' (Marimuthu 1971).

In sum, not only is the plantation cut off from the mainstream of the greater Malaysian society, essentially becoming an alienated community, but within the estate itself, isolation and segregation by race, caste, and socio-economic class rooted in mode of subsistence, and reinforced by vernacular schoolings becomes the norm. While the estate 'totalistic' environment acts as the informal setting for indoctrination into the membership of an alienated community within the greater Malaysian nation state, the estate vernacular school sets the tempo for locating and ensuring role and social status within that alienated community.

Fixed in status by their vernacular education system, occupation (mode of subsistence) and meagre income, Indian parental expectations toward their children's education soon pave the way for their transition from the few years of vernacular schooling on the estate to wielding their father's knife among the rubber trees. Thus, the self perpetuating cycle continues. All of this transpires in an environment dominated by bureaucratic managerial authority, patronage and paternalism, the estate vernacular schools being but one act of patrimony. In his text dealing with the persistent poverty of third world plantation economies, Beckford (1969) accurately portrays this unending cycle of poverty and social injustice:

The nature of social and political arrangements creates several biases toward a continuous state of underdevelopment. Inherent social instability impedes investment; the rigid pattern of social stratification restricts mobility; the concentration of social, economic and political power prevents the emergence of a highly motivated population; and racial discrimination inhibits the fullest use of the society's human resources.

Today, tensions are mounting on Pulau Estate as the number of unemployed youth, especially of Indian descent, abounds. As Marimuthu (1971) observed, "These youth consider themselves as 'double failures' – unable to make the grade at school and unable to find employment both within and without the plantation world." Whereas the plantation system has been traditionally perceived as a stepping stone to the outside world by the Chinese (Ness 1967), it has been viewed as the only world by the labouring Indians. But with the increased hiring of Malays as estate labourers, a form of Indian social mobility derived of forced emigration into urban centres might occur. Where the vernacular schools failed to promote social mobility, changed political-economic conditions may indeed force this mobility through emigration. It is this subtle process that leads one to believe that contrary to traditional educational dictum, changing the curriculum may be a necessary step to social change, but not sufficient in itself. For it is the estate economic environment that conditions education, and it is totally impossible to change that environmental social structure through the schools, because the schools supply what the environment demands. In the past, the need has been for docile unskilled labourers. But what of the future?

The above discussion leads us to another emerging issue for the Indian estate labourer, that is, concomitant with the changing economic patterns, Malaysia has arrived at a political policy of national integration through the promotion of a common national consciousness. Within this larger objective, the schools have now been chosen as an instrument for political indoctrination and the realization of a national Malaysian identity. But the problem for the Indian population so persistently concerned with the preservation of their cultural identity through vernacular schooling, is that the manifestations of this new national policy in terms of curriculum changes had resulted in the introduction of a compulsory Malay exam, Malay language instruction and a common syllabus which has the combined effect of making national identity more or less 'Malay based' and in conflict with sub-cultural identification.

As Arasaratnam (1970) found, although the Indian English-educated commercial class view Malaysia as their permanent home, the labouring estate class has continually existed in a tenuous position of 'non-citizenry', the parents frequently sending money back to India, not knowing when they will be released from work with the fluctuation of world rubber prices. Their children who have only known life in Malaysia are beginning to doubt 'who they are' and 'where they belong'. In a true sense they are the children of an uprooted people, with their only insurance of maintaining ties with their heritage, the vernacular school process, now being challenged by national governmental policy. Thus, the very Indian vernacular schools which at best transmitted the cultural heritage, and at worst insured Indian labouring children a low social status, now threatens to wipe out the only thread of meaning for the labouring Indian class through the introduction of a national language and Malay-based syllabus. The question still remains as to whether these changes will result in an opening up of channels for social mobility for the Indian labourer's child. The possibilities are doubtful as long as the school remains within the estate context, serving only the labouring class.

Cynthia Enloe (1970), in her study of the role of education in multiethnic politics in Malaysia, points to the primary Malaysian dilemma as being that of "nation-building: the tension between the requisites of economic development and national identity." This author would be more direct in saying that the evolving problems of nation-building in Malaysia today, as evidenced in the plantation frontier, appear to exercise themselves more in the tension between social class formation and the preservation of cultural identity (cultural pluralism). Education for national consciousness may indeed mean the eventual devolution of the previous emphasis on cultural pluralism, but there is little indication that it will mark the public acknowledgement of the role of education in the allocation of social class status.

The functions of schooling seem to be reversing themselves in the government priority system and in the public purview[15] as the previously latent function of vernacular schooling as a social class broker becomes a manifest function of the National type school, while the old manifest function of promoting cultural pluralism through vernacular schooling becomes a latent concern of government bureaucrats and a simmering powder keg for communal strife.

Similar to the historical development of schooling in America's plural immigrant society, the National type recalls the 'common school' of the 1800's when American government policy was projected at assimilating the immigrant masses (Katz 1968). That policy resulted in the debate of the last two decades on the role of education in social class formation and the whole issue of 'equality of educational opportunity'. Ironically, America has gone full circle and the movement of the seventies portends a search for the roots not found in political upheaval of the sixties through the stress on ethnic studies programmes and training teachers to be cognizant of cultural differences. As American history seems to be engaged in rewriting itself, what this means for the Malaysian experience only history will recollect, and that obviously will be strongly determined by 'who' writes that history.

With regard to national identity in Malaysia, Manning Nash's (1972) observations provide much insight into what may be in store:

> Schools promote value consensus when they are effectively tied to the central values and institutions, but it is the organization of political and economic life that provides integration in a modernizing society. Therefore, it is the reconstruction of politics and economics that reduces the ethnic component in competition, not the mere establishment of common values, aims, and orientation. In a modern society it is as much procedure as culture that holds it together in the fragile and instrumental manner that complex societies are held together.

Returning to our specific group under study, if the orientation of the Malaysian governmental educational policy since independence has been as Bock (1971) proclaims, "First, to view the schools as the primary socializing agencies for transmitting those values and attitudes deemed crucial to the creation of an allegiant, integrated young citizenry, and second, to manipulate the school system as an instrument for sponsoring the mobility of the indigenous Malay population," then it would seem that the emerging conflict for Pulau Estate Indian labourers between cultural identity and social mobility has relatively little meaning if the estate Indian population is discarded to wallow in the estate conditions of poverty. Even the Murad study (1973) in its nationwide survey, placed the poor Indian estate child in a category of 'rural' and emphasized the Malay nature of this rural category, which in effect hid the conditions of Indian vernacular schooling by blending them with the problems of rural (Malay medium) education in general.

Ignored by government policy, hidden from the eyes of mainstream Malaysian society, the plantation Indian labour force has indeed become Malaysia's forgotten people. Enmeshed in the entangled conflicts of social class, caste, and cultural identity, the Indian labourers remain locked in time and space as victims of a vicious cycle of poverty, ensured of this fate by the dysfunctional nature of the Indian estate vernacular school as seen in the context of the larger Malaysian society. It would be tragic and bitterly unjust, should they remain so remembered as a footnote in history, or a subject merely for theoretical banter at some academic symposium.

## References


Ampalavanar, Rajeswari
1972 "Class, Caste and Ethnicism among Urban Indians in Malaya, 1920–1941." *Nusantara* 2: Kuala Lumpur.

Arasaratnam, Sinnappah
1970 *Indians in Malaysia and Singapore.* Kuala Lumpur: Oxford University Press.

*Barnes Report on Malay Education*
1951 Kuala Lumpur: Government Press.

Bock, John C.
1971 "The conflict between contest and sponsored mobility in the Malaysian Educational system." Paper presented at the *Comparative and International Education Society*, 1971 annual meeting: San Diego, California.

Beckford, T.
1969 *Persistent Poverty: Underdevelopment in plantation economies of the Third World.* London: Oxford University Press.

Chelliah, D. D.
1960 *A Short History of Educational Policy in the Straits Settlements.* Singapore: G. H. Kiat.

Coleman, James S.
1966 *Equality of Educational Opportunity.* Washington, D.C.: U.S. Government Printing Office.

Emerson, Rupert
1964 *Malaysia. A Study in Direct and Indirect Rule.* Kuala Lumpur: University of Malaya Press.

Enloe, Cynthia H.
1970 *Multi-Ethnic Politics: The Case of Malaysia.* Research Monograph no. 2, Center for South and Southeast Asia Studies, Berkeley: University of California.

Fenn-Wu
1951 *Chinese Schools and the Education of Chinese Malayans.* Kuala Lumpur: Government Press.

Furnivall, J. S.
1956 *Colonial Policy and Practice: A Comparative Study of Burma and the Netherlands Indies.* New York: New York University Press.

Gagliano, Felix V.
1970 *Communal Violence in Malaysia 1969: The Political Aftermath.* Athens, Ohio: Ohio University Center for International Studies.

Goffman, Erving
1961 *Asylums.* Garden City, New York: Doubleday-Anchor.

Gordon, Shirle
1970 "The Condition of Our Plantation Workers-the Fathers and Mothers of the Children." *Intisari* 3 (4). Singapore: Malaysian Sociological Research Institute.

Hanrahan, Gene Z.
1971 *The Communist Struggle in Malaya.* Kuala Lumpur: University of Malaya Press.

Jackson, R. N.
1961 *Immigrant Labour and the Development of Malaya 1786–1920.* Kuala Lumpur: Government Press, Federation of Malaya.

Jain, Ravindra K.
1970 *South Indians on the Plantation Frontier in Malaya.* New Haven: Yale University Press.

Katz, Michael B.
1968 *The Irony of Early School Reform.* Boston: Beacon Press.

Kondapi, C.
1947 *Straits Times* April 1947: Singapore.

Lim-Chong-Yah
1967 *Economic Development of Modern Malaya.* London: Oxford University Press.

Maday, Bela et al.
1965 *Area Handbook for Malaysia and Singapore.* Washington, D.C.: U. S. Government printing office, July.

Mahajani, Usha
1960 *The Role of Indian Minorities in Burma and Malaya.* Bombay, India: Vera and Co.

Maliamauv, Joseph Paul
*Some Aspects of the Education of Plantation Workers' Children.* Graduation Exercise, Faculty of Economics and Administration. Kuala Lumpur: University of Malaya.

Marimuthu, T.
1971 "Education, Social Mobility and the Plantation Environment: Proposal for Enquiry." *Journal Pendideken* 2, Kuala Lumpur.

Mills, C. Wright
1959 *The Power Elite.* New York: Oxford University Press.

Murad bin Mohd. Noor
1973 *Kajian Keciciran* (*Dropout Study*). Kuala Kumpur: Ministry of Education, Malaysia.

Nash, Manning
1972 "Ethnicity, Centrality and Education in Pasir Mas, Kelantan." *Comparative Education Review* 16 (1).

Ness, Gayl D.
1967 *Bureaucracy and Rural Development in Malaysia.* Berkeley, California: University of California Press.

Persatuan Kemajuan Ra'ayat
1971 *Up To Us.* A three year effort in self-development by plantation workers in Negri Sembilan, Malaysia, Seremban, Malaysia: Chang Press.

Ponniah, S. M.
1970 "Multi-lingual education: the disinheritance of the Tamil workers's child." *Intisari* 3 (4). Singapore: Malaysian Sociological Research Institute.

Ponniah, S. M.
1971 "Preface to An investigation Into the Problems of Tamil Education in West Malaysia." (mimeo proposal for research) Kuala Lumpur.
Radhakrishnan, K. P.
1969 *National Integration and Estate Indian Proletariat.* (Graduation Exercise). Kuala Lumpur: Faculty of Economics and Administration, University of Malaya.
*Razak Report of the Education Committee*
1956 Kuala Lumpur: Government Printing Office, Malaysia.
Ryan, N. J.
1962 *The Cultural Heritage of Malaya.* Singapore: Longman Malaysia Ltd.
Sandhu, Kernial Singh
1969 *Indians in Malaya (some aspects of their immigration and settlement, 1786–1957).* Cambridge: Cambridge University Press, England.
*Second Malaysia Plan, 1971–1975*
1971 Kuala Lumpur: Malaysian Government Press.
*Seminars on Tamil Education* held at the University of Malaya:
1967, 1971, and 1972. Sponsored by the NLFC and the Tamil Language Society.
Shils, Edward
1961 *Theologic of Personal Knowledge.* London: Routledge and Kegan Paul.
Smith, R. T.
1967 "Social Stratification, Cultural Pluralism and Integration in West Indian Societies, "in S. Lewis and T. G. Matthews (eds.), *Carribbean Integration,* Puerto Rico.
Subramaniam, P.
1970 "Pioneers educated sons of workers must revolutionize plantation education." *Intisari* 3 (4). Singapore: Malaysian Sociological Research Institute.
*Talib Report* of the Education Review Committee
1960 Kuala Lumpur: Government Press.
The Indian Education Committee
1951 *Memorandum on Indian Education in the Federation of Malaya,* Kuala Lumpur: Malayan Printers.
Thompson, E. T.
1943 "Comparative Education in Colonial Areas with Special Reference to Plantation and Mission Frontiers." *American Journal of Sociology* 48 (6).
Thompson, E. T.
1965 *Plantation Systems of the New World.* Washington.
Thompson, Virginia and Richard Adloff
1955 *Minority Problems in Southeast Asia.* Stanford, California: Standford University Press.
Vadiveloo, C.
1972 "Tamil Education and Facilities Available for It." Paper presented

at the *Tamil Language Society*, University of Malaya, April 1972: Kuala Lumpur.

Wong, Francis Hoy Kee and Ee Tiang Hong
1971 *Education in Malaysia.* Singapore: Heinemann Educational Books (Asia) Ltd.

Zain, Tan Sri Abdul Aziz bin Mohd
1971 *Revised Report of the Royal Commission on the Teaching Services, West Malaysia.* Kuala Lumpur.

## Notes

1. The project was designed and directed by the author, then Visiting Lecturer at the Science University of Malaysia. The research team consisted of students from the Science University of Malaysia: V. Palanisamy, Ilan Govan Supiah, Navasathy Francis, Hamima Dona Mustapha, Rustam Mohd. Isa, Wong Ah Sung, and Siau Lean Sim.
2. The name of the estate was changed as a condition of access to the estate persons and reccords. It should be noted that it is not easy to gain entry to, and raise questions on, a Malaysian plantation. Although quite willing initially, as it became evident that the investigation was going beyond a mere look at the schools to the entire estate socio-economic environment, cooperation lessened substantially.
3. A detailed description of the research design and methodology is housed in the office of the Director, Centre for Educational Studies, Science University of Malaysia, Penang, Malaysia. The study was funded by the Centre and would have been impossible without its generous assistance.
4. Manning Nash (1972) employs the Shilsian (1961) concept of 'centrality' in discussing this elite when he states: "In its simplest sense 'central' institutions and 'central' values refer to those values held by persons and groups who are the legitimate elite of the society and who occupy the commanding heights of political and economic power controlling through a set of institutions (politics, schools, communication media, religious codes, etc.) the macro levels of the society." This concept is not dissimilar from C. Wright Mills' (1959) notion of 'the power elite.'
5. For a detailed account of the internal struggle in Malaysia which followed the defeat of the Japanese read Hanrahan's book, *The Communist Struggle in Malaysia* Kuala Lumpur: University of Malaya Press, 1971.
6. For an expanded account read Gagliano's *Communal Violence in Malaysia, 1969: The Political Aftermath.* Athens, Ohio: Ohio University Center for International Studies, 1973.
7. Although demographic records are kept and date back a number of years, it is our experience that they are not totally accurate, therefore, all figures herewith should be taken as estimates of prevailing conditions.
8. On one occasion the manager attempted to integrate some quarters by race and found that within the week the individuals involved had exchanged housing assignments such that the previously ethnically segregated pattern was reestablished. It might be further noted that the pariah or lower caste all dwell in a common line-site segregated from other higher caste but equivalent social class labourers.
9. The staff may be further differentiated into specialized occupational roles

revolving around the hospital, office, factory, and field. An additional sub-class of 'officially unemployed' consists primarily of youth who work as sub-hired 'collects' or latex cup scrapers for regular tappers endeavouring to enhance their income by conserving every ounce of latex and paying a commission to those who would assist – the 'collects.' This group also increases its income by periodically turning to deviant acts such as gambling, smuggling, and setting fires and might be synonymous to the Marxist sub-class of 'lumpen-proletariat.'

10. One example of this is the case of the present assistant chargeman, who has been schooled in Kulim and has returned to act as assistent to his father, the estate chargeman.
11. For a discussion of the notion of a 'total institution' see Goffman's (1961) book, *Asylums*. For an application of the concept to the plantation environment see Jain (1970), Marimuthu (1971) or Smith (1967).
12. The manager's similar disgust with the Headmaster was apparent throughout the project. One could almost surmise that his initial openness to the project was tied to his deepest hope that somehow the research might turn up enough evidence to warrant his removal. The tension could always be felt when around both of them together.
13. Arasaratnam (1970) has recently argued that, "The paternalism of the planter and the labour officer may be replaced by the paternalism of the union officials, the major deterrent being a wakening of 'true' consciousness among the workers."
14. In effect, management largesse not only functions to enhance the dependent, superordinate/subordinate relationship, but also serves to break up Indian families when the husband is forced to seek increased wages in the towns, while the wife remains working on the estate so that the large family might maintain the housing, medical and other management-supplied entities. In this situation, with the mother having to work in order legally to maintain estate residency, the children often go unattended, are sent off to the impersonal crèche, or tended by an elder daughter, herself having to drop out of school to serve as pseudo-mother. This physical separation between parent and child and husband and wife further leads to child negligence, marital infidelity and a general breakdown of the family structure.
15. It is difficult at this time to say just how public the movement away from social structure rooted in the notion of cultural pluralism toward one based on social class differences will be. It already appears that a culturally heterogeneous political elite is forming as the apex of the government and is more than willing to preserve its own social status by promoting a continuing mythology of cultural diversity while attempting within its political influence (e.g. media control) as far as possible to block the rise of class consciousness. With the data in this study pointing toward the growth of a multi-cultural estate labour force, there is little doubt that the seeds of class struggle in Malaysia are evolving.

# Sex Discrimination: Theory and Research

CONSTANTINA SAFILIOS-ROTHSCHILD

CONSTANTINA SAFILIOS-ROTHSCHILD is a Greek Sociologist who received her Ph.D. in Sociology from Ohio State University in 1963. She is at present a Professor of Sociology and Director of the Family Research Center at Wayne State University in Detroit, Michigan.

She is an Associate Editor for the American and International *Journal of Marriage and the Family*, *Journal of Comparative Family Studies*, and the *Journal of Health and Human Behavior*.

She has conducted research in Detroit, Michigan and Athens, Greece, on Family Dynamics, the Familial and Social Dynamics of Fertility, Work Commitments, the Options of Men and Women as well as on Attitudes toward Mental Illness.

Under a large contract with the National Institute of Education, she reviewed and synthesized for 1974 through 1976 literature on sex role socialization, sex discrimination as well as other types of discrimination since 1960. On the basis of the synthesis of this literature, she is now in the process of building conceptual models to explain sex discrimination.

In November, 1975, under a Ford Foundation grant, she organized a working conference on Family and Sex Roles and is now editing the volume resulting from this conference.

She is a member of many professional societies, and has taught in a number of Universities in North America and Europe. She is the author of a number of books including *Toward a Sociology of Women*, Lexington, Mass: Ginn & Co., (Xerox College Publishing), January, 1972; *Women and Social Policy*, Englewood Cliffs, N.J.: Prentice-Hall, January, 1974; *Sex, Love, and Sex Roles*, Spectrum Books, Prentice-Hall (forthcoming in Fall, 1976); and *Socialization is Destiny*, University of California Press (forthcoming).

# Sex Discrimination: Theory and Research

CONSTANTINA SAFILIOS-ROTHSCHILD

Sex is the basis of discrimination in all societies. Everywhere, sex stratification systems make for an unequal distribution of wealth, power, and prestige on the basis of gender. Since women usually occupy the inferior position, they are the ones who receive a lesser (or no) share of the valued societal goods. Of course, men may also be discriminated against on the basis of their gender in some areas (such as, child custody) but never with respect to the most valued goods: wealth, power, and prestige.

However, because several salient stratification systems co-exist in most societies, each individual occupies a position in each one of them. These different stratification systems may include: social (class), racial, religious, ethnic, age, height, and health stratification. Most often the profile of each individual's statuses in all these stratification systems is uneven in that the individual may occupy the subordinate position in one or more systems, the superordinate position in another system, and a middle status in other stratification systems. A woman, for example, may be black, middle-class, young, and disabled. And another woman may be white, working-class, Jewish, old and healthy. Thus, the degree of discrimination directed against different women is, in fact, determined not only on the basis of gender but also on the basis of a number of interacting statuses they occupy on all salient stratification systems. Some of these other statuses may compound the degree of discrimination directed against women and other statuses may neutralize their sex-status so as to minimize sex discrimination.

While the extent to which any individual is discriminated against depends upon the unique combination of statuses he (she) occupies on the different overlapping stratification systems, there is no theory that systematically treats this problem, and little empirical relevant evidence is available. Hraba and Braito (1974), in a pioneer article, have dealt with the overlapping race, sex, and class statuses and the individual's consciousness of relative discrimination on the basis of each of these characteristics. They claim that individuals tend to attribute experienced social inequality to the one criterion that explains their status incongruency or status inconsistency (Hraba and Braito, 1974). Working-class women, for example, who become educated but whose education does not translate into economic, prestige, or power gains as it does for men in the same economic class, will tend to (accurately) attribute experienced inequality to their gender rather than to their class position (Blum and Coleman, 1970; Harbeson, 1971; Fuchs, 1972). Evidence from a recent study of adolescents supports Hraba and Braito's (1974) contention. This study showed that the earliest self-placement into social identities was made in terms of gender rather than on the basis of race or class position. Gender was the second most salient social identity following age for both black and white ninth grade students, while race ranked seventh by black students and tenth by white students and class identity had the lowest saliency of all social identities (Wellman, 1971).

Probably the best studied overlapping stratification systems and the varying degree of ensuing discrimination are the race and sex stratification systems and to some extent the class stratification system in addition. All available evidence indicates that, at least within the American society, occupying the double superordinate position of a *white male* gives one extraordinary advantages of opportunity and access to valued societal goods, regardless of one's merits (Safilios-Rothschild, 1974a).

In one study, for example, several transcripts reflecting different levels of performance, ability, and grades were sent to universities and colleges all over the United States to be evaluated and considered for admission. Accompanying each transcript were names and pictures identifying the transcript as belonging to a male or female, white or black, with the identifying characteristics varied so as to represent each race-sex group at each level of scholastic ability and achievement. The results showed that among males, the white ones were clearly chosen regardless of the applicant's ability. Furthermore, low-ability and achievement white males were also chosen over white or black females of equal or even higher ability, unless the women were quite obviously superior (Walster, McCleary, and Clifford, 1970). Thus, among men, the superordinate position in the race stratification system is the determining factor in the access to valued goods. For women, their subordinate position in the sex stratification system seems to be so pervasive that they are consistently discriminated against regardless of race, unless they have such an outstanding scholastic achievement that gatekeepers are willing to let them in the circle of the "chosen few."

There is also considerable evidence from developing societies that high social status women experience little sex discrimination due to their status (Safilios-Rothschild, 1974a). Their superordinate position in the class stratification system exempts them from the restrictions and constraints of sex role stereotypes and ensures them, almost equally with men, access to and control of the valued goods of wealth, prestige, and power. High social status can neutralize the inferior sex status only in societies in which the prevailing class stratification system tends to be rigid. There is little upward social mobility in these societies, and the prevailing criteria are particularistic and even familistic. High status men favour high status women over the lower status men, thus safeguarding that wealth, prestige, and power will remain within the class confines.

Black women seem to have attracted considerable attention and research interest partly because they represent a clear-cut case of a "double minority status" and because research evidence shows that in some circumstances their low status in both the race and sex stratification systems becomes an advantage (Epstein, 1973; and Bock, 1969). Epstein (1973), for example, found that black professional women who entered prestigious occupations stereotyped as "masculine" within the American society (such as law, medicine, or engineering), managed to obtain higher income and status than black professional men or white professional women. Her explanation was that these black women were non-threatening to white men and were allowed access to prestigious "masculine" fields and even a considerable extent of occupational achievement. These black women were non-threatening to white men because their double minority status placed them outside the realm of institutionalized rules of exchange since they could not up to now exchange sexual attractiveness for the right to enjoy desired goods. Their sexual possession by white men in no concrete way enhanced their status since high status white men could have sexual access to black women, if they wished, without having to offer in return income and status through marriage. Up to very recently, the black woman was supposed to be psychologically and socially rewarded by the mere fact that a white man was interested in a sexual association with her.

Actually, it is important to note that, at least income-wise, black professional women earn on the average more than white professional women (Sorkin, 1972). This is partly due to the fact that black women seem to have been less restrained from entering high-pay "masculine" occupations and partly because of the black women's lower geographical mobility and hence greater seniority (Sorkin, 1972). Almquist (1973), however, found that after standardizing for education and occupation, no race discrimination in terms of wages is evident between white and black women. When, however, the black female's income is standardized to that of the black male, the income difference due to sex discrimination is high (namely, $2,501). Furthermore, white females standardized in terms of education and occupation to white males, earn on the average $ 4,470 less than white males, while the income difference (due to race discrimination) between black and white males is only $ 1,772 (Almquist, 1973). Thus, while it seems that being black may be indirectly an asset to highly educated women over similarly highly educated white women, black women who are not well educated may suffer an economic double penalty from their double minority status. In general, sex discrimination seems to exceed race discrimination since after controlling for education and occupation (access to which is greatly inhibited by sex and race discrimination), income discrepancies are larger between black men and women rather than between black and white women or between black and white men.

Despite the many different overlapping stratification systems and the fact that the degree of discrimination that any woman experiences is determined by the particular configuration of statuses she occupies in these stratification systems, much of the theorizing and the large majority of research studies have abstracted sex discrimination and deal exclusively with it. Possibly a definition of sex discrimination is at this point necessary. *Sex discrimination* refers to *the differential treatment of women and men on the basis of their categorical membership, that is, on the basis of their gender, and without consideration of individual differences in terms of ability, competence, inclination, and commitment.*

The sex stratification system is maintained and women are assigned and kept at the subordinate position by means of sex role socialization as well as by sex discrimination. *Sex role socialization* refers to *the cognitive and learning processes by which women (and men) internalize the sex role ideology, that is, a complex body of stereotyped beliefs about the "nature" (inferior and "weak") of women, and the sex appropriate means for sharing in the distribution of valued goods (that is, income, status, and power).*

Successful sex role socialization guarantees the bringing up of sexist individuals who will discriminate on the basis of gender, will uphold sexist, prejudiced values, and will maintain the sex stratification system. The existence of a sex stratification system is and has been legitimized by respected and influential ideologies, *religious*, *moral*, or *scientific*, or by some combination of such ideologies. Depending upon the type of society and the prevailing degree of social differentiation and complexity, the type of legitimizing ideology varies. The more "closed" a society in terms of social mobility and the less socially differentiated and complex, the more the legitimation of women's subordinate position is derived from practically immutable religious and/or moral ideologies. The more, on the contrary, a society is "open," socially differentiated and complex, the more the legitimation is predominantely derived from scientific ideology, which can be potentially attacked for its correctness on more "objective," scientific (and hence subject to proof and change) grounds.

## I. Sex Prejudice

Turning now to examine the nature of sex prejudice (or sexism) and its behavioural correlates, the existing literature deals mainly with race prejudice and only inferences can be made as to the extent that the existing theories and research findings are equally applicable to sexism. The belief theory of prejudice, for example, suggests that when it is perceived that an individual is black or a woman, the tendency is to make assumptions about his or her different beliefs, assumptions which account for our negative feelings and discriminatory actions toward that individual. The assumption that another individual will not validate one's belief systems, tends to dispose one negatively toward that person (Banks, 1974). Furthermore, it seems that prejudice, racism or sexism, is the outcome of a combination of the tendency on the part of those who are already prejudiced to perceive blacks or women as dissimilar from themselves and of the tendency for this perception of dissimilarity to trigger off a greater extent of prejudice.

In fact, the belief theory can explain some aspects of sexism that are expressed by means of overt, blatant sex discrimination. In societies and in periods in which the type of dress, the overall appearance, the language as well as the existing norms about behaviour established and accentuated differences between men and women, one can find the most blatant sexism and sex discrimination directed against women. The veils worn by women in Muslim countries provide a striking example of the creation of and accent placed upon a most visible difference between men and women. Since, however, differences could, at least theoretically, result in sex discrimination in either direction, it is the content of the accentuated differences that helps to underline women's subordinate, dependent position. The crinolines, the corsets, the long narrow skirts, the dainty shoes, the long hair, all helped underline not only the existence of two separate worlds – the "man's world" and the "woman's world" – but also the weak, helpless, and dependent "nature" of women.

It must be pointed out, however, that the present trend in the United States and most West European countries toward unisex clothes, hair styles, and appearance, especially among the young, is a helpful and necessary but not sufficient condition to break down sexism and sex discrimination. Most probably overt, blatant sex discrimination is affected by this unisex tendency that plays down the anatomical and physical differences between men and women. And it is again this openly proclaimed type of sex discrimination, the overt, blatant type, that is first and most affected by non-discrimination legislation, policies, and ideologies. But unless psychological sexism is eradicated, sex discrimination goes underground and becomes more disguised, more subtle, but no less invidious. And because of its new subtlety, more deadly and more persistent.

Other studies have shown that highly prejudiced individuals tend to make grosser discriminations under stress (than in more neutral situations), to include the subject of their prejudice in the same category with an innocent bystander and to project their hostility on to the latter. Less prejudiced people, on the contrary, react to stress with a tendency to make finer differentiations (Berkowitz, 1961). These findings from race prejudice become very relevant since they agree with observations that under the present stressful conditions of unemployment, inflation, and severe budget cuts, men and women who are highly sexist tend to make more gross sexist evaluations, judgments, and decisions than before, especially if they are personally involved in potentially threatening situations in terms of income, employment, promotion, tenure, or access to power.

The important issue, however, is to what extent is sexism translated into sex discrimination; what type of sex discrimination as well as what the conditions are that tend to enhance or depress the acted out degree of sex discrimination. Available studies concerning the relationship between race prejudice and race discrimination have shown that reported attitudes and actual behaviour are not consistent (Merton, 1949; Rose, 1956; Simpson and Yinger, 1958; and Westie, 1964). Highly prejudiced individuals tend to be more inconsistent because they are affected by a number of conditions and social constraints, such as prevailing values regarding the nature, rights, and treatment of blacks or women, and the type of relationship and interaction with the woman in question (Linn, 1965; DeFriese and Ford, 1968; Warner and Dennis, 1971). Non-prejudiced individuals are quite concerned about and influenced by how they think others will interpret, evaluate and react to their behaviour vis-à-vis blacks or women (Linn, 1965; Fendrich, 1967; and Warner and Dennis, 1971). This explains why, once the women's liberation ideology became widespread in the U.S., the Scandinavian, and some other Western European nations, some men – who were never sexist – felt free to treat women as equals and as individuals and to discontinue discriminatory behaviours they adhered to in the past due to perceived social constraints (Safilios-Rothschild, 1974a).

The present, persisting poor agreement between sexism and sex discriminatory behaviour may be accounted for by the following principal reasons:

(*a*) Prejudiced people may appear to be sexism-free according to standard attitude measures, especially if they are well-educated and can, therefore, effectively dissimulate socially "undesirable" attitudes such as, sexist attitudes. As sexism is increasingly becoming something "nice" people should not feel subtle measures are needed to tap the dimensions involved. Thus, apparent inconsistencies between attitudes and behaviour may be only measurement artifacts and may in fact represent a good fit between sexism and sex discriminatory behaviour.

(*b*) Because in many educational and occupational settings in the U.S. and a few other European societies there are psychological, social and occasionally economic sanctions imposed for demonstrated sex discrimination, even highly prejudiced individuals – especially, those in prominent, decision-making positions – have often to mask their prejudice and to refrain from overt sex discrimination or are required to take action against on-going overt sex discrimination. This situation creates cognitive dissonance in them, since they remain as prejudiced as ever but, at least some of them, cope with the resulting stress by re-examining their beliefs about women and by in fact lessening the degree to which they are sexist (Safilios-Rothschild, 1974a).

(*c*) Some individuals who are not sexist may discriminate against women in one context and not discriminate against them in another context. Because sex prejudice is not unidimensional, some men may be free of prejudice with respect to women's educational and occupational rights and options but may be unwilling to treat women as equals in the familial, sexual, and affective contexts (Safilios-Rothschild, 1972a).

In general, it must be emphasized that it is very difficult to draw conclusions regarding the degree of agreement between sexist attitudes and beliefs and sex discriminatory behaviour partly because it is increasingly difficult accurately to measure sexist attitudes. And partly because research hitherto has seldom tapped varieties of sexist behaviour beyond the overt, blatant type of sex discrimination. Inconsistencies are, therefore, most probably due to measurement shortcomings rather than to actual, meaningful discrepancies.

## II. A Typology of Sex Discrimination

Sex discrimination may be expressed and acted out differently according to the type of society, the prevailing values about equality and freedom, the social desirability of sex discrimination, the degree of sex prejudice, the acting individual, the value attached to the "goods" at stake, as well as the characteristics of the woman toward whom the sex discrimination is directed. While we shall consider in some detail the effect of each of the above factors on the type and intensity of sex discrimination, it is helpful to start with a concise typology of sex discrimination:

*Typology of Sex Discrimination*

A. Formal Sex Discrimination
I. Indirect Sex Discrimination
II. Institutional Sex Discrimination
a. Overt Sex Discrimination
b. Disguised Sex Discrimination
B. Informal Sex Discrimination

*Formal sex discrimination* refers to sexist behaviours that have been in some way formalized as policies, laws, rules, or precedents and are followed as "due process." Formal sex discrimination may vary according to the degree of directness and the degree of overtness of the discriminatory actions. *Indirect sex discrimination* refers to sex discrimination that can take place at one level or setting on "objective" grounds because overt and informal sex discrimination was successfully carried out at previous levels or in other contexts. For example, considerable sex discrimination at the university level, as will be seen later, is indirect because overt and informal sex discrimination at the elementary and high school level as well as within the family have already eliminated many options and shaped aspirations, likes and dislikes, stifled talents and potentials, and instilled sex appropriate fears and controls.

*Institutional Sex Discrimination* refers to sex discriminatory behaviour that has been built into the formal policies of institutions. This type of structural, institutionalized sex discrimination tends to be perpetuated by prejudiced and non-prejudiced persons alike (Burkey, 1971; Blauner, 1972; Berkanovic, 1973; Butsch, 1974; and Benokraitis and Feagin, 1974). Isolated non-prejudiced individuals in powerless positions cannot go effectively against institutional sex discrimination, even if their consciousness is raised significantly to recognize sex discriminatory practices. Many non-prejudiced individuals are not, however, conscious of the sex discriminatory nature of many policies they follow and practices in which they engage. When, however, many individuals within an institution are non-prejudiced and become conscious of sex discriminatory institutional processes, they can change these processes, especially if at least some of them have power and societal and/or legal support. It can be argued, however, that some structural aspects of institutions which are directly and indirectly overtly sex discriminatory are to a large extent beyond the control of individual institutional members, regardless of their degree of sex prejudice. Taking the educational institution as an example, structural features such as sex-differentiated curricula and fields (determined by centralized higher authorities and prevailing values), sex-ratio of teachers or professors and school or college administrators, sex-segregated schools and colleges represent discriminatory features against which considerable legal and popular polemics must be aroused before they can be attacked and changed. Institutional members, however, such as teachers, school administrators, and vocational counsellors can, to some extent, counteract the sex-differentiation of curricula and fields, if they do not themselves endorse the appropriateness of such sex-differentiation.

Institutional sex discrimination may be *overt*, if the institutional processes and policies openly discriminate on the basis of gender, or *disguised*, if sex discrimination takes place under the disguise of another more "universalistic" and socially acceptable criterion such as age limit for college admissions, undesirability of credit transfers, or exclusion of part-time students from graduate and professional schools (that discriminate almost entirely against women college students). In some cases, the disguise used for sex discrimination is ridiculous as when, for example, university policies excluded pregnant students from research assistantships (and other financial aid to graduate students) on the basis of their "pregnancy rather than on the basis of gender!!!"

Finally, *informal sex discrimination* refers to sex discriminatory practices and behaviours of prejudiced individuals that may vary considerably with respect to the degree of overtness or subtlety. Since informal sex discrimination is carried out by prejudiced individuals, it may take place regardless of the degree of institutional sex discrimination present. In its subtlest forms, informal sex discrimination can be successfully practised even when the formal policies and rules of an institution are not only non-discriminatory but clearly forbid and even punish sex discrimination.

While usually all types of sex discrimination are found in all societies, different types of discrimination are more relied upon in different societies. One of the important societal differences is the explicitness and thoroughness of the prevailing sex role socialization process. The more "closed" is a society and the more "equality" is not highly valued and legitimized by influential political and social ideologies, the more sexism can be overt and the more the socialization of children can explicitly and systematically prepare them to "fit" in a rigid sex stratification system. Little girls are made to feel less important and valuable than their brothers in all circumstances. Parents are proud of their sons and brag about them to friends and relatives. Even when they have to punish them harder and more frequently, it is clear that they have an admiration and a weakness for them and for their rough, unruly, "masculine" behaviour. Boys are given the best morsels of food and in cases of food scarcity, they are given most of the food while girls suffer from malnutrition. Girls observe the subservient position of their mothers who take orders from their fathers, are shouted at when they have disobeyed these orders, and are treated as servants and objects.

Girls also witness the family drama when another girl is born instead of an expected and hoped for boy. Everybody is unhappy, tears are shed, and not infrequently the father is angry and turns his anger against his wife who "can only bear girls ..." Furthermore, the message that the subordinate position is the girls' rightful place in the sex stratification system gets across to them by the fact that brothers (even those younger than their sisters) become the protectors, controllers, and overseers of their sisters, and have the right to beat them up, to embarrass them, to shout at them, and to run their lives. With such clear-cut, explicit, and poignant sex role socialization experiences, girls have to be born rebels to attempt or be able to escape their "natural" subordinate position in the sex stratification system.

In "closed" societies in which relatively little upward social mobility takes place, people do not have aspirations and expectations to change their lives significantly from that of their parents and tend, therefore, to accept their assigned "place." In such societies, a particularistic rather than a universalistic orientation accentuates women's inability to escape traditional sex role stereotypes and sex stereotyped options since decisions and evaluations are made on the basis of who one is ("a woman") rather than on the basis of what one can do (individual abilities, talents, and competence).

In such societies, because sex role socialization is so explicit, pervasive, and thorough and because sex discrimination is also self-understood, clear-cut, and overt, there is no need for elaborate and subtle sex discrimination. Thus, there is no need to rely upon disguised institutional or informal sex discrimination. And because sex role socialization and overt sex discrimination are so overwhelming and devastating, there is no need for systematic societal checks at different critical points in order to screen out women who may have slipped through. Because of this, the very few women who escape the sex role socialization can, if they are highly intelligent or high status, beat sex discrimination by using their particularistic characteristics (high intelligence, or social status) and manage to reach high positions and enjoy considerable power.

The more on the other hand social mobility becomes possible or expected in a society, the more universalistic rather than particularistic criteria are (in fact or ideally) used and the more equality becomes valued and legitimized by major ideologies, the more sex role socialization and sex discrimination tend to become subtle and disguised under other more acceptable pretences. Girls are told that they are different from boys but equally important while at the same time parents, teachers, the media, admire and emphasize masculine pursuits, masculine characteristics, masculine achievements, and male heroes. Girls are encouraged to do well in school but the message is clear that if they are too intelligent and too highly achieving, boys will not be interested in taking them out and will not fall in love with them. Girls are brought up with the rhetoric that they are free to do whatever they wish but are carefully indoctrinated and steered to do the "right things" that is, to accept the constraints of feminine stereotypes in order to be loved and accepted.

Since, however, it is possible that this type of more subtle and "psychological" sex role socialization may not be consistently successful or always expertly carried out, and because sex discrimination cannot be blatant, a great wealth of techniques and means to discriminate proliferate as checks at different critical points of access. Thus, elaborate indirect means of sex discrimination, disguised sex discrimination and informal sex discrimination techniques are used, the last being the most relied upon for controlling "deviants" from sex stereotyped options and behaviours. Some informal sex discrimination techniques require actors who are aware of their sexism; in others, the sexism may be unconscious. The fact that often unknowingly sexist individuals successfully use informal techniques of sex discrimination was clearly demonstrated in the United States after the widespread dissemination of the Sex Role Ideology. When some teachers, professors, parents, vocational counsellors, administrators, employers, or therapists realized how sex discriminatory were many of their techniques, arguments, advice or suggestions, they became most anxious to change them since they were not in fact aware of their sexist behaviour.

The important feature of sex discrimination in "open," universalistic-oriented societies is that sex discrimination in all its forms is pervasive of all societal structures and institutions and at all levels. Even women who have managed to escape the limitations of an effective sex role socialization cannot get through the many sex discriminatory checks built-in in all important access points. Furthermore, the more "open" and universalistic the society purports to be, the more women and men are given the impression that they are making free choices and that decisions concerning them are made on the basis of objective, universalistic criteria. As long as no particular social movement has made "gender" a suspect criterion, it continues to be used as a valid, substantive criterion for differentiating "appropriate" fields, positions, promotions, salaries, and other options for men and women.

After, however, as a result of a Women's Liberation Movement and the ensuing Sex Role Ideology it becomes clear that "gender" is a suspect criterion on which to base valid decisions, sex discrimination becomes illegal, but it does not disappear, it only goes underground. New subtler, more sophisticated strategies and techniques are devised in order to disguise sex discrimination or in order to enact sex discrimination while officially complying with non-discriminatory rules and policies. The most well-known technique is "tokenism" by which the complying institution admits only *one* (or two) female students or hires *one* (or two) female employees, professors, or administrators in an all-male field. It is only recently, however, that research showed the dynamics by which such tokenism truly constitutes sex discrimination.

Research, for example, on the type of role models that token faculty women serve to female students has shown that such token faculty women tend to accentuate the marginality and inappropriateness of women in the professional field involved. Women, therefore, are discriminated against in that they do not feel encouraged to opt for masculine fields and the available research findings show that in fact they choose these fields much less often in universities and departments in which there is a lack of a sufficient number of women faculty models to normalize their professional choice. Furthermore, token women faculty members may occasionally serve as negative models due to their own peculiar idiosyncracies or life styles which again tend to stand out instead of being normalized within a larger group of faculty women (Litton Fox, 1973). Token women faculty members have in the past acted (and are still occasionally acting) as negative models through the "queen bee" syndrome that is, by actively discouraging women from entering the field, by being hostile toward women, and by actively discriminating against them through grades and research opportunities. Thus, Departments of Engineering or Physics can comply with affirmative action by adding one or two women to their faculty without in fact diminishing in any way the degree of indirect discrimination against women students.

Tokenism in student admissions at different levels has been proven to be even more discriminatory and destructive for the women students involved. A recent study examined, for example, the nature of interactions that take place when a "solo" woman finds herself in a professional peer group such as a group of psychiatric residents or a group of psychiatric graduate students and the effect of these interactions for the training and integration chances of the women (Wolman and Frank, 1973). The study showed that in each of the six peer groups observed, the men reacted negatively to the woman "intruder" in their all-male group and used a variety of techniques in order to neutralize her presence and preserve the "all-male" atmosphere and quality of interaction. Men continued to talk between themselves, intellectualizing feelings rather than expressing them as they are required to do during psychiatric training, since in this way they could emphasize their masculinity. Also men avoided pairing or in any way allying with the lone woman in order not to disrupt the cohesiveness between the male members and in order not to share her deviant and marginal role. The possibility for sexual attraction made the woman's presence even more threatening since such an occurrence would constitute a highly disruptive element in the male relationships and friendships. Men handled this potentiality for sexual attraction by completely ignoring the woman's sexuality and by condemning her to a low and marginal status. Consistently the "solo" woman is always defined as deviant, is isolated, and made peripheral and marginal regardless of her behaviour, her personality, or the type of copying techniques used. Thus, women are discriminated against by their male peers since their forced marginality seriously interferes with the outcome of their training. Some become so discouraged that they drop out altogether and others enjoy limited training experiences because they are excluded from the group (Wolman and Frank, 1973).

Some recent evidence is even more disturbing since it indicates that even when larger numbers of women are admitted to previously masculine professional schools such as medical schools, institutional policies that require the sub-division of students into smaller groups serve to reduce the presence of woman to a "solo" presence in each group. A recent survey of women medical students showed that they were told informally but firmly that no more than one girl should belong to the same small instructional group of usually 7–8 students (Campbell, 1973). Sometimes the reason for this dispersion of women was clear and explicit: "women shouldn't get together, so they start protesting, agitating, and all this Women's Lib nonsense." But even when the rationale was not explicitly stated, the results were clearly discriminatory against the women, as a recent study of such groups of medical students in the anatomy class showed (Frank, 1975). Similar to the fate of the "solo" psychiatric trainee, the "solo" female medical student in the instructional small groups in the anatomy class was totally ignored and left out from the topical conversation by her fellow medical students, was made marginal and had little chance to participate in the crucial training experiences (Frank, 1975).

All the above recent evidence from small group research in the United States suggests that when overt sex discrimination becomes illegal, prejudiced individuals revert to subtler, informal sex discrimination that can be documented and combatted only with great difficulty. This is the price that societies pay when legal and social changes take place before the large majority of individuals have values and attitudes consonant with these changes. It is interesting to speculate as to the form that sex discrimination will take now that even these subtler techniques have been uncovered and made public. Will sexist people give up or try to become even more ingenious?

## III. The Content of Sex Discrimination

Turning now to the content of sex discrimination, we shall examine the accumulated evidence from a considerable number of research studies which have shown the dynamics of sex discrimination within the context of concrete settings. We shall limit our presentation to the educational and occupational setting for which there is sufficient research evidence. Most of the relevant research has taken place in the United States and Canada, especially with regard to sex discrimination at the elementary school level. Whenever relevant research is available from U.S.S.R., Sweden, Poland, or other countries, it will be incorporated in the discussion.

### *A. Sex Discrimination at the Elementary and High School Level*

At these levels, sex discrimination may be indirect, overt institutional, or informal. *Indirect sex discrimination* at the elementary school level has been mainly accomplished outside the schools in the family and by the mass media. Available research evidence has amply documented that mothers and fathers behave differently toward daughters than toward sons from the time of birth (Lynn and Sawrey, 1962; Droppleman and Schafer, 1963; Moss, 1967; Moss, Robson and Pederson, 1969; Goldberg and Lewis, 1969; Lewis, 1972). Some of these sex-differentiated parental behaviours are of great interest because of the implications they have for the long-range educational behaviour and achievements of daughters and sons. Boys, for example, are given more and earlier independence training (Collard, 1964); more punishment (Droppleman and Schafer, 1963); and are encouraged more in intellectual curiosity than girls (Lynn and Sawrey, 1962). Mothers maintain physically close and affectionate relationships with their daughters for a longer period of time than with their sons (Lewis, 1972); they reward them more and they punish them less. Daughters, therefore, tend to receive much more affection and approval while sons receive a better balance of positive and negative reactions from their mothers. Actually, girls seem to suffer from too much love and maternal concern. Some psychologists have pointed out that mothers and fathers tend to be much more anxious and protective toward their daughters than toward their sons and, therefore, even to encourage dependency in them as a guarantee that they will remain protected by the parents (Wladis Hoffman, 1974). Thus, despite the greater maturity and sturdiness of the female infant (Garai and Schienfeld, 1968), parents are anxious about the independent behaviours of girls and happy and relaxed over similar behaviours on the part of boys.

As Wladis Hoffman (1974) had concluded a maternal sex-differentiated behaviour that could be labelled "overhelp" may be the most detrimental behaviour for daughters' development of independence and achievement motivation. If the parent responds to the child's crying or asking for help too quickly, the child never has a chance to develop the ability to tolerate frustration, to tackle by itself the problem and to explore possible solutions. And there is evidence that mothers tend much more quickly and frequently to help girls than boys when faced with some kind of a difficult task (*ibid.*). Thus, girls learn to be dependent upon adults for help rather than trying to cope with problems and difficult situations and to explore solutions by themselves.

Furthermore, mothers place a greater degree of pressure for achievement and independence on their pre-school-age boys than on girls of the same age. In addition, mothers tend to reward boys' aggression as appropriate "masculine" behaviour while girls' aggression is never rewarded and only indirect expressions are at best tolerated. Furthermore, mothers place pressure on girls for "feminine" neatness, obedience and conformity while the pressure on boys is for independence and achievement (Hatfield, Ferguson, and Alpert, 1967). Another observation study showed, similarly, that fathers positively reinforce significantly more often dependent rather than independent daughters (Osofsky and O'Connell, 1972).

Finally, it seems that high achievement motivation in girls is fostered by exactly those parental behaviours which are the opposite of those fostering "femininity." Namely, achievement motivation is higher in girls when their mothers are less affectionate and less nurturant and when they set high standards for their daughters' intellectual achievement. Furthermore, daughters are more proficient in both reading and arithmetic achievement tests when their mothers hold high achievement expectations (Crandall, Dewey, Katkovsky, and Preston, 1964). It seems, therefore, that while the best condition for fostering "femininity" in girls is maternal affection and nurturance (Hetherington, 1967), the best type of maternal behaviour for high achievement socialization is a balance of warmth combined with some punishment and distance on the part of mothers as well as high expectations for achievement and independence (Berens, 1972; Stein and Bailey, 1972). Thus, mothers' "over-affection" lavished on their daughters represents the subtlest and "sweetest" but also probably one of the most potent types of sex discrimination. All these socialization studies, most of which are observational, suggest that girls and boys are differentially conditioned by their parents so that by the time they go to school, they: (*a*) are aware of existing sex role stereotypes and sex-appropriate behaviours; (*b*) have already been influenced by their parents' sex-differentiated behaviours so that girls have a greater tendency to be obedient, neat, passive, and dependent and boys a greater tendency to be aggressive, disobedient, independent, exploring, and creative. These tendencies instilled in children by parental sex role socialization and reinforced through all the books and comics they read and all the television shows and advertisements they see constitute a significant indirect sex discrimination since they pave the way for sex discrimination in school.

It must be further pointed out that the more children advance in school, the more indirect sex discrimination builds up from grade to grade. The more intense the informal and institutional sex discrimination on the part of teachers, curricula, readers, and school structures has been in early grades, the more indirect sex discrimination operates in later grades. Boys and girls tend increasingly to behave according to sex role stereotypes and further to justify teachers' sex-differentiated behaviours and expectations and all types of ongoing sex discriminatory practices.

Once boys and girls start going to school (from kindergarten on), they are faced with a number of *institutional* sex-discriminatory features, most of which are quite *overt*. The first such feature is the sex-composition of the faculty which in most countries is quite skewed toward the female sex at the lower grades and increasingly toward the male sex at higher grades and in administrative positions. Probably the American case represents an extreme since only two percent of the elementary school teachers are male while very few women are school administrators but similar situations are replicated in several societies. Such a clearly sex-differentiated school hierarchy clearly transmits the message to girls that women, even when they work, occupy subordinate positions in which they must obey men and abide by their decisions. Such a message is quite powerful in helping consolidate the effects of the continuous informal sex discriminatory practices to which girls (and boys) are subjected.

Furthermore, children are exposed to sexist books and illustrated material even before they can read and clearly to sexist texts from the time they can read. Content analyses of elementary school texts of all types (history, literature, and even arithmetic) carried out in the United States (DeCrow, 1972; Saario, Jacklin, and Tittle, 1973; Taylor, 1973; Frazier and Sadker, 1973; Levy and Stacey, 1973; Stacey, Berand, and Daniels, 1974; in Sweden (Fredriksson, 1969; Westman Berg, 1969); and in Norway and Finland (Westman Berg, 1969) show that readers not only reflect the sex stratification system in the society but even surpass reality by portraying an even more sexist society than is true at present. Fathers are presented as the sole breadwinners and decision-makers and as exclusively involved in traditional stereotyped male activities. Mothers are depicted virtually exclusively as homemakers and nurturers and *when* they are shown as working women, they are nurses, teachers, or secretaries. Mothers are, furthermore, presented as dull, ineffectual, almost totally preoccupied with housework and shopping, incapable of problem solving and even stupid.

The sex discriminatory power of such sexist school readers is enormous since children learn within the context of a "lesson," hence within the context of official knowledge and wisdom, the appropriateness and even desirability of a sex stratification system in which women *must* occupy the subordinate position. Thus, all their previous perceptions regarding such a sex stratification system become solidified with the seal of education and "science." Furthermore, these sexist readers make children (and especially boys) feel that sex discrimination is a "natural" process that everybody follows.

But probably the most effective type of sex discrimination to which school-children are subjected is the *informal* set of sex discriminatory behaviours on the part of teachers. It must be emphasized that, as is often true with informal sex discrimination, those who practise it may not be conscious of the nature of their behaviour or of its implications and consequences for the students involved. This may be due partly to naïveté as to what behaviour constitutes sex discrimination and partly to lack of understanding of the dynamics involved in the translation of a teacher's behaviour or expectation into a student's behaviour. A recent study (Chasen, 1974) illustrates well the above points. The interviewed elementary school teachers felt that they treated school-girls and school-boys equally in the classroom and resisted the implication of possible sex stereotyping in their behaviours or thoughts regarding their students. When asked, however, specific questions regarding their beliefs and behaviours, it became clear that they held sexist beliefs and exhibited sex-differentiated behaviours that were discriminatory toward girls. They reported, for example, that they believed that boys are innately more aggressive while girls are innately more passive while they also admitted that they were actively discouraging aggressive behaviour in girls (but not in boys), thus facilitating a self-fulfilling prophecy. Teachers also reported that aggressive behaviour in the teacher-child interactions was encouraged more in boys than in girls. Furthermore, teachers reported feeling boys' muscles more frequently than girls' muscles and telling boys more often than girls that they were strong and that they encouraged boys to do wood-working, while girls were mostly encouraged to do collage, a sedentary, passive activity. More specifically, the majority of the teachers said that they often encouraged boys to play with blocks or to do wood-working while only a few of them encouraged boys to play with dolls. Furthermore, it is interesting to note that there was emotional resistance on the part of the teachers to boys' playing with dolls or to girls' playing with blocks (Chasen, 1974).

A number of observation studies conducted in American elementary and high schools have documented the teachers' sex-differentiated behaviours that constitute a different type of sex discrimination directed toward boys and girls. The findings of these studies can be grouped into categories:

(*a*) Findings showing that teachers praise as well as criticize more frequently boys than girls. One observation study, for example, concluded that boys were asked more direct questions by the teacher than girls. They were also praised more frequently when they gave correct answers and criticized more often for incorrect answers or failures to respond (Brophy and Good, 1970). These findings are significant because they indicate that the teachers' sex-differentiated behaviour tends to place a greater pressure on boys rather than on girls to achieve a pattern that tends to reinforce that produced by similar sex-differentiated parental behaviours.

(*b*) Findings indicating that teachers interact much more often with boys than with girls, these interactions being both positive and negative. One observation study concluded that boys were found to have more interactions with the teacher than girls and appeared to be generally more salient in the teacher's perceptual field (Brophy and Good, 1970). Another observation study of seventh and eighth grade classrooms concluded that boys were more active and interacted more frequently with teachers and that boys received more contacts from teachers, both positive and negative while girls received less contacts but proportionately more positive ones (Good, Sikes, and Brophy, 1973). In terms of these findings, girls seem to be sex discriminated in that they have less contact and interactions with the teacher and are experiencing a less stimulating school environment than boys.

(*c*) Findings indicating that girls tend to be more approved of by teachers than boys because they fit better the desirable institutional-type behaviour of dependent, docile, passive, obedient children that do not disrupt the classroom routine. One study, for example, showed that student teachers prefer students described as dependent, passive, and acquiescent and react less favourably to students portrayed as independent, assertive, and active. In fact, all student teachers, men and women, assign the highest mean preference rating to conformist, rigid girls while the independent girls receive the lowest ratings (that is, even lower than independent boys who seem to be better tolerated) (Good and Grouws, 1972). Thus, it seems that the teachers' ideal of a schoolchild coincides with the "feminine" stereotype, a fact that may appear to be beneficial to girls at a short-range but which is clearly detrimental to them in the long-range. Already socialized at home and by the media to behave according to sex role stereotypes, girls receive a very powerful reinforcement to do so through the teachers' approval and rewards, including good grades. This process, however, proves to be detrimental to girls after a few years since they, thus, become locked into their sex role and socialized to habitual modes of behaving which are essentially incompatible with autonomy, independence, and assertiveness, characteristics associated with achievement and with competent and effective adult functioning (Grambs and Waetjen, 1966; Sadker and Sadker, 1972; Lee, 1973). Boys, on the other hand, because of their "masculine" socialization, already begun at home, tend to displease teachers and attract their punishment and criticisms but are, thus, able to maintain their high level of activity as well as their autonomy, independence, assertiveness, and intellectual curiosity. Boys can, thus, attract a greater share of the teacher's attention and possibly become further stimulated by such interactions. Furthermore, teachers' tendency to give lower grades to boys than to girls (partially as a punishment for disruptive behaviour) may, in some cases, tend to reinforce boys' relatively greater emphasis upon learning rather than upon pleasing the teacher or obtaining good grades.

(*d*) Findings indicating that gender and scholastic achievement are mutually interactive variables that affect the teacher's behaviour vis-à-vis the students. More specifically, the available research evidence indicates that teachers tend to tolerate low level scholastic achievement better in girls than in boys since, according to sex role stereotypes, boys are clearly supposed to be leaders and to achieve highly (Lippit and Gold, 1959; Good, Sikes, and Brophy, 1973). Because of teachers' high expectations for boys, their failure to achieve is punished with disapproval and rejection while the teachers behave somewhat more cordially to girls with similar low achievement levels (Lippit and Gold, 1959). The more recent study (Good, Sikes, and Brophy, 1973) showed that low achievement boys are especially likely to be highly criticized by teachers, to receive little teacher feedback about their academic work, and little opportunity to respond. The study further showed that while high achievement boys have more frequent and more supportive contacts with teachers than high achievement girls, low achievement boys have fewer and more negative contacts with teachers than low achievement girls (Good, Sikes, and Brophy, 1973). Low achievement girls have social approval for "being nice" as an alternative to high scholastic achievement, while the only alternatives open to low achievement boys is athletic prowess or aggressive behaviour (Caplan and Kinsbourne, 1974). Thus, girls are again discriminated against whether they are high or low achievers. When they are high achievers, they have less interaction with and less supportive feedback from teachers than high achieving boys. When they are low achievers, they are under less pressure to strive toward a higher level or alternative types of achievement since they are still liked and approved of by the teacher, as long as they stay quiet, compliant, and dependent. It seems, however, that low achieving boys are also discriminated against by the extreme pressure placed upon them to achieve and the painful social rejection inflicted upon them when they fail to fulfill the sex-appropriate level of achievement.

### *B. Sex Discrimination in Higher Education*

At this level, *indirect* sex discrimination becomes very important because of the considerable sex discrimination that has already taken place at lower levels. Because, for example, women are "cooled out" of science and mathematics courses in high school, most of the "masculine," high prestige academic fields in college are closed to them due to their poor background (Flanagan, 1966). Also, because vocational counsellors in high school as well as parents have already discouraged girls from entering high prestige, "masculine" fields, there is often no need to apply further sex discriminatory rules and practices at the college level. Women have been convinced to stay in "their place," that is, to enter the few appropriate "feminine" fields, if they go to college at all.

Another type of indirect sex discrimination at the college level takes place because women are discriminated against when they get married or they have children. Their discrimination in this area results from the fact that they are assigned the major (if not the exclusive) responsibility for household tasks and child care. Thus, a high school marriage or a marriage right after high school graduation drastically diminishes women's chances of attending college (Ludeman, 1961). Also, married women in general enroll as graduate or undergraduate students in smaller numbers than single women and tend to drop out of college in larger numbers than single or divorced women (Feldman, 1973; Lord, 1968). Also, because women have to follow their husbands wherever their job or education takes them, they usually lose credit hours in transferring from one university to another and have their training lengthened by having to satisfy different sets of requirements (Pullen, 1970; Ruslink, 1969; Shoulders, 1968; Chess, 1969).

Up to very recently in the United States and many other nations, *overt* institutional sex discrimination was best illustrated by the sex-segregated colleges and universities. Repeatedly courts had been reluctant to recognize sex segregation as similar to race segregation and to outlaw sex admission policies at the college and university level (Shaman, 1971). The arguments were that there are many different women's as well as co-educational colleges and universities that women can attend and that many of the women's colleges are of high quality. And even when a college is not accessible to a woman in the town or city where she lives, she can always go to a college in another city (Shaman, 1971). Both of these arguments are not valid. In most societies sex segregation at the higher education level constitutes sex discrimination because men's colleges are usually more richly endowed, offer a greater variety of courses and curricula – including those preparing students for high prestige, "masculine" fields, – have better teachers and enjoy a better academic reputation (Shaman, 1971; Bunting, 1961). Furthermore, moving to another city or another state in order to be able to attend a college that offers the desired curriculum makes education much more expensive for women (since they can no longer live at home) or outright impossible, when they are married and cannot move away (Shaman, 1971; Ewald, 1971).

A different type of blatant institutional sex discrimination is represented by the practice of quotas limiting the number of women admitted to engineering, medical, law schools, as well as graduate programmes (Cross, 1971; Phelps, 1973; McBee and Suddick, 1974). Thus, women are discriminated against regardless of whether they are qualified or not. Only outstanding women are admitted; otherwise men are preferentially admitted even if less qualified than many of the women applicants (Cross, 1971; McBee and Suddick, 1974). And clearly, average women do not stand a chance (Werts, 1966; Waltser, Clearly, and Clifford, 1971; Hunter, 1967). The degree of discrimination against women applicants is, furthermore, much greater in prestige universities than in other universities (Solmon, 1974).

There are, furthermore, a number of discriminatory policies with regard to some types of financial aid available to men and women college students. First, a number of fellowships and scholarships connected with athletics or ROTC are open only to men. Second, fewer women are given part-time research assistantships that not only provide them adequate financial aid but also with valuable research apprentice experience (Solmon, 1974). Third, in "masculine" fields women are less often appointed teaching assistants since there is a reluctance in having women teach men students (Harris, 1970). Finally, discriminatory university policies exclude women but not men fellowship applicants on the basis of their spouse's income, policies that seriously discriminate against middle-income married women who want to attend graduate school. Such women, regardless of merit, must either work part-time (something often very difficult because of their familial responsibilities) or be financially dependent upon their husbands, who often at least mildly disapprove of their attending graduate school.

*Disguised* sex discrimination has been increasingly relied upon during the last decades in societies such as the United States, since it tends to be more socially acceptable than overt sex discrimination. The best examples of such discrimination at the university level are:

(*a*) The existence of a more or less formal age limit at 35 years of age in admissions that discriminates primarily against women who return to college (at the undergraduate or graduate level) at that age due to the prevailing discriminatory division of labour within the family (Blackwell, 1963; Lyon, 1964; Randolph, 1965; Johnstone and Rivera, 1965; Hunter, 1967).

(*b*) Strict rules and policies regarding the transfer of credit hours that again discriminate primarily against women who must transfer often due to their husbands' moves (Shoulders, 1968; Chess, 1969; Ruslink, 1969; and Pullen, 1970).

(*c*) Requirements of full-time attendance throughout the entire training (or at least for 1–2 years) in graduate programmes and professional schools act as powerful barriers to women's entry to such programmes and schools (Myers, 1964; Riesman, 1965; Hembrough, 1966; Chess, 1968; Bunting, Graham, and Wasserman, 1970). Women's frequent inability to attend full-time is again due to indirect sex discriminatory (discriminatory division of labour) within the family and to some extent also to their lesser access to scholarships and fellowships due to overt or informal sex discrimination. Thus, many qualified and interested women cannot become physicians, lawyers, pharmacists or researchers and university professors when they are young but have to postpone their studies until their children are grown up, at which time they are discriminated against on the basis of their age.

When all other types of sex discrimination have not been successful in keeping women out of the university, or out of "masculine" fields or the graduate programme sexist faculty and administrators can still screen women out by means of *informal* sex discrimination. Women are cooled out by means of a number of techniques and strategies that can be grouped into three major categories:

(*a*) Humiliation or severe psychological harassment and intimidation (Bikman, 1970; Campbell, 1973).

(*b*) Belittling (Bikman, 1970); ignoring the existence of women students, even when they represent 25 percent of the student body in a masculine field like medicine; and rejection of women as intellectual beings (Campbell, 1973). A study at the University of Southern California at Berkeley reported that women students were significantly less often than men treated as colleagues or apprentices by their professors not only in more "masculine" fields as mathematics and the biological sciences but also in psychology, sociology, history, or anthropology. The same study also showed that women students are taken less seriously professionally by their professors even in the advanced years of graduate school and that these subtle but potent discriminatory behaviours constitute the underlying reason for women's dropping out of graduate school (Sells, 1973).

(*c*) Preferential treatment of men with regard to research assistantships and opportunities for research experience.

After all the types of discriminatory practices and rules at the university level have been presented, it becomes clear that the only women who have a chance to enter in and, more important, to graduate especially from "masculine" fields, professional schools, and graduate programmes are the highest qualified women, the most stubborn and resilient women, with strong nerves and a "thick skin," and those with a sufficient income that allows them to attend on a full-time basis (when they are not granted a fellowship) by hiring help for their familial responsibilities. This portrait of the woman who can make it to professional schools, to graduate programmes, and "masculine" fields makes it abundantly clear that women are overwhelmingly discriminated against in many ways at the university level.

### *C. Occupational Discrimination*

In most countries educational discrimination diminishes before occupational discrimination, in terms of both attitudes and behaviours. In a country like Greece, for example, it is widely accepted by now that women should have equal educational opportunities with men at all levels (Safilios-Rothschild, 1972a) and, in fact, an equal percentage of men and women complete high school while 31.6 percent of women attend college (Statistical Yearbook of Greece, 1972). When, however, it comes to women's employment, only about one-third of men and women think that married women should work (Safilios-Rothschild, 1972a) and, in fact, only 27.8 percent of Greek women do work (Statistical Yearbook of Greece, 1972). Thus, women are often not allowed *entry* into an occupation, even when they are qualified to do so and, furthermore, if they manage to enter an occupation, they are invariably discriminated against in a variety of ways (*treatment* discrimination – Terborg and Ilgen, in press; Levitin, Quinn, and Staines, 1971).

A basic *entry* type of occupational sex discrimination carried out by means of indirect, institutional, overt, and informal strategies, policies, and rules refers to the labelling of occupations as "masculine" and "feminine." This labelling is discriminatory because in all societies and periods the occupations which are classed as "feminine" are the low status, low pay, auxiliary occupations or monotonous, routine jobs that men are willing to relegate to women. Men, on the other hand, keep for themselves the occupations of higher prestige and pay as well as the more interesting and those with access to power positions. Furthermore, whenever an initially low status and low pay occupation, due to ongoing social changes, becomes more prestigious, better paid, or vested with some power, it becomes re-classified as "masculine" and men start to dominate it, while an occupation becomes re-classified as "feminine" in the reverse situation. The occupation "secretary" represents a good illustration of an occupation which in many African countries is still relatively well paid and prestigious and is dominated by men. In western societies, on the other hand, where it carries little prestige and administrative positions are better paid and more promising, secretarial jobs are held by women while men with the same educational qualifications can enter administrative jobs labelled "masculine" (Safilios-Rothschild, 1974a).

It is important to note that the sex labels attached to occupations are usually justified on the basis of sex role stereotypes and varying interpretations of sex-related characteristics. In the U.S.S.R., medicine is labelled a "feminine" occupation because it is a relatively low status and a low paying occupation, but the label is justified in terms of women's nurturant "nature" (Power Goldberg, 1972; Dodge, 1966). In the U.S., however, where medicine is a highly prestigious and a very well paying occupation, it is labelled "masculine" and the label is justified on the basis of the high degree of commitment necessary that women cannot make due to their familial responsibilities. Actually, of course, the usual justification of the built-in flexibility in occupations labelled "feminine" (such as, teaching at the elementary school) is false since, in fact, many of the occupations labelled "masculine" do have much more flexibility (Safilios-Rothschild, 1972b). Occupations such as medicine, dentistry, pharmacy, research work, or teaching at the university level, occupations labelled "masculine" in the United States and several other societies, can provide considerable flexibility since the professional can largely set his own hours and can work fewer than 40 hours per week in an office setting. In some societies, of course, such as Finland, Hungary, Poland, the U.S.S.R., Denmark or Greece, pharmacy and dentistry have recently become predominantly "feminine" occupations (or equally open to both sexes) partly because of this built-in flexibility (Safilios-Rothschild, 1971).

Once, however, due to their outstanding qualifications or different combinations of circumstances women become trained for a masculine field, *entry* discriminatory practices tend to screen them out or to relegate them to lower positions with less pay and advancement probabilities than men. Studies of university administrators (Simpson, 1970; Fidell, 1970) and bank supervisors (Rosen and Jerdee, 1974) have shown that qualifications being equal, a male candidate would be chosen over a woman unless the woman was clearly superior. Furthermore, women may not have access to prestigious positions simply because they lack the information about these jobs and because they are not recommended for these jobs by powerful, top-ranking men in the field. Most of the jobs in academia as well as industry at high levels, especially the "plums," have been always filled through the informal "buddy" communication network between males (Epstein, 1970). But the existence of similar buddy systems between salesmen, skilled workers, construction contractors, union leaders, and so on, has been all too powerful in keeping women out of a wide range of positions in all types of masculine occupations. The recent requirement in the U.S. and some other societies for wide advertisement of openings has, to some extent, mitigated, but by no means neutralized, this type of occupational sex discrimination. Probably the development of an equally powerful women's communication network can help fight effectively this type of sex discrimination, as the recent experience of American professional women has proven.

Finally, an *indirect* type of sex discrimination in the family system, resulting from the wife's (legal and social) obligation to go where her husband's job takes him, has and is still drastically limiting women's geographic mobility and hence, her degree of access to jobs, particularly desirable jobs. Despite the few sensational reported cases in which professional couples in the United States or Sweden live in different cities in order for both to be able to hold the jobs they wish and despite the fact that some men in the academic field and industry will not consider an offer unless job opportunities (or more rarely, an offer) are available to their wives, these cases appear to still represent the minority. A recent study of women microbiologists reported that 93 percent of the women doctorates would be willing to move only if their husband could find a satisfactory position in the same location before moving, but only 20 percent of the men made such conditions for their wives' employment (Kashket, *et al.*, 1974).

But even when women are hired, *treatment* sex discrimination continues. The available evidence indicates that they are consistently offered, on the average, lower salaries than men regardless of their qualifications (Terborg and Ilgen, in press). These salary differentials may represent partly blatant and partly indirect sex discrimination due to women's older average age, recommendations from less powerful people, graduation from less prestigious schools or lack of valuable research or apprentice experience. With respect to advancement and promotions, all types of sex discrimination continue to operate and to become more overt and clear-cut, the more women do well and aspire to top decision-making and policy positions (Miller, Labovitz, and Fry, 1974). Women are, in fact, most often bypassed, either openly or increasingly under some socially acceptable pretext, for promotions that would place them in supervisory positions over men, even when they are the best qualified for these positions (McCune, 1970; Kashket, *et al.*, 1974).

Promoting a woman to a supervisory position over men would, in fact, break down the prevailing sex stratification system and that is why the reluctance to do so is great and the resistance very strong. Several studies of male managers (Bass, *et al.*, 1971; Gilmer, 1961) or of bank supervisors (Rosen and Jerdee, 1974) showed that not only do they hold stereotypic views of women but they also have less confidence in the ability of a female supervisor than a male supervisor and they would feel uncomfortable with a woman supervisor. These strong resistances to having a woman supervisor explains why men occupy the top administrative (or all administrative) positions even in occupations dominated by women such as social work, elementary school teaching (Lyon and Saario, 1973), or librarianship. A recent American study showed that among librarians only in sub-specialties such as school librarianship, in which only six percent are men, women can get promoted to top positions and have power. In other sub-specialties such as academic librarianship in which one-third are men, this minority controls all top positions of power in the field (Kronus and Grimm, 1971). Similar patterns have been documented for Poland (Sokolowska, 1965) and the U.S.S.R. (Dodge, 1966).

Often, however, women can be bypassed for promotions because by means of a variety of discriminatory practices and behaviours, they have not been given the opportunity to acquire the necessary qualifications and experience; they are given less chances to gain experience in challenging responsible assignments (Terborg and Ilgen, 1974; Kay, 1972); to participate in management training (Rosen and Jerdee, 1974); they are less often invited to present papers (Yokopenic, Bourque, and Brogan, 1974), to write chapters in influential books, to become visiting lecturers, to serve on review and editorial boards (Kashket, *et al.*, 1974); and temporarily to take the place of the sick foreman, or the absent boss. Thus, eventually they can be more "objectively" discriminated against in terms of raises, promotions, and other occupational rewards.

One of the most painful and effective *informal* techniques of occupational sex discrimination to which women are subjected is rejection and an atmosphere of "cold war," the intensity of which increases as they prove to be more competent, ambitious, and successful (Hagen and Kahn, 1974). The more women improve their position in an organization, the more they tend to lose the friendship and respect of their colleagues (Miller, Labovitz, and Fry, 1974). Thus, when men have to recognize a woman's competence and allow her to achieve significantly, they punish her psychologically for her deviance by withdrawing their friendship, approval, and liking for her, thus forcing her to a painful isolation that dampens her success.

It seems, therefore, that a woman who attempts to break through the existing sex stratification system by entering a "masculine" field or by aspiring and achieving highly (and, thus, acquiring prestige and possibly also power and a higher income) has to be a very unique being in order to be able to survive through all types of sex discrimination to which she will be subjected. She must be a very strong person not to bend under the harassment or the derogatory remarks of teachers and peers; intelligent, competent, and hard-working in order to be able to make it without any encouragement or help and so that she can continuously prove that she is superior to most men; and independent enough to be able to go on despite psychological rejection and active dislike on the part of colleagues and acquaintances. This exactly has been the essence of sex discrimination: while many men, even mediocre ones, can enter prestigious fields, can compete, aspire, and achieve as highly as they can, it is only the unusual woman, intellectually and psychologically that can enjoy the same options.

## References


Almquist, Elizabeth
1973 "The Income Losses of Working Black Women: Product of Racial and Sexual Discrimination," Paper presented at the annual meeting of the American Sociological Association, New York.

Banks, W. Curtis
1974 "Toward an Attributional Model of Prejudice," Paper presented at the annual meeting of the American Psychological Association New Orleans.

Bass, B. M. *et al.*
1971 "Male Managers' Attitudes Toward Working Women," *American Behavioral Scientist*, 15: 221–236.

Benokraitis, Nijole and Joe Feagin
1974 "Institutional Racism: A Review and Critical Assessment of Literature," Paper presented at the annual meeting of the American Sociological Association, Montreal.

Berens, Anne E.
1972 "Socialization of Need for Achievement in Boys and Girls," *Proceedings of the Annual Convention of the American Psychological Association*, 7 (part 1): 273–274.

Berkanovic, Emil
1973 "Some Implications of Professionalism for Institutional Racism," Paper presented at the annual meeting of the American Sociological Association, New York.

Blackwell, Gordon W.
1963 "The College and the Continuing Education of Women," *Educational Record*, 44 (January): 33–39.

Blauner, Robert
1972 *Racial Oppression in America*, New York: Harper and Row.

Blum, Z. D. and C. S. Coleman
1970 *Longitudinal Effects of Education on the Income and Occupational Prestige of Blacks and Whites*, The Johns Hopkins University, The Center for the Study of Social Organization of Schools.

Bock, E. Wilbur
1969 "Farmer's Daughter Effect: The Case of the Negro Female Professionals," *Phylon*, 30 (1): 17–26.

Brophy, J. and Good, T.
1970 "Teachers' Communication of Differential Expectations for Children's Classroom Performance: Some Behavioural Data," *Journal of Educational Psychology*, 61: 365–374.
Bunting, J. Whitney
1961 "The Relation of Business to Women's Higher Education," *Educational Record*, 42 (October): 287–295.
Bunting, Mary, Patricia A. Graham and Elga Wasserman
1961 "Academic Freedom and Incentive for Women," *Educational Record*, 51 (Fall): 386–391.
Burkey, Richard M.
1971 *Racial Discrimination and Public Policy in the United States.* Toronto: D. C. Heath and Co.
Butsch, Richard J.
1974 "Some Dynamics of Racial Stratification in the United States." Paper presented at the annual meeting of the American Sociological Association, Montreal.
Campbell, Margaret A.
1973 *Why Would A Girl Go Into Medicine?*, Monograph, November, New York.
Chasen, Barbara
1974 "Sex Role Stereotyping and Pre-kindergarten Teachers," *Elementary School Journal*, 74 (January): 225–230.
Chess, Elizabeth
1969 "A Modest Proposal for the Educating of Women," *American Scholar*, 38 (Autumn): 618–627.
Collard, E. D.
1964 "Achievement Motive in the Four-Year-Old Child and Its Relationship to Achievement Expectancies of the Mother," Unpublished Doctoral Dissertation, University of Michigan.
Crandall, V. J., R. Dewey, W. Katkovsky and A. Preston
1964 "Parents' Attitudes and Behaviors and Grade School Children's Academic Achievements," *Journal of Genetic Psychology*, 104: 53–66.
Cross, K. P.
1971 *The Undergraduate Women*, Research Report No. 5, Washington: American Association for Higher Education.
DeFriese, G. and W. S. Ford
1968 "Open Occupancy – What Whites Say, What They Do," *Transaction*, 5 (April): 53–56.
Dodge, Norton J.
1966 *Women in the Soviet Economy*, Baltimore, Md.: The Johns Hopkins Press.
Droppleman, Leo F. and Earl S. Schaefer
1963 "Boys' and Girls' Reports of Maternal and Paternal Behavior," *Journal of Abnormal and Social Psychology*, 67 (6): 648–654.
Epstein, Cynthia
1970 "Encountering the Male Establishment: Sex Status Limits on

Women's Careers in the Professions," *American Journal of Sociology*, 75 (May): 965–982.

Epstein, Cynthia Fuchs
1973 "Structuring Success for Women: Guidelines for Gatekeepers" *National Association for Women Deans, Administrators, and Counselors Journal*, Fall: 34–42.

Ewald, Linda S.
1971 "Sex Discrimination in Higher Education: Constitutional Equality for Women?" *Journal of Family Law*, 10 (3): 327–343.

Feldman, Saul D.
1973 "Impediment or Stimulant: Marital Status and Graduate," *American Journal of Sociology*, 78: 982–994.

Fendrich, J. M.
1967 "A Study of the Association Among Verbal Attitudes, Commitment, and Overt Behavior in Different Experimental Situations," *Social Forces*, 45 (March): 347–355.

Flanagan, John C.
1966 "Quality Education for Girls," *Women's Education*, 5 (4): 1–7.

Fox, Greer Litton
1973 "'Nice Girl': The Behavioral Legacy of a Value Construct," Paper presented at the National Council on Family Relations, Toronto, October.

Frank, Harold
1975 "The Socialization of Freshwomen Medical Students," Paper presented at the annual meeting of the American Educational Research Association, April, Washington.

Frank, Harold H. and Wolman, Carol
1973 "Gender Deviancy in Male Peer Groups," *Proceedings of the 81st Annual Convention of the American Psychological Association*, 8: 1067–1068.

Frazier, Nancy and Myra Sadker
1973 *Sexism in School and Society*, New York: Harper and Row.

Fredriksson, Ingrid
1969 *Konstroller i larobocker*, Stockholm: Swedish Joint Female Labour Council.

Garai, Josef and M. Schienfeld
1968 "Sex Differences in Mental and Behavioral Traits," *Genetic Psychological Monographs*, 77: 169–299.

Gilmer, B.
1961 *Industrial Psychology*, New York: McGraw-Hill.

Goldberg, Susan and Michael Lewis
1969 "Play Behavior in the Year-Old Infant: Early Sex Differences," *Child Development*, 40: 21–31.

Good, Thomas and D. Grouws
1972 "Reaction of Male and Female Teacher Trainees to Descriptions of Elementary School Pupils," Technical Report No. 62, Center for Research in Social Behavior, University of Missouri at Columbia.

Good, Thomas L., J. Sikes and J. Brophy
1973 "Effects of Teacher Sex and Student Sex on Classroom Interaction," *Journal of Educational Psychology*, 65 (1): 74–87.
Grambs, J. and W. Waetjen
1966 "Being Equally Different: A New Right for Boys and Girls," *National Elementary Principal*, 46: 59–67.
Hagen, Randi and A. Kahn
1974 "Discrimination Against Competent Women," Abstract, Unpublished Paper, Iowa State University.
Harbeson, Gladys Evans
1971 *Choice and Challenge for the American Women*, Cambridge: Schenkman Publishing Co., Inc.
Harris, A. S.
1970 "The Second Sex in Academy," *American Association of University Professors Bulletin*, 56: 283–295.
Hatfield, J. S., L. R. Ferguson and R. Alpert
1967 "Mother Child Interaction and the Socialization Process," *Child Development*, 38: 365–414.
Hembrough, Betty
1966 "A Two-Fold Educational Challenge: The Student Wife and the Mature Woman Student," *National Association of Women Deans, Administrators and Counselors*, Summer: 163–167.
Hetherington, E. Mavis
1967 "The Effect of Familial Variables on Sex Typing, on Parent-Child Similarity, and on Imitation in Children," in John P. Hill (Ed.), *Minnesota Symposium on Child Psychology*, Vol. 1, Minneapolis: The University of Minnesota Press, pp. 82–107.
Hraba, Joe and Rita Braito
1974 "Social Formation of Consciousness of Kind: Race, Sex and Class," Paper presented at the annual meeting of the American Sociological Association, Montreal.
Hunter, Thelma
1967 "The Status of Women in Australia," *Indian Journal of Social Work*, 28 (2): 161–167.
Johnstone, J. and R. Rivera
1965 *Volunteers for Learning*, Chicago: Aldine.
Kashket, Eva Ruth, *et al.*
1974 "Status of Women Microbiologists," *Science*, 183 (4124); 488–494.
Kay, M. Jane
1972 "A Positive Approach to Women in Management," *Personnel Journal*, 51 (1): 38–41.
Kronus, Carol L. and Grimm
1971 "Women in Librarianship: The Majority Rules?" Paper presented at the annual meeting of the American Sociological Association, Denver.
Lee, Patrick C.
1973 "The Early Classroom Experience: Masculine or Feminine?" *Perspectives on Education*, 6 (Fall): 10–15.

Levitin, Teresa, Robert P. Quinn and Graham L. Staines
1971 "Sex Discrimination Against the American Working Woman," *American Behavioral Scientist*, 15 (2): 237–254.
Levy, Betty and Judith Stacy
1973 "Sexism in the Elementary School: A Backward and Forward Look," *Phi Delta Kappan*, 55: 105–109.
Lewis, Michael
1972 "State As An Infant-Environment Interaction: An Analysis of Mother-Infant Behavior as a Functioning of Sex," *Merrill-Palmer Quarterly*, 18: 95–121.
Linn, L. S.
1965 "Verbal Attitudes and Overt Behavior: A Study of Racial Discrimination," *Social Forces*, 43 (March): 353–364.
Lippitt, Ronald and Martin Gold
1959 "Classroom Social Structure as a Mental Health Problem," *Journal of Social Issues*, 15 (1): 40–49.
Lord, M. E. M.
1968 "Mature Women and the Degree of Doctor of Philosophy," Unpublished Doctoral Dissertation, University of Wisconsin.
Ludeman, W. W.
1961 "Declining Female College Attendance: Causes and Implications," *Educational Forum*, 25 (May).
Lynn, David B. and William L. Sawrey
1962 "Sex Differences in the Personality Development of Norwegian Children," *Journal of Genetic Psychology*, 101: 367–374.
Lyon, C. and T. Saario
1973 "Women in Public Education: Sexual Discrimination in Promotions," *Phi Delta Kappan*, 54 (2): 15–20.
Lyon, R.
1964 "Married Women and the Academic Tradition," *Journal of Higher Education*, 35: 251–255.
McBee, Louise and E. D. Suddick
1974 "Differential Freshman Admission By Sex," *National Association for Women Deans, Administrators and Counselors Journal*, 37 (2): 75–77.
McCune, Shirley
1970 "Discrimination of Women as Viewed by Female ASTD Members," *Training Development Journal*, 23 (11): 24–36.
Merton, Robert K.
1949 "Discrimination and the American Greed" in Robert M. MacIver (Ed.) *Discrimination and National Welfare*, New York: Harper.
Miller, Jon, Sanford Labovitz and L. Fry
1974 "Differences in the Organizational Experiences of Women and Men: Resources, Vested Interests, and Discrimination," Paper presented at the annual meeting of the American Sociological Association, Montreal.
Moss, H. A.
1967 "Sex Age and State as Determinant of Mother-Infant Interaction," *Merrill-Palmer Quarterly*, 13: 19–36.

Moss, H. A., K. S. Robson and F. Pedersen
1969 "Determinants of Material Stimulation of Infants and Consequences of Treatment for Later Reactions to Strangers," *Developmental Psychology*, 1: 239–246.
Myers, George
1964 "Labor Force Participation of Suburban Mothers," *Journal of Marriage and the Family*, 28 (3): 306–311.
Osofsky, Joy D. and Edward J. O'Connell
1972 "Parent-Child Interaction: Daughter's Effects upon Mothers' and Fathers' Behaviors," *Developmental psychology*, 7 (2): 157–168.
Phelps, M. W.
1972 "Does Sex Make a Difference?" *College and University*, Winter: 40.
Power Goldberg, Marilyn
1972 "Women in the Soviet Economy," *The Review of Radical Political Economics*, 4 (3) July.
Pullen, D. L.
1972 "The Educational Establishment: Wasted Women," in M. L. Thompson (Ed.), *Voices of the New Feminism*, Boston: Beacon Press.
Riesman, David
1965 "Some Dilemmas of Women's Education," *Educational Record*, 46 (Fall): 424–434.
Rose, Arnold M.
1956 "Intergroup Relations United States Prejudice: Pertinent Theory for the Study of Social Change," *Social Problems*, 4 (October): 173–176.
Rosen, B. and T. H. Jerdee
1974 "Influence of Sex Role Stereotypes on Personnel Decisions," *Journal of Applied Psychology*, 59: 9–14.
Ruslink, D. H.
1969 "Married Women's Resumption of Education in Preparation for Teaching," Unpublished Doctoral Dissertation, New York University.
Saario, Terry N., Carol Nagy and Carol Title
1973 "Sex Role Stereotyping in the Public Schools," *Harvard Educational Review*, 43 (August): 386–413.
Sadker, Myra and Sadker, David
1972 "Sexual Discrimination in the Elementary Schools," *The National Elementary Principal*, October: 41–45.
Safilios-Rothschild, Constantina
1972a "The Options of Greek Men and Women," *Sociological Focus*, 5 (2): 71–83.
Safilios-Rothschild, Constantina
1972b *Toward a Sociology of Women*, Lexington, Mass.: Xerox College Publishing.
Safilios-Rothschild, Constantina
1974a *Women and Social Policy*, Englewood Cliffs, New Jersey: Prentice-Hall.

Safilios-Rothschild Constantina

1974b *Development of Models for Understanding the Processes Involved in Sex Discrimination*, National Institute of Education Contract NIE-C-74-0139.

Sells, Lucy

1973 "Sex Differences in Graduate School Survival," Paper presented at the annual meeting of the American Sociological Association, New York.

Shaman, Jeffrey M.

1971 "College Admissions Policies Based on Sex and the Equal Protection Clause," *Buffalo Law Review*, 20 (3): 609–623.

Shoulders, J.

1968 *Junior College – An Attraction to Women*, Columbia, Missouri: University of Missouri.

Simpson, G. E. and J. M. Yinger

1958 *Racial and Cultural Minorities*, New York: Harper.

Sokolowska, Magdalena

1965 "Some Reflections on the Different Attitudes of Men and Women Toward Work," *International Labor Review*, 92 (July–December): 35–50.

Solmon, Lewis

1974 "Do Women Graduate Students Get a Raw Deal?" Paper presented at the meeting of the Public Choice Society, March 21.

Sorkin, A. L.

1972 "Education, Occupation, and Income of Nonwhite Women," *Journal of Negro Education*, 41 (4): 343–351.

Statistical Yearbook of Greece

1973 National Statistical Service of Greece, Athens, Greece, June.

Stein, Aletha and Margaret M. Bailey

1973 "The Socialization of Achievement Orientation in Females," *Psychological Bulletin*, 80 (5): 345–366.

Taylor, Marjorie E.

1973 "Sex Role Stereotypes in Children's Readers," *Elementary English*, 50 (7): 1045–1047.

Terborg, James R. and Daniel R. Ilgen

1974 "A Theoretical Approach to Sex Discrimination in Traditionally Masculine Occupations," Paper presented at the annual meeting of the American Psychological Association, New Orleans.

Walster, E., T. A. Cleary and M. M. Clifford

1971 "The Effect of Race and Sex on College Admission," *Sociology of Education*, 44: 237–244.

Warner, Lyle G. and Rutledge Dennis

1971 "Prejudice Versus Discrimination: An Empirical Example and Theoretical Extension," *Social Forces*, 48 (4): 473–484.

Wellman, Barry

1971 "Social Identities in Black and White," *Sociological Inquiry*, 41 (Winter): 57–66.

Werts, Charles E.
1966 "Sex Differences in College Attendance," *National Merit Scholarship Corporation Research Report*, 2 (6): 11p.

Westie, F. R.
1964 "Race and Ethnic Relations," in Robert E. L. Faris (Ed.), *Handbook of Modern Sociology*, Chicago: Rand McNally: 576–619.

Westman Berg, Karin
1969 "Schoolbooks and Roles of Sexes," *Hertha*, No. 5: 48–57.

Wladis Hoffman, Lois
1975 "Early Childhood Experiences and Women's Achievement Motives," Unpublished Doctoral Dissertation, Department of Psychology, University of Michigan.

Yokopenic, P. A., Linda B. Bourque and D. Brogan
1974 "Professional Communication Networks: A Case Study of Women in the American Public Health Association," Unpublished manuscript, University of California, Los Angeles.

# The Changing Context of American Race Relations: Urban Blacks and Structural Shifts in the Economy

WILLIAM J. WILSON

WILLIAM J. WILSON is a Professor of Sociology at the University of Chicago. He was previously an Associate Professor of Sociology at the University of Massachusetts, Amherst and a Visiting Associate Professor of Sociology at Harvard University. He holds a 1966 Ph.D. in Sociology from Washington State University. Professor Wilson is the author of *Power, Racism, and Privilege: Race Relations in Theoretical and Sociohistorical Perspectives* (Macmillan Co., 1973 and a Free Press Paperback, 1976); *American Blacks: From Racial Oppression to Class Subordination* (Random House, forthcoming, 1977); and co-editor of *Through Different Eyes; Black and White Perspectives on American Race Relations* (Oxford University Press, 1973). He is also the author of over twenty articles published in professional journals and books, including *The American Sociological Review, American Journal of Sociology, Sociology and Social Research, Journal of Social Issues, Pacific Sociological Review, Phylon: The Atlanta Journal of Race and Culture,* and *Sociological Forces.* He is a member of the Editorial Board of the *American Journal of Sociology;* Associate Editor of *The American Sociologist* and the *International Journal of Contemporary Sociology;* past member of the Social Sciences Research Review Committee of the National Institute of Mental Health; and Executive Secretary of the Research Committee on Ethnic, Race and Minority Relations of the International Sociological Association.

# The Changing Context of American Race Relations: Urban Blacks and Structural Shifts in the Economy

WILLIAM J. WILSON

Few people would disagree with the assertion that as the black population in America became more urbanized, they were increasingly able to improve their general economic situation. Prior to 1910, Negroes had been denied entry into even the most menial jobs in the manufacturing sector but, beginning with World War and throughout the 1920's, they could at least procure unskilled jobs in the growing automobile and steel industries. However, the real break-through occurred during the World War II period, when President Roosevelt's executive order banning discrimination in defence plants and in government agencies, when an acute nationwide labour shortage, and when government subsidized training programmes all enabled blacks to move into jobs heretofore denied to them, primarily semi-skilled jobs in manufacturing. In fact, they even made entry into a variety of white collar positions.

Although some blacks lost jobs following World War II because of cutbacks in the defence industries and the re-entry of white veterans into the civilian labour force, the continual expansion of the economy following the War, partly because of successful government attempts to avoid a postwar recession, created a relatively favourable job market for black workers. Indeed, the steady stream of black migrants from the rural South was easily absorbed into the urban labour market throughout the 1940s and early 1950s. However, after 1954, structural changes in the American economy, interacting with demographic

---

This paper is part of a larger study to be published in 1977 as a volume in the Random House series on Ethnic Groups in Comparative Perspective. The research for this paper was supported by a Ford Foundation grant in Urban Studies, awarded to the University of Chicago's Department of Sociology. Appreciation is expressed to Katherine O'Sullivan. See for her helpful comments on a previous draft of this paper.

changes in the urban black population, caused serious labour market problems for a large segment of the black population.

## I. The Increase in Black Unemployment

Although labour economists have frequently noted the limitations of using official unemployment rates as one of the indicators of a group's economic well being, nonetheless, "they have come to be generally accepted as the most significant single measure of relative disadvantage."[1] It is therefore important to note that the two-to-one unemployment ratio between blacks and whites since 1954 has shown very little change despite shifts from good to bad economic years since then (see Table 1). Blacks actually fared better in relation to white unemployment prior to 1950. A black/white unemployment ratio of 0.9 was reported in the 1930 Federal Census Report, and only 1.18 in the 1940 Report.[2] And in 1948 and 1949, the first two years that official annual employment statistics were recorded, the rates were 1.68 and 1.59 respectively.

If unemployment has become a chronic problem for the black population generally, it is reaching disastrous proportions for young blacks in the labour force. In 1954, the black teenage unemployment percentage was only slightly greater than the white rate. However, each year since 1966, a greater than two-to-one black-white unemployment ratio has been officially recorded. From 1970 to 1974, black teenagers' unemployment has averaged 32 percent, and the 1974 rate of 32.9 percent was close to two-and-a-half times greater than the recorded white teenagers' unemployment (see Table 2).[3] At the time of this writing, the most recent Bureau of Labor statistics figures reveal that for the first quarter of 1975, the unemployment percentage for black teenagers jumped to 39.8 and for white teenagers to 18.0.[4]

The high rates of unemployment for black teenagers in the 1970s are to some extent related to the general slowdown in the American economy. However, even in the relatively high business activity year of 1969, the rate of unemployment for black teenagers was 24 percent.[5] Moreover, in 1974, the percentage of unemployment for black teenagers was almost five times as high as that for black adults (whose rate of 7.5 nearly doubled the white adult rate of 4.2), whereas twenty years earlier, black teenagers had been unemployed at a rate (16.5) only slightly less than twice the black adult rate (9.4).[6] Even the very high official unemployment figures, however, do not capture the real

TABLE 1. *Unemployment Rates by Race for Persons 16 Years and Over: 1948–1974*

| *Year* | *Unemployment Rate** | | *Ratio: Black and other races to white* |
|---|---|---|---|
| | *Black and other races*** | *White* | |
| 1948 | 5.9 | 3.5 | 1.69 |
| 1949 | 8.9 | 5.6 | 1.59 |
| 1950 | 9.0 | 4.9 | 1.84 |
| 1951 | 5.3 | 3.1 | 1.71 |
| 1952 | 5.4 | 2.8 | 1.93 |
| 1953 | 4.5 | 2.7 | 1.67 |
| 1954 | 9.9 | 5.0 | 1.98 |
| 1955 | 8.7 | 3.9 | 2.23 |
| 1956 | 8.3 | 3.6 | 2.30 |
| 1957 | 7.9 | 3.8 | 2.07 |
| 1958 | 12.6 | 6.1 | 2.07 |
| 1959 | 10.7 | 4.8 | 2.33 |
| 1960 | 10.2 | 4.9 | 2.08 |
| 1961 | 12.4 | 6.0 | 2.07 |
| 1962 | 10.9 | 4.9 | 2.22 |
| 1963 | 10.8 | 5.0 | 2.16 |
| 1964 | 9.6 | 4.6 | 2.09 |
| 1965 | 8.1 | 4.1 | 1.98 |
| 1966 | 7.3 | 3.3 | 2.21 |
| 1967 | 7.4 | 3.4 | 2.17 |
| 1968 | 6.7 | 3.2 | 2.09 |
| 1969 | 6.4 | 3.1 | 2.06 |
| 1970 | 8.2 | 4.5 | 1.82 |
| 1971 | 9.9 | 5.4 | 1.83 |
| 1972 | 10.0 | 5.0 | 2.00 |
| 1973 | 8.9 | 4.3 | 2.07 |
| 1974 | 9.9 | 5.0 | 1.98 |

Source: U.S. Department of Labor, Bureau of Labor Statistics, Handbook of Labor Statistics, 1975.

* The unemployment rate is the percent of the civilian labour force that is unemployed.

** "Black and other races" is a United States Census Bureau designation, and is used in those cases where data are not available solely for blacks. However, because about 90 percent of the population "Black and other races" is black, statistics reported for this category generally reflect the condition of the black population.

condition of black teenage joblessness. A 1971 study conducted by the United States Department of Labor showed that while the black teenage unemployment rate increased by 10 percentage points from

TABLE 2. *Unemployment Rates by Race for Persons 16–19 Years Old: 1954 to 1974*

| *Year* | *Unemployment Rate* | | *Ratio: Black and other races to white* |
|---|---|---|---|
| | *Black and other races* | *White* | |
| 1954 | 16.5 | 12.1 | 1.27 |
| 1955 | 15.8 | 10.3 | 1.53 |
| 1956 | 18.2 | 10.2 | 1.78 |
| 1957 | 19.1 | 10.6 | 1.80 |
| 1958 | 27.4 | 14.4 | 1.90 |
| 1959 | 26.1 | 13.1 | 1.99 |
| 1960 | 24.4 | 13.4 | 1.82 |
| 1961 | 27.6 | 15.3 | 1.80 |
| 1962 | 25.1 | 13.3 | 1.89 |
| 1963 | 30.4 | 15.5 | 1.96 |
| 1964 | 27.2 | 14.8 | 1.84 |
| 1965 | 26.2 | 13.4 | 1.96 |
| 1966 | 25.4 | 11.2 | 2.26 |
| 1967 | 26.5 | 11.0 | 2.41 |
| 1968 | 25.0 | 11.0 | 2.27 |
| 1969 | 24.0 | 10.7 | 2.24 |
| 1970 | 29.1 | 13.5 | 2.16 |
| 1971 | 31.7 | 15.1 | 2.10 |
| 1972 | 33.5 | 14.2 | 2.36 |
| 1973 | 30.2 | 12.6 | 2.37 |
| 1974 | 32.9 | 14.0 | 2.35 |

Source: U.S. Department of Labor, Bureau of Labor Statistics, *Handbook of Labor Statistics, 1975*.

the first quarter of 1970 to the second quarter of 1971, their rate of participation in the labour force declined by more than 7 points from 51.2 to 43.8 percent. These figures suggest that the higher the unemployment, the more that black teenagers give up looking for work altogether.

Among the factors that have contributed to the joblessness among Negro teenagers has been their sharp rise in the population. The number of central city black youths aged 16 to 19 increased by almost three-fourths in less than a decade (1960 to 1969), compared with an increase of only 14 percent for white teenagers of the same ages. Furthermore, black young adults (aged 20 to 24) increased in number by two-thirds, three times the population increase for their white counterparts.[8] It is, then, nearly an understatement to say that the increase of younger blacks in the central city constitutes a population explosion.[9] It hardly needs emphasizing that what observers call the "central city crisis" derives in part from the unprecedented increase in younger blacks, many of whom are not enrolled in school, are jobless, and are a source of delinquency, crime and unrest in the ghettos.[10] This population explosion of young blacks has occurred at the very time when structural changes in the economy pose serious problems for unskilled Negroes in and out of the labour force.

## II. The Effect of Structural Change in the Economy on Central City Employment

Following World War II, fundamental technological and economic changes facilitated the increasing decentralization of American businesses. Improvements in transportation and communication have made the use of open and relatively inexpensive tracts of land outside central cities more feasible, not only for manufacturing, wholesaling and retailing, but also for residential development. With the introduction and diffusion of single-level assembly line modes of production, the traditional central city multi-story factories have been rendered obsolete. At the very time that the high cost and limited availability of land, rising tax rates, increasing traffic congestion and mounting rates of vandalism and other crimes have increased the operating costs of city industries, many firms, previously restricted to the central city locations near ports, freights and passenger facilities, began to rely more heavily on truck transportation, and therefore to locate in outlying sites near interchanges, the expanding metropolitan expressway system and new housing construction. Moreover, the increasing use of the automobile has freed firms from the necessity of locating near mass transportation facilities in order to attract a labour force. Consequently, industry savings in transportation and communication are no longer necessarily associated with central city locations. Indeed, in the nation's twelve largest metropolitan areas, the central city's proportion of all manufacturing employment dropped from 66.1 percent in 1947 to less than 40 percent in 1970.[11]

This remarkable shift in industry concentration has occurred despite the fact that the numbers of central city businesses "actually moving to the suburbs have been relatively small."[12] The problem for the central city is not so much the loss of industry as it is the lack of industrial growth or expansion. Manufacturing employment has tended to expand outside central cities, especially in the new aircraft, aerospace and electronics industries. In a recent study of ten large metropolitan areas, 79 percent of the employment growth in manufacturing from 1959 to 1967 occurred outside the central city (see table 3). Furthermore, the growth of retail and wholesale trade took place overwhelmingly in the suburbs.

Whereas the economic stalemate in the central city manufacturing sector has meant limited opportunities for those seeking better paying blue-collar jobs, the developing service-producing industries have ef-

TABLE 3. *Employment Outside the Central City in 10 Large Metropolitan Areas, by Industry, 1959 and 1967*

| *Area and Industry* | *Percent of SMSA employment outside central city* | | *Percent of SMSA employment growth outside central city, 1959 to 1967* |
|---|---|---|---|
| | *1959* | *1967* | |
| Average, 10 areas | 28 | 32 | 54 |
| Atlanta | 22 | 27 | 36 |
| Baltimore | 30 | 37 | 72 |
| Boston | 61 | 62 | 73 |
| Houston | 7 | 6 | 5 |
| Kansas City | 26 | 28 | 37 |
| New Orleans | 18 | 24 | 40 |
| New York | 15 | 19 | 49 |
| Philadelphia | 40 | 46 | 79 |
| St. Louis | 42 | 49 | 85 |
| Washington, D.C. | 39 | 49 | 70 |
| Average, all industries | 28 | 32 | 54 |
| Manufacturing | 37 | 41 | 79 |
| Retail Trade | 32 | 41 | 78 |
| Wholesale Trade | 16 | 22 | 68 |
| Services | 23 | 29 | 42 |
| Finance, insurance, and real estate | 13 | 18 | 42 |
| Other | 27 | 28 | 31 |

Adapted from: *Manpower Report of the President*, Washington, D.C.: U.S. Government Printing Office, 1971.

* The standard metropolitan statistical areas (SMSA's) covered are those for which the central-city county was substantially co-terminous with the central city. The definition for each area for 1959 was corrected to 1967 boundaries, for comparability. Excludes government workers and the self-employed.

fected a rapid expansion of white-collar employment. In the last several decades, the national economic structure has shifted gradually from a basis in goods-producing industry (manufacturing, construction, mining and agriculture) to a concentration on service-producing industry (transportation, service, government, public utilities, trade and finance). In 1947, the majority (51%) of American workers were located in the goods-producing sector of the economy; by 1968, sixty-four percent of American workers were employed in the service-producing industries; and by 1980, that figure will increase to sixty-eight percent.[13] The nationwide shift from goods to services has been most pronounced in the central cities. Furthermore, the expanding employment opportunities in the clerical, professional, and administrative positions associated with finance, insurance and real estate firms, professional and business services, and federal, state and local government agencies have higher educational and training requirements than those associated with blue-collar employment (except possibly for the skilled crafts).[14] It is true that the service industries that employ low-skilled workers (in jobs ranging from hospital orderly to dishwasher) have also grown substantially. But, such jobs are poorly paid, menial and dead end. Accordingly, the lack of job expansion in the manufacturing sector and the fact that the desirable jobs in the service industries require education and training means that

> employment in the more desirable better paid jobs which workers can enter without a high school education or special skill is decreasing in central cities, in relative terms and sometimes also in absolute numbers.[15]

The structural changes in the job market are not unrelated to the increase in the black-white unemployment ratio and to the sharp increase in the black teenage unemployment rates over the last decade.

## III. The Dual Labour Market Theory and the Employment Problem of Urban Blacks

In one interpretation of the relationship between joblessness and structural changes in the economy, Charles C. Killingsworth (1968) maintains that, in recent years a "twist" in the demand for different types of labour has occurred.[16] More specifically, there has been a long run decline in the demand for low-skilled, poorly-educated workers and a long run rise in the demand for high-skilled well-educated workers; and that this twist has proceeded farther and faster than adjustments in the supply of labour, resulting in a growing imbalance in the labour market.[17]

From this, Killingsworth concluded that

the declining participation rates among the less educated must reflect in some measure a form of 'hidden unemployment' – that is, workers who had abandoned an active search for work because of discouragement, but who were nevertheless willing and able to work.[18]

It certainly does not need a great deal of imagination to see the relevance of this argument for the black population, particularly in view of their disproportionately high representation in the category of low-skilled and poorly-educated workers, and in the increasing number of discouraged workers who have given up actively seeking work (the Department of Labor reports that "among persons not in the labour force in early 1975, 4.4 percent of the black and other races and 1.6 percent of whites were discouraged workers.")[19]

However, another interpretation of the labour market problems of blacks, especially with respect to the central city, suggests that the problem is not one of a declining number of available jobs, but a decrease in the number of stable higher paying jobs. In this vein, Doeringer and Piore report that

in many cities it appears that those employment and income problems do not reflect absolute barriers to employment so much as a deficiency of high rate or otherwise preferred employment opportunities. For example, a study of the low wage labour market in Boston showed that employment in hospitals, hotels, warehouses, building maintenance services, industrial sweatshops, and so forth, is readily available to the disadvantaged. But, attractive high wage employment – jobs which constitute, in the current language of manpower, 'meaningful employment opportunities' – were much less accessible.[20]

This observation deserves brief review because it relates explicitly to the theory of the "dual labour market," a theory which seems to have particular application to the employment problems of the black population.

The basic assumption of the dual labour market theory is that the American labour market can be readily separated into a primary sector and a secondary or low-wage sector, a division which parallels Averitt's separation of the United States economy into the "central" firms (identified as the centre of the new American economy, firms with vertically integrated production processes and technologically progressive systems of production and distribution) serving national and international markets and the "periphery" firms (characterized by labour-intensive technology, low profit and retaining earnings, and economic crises that often result in severe financial retrenchment) serving restricted local markets.[21] Jobs in the primary labour market are distinguished by stable employment, high wages, good working conditions, advancement opportunities, and due process and equity in the administration of work rules. On the other hand, jobs in the secondary sector tend to be dead-end and to have high labour turnover, low wages, inadequate fringe benefits and capricious and arbitrary supervision.[22]

Although there is some movement of workers from the secondary sector to the primary sector and vice versa, the theory suggests that the more disadvantaged the worker in terms of, say, education, training and race, the more likely he is to be locked in the secondary labour market; that factors such as discrimination, inadequate skills, poor workers history, and residential location combine to hamper severely the disadvantaged worker's entry into the primary labour market.

As indicated above, this theory seems to have particular relevance to the employment problems of urban blacks. For example, three out of every five black men employed in the central cities in 1970 were in the comparatively low level job categories of non-farm labourers, service workers and operatives, as opposed to only one out of every three white males. Moreover, almost three out of five black women were in service or operative jobs, twice the rate for white women.[23] Although some of the jobs included in these aggregate statistics are probably part of the primary sector (particularly the operative positions which tend to be among the higher paying semi-skilled jobs usually associated with the manufacturing industries), they provide a rough estimate of the heavy concentration of blacks in the secondary labour force of central cities. They likewise help to explain the very heavy unemployment rates in the black ghetto.

The high unemployment rates in the central city ghettoes are directly related to high labour turnover rates in the secondary market. Recent data on employer and worker attitudes clearly indicate the instability of the secondary market.

Employers complain of lateness, absenteeism and turnover among workers. Workers are especially bitter about arbitrary management, low wages, and job insecurity. As these comments suggest, the instability appears to be characteristic of both jobs and workers. Certain of the jobs available to the disadvantaged – jobs in hospitals and hotels for example – although menial and low paying, are stable, but turnover among the employees who hold them is relatively high. Other jobs – in non-union construction, seasonal manufacturing and the like – are very unstable and are not organized to provide continuous employment. Whatever its cause, however, the amount of job changing which occurs means that any given level of employment in the secondary sector is associated with a higher level of frictional unemployment than in the primary sector. In a sense, therefore, high levels of turnover and frictional unemployment may be taken as the salient characteristic of the secondary market.[24]

High rates of unemployment in black ghettoes serve to preserve and reinforce the secondary labour force. Because of the legions of unemployed black workers, particularly under 21, wages are kept low and employers are able to replace workers at any time. Moreover, lack of union organization provides little insulation against the supply and demand pressures in the labour market, therefore further depressing wages.[25]

## IV. Barriers to Black Employment in Central Industries

On the one hand, it is clear that many ghetto workers are denied jobs in the primary labour market because of lack of training and education. As already indicated, job opportunities in the expanding white collar service and professional arenas demand educational prerequisites that exceed those of many central city black residents. On the other hand, the limited black participation in the higher blue-collar jobs of the central industries for which they do qualify suggest that there are other barriers to employment in the primary labour market. Most certainly, the concentration of blacks in relatively isolated ghettoes severely limits their access to the diversified urban labour market. Nearly half of all blacks in metropolitan areas of 250,000 or more lived in poverty areas (in contrast to 10 percent of whites).[26]

Ghetto isolation in itself makes it difficult for low-status black workers to learn about the better paid jobs in other areas of the metropolis, and to travel to these jobs, because of high transportation costs or inadequate transit systems.[27] However, a far more salient factor is employment discrimination. Recent research of unemployment and discrimination in 30 of the nation's largest cities revealed that blacks do not experience employment barriers in low-paid menial and casual jobs of the secondary labour market, but rather in the more desirable, higher paying jobs in the manufacturing, construction and finance industries.[28] In fact, the greater the proportion of city jobs found in these industries, the higher the unemployment rate in the slums.[29] Again, it is probably true that lack of education, experiences and limited skills were influential in excluding slum residents, especially non-whites, from jobs in these industries, but it is equally likely that discrimination was a significant factor in this exclusion. It is interesting to note that the same study revealed that the larger the city employment in the government sector, the lower the slum unemployment rate. Because of enforcement of anti-discrimination statutes by Federal, state and local officials and also because of vigorous efforts to attract and hire qualified black workers, blacks have been able to get respectable government jobs in contrast to their limited inclusion in private industry.[30] And, since the government sector has undergone substantial employment growth in the last several years, black representation in valued government jobs has increased far more rapidly than in the desired jobs of the private sector. Indeed, from May 1973 to May 1974, 64 out of every 100 new federal employees came from racial minority groups.

The industries which are associated with the highest black unemployment are, co-incidentally, dominated by a white elite labour force, who through effective unionization, have solidified their hold on the higher paying and respectable blue-collar jobs in the primary sector. The unions in the central firms have successfully pressed for consistent wage increases, increased fringe benefits and generated a protective private welfare state, financed by management. The net effect is the virtual elimination of the employability of a floating transient labour force. Employers who hire additional workers in high-demand periods find themselves penalized because of changes in compensation and work rules promoted by trade unions and supplemented by legislation. Thus, employer expenditures for unemployment insurance, social security, worker's compensation insurance, and other fringe benefits have made labour cost more a function of the number of workers employed than of the number of hours worked. Accordingly, central firm management finds it cheaper simply to pay their regular work force overtime than to hire additional employees under the welfare umbrella; consequently, even when demand is high, transient workers are forced to remain in the periphery economy or to join the ranks of the unemployed. Meanwhile, in the face of continuing automation, the labour unions seek to preserve the interests of the nuclear work force by supporting a policy that gradually reduces the number of less senior workers when demand is low, thereby increasing the transient work force. In short, the pattern of over-employment for senior workers reinforces the pattern of unemployment for junior or transient workers in the higher paying central industries of the United States economy.[31]

These central industry employment patterns have all but eliminated the importance of race in labour-management strife. In the past, management was able to exacerbate tensions between white and black workers by creating a split labour market – split in the sense that black labour was considered cheaper than white labour, regardless of the work involved.[32] These tensions often erupted into violence when blacks were used as strike breakers to undercut white workers. However, although the split labour market thesis seems to have had considerable relevance in previous periods, especially in the nineteenth century and early twentieth century, it is not very applicable in accounting for black exclusion from the primary labour market today. This is not to suggest that the elite white labour force is no longer concerned about being undercut by black workers, but that because of the nationwide equal employment legislation of the 1950s and 1960s (including the Federal Civil Rights Law of 1964), employers are no longer able to undercut the white labour force by hiring lower-price blacks. Prior to the passage of equal employment legislation, employers had little hesitation in hiring blacks at pay scales below those paid to whites with similar qualifications or abilities. Moreover, in situations where white workers had sufficient power to resist the hiring of blacks at either similar skill levels, higher skill levels, or at the supervisory levels, management often employed blacks in jobs below their skill level or established segregated work forces with depressed wages.[33] In a slack labour market today, however, there is no economic incentive to hire blacks who together with other minorities, must receive equal pay for equal work. Accordingly, the problems blacks are now facing in the primary labour market may have more to do with discrimination in hiring than with discrimination in pay scales. Indeed, there is some evidence that the recent increases in the black-white unemployment ratios are related to the passage of equal employment legislation. The 1975 Economic Report of the President points out that

> empirical studies have estimated the extent to which differences in State laws requiring 'equal pay for equal work' (prior to the national Civil Rights Act of 1964) affect race differences in income and unemployment, when other

economic variables are held constant. The result indicates that State equal pay laws reduced the gap between the wage rates of equally skilled blacks and whites, but increased the difference in unemployment.[34]

## V. The Lower-Class Black Worker and the Secondary Labour Market

If the association between the higher unemployment rates and the passage of equal employment legislation is at least partly due to the removal of the economic incentives to hire blacks, then this relationship probably has greater relevance in the primary labour market than in the secondary market; greater application, in other words, in jobs that are competitive, higher paying and desirable, than in jobs that are undesirable, low paying and menial. Jobs in the secondary sector, particularly in urban areas where most blacks are concentrated, have a considerably lower percentage of white workers and a substantially higher percentage of black workers than jobs in the primary sector. Indeed, such jobs have come to be identified with the lower-class non-white urban labour force. It is not surprising therefore that recent studies of unemployment in the urban core reveal that blacks do not experience any special employment barriers in the casual, low-paid and menial jobs of the secondary sector.[35] In fact, many of these jobs remain unfilled, despite the extremely high unemployment rate of blacks in the inner city. Employers constantly complain of the difficulty of attracting and keeping a stable work force and often comment that some blacks seem to be more willing to go on welfare than to accept available work.

However, the situation for inner city black workers is far more complicated than such observations suggest. Research on black employment problems has consistently shown that poor blacks tend not only to value work, but also to feel that self-respect and employment are inseparable. Enduring lack of success in the labour market lowers their self-confidence and promotes feelings of resignation that can lead to abandoning the job search temporarily, if not permanently.[36] Nowhere is this more clearly demonstrated than in Elliot Liebow's sensitive study of streetcorner men in a Washington, D.C. ghetto. Liebow states:

> The most important fact is that a man who is able and willing to work cannot earn enough money to support himself, his wife, and one or more children,

A man's chances for working regularly are good only if he is willing to work for less than he can live on, and sometimes not even then. On some jobs, the wage rate is deceptively higher than on others, but the higher the wage rate, the more difficult it is to get the job, and the less the job security.[37]

Liebow's research reveals that the attitude of lower status black males toward low-paying and menial jobs is a reflection of the general societal attitude, namely one of contempt. The jobs filled by low-status inner city blacks tend to be underpaid, uninteresting, dirty and hard; they do not provide respect, status, opportunity or advancement; they represent, in short, the lowest rungs of the occupational ladder. It is not surprising that, like the rest of society, the low-status black male disdainfully views such employment. As Liebow observes:

He cannot do otherwise. He cannot draw from a job those values which other people do not put into it.[38]

Liebow's research was conducted in the early sixties. Since then, as the foregoing discussion has shown, the job market situation for residents in ghetto communities has actually deteriorated. In the Oakland community of Chicago's South Side, for instance, 32 percent of the neighbourhood's work force of 4,323 were unemployed in early 1976. As an unemployed worker on the South Side observed,

Times are hard. You go in for a job interview and they tell you they can give you $2.00 an hour. Now what can you do with $80.00 a week these days? But, when you say you want more money, they say you don't want to work.[39]

It is no doubt true that in recent years attitudes concerning low-status work have changed. Workers today are less willing to accept the kinds of low-paying and menial jobs that their grandfathers or fathers readily accepted. To some extent, this change in attitudes is related to a revolution of rising expectations, not only for the black poor, but for all citizens of America, expectations generated by economic progress and by the democratic welfare states' official recognition of human suffering. Moreover, many of the black poor have internalized the values emanating from the civil rights and black protest movements, values that promote black pride and that explicitly reject the view that disadvantaged minorities should be content with a system of unequal rewards. Furthermore, unlike the situations experienced by their fathers or grandfathers, the low-status dishwasher, or hospital orderly, or janitor need not attach himself permanently to a specific job. There are other low-status jobs available; and, there are alternative income sources in welfare and illegal activities which, in combination with attitudes disdaining low-status work, contribute to the instability of the low-wage work force. Peter B. Doeringer's empirical study of the ABCD Federal manpower project in Boston revealed that workers, when asked why they quit ABCD jobs,

> mentioned the low wages, the poor working conditions and the lack of advancement opportunities. These workers know that menial jobs are always available and that the accumulation of an erratic work history would not be a barrier to obtaining menial jobs in the future.[40]

The underclass also know that illegal activities, in many respects, provide a more lucrative alternative to low-wage employment. It was estimated in a recent study that roughly 20 percent of the adult residents in Harlem lived entirely on illegal income in 1966.[41] This same study also reported the results of intensive interviews with 28 black youths, aged 18 to 24, many of whom regarded illegitimate hustling activities (e.g., numbers, gambling, narcotic sales and prostitution) as an easier, more desirable mechanism for achieving status and success in their neighbourhoods than pursuing legitimate but low-level employment.[42]

Finally, welfare provides another substitute for low-wage and menial employment. Recent data on public assistance in six of the largest northern metropolitan areas in the United States reveals that contrary to conventional beliefs,

> the rapid rise that occurred during the 1960's in the number of persons on welfare resulted mainly from an increase in the number of urban non-migrants applying for welfare.[43]

Blacks born in the North were more likely to adopt the welfare alternative than blacks born in the South. This was true despite the fact that the level of education of northern-born blacks was higher than the level of education of southern-born blacks. Moreover,

> the migrants (both men and women) have tended to have higher labour force participation rates and lower unemployment rates than black natives in the cities in question.[44]

Data such as these have to be interpreted cautiously, however, because the lower welfare and unemployment rates and the higher labour force participation rates of the southern migrants may be partly related to the fact that many southern-born blacks who would be likely candidates for the unemployment and welfare rolls, simply return to the South if they are unsuccessful in finding work, thereby creating the possibility that the migrants who remain tend to be those who have experienced greater success in obtaining employment. On the other hand, the hypothesis can be entertained that blacks who leave the South in search of better economic opportunities are more willing to accept the kind of menial work that northern-born blacks have come to reject, more willing to adapt to an economic arrangement which seems to have created permanent economic proletariats out of a substantial percentage of lower city residents. If so, this is not unlike the behaviour of those migrants from other parts of the world who leave a poorer economy for a more developed economy, who, in hopes of improving their standard of living, tend willingly to accept the kinds of work that the indigenous workers have come to reject.

## VI. Conclusion

William K. Tabb remarked recently that

> In the past, an understanding of race was central to a comprehension of the position of black Americans. In the future, as racist barriers are overcome by a significant number of blacks, it may be that race and class analysis will become more important.[45]

It would be extremely difficult to comprehend the plight of inner-city blacks in the United States by focusing solely on racial oppression, that is, the overt and explicit efforts of whites to keep blacks in a subjugated state. In the past, racial oppression was designed, overt, and easily documented, ranging from slavery to segregation, from the endeavours of the white economic elite to exploit black labour to the actions of the white masses to eliminate or neutralize black competition, particularly economic competition.[46] As the United States has entered the latter half of the twentieth century, however, many of the traditional barriers have crumbled under the weight of the political and social changes of the civil rights era. A new set of obstacles have emerged from basic structural changes in the economy. They are therefore impersonal; but, they may prove to be even more formidable than the exclusively racial barriers for certain segments of the black population. In other words, whereas the old barriers were usually designed to control and restrict the entire black population, the new barriers create hardships only for the black under-class; whereas the old barriers were based explicitly on racial motivations derived from intergroup contact, the new barriers have racial significance only in their consequences, not in their origins; in short, whereas the old barriers helped to define racial oppression, the new barriers depict class subordination within race.

It would certainly be misleading and oversimplified to argue that categorical racial oppression has disappeared in present day America, because blacks of all social classes continue to experience racial discrimination, albeit to a lesser extent. Nonetheless, it is increasingly clear that in the economic order, talented and educated blacks are now entering positions of prestige and influence at a rate comparable to or, in some situations, exceeding that of whites with equivalent qualifications (e.g., from 1964 to 1974, the proportion of black male workers in white-collar positions increased from 16 to 24 percent, with the bulk of this increase occurring in the higher level professional, technical and administrative positions. On the other hand, the proportion of white males in white-collar positions remained slightly over 40 percent during this period).[47] As the black middle class is riding on the wave of political and social changes and benefiting from the growth of employment opportunities in the growing white-collar sector of the economy, the black under-class is entangled in a hopeless mire of economic stagnation. A history of racial discrimination and oppression created the huge black under-class and the recent technological and economic revolutions have combined to ensure it a permanent status.

In response to the black protest movement of the 1960s, the economic and political systems in the United States have shown remarkable flexibility in incorporating talented blacks into positions of greater prestige and higher income. At the same time they have demonstrated a persistent rigidity in handling the problems of lower-class blacks. Accordingly, for the first time in American history, class issues can now seriously compete with race issues in the way blacks develop or maintain group positions.

## Notes

1. Charles C. Killingsworth, *Jobs and Income for Negroes*. Ann Arbor: University of Michigan Press, 1968, p. 11.
2. *Ibid.*
3. These figures for black youths are based on those computed for "blacks and other races" in which about 90 percent are black. However, in 1973, the U.S. Department of Labor bgan to collect data on blacks alone, and they indicate

that when this is done, official unemployment rates for blacks (adults and teenagers) actually increase. In the case of teenagers, the black unemployment rate increases from 32,9 percent to 34.9 percent in 1974 and the black/white teenage employment ratio increases from 2.4 to 2.5.

4. The unemployment figure for black teenagers is based on the rate computed for "blacks and other races." U.S. Bureau of the Census, Current Population Reports, Special Studies, Series P-23 No. 54, *The Social and Economic Status of the Black Population in the United States*, 1974, p. 2.
5. *Manpower Report of the President*, Washington, D.C.: U.S. Government Printing Office, 1972, p. 85.
6. These figures are based on *Handbook of Labor Statistics* 1975, Washington, D.C.: U.S. Department of Labor, Bureau of Labor Statistics, U.S. Government Printing Office, 1975.
7. *Manpower Report of the President*, Washington, D.C.: U.S. Government Printing Office, 1971, p. 85.
8. *Manpower Report of the President*, 1972, *op. cit.*, p. 85.
9. See Killingsworth, *op. cit.*, for a fuller discussion of this problem.
10. *Manpower Report of the President*, 1971, *op. cit.*, p. 85.
11. See John F. Kain, "The Distribution and Movement of Jobs and Industry" in *The Metropolitan Enigma: Inquiries into the Nature and Dimension of America's "Urban Crisis."* Cambridge: Harvard University Press, 1968, p. 3; *Manpower Report of the President*, 1971, *op. cit.*, p. 88; and Raymond C. Hummel and John M. Nagel, *Urban Education in America: Problems and Prospects*, New York: Oxford University Press, 1973, p. 214.
12. *Manpower Report of the President*, 1971, *op. cit.*, p. 88.
13. See Daniel Bell, *The Coming of Post-Industrial Society: A Venture in Social Forecasting*. New York: Basic Books, Inc., 1973, p. 131.
14. The association of white-collar jobs with the growing service producing sector of American society is not to overlook the fact that there are blue-collar and white-collar positions in both the service- and goods-producing sectors of our economy. However, even in the goods-producing sector, the proportion of blue-collar jobs is losing ground to white-collar positions. Daniel Bell has commented on this situation: "The spread of services, particularly in trade, finance, education, health and government, conjures up the picture of a white-collar society. But all services are not white-collar, since they include transportation workers and auto-repair men. But then, not all manufacturing is blue-collar. In 1970, the white-collar component within manufacturing – professional, managerial, clerical, and sales – came to almost 31 percent of the work force, while 69 percent were blue-collar workers (6,055,000 white-collar and 13,400,000 blue-collar). By 1975, the white-collar component will reach 34.5 percent. Whithin the blue-collar force itself, there has been a steady and distinct shift from direct production to non-production jobs, as more and more work becomes automated and in the factory, workers increasingly are employed in machine-tending, repairs, and maintenance, rather than on the assembly line." Bell, *op. cit.*, p. 133.
15. *Manpower Report of the President*, 1971, *op. cit.*, p. 91.
16. Charles C. Killingsworth, Jr., "The Continuing Labor Market Twist," *Monthly Labor Review*, September, 1968.
17. *Ibid.*
18. *Ibid.*, p. 12.
19. U.S. Bureau of the Census, Current Population Reports, Special Studies, Series P-23 No. 54, *The Social and Economic Status of the Black Population in the United States*, 1974, p. 52.

20. Peter B. Doeringer and Michael J. Piore, *Internal Labor Markets and Manpower Analysis*, Cambridge: Harvard University and Massachusetts Institute of Technology, 1970, Chapter VIII, pp. 2–3.
21. Robert T. Averitt, *The Dual Economy*. New York: Norton, 1968.
22. For a discussion of the dual labor market theory, see Harold Baron and Bennet Hymer, "The Negro in the Chicago Labor Market," in Julius Jacobsen, ed., *The Negro and the American Labor Movement*, New York: Doubleday Anchor books, 1968; Barry Bluestone, "Low Wage Industries and the Working Poor," *Poverty and Human Resources Abstracts*, March-April, 1968; Barry Bluestone, "The Tripartite Economy: Labor Markets and the Working Poor," *Poverty and Human Resources*, July-August 1970; Peter B. Doeringer and Michael J. Piore, "Unemployment and the Dual Labor Market," *The Public Interest* 38, Winter 1975; Peter B. Doeringer and Michael J. Piore, "Equal Employment Opportunity in Boston," *Industrial Relations*, May, 1970; Peter B. Doeringer and Michael J. Piore, *Internal Labor Markets and Manpower Analysis*, *op. cit.*; Peter B. Doeringer, ed., *Programs to Employ the Disadvantaged*. Englewood Cliffs, N.J.: Prentice-Hall, 1969; Louis A. Ferman, "The irregular Economy: Informal Work Patterns in the Ghetto," University of Michigan, mimeograph copy, 1977; David M. Gordon, *Theories of Poverty and Underemployment*, Lexington, Mass: Heath Lexington, 1972; Michael J. Piore, "On the Job Training in the Dual Labor Market," in Arnold Weber et al., *Public Private Manpower Policies*, Madison, Wis.: Industrial Relations Research Association, 1969; Michael J. Piore, "The Dual Labor Market: Theory and Implications," in David M. Gordon, ed., *Problems in Political Economy; An Urban Perspective*. Lexington, Mass: D.C. Heath, 1971; Thomas Vietorisz and Bennet Harrison, *The Economic Development of Harlem*, New York: Praeger, 1970; Howard M. Wachtel, "The Impact of Labor Market Conditions on Hard-Core Unemployment: A Case Study of Detroit," *Poverty and Human Resources*, 1968: and *Manpower Report of the President*, 1971, pp. 96–99.
23. *Manpower Report of the President*, 1971, *op. cit.*, p. 87.
24. Doeringer and Piore, 1970, *op. cit.*, Chapter VIII, pp. 5–6.
25. Daniel R. Fusfeld, *The Basic Economics of the Urban Racial Crisis*, New York: Holt, Rinehart and Winston, 1973, p. 31.
26. *Manpower Report of the President*, 1971, *op. cit.*
27. *Ibid.*, p. 93; also see John F. Kain, "Housing Segregation, Negro Employment and Metropolitan Decentralization," *Quarterly Journal of Economics*, May 1968.
28. Stanley L. Friedlander, *Unemployment in the Urban Core*, New York: Praeger, 1972; also see Alice Handsaker Kidder, "Racial Difference in Job Search and Wages," *Monthly Labor Review*, July 1968.
29. Friedlander, *op. cit.*, p. 119.
30. *Ibid.*
31. Averitt, *op. cit.*
32. Edna Bonacich, "A Theory of Ethnic Antagonism: The Split Labor Market," *American Sociological Review* 37, 1972; "Split Labor Markets in the United States 1830–1863," *American Journal of Sociology* 81, 1975; "Advanced Capitalism and Black/White Relations in the United States: A Split Market Interpretation," *American Sociological Review* 41, 1976.
33. *Economic Report of the President*, Washington, D.C.: United States Government Printing Office, 1975, p. 113.
34. *Ibid.*
35. Stanley Friedlander, *op. cit.*, and Doeringer and Piore, 1970, *op. cit.*
36. Elliot Liebow, *Tally's Corner: A Study of Streetcorner Men*, Boston: Little, Brown and Company, 1967, pp. 29–71; Leonard Reissman, "Readiness to Succeed:

Mobility Aspirations and Modernism Among the Poor," *Urban Affairs Quarterly*, March, 1969, pp. 379–395; *Manpower Report of the President*, 1971, p. 107.
37. Liebow, *op. cit.*, pp. 50–51.
38. *Ibid.*, p. 59.
39. *Chicago Tribune*, Thursday, January 29, 1976, section 7.
40. Peter B. Doeringer, ed., "Low-Income Labor Markets and Urban Manpower Programs: a Critical Assessment," Report submitted to the Office of Manpower Research, United States Department of Labor, January, 1969.
41. Friedlander, *op. cit.*, p. 187.
42. Ibid. Also see *Manpower Report of the President*, 1971, *op. cit.*, pp. 98–99.
43. *Manpower Report of the President*, Washington, D.C.: U.S. Government Printing Office, 1974, p. 95. The six metropolitan areas include New York, N.Y., Philadalphia, Pa., Washington, D.C. – Md.-Va., Chicago, Ill., Detroit, Michigan, and Los Angeles-Long Beach, Calif.
44. *Ibid.*
45. William K. Tabb, "Race Relations Models and Social Change," *Social Problems* 18, Spring, 1971, pp. 431–444.
46. William J. Wilson, *Power, Racism and Privilege: Race Relations in Theoretical and Sociohistorical Perspectives*, New York: The Free Press, 1976.
47. U.S. Department of Commerce, The Social and Economic Characteristics of the Black Population in the United States, 1974, Current Population Reports, Special Studies Series P-23, Washington, D.C.: U.S. Government Printing Office, 1957, p. 57.

# Racism in Britain: Management Concepts, 1948-1975

CHRIS MULLARD

CHRIS MULLARD, born in England in 1944, is a research member of the Department of Sociology, Durham University, working on a study of race, power and resistance in the United Kingdom. He received his M.A. degree in Sociology from Durham University. He was a member of the National Association of Community Relations Officers from 1969 to 1973, and since 1973 he has been a member of the Institute of Race Relations.

As an 'activist' as well as an academic in the field of race relations he was the Tyneside Regional Secretary of the Campaign Against Race Discrimination between 1967 and 1969; and the Community Relations Officer for Tyne and Wear between 1969 and 1973. From 1970 to 1976 he was a Visiting Lecturer in Race Relations at Newcastle-upon-Tyne Polytechnic.

During 1974 he was invited by the National Aboriginal Forum to undertake a study of Aboriginal/Euroaustralian relations and a lecture tour of Australian Universities.

Over the last ten years Chris Mullard has contributed many reviews, articles and papers to newspapers, magazines and academic journals, including *The Times*, *Atlas Magazine*, *Race Today*, *Race and Class* and *Sociology*. Relevant books include *Black Britain*, 1973, (revised and published in America under the title *On Being Black in Britain*, 1975); and *Aborigines in Australia Today*, 1974.

# Racism in Britain: Management Concepts, 1948-1975

CHRIS MULLARD

Britain's black population has known the hardship of discrimination, prejudice and control for more than four centuries. In 1596 Elizabeth I objected to the number and presence of black slaves in Britain, and instructed that they 'should be sent forth of the lands'.[1] Dissatisfied with the response, five years later she issued a Royal (Repatriation) Proclamation, which renewed a licence to Casper van Senden, a Lubeck trader, to transport Negroes and Blackamoors 'out of this Her Majesty's realm'.[2]

By 1764 London's growing black community was again the centre of controversy; a writer in the *Gentleman's Magazine* declared that:

> The practice of importing negro servants into these kingdoms is said to be alreadie a grievance that requires a remedy, and yet it is every day encouraged, insomuch that the number in this metropolis only is supposed to be near 20,000: the main objection to their importation is that they cease to consider themselves as slaves in this free country, nor will they put up with an inequality of treatment, nor more willingly perform the laborious duties of servitude than our own people, and if put to it, are generally sullen, spiteful, treacherous, and revengeful. It is therefore highly impolitic to introduce them as servants here where that rigour and severity is impracticable which is absolutely necessary to make them useful.[3]

Endorsing the general belief that Negroes belonged to a sub-human species, Edward Long in 1774, when the black slave population in Britain had increased to more than 30,000, proclaimed with the authority of an established historian and respected man-of-letters: 'I do not think that an orang-outang husband would be any dishonour to an Hottentot female'.[4] With the sexual identification and equation made, and the final belittlement of blacks completed, he then proceeded to advocate that 'some restraint should be laid on the unnatural increase of blacks imported'.[5] Nearly two hundred years later this plea for Black influx control, in a somewhat different disguise, was reaffirmed and expressed in the 1968 speeches of the Right Honourable Member of Parliament for Wolverhampton South West.

In his Walsall speech, Enoch Powell identified 'the problem facing Britain' as the 'inflow of (coloured) immigrants', pointing out that:

> Some problems are unavoidable. Some evils can be coped with to a certain extent, but not prevented. But that a nation should have saddled itself, without necessity and countervailing benefit, with a wholly avoidable problem of immense dimensions is enough to make one weep. That the same nation should stubbornly persist in allowing the problem, great as it already is, to be magnified further, is enough to drive one to despair.[6]

By April 1968 the tears of despair had driven him down the same scapegoat path that Elizabeth had deftly pirouetted four centuries earlier. According to the classical scholar of vision, black immigrants placed an intolerable strain on the social services they had been recruited to man, and, 'to the great annoyance of (our) own liege people that covet the relief which these people consume',. they consequently deprived 'others' from the benefits and services provided by the Welfare State. Similarities with the Elizabethan understanding of 'the problem' did not end with the pinpointing of a scapegoat community to take the blame for those 'greatly distressed in these hard times of dearth':[8] he too considered that repatriation was the only permanent solution to the evil:

> The resettlement of a substantial proportion of the Commonwealth immigrants in Britain is not beyond the resources and abilities of this country, if it is undertaken as a national duty, in the successful discharge of which the interests both of the immigrants themselves and of the countries from which they came are engaged. It ought to be, and it could be, organised now on the scale which the urgency of the situation demands, preferably under a special Ministry of Repatrition or other authority charged with concentrating on this task.[9]

Although such a Ministry has not yet been created formally, Powell's suggestions, treated seriously by many, coupled with Elizabethan and eighteenth century policies, indicate that British attitudes towards blacks have been far from tolerant. In fact the work of Walvin[10] and Shyllon[11] would suggest that what Ruth Glass has termed bashfully 'the all pervasive British ambivalence towards colour' would be better reformulated as the all pervasive existence of British racism.[12] Their historical studies, and particularly those of Walvin, show quite conclusively that a racist ideology was both fashionable and necessary for colonial development; and that without it few, if any, blacks would be in Britain today.

A weakness portrayed in their work, and, indeed, in many British race relations studies, is that they fail to show how racist ideas and patterns of discrimination have become securely institutionalised in British society. Even studies of a more sociological flavour, such as the monumental work of Rose *et al.*, seem to see racial discrimination as an isolated phenomenon, non-related to the prevailing idea and actions of those who shape society.[13] The net result is that the discriminatory policy proposals advocated in sixteenth-, eighteenth-, and twentieth-century Britain have tended to be viewed either as the rantings of intelligent but prejudiced individuals (Powell); proposals for the solution of problems other than race (Elizabeth); or, like the 1971 Commonwealth Immigration Act, which redefined and formalised controls on black immigration, as policies designed to encourage internal racial harmony and 'good' race relations.

Even the 'race professionals'[14] appear, on the surface at least, unable to accept that whites, rather than blacks, are responsible for 'the problem'; that racism, manifested in the form of institutionalised discrimination, rather than individual prejudice or discrimination, constitutes the more significant threat to racial harmony and justice; and, finally, that a race relations industry which operates on racist assumptions presents not what Katznelson calls a buffer institution but a model of management and control.[15] The almost complete inability to acknowledge this has led, over the last two decades, to the further institutionalisation of racism, and the (re)birth of policies designed to manage rather than erase it.

With a focus on white rather than black society, on race and immigration policies, I shall then attempt to examine in this paper the nature of current racism and how it has been managed by successive Governments since June 1948, when 492 Jamaicans aboard the Empire Windrush arrived in the 'Mother Country' to find open hostility, menial jobs and a warm welcome at Clapham Common Underground Station where 242 of them were temporarily housed. Rather than offering an expansive history of British racism, I propose here to restrict discussion to an examination of what I consider to be the two central policy concepts of 'citizenship', and 'patriality', on which debates and legislation have been based.

## I. Citizenship

From our discussion so far it is clear that control policies, in one form or another, have featured crotchet-like in the British repertoire of race and immigration policy. The only periods in which they were abandoned for unrestricted importation and free immigration were during the two centuries which immediately followed Elizabeth's 1601 Proclamation, and, again, between 1948–1961. In both cases they were lifted for reasons which held definite advantages for the economy. The demand for cheap slave labour in seventeenth and eighteenth century England to cater for the needs of the rich and to man the slaving vessels which plied the triangular trade routes militated against any form of control other than that which existed for the importation of 'personal property'. The demand for less cheap but equally dependent workers in the mid-twentieth century also escaped the critical eye of immigration and custom officials, for these workers, no longer perceived as 'personal property', were now 'migrants'.

Unlike the importation practices employed before the abolition of slavery in 1807, the 'open-door' policy pursued between 1948–1961 was based upon a number of notions concerning this new status. The first sprang from the political realisation that Commonwealth relations, improved in part by wartime co-operation and comradeship, needed cementing before colonial independence movements severed them altogether. A second reflected 'the Commonwealth ideal': the belief that the credibility of a proclaimed multi-racial society rested upon the *de jure* equality of all regardless of colour or creed. Yet a third factor which influenced the debate on status amounted to the paternal recognition of British responsibility for the colonised, and especially for those who were attracted to the 'Mother Country'. All these considerations together with the acute post-war labour shortage, were eventually taken into account when the social and political status of migrating black workers was redefined in 1948.

Under the British Nationality Act which came into effect on 1st January, 1949, full citizenship rights, including the right to enter the United Kingdom 'without restrictions of any kind', were guaranteed to all those 'of the United Kingdom and colonies'.[16] In short this meant that black workers migrating to Britain could now be treated in exactly the same way, for the purposes of nationality and citizenship, as white British born citizens. It conferred upon them not only the full rights of citizenship, but also the theoretical right to free themselves, from a colonial relationship which had imprisoned them for three or more centuries.

## A. *Black 'Citizens': Migration and Settlement*

Shrugging off the stigma of oppressive labels, black workers, as equal 'citizens', were officially encouraged, after the 1948 Act, to join those brought by the Empire Windrush. In the space of a decade their numbers rose from an estimated 74,500 in 1941 to 336,600 in 1961. At the same time it was generally believed that the reasons for increased migration were 'fairly evident'. In the West Indian case Ruth Glass identified them as 'the pressure of population' in the Caribbean, the high level of unemployment and under-employment, and the effect of the 1952 Walter McCarran Act which had reduced the flow of West Indians to America 'to a mere trickle'.[17] Together with the additional factors of religious and caste persecution, students of Asian migration offered similar explanations.[18] Apart from the early work of Senior in which he maintained Britain had 'called upon her colonies and territories to help resolve man power shortages', little reference was made to what I term the double attractive migration principle: the purchase of *needed* labour with the currency of citizenship.[19]

Long after Senior's study, scholars of the calibre of Patterson continued to emphasize the 'push' rather than 'pull' migration factors.[20] The realisation that Britain *needed* additional workers to fill new jobs and vacancies created by an expanding economy did not really dawn until after the publication of Peach's notable study on 'West Indian Migration to Britain'.[21] Straitjacketed by a predisposition towards studying the 'newcomers', 'strangers', and 'guests' appeared to entail the exclusion of any but a tentative consideration of the nature of British racism, the needs of the economy, or, for a 'Mother Country', the uncomfortable possibility that Britain required more assistance than she was able to give.

Driving this point home by turning the whole 'push-pull' thesis inside out, Peach concluded that the 'push' factors listed by Glass and others were 'passive' rather than 'dynamic'; and that 'trends in migration were governed by factors external to the West Indies'.[22] The major external and dynamic factor was that the expansion of the metropolitan economy had created gaps at the lower end of the occupational and residential ladder 'to which West Indians and other coloured immigrants were drawn in as a replacement population'.[23]

Whereas the Government continued to maintain the myth that there was no direct correlation between black migration and labour needs, British industry viewed the issue quite differently. Suffering from acute labour shortages, the British Hotels and Restaurants Association, the Regional Hospital Boards, and, in India and Pakistan, individual representatives from the textile industry all appointed agents or launched campaigns in black Commonwealth territories and colonies to recruit the kind of labour required.

It was therefore with no surprise that industry greeted the Smethwick Labour Exchange Report, which stated clearly and candidly that:

> Shortage of labour is the concern of almost every employer in the town. A policy of importation is now being pursued ... Coloured labour from the Commonwealth is greatly easing the labour shortage. The labour turnover among these immigrant workers is lower than the average ... The employers would be very worried if coloured labour were withdrawn. All employers readily pay tribute to the valuable contribution this type of labour is making towards industrial output.[24]

Patterns of settlement also reflected the relationship between labour demand and supply. They suggested that the second component in the attractive migration principle, the currency of citizenship, was as important as the knowledge that jobs existed.

The need, on the employers' part, to purchase cheap labour for an outmoded, undercapitalised, and, almost, bankrupt textile industry, centred in West Yorkshire and South-east Lancashire, led personnel officers, often with colonial and wartime experience, to Pakistan; the belief of Pakistanis, on the other hand, that they would be accorded full rights as citizens, and that hostel or lodging-house accommodation in cities such as Bradford was plentiful, helped to complete the exchange – citizenship for labour, jobs for rights.

West Indians attracted to the Greater London area were offered very much the same package. The London Transport Executive medical officer and interviewer, who went to Barbados in 1956, pointed out to potential applicants that besides a job they could expect no racial discrimination, full citizen rights, and a 'sunny future' in the Mother Country. Those invited to the Midlands to begin and stay 'at the lower end of the occupational ladder' received similar pledges either directly through employers or indirectly through the projected image, fostered and maintained in the West Indies by the colonisers, of the Mother Country's benevolence and recognition of rights to all those who wished to migrate.

In the case of Indians, mainly Sikhs and Hindus from the Punjab, West Bengal and Gujarat, the exchange contained an added significance which resulted from the role Indians had played in the development of the British Empire. The relationships established between officers and men in the Indian Army, administrators and clerks in the Indian Civil Service, and colonial administrations in Africa and the West Indies, and those which defined the 'buffer' role between white colonisers and black colonised in every corner of the Empire, all encouraged migrants to believe that their boat had come home. For services rendered in the past, they were now to receive, at long last, not only jobs in their 'beloved country' but the same privileges and rights enjoyed by those who were once their masters. Like the West Indians in the early fifties, the Indians who arrived towards the end of the decade began work in *their* country with a dedication and optimism that befitted their status as full citizens.

Of the total migrant population, London and the West Midlands attracted 47% and 14% respectively, and the remaining 69% settled in the conurbations of South-east Lancashire, West Yorkshire, Merseyside, and Tyneside. The picture that finally emerged showed that blacks were pulled initially towards areas in which there were jobs, and later, in the seventies, when the population had exceeded 1,500,000, to areas where there existed both jobs and established communities. A belief that possession of full citizenship automatically entailed equal rights went unquestioned.

### B. *Discrimination and Disillusionment*

That the concept of citizenship was based on a false assumption, namely that it applied to all, irrespective of ethnic origin or religion, also appeared to go unnoticed. To have recognised the dismal reality that many of the new citizens possessed few rights would not only have upset the delicate equilibrium the Government attempted to maintain between labour demand and supply, but it would also have involved the acceptance that excessive discrimination existed. It was thus in the interest of the Government, and through it the economy, that the facade of equality accompanied by the myth of citizenship should be maintained.

The Senior and Manley Report in 1955, which exposed shop floor discrimination, was consequently played down by both Government and employers.[25] Richmond's conclusion in the same year that 'one-third (of the white population) was tolerant of coloured people, one third was mildly prejudiced, and one third was extremely prejudiced' received much the same fate.[26] A Gallup Poll survey carried out in 1958 which indicated that 10% of the sample were severely prejudiced, 75% partially prejudiced, and only 15% tolerant was considered to be unrepresentative and unreliable, as the survey had been conducted during a time of abnormal racial tension – in London on the 3rd and 4th September, the same week as the Notting Hill race riots! Further findings which showed that 71% of the population objected to mixed marriages, 60% would move if black citizens came to live in their neighbourhoods, and that 54% believed that black citizens should not be admitted to council housing lists on the same conditions as white citizens, were interpreted by many as expressions of individual choice, rather than of prejudice.[27]

The 'Sorry, No Coloureds', and 'Coloureds need not apply' advertisements which appeared with regular monotony in the daily and weekly press also fell under the apocryphal heading – 'freedom of choice'. Personal testimonies of racial discrimination were treated with utter contempt: Blacks were not to be trusted for they had 'chips larger than mountains' on their shoulders. Thus all black views, including those that follow, were seen as biased accounts of the migrants' experience, rather than as accurate statements,illustrative of both the existence of personal and institutionalised discrimination.

We found that we were unable to get good housing facilities, only to be turned away because we are black, so we had to take run-down houses. The various councillors turned a blind eye and applications to the council were met with the same disregard, leaving us in rat-infested houses, bad sanitation, and no heating. Subsequently it was made to look as though we are the ones who brought the house in that condition, whereas we were forced into them in that deplorable manner.[28]

What we had to put up with in those days was very bad. We were treated like filth, not good enough to lick their arses. I remembered being told at an engineering firm I worked for to do, I think it was, to clean out the toilets. I told the charge-hand it wasn't my job and that I wouldn't do it. The next thing I knew I was pounced on by half a dozen louts, kicked in the balls, and thrown down the toilet . . .[29]

Intensified by the dehumanising effects of discrimination, the sham of citizenship brought disillusionment. Compounded with a deep sense of betrayal, and expressed in the form of shattered hopes and pleas to return to a former place and state of relative happiness, a Trinidadian recalled his experience as follows:

I thought the people will be friendly because in the West Indies white and black get along very well, so I thought to myself that there would be no problems. This shattered in a few weeks, and the dreams of making it in the Mother Country was gone, not for a while but for ever.[30]

Another black citizen, conscious of the occupational downgrading current in the fifties, justifiably complained:

I was a cabinet-maker in Jamaica, but here they say not good enough. I'm 45 and I get only labouring. Every time sent away because I'm black. I work hard but always there is trouble and they say I go. It says on my passport I'm a citizen of England. But that don't help me . . . It's hard, man . . . No one believes a black man. I'm citizen of England. I like to go home.[31]

Overtly expressed attitudes (prejudice) and actions (discrimination), in the Trinidadian's case, appeared to reflect the white populations' reluctance to accept black citizens as equals, combined with the beliel that they had no right to remain in Britain and masquerade as fulf citizens. The covert practices and adoptive stances of the latter recognised the economy's need for cheap and dispensable labour, whilst at the same time assured, through occupational downgrading, colour-code systems at Labour Exchanges and housing departments, and through institutionalised attitudes which embodied and projected notions of racial superiority, that black citizens were in, but not part of British society. Although both expressions of discrimination complemented each other, their social effects were neither truly acknowledged, nor discerned as being manifestly harmful to the individual or the society in general.

By definition, then, citizenship precluded any recognition at all of racism, as it depended upon the fallacious dogma that all British citizens, regardless of race or belief, had always enjoyed full equality of rights before the law. Pointing to the famous case of *Constantine v Imperial London Hotels Ltd.*, in 1944, which raised the issue of racial discrimination, but provided no precedent for its illegality, those who believed in the 'reality' of citizenship held it up as evidence that Britain was both a just and non-racist society. Despite Mr. Justice Birkett's pronouncement, "... that *although* (Constantine) *was a man of colour* no ground existed on which they were entitled to refuse to receive and lodge him',[32] many still thought that the payment of citizenship had rendered colour irrelevant.

### C. *Citizenship as a Management Concept*

From the evidence of Peach and Foot it would appear that racism continued to occur precisely because the state's role as protector demanded the acceptance of certain priorities. Previous commitments to those born here, together with a history of racist ideas and attitudes stretching back to Elizabeth's Royal (Repatriation) Proclaimation in 1601, irrationally dictated that the economic rights of indigenous employers should supercede the evil and social rights of those considered as 'newcomers', 'strangers' or 'coloureds'.

In this way the superior rights of landladies, pub landlords, hoteliers, cinema proprietors, club owners, estate agents, insurance brokers, bankers, and so on *ad infinitum*, covering all areas of public social life, were protected by the right to exercise preference. In other words the right to discriminate on the basis of colour, religion, or ethnic origin was one endorsed by the state and sanctioned in law, in as much that both the state and law simply ignored the existence of discrimination.

> When the other fellow's skin happens to be coloured, then the Britisher's gift for underestimating him becomes all the more pronounced. The Colonial administrator and trader (and ordinary white citizen) have been so accustomed to feeling a superior being among 'the natives' that they have grown almost incapable of treating them on equal terms – either as foe or friend.[33]

The status accorded to black citizens thus appeared qualitatively quite different from that enjoyed by white citizens. In practice, negative legal sanctions and role ascriptive systems created both second class citizenship and a culture of racism. Both seemed necessary in order to satisfy the labour needs of an expanding economy; both were imperative for the public's support of an 'open-door' policy which, historically and emotionally, conflicted with an ethnocentric definition of 'Britishness'.

Acceptance could only be gained for such a policy if it were seen that the colonial relationship, despite altered geographical circumstances, still remained intact; and that the economic advantages the relationship symbolised and was constructed to yield still accrued. The exploitation of black workers in the form of low wages, promotion bars, exceptionally long hours, slum accommodation, and trade union unwillingness to take action 'not only on the level of disputes and compensation, but also on the general level of discrimination' epitomised the unequal basis of the relationship.[34] Housing discrimination, later described by Rex, Moore,[35] and Burney, and the social deprivation it both fostered and contained, further suggested that the relationship in practice operated on concepts of second class citizenship rights.[36]

But whilst a general belief existed that all citizens possessed equal rights, neither an examination of this racist relationship, nor a political recognition of discrimination proved necessary: the 'opendoor' policy together with racism could progress unimpeded as long as both resulted in advantages for the economy.

Thus as a management concept, citizenship performed a number of functions essential to the well-being of the state and economy. In the first place it allowed for, and indeed, helped to encourage the unrestricted migration of black workers from the Commonwealth. Through purchasing needed labour with the currency of full citizenschip rights it gave birth to the myth, soon shattered by experience, that Britain was a non-racist society. Thirdly, it was able to maintain the cherished notion that the Mother Country, a living example of a truly multiracial society at work, provided golden opportunities for all those prepared to walk her pavements. Fourthly, it managed to subsume the colonial relationship under the humbug of high-principled rhetoric: by emphasising the 'push' rather than 'pull' migration factors, and pointing out that a paternally benevolent hand should be extended to less fortunate citizens coming from impoverished, over-populated, disease ridden, and lamentably backward parts of the Commonwealth. And, fifthly, as we have seen, the myth of equality it embodied appeared to protect the state from racist accusations, whilst at the same time allowing institutions, employers, and white citizens to exercise their right to discriminate on the basis of colour, religion, and ethnic origin. In other words, as the conceptual cornerstone of British race relations policy for more than a decade, the idea of citizenship and the way in which it was used achieved the distinction of being able to manage racism without acknowledging its existence.

## II. Patriality

By 1960, demands for independence in African and West Indian colonies, Suez, an economic slump, and the 1958 and 1959 riots in Nottingham and Notting Hill had heralded a change in Government and public thinking. Demands for independence had brought into sharp relief the respective statuses of both 'migrant' and 'colonial' blacks; the farce of Suez had questioned the future of Britain's role as a colonial nation; the economic slump had called for a practical reassessment of labour requirements; and race conflict and rioting in major English cities had revealed that the official ostrich-headed stubbornness towards racism could no longer be maintained. At the end of the decade as the cry "Keep them Out" could be heard in many parts of the country the issue was debated in Parliament.

Against the background of racist innuendo, race rioting, and the stabbing to death of Kelso Cochrane, a West Indian carpenter, in May 1959, the first publicly acknowledged British debate on 'race' concluded with the assertion that blacks constituted 'the problem', that numbers rather than colour presented an obstacle to racial harmony. Apart from the sincere but abortive attempts made by Fenner Brockway and his supporters, the issue of racial discrimination hardly featured at all, except to confirm that restrictions on black migration would eradicate it.

As well as the muddled logic and racist assumptions it exposed, the debate also represented an attempt to reconcile three basic conflicts. On the one hand, assuming tautologically, that blacks were both the cause and effect of 'the problem', the economy still required a supply of cheap labour, but yet, on the other hand, the public had clearly demonstrated in Notting Hill, the press, and in the activities of political movements such as Mosley's and the various regional Immigration Control Associations dotted over the country like ink blots on white paper, that blacks were not welcomed in 'this green and pleasant land'. The third, but less important conflict arose out of the problematic definition of citizenship as extended to all migrants. How could a citizen in theory, with freedom of mobility and full equal rights, be a non-citizen in practice, with restricted mobility and few, if any, rights? The answer that emerged was one that was to be articulated more clearly a decade later in the 1971 Commonwealth Immigration Act – 'patriality'.

### *A. The Special Relationship*

Based on the joint notions that a special- familial or patrial – relationship existed between the Mother Country and its (in)dependent colonies, and that some kind of control was necessary for internal racial harmony, the concept of patriality satisfied, to some extent, all concerned parties other than the migrants themselves. Many Commonwealth idealists, enraged by the demands of the British racist lobby, were thankful that their ideas of the special relationship which included preferential and favourable trade agreements with the Commonwealth, had been preserved. Employers welcomed the proposed provisions which allowed black migration to be regulated to the needs of the economy in a controlled rather than a laissez faire way. The self-confessed racists found a measure of consolation in the fact that official policy makers had in part adopted their ideological position on race by showing a willingness to close the door. And those concerned with promoting racial harmony, although disappointed with the lack of positive provisions, by and large believed that the new thinking and approach would greatly alleviate racial tension.

As a vague concept, based on a sense of shared historical experience, familial ties, and a commitment to preserve the memory of Empire, this special relationship lacked sufficient precision for the purposes of policy. It needed to be spelt out in much clearer terms; thus the whole decade that followed the debate on 'race' addressed itself to this task. The discussions held and the legislation passed then, form today, the current basis of race and immigration policy, as well as the setting in which British racism found political and social support.

### B. *From 'Migrant' to 'Immigrant'*

With the migrant now firmly identified as 'the problem', rather than the existence of rampant discrimination and racist beliefs, the first task, was to formalise the reality of sham citizenship. The core idea of the special relationship – patriality – was thus used to distinguish the respective statuses of two groups of 'migrants'. Those who looked as if they had familial ties were still considered as migrants, people moving from one part of the Commonwealth to another; whereas those who did not were cast as 'immigrants'. In effect this only amounted to the official and political recognition of the black migrant's situation, for, discriminated against, he had always been seen as an 'immigrant'.

From migrant to immigrant, from migration to immigration, the operationalised concept of patriality also encompassed, through what Lord Mancroft had termed 'administrative measures', the question of citizenship. Justified on the basis that black immigrants neither possessed any *real* ties with Britain, nor fell within the provisions 'in respect of British protected persons and citizens of the Republic of Ireland', the automatic right of citizenship was withdrawn under the *1962 Commonwealth Immigrants Act.* It was:

> An Act to make temporary provision for controlling the immigration into the United Kingdom of Commonwealth citizens; to authorise the deportation from the United Kingdom of certain Commonwealth citizens convicted of offences and recommended by the court for deportation; to amend the qualifications required of Commonwealth citizens applying for citizenship under the British Nationality Act, 1948.[37]

The deportation clause gave legal expression to the opinion that black workers were considered no longer to be either in or part of British society. Although granted notional citizenship, they were to be treated as immigrants, people with fewer rights than migrants, and more stigmatised than aliens.

Further the voucher system introduced under the Act eliminated any fanciful notion harboured, by blacks or whites, once enthused with the Commonwealth ideal, that they were required for any purpose other than for their labour. Issued on the initiative of British employers, Category A vouchers were confined only to those who had a specific job to come to; Category B vouchers were restricted to those with recognised skills and qualifications in short supply in Britain; and, with preference shown to those with war service, Category C vouchers were reserved for all other workers. Defined in terms of their usefulness to the economy, voucher-holders, as they do today, came to Britain not as migrating citizens but as immigrant workers.

### *C. Black Immigration Control*

Geared to labour requirements and a tolerable level of racism, patriality, as a management concept, depended upon effective black immigration control for vindication; not just because it arose from such demands, but also because it was based upon a principle of distinction, the difference between those who had a special relationship with Britain and those who did not. Although the 1962 Act had affected a change in status and citizen rights, it had not attempted to define in any way what was meant by the special relationship, or, indeed, just how many black immigrants should be admitted. This was to come three years later in the form of a Labour Government' White Paper, *Immigration from the Commonwealth.*[38]

By putting a limit of 8,500 on vouchers issued in any one year and abolishing Category C vouchers taken up previously by manual and unskilled workers, the 1965 White Paper reiterated officially that economic usefulness coupled with the added criteria of educational attainment now formed part of this special relationship. Translating a control theory based upon suspect principles into administrative action, the White Paper allowed for the regulated entry of:

Doctors, dentists, and trained nurses; teachers who are eligible for the status of qualified teacher in this country; graduates in science and technology who have had at least two years' experience in suitable employment since graduation; non-graduates with certain professional qualifications who have had at least two years' experience in suitable employment since qualifying; and applicants who have a specific job to come to in this country.[39]

Removing the emphasis away from the 'historical' Commonwealth special relationship, and relating it to economic and educational suitability, the White Paper guaranteed the rigorous control of the non-wanted, as well as defining those who were. A third provision for doing this concerned the practical application of a principle based on the moral and social desirability of individual immigrants. In the words of the White Paper:

The government regard it as important that there should be a speedy and effective power to repatriate immigrants who in one way or another, e.g. by obtaining entry by misrepresentation or by flouting the conditions on which they were admitted, evade the stricter control over immigration that is now envisaged. Without it the effectiveness of the control would be greatly weakened. It is therefore the Government's intention to seek for the Home Secretary a general power – in addition to his power to act on the recommendation of a court – *to repatriate such Commonwealth citizens if he considers the public interest to require it.*[40]

Stripped of automatic citizenship, black immigrants were to be tolerated only as long as it was in the public interest. Thus five years before Powell's Eastbourne speech, those convicted of imprisonable offences, those suffering from mental disorders, or who were 'otherwise undesirable for medical reasons', and those admitted, 'in the opinion of the Secretary of State, contrary to the interests of national security', were, under the 1962 Act, rendered liable for immediate deportation, either by immigration officers at the port of entry, or by Judges and Magistrates sitting in the more rarified atmosphere of a British courtroom.[41]

The extension of this power to all those deemed undesirable in 'the public interest' meant that the special relationship, muzzled further by a repatriation policy, was one in fact defined and set in motion by a racist-receiving public. What the public had considered to be against its interest in 1965 paved the way for more stringent immigration controls in 1968 and 1971, the racial formulation of patriality, and an internal race relations policy founded on a conundrum, inspired not by the 'pervasive British ambivalence towards colour' but the realisation that:

> The United Kingdom is already a multi-racial society and Commonwealth immigrants make a most valuable contribution to our economy . . . At the same time it must be recognised that the presence in this country of nearly one million immigrants . . . with different social and cultural backgrounds raises a number of problems and creates various social tensions in those areas where they have concentrated.[42]

Spelt out, the conundrum appeared to ask: How could British racism be best managed? The answer contained in the White Paper suggested that, as black immigrants were responsible for it, the best policy to pursue was to restrict entry, and make nominal provision for the 'integration' of those already here. Financial assistance to local authorities, Voluntary Liaison Committees, and the National Committee *for* Commonwealth Immigrants, chaired by the Archbishop of Canterbury, invalidated, or so it was claimed, any criticism that the policy as a whole amounted to an endorsement of racist ideas, the official creation and approval of a colour bar, and the equation that 'colour plus numbers equals problem'. But these provisions, together with those in the 1965 Race Relations Act, which outlawed discrimination *only* in 'public places', were a consequence of a policy 'relating to control on the entry of immigrants so that (they do) not outrun Britain's capacity to absorb them.[43]

In other words the 'positive measures designed to secure for the immigrants and their children their rightful place in our society, and to assist local authorities and other bodies in areas of high immigration in dealing with certain problems which have arisen', were of secondary rather than of primary or equal importance.[44] 'Their rightful place in our society' had already been determined during the 'open-door' years, and by the belief, underpinning control on legislation, that, at best, they were dispensable units of labour, and, at worst, candidates for repatriation.

### *D. The Grandfather Clause*

By 1968 this belief in their sub-human worth reached a new zenith. Daniel reported that there was:

> Racial discrimination varying in extent from the massive to the substantial ... moreover, the more different a person is in his physical characteristics, in his features, in the texture of his hair and in the colour of his skin, the more discrimination he will face ... and prejudice against Negroes (and Asians) is most deep-rooted and widespread.[45]

Seventy-two percent of the immigrants interviewed believed that employers discriminated; 45% of the West Indians interviewed, 35% of Indians, 34% of Pakistanis, and, significantly, only 6% of the Cypriots, revealed that they had been discriminated against. Without any real assessment of the candidate on the basis of merit, qualifications, or general suitability, many were rejected because of their race or colour. In the case of housing just over 66% of the total sample believed that landlords discriminated; 88% of the West Indian sample, 55% of the Indian, and 44% of the Pakistani sample. The P.E.P. Report confirmed one of the major findings of the Milner Holland Report in 1965 which stated that in the London area 89% of all private rented accomodation vacancies advertised *excluded* black tenants: the existence of 'massive' racial discrimination determined not only the areas in which black immigrants could find accommodation, but also the poor conditions in which they had, and still have to live. Confirming much that was already known or suspected, the survey concluded that discrimination was highest among those with qualifications, including English trade, professional and school-leaving certificates; those with a good knowledge of the language; those who had been in full employment before arrival; and those who had been in the country for a relatively long period.

In other words the partly anglicised, those who presented a direct threat to individual Englishmen, to a metropolitan oriented labour-system, to a society which believed, in the face of contradictory empirical evidence, that it was non-racist, suffered most. Further, the knowledge that the relationship between racist ideas and the social structure was one that could not easily be broken by platitudes, good intentions, or even legislation of the limited scope of the Race Relations Acts, also brought a profound sense of alienation.

Powell's speeches and the debate which accompanied the 1968 Commonwealth Immigration Bill through both Houses helped to consolidate this sense by giving explicit expression to the racist basis of intended legislation.[46] For, besides restricting the number of vouchers to 1,500 for Kenyan Asians possessing British citizenship, the 1968 Act, passed and granted Royal Assent in an unprecedented forty eight hours, spelt out unequivocably what the Government and, indeed, the British public, whose interests it protected understood by patriality.[47] Simply, the right of entry was conferred on those with 'at least one of his parents or grandparents born in the United Kingdom'. Others who had been born, naturalised, adopted, or registered in the United Kingdom also obtained a similar right.

Unless applicants for vouchers had one of these 'substantial connections' with Britain, they, as U.K. passport holders, were denied entry. They were either shuttlecocked around the world as stateless persons by international airlines, imprisoned in the special detention centres at British airports, or driven directly to Pentonville prison, where they remained in a special wing until deported or allowed conditional entry.

Defined to establish a mainly white-only immigration policy, the patriality or 'grandfather-clause' epitomised what Moore has termed 'the most overtly racial measure on the statute book'.[48] It exposed the governmental pretence of non-racial bias in respect of immigration legislation; it confirmed the view propounded by Powell and others that in times of economic and social decline blacks, as workers, were not required; it articulated the special relationship in the clearest terms possible; and it portrayed convincingly that a racist immigration policy reflected the wishes of the electorate in general and white workers, local authority officials, and the police in particular. It afforded a kind of political consumation to the relationship between racist ideas and the social structure.

Posing as a political sop to the outraged left on the one hand, and a determined effort to combat discrimination by the right on the other, the 1968 Race Relations Act which immediately followed was in fact no more than a pawn in the defence of a racist society; a society which had legally sanctioned the ideas and beliefs that had steered it through

Empire, via post-war metropolitan rioting, and into an epoch which is only now realising the unanticipated effects of British colonialism – the arrival and presence of approximately 2½ million ex-colonial subjects, all in one way or another demanding a slice of *their* cake together with the right of equal treatment, respect and status. The well documented evidence that now exists on the working of the 1968 Race Relations Act, which set up the Community Relations Commission and extended the scope of the 1965 Act to include employment, housing, education, and other services, all points to the conclusion that the Act was never intended to work.[49] Even the Select Committee on Race Relations and Immigration in its 1974–75 Report on *The Organisation of Race Relations Administration* considered that in its opinion:

The Race Relations Board and the Community Relations Commission have both failed to make sufficient impact or gain the confidence of the ethnic communities. Indeed, both the Board and the Commission themselves emphasised this lack of confidence. The Commission indeed complained that 'it can urge the Government to do things, but if when it urges them to do things there is really very little response, its credibility and authority are inevitably diminished.' This lack of confidence is aggravated by the unsatisfactory procedures afforded to the Board and the unsatisfactory terms of reference given to the Commission. They have not been given the tools to do the job and have been prejudiced by lack of resources and lack of authority.[50]

The Select Committee concluded, like Richmond in the mid-fifties, Daniel in the late sixties, and the most recent Political and Economic Planning national survey on discrimination, carried out in 1973, that:

Race discrimination and race prejudice are still widespread . . . Consequently there is a risk of the communities becoming permanently alienated. What is needed, above everything else, is a clear and demonstrable Government commitment to equal rights.[51]

In retrospect and taken together, the 1968 Commonwealth Immigration Act and existing Race Relations Act coated a moral and social felony with the marzipan of political respectability. In the case of the first it reasoned emotionally 'that it is both right and natural to give easy access to Britain to all those with close and recent family ties with this country';[52] in the case of the second it accepted the harmful effects of racial discrimination without providing 'the tools to do the job'; and in the case of both, the concept of patriality used to manage British racism mapped out with the ease of a cartographer's pen the acceptable contours of black-white relations.

### *E. Non-patrial Aliens*

What the 1968 Immigration Act had omitted, the 1971 Commonwealth Immigration Act included. It extended and formalised the racial basis of legislation by articulating the operational principle of patriality more clearly. By turning what Roche has called 'the key in the lock', and slamming the door on more or less all future black immigration, the Act stabilised British racism, in as much that it blocked off what the majority of white British citizens still considered to be the source of 'the problem'.[53] The problem, it was believed, would disappear, uncovering the fact that discrimination and prejudice was largely the result of negligent or unintended actions, rather than the systematic expression, in the form of racially conceived immigration laws, of ideas and values firmly embedded in the social structure.

By creating two separate categories of immigrants – the patrials and non-patrials – the Act ascribed two kinds of status and rights to prospective immigrants. Patrials or persons with a parent or grandparent born, naturalised, adopted or registered in the United Kingdom possessed the right of free entry and status accorded to full citizens. The non-patrials, on the other hand, were, as aliens for all practical and administrative purposes, subjected to strict control, and if allowed entry, humiliated by the conditions attached: medical examinations, registration with the Department of Employment, notification to the appropriated authorities of any change of address or job, and, if they wished to apply for citizenship after five continuous years of residence, proof of their 'good conduct' together with a reasonable command of English.

In practice such conditions meant in 1973, when the Act came into force, that the non-patrials' negative status virtually precludes them from buying a house, raising capital, starting up businesses, taking part in active union affairs, demonstrating, or even taking part in the political life of their own or the wider community.[54] Consequently, the kinsfolk of those black citizens, Government and industry wooed to the Mother Country during the open-door policy years 1948–1961, no longer possess automatic citizenship, the social, political, civil, and economic rights associated with it, or even the rights of a white immigrant from Germany, France, or Holland: the concept of patriality and how it has been applied has today stripped them of everything except their British passports.[55]

Legalised, it has affected a metamorphois in status from black wanted citizen to black unwanted non-patrial alien; it has managed racism jointly by redefining 'the problem', pandering to an ethnocentric conception of Britishness, and redirecting attention away from discrimination and prejudice to the 'boatloads of wogs' landing illegally on silvery beeches in midnight fog. Moreover, in the understating words of Baroness White it has given 'the appearance to people overseas of Britain being racially biased'.[56]

Neither sure of their status nor of when the next hatchet will fall, the future looks bleak for blacks already settled here, but for black non-patrials attempting to enter, the future must look even bleaker. Moore and Wallace have reported that:

> One (black non-patrial) passenger went from London to East Africa, on to Burundi, Ruanda, South Africa, Mauritius and Sydney. *Return to Sender* reported the case of a twenty-one year old man who left Entebbe and came to Dover via Athens and Frankfurt. He was held in two British jails and then deported; Frankfurt, Cairo, Entebbe, (where, of course, he was not let in), Nairobi, Dar es Salaam and Port Louis (Mauritius). He came back the same way and less than a month after leaving Entebbe he was again in Pentonville prison.
>
> Some of this shuttlecocking involved whole families, with children. In February 1975 a sick woman and two children were admitted temporarily after two years shuttlecocking. The record for *time in flight* (as distinct from custody or airport lounges) is one month. The record stay in one airport lounge was achieved by three brothers who in fact had Ugandan passports but were denied this citizenship. They arrived before the beginning of the mass exodus, in April 1972. They had a grandfather and two uncles in the U.K. They were refused entry and returned to India from where they had come. They arrived at St. Cruz airport on April 26 and stayed two months in the lounge before returning to the U.K. on June 26. They were held for a month and returned to India.[57]

Besides creating a class of shuttlecock non-patrials, the concept of patriality should also be seen as the culmination of racist ideas expressed in law. What started as a 'temporary provision' in 1962, gained momentum and definition between 1965 and 1968, and inhumane enforcement in 1973, was thus not the control of black immigration, although it most certainly manifested itself in the form of controls, but was, in fact, the management of racism. Whereas the concept of citizenship depended upon the myth of just and actual equal rights, patriality, in contrast, accepted that such rights should only be technically reserved for those with familial ties in Britain. In my opinion, although technically this includes many blacks born, adopted, naturalised, or registered here, in practice familial ties, which only thinly veil the colour definition of patriality, exclude these groups. Their colour both defines them as immigrants and determines their social fate as non-wanted aliens in times of social and economic depression, and wanted *Gastarbeiter* in times of prosperity.

The policy pursued with inordinate rigour since 1962 has thus tended to legitimise racism. The relations it has established today provide a legitimate structure – immigration controls – through which racist ideas and actions can be expressed. Thus the National Front's and Enoch Powell's calls for total repatriation, and the Select Committee's recommendations for improved race relations legislation are now quite compatible: for in the public mind one cannot be achieved without the other.

## III. Conclusion

In this paper I have argued that the plight of British blacks, whether they be shuttlecock non-patrials, non-patrials, immigrants, migrants, or citizens resident here, must be seen in a wider perspective than the mere presence or absence of racial discrimination. Such a perspective should encompass a review of British ideas, attitudes, and actions towards blacks, as well as an attempt to unravel the inter-relationships between them. It has been a central part of my argument that inter-relationships do in fact exist, that the nature of legislation and forms of discrimination practised reflect this, and that the evolution and operation of the two concepts designed to manage rather than erase racism indicate that the real problem – racism – is neither a temporary evil, nor a social inkspot located outside the social structure to be blotted up by existing or, proposed race relations legislation. For, until the racist immigration controls, with the roles and statuses they ascribe to *all* blacks, are as effectively dismantled as they were constructed, no amount of envisaged remedial action can help. In fact it can only but compound and institutionalise further the problem of British racism.

## Notes

1. *Acts of Privy Council*, XXVI, 1596–7, p. 16.
2. See J. L. Hughes and J. F. Larkin (ed.), *Tudor Royal Proclamations, 1588–1603*, Yale University Press, 1969, p. 221, or James Walvin, *The Black Presence*, Orbach and Chambers, London, 1971, pp. 64–5 for full text.

3. *The Gentleman's Magazine*, vol. XXXIV, 1764, p. 492.
4. Edward Long, *History of Jamaica*, London, 1774.
5. Edward Long, *Candid Reflections ...*, London, 1772, p. 46.
6. B. Smithies and P. Fiddick, *Enoch Powell on Immigration: An Analysis*, Sphere Books, London, 1969, p. 19.
7. J. L. Hughes and J. F. Larkin, *op. cit.*, 1969, p. 221.
8. *Ibid.*, p. 221.
9. B. Smithies and P. Fiddick, *op cit.*, p. 77.
10. James Walvin, *op. cit.*, and *Black and White: The Negro and English Society, 1555–1945*, Allen Lane, The Penguin Press, London, 1973.
11. F. O. Shyllon, *Black Slaves in Britain*, Oxford University Press, London, 1974.
12. Ruth Glass, *Newcomers: The West Indians in London*, Centre for Urban Studies and George Allen and Unwin, London, 1960, p. 146.
13. E. J. B. Rose and Associates, *Colour and Citizenship: A Report on British Race Relations*, Oxford University Press, London, 1969.
14. The phase 'race professionals' was coined by B. W. Heineman, Jr., *The Politics of the Powerless: A Study of the Campaign Against Racial Discrimination*, Oxford University Press. London, 1972, pp. 126–8. He uses the term, as I do here, to describe academics, members of official or semi-official organisations, activists in 'immigrant groups', who worked both within and outside the Government.
15. Ira Katznelson, *Blackmen, White Cities: Race, Politics, and Migration* in the United States, 1900–30 and Britain, 1948–68, Oxford University Press, London, 1973, Chapter Eleven, pp. 175–188.
16. *British Nationality Act*, 1948, HMSO, London.
17. Ruth Glass, *op. cit.*, pp. 6–7.
18. See Dilip Hiro, *Black British, White British*, Eyre and Spottiswood, London, 1973; Kushwant Singh, *A History of Sikhs*, vol. 2, 1839–1964, Princeton University Press, Princeton, 1966 for general background; and for the particular reference R. Desai, *Indian Immigrants in Britain*, Oxford University Press, London, 1963, p. 2.
19. Clarence Senior, Race Relations and Labour Supply in Great Britain, *Social Problems*, vol. 4, no. 4, April 1957, pp. 302–312.
20. Shiela Patterson, *Dark Strangers: A Study of West Indians in London*, Tavistock Publications, London, 1963.
21. Cori Peach, *West Indian Migration to Britain: A Social Geography*, Oxford University Press, London, 1968.
22. *Ibid.*, p. 36.
23. *Ibid.*, p. 92.
24. Paul Foot, *Immigration and Race in British Politics*, Penguin Books, Harmondsworth, 1965, p. 63.
35. Clarence Senior and Douglas Manley, *A Report on Jamaican Migration to Britain*, Kingston, 1955. An abridged version of this report is to be found in the Fabian Research Series, no. 179, London, 1956.
26. Anthony H. Richmond, *The Colour Problem: A Study of Racial Relations*, Penguin Books, Harmondsworth, 1955, p. 245. It should, however, be noted that in 1959 Michael Banton disputed Richmond's findings on the basis that the maintenance of social distance is a customary British trait, and one not neccessarily actuated by prejudice; thus 'when people say that others of their acquaintance would dislike working with a coloured man, or having one as a neighbour or visitor, they are saying that this would be contrary to the group's norms of conduct, not that each one of these people, individually, is unfavourably disposed.' On the basis of the evidence he produces alone, Professor Banton's claim is quite unconvincing. For a full account see his *White and Coloured*,

Johnathan Cape, London, 1959, together with an earlier statement in Economic and Social Position of Negro Immigrants in Britain, *The Sociological Review*, vol. 1, no. 2, December, 1953.

27. See Ruth Glass, *op. cit.*, pp. 122–127, and Appendix B, pp. 246–60 for a detailed analysis of the 1958 Gallup Poll. Although the accuracy of this and the Richmond Survey is open to dispute, what is significant, I believe, is not the exact percentage of recorded prejudiced responses, but the fact that a substantial amount existed. On this point most researchers at the time were in agreement.
28. Quoted in Chris Mullard, *Black Britain*, George Allen and Unwin, London, 1973, p. 42.
29. *Ibid.*, p. 44.
30. *Ibid.*, p. 41.
31. Ruth Glass, *op. cit.*, pp. 69–70.
32. Law Report, *The Times*, 29 June, 1944; my italics.
33. Quoted in Kenneth Little, *Negroes in Britain: A Study of Racial Relations in English Society*, Routledge and Keegan Paul, London, 1972, p. 245; but first published in 1948.
34. See Sheila Allen, Study of *Pakistanis in Employment: Bradford*, Institute of Race Relations, London, 1968 for a thorough analysis of employment practices; and for a more general demographic picture of the West Riding consult Eric Butterworth, (ed.), *Immigrants in West Yorkshire*, Institute of Race Relations (Special Series), London, 1967.
35. John Rex and Robert Moore, *Race, Community and Conflict: A Study of Sparkbrook*, Oxford University Press, London, 1967.
36. Elizabeth Burney, *Housing on Trial: A Study of Immigrants and Local Government*, Oxford University Press, London, 1967.
37. *Commonwealth Immigrants Act*, 1962, HMSO, London, p. 1.
38. For a good and detailed discussion on the 1965 White Paper see Sheila Patterson, *Immigration and Race Relations in Britain, 1960–1967*, Oxford University Press, London, 1969, Chapter Two.
39. *Immigration from the Commonwealth*, Cmnd 2739, HMSO, London, 1965, para 16(i) and (ii).
40. *Ibid.*, 1965, para. 25.
41. *Ibid.*, 1962, para. 4(a) (b) and (c) in conjunction with Part 11 paras 6–11 inclusive.
42. *Ibid.*, 1965, para. 32.
43. *Ibid.*, 1965, para. 1.
44. *Ibid.*, 1965, para. 1.
45. W. W. Daniel, *Racial Discrimination in England* (Based on the PEP Report) Penguin Books, Harmondsworth, 1968, p. 209.
46. *Parliamentary Debates*, House of Commons, 27 February, 1968, cols 1303, 1342.
47. *Commonwealth Immigrants Act 1968*, HMSO, London.
48. Robert Moore, *Labour and Colour 1965–1968*, *Venture*, September, 1968.
49. Chris Mullard, 1973, *op. cit.*, pp. 75–88.
50. *The Organisation of Race Relations Administration*, Select Committee on Race Relations and Immigration, HMSO, London, 1975, para. 22.
51. *Ibid.*, 1975, para. 64.
52. *Parliamentary Debates*, House of Commons, 21 February, 1973, col. 598. In the debate the then Home Secretary, James Callaghan, enunciated three principles on which policy was based: a) only the inescapable minimum' can be allowed entry into this already crowded island; b) priority must be given to those whom Britain has a 'continuing responsibility' towards; and c) it is only right and natural to give easy access to those with family ties in Britain. Taken as a whole

this policy, as Hannah Rose points out, is quite irrational. For her comment see "Towards a Rational Immigration Policy?", *New Community*, vol. 11, no. 2, Spring, 1973, pp. 159–167.

53. T. W. E. Roche, *The Key in the Lock*, John Murray, London, 1969; and also Robert Moore and Tina Wallace, *Slamming the Door: The Administration of Immigration Control*, Martin Robertson, London, 1975.
54. The year by year registration rule not only makes the non-patrials a poor risk for building society or bank loans, but it also helps to intensify their own feelings of insecurity. The good conduct qualification inhibits the full expression of 'political' interests, and thus of themselves as individuals. In some cases known personally to me, it in fact makes for total passivity, based on a fear that they may be deported or repatriated at any time.
55. Since 1968, British Passports held by many black immigrants merely express that they were once accorded full citizenship: in practice their worth is devalued by the scope and degree of racist legislation. See Mariyam Harris, *The D Valued Passport*, Christian Action, London, 1971.
56. *Parliamentary Debates*, House of Lords, 339, col. 545.
57. Robert Moore and Tina Wallace, 1975, *op. cit.*, p. 64. For a detailed account account of the 'shuttlecocks' see Mary Dines, *Return to Sender*, JCWI Report, London, September, 1970.

# Holocaust in Burundi, 1972

STANLEY MEISLER

STANLEY MEISLER was born in New York City in 1931. He graduated from the City College of New York with a Bachelor of Arts degree in English. He did graduate work in English and in African Studies at the University of California in Berkeley. In 1962 he was awarded the Ford Foundation area research training fellowship for study in Africa. He is a former deputy-director of the office of the Evaluation and Research of the United States Peace Corps. Since 1967 he has been serving as Foreign Correspondent for the *Los Angeles Times* in Africa, Latin America and Spain. His articles have appeared in various magazines, including the *Atlantic* and the *Nation.*

# Holocaust in Burundi, 1972

STANLEY MEISLER

In 1972, the government of Burundi, controlled by the minority Tutsi tribe, tried to eliminate the entire modern class of the majority Hutu people. All those with some education, government jobs or money were to be killed. The Hutus then made up 85 percent of the population in this central African country. But they offered little resistance. The government probably killed somewhere between 100,000 and 200,000 Hutus that year.

It was not easy for the rest of the world to find out what was going on. But the news did seep out. Six months later, there could be no doubt of the enormity of the horror. Yet, even when the facts were beyond dispute, the rest of the world did little to condemn Burundi or to prevent more violence. In 1973, in fact, new massacres began.

The situation was a complex one, and several questions need to be considered. What were the forces that pushed the government of Burundi to such large scale murder? What happened? Why did the rest of the world simply turn away?

## I. Historical Background: Burundi and Rwanda

The history of Burundi cannot be separated from that of its neighbour, Rwanda. There had been mass tribal killing in Rwanda and Burundi for more than a decade, the killing on one side sometimes provoking the killing on the other. The two neighbours have similar traditions and problems. Each about the size of the American state of Maryland, each with almost four million people, Burundi and Rwanda are the most densely populated countries in Africa and among the poorest in the world. Their people graze cattle and farm on a myriad of lovely, verdant hills along Lake Kivu and Lake Tanganyika. In colonial days, the two countries were ruled together as Rwanda-Urundi, a colony of the Germans from 1885 until World War I and a mandate and trust territory of the Belgians from then until independence. Both were feudal kingdoms with masses of Hutu people ruled by Tutsi lords and kings.

More than four hundred years ago, the Tutsi people (better known by the African plural, Watutsi) came down to Rwanda and Burundi from the north, probably Ethiopia. They were cattle people, probably Hamitic, with slender features and skin somewhat lighter than most other Africans. The Tutsis were tall, some well over six feet. Rwanda and Burundi were already inhabited then by a few pygmies and by many Hutu people. The Hutus were farmers who lived by their hoes. They were Bantu people, short, stocky, dark, with negroid features.

Over the years, the small group of Tutsi immigrants subjugated the masses of Hutus into a kind of feudal system by exchanging their cattle for subservience. Much as in medieval Europe, a pyramid developed with Tutsi lords giving their own loyalty to more important Tutsi lords in exchange for protection. A mwami, or Tutsi king, ruled at the top of the pyramid in each country.

There were all kinds of variations in the basic feudal scheme. But one thing was clear. Centuries of tradition made the Tutsis feel like a privileged, superior people and the Hutus feel like a subjugated, inferior people. The Tutsis looked on themselves as intelligent people capable of leadership and scorned the Hutus as no more than hard-working and dumb peasants. The Hutus tended to agree.

The Tutsi attitude, nurtured by tradition, was expressed to the writer after the massacres by a young American-educated Tutsi of Burundi, the son of a lord. "I know the Hutus," he said. "They will never take over. The Hutu peasant does not care anything about politics. And, what if he took over the government? He could never run it. Throughout the world, the ruling class is always made up of no more than one to five percent of the population. Why should it be different in Burundi?"

Such feelings of innate Tutsi superiority and the feudal structure of Rwanda and Burundi were challenged in the early 1960s by many of the ideas generated during the rush to independence in black Africa. Only 15 percent of the population in Burundi and 10 percent in Rwanda, the Tutsis began to feel deep fears about their place in societies where power might go to the majority tribe. The feelings of inferiority by the Hutus and of fear by the Tutsis probably account for most of the terrible bloodshed.

The first troubles took place in Rwanda. In early 1961, the Hutu leaders, with the connivance of Belgian colonial officials, overthrew the mwami of Rwanda. Rwanda became independent in 1962 as a republic run by Hutus. This revolution was accompanied by continual persecution of the Tutsi minority which reached its peak in 1963 and 1964. At that time, the late English philosopher Bertrand Russell called the killings "the most horrible and systematic human massacre we have had occasion to witness since the extermination of the Jews by the Nazis." It is probable that since the mwami of Rwanda was overthrown, the Hutus have killed more than 20,000 Tutsis and forced 200,000 to take refuge in neighbouring Uganda, Zaire and Burundi.

This could hardly reassure the Tutsis of Burundi. Unlike Rwanda, Burundi became independent in 1962 as a kingdom with a mwami still ruling. But he lasted only four years. He was overthrown in 1966, not by Hutus, but by Tutsi army officers from a non-royal clan led by Michel Micombero, now president. Since independence, Hutu rebels have tried to take over Burundi in a succession of coups, plots or uprisings. Each attempt has been met by Tutsi reprisals. The most terrible reprisal came in 1972 after the most serious Hutu uprising.

## II. The Great Killings of 1972

It would be misleading to blame all of the 1972 killing on a savage frenzy of Tutsi fear. Some Hutus were killed in wild, indiscriminate rampages. Others were victims of personal vendettas. But most were wiped out in a cold and calculated way by a Tutsi government that seemed to make the decision that it could guarantee itself power for at least another decade by eliminating all potential leaders of the majority tribe. It is this coldness that made the events of Burundi different from the earlier bloodshed in Rwanda.

The killings began in late April, reached their height in May and ended, more or less, by August. The government did not try to deny that great killing had taken place. But it issued a self-serving interpretation of the events. According to a government white paper, issued in June, a force of 25,000 Hutus, many led by former Congolese rebels in exile in East Africa, had attacked four sectors of Burundi on the night of April 29th. Their aim, according to the Tutsi government, was genocide of the Tutsi people.

The government said that bands of Hutus pillaged the countryside and murdered Tutsis. The Hutus, according to the white paper, were armed with poisoned machetes, clubs, automatic rifles, and Molotov cocktails. The invaders and rebels were drugged into a state of ferocious excitement. They were convinced their skin was impermeable, that bullets coming at them would turn to water. Before the Burundian army could defeat them, the government insisted, the Hutu rebels massacred 50,000 people, almost all Tutsis.

President Micombero said that his army found lists of Hutu plotters on the defeated rebels. These lists, he said, were used by the government to track down and execute the plotters. "Only the guilty have been punished," he said, "The innocent were not troubled at all." The president estimated that the death toll could have reached 100,000.

The government's version of the events, however, was rejected by all foreign sources in Burundi who spoke to the writer several months later. Many foreigners were reluctant to talk with a visiting newsman. They were afraid of expulsion, fearful of being overheard by government security men. They sometimes used the euphemism of "talls and smalls" to describe the Tutsis and Hutus. But, reluctant or not, all foreign sources said that the government had not sought out plotters. Instead, it had attempted a systematic elimination of the modern Hutus.

Many sources agreed that the troubles began with some kind of Hutu uprising. But they said that the Hutu rebels killed a few thousand Tutsi at most, not 50,000. The uprising, the sources went on, became a trigger or an excuse for the government onslaught.

A few sources, in fact, speculated that the government knew about the intended uprising but did not try to prevent it. The Tutsis wanted an excuse, according to these sources, to begin their long-planned drive against the Hutus. Victor D. Du Bois has suggested that the Hutu revolt was, in fact, provoked by the Tutsis.

According to most sources, the government had lists of intended victims. The lists were not exclusive. More Hutus died than were listed. But the lists were taken seriously. There are stories of Hutus begging Tutsi friends to check the lists in government offices to see which Hutus were on it. One source said a Tutsi official tried to reassure the wife of a missing Hutu by showing her a government list without her husband's name on it. But he had been killed anyway.

Although many Hutus were taken away from their homes at night, a large number simply received a summons in an orderly way to report to the police at a certain time. In Bujumbura, the capital, many victims were killed in prison. Many foreigners later had all kinds of grisly stories about the methods of execution, all difficult to verify. But most sources agreed with a diplomat who said, "They did not use many bullets."

The bodies were thrown on trucks that drove from the city to a field near the airport. In the first few days, the trucks rumbled through town in daylight. But the government later decided to try to hide what it was doing. The trucks were shifted to night runs. Under heavy lighting, bulldozers dug mass graves at night and covered them over.

There seemed to be three kinds of victims. First, the government tried to kill almost every Hutu who had a government job, including Hutu soldiers. Many of the death lists were simply lifted from civil service rolls that evidently had been prepared a few months earlier.

Second, the government tried to kill all Hutus who had enough wealth for potential leadership. Wealth is a very relative term in Africa. Many sources said that the so-called wealthy Hutus were any who owned a shop, had a bank account, or lived in a house with a corrugated iron roof instead of a thatched one.

Finally, the government tried to kill all educated Hutus. Education was probably defined differently by officials in different parts of the country. But almost all Hutu university students, many Hutu secondary school students, and perhaps half the country's Hutu teachers were killed. In one incident, six women teachers were killed in front of their students.

The categories of victims explained why a visitor later could hardly find a Hutu inside Bujumbura but could see many trudging along the roads in the countryside, their hoes on their shoulders. Bujumbura, a city of 70,000, was never a Hutu city. The Tutsis, who controlled the wealth and power of Burundi, dominated the capital. But there were thousands of Hutus living there, the Hutus who had left their traditional peasant life in the countryside to join the modern world of the big town. These modern Hutus – all in the money economy, some educated, many in government jobs – were the prime targets of the onslaught.

It is difficult for an outsider to understand how the government was able to inflict so much punishment on the Hutus in a tiny country where they make up the great bulk of its population. They outnumbered the Tutsis almost six to one. Yet the Hutus were cowed by an army that numbered no more than 4,000 at the start of the troubles and far less after it had purged itself of Hutus.

75,000 Hutus fled Burundi and took refuge in Zaire, Tanzania and Rwanda. But thousands more remained behind and took their punishment without much resistance.

There were stories of Hutus accepting their summonses and reporting to the police at the scheduled time even though they knew death awaited them. There were other stories of officials loading Hutus on trucks and, when the trucks were full, ordering the remaining Hutus to come back the next day. The Hutus obeyed. One Hutu minister was overseas when the troubles erupted, yet flew home to his execution. Some Hutus escaped, according to one story, only after Europeans forced them against their will into a truck and drove them across the border.

Some observers said that even Hutus trying to escape did so half-heartedly. "They were pathetic," said one foreigner who had worked with Hutus for many years. "Any kid with a third-grade education in the United States has read enough funny books to know how to escape. But they would walk to the border down the main road. If one gendarme stopped them, they would turn back."

Foreigners who knew the Hutus well blamed their strange acquiescence on a strong streak of fatalism in the Hutu personality and an intense psychological dependence on their Tutsi lords. Much like the serfs in medieval Europe, the Hutus for centuries had given their loyalty to the Tutsis in exchange for protection. Caught in a terrifying crisis in 1972, most did as they were told.

## III. World Reaction

The reaction by outsiders to this killing was feeble. Missionaries kept quiet or muted their concern. Most foreign governments refused to protest in public. Two African countries even rushed military help to Micombero's government. Almost all foreign aid continued to flow. European businessmen kept playing golf in Bujumbura.

It is not difficult to imagine the outcry in the rest of the world if the whites who run the government of South Africa had decided to put down a rebellion and guarantee their continued control by killing all black South Africans with some education, wealth or potential for leadership. Yet the events in Burundi, roughly analogous, provoked few protests. It was almost as if all foreigners had banded together in a conspiracy of silence.

Actually there was no conspiracy. For a variety of reasons, all institutions that might have protested – churches, governments, international organizations – made separate decisions to look the other way. Each decision seemed logical and right to those who made it. But, as a result, the Burundi government escaped any punishment or even condemnation.

Missionaries and other religious leaders showed the most surprising restraint, for, in the past, they have been in the forefront of those exposing injustice in Africa. During the Nigerian and Sudanese civil wars, for example, church groups played a major role in publicizing the pains of Biafra and the southern Sudan.

Burundi is one of the most Christian countries in Africa, for more than half of its population is Christian, mostly Catholic. It might seem that this strength would make churchmen forthright in their condemnation of the killing. But it actually made most missionaries hesitant. They were afraid that if they spoke out they might lose their hold on Burundi. They believed that silence was the price they had to pay to expand Christianity. Some reasoned that protest would have been futile anyway. In the long run, they told themselves, their silence and the spread of Christianity might give them more influence to prevent the recurrence of such a holocaust.

Some of the tortuous reasoning came through in an interview that an American Protestant missionary reluctantly granted. He said that Protestant missionaries were in a precarious position in Burundi. Government leaders, mainly Catholic, suspected them of stirring up troubles among the Hutus. He paid tribute to the American embassy in Bujumbura for trying to keep stories about the massacres away from the American press when they began. He said that if the news had been splashed in American newspapers, the Burundi government might have blamed the 100 American Protestant missionaries in Burundi and expelled them.

Yet, a few minutes later, the missionary deplored the fact that the rest of the world had ignored what had happened in Burundi. The inconsistency was quickly pointed out. How could he praise the U.S. embassy for withholding the news and then deplore the fact that the news was ignored? The missionary shrugged.

He was asked how he could continue to work in Burundi. Many

victims had been Protestant. The government had slaughtered Hutus that he had trained for years. Why convert people to Christianity and educate them in a country that might slaughter them just because they were educated? Put on the defensive, the missionary laughed nervously. "I suppose you could say that's our job," he said, "preparing people to die."

Catholic leaders also found themselves caught between their conscience and politics. Much of the Catholic clergy was Tutsi. Almost all the Tutsi leaders of government, including the president, who came to confession several times a week, were Catholic. The Catholic clergy did not remain silent, but it did not say very much either.

Soon after the killing began, the Bishop of Bujumbura, a Tutsi, urged the government to be judicious in punishing those Hutus accused of plotting against the government. A few weeks later, Pope Paul VI, speaking to a Sunday crowd at St. Peter's Square, called for a solution to the "pitiless and ferocious strife." The Papal Nuncio in Bujumbura delivered a note to the Burundi government urging restraint. In January 1973, the five bishops of Burundi – two Tutsi, two Hutu, and one Belgian – issued a pastoral letter describing the country as "drowned in blood" but blaming the troubles on "the egoism of both Hutu and Tutsi elites," not tribalism. Against the enormity of what happened in Burundi, all these Catholic pronouncements seemed ineffectual.

The reaction of the U.S. government to the events was typical of most foreign governments. Ambassador Thomas P. Melady believed that his first responsibility was protection of the 150 Americans in Burundi, mostly missionaries. When the massacres began, the U.S. embassy in Kenya, receiving reports from Melady, began briefing American correspondents on what was going on. The correspondents, based in Nairobi, had been unable to obtain visas for Burundi. Melady immediately rebuked the embassy in Nairobi and demanded that it stop the briefings. He feared that news reports in American newspapers would be traced easily by the Burundi government to the U.S. embassy in Bujumbura and its main sources, the American missionaries. The clamp down on the news became so tight that Senator Edward M. Kennedy complained in June that the State Department was withholding its information on the massacres from Congress.

The U.S. government never publicly rebuked the Burundi government. In the fall of 1972, Assistant Secretary of State David Newsom secretly called the Burundi ambassador to the State Department and expressed American concern over the troubles. But this concern was never communicated in person in Bujumbura to President Micombero by either Melady or his successor, Ambassador Robert L. Yost. Melady, in fact, accepted an award from Micombero before he left Burundi in late May 1972 to become Ambassador to Uganda.

According to a report by the Carnegie Endowment for International Peace, a State Department officer did propose that the United States, as a sign of its displeasure, stop buying coffee from Burundi. An American firm, Folgers, buys more than 80 percent of Burundi's coffee, its main export, accounting for 65 percent of Burundi's earnings of foreign exchange. The officer proposed that the U.S. government either place an embargo on purchases of coffee or persuade Folgers to stop buying on its own.

But this proposal, according to the Carnegie report, was dropped without even serious consideration. American policy-makers were persuaded that protest was futile in any case and that the troubles ought to be treated as an African problem. If African governments chose to ignore the massacres, the U.S. officials reasoned, why should the American government make an issue of it.

The United States did suspend a fund of $ 25,000 that the office of the ambassador had available for small self-help projects within Burundi. But the U.S. government supplied $ 300,000 worth of relief in 1973, mostly in surplus food. American officials insisted that this food was distributed only to the widows and orphans of the victims. But, according to the Americans actually distributing the food, it went to all people of all tribes throughout the country without discrimination.

Belgium was the only western country to react differently from the United States. The former colonial power in Burundi, Belgium was the largest donor of foreign aid and had the most nationals living there, about 3000. In May, Premier Gaston Eyskens denounced the massacres as "veritable genocide." His government announced it would review continuation of its four and a half million dollars a year foreign aid programme. This set off a storm of anti-Belgian invective from the Burundi government, which even accused the Belgians of starting all the troubles in the first place.

In the end, Belgium did not carry out its threat. It withdrew 35 advisers from the Burundi army, but this was less to punish Burundi than to placate Belgian public opinion. It was hard to justify keeping advisers in an army that was killing the elite of the majority tribe. The Belgians also refused to replace 50 technicians who were expelled by the Burundi government after the massacres, evidently because they had expressed disapproval of what was going on.

But, in general, Belgium neither withdrew nor substantially cut its foreign aid. It may have decided against planning new programmes, but that is something that Burundi would not perceive as a rebuke. Belgian officials took the view of most foreigners involved in foreign aid in Burundi. They insisted that punishing the government by withdrawing aid would only hurt the masses. "Foreign aid must be maintained," said a Belgian official. "This, with Rwanda, is the poorest country in the world." "If we cut foreign aid," said a foreign aid official from another country, "you will only have more misery here. If you put a curtain around this country, it will be worse." As a result, the United Nations, France, the Common Market, and West Germany all maintained their foreign aid programmes.

Almost all African governments reacted in a predictable way. As usual in cases of African disorder, the governments either ignored the massacres or pledged support to the government. Deluded by the claim that the original Hutu uprising had been led by former Congolese rebels now exiled in Tanzania, President Mobutu Sese Seko of Zaire (the former Congo) even sent troops to Bujumbura and President Julius Nyerere of Tanzania sent ammunition. In May, Diallo Telli, then secretary-general of the Organization of African Unity (OAU), flew to Bujumbura and announced "the total solidarity of the secretary-general of the OAU with President Micombero." At its annual summit conference in June, the OAU refrained from any public statement on the massacres.

Only Rwanda departed from the African line. In June, President Gregoire Kayibanda of Rwanda sent a letter to Micombero asking him to "halt the killing that does Africa no good." But the Burundi government, without making the letter public, described it as an endorsement of the government's policies. Rwanda then dropped the matter.

While governments and institutions kept quiet about the massacres, most of the 6,000 foreigners in Burundi also made little protest. Few demonstrated their disgust by leaving. They, like their governments, probably felt that protest was futile.

Some foreigners also reported that it was possible to ignore what was going on. Most of the killings and arrests took place at night far from the offices where expatriates worked. Trucks went through streets at night, but only a few whites actually saw the bodies in them. Expatriates were often not on close terms with Africans anyway. Seven workers might disappear from an office one week. That would be terrible and regrettable but not heart-rending. Moreover, the government was careful not to harm foreigners. For a white expatriate, it was possible to remain in Burundi and keep playing golf. There was another reason for the lack of outcry. Most westerners and their governments reacted to the disorders as if they believed slaughter was a way of life in this part of Africa, best ignored, at least until time and civilization tamed the savages. The slaughter of thousands of blacks by blacks was not really considered a holocaust by most white governments. Ironically, African governments seemed to agree.

## IV. Reaction in Rwanda

Events since 1972 did not indicate much hope for an end to turmoil in the area or to a change of mood among outsiders. The bloodshed spread to neighbouring Rwanda by the first months of 1973. There, the ruling Hutus unleashed their resentment against their former Tutsi lords. Hutus forced private employers to dismiss Tutsi workers and frightened Tutsi students away from the university and secondary school. Hutus began rioting and murdering Tutsis on the hills in the countryside. The bloodshed, however, was not on the scale of the earlier massacres in Rwanda or of the 1972 holocaust in Burundi. Foreign sources in Kigali, the capital of Rwanda, estimated that between 750 and 3,000 Tutsis died in Rwanda in 1973.

In May 1973, Hutu refugees crossed the borders from Rwanda and Tanzania into Burundi in an attempt to avenge the 1972 massacres and overthrow the Tutsi government. The Hutus failed. But the frightened Tutsi government organized youth patrols to guard Bujumbura, now an all-Tutsi city, from the Hutu countryside. Soldiers and youths then began reprisals against Hutus.

According to a report in *Africa* magazine, the killing again became systematic but was aimed this time at the masses, not just the educated. The magazine, quoting Swiss journalist Jean Ziegler, said that Tutsi soldiers and youths would surround Hutu villages suddenly, sack them, and torture and murder the inhabitants.

Despite this new evidence of massacres, the United States, according to Roger Morris of the Carnegie Endowment, decided in early 1974 to normalize its relations with Burundi and begin a formal aid programme. Morris attributed this to the discovery of $ 14 billion worth of nickel in Burundi by a U.N. survey team in the summer of 1973. Morris said the U.S. government did not want American companies to lose in the competition for the right to mine this nickel.

With thousands of embittered Hutu refugees in camps across the borders, with the fearful Tutsi rulers still far outnumbered, with governments like that of the United States more interested in nickel than murder, the outlook was for more turmoil and more neglect.

## References

Much of this material, in different form, has appeared in the *Los Angeles Times* and the *Atlantic* magazine. Conclusions are based mainly on interviews with foreigners and Burundians who must remain anonymous. Historical and cultural background is drawn from Rene Lemarchand's *Rwanda and Burundi* (London: Pall Mall Press) and Victor D. Du Bois's *To Die in Burundi*, his reports in the American Universities Field Staff series, September 1972. The Burundi government's version of the massacres was detailed in its ministry of information's report, *Livre Blanc sur les Evenements Survenus aux Mois d'Avril et Mai 1972*. The Carnegie Endowment published its analysis of the American reaction in its pamphlet, *Passing By: The United States and Genocide in Burundi, 1972*. Project Director Roger Morris added to this in an article in the *New York Times*, March 3, 1974. An account of the 1973 troubles appears in the September 1973 issue of the London-based magazine, *Africa*.

# Bangladesh: A Profile of 20th-Century Genocide

ANTHONY MASCARENHAS

ANTHONY MASCARENHAS was born in Belgium, now in the South Indian State of Mysore, 1928. A Goan Christian, after graduation, he joined Reuters in Bombay in 1947. He settled in Karachi in 1948 and served on the Associated Press of Pakistan from 1949–1954. His next journalistic stint was Reuter Correspondent in Pakistan for two and a half years, followed by stringing for the *New York Times* and *Time/Life* for seven years, while freelancing for various Pakistani publications. He joined the *Morning News*, Karachi, as chief reporter in 1961, and represented this newspaper in New Delhi from July 1963 to November 1965. On return to Pakistan he became an assistant editor of *Morning News*, a position he held until he decided to quit Pakistan in May 1971 in protest against the crimes against humanity committed by the military junta in East Bengal.

The London *Sunday Times* published his eye-witness accounts of the horrors perpetrated in East Bengal. These articles and his subsequent book *The Rape of Bangladesh* created a world-wide sensation. In 1972 he won the Granada Special Award (What The Papers Say) and the Special Award from the International Publishing Company for reporting the genocide in Bangladesh. He is currently a foreign news writer with the *Sunday Times*, specialising on the Indian Sub-Continent, and he is preparing for publication a book documenting the murder of Sheikh Mujibur Rahman and the subsequent events leading to the establishment of military rule in Bangladesh.

# Bangladesh: A Profile of 20th-Century Genocide

ANTHONY MASCARENHAS

> Before God we tried to preserve this nation of Pakistan in spite of the oppression, neglect and servitude inflicted upon us by your rulers these 23 years. But your leaders would neither tolerate the idea of sharing power with us nor would they let go of us sufficiently to let us control our own destinies.
>
> *Tajuddin Ahmad, Prime Minister of The provisional govt. of Bangladesh*

The creation of Pakistan in 1947, a novel experiment in statehood, posed the question whether religion, Islam in this case, could provide bonding sufficiently strong to overcome the stresses of a plural society whose complex cultural differences were further compounded by economic disparities and a vast geographical separation. In the event religion proved unequal to the task. The discrimination practised by the Punjab-dominated West Pakistan against the Bengalis of East Pakistan (now Bangladesh) was pervasive, even to the denigration of the piety of the province's 60 million Bengalis. Thus on 16th December 1971 Pakistan's Eastern province with 60% of the population broke away to form the Republic of Bangladesh.

The exercise was tragically exorbitant in human terms. Bangladesh leaders claim that the Pakistan army's nine-month campaign of genocide killed almost two million people in the attempt to crush Bengali nationalism. Another 10 million refugees fled to temporary safety in India. In a wider perspective the 1971 cataclism affected more than 700 million people because it shattered the economies of Bangladesh, Pakistan and India. It is easily the greatest human disaster in modern times.

## I. Background to Conflict

Pakistan (the term, in Urdu, means "Land of the Pure") was created with built-in conflict. The historic upsurge of Muslims in the old British Indian empire seeking the shelter of a separate homeland against what they felt – and not without reason – to be domination by the Hindu majority had been eminently purposeful for the partition of the sub-continent into separate states of India and Pakistan. But it was not in itself sufficient to cement the disparate and geographically separated economic and cultural entities that emerged to form Pakistan. Not only did 1,000 miles of hostile Indian territory stand between the two wings of the country, but East and West Pakistan were different in every way. In West Pakistan nature had fostered energetic, aggressive peoples – hardy hill men and tribal farmers who have constantly to strive for a livelihood in relatively harsh conditions. They were a world apart from the gentle Bengalis of East Pakistan who had an easy abundance in their delta homeland. West Pakistanis and East Pakistanis lived different lives in entirely different environments. They spoke and thought differently; they ate and dressed in their own distinctive fashions; even their sports were different. Although there was a constant mixing of the four broad racial groups within West Pakistan, the peoples of the East and West seldom married.

Politically also the two parts of the country were on different wavelengths. West Pakistan considered itself part of the Middle East and looked in that direction. For its part East Pakistan was very much involved with its neighbours in South-East Asia where it found a natural affinity. It had never been enthused by West Pakistan's international pre-occupations. One of these was a proposal in 1958 for a confederation with Afghanistan and Iran. The prime reason underlying this extreme measure was to offset what West Pakistanis thought was an intolerable political weight of the millions of East Pakistan. It was abandoned after both Afghanistan and Iran rebuffed the idea. The relationship between East and West Pakistan was thus as tenuous as perhaps the ties would be if Britain and Bulgaria suddenly decided to come together in a new state.

Islam, of course, was the common factor linking East and West Pakistan. But the 23 year history of their association has shown that religion made a poor binding without the resin of a common hatred. The partition of India undermined this when it removed the ideological conflict with the Hindus – the only real basis of Indian (and Pakistani) Muslim unity. Denied this cohesive factor, the new Muslim entities of East and West Pakistan began to seek separate channels of self-interest after the first flush of creation had faded. For very real reasons of survival and advancement, the more aggressive West Pakistan began to dominate the naturally prosperous and more populous East. For its own survival, East Pakistan began to resist this domination.

Religion took a back seat before the economic, cultural and political issues. The conflict began to escalate.

## II. The Seeds of Conflict

### *A. Political Discrimination*

One of the key factors in Bengali sensitivity about the "colonialism" of West Pakistan was the unceasing efforts of the leaders from the western wing to demolish the political weightage East Pakistan could have hoped to enjoy due to its greater population. These efforts came in the form of a series of constitutional, administrative and financial contrivances over the years and designed to maintain effective power in the West.

From the start the first prime minister, Mr. Liaquat Ali Khan, proposed that East and West Pakistan should have equal representation in the central legislature which would have two chambers. The proposal ignored the fact that the Bengalis then constituted 56% of the total population and they strongly opposed it. Despite these objections the idea was pursued in a variety of permutations in the eight years it took to write Pakistan's first constitution. Agreement on equal representation in the legislature was finally reached at a price: the promise that the Bengalis would also have equal representation in the central administrative service and in the armed forces. The promise was never fulfilled though the "parity" formula, as the agreement was called, was incorporated in the 1956 and 1962 constitutions. East Pakistan's share of the senior administrative posts never exceeded 36% and even as late as 1969 President Yahya Khan could find only three Bengalis among the 19 department heads in the central government. Bengali representation was immeasurably less in the armed forces. In 1970 there was only one Bengali Lt. General in the Pakistan army. No Bengali ever held an equivalent position in the navy or air force. This under-representation was made all the more intolerable for the Bengalis by the fact that from 1950 till the secession Pakistan was ruled by a Punjab-dominated bureaucratic-military oligarchy.

The country never had a real tradition of democracy. The Muslim League, which spear-headed the movement for Pakistan, was dominated by a landed aristocracy and an educated elite. The aristocrats were the feudal landlords of the Punjab and Sind, the Khans of the North-West Frontier province and Baluchistan. The educated elite comprised the petty chieftans and senior politicians of the United Provinces (in Northern India) and the shrewd barristers of Bombay. Among the latter was the towering, autocratic Mr. Mohammad Ali Jinnah, the "Quaid-i-Azam" (Great Leader) who founded the new state. They influenced the big decisions. They conducted the negotiations with the departing British. They assumed and maintained a monopoly of power in the young Muslim state. On the other hand the Bengalis, whose mass support had played a decisive role in the attainment of Pakistan, were sharply divided at the top, hopelessly outnumbered and rendered ineffective. Bengali stalwarts such as Mr. A. K. Fazlul Huq and Mr. H. S. Suhrawardy found themselves isolated from the Muslim League and out of official favour within three years of the birth of Pakistan.

In the years after independence the ruling circle in Pakistan was compacted. Power became the preserve of the Punjabis and their blood relatives, the Hazara Pathans. This was effectively exercised for more than 20 years by a small coterie of civil servants, politicians and ambitious army men operating behind a facade of democracy. The seven prime ministers who held office in the first 11 years were removed not by electoral process but by violence and the fiat of the bureaucratic-military establishment. During this time the national parliament met for only 338 days – an average of just over 30 days a year. It enacted 160 laws whereas the Governors General/Presidents issued 376 major ordinances which became law by decree. Since these autocratic heads of state were uniformly from West Pakistan, it was inevitable that the Bengalis should feel excluded from the decision-making process. The disenchantment grew with the years. It is also a matter of record that over the years second-line Bengali politicians willingly lent themselves as the instrument of this discrimination.

### *B. Linguistic Discrimination*

The Bengali language, always a cherished medium of cultural expression of the people, was from the start a target of West Pakistan discrimination. On his one and only visit to East Pakistan in February, 1948, the "Quaid-i-Azam" Mr. Mohammad Ali Jinnah declared "Urdu and Urdu alone" would be the state language of Pakistan.

This insistence on Urdu was a curious attitude for the founding father to take. Less than 10% of the population of the country had any knowledge of the language. On the other hand Bengali was spoken by 60%. The other provinces had their own well-developed languages. But there was Mr. Jinnah insisting that all should speak Urdu.

His words came as a cold shower to the sensitive Bengalis. It provoked a series of riots. Thousands of students were arrested for pressing the demand for Bengali to be given official recognition. One of them was Sheikh Mujibur Rahman who after this first experience of jail went on to become the father of Bangladesh independence.

As the agitation developed new forms of grievance arose. Bengali members of the constituent assembly were denied permission to speak in their mother tongue. When they protested, Prime Minister Liaquat Ali Khan replied "Pakistan is a Muslim state and it must have as its lingua franca the language of the Muslim nation ... It is necessary for a nation to have one language and that language can only be Urdu."

The assertion that Urdu was the "language of the Muslim nation" was an outrageous contortion of ideology. Arabic, not Urdu, is the language of the Koran, the holy Book of Islam. The "non-Muslim' or infidel innuendo implicit in the Prime Minister's statement did not apply to Punjabi, Baluchi, Sindhi and Pushto spoken in the provinces of West Pakistan. It was solely directed against Bengali. Others went so far as to ludicrously suggest that since Bengali was also the language of Hindus living in the Indian state of Bengal, it was a "Hindu language" and hence "anti-Muslim." Punjabi is spoken equally by the Muslims of the Pakistan province of the Punjab as it is by the Hindus across the border in the Indian state of the same name. Punjabi however has never suffered the same reproach. There was no rationale whatsoever for this discrimination against Bengali, only blind prejudice.

The agitation in support of the Bengali language reached a climax in a series of bloody riots in 1952. The central government, dominated by West Pakistanis, first gave grudging recognition to the importance of Bengali, but asked that it be written with the Urdu script. Ultimately it was forced to place it on a par with Urdu and English as the official languages of the state. By then the language issue had become a key factor in Bengali nationalism.

### *C. Economic Disparity*

The economic disparities were always the principal issue clouding the relationship between the two wings of Pakistan. West Pakistan by no means an area of affluence, was nevertheless a far cry from the unrelieved poverty manifest throughout East Pakistan. Statistics are not the best yardstick to prove an argument for they can be advanced with equal force by either side. In 1971, however, a group of Bengali economists such as Mr. Rehman Sobhan and Mr. Kabiruddin Ahmad, and a group of three Harvard economists, Edward S. Mason, Robert Dorfman and Stephen A. Marlin, separately marshalled imposing documentation of the manner in which East Pakistan had been kept as a virtual colony of the West wing. Their revelations were startling Among them were:

(a) The per capita income in West Pakistan in 1969–70 was 61% higher than in East Pakistan and double what it was 10 years earlier.

(b) In 1950–55 East Pakistan received only 20% of development expenditure and West Pakistan 80%. In 1965–70 despite promises of the central government, East Pakistan with 54% of the population received 35% of the total expenditure on development, while West Pakistan got 65%.

(c) East Pakistan's export surplus with the outside world (mainly from jute and jute products) had been to a large extent used to finance deficits in West Pakistan, resulting in a nett drain of real resources from East to West. The total transfer of resources in this manner in the 20 years ending 1968–69 was computed at US $ 2,100 million at the then open market rate of exchange. At the same time between 40 and 50% of all West Pakistan exports were sold in what had become a captive market in East Pakistan.

(d) Contrary to official arguments about a population explosion which were used to justify a slower income growth for East Pakistan, the province had a slower rate of population growth than the West. East Pakistan's population rose from 41 million in 1949–50 to 53 million in 1959–60 and 69 million in 1969–70, registering an annual increase of 2.9% in the first decade and 3% in the second. In West Pakistan the population increased from 32 million in 1949–50 to 45 million in 1959–60 and 59 million in 1969–70 for an increase of 4% in the first decade and 3.1% in the second.

These assertions undoubtedly helped to substantiate the charges of economic strangulation by West Pakistan which were advanced by Bengali nationalists to promote the political and economic emancipation of their province.

Other evidence of exploitation came from the profusion of West Pakistani business houses which almost exclusively monopolised the economy of the East wing. They controlled jute and cotton textile factories, tea gardens and processing plants, banks, insurance houses, car assembly plants and some of the major import-export businesses. It was therefore understandable that the Bengali should complain when he found himself constantly having to seek out "West Pakistani outsiders" for the job he wanted, the clothes he wore, the goods he bought in the market and the money he required to borrow. Even the "burra sahib" (boss) in the government offices was not unusually a civil servant from the West Wing or a non-Bengali refugee from India.

All this led Sheikh Mujibur Rahman to chide West Pakistanis with the words "... in a family, eating by one member does not fill the stomach of another. So how and with what conscience do you call us selfish for demanding our share ... you who are not only enjoying your own share but devouring the share of your brothers?" (The Awami League manifesto, "Our Right to Live.")

### *D. Religious Discrimination*

It could have been readily assumed that a state whose raison d'être was a faith shared with equal fervour by its culturally diverse and geographically separated components, would be immune to religious discrimination within the dominant group. Unfortunately this was not so in Pakistan. The West Pakistani discrimination against the Bengali language in the context of blind religious prejudice has already been mentioned. There were other manifestations of such perverted logic, if the term can be used at all, despite the obvious realities. The Bengalis were perhaps a little more devoted to the orthodox practice of Islam than their co-religionists in West Pakistan. They rigidly observed the dawn to dusk abstention from food and water during the fasting month of Ramadan. So also was the enforcement of prohibition which had a more relaxed application in West Pakistan. Dacca, the capital of the old eastern province, took pride in claiming to be a "city of mosques" with over 1,000 such places of worship. Nevertheless there were over the years some notable examples of the denigration of the piety of Bengali Muslims which were extremely offensive to them. One such was a remark attributed to a Punjabi governor of East Pakistan who is alleged to have said that the Bengalis were "half Muslims" who did not bother to '*helal*' (kosher) their chickens. The reported insult provoked a counter-blast from Maulana Bashani, a leading religious and political personality. "Have we to lift our *lungis* (sarongs)" the Maulana asked, "to prove we are Muslims?" (The reference was to the Muslim requirement of circumcision).

An underlying cause of this denigration was a complex that some West Pakistanis had about the cultural affinity Muslim Bengalis had with the hated Hindu Bengalis across the border in India. This was somehow assumed to have diluted the Pakistani (and Muslim) identity of the Bengali Muslims. In 1971 when new moves to extend the domination of East Pakistan came unstuck in an upsurge of Bengali nationalism, this underlying West Pakistani bigotry was to explode in a terrifying orgy of violence.

## III. The Development of Conflict

In the spring of 1969 two far-reaching developments created a political shambles in Pakistan. The first was a nation-wide upsurge against the undisguised dictatorship of General Mohammad Ayub Khan who had seized power 10 years earlier. This had delivered a savage body blow to the Punjab dominated military-bureaucratic combine holding the monopoly of power. The second was the polarisation of the competing ambitions of East and West Pakistan. For the first time political groups in East Pakistan united in their opposition to the discrimination by the West. The combination of these circumstances and the increasingly violent attempts by the ruling elite to re-assert itself resulted in the secession of Bangladesh two years later.

### *A. The Upsurge against Dictatorship*

On 7 October, 1958, the Pakistan army led by General Mohammad Ayub Khan finally ended the charade of parliamentary government. The General, who promoted himself to Field Marshal, dismissed the Prime Minister, the national assembly and his old friend, President

Iskander Mirza, to usher in an era of unconcealed dictatorship.

The excuse was the restoration of political and economic stability – and there was undoubtedly need for this. But what in fact had happened was that the power-hungry monster lurking within the body politic of Pakistan had finally broken out. By demolishing even the facade of democracy maintained over the years, the military-bureaucratic combine brought the people face to face with their real oppressor. The development ultimately proved to be its undoing. But for the next decade, until the spring of 1969, Pakistan was to be ruled with an iron fist.

Seldom has there been a more vivid demonstration of Lord Acton's dictum, "... absolute power corrupts absolutely." The military-bureaucratic elite, as the principal instrument of Field Marshal Ayub's power, achieved an eminence beyond its wildest dreams. It totally demoralized Pakistan. Servility, sychophancy and corruption in its many forms became a way of life. Indeed, political, professional, and business advancement was inconceivable without the necessary obeisance in the right direction and the liberal application of grease. Never had the people of Pakistan been so debased.

Towards the end of 1968 particularly savage police excesses against a group of young college boys in Rawalpindi sent a wave of revulsion throughout the country. Ayub's efforts to control the situation were singularly inept. In a matter of weeks it had developed into an unprecedented mass upsurge against the ageing Field Marshal's dictatorship. The pent up frustrations of a nation had finally exploded. After a series of retreats Ayub Khan was forced to resign as much by the public pressure as by a desperate act of self-preservation by the military-bureaucratic establishment. For the moment it appeared that the people had finally come out on top.

### *B. Polarisation of the East Pakistani Opposition*

The traumatic events in West Pakistan had come as a heaven-sent opportunity to the opposition forces in the East wing. Field Marshal Ayub Khan, like others before him, had relied on middle-line Bengali politicians from religious parties to hold down the mounting unrest in East Pakistan. With Ayub's exit, these instruments of West Pakistan power were eclipsed. The way was opened for Bengali nationalist groups to press for the redress of East Pakistan's grievances. Heading the movement was Sheikh Mujibur Rahman and the Awami League (People's league), once the principal targets of Field Marshal Ayub Khan's repression.

Bengali interest in the Awami League was centred on the party's manifesto. It was a six-point demand intended to remove the political and economic disparities suffered by East Pakistan. The emphasis was on regional autonomy. The Bengalis wanted opportunity to pursue their own development. Proposed was a federal structure with the federating units (East and West Pakistan) independently controlling their own economic development through separate legislative and fiscal systems embracing currency, banking, public accounts and foreign trade. The federal government would be responsible only for defence and foreign affairs. The federating units would be represented in the federal parliament on the basis of their population and would also be empowered to maintain their own militia or para-military forces.

While it was intended that these contrivances should help to remove East Pakistan's grievances, the Awami League's manifesto was a curious, if unintentioned, throw-back to the concept of Pakistan enunciated in the historic Muslim League resolution at Lahore in 1940. It required that the areas in which the Muslims were numerically in the majority, as in the north-western and the eastern zones of India, should be grouped to constitute independent *states* in which the constituent units would be autonomous and sovereign. The good sense of this arrangement answered the challenges of geographical separation of the two wings of Pakistan. But it did not conform to the ambitions of the landlord class and the Muslim elite who dominated the Muslim League. Six years later the plurality was claimed to be a secretarial error and suitably amended to the singular. Pakistan would be not two, but one state. In 1969 the Awami League appeared to be trying to restore the original concept of plural states, albeit in diluted form, in the endeavour to redress grievance and preserve the Pakistan entity. Punjabis however saw it as the thin end of a secessionist wedge. As their opposition to the autonomy plan grew, so did Bengali unity consolidate under the Awami League banner. In the spring of 1969 the polarisation was complete.

### *C. The Pakistan Army's Riposte*

On 26th March, 1969, President Ayub Khan, the ageing Field Marshal, finally bowed to the inevitable and resigned. He was replaced by the commander-in-chief of the Pakistan army, General Agha Mohammad Yahya Khan. General Yahya's new command was a shambles. The nation-wide upsurge against Ayub had resulted in a break-down of law and order. Rioting, arson and looting were reported from the main towns where the police found themselves overwhelmed. The collapse of Ayub's highly personalized style of government had brought the administration to a standstill. Strikes and disturbances were shattering the economy. The success of the popular revolt against the tyrant, Ayub, had bred a dangerous mood of recklessness among the politicians and students of West Pakistan and in the Eastern wing what the intelligence agencies reported was an alarming secessionist movement.

After placing the country under martial law, General Yahya told the people:

> My sole aim in imposing martial law is to protect life, liberty and property of the people and put the administration back on the rails . . . I wish to make it absolutely clear to you that I have no ambition other than the creation of conditions conducive to the establishment of a constitutional government. It is my firm belief that a sound, clean and honest administration is a pre-requisite for sane and constructive political life and for the smooth transfer of power to the representatives of the people elected freely and impartially on the basis of adult franchise. It will be the task of these elected representatives to give the country a workable constitution and find a solution of all other political, economic and social problems that have been agitating the minds of the people.

There was no ambiguity about General Yahya's statement. It was, however, patently in the tradition of new dictators. The obvious questions before Pakistanis on that spring day in 1969 were: (a) was the new President sincere about the promise of democracy? and; (b) had the Punjab-dominated military-bureaucratic establishment finally relinquished the effective power it had controlled for more than 20 years?

Perceptive observers could have found the answers, as some of us did, in the manner in which General Yahya Khan had become President.

The constitution required that the Speaker of the national assembly act as President if the latter found himself unable to function through absence abroad or any other reason. Thus the Speaker should have stepped into Ayub's vacant seat. But the Field Marshal relinquished authority, not to the Speaker, but to the commander-in-chief of the army. The assumptions were inescapable: the army was still the final arbiter in Pakistan; and that army was essentially a Punjabi army reflecting the unchanging values and ambitions of the Punjabi feudal class.

In their euphoria the people did not realise that their struggle for democracy was far from over. They had, indeed, won a major battle – Ayub and his officers and political henchmen had been sent packing – but the war itself was another thing. Power still lay very much in the hands of the army and its civilian advisers. Admittedly the old guard had been swept away and the newcomers would have to be demonstrably more responsive to public demand; but they were undeniably of the same ruling stock. In practical terms only another change had been rung in the interminable musical chairs that had characterised Pakistan politics since the founding of the state.

General Yahya Khan was not a Punjabi, nor a man from the neighbouring Hazara district as Ayub Khan was. The new president was a Pathan from Peshawar addicted to a high and free style of living. It was, perhaps, these qualities and an apparent subservience to his chief, that made him for Ayub an ideal choice for the job of commander-in-chief of the army. Now Yahya Khan had moved into the President's chair by virtue of his army command. In these circumstances the general knew, perhaps better than most others, that the army had no intention of abdicating the real power it exercised. To secure his position he would have to conform to the rules of the club; but he was astute enough to realise the need for caution.

The turbulent events of the previous six months had underscored the need for broader public participation in the government. Ayub's scrapping of the parliamentary system had proved to be a costly mistake. There had also been no general elections in the 22 years of independence. Thus it was abundantly clear to General Yahya and his group that unless elections and some form of "parliamentary democracy" was conceded as a sop to the public, the battered establishment could be entirely wiped out.

Events have proved that what General Yahya Khan intended in his broadcast on 26th March, 1969, was not the real transfer of power to the people through their elected representatives, but the delegation of some authority to a civilian government with himself, backed by the army, holding the whip hand. Diehard opponents of Bangladesh have justified this obvious lack of sincerity on the grounds of "national interest." They claim that the Pakistan experience had shown its politicians to be perfidious, that the people had to be protected against their own excesses and that the army had "an inherent responsibility greater than any constitution." In this context General Yahya's promise of the transfer of power meant the transfer of power with the "accepted reservations." The army had no misunderstanding about this. The misunderstanding was elsewhere. This perverted thinking made for confrontation between East and West Pakistan and the inevitable breakaway of the Bengalis for the creation of Bangladesh.

## IV. Confrontation

Pakistanis went to the polls in December, 1970, to elect a constituent assembly which was intended to give the country a new constitution. It was, indeed, a free expression of the public will based on general adult franchise. In the circumstances, General Yahya would have been unwise to try to tamper with the elections. But what he did do from the start was to try to pre-determine the constitutional pattern so as to leave his own (and the army's) over-riding position untouched. The contrivance employed for this purpose was the Legal Framework Order.

The operative clauses in the Order were Articles 25 and 27 and No 4 of the "fundamental principles" on which the new constitution was to be based. Article 25 specified:

> The constitution bill, as passed by the national assembly, shall be presented to the President for authentication. The national assembly shall stand dissolved in the event that authentication is refused.

Article 27 said:

> (1) Any question or doubt as to the interpretation of any provision of this order shall be resolved by a decision of the President, and such decision shall be final and not liable to be questioned in any court. (2) The President and NOT the assembly shall have the power to make any amendment of his order.

If the Presidential veto was specifically spelled out, the basic pattern of the constitution enunciated in the "fundamental principles" of constitution making were woefully ambiguous. No. 4 of these principles decreed:

All powers, including legislative, administrative and financial, shall be so distributed between the federal government and provinces that the provinces shall have maximum autonomy, that is to say, maximum legislative, administrative and financial powers, but the federal government shall also have adequate powers, including legislative, administrative and financial powers, to discharge its responsibilities in relation to external and internal affairs and to preserve the independence and territorial integrity of the country.

It did not require a dictionary to expose the absurdity of such a dispensation. The maximum autonomy, legislative and financial powers allowed the provinces would inevitably conflict with the *adequate* legislative and financial powers concurrently required for an effective federal government. So also would the federal government's over-riding responsibility in *internal* affairs clash with the *maximum* autonomy to be enjoyed by the provinces.

General Yahya's gambit became obvious to everyone. In essence it was to ensure a deadlock in the assembly's constitution making; then through the exercise of wide veto powers to nudge it into framing a constitution within limits acceptable to him. Of course the elections would be free and fair. In terms of the constitution he desired General Yahya (and the army) would be home and dry.

This elaborate scheme, however, had a fundamental flaw which proved to be its undoing. It was based on the assumption that the elections would throw up a patch-work of political parties and groups which could be manoeuvred as the President required. The history and current experience of political discord encouraged General Yahya in this belief. So he did not hestiate in allowing the provinces to be represented in the national assembly on the basis of their population. The measure gave East Pakistan 169 of the assembly's 313 seats and a permanent majority in the House. Yahya and his political advisers thought it inconceivable that East Pakistan would speak with a single voice. Here he gravely miscalculated. Seizing the heaven–sent opportunity of a built–in political advantage, Sheikh Mujibur Rahman astutely made the Awami League's six point manifesto a Magna Carta for the redress of East Pakistan's grievances. With this he turned the elections into a referendum on Bengali nationalism. When the votes were counted West Pakistan indeed presented a patch-work of parties. But in East Pakistan the Awami League romped home with 167 seats – more than enough to put its own stamp on the proposed constitution. To drive home the point Sheikh Mujibur Rahman on December 9,

1970, bluntly told Yahya Khan that East Pakistan would accept nothing less than the Awami League's six-point autonomy demand.

What happened next is best explained by a speech made by Professor G. W. Chowdhury, unofficial constitutional adviser to President Yahya Khan, at a meeting of the Pakistan Society in London on 10 September, 1970. (Society's Bulletin No 31, pp. 46–56)

COL. G. L. HYDE: On the basis of 'one man, one vote' the election will result in a constituent assembly. Will the constituent assembly have a majority of members from East Pakistan?

PROF. CHOWDHURY: Yes ...

COL. HYDE: So that means there will always be an East Pakistan majority?

PROF. CHOWDHURY: Well, if one believes in democracy one has to accept this 'one man, one vote', and we believe and we hope that there will be no such thing called East and West Pakistan in the federal legislature. This will instead develop on the basis of parties. Whichever party comes to power this general distinction, we hope, will not remain. So there is no question of East Pakistan members forming one single group in confrontation – *if that comes then it means that the State comes to an end.* (author's emphasis.)

MR. AZAM: What action will the government take in case they find that everything is being decided on the basis of East Pakistan versus West Pakistan?

PROF. CHOWDHURY: *That would certainly not be acceptable to West Pakistan.* (Author's emphasis.)

Professor G. W. Chowdhury, a Bengali and close confidant of President Yahya, had thus clearly stipulated *three* months before the election that: (a) West Pakistan would not accept the democratic verdict if the country's major population group living in East Pakistan chose to speak with one voice; and (b) Should such a confrontation occur, it would be resisted by West Pakistan, even to the undoing of the state. That confrontation did take place on December 9, 1970, when the election results became known.

## V. GENOCIDE

The tragedy that followed the general elections in December, 1970, can be summed up in a single sentence: the Bengalis under the banner of the Awami League won the elections and for the first time were in a position to assert themselves through projected new state institutions; the Punjab-oriented ruling coterie which dominated Pakistan from 1948 would not let them – and had the army to back it up.

General Yahya Khan could have accepted the popular verdict, but he chose to ignore it and in doing so he found an accomplice in Mr. Zulfiquar Ali Bhutto whose Pakistan People's Party had won 81 seats. (Mr. Bhutto became Pakistan's new strong man after Bangladesh's secession.) The sequence of events is conclusive:

January 13 (1971): General Yahya Khan meets Sheikh Mujibur Rahman in Dacca, tells reporters he is the "future prime minister."

January 29: Sheikh Mujibur Rahman and Zulfiquar Ali Bhutto have an inconclusive meeting in Dacca when they discuss plans for the new constitution.

February 11: Bhutto, after a party meeting, tells reporters in Multan (Punjab) only "the finishing touches remain" for his draft of the constitution.

Februart 12: Bhutto has a lengthy meeting with Yahya in Rawalpindi and apparently changes his mind about the constitution draft.

February 13: General Yahya announces that the national assembly will meet in Dacca on 3 March. Bhutto flies on to Peshawar and at a cocktail party electrifies the gathering with the words "Bhutto is once again in the saddle. It has been decided by the powers that are. Mujib is out. I'm to be Prime Minister."

February 14: Bhutto tells Wali Khan, the Pathan leader, "... not even my party knows it, but I'm not going to Dacca for the national assembly session."

February 15: Bhutto announces he will boycott the assembly meeting unless he could "safeguard West Pakistan interests" by a prior understanding with Sheikh Mujib.

February 21: General Yahya dissolves his civilian cabinet and calls a meeting of the military governors and other army leaders in Rawalpindi. Military preparations are noticed in Rawalpindi, Karachi and Dacca.

February 28: Bhutto publicly calls for a postponement of the assembly session.

March 1: General Yahya Khan, without consulting the leader of the major party (Sheikh Mujib) postpones indefinitely the assembly session. The official excuse: East West Pakistan confrontation and Bhutto's boycott of the assembly.

March 1–25. Civil disobedience mounts on massive scale in East

Pakistan which is totally shut down. Two divisions of the Pakistan army are airlifted from Karachi to Dacca, the East Pakistan capital.

March 25: The Pakistan army launches massive crackdown on Bengali dissent.

Within two weeks of the army crackdown in East Pakistan, evidence began to emerge that it was a well-defined campaign of genocide. The targets were: (a) Bengali military men, Bengali policemen and para-military troops; (b) The Hindus; (c) everyone connected with the Awami League; (d) Students – college and university boys and girls; and (e) Bengali intellectuals such as professors, teachers, journalists involved in the nationalist movement. In many cases troops carried lists of intended victims when they went on special assignments. Otherwise there was indiscriminate killing of target types. The Hindus were marked out because the regime considered them to be "Indian agents" who had subverted the Muslims of East Pakistan. The Bengali military men and police represented the only trained cadres capable of resisting the Pakistan army. The others were designated targets because it was thought that their political ambitions were a direct threat to the integrity of the state.

The author was told in the 16th Division Headquarters in Comilla:

> We are determined to cleanse East Pakistan once and for all of the threat of secession, even if it means killing off two million people and ruling the province as a colony for the next thirty years.

That was the end of Pakistan as it was conceived in 1947, and the birth of Bangladesh. Discrimination and then genocide made secession inevitable.

# Mexican Americans in the United States: The Evolution of a Relationship

RUDOLPH O. DE LA GARZA

RUDOLPH O. DE LA GARZA is a graduate of the University of Arizona, where he earned a Ph.D. in Government and a Master of Arts degree in Latin American Studies. He is now the Assistant Dean of the Colorado College, and as Assistant Professor he lectures on Chicano Politics, Minority Politics, Latin American and Mexican Politics.

He has presented papers on various aspects of the Chicano situation, and other social problems, at a number of seminars and conventions. Several of these papers are on the list of forthcoming publications. He has also published many articles in leading journals and magazines.

For two years he served as Student Affairs Officer and Assistant Director of the bi-national centre, United States Information Agency in Cochabamba, Bolivia.

# Mexican Americans in the United States: The Evolution of a Relationship

RUDOLPH O. DE LA GARZA

In the 1960's Mexican American political activists began openly accusing American society of being racist and anti-Mexican and demanded an immediate end to all discriminatory practices affecting their community. This challenge came as a surprise to most Anglo Americans because, with notable exceptions, few were aware of the conditions in which Mexican Americans lived, much less of how they were discriminated against. Moreover, most South-western communities celebrated "Spanish" holidays and community leaders invariably included citizens of Mexican ancestry. Thus, few Anglo Americans recognized the legitimacy of Chicano protests, and some Spanish-surnamed citizens have been equally puzzled and alienated by Chicano militancy. The objective of this paper, therefore, is to describe the relationship between Mexican Americans and Anglo American society and explain why members from both communities fail to recognize the subordinate and exploited situation of the Mexican American people. Particular attention will be given to the origins of the relationship, to the mechanisms used by Anglo American society to maintain the relationship, to how Mexican Americans have responded to these measures, and to how and to what degree the relationship has changed in recent years.

## I. Mexican Americans: A Unique Minority

Mexican Americans, it should be noted at the outset, share with Native Americans the distinction of being the two only territorial minorities in the United States.[1] They lived in viable communities in what is now the American South-west [i.e., Arizona, Colorado, Texas, California, and New Mexico] long before the Anglo American conquest. Thus, they cannot be considered an immigrant group comparable to the

Irish or Italians; they are a conquered people, and this legacy conditions all aspects of their relationship to Anglo America.

Although Mexicans did settle the American South-west, it would be incorrect to assume that all Mexican Americans living in this region are descendants of those early settlers. In fact, as of 1848 there were only 75,000 in this area,[2] and the great majority of today's seven million Mexican American residents are post-1848 migrants. What must be noted, however, is the psychological, geographical and cultural linkage that bonds the first settlers with the more recent arrivals. Unlike the European immigrants who uprooted themselves and came to the United States committed to remaining and developing a new way of life, Mexicans who came and continue to enter the United States have separated themselves far less from their origins. From an ecological perspective there was and is little difference between Northern Mexico and the South-western United States. Most settled into institutionally complete communities that shielded them from contact with Anglo American society and thus culturally and politically the border has been of dubious significance.[3] For decades the border was unguarded and Mexicans had easy access to El Paso, Tucson, San Antonio, Los Angeles, and other South-western cities. Having arrived in those cities and joined the Mexican American communities there was little opportunity to participate in politics and thus the possibility of learning new political norms was minimal at best. Furthermore, because of the ease of access and return, many Mexicans came with no intention of staying. While many did return to Mexico, many others did not, even though they continue to this day to talk about going home. Even though this migration experience was not as traumatic as that of the European immigrants, it would be incorrect to assume that the move from Mexico to the United States was painless. The migrants left and continue to leave primarily because of the scarcity of job opportunities available to them in Mexico. They did not, however, leave their traditions, language and values. The Mexican migration also differs from the European experience in that it continues through today. While European immigration came in a great wave during the latter part of the 19th and early 20th centuries, Mexican migration has been a continuous process punctuated by high points in 1910, the 1920's, 1940's, and 1950's. European immigrants have been cut off from their parent populations and find it difficult to maintain their ethnic identities, and thus increased interaction with Anglo American society becomes perhaps natural and inevitable. Large numbers of Mexican migrants, on the other hand, are constantly joining Mexican American communities, thus preventing the atrophy of cultural traditions. Clearly, then, there are key differences between the European and Mexican experiences. Perhaps the most significant of these is that the former psychologically and physically uprooted themselves in coming to America. Mexicans, on the other hand, came to the United States without having to separate themselves socially, culturally, psychologically or linguistically from their native communities. They are, therefore, more accurately conceived of as migrants than as immigrants, and thus even though these relatively recent arrivals are in most cases not the physical descendants of the region's early settlers, they are the cultural heirs of the South-west. It is because of these intimate bonds that these recent arrivals can join with the descendants of the early settlers to protest against efforts to treat them as immigrants and "Americanize" them. These bonds also move recent migrants to support the heirs of the early settlers in their struggle to reclaim lands lost to Anglo American conquerors. For all of these reasons, then, Mexican Americans are unique among America's minority groups, and the relationship Mexican Americans have with Anglo American society is different from that experienced by any other American minority population.

## II. Mexican American History: A Brief Review

The government of the United States from its earliest days considered expanding its territorial boundaries to what is now the American South-west. This imperialistic objective, legitimized under the euphemism of "Manifest Destiny," began to be realized in 1835 when Anglo Americans in Texas saw themselves in danger of becoming the alien subjects of a people to whom they deliberately believed themselves morally, intellectually, and politically superior. The racial feeling, indeed, underlay and coloured Texan-Mexican relations from the establishment of the first Anglo American colony in 1821.[4] These Texans rebelled and, after initial defeats at the Alamo in San Antonio, and Goliad, the Texans defeated the Mexican forces at the battle of San Jacinto in 1836. With this victory the Texans declared themselves independent from Mexico. The Mexican government never recognized the independence of Texas, so when the United States government in 1845 granted statehood to Texas, Mexico had no choice but to break relations with the United States. Both nations increased their military activities in the disputed area. On May 13, 1846, the United States' Congress declared war. The United States triumphed easily, and the signing of the Treaty of Guadalupe Hidalgo on Feburary 2, 1848, officially ended the war.

Despite its powerless position, Mexico attempted to protect the well being of its former citizens who chose to remain in the newly conquered territory by including in the Treaty provisions protecting them. The Treaty guaranteed that "property of every kind, now belonging to Mexicans, not established there, shall be inviolably respected. The present owners, the heirs of these, and all Mexicans who may hereafter acquire said property by contract, shall enjoy with respect to it, guaranties equally ample as if the same belonged to citizens of the United States." The Treaty also guaranteed that these Mexicans would be admitted "to the enjoyment of all the rights of citizens of the United States according to the principles of the Constitution; and in the mean time shall be maintained and protected in the free enjoyment of their liberty and property, and secured in the free exercise of their religion without restriction."[5] Anglo society did not respect these guarantees, however, and consequently from 1848 until at least the early part of the 1970's the relationship between Mexican Americans and Anglo Americans has been characterized by two distinct patterns. Anglo Americans have systematically denied Mexican Americans their rights and privileges, legally and illegally opposed and repressed efforts by Mexican Americans to participate fully in American society, and prevented Mexican Americans who identified with their community and maintained cultural characteristics such as distinct language patterns or living styles from attaining politically powerful or socially prominent positions. Anglo American society has simultaneously rewarded economically, politically, and to a lesser degree socially, those Mexican Americans who were willing to discard their cultural heritage and serve the dominant sector against the Mexican American community. The consequence of this has been to separate Mexican Americans from Anglo American society and to cleanse Mexican cultural influences from all major societal institutions. Mexican Americans, meanwhile, have continuously attempted to participate in American social, economic and political life to the extent that they could without sacrificing their cultural identity. Because such possibilities have been limited, Mexican Americans have focused their energies on maintaining their own community apart from Anglo American society. Thus, the tension that exists between Anglo Americans and Mexican Americans is a result of these conflicting patterns, and the history of the Mexican American people can be succinctly described as the continuous effort to overcome the barriers erected by Anglo society and participate in and share the privileges, rights and responsibilities of American citizenship while maintaining cultural integrity.

Anglo Americans dealt with the Mexican inhabitants of the South-west in a racist manner from the moment of initial contact. While it has been argued that they felt justified in viewing the Mexicans as inherently inferior because of the ease with which the United States defeated Mexico and because the overwhelming majority of Mexicans they encountered were illiterate and unsophisticated peasants,[6] in fact, Anglo Americans had such stereotypes of the Mexican people long before they met them. Blinded by their biases, Anglos forced what they encountered into their preconceived moulds. From the outset, Anglos saw the Mexican people as inherently inferior, lazy and cowardly. This racism was so intense that one scholar suggests that it was a principal factor behind the Mexican war. Without this racist motivation, he argues, the United States would likely have been satisfied to have established economic hegemony over Mexico and would have resisted the temptation of military conquest.[7]

This attitude elicited and legitimized the use of violence by Anglos from the 1830's onward as they strove to establish, enforce and maintain control of the newly conquered lands and people. Vigilante groups such as the Texas Rangers were founded to "keep the Mexicans in their place," and the violence was so widespread that there were more lynchings of Mexican Americans in the South-west from 1865 to 1920 than of Blacks in the South-east during the same period.[8] Because the style and pervasiveness of this repression varied according to local conditions, scholars have tended to de-emphasize the central role that the violence initiated by public institutions as well as private individuals played in shaping the relationship between Mexican Americans and Anglo Americans. What must be understood is that Anglo Americans were as repressive as necessary to insure their domination, and that everywhere in the South-west Anglo American control was instituted and protected through the widespread and often indiscriminate application of force.

Violence was particularly common in Texas. Memories of defeats at the Alamo and Golida made "Mexicans" easy targets, and the treatment meeted out by Texas' legendary Rangers illustrates the abuse suffered by the Mexican American community in that state. The Rangers "often killed Mexicans who had nothing to do with the criminals they were after. Some actually were shot by mistake ... But perhaps the majority of the innocent Mexicans who died at Ranger hands were killed much more deliberately than that." They were probably killed to terrorize the community and make it more submissive.[9] The Texas gunslinger who bragged that he had killed 37 men, "not counting Mexicans,"[10] further suggests how commonplace such violence was.

Although it has been argued that the conquest of New Mexico was bloodless, violence, in fact, also played a major role in ensuring Anglo American hegemony. Nearly 300 Mexicans were killed in resisting the Anglo take-over. Once the conquest was effected and Hispanos began to lose their lands and rights, they organized guerilla groups to defend their interests. Their efforts again failed, and by the end of the 19th century New Mexico had been pacified.[11]

In California, Anglo Americans again resorted to violence whenever necessary. As in Texas, they used violence to terrorize the community into submission. Vigilantes drove Mexican miners away from their claims, and a Foreign Miners' Tax was passed in 1850 to help dispel the Mexicans. The author of this legislation boasted that he would "maintain a better stomach at the killing of a Mexican" than at the crushing of a louse.[12] Perceived as irresponsible and criminal by nature, the Mexican community was subjected to continuous abuse and attack until Anglo Americans consolidated their positions and Mexican American resistance had been broken.[13] By the 1900's most Mexican Americans understood their situation. They knew that so long as they "stayed in their place" they would be left relatively alone. They would not, however, be allowed to exercise their rights as citizens, much less benefit from the guarantees of the Treaty of Guadalupe Hidalgo. Unable to resist Anglo domination any longer, the Mexican American community withdrew from active interaction with Anglo society. This withdrawal has been incorrectly interpreted as apathetic; it reflects, instead, a deep seated alienation.

By the 1920's a small segment of the Mexican American community had improved its socio-economic status and had begun to consolidate its gains. This new middle class willingly accommodated itself to extant racist norms and practices. The relatively affluent sought above all to be recognized as Americans, and they made every effort to ensure that, as Americans, they were not confused with new Mexican immigrants who were entering the United States in ever increasing numbers. The attitudes and behaviour of this group are illustrated in the activities of the League of Latin American Citizens (LULAC), a Mexican American middle class group founded in Texas in 1929. An explicitly accommodationist organization, LULAC had as one of its primary objectives the development "within members of our race the best, purest and most perfect type of a true and loyal citizen of the United States of America." LULAC, and this new middle class in general, chose to consolidate newly achieved status rather than press for cultural pluralism and the expansion of economic and political opportunities for the Mexican American community at large. Although groups such as LULAC were the most active and best known of this period, they represented only a small segment of the Mexican American people. The great majority of Mexican Americans remained uninvolved with the mainstream of society.

Between the 1920's and the end of World War II the socio-economic conditions of the Mexican American community improved noticeably. For many, particularly LULAC members and their sympathizers, these improvements were evidence of the success of the accommodationist approach. Actually, these advances were primarily a result of the programme initiated by the Roosevelt administration to overcome the problems caused by the Great Depression and of the increased opportunities available to Mexican Americans as a result of the nation's wartime economy. During this period Mexican Americans enjoyed greater opportunities and mobility than ever before. They were hired for jobs that previously had been denied them, and those who served in the military were treated more fairly and were offered more opportunities than they had ever enjoyed previously. By the end of the war a renewed faith in the American system had begun displacing the alienation of earlier generations. The end of the war, however, brought an end to many of these opportunities. Anglo American veterans returned to their jobs and displaced the recently hired Mexican Americans; Mexican American veterans had no jobs to which they could return. Two incidents document the fact that the material gains made during these years were the result of special circumstances rather than of firmly grounded changes in societal attitudes and structures. The first is California's "Zoot suit" riots of 1943 in which police watched while Anglo American servicemen attacked and beat Mexican American youths. California newspapers applauded these attacks, and no charges were ever brought against the attackers. The second was the refusal in 1948 of public officials to allow a Mexican American veteran of the Philippine campaign to be buried in the local cemetary in Three Rivers, Texas. These examples are particularly significant of Anglo American attitudes because both incidents resulted from the decisions made by public officials, and public opinion supported both decisions.

The realization that little had changed prompted many middle class Mexican Americans to abandon the LULAC approach in favour of an explicitly political tactic. The essence of this new approach was to mobilize the community at large in order to create the political resources necessary to deal with the system from a position of strength. Implicit in this new approach was the insistence on the maintenance of cultural identity and the belief that Anglo American politicians would respond to the demands of a mobilized Mexican American community. From Texas to California organizations reflecting this new attitude were born. The leaders of these new organizations genuinely believed this approach would prove successful, and thus these organizations either included Anglo Americans within their ranks or worked closely with Anglo American sympathizers. The principal organizations established during this period were the California-based Community Service Organization; the Texas-based American G. I. Forum, founded in 1948 as a result of the incident in Three Rivers, Texas described earlier; the Mexican American Political Association (MAPA), founded in California in the late 1950's; and the Political Association of Spanish Speaking Organizations (PASSO), founded in Texas in 1958. These organizations attacked basic problems such as job discrimination and poor housing, and they worked within the existing political system to help elect those individuals who were most likely to defend their interests. After modest electoral successes, MAPA helped elect a Mexican American Congressman in Los Angeles, and PASSO was instrumental in assisting Mexican Americans to win control of Crystal City, Texas in 1963, this approach proved ineffectual. For reasons which will be described shortly, this tactic did not result in the election of many Mexican Americans. More importantly, those few Mexican Americans who were elected were unable to shape public policy to meet the needs of the Mexican American community. The failure of this tactic was particularly significant because the promises of President Kennedy's New Frontier and of President Johnson's Great Society inspired the Mexican American people. The failure of societal institutions to respond to the needs of the Mexican American people after so greatly raising their expectations deeply alienated the Mexican American community, and many became convinced that the only way to effect change was through the politics of confrontation. Thus the foundation for the Chicano Movement was laid.

The emergence of the Chicano Movement in the middle 1960's set a new tone for Anglo American-Mexican American relations. Emulating the style of Black militants, Chicanos threatened to resort to violence if their demands for improved education, job opportunities and political representation were not met. Equally significant, these were not the reiteration of past requests for increased opportunities to participate in the mainstream of American society, but were instead demands for policies and programmes which would improve socio-economic conditions while maintaining and reinvigorating cultural patterns. Almost simultaneously Chicano militants across the South-west mounted their protests. They walked out of schools to protest against racist educational policies; they denounced police violence and openly threatened to respond in kind unless new police procedures were instituted; they developed *La Raza Unida*, a Chicano political party, so as to give Mexican Americans the opportunity to elect their own representatives and shape their own policies.

Within a few years the Chicano Movement had convinced most Anglo leaders that Mexican Americans had become a political force which had to be respected. It is noteworthy that the Movement achieved this status without having recruited large numbers to its ranks. The activists probably have never totalled more than five percent of the total community. They speak, however, in the interests of the majority of the community, and even those who do not support the Movement's tactics and rhetoric agree on the need for change and empathize with the frustration and anger of the militants. Thus Chicano activists, like the Black rioters of the 1960's, have the unarticulated support of their community. It is because of this potential widespread support that Chicanos have become a political force. In Texas La Raza Unida, under the leadership of Jose Angel Gutierrez, mobilized this potential support and used the electoral process to take over all governmental offices in Crystal City, Texas. Once in power La Raza Unida officials immediately initiated programmes which began to address the needs of the Mexican American community while simultaneously infuriating Texas Anglo Americans.[14] These events combined with the more militant but less successful efforts of Rodolfo "Corky" Gonzalez in Colorado and with the movement led by Reyes Lopez

Tijerina to physically reclaim lost New Mexican land grants to convince Anglo American leaders that the Movement indeed had the potential to mobilize widespread support.[15] Such a mobilization would clearly threaten the stability of South-western society, and the desire to prevent such a destabilization was surely one of the factors that led Anglo American leaders into dealing seriously with and responding to the demands of the Mexican American community.

The Chicano Movement has not achieved all or even most of its objectives. While the socio-economic status of Mexican Americans has improved in absolute terms as well as relatively vis-à-vis Anglos, Mexican Americans continue to be disproportionately of the lower classes. In Texas in 1960 Mexican American male operatives earned 68 percent of Anglo operatives' incomes; in 1970 this had increased to 82 percent. Mexican American foremen in 1970 earned only 67 percent of Anglo foremen's incomes, but in 1960 they earned only half of what Anglo foremen earned.[16] Median family income for Mexican Americans in the South-west had increased from $4,164 in 1959 to $9,600 in 1975, but during the same period all family income increased even more and went from $6,448 to $12,800.[17] Overall, Mexican Americans remain significantly behind Anglo Americans, and this difference is exacerbated by the fact that Mexican American families are usually much larger than Anglo families. Furthermore, 29 percent of Mexican Americans live below the poverty line while only 13 percent of all American families are in this condition.[18] There have also been increases in Chicano political representation, but the increases vary from state to state and overall Mexican Americans continue to be under represented. The major gains have been the election of Mexican American governors in Arizona and New Mexico. Significantly there has been no increase during the last fifteen years in the number of Chicano national representatives, and increases at the state legislative levels have been few, yet important. These improvements are evidence of the changed relationship. It is unclear, however, whether such changes will continue, or whether in fact Mexican Americans have exhausted their ability to win concessions from societal institutions.

The slow pace of change and the uncertainty of continued improvement result from the deeply rooted institutional patterns which subordinate Mexican Americans. It is these patterns which will next be described.

## III. Anglo American Institutions and Mexican American Subordination

The Anglo defeat of Mexico and the subsequent purchase of Northern Mexican territory resulted in the internal colonization of the Mexican American people.[19] As was true of the colonial experiences in Africa and Asia, the internal colonization of the American South-west was effected through institutional arrangements designed to institute and preserve the economic, racial-cultural and political domination of the Mexican American people. In other words, the discrimination and violence inflicted on Mexican Americans were not the haphazard results of individual racists or avaricious empire builders; this treatment was the direct result of the perceptions Anglo Americans had of Mexican Americans and of the institutional structures imposed on them.

The foundation of this structure was the racism with which Anglo Americans viewed the Mexican American. As stated previously, Anglo Americans considered the Mexican people inferior prior to encountering Mexicans in the South-west. While these attitudes were most virulent during the 19th century, they have continued into the 1970's, even if voiced less frequently and held less passionately by most people. It is important to add that it is largely irrelevant whether these attitudes are the result of cultural misunderstanding or of the Anglo American's overt desire to dominate. Whatever their origin, these attitudes are used to justify the subjugation of the Mexican American people. In the 19th century, Anglo Americans voiced their views unabashedly. A veteran of the Mexican war described Mexicans by stating that "... a pastoral life, generally so propitious to purity of morals and strength of constitution, does not appear to have produced its usually happy effect upon that people ... vile rancheros, the majority of whom are so vicious and degraded that one can hardly believe that the light of Christianity has ever dawned upon them."[20] Walter Prescott Webb, one of America's foremost historians, wrote: "Without disparagement, it may be said that there is a cruel streak in the Mexican nature ... This cruelty may be a heritage from the Spanish of the Inquisition; it may, and doubtless should be attributed partly to the Indian blood ... The Mexican warrior ... was, on the whole, inferior to the Comanche and wholly unequal to the Texan ... For making promises – and for breaking them – he had no peer."[21] Anglo Americans in California voiced similar sentiments:

Devoid of intelligence sufficient to appreciate the true principles of free government; vicious, indolent, and dishonest, to an extent rendering them obnoxious to our citizens; with habits of life low and degraded; on intellect but one degree above the beast of the field, and not susceptible of elevation; all of these things combined to render such classes of human beings a curse to any enlightened community.[22]

By the turn of the century these attitudes were voiced in more elegant terms:

Socially and politically the presence of large numbers of Mexicans in this country gives rise to serious problems ... they lack ambition, are to a very large extent illiterate in their native language, are slow to learn English, and in most cases show no political interest .... But their most unfavourable characteristic is their inclination to form colonies and live in a clannish manner .... Their low standards of living and of morals, their illiteracy, their utter lack of proper political interest, the retarding affect of their employment upon the wage scale of the more progressive races, and finally their tendency to colonize in urban centres, with evil results, combine to stamp them as a rather undesirable class of residents.[23]

Anglo Americans used these false images of Mexican Americans to defend their argument that by conquering the region they were in fact civilizing it. They saw Mexican Americans as their mirror image and they could thus rationalize any act as the natural consequence of the conflict between civilization and barbarism, between good and evil. "Whenever the colonizer adds, in order not to fall prey to anxiety, that the colonized is a wicked backward person with evil, thievish, somewhat sadistic instincts, he thus justifies his police and his legitimate severity."[24] Armed with these attitudes, it is not surprising that Anglos treated Mexican Americans as they did. The crass racism and violence of the 19th century gave way to more subtle but equally pervasive discrimination in the 20th century. The epithets with which the uneducated pioneers described the Spanish speaking were replaced by social science concepts which, however elegantly phrased, perpetuated and legitimized the subordination of Mexican Americans. Social scientists, in the tradition of their less educated precursors, continued to cite cultural values as the cause of the Mexican Americans' poverty and uneducated state, and they echoed the 19th century views of Mexican American living styles.[25] "Some retreat to the security of the conservative Mexican American world." They concluded that Mexican Americans were by nature passive, indolent and hateful. "For many years, the immigrants and his sons made no effort to free themselves. They burned with resentment over a thousand slights, but they did so in private ... The Spanish speaking person is more likely to accept and resign himself to whatever destiny brings him." Furthermore, this "fatalistic philosophy produces an attitude of resignation which often convinces the Anglo that the Latin lacks drive and determination. What the Anglo tries to control, the Mexican-American tries to accept." Going one step further, one social scientist explicitly blamed Mexican Americans for consciously hindering their own development. "While the Anglos try to keep up with the Joneses, the Latins try to keep the Garcias down to their own level." Thus, as was true of African and Asian colonial subjects, the Mexican American is seldom seen or described as an individual. Instead, all Mexican Americans are presumed to hold identical values, and it is these values that inhibit their progress. While Texas Rangers might have said, "If you have seen one Mexican, you've seen them all," social scientists posit that Mexican Americans exhibit a "marked lack of internal differentiation" and are an "unusually homogeneous ethnic group."[26] Social scientists suggest that perhaps the most significant value Mexican Americans lack is self discipline. Lacking this, they are unable to adhere to schedules or conform to societal rules. "The combination of stress on work and rational use of time ... forms little or no part of the Mexican American socialization process ... [They have no] habits of self discipline, [and] few Mexican American homes stress higher education. It may be suggested that the excess of juvenile delinquents among Mexican Americans ... is not composed of deviants from the cultural pattern of the Mexican American population but rather of boys who over-conform to this pattern." Mexican Americans know that Anglo Americans consider them inferior, and they also know that these attitudes are so deeply ingrained that many Anglo Americans do not recognize and cannot admit to them. Thus, many Anglo Americans have been willing to state that Mexican Americans should be treated as equals while also indicating that they are essentially inferior, and they do not recognize the inherent contradiction between these attitudes. In actual practice, the latter belief has been the more powerful and has permitted "rationalizing the Anglo American practice of excluding Mexicans from any situation that involves close or allegedly close contact with Anglo Americans, as in residence, and the common use of swimming pools and other recreational facilities."[27] Continued exposure to these images in time influences the Mexican American's self perception. "The accusation disturbs him and worries him even more because he admires and fears his powerful accuser. 'Is he not partially right', he mutters. 'Are we not all a little guilty after all? Lazy, because we have so many idlers? Timid, because we let ourselves be oppressed'. Willfully created and spread by the colonizer, this mythical and degrading portrait ends up by being accepted and lived with to a certain extent by the colonized."[28] As Memmi suggests, the Mexican American has internalized Anglo American stereotypes and views himself in almost exclusively negative terms. In a study conducted in the 1960's, eleven of the twelve self-images Mexican Americans born in the United States agreed on were negative; significantly, however, ten of the twelve self-images Mexican Americans who had been born in Mexico and migrated to the United States selected to describe themselves were positive. While the native born respondents saw themselves as authoritarian, emotional, lazy and unconcerned with education, the respondents born in Mexico considered themselves as practical, proud, gregarious and well adjusted.[29] These findings illustrate the importance of racism and Anglo American control of major societal institutions in shaping the relationship between Anglo Americans and Mexican Americans. Above all, they indicate that many older Mexican Americans have been socialized into accepting their subordinate status. The effectiveness of this socialization is manifested by the willingness of past generations of Mexican Americans to deny their cultural heritage and identify as Spaniards, or, in more extreme cases, to discard all possible cultural characteristics and identify merely as American.[30] How this socialization has been and continues to be effected can be seen in how educational, political and judical institutions have dealt with Mexican Americans.

## IV. Education as a Subordinating Process

It has become popular in recent years to point out that American education has failed the minority student. From the Mexican American perspective it would be more accurate to indict the system for having successfully achieved its objective of legitimizing and reinforcing the subordination of Mexican Americans. The primary educational objective of South-western schools vis-à-vis Mexican American children was not to aid them in developing the skills necessary for acquiring political and economic power, but instead was to provide them with the knowledge and skills appropriate to maintaining their low status positions.[31] School systems realized this objective through the implementation of policies which emphasized the social inferiority of Mexican Americans and which guaranteed that Mexican American children would receive an inferior education.

Educators worked with political leaders to establish segregated school systems to insure that the extant social order be maintained. In 1934 a Texas school board member stated, "I don't believe in mixing. They are filthy and lousy, not all, but most of them." A colleague added, "We segregate for the same reason that southerners [sic] segregate the Negro. They are an inferior race, that is all . . ."[32] A California school principal in the 1960's reiterated these views. "Given time and library resources, it would be possible to make a strong case that racially these people are inferior."[33] This pattern of segregated schools continues today. A recent study found that Mexican American students across the South-west were "severely isolated by school district and by schools within individual districts."[34] Furthermore, Mexican Americans are greatly under represented on the staff and boards governing these schools, and the majority of Mexican Americans serving in these capacities are found in districts which are primarily Mexican American.[35] It is noteworthy that, unlike Blacks, Mexican Americans have never been legally segregated. Instead, segregation has been maintained through the extra-legal maintenance of residential patterns.[36] In California, where residential patterns were not as rigid, the same ends were accomplished through continuous redefining of school zone boundaries. When even this proved ineffective, school authorities transferred students across zones in order to maintain segregated school systems.[37] The impact of this segregation is exacerbated by the fact that Mexican American school districts are unable to finance quality programmes. They use non-graduate teachers and temporary staff far more than do Anglo American schools, and they also have a much higher student-teacher ratio. Yet, "it is obvious that residents of predominantly Mexican American neighbourhoods are paying proportionately more of their income to property taxes to support the education of their children than residents in primarily Anglo districts."[38] Mexican American parents have to date sued unsuccessfully to correct this inequity. Mexican American schools also have inferior physical plants, and one Anglo American official defends this by arguing that providing good facilities would only frustrate Mexican Americans since they will never be able to acquire fine facilities in their personal world.[39]

South-western schools have also used their curriculum and instructional style to socialize Mexican American children into a submissive, subordinate class. Mexican American children "are expected to internalize the national American culture, including such basic values as equality, at the same time they are learning the different and unequal roles expected of them by local society."[40] This differential role socialization begins when schools systematically degrade and ignore Mexican American culture. Until recently, schools discouraged students from speaking Spanish and punished those who disregarded these instructions. As late as 1970, it was a crime for teachers in south Texas to use Spanish in ordinary school activities.[41] In part this policy has been justified on the grounds that "their Spanish is of such an inferior quality that it does not warrant classification as a language."[42] Others want to eliminate the use of Spanish because it "fosters anti-Americanism," and because of the belief that children from Spanish-speaking homes are "*ipso facto*, less than normally intelligent."[43]

Schools have complemented this socialization by the way in which they generally treat Mexican American culture. Throughout the Southwest schools have refused to offer courses about Mexican Americans. Only 4.3 percent of elementary schools and 7.3 percent of secondary schools include Mexican American history courses in their curriculum. When Mexican American themes are included the result is to reinforce negative stereotypes. Instead of focusing on fundamental historical and cultural issues, schools highlight fiestas, costumes and eating habits.[44] Even then, however, cultural traits are disparaged by comments such as "a person just can't eat a tortilla among nice people."[45] These practices are reinforced by the way in which school officials treat Mexican American students in general. Mexican American students receive less praise and encouragement than do Anglo Americans in the same classroom,[46] and Mexican American students participate less in extra-curricular activities than do Anglo Americans.[47] Mexican American students soon learn that they will be "rewarded in school and in church when they look and act like Anglos, and punished (or ignored) if they look and act like Mexicans." For this reason Mexican American children tend to choose Anglos for role models and as candidates for leadership positions.[48] The way schools shape such behaviour is illustrated in the explanation given by an Anglo American teacher for selecting an Anglo student to be playground leader. "... I think Johnny needs to learn how to set a good example and how to lead others. His father owns one of the big farms in the area and Johnny has to learn how to lead the Mexicans. One day he will be helping his father and he will have to know how to handle Mexicans. I try to help him whenever I can."[49] It is because of these policies that Mexican Americans are educationally deprived. Approximately half of all Mexican American children entering school do not speak English as well as Anglo American children, and the negative impact schools have on them is suggested by the fact that their academic problems increase the longer they remain in school.[50] Given this hostile environment, it is not surprising that Mexican Americans have the highest educational attrition rate among major ethnic groups in the South-west, and that a lower percentage of Mexican Americans goes to college than of any of these other groups.[51] The frustration such policies produce are evidenced in how students react to them. "Schools try to brainwash Chicanos. They try to make us forget our history, to be ashamed of being Mexicans, of speaking Spanish. They succeed in making us feel empty, and angry inside."[52] Thus, the educational system has functioned to train Mexican Americans for low status positions. While it is true that some Mexican Americans have attained high educational status, they have done so either because they accommodated themselves to the system, i.e., Anglicized themselves, or because they escaped the system. The lack of technical and professional skills within the Mexican American community would thus clearly seem to be the result of educational policies designed to prevent Mexican Americans from developing these skills and to socialize them into accepting their subordinate status.

## V. The Political Process as a Subordinating Agent

The political system has complemented the educational process by effectively preventing Mexican Americans from participating fully in American political life. Mexican Americans vote less, are less likely to be involved in party activities, have less political information, run for office less, and hold fewer public offices than Anglo Americans. Numerous scholars incorrectly suggest that this lack of involvement is the logical consequence of the apathy and passivity of the Mexican American people. It is instead the result of Mexican Americans having been socialized into not becoming politically involved as well as the result of obstacles which minimize Mexican American participation even when they do mobilize.

Numerous devices have been used to disenfranchise the Mexican American. Historically, violence was used regularly to intimidate would-be voters; in more recent years Mexican American voters have been threatened with the loss of their jobs or the loss of welfare pensions or food stamps.[53] English literacy requirements, common in the Southwest, prevented many Mexican Americans from voting. This requirement was invalidated in 1970. Residency requirements disenfranchised migrant workers, and this had particular significance in south Texas where rural communities left almost en masse to harvest northern crops. Until recently, counties in south Texas also registered voters only on week days from 8:00 A.M. to 5:00 P.M., thus making it difficult for the working class (i.e., almost all) Mexican Americans to register. The fact that felons are legally disenfranchised also affects Mexican American voting strength disproportionately. Mexican Americans are overrepresented in prisons as a result of "inter-related institutional discriminatory practices that result in more Mexican Americans being arrested ... than middle class persons ..."[54] Many potential voters are thus permanently disenfranchised. The effect of these practices is exacerbated by the fact that most Mexican Americans are of low socio-economic status which is highly correlated with low levels of political participation. Given that most Mexican Americans have been unwilling to sacrifice their cultural identity in exchange for the right to participate in political life and instead live almost exclusively within their own community, it is not surprising that Mexican Americans admit they do not understand the political process[55] and that they are less concerned with and less informed about public issues than Blacks or Anglo Americans.[56] This lack of interest also reflects the alienation Mexican Americans feel as a result of the system's unresponsiveness. When asked if "people like themselves have a great deal to say about government," 35 percent of Los Angeles respondents and 40 percent of San Antonio respondents said no; 47 percent of San Antonians and 44 percent of those in Los Angeles further believed that public officials did not care about their constituents. Ironically, the overwhelming majority of respondents in both cities agreed that "voting decides what happens."[57] This response suggests the degree to which Mexican Americans have internalized American political rhetoric, which in turn suggests why so few Mexican Americans openly support the Chicano Movement. Despite these attitudes and these obstacles, Mexican Americans have attempted to participate in the electoral process when they have perceived political activities to be in their interest. In 1960, Mexican Americans turned out at record levels and gave 85 percent of their votes to John Kennedy. Their votes enabled him to carry Texas and New Mexico. Since 1960, however, Mexican American participation in national elections has decreased significantly. Chicano voting patterns at congressional and state levels provide greater insight into how the electoral process works against the Mexican American community. With a few exceptions in New Mexico, there had been no Mexican American candidates for state-wide office until 1970 when Raul Castro ran for governor in Arizona. The reason for this paucity of candidates is that neither dominant political party would nominate Mexican Americans for such offices. Castro won the nomination over the objections and without the support of party leaders.[58] Mexican Americans are much more successful in district and local elections where it is difficult to prevent their triumph. Even here, however, victories have only recently become widespread. In California, between 1849 and 1973 only nine Mexican Americans served as senators and twenty-four as assemblymen. In 1974 a Mexican American was elected to the state senate for the first time in sixty-two years.[59] A similar pattern exists in Colorado, Texas and Arizona. Those who have won office have been elected almost exclusively from areas with highly concentrated Mexican American populations. Although these "safe districts" allow Mexican American legislators to gain seniority and become influential within their respective chambers, in all but New Mexico these state legislators have been unable to have legislative programmes approved which would materially benefit their constituencies. Surprisingly, perhaps the greatest under representation exists at the local levels. In Tucson, Arizona, over the twenty-five year period from 1945 to 1969, of 111 candidates for city councilman only five were Mexican American, and from World War II until today there has been no Mexican American mayoral candidate.[60] Even more severe patterns of exclusion exist in Texas.[61] The extent to which Mexican Americans are excluded is manifested by conditions in California

TABLE 1: *Chicano Representation In State Legislatures March, 1973*

| *State* | *Total # of Legislators* | *# of Chicano Legislators* | *% of Total Legislators that are Chicano* | *% of Total Population that is Chicano* |
|---|---|---|---|---|
| Arizona | 11 | 90 | 11.1 | 18.8 |
| California | 5 | 118 | 4.2 | 15.5 |
| Colorado | 4 | 100 | 4.0 | 13.0 |
| New Mexico | 32 | 112 | 34.0 | 40.1 |
| Texas | 10 | 181 | 5.5 | 18.4 |

TABLE 2: *Chicano Representation in City Councils in Selected Texas Cities, 1970**

| | *% Mexican American Population* | *% of Mexican American City Councilmen* |
|---|---|---|
| Austin | 16.0 | 0 |
| Beaumont | 4.5 | 0 |
| Corpus Christi | 40.5 | 14.3 |
| Dallas | 6.7 | 1.3 |
| El Paso | 58.1 | 11.4 |
| Ft. Worth | 9.2 | 0 |
| Lubbock | 16.0 | 0 |
| San Antonio | 52.1 | 27.0 |
| Waco | 7.4 | 0 |

* Charles L. Cotrell, "The Effects of At-Large Elections on the Political Access and Voting Strength of Mexican Americans," (Paper presented at the Rocky Mountain Social Science Association Meeting, April, 1974), p. 60.

TABLE 3: *Mexican American Representation on State Boards of Education**

| | *# of Mexican Americans* | *Total # Board Members* | *% of Total Board Members that is Mexican American* | *% of Mexican American Students* |
|---|---|---|---|---|
| Arizona | 0 | 9 | 0 | 19.5 |
| California | 1 | 10 | 10.0 | 16.5 |
| Colorado | 0 | 5 | 0 | 13.7 |
| New Mexico | 3 | 10 | 30.0 | 39.4 |
| Texas | 2 | 24 | 8.3 | 22.6 |

* U. S. Commission on Civil Rights, *Toward Quality Education for Mexican Americans, Report VI, MexicanAmerican Education Study*, February, 1974, p. 13.

as of 1970. Less that two percent of all elected and appointed officials at municipal, county, state and federal levels were Mexican American.[62] The extent and level of under representation is documented in Tables 1, 2, and 3. This lack of representation is the result of numerous practices designed to minimize the impact of Chicano voting. In California, gerrymandering is most commonly used. Rather than allow Mexican American communities to elect their own representatives, the Mexican American areas are cut up so that no electoral district includes a majority of Mexican American voters. East Los Angeles, with a population in excess of 1,000,000, has been divided into nine state assembly seats, seven state senate districts, and six congressional seats. State Democratic leaders have refused to revise district boundaries in this area, and thus the U.S. Commission on Civil Rights concluded that "the Mexican American in California has been gerrymandered out of any real chance to elect his own representatives to the State Legislature or the United States Congress in a proportion approaching his percentage of the State population."[63] At-large elections and multi-member districts have been equally effective in preventing Chicano electoral triumphs. These districts have large Anglo American majorities which makes it unlikely for Mexican Americans to be nominated by a major party so as to even contest the election. When they are nominated defeat is almost inevitable. At-large elections allow Anglo American voters two opportunities to defeat Mexican Americans. These elections usually involve a run-off election, and if a Mexican American has made it to the run-off, Anglo American voters almost always mobilize behind and elect the Anglo American candidate.[64] At-large districts are used extensively in school board elections, city council elections, and elections for state representatives. Multi-member districts allow one group of citizens to elect all the officials from a given district. Districts utilizing this arrangement usually have Anglo American majorities, and thus this group is able to elect an entire slate of candidates supporting its interests. Elected officials, therefore, seldom feel politically obligated to the Mexican American community, and Mexican Americans are in no position to hold these officials accountable. Consequently, Mexican Americans are left with no representation. For these reasons federal courts have recently declared that multi-member districts are a device for diluting Mexican American voting strength and have ruled against their continued use. These electoral devices are reinforced by the attitudes with which Anglo Americans view Mexican American candidates. In Lubbock, Texas, twenty-four percent of Anglo voters opposed Mexican Americans serving in the State Legislature, thirty-eight percent opposed one serving as governor, and forty-four percent opposed the idea of a Mexican American president.[65] While Lubbock may not be a representative city, that many Anglo Americans in other cities share these attitudes is suggested by their behaviour. Texas Democratic and Republican party chairmen admit that whisper campaigns are used to mobilize voters against Mexican American candidates.[66] For these reasons Mexican Americans almost automatically confront a united Anglo American opposition. In El Paso, Texas, for example, Mexican American candidates are accused of representing "special interests," while any candidate supporting affluent Anglo American sectors are described as "candidates of all the people."[67] It is because of such attitudes and devices that Mexican Americans are elected almost exclusively from districts with overwhelming Mexican American majorities. Both political parties have supported this pattern. Given that the Democrats have been more powerful in the South-west and that Mexican Americans have consistently voted Democratic, the Democrats' disregard of Chicano demands is particularly noteworthy. In Texas, Democratic leaders refused to abandon multi-member districts until legal action made this obligatory. Texas Democratic leaders have also objected vigorously to having the state come under the federal voting rights act extension of 1975. California's Democrats have been equally resistant to demands for redistricting notoriously gerrymandered areas which have kept Mexican Americans out of office for decades. Even more significant is the fact that in no state have Anglo American Democratic party leaders formulated public policy designed to address the major problems confronting the Chicano community. As the weaker party the Republicans have not been in a position to block Mexican American political gains. It is significant however, that Republicans have not attempted to recruit Mexican Americans into their party. Instead, they have either ignored or opposed any policy proposals designed to aid Mexican Americans, made token Mexican American appointments which have insulted rather than placated the Mexican American community, or attempted to attract Mexican American voters with false promises only to ignore those promises following the election. Even though neither party has been responsive to Chicano needs, it would be incorrect to conclude that both have treated Mexican Americans equally. While Democrats have not responded to demands for change, the Republicans have, when in power, openly attacked the Mexican American community. Governor Jack Williams of Arizona offended all Mexican Americans when he refused to reconsider legislation affecting Mexican American farmworkers and stated in effect that, "As far as I'm concerned these people don't even exist." Ronald Reagan and Richard Nixon showed themselves to be equally callous by their ostentatious support of grape growers at the height of Cesar Chavez' grape boycott. No Democrat has been this crass in his dealings with Mexican Americans, and some, including Governor Brown of California and Governor Lamm of Colorado, have made efforts to assist Mexican Americans. In summary, then, the political process has reinforced the lesson educational institutions taught to Mexican Americans. Mexican Americans have been discouraged from becoming politically active, and when they do become active they face almost insurmountable barriers which are designed to frustrate their efforts. Consequently, public policy has not been designed to meet the needs of the Mexican American people. As is true of educational institutions, political institutions function so as to subjugate the Mexican American people, and historically only those Mexican Americans willing to abandon their cultural traditions have been allowed to participate and succeed within the political process.

## VI. Law Enforcement as a Process of Political Subjugation

In principle, the nation's judicial system is designed to correct wrongs perpetrated against citizens by the state or by other citizens, and the police should be impartial servants of the public interest. In fact, however, members of the judiciary and police, like any other citizens, internalize and share the biases common to American society. It is not surprising, therefore, that these agencies have dealt with Mexican Americans in the same way that other institutions have. These institutions, however, have a greater role in maintaining the subordinate status of Mexican Americans because it is only the police and the courts that are in a position to correct the problems created by schools, political bodies, and the economic sector. Like sociologists and educators, police have traditionally viewed Mexican Americans as inferior and crime prone. The official report on the 1943 "Zoot suit" riots concluded that Mexican Americans had initiated the violence, and that this was a result of "... his [the Mexican American's] desire ... to kill, or at least to let blood ..." In 1960, the Los Angeles police chief echoed these views: "The Latin population that came in here presented a great problem ... because of some of these people being not too far removed from the wild tribes of the district of the inner mountains of Mexico. I don't think you can throw the genes out of the question when you discuss behaviour patterns of people."[68] In 1970, J. Edgar Hoover ascribed similar instincts to Mexican Americans. "You never have to bother about a president being shot by Puerto Ricans or Mexicans. They don't shoot very straight. But if they come at you with a knife, beware."[69] These attitudes are at least partially responsible for job requirements which are unrelated to job performance but which have functioned to exclude Mexican Americans from South-western police forces. The U.S. Commission of Civil Rights found that Mexican Americans comprised 5.7 percent of South-western police departments whereas they comprised 11.7 percent of the total population. Comparable under representation exists on sheriff's departments, andMexican Americans have even less representation on state police agencies.[70] The combined effect of these factors results in Mexican Americans being denied equal protection under the law. Police have often refused to protect Mexican Americans. During the "Zoot suit" riots Los Angeles police stood by while sailors and soldiers viciously and indiscriminately attacked Mexican Americans. Police have been particularly negligent in protecting Mexican American protesters and organizers. In 1932, a California sheriff explained why police took such actions. "We protect our farmers here in Keen County. They are our best people. They are always with us. They keep the county going. They put us here and they can put us out again so we serve them. But the Mexicans are trash. They have no standard of living. We herd them like pigs."[71] Police attitudes and behaviour toward Mexican American farmworkers have not changed much since then. In 1967 Texas Rangers harassed and arrested United Farm Worker organizers and their tactics intensified as the organizational efforts succeeded. United Farm Worker organizers in California and Texas voice similar complaints today. In El Paso, Texas, police involved themselves in a Chicano protest against a landlord. Instead of maintaining order, the police insulted the demonstrators and threatened to arrest them.[72] Furthermore, police have themselves acted against the Mexican American community. Their perception of Mexican Americans as crime prone results in "police-induced" crime, that is, policing Mexican American barrios so heavily that high arrest rates naturally result. Police patrol barrios far more heavily than Anglo American neighbourhoods, even though the latter have higher crime rates.[73] This harassment extends to arresting Mexican Americans for traffic violations that are overlooked when committed by Anglo Americans.[74] Even more significant is the willingness of police to use force against Mexican Americans. The Texas Rangers are the most notorious offenders, and their century-old tradition is still alive. In south Texas, many Mexican Americans are fearful of the Rangers. This fear is so deep that a Mexican American doctor testified that he is afraid to be alone on the highway if the Rangers are around.[75] New Mexico police generated similar reactions when they crushed the northern New Mexico movement to reclaim lost land grants.[76] In California, police brutally attacked Chicano anti-war demonstrators and their indiscriminate use of violence resulted in many injuries and the death of a major Chicano journalist. The Los Angeles *Times* condemned these actions and asked, "Why, above all, were those deadly wall-piercing cannon shells used in a situation they were not designed for ... Who authorized their use?"[77] No police were indicted. The courts perpetuate rather than correct this pattern. Mexican Americans have been almost completely excluded from grand juries, which determine if there is sufficient evidence to hold a trial, as well as from trial juries. Seldom are Spanish speaking officials present in court, and consequently many Mexican Americans are tried without understanding what is being said. Finally, Mexican American judges are almost non-existent outside New Mexico.[78] These court practices and police procedures combine with public attitudes to explain why Mexican Americans are so over represented within penal institutions.

## VII. Conclusion

The interlocked functioning of educational, political and judicial institutions illustrates how Mexican American subordination is maintained. Schools teach Anglo American children that they are superior, and Mexican American children are taught that they must become Anglicized if they are to succeed. The political process has been structured to prevent Mexican Americans from reordering the relationship and to minimize the possibility of Mexican American demands being heard or answered. Judicial and police agencies stand behind the actions of other institutions and leave the Mexican American people with no clearly viable recourse. The institutional practices and public attitudes described here also clearly indicate that Mexican American subordination is the result of how Anglo American society is structured and how it functions. It is not because individual Anglo Americans are prejudiced that Mexican Americans suffer discrimination. It is, instead, because Anglo American society has taught itself that Mexican culture is inferior and therefore, knowingly and unknowingly, Anglo Americans systematically attempt to eliminate any influences Mexican American values might have on American society. Part of this strategy includes allowing Mexican Americans to live their own life styles so long as they do so within their own communities and apart from mainstream society. Anglo Americans are convinced, furthermore, that they do not discriminate against Mexican Americans as they admit they have against Blacks because some Mexican Americans, unlike Blacks, have attained relatively high social as well as economic positions. What Anglo Americans do not recognize is that they have accepted Mexican Americans who for the most part have internalized Anglo American values. Anglo American society, in other words, has been willing to accept competent, acculturated Mexican Americans, but it has not been willing to accept as equal Mexican American cultural values.

The Chicano Movement began in reaction to this attitude and the consequent subordination of Mexican Americans. To date the Movement has been a major force in legitimizing Mexican American values and in creating conditions within which institutions would recognize and begin to respond to the needs of the Mexican American people. Recent changes in institutional practices suggest the Movement has enjoyed some success. Primarily as a result of Chicano pressures, South-western school systems have initiated numerous programmes to meet Mexican American needs. Bilingual education is now offered in numerous schools across the South-west, but its impact is unclear because Anglo American administrators initiated these programmes reluctantly and are implementing them improperly. Experts on bilingual education criticize these programmes because they are speeding assimilation rather than reinforcing cultural identity and maintaining cultural traditions as was originally intended. Similarly, Mexican American teachers continue to protest that few Mexican Americans are in key administrative positions even though schools have hired increasing numbers of Mexican Americans as teachers. Similar complaints are voiced against colleges and universities where Mexican American professors have often been relegated to non-permanent positions and where Mexican American students are recruited but little is done to assist them once they are on campus. The impact of the Chicano Movement is most evident in the political arena. The creation of a Chicano political party, La Raza Unida, and Raza Unida's take-over of Crystal City Texas, are dramatic evidence of increased Chicano political and social power. More significant than these events, however, is the fact that extant political institutions have modified many of their practices in an attempt to mollify Chicano demands. Thus, political parties are increasingly willing to nominate and support authentic (as opposed to token) Mexican American candidates, and Mexican Americans are holding an increasing number of key positions across the South-west. Among the most important of these are the Speaker of the House in

Colorado, the Senate Majority Leader in Arizona, and New Mexico's governorship. These and other officials have been instrumental in formulating policies designed to aid the Mexican American people. Not all of this has been enacted, but for the first time in history Mexican American demands are being debated and policy changes, admittedly incremental, are being effected. The election of these officials and these modest policy changes would surely not have come about when they did without the Chicano Movement, and it is possible that they might never have come about had it not been for the pressures generated by Chicano activists. This is not to say that these pressures alone produced these changes, but it is difficult to imagine how Anglo American society would have moved in this direction in and of itself. Ironically, these changes have eroded the Movement's support. The Movement could mobilize the Mexican American community as long as it could point to society's unwillingness to respond to Mexican American needs. As institutions respond, Chicano activists lose credibility. Thus, Chicano militants have been unable to expand their support because they played such an important role in restructuring political relationships so that Anglo American decision makers would regularly consider and sometimes respond to Mexican American needs. The Movement has also influenced judicial practices. Mexican Americans are no longer excluded so effectively from juries. College recruitment efforts will soon result in a large increase in Mexican American lawyers, and police forces across the South-west are making increasing efforts to recruit Mexican Americans. It is still too early to determine whether such changes will lead to substantial improvement in how police and courts deal with Mexican Americans. What is clear is that the relationship between Mexican Americans and Anglo Americans has permanently changed. It seems extremely unlikely that Mexican Americans will ever again accept denying their cultural heritage as the price for full participation in American society. Furthermore, the Chicano Movement has helped produce a new leadership class that identifies with the community while also having the skills necessary for dealing with Anglo American decision makers. Such leaders will continue to press Mexican American demands and decision makers will have to deal with them forthrightly. Some progress, as has been shown, has already been achieved. Mexican Americans will press for increased changes however, and how Anglo American society responds to these pressures will provide a most important insight into the nature of American pluralism and the ultimate responsiveness and openness of American society.

## Notes

1. For a discussion of the concept of "territorial minorities," see, Rudolph O. de la Garza, Z. Anthony Kruszewski, and Tomas Arciniega, eds., *Chicanos and Native Americans: The Territorial Minorities* (Englewood Cliffs: Prentice Hall, 1973).
2. Carey McWilliams, *North From Mexico* (New York: Greenwood Press, 1968), p. 52.
3. Rodolfo Alvarez, "The Psycho-Historical and Socioeconomic Development of the Chicano Community in the United States," *Social Science Quarterly*, Vol. 53, No. 4 (March, 1973), pp. 920–942, interprets the meaning of the border from this perspective.
4. As quoted in Rodolfo Acuna, *Occupied America: The Chicano's Struggle Toward Liberation* (San Francisco: Canfield Press, 1972), p. 15.
5. "The Treaty of Guadalupe Hidalgo," in Wayne Moquin and Charles Van Doren, eds., *A Documentary History of the Mexican Americans* (New York: Praeger Publishers, 1971), p. 184.
6. Matt S. Meier and Feliciano Rivera, *The Chicanos: A History of Mexican Americans* (New York: Hill and Wang, 1972).
7. Interview with David Weber, Fall, 1975.
8. Moquin, *Documentary History* . . ., p. 181.
9. Americo Paredes, *With His Pistol in His Hand* (Austin: University of Texas Press, 1959), p. 26.
10. McWilliams, *North From Mexico*, p. 98.
11. These events are thoroughly discussed in Acuna, *Occupied America*, pp. 57–76.
12. As quoted in Leonard Pitt, *Decline of the Californios* (Berkeley: University of California Press, 1966), p. 61.
13. Pitt, *Decline* . . ., offers the most complete description available of the California experience.
14. The Chicano take-over is well described in John Shockley, *Chicano Revolt in a Texas Town* (South Bend: University of Notre Dame Press, 1974).
15. For further discussion of these individuals see Tony Castro, *Chicano Power* (New York: Saturday Review Press, 1974).
16. Lyle W. Shannon and Judith L. Mckim, "Mexican American, Negro and Anglo Improvement in Labor Force Status Between 1960 and 1970 in a Midwestern Community," *Social Science Quarterly* (June, 1974), p. 99.
17. Leo Grebler, Joan Moore and Ralph Guzman, *The Mexican American People* (New York: Free Press, 1970), p. 181; Selected Characteristics of Persons of Spanish Origin in the United States, Advance Report, U. S. Department of Commerce, Bureau of the Census (March, 1975).
18. Selected Characteristics of Persons and Families of Mexican, Puerto Rican, and other Spanish Origin, U. S. Department of Commerce, Bureau of the Census (March, 1972), p. 9.
19. Joan Moore, "Colonialism: The Case of the Mexican American," *Social Problems*, Vol. 17, No. 4, pp. 463–471; Guillermo V. Flores, "Race and Culture in the Internal Colony: Keeping the Chicano in his Place," in Frank Bonilla and Robert Gulig, eds., *Structures of Dependency* (Stanford, 1973).
20. As quoted in Paredes, *With His Pistol in His Hand*, p. 17.
21. *Ibid.*
22. As quoted in Acuna, *Occupied America* . . ., p. 107.
23. As quoted in Moquin, *Documentary History* . . ., pp. 258–259.

24. Albert Memmi, *The Colonizer and the Colonized* (New York: Orion Press, 1965), p. 81.
25. All of the quotations in this paragraph are taken from an excellent review of the literature by Octavio Romano-V, "The Anthropology and Sociology of the Mexican-Americans," in *Voices: Readings from El Grito – 1967–1973* (Berkeley: Quinto Sol, 1973), pp. 43–56.
26. Quotations in this paragraph are also from Romano-V, "Anthropology and Sociology ..."
27. Ozzie G. Simmons, "The Mutual Images and Expectation of Anglo Americans and Mexican Americans," in John H. Burma, ed., *Mexican Americans in the United States* (Cambridge, Mass.: Schenkman Publishing Company, 1970), p. 385.
28. Memmi, *Colonizer and Colonized,* pp. 88–89.
29. Anthony Gary Dworkin, "Stereotypes and Self-Images Held by Native-Born and Foreign-Born Mexican Americans," in Burma, *Mexican Americans ...,* pp. 402–403.
30. McWilliams, *North From Mexico,* discussion on the "Fantasy heritage of the Southwest" is insightful on this point.
31. Thomas P. Carter, *Mexican Americans in School* (New York: College Entrance Examination Board, 1970), forcefully makes this argument.
32. U. S. Commission on Civil Rights, *Mexican American Education Study,* Report 1 (April, 1971), p. 12.
33. Carter, *Mexican Americans ...,* p. 48.
34. *Mexican American Education Study,* Report I. pp. 21–40.
35. *Ibid.,* pp. 41–52.
36. These practices are described in Charles L. Cotrell, "Municipal Services Equalization and Internal Colonialism in San Antonio, Texas: Explorations in 'Chinatown," a paper presented at the Rocky Mountain Social Science Convention, April, 1975.
37. *Mexican American Education Study,* Report I, p. 13.
38. U. S. Commission on Civil Rights, *Mexican American Education Study,* Report IV (August, 1972), p. 29.
39. As quoted in Carter, *Mexican Americans ...,* p. 125.
40. *Ibid.*
41. U. S. Commission on Civil Rights, *Mexican American Education Study,* Report III (May, 1972), p. 14.
42. Carter, *Mexican Americans ...,* p. 52.
43. *Mexican American Education Study,* Report III, pp. 20, 13.
44. *Ibid.,* pp. 31–33.
45. Carter, *Mexican Americans ...,* p. 93.
46. U. S. Commission on Civil Rights, *Mexican American Education Study,* Report V (March, 1973), p. 17.
47. U. S. Commission on Civil Rights, *Mexican American Education Study,* Report II (October, 1971), p. 39.
48. Carter, *Mexican Americans ...,* p. 82.
49. *Ibid.,* p. 83.
50. *Ibid.,* p. 18; *Mexican American Education Study,* Report V, p. 24.
51. *Mexican American Education Study,* Report II, pp. 10, 22.
52. *Mexican American Education Study,* Report III, p. 11.
53. Shockley, *Chicano Revolt ...,* describes these incidents.
54. U. S. Commission on Civil Rights; *Mexican Americans and the Administration of Justice in the Southwest: A Report,* 1970, p. 15.
55. Grebler, *et. al., Mexican American People,* p. 567.

56. Clifton McCleskey and Bruce Merrill, "Mexican American Political Behavior in Texas," *Social Science Quarterly* (March, 1973), pp. 785–798.
57. Grebler, *et. al., Mexican American People*, p. 567.
58. Personal interview, Spring, 1972.
59. Fernando V. Padilla and Carlos B. Ramirez, "Patterns of Chicano Representation in California, Colorado and Nuevo Mexico," *Aztlan*, Vol. 5, No. 1 and 2 (Spring and Fall, 1974), p. 189.
60. John Crow, "Mexican American Wards and Tucson City Elections," Unpublished, undated paper, University of Arizona, pp. 3–4.
61. Charles L. Cotrell, "The Effects of At-Large Elections on the Political Access and Voting Strength of Mexican Americans and Blacks in Texas," a paper presented at the Rocky Mountain Social Science Association Meeting, April, 1974.
62. *Political Participation of Mexican Americans in California: A Report of the California State Advisory Committee to the United States Commission on Civil Rights*, August, 1971, p. 61.
63. *Political Participation* . . . .
64. This pattern is described in Rudolph O. de la Garza, "Voting Patterns in 'Bi-Cultural El Paso': A Contextual Analysis of Chicano Voting Behavior," *Aztlen*, Vol. 5 (Spring and Fall, 1974), pp. 235–260.
65. Frank L. Baird and Jesus F. Guzman, Jr., "Mexican Americans in Lubbock: Political Subculture and Mexican American Political Behavior," a paper presented at the Rocky Mountain Social Science Association Meeting, April, 1973.
66. Cotrell, "The Effects of At-Large Elections . . .," p. 50.
67. *Ibid*.
68. Grebler, *et. al., Mexican American People*, pp. 529–530.
69. *Time*, Dec. 14, 1970.
70. *Mexican Americans and the Administration of Justice*, pp. 78–83.
71. Grebler, *et. al., Mexican American People*, p. 533.
72. *Mexican Americans and the Administration of Justice*, p. 17.
73. Armando Morales, "Police Deployment Theories and the Mexican American Community," *Voices* (Berkeley: Quinto Sol, 1971), pp. 167–179.
74. *Mexican Americans and the Administration of Justice*, p. 9.
75. *Ibid*., p. 16.
76. *Mexican Americans and the Administration of Justice*.
77. Albert Herrera, "The National Chicano Moratorium and the Death of Ruben Salazar," in Ed Ludwig and James Santibanez, eds., *The Chicanos: Mexican American Voices* (Baltimore: Penguin Book, 1971), p. 241.
78. *Mexican Americans and the Administration of Justice*, Chapters 5–7.

# Institutionalised Inequality and Differentiation: An Evaluation of Race Discrimination in South Africa

LAWRENCE SCHLEMMER

PROFESSOR LAWRENCE SCHLEMMER, of the University of Natal in Durban, South Africa, was born in Pretoria in 1936. He received his early training at the University of Pretoria and the University of South Africa. After some years as a social worker, he became a research assistant in the Department of Sociology at the University of the Witwatersrand, where he was later to be appointed as a lecturer. In 1964 he took the post of Senior Research Fellow in the Institute for Social Research in Durban, and was appointed Director of the Institute and Professor in 1972.

Professor Schlemmer has published some 50 articles, reports and monographs in the fields of race relations, political sociology, industrial sociology and the sociology of planning. He is Honorary Vice President of the South African Institute of Race Relations, Chairman of the Institute for Industrial Education, which runs a trade union education and research programme, and a member of the official Planning Advisory Committee for KwaZulu. He has delivered papers at three international conferences on race relations and Southern African affairs: at a conference convened by the University of Denver at Lake Como in Italy in 1972; at Dalhousie University, Canada, in 1973; and at a conference organised by Yale and Wesleyan Universities in New York in 1974.

# Institutionalised Inequality and Differentiation: An Evaluation of Race Discrimination in South Africa

LAWRENCE SCHLEMMER

South Africa is pre-eminently associated with the word "Apartheid," a term which was formerly part of official policy nomenclature in South Africa, and which has come to be used as an international catch-phrase for legally enforced racial discrimination of many different kinds.

Amidst many other cleavages and conflicts in international affairs, there is very widespread consciousness of colour differentiation in world society; the wealthy Western nations are in some ways perceived as an international pigmentocracy. To many people South African society quite understandably epitomises this perception of differentiation in mankind's ranks in present times. A coincidence of distinctions in wealth and colour in South Africa also symbolises very dramatically the major patterns of differentiation in world economic development. Perhaps most important of all, however, is the fact that South Africa is justifiably seen to have set its policies against the direction of world-wide attempts, however ineffective or merely token in nature, to reduce racial discrimination.

South Africa is a relatively small society in which nearly all the dominant tensions of the world are writ very large. This makes it particularly important to attempt to understand the precise nature of South African society. An understanding of the basis of discrimination in South Africa may add to our insight into the problem of racism wherever it occurs.

## I. An Evaluation of the Origins and Proximate Causes of Race Discrimination in South Africa

It is insufficient to attempt nothing more than a description of race discrimination as it exists currently; such descriptions lend themselves to a wide variety of different (and sometimes superficial) interpretations. It is felt to be necessary to evaluate the factors underlying "Apartheid" in a historical time perspective. A word on the level of analysis appropriate to such an evaluation is necessary.

In any attempt to understand a *social system* of discrimination, one has to avoid a dominantly psychological conceptual approach. As Schermerhorn puts it, "... prejudice too often monopolised attention to the neglect of societal and structural conditions ... If research has confirmed anything in this area, it is that prejudice is a product of *situations*, historical situations, economic situations, political situations; it is not a little demon that emerges in people simply because they are depraved."[1] To search for a psychology of White South Africanism at the base of Apartheid will not reward us; psychological characteristics are likely to be the product of socio-historical forces. Social psychological research among South African Whites tends to corroborate this. On the basis of careful empirical observations, Orpen says that "... the results so far indicate that the view ... that prejudice is mainly an expression of inner needs and conflicts just does not hold up in South Africa ... personality factors should *not* be stressed in the explanation of prejudice in relatively 'prejudiced' situations."[2]

One must trace the origins of South Africa's present social order to the history of White settler colonialism. It needs to be noted in this regard that prior stereotypes of African aboriginals as cannibals and barbarians had existed in Europe and that the settlers probably arrived with unfavourable images of Black people.[3] At the time of the initial settlement by the Dutch, various factors reinforced stereotypes and made a social cleavage between the settlers and the Khoi people of the Cape more or less inevitable. There were differences in culture, appearance and personal habits (made wider still by mutual ignorance and partial, segmental contact) distinctions between heathen and protestant Christian which were important to the Whites because their own ethnic and national identity was closely bound up with protestant concepts of salvation,[4] and, very importantly, a polarity of material interests arising out of the issues of rights over land and the terms of the cattle trade conducted between the two groups.

In the Cape Colony, a racially-mixed community, the Coloured people, emerged out of biological contact between Khoi peoples, Malay slaves and White settlers. This community was a social segment on the fringe of the settler society. Some early penetration of Coloured people (mainly freed slaves who had been baptised) into the White settler society took place, but, partly because of the settlers' interest in conserving slave labour, the process did not gather momentum.[5] Hence, even the people of mixed blood tended to become viewed as a separate community, almost similar in status to the indigenous Khoi peoples; a plural situation based not only on culture but on the convergence of the factors of skin colour, religious identity and economic interests had been firmly established. Even when British policies in later years – namely the emancipation of slaves and the introduction of a qualified franchise for "non-Whites" – encouraged the emergence of the so-called "liberal tradition" in the Cape, this tradition did not become sufficiently strong or pervasive among White settlers to produce any significant movement towards a close social integration of White and Coloured people.[6]

The emergence of sharp cleavages along racial lines in the cradle of South African history, the early Cape, is important to our understanding of racism in South Africa because the Cape offered perhaps the most favourable opportunities for non-racial communities to emerge. The odds against non-racial development were even greater in the wider setting of White contact with African societies on the Eastern frontier and in the interior. In the course of this history, a large number of indigenous societies whose technology (initially) did not include firearms, horses, wagons, facilities for food storage and other techniques useful in warfare, were conquered, subjugated or displaced by Dutch and British metropolitan and settler forces. In some parts of South Africa, vacant land or land temporarily vacated by indigenous people fleeing the effects of inter-tribal warfare (the so-called "Difaquane" wars after 1822) was settled by Whites. As Leftwich's arguments suggest, until the discovery of diamonds and gold stimulated industrial development (in itself a major factor leading to eventual unification of territories) there was a series of uneasily co-existing *societies*, with the indigenous societies subjected to lesser or greater degrees of external control by different regimes.[7] Thus an essentially plural social framework (structurally, socially and culturally) conditioned the emergence of South Africa's industrial society.

Pluralism as a guiding feature of the emerging society must, however, not be understood in purely socio-cultural terms. Different "national identities" and cultural patterns had high salience initially and were dramatised by sentiments aroused in armed conflict. But after conquest, the possibilities of acculturation and integration would have been ever-present had it not been for other factors; factors which reinforced or created inequality of such an order that cultural and ethnic differences came to coincide with socio-economic distinctions. In the popular settler mind, all these differences came to be seen in dominantly racial terms; the racial factor being the most visible and easily conceptualised index of group differentiation.

The discovery of diamonds and gold in the late 19th century marked the beginning of South Africa's industrial revolution; a process which was to mould race relations more powerfully than any events in the previous history of the region. The diamond diggers and gold miners, initially, were British and European immigrants; and the former in particular came to work in South Africa with a strongly imbedded "craft-union" tradition of economic protectionism. The existing social structure of the society gave these workers a distinctive identity and privileges as Whites, and as workers they saw themselves as a class distinct from the class of owners but also distinct from African (and to a lesser degree) Coloured workers. Their ranks were swelled by impoverished, poorly-educated White Afrikaners moving off the land, who had only their White skins to protect them against labour competition from Africans. Both groups saw Africans as a threat, and White worker pressure for protection was rewarded in 1904 with the passing of Ordinance No. 17 (Transvaal) which excluded African miners from skilled jobs, and in 1924 with the passing of the Industrial Conciliation Act, which laid a basis for industrial negotiation between management and employee but which excluded Africans from the definition of employees.[8] The Industrial Conciliation Act of 1924 laid a foundation for a basic pattern of collaboration between White management, White labour and the Government (albeit overlaid with sharp, but less basic, conflicts) in protecting White privilege, initially in the name of the so-called "civilized labour policy."[9]

Another vital theme which impinges on industrialisation in South Africa's history is the land issue. From the time of earliest settler colonialism competition for land had been fierce. After various "squatters' laws" enacted before Union in order to limit African penetration of "White" land, the 1913 Land Act reserved 7% of the total area of the country for African occupation and imposed limitations on acquisition of land by Africans and on African farming of land outside the "native reserves." The Beaumont Land Commission of 1915 observed that the land set aside for Africans was seriously overcrowded and could reasonably accommodate only one-half of the total African population. The 1913 Act was not completely effective in preventing all acquisition by indirect means of "White" land by Africans, and in 1936 the Native Trust and Land Act was promulgated to tighten the formal segregation of the land. This act made provision for more land for African reserves (over 12% of the land area) as a compensation for the removal of qualified Africans from the common franchise in the Cape. However, the overcrowding of the African land area became more and more serious, undermining the pre-capitalist tribal economy. This, together with Poll or Hut Taxes (later, Bantu General Tax) imposed on Africans, forced increasing numbers of Africans off the land into urban and White agricultural employment.

One can see, therefore, that as a consequence of the way in which privileged White access to land was secured, the well-known problem of "migrant labour" was exacerbated. The policy of "segregationism," which included the land acts referred to above, the Native Affairs Act of 1920, the Native (Urban Areas) Act of 1923 (defining the entry of the mass of Africans to urban areas to be for purposes of employment only) and other legislation essentially defined the bulk of the African population as people *external to* the core society of South Africa. The "Influx Control" laws, the system of labour compounds for African workers in the cities, the Masters and Servants laws (going back to long before Union) and after Union the Bantu Labour Regulations Act of 1911, and the Bantu Service Contract Act of 1937, as well as other legislation, had as a consequence the emergence of what has been termed "unfree" labour; labour which was powerless and easily exploitable.

Facts like these have been analysed in greater detail by sociologist-historiographers like Legassick and Wolpe[10] who have sought to explain segregation and later, Apartheid, in terms of the policy response to the needs and interests of capital accumulation, initially in White agriculture and mining and later in secondary industry. No adequate explanation of Apartheid is possible without taking account of this (materialist) analytical perspective. This approach, however, requires to be complemented in order to explain the particular nature of South African Apartheid. If one assumes that capital accumulation, coercive control of labour and other material interests are more or less *exclusive* features of the socio-political dynamic producing the race-oligarchical state form and the policies of government, one has considerable difficulty in explaining the remarkable rigidity of institutionalised race discrimination in the society. Status mobility and assimilation into the dominant group of small numbers of, say, better-educated members of the colonised groups is not necessarily contradictory to the maintenance of extreme forms of labour exploitation. In fact it can be argued that by a process of "selective co-optation" or better still, social incorporation of Black elites, the productive system, seen in isolation from the broader political economy, could have strengthened its basis of legitimacy. Since the Union of the various territories in 1910, and particularly since 1948, the "marginal" Blacks (Coloured people and qualified Africans in the Cape) have, however, been progressively disenfranchised.

One way of defending the exclusively class-orientated explanation is to argue that the structure of capitalism in South Africa required, or had as a consequence, a variety of social norms, stereotypes and beliefs which led to the social formations characteristic of segregation and later Apartheid. This argument would see social and political policies as evidence of the "hidden hand" of forces of production in the "superstructure" of the society – its cultural values, social patterns and legitimising ideologies. Another view would be to assert that the state form articulates with the mode of production in such a way as to ensure the *long-term* survival of the system of exploitation, *via* rigid race discrimination, some of which may appear irrational from a short-term or superficial economic perspective. Both these views, however, tend to assume an undimensional simplicity in the social dynamics of a society which is impossible to reconcile with empirical observation.

Yet another explanation, which would deviate from the materialist view would be that the issue is primarily one of the maintenance of *power* by the dominant White group and that the safeguarding of this political hegemony requires rigid racial differentiation in terms of status and privileges. Under the privileges consequent upon power would be subsumed the important advantages to the Whites of the maintenance of the particular economic mode of production, but the range of privileges would extend beyond narrowly-defined material advantages to include enhanced racial status, esteem and ego rewards, the benefits of relatively elaborate life-styles even among less affluent Whites and the protection of a major share of social goods and facilities. Yet, even the maintenance of power is not inconsistent with some blurring of racial boundaries and selective assimilation of Blacks who could share the interests of Whites. Many Caribbean and Latin American societies, for example, display gradations of privilege corresponding with gradations in pigmentation.[11]

Why the rigidity of separation in South Africa? What theoretical perspective can adequately account for it? It has already been argued that to reduce the level of explanation to the psychology of prejudice is to attempt to explain the system in terms of one of its consequences at the level of individual actors – a tautological exercise. Is it the *fear* among Whites of being "swamped" – socially eclipsed – by overwhelming numbers of Blacks which is at the root of the rigid separation? This argument is not to be overlooked[12] and the demographic factor is one which certainly makes the South African situation demand a different kind of evaluation than the situations of inter-group tension say in the U.S.A., Europe, Australia and other places elsewhere. Such fear, however, requires the out-group to be perceived as "alien," with incompatible values (the relevance of such perceptions has been demonstrated empirically at the social psychological level by Rokeach.[13] This may have been a root cause of breakdown in inter-group communication at the time of frontier contact, but after 300 years of colonisation the mutual alienation of communities must also be seen as rather more of a consequence of the system than as its cause.

A popular argument, of course, is that the Whites brought civilisation, Christianity and technology to Southern Africa and that their dominance in the society is an indication of their civilising and developmental role even today, and that this calling is a justification for racial differentiation and a policy of gradual (apparently interminable) preparation of Black people for equal participation or self-determination in a modern society. This argument is as old as colonialism itself, and even the most cursory consideration of the inequalities of access to education and the means of development (see Section II) gives the lie to this kind of explanation.

One is still faced, then, with the problem of explaining the emergence of Apartheid (more recently termed "Separate Development") as a pervasive system of institutionalised differentiation and inequality between races in South Africa. Inequality between groups in societies and discrimination of all kinds are universal phenomena, but rarely are so many aspects of differentiation in a single society secured or reinforced by legal enactments as is the case in South Africa.

The notion of the "plural society" can be of assistance in attempting this explanation. Pluralism in South Africa comes into sharpest focus when considering the role of Afrikaans nationalism and its accompanying political ethos, particularly after 1948. While a continuation of policies of segregation and the social mix of formal and informal differentiation which were characteristic of earlier government policies had broadly the same consequences as Apartheid for the *majority* of Black people the effects of Apartheid have been dramatic at the margins of racial boundaries and of the status cleavages associated with race. Apartheid to a significant extent has unblurred these boundaries in the South African plural society, and many "grey areas" of interracial interaction have been partly or wholly removed.

In this paper it is impossible to attempt a chronological description of the origins, growth and emergent characteristics of the vitally important movement of Afrikaans nationalism. A brief listing of the factors contributing to its emergence will have to suffice; this outline is based on a variety of sources.[14] It needs to be noted that Afrikaner nationalism as a basis for popular political motivation among a strong majority of Afrikaners only manifested itself in the late Thirties and Forties of this century, culminating, of course, in the 1948 election victory for Afrikaans nationalism. This movement had its early origins in a Calvinist/puritan religious identity and the relative isolation of Afrikaner rural communities on the shifting frontier. Intellectual inspiration for the movement emerged in the language-cultural movement which ultimately led to Afrikaans supplanting Dutch as the recognised language of Afrikaners. Like most nationalisms of substantial intensity, a protracted sense of collective threat was experienced. First of all there were clashes with indigenous African warrior groups on the expanding frontier, and then successive political confrontations and military clashes with British forces culminating in the Anglo-Boer War. British imperialism continued to threaten Afrikaner group integrity after the war in the form of vigorous Anglicanisation policies pursued by Lord Milner. In the Twenties and Thirties of this century, Afrikaner poverty in the cities and other forms of social dislocation caused by rural-urban migration of Afrikaners led to a mobilisation of Afrikaner organisations to rehabilitate poor Afrikaners, to redress the economic imbalance between English and Afrikaans-speaking White communities, and to facilitate capital accumulation by Afrikaner economic bodies. During the same period there was a cultivation by members of the Afrikaner Church and intellectual elite of a distinctive consciousness of Afrikaner history, destiny and religious calling which became part of popular self-concepts towards the end of the 1930s. By this stage, an emergent "bureaucratization" of Afrikaner social, political and economic life, with interlocking and inter-penetrating organizations and interchangeable leadership produced an increasing measure of "elite consensus," which was to consolidate itself and mobilize further popular support in the period following the 1948 election victory for the Nationalist and Afrikaner Parties.

Thus, from 1948 onwards, the White Afrikaans segment of the population has dominated South African politics as a *corporate group* with a high degree of internal coherence and a well-developed popular sense of corporate group identity. The political policies of the Afrikaans Nationalist Party as regards the "non-White question," while not discontinuous with the earlier policies of segregation, began to reflect a set of principles congruent with the core ethos of Afrikaner group identity. As du Toit says, "Apartheid differed from the rather eclectic ways of segregation above all in the insistence on the consistent application of a few basic principles, primarily that of separation aimed at ensuring White survival and Afrikaner Identity."[15]

This discussion reflects one level of analysis of Apartheid – and as such presents a crucial set of insights. There is, however, another level at which the policy must be perceived as well in order to reach some sort of an understanding of certain ambiguous features of the policy which will be described in Section II of this essay. What is referred to here is the fact that the policy motivations are not only *cynical* or *justificatory*, but also (perhaps for no more than a section of supporters of the policy) a reflection of *idealism* nurtured in the struggle of Afrikaners for emancipation and political self-expression. This idealism has been reflected empirically, for example, in a study of attitudes conducted by this author, in which some roughly one-fifth of Afrikaners in Durban were found to combine an insistence on race separation with almost as much willingness to grant Blacks access to economic resources and opportunities for development as was encountered among White liberals.[16] Thus "enlightened pluralism" certainly exists among Afrikaans Nationalists, even outside the circles of university and some religious intellectuals. To some extent (perhaps a considerable extent) the enlightened pluralism may involve a projection on to Blacks of the Afrikaner's own aspirations and experience of group emancipation.[17] Certainly, the policy of Apartheid or Separate Development seems to involve a basic mode of political thinking or response in terms of corporate ethnic or "national" categories (which is less crystallised among English-speaking Whites) and which is not *necessarily* synonymous with an exploitative or dominating orientation vis-à-vis Blacks; Rhoodie demonstrates this point effectively.[18] Another relevant basic political orientation among some Afrikaner nationalists is perhaps a relatively pronounced degree of romantic idealism centred around a basic political precept, reminiscent of the German romantic idealism of a previous era.[19]

Whatever the relative importance of the elements of Afrikaner nationalism are, both the justificatory and idealistic components have facilitated a policy approach in terms of more or less "total blueprints" for dealing with the colour issue in South African society. Initially, at any rate, policy development is not conceived as a process of pragmatic adaptation to short-term pressures and needs – moving from precedent to precedent, which is typical of liberal or moderate conservative policies – but as a plan for the fundamental resolution of large issues.

The Afrikaners in the South African setting have become *the* corporate group among corporate groups in South Africa, and the policies of the past 28 years reflect this structure. Yet, looking back on earlier history, and at, say, the history of Natal (the British, the Zulus and the Indians, all involved in more inter-ethnic conflict or competition than co-operation) one realises that even without the Afrikaners, cleavages in economic interests and corporate boundaries would have come to coincide. Even the tenuous laissez-faire liberalism of the Cape before and for a while after Union held out no guarantee of a reduction in material inequality between the *majorities* in the different racial groups, or of the emergence of a non-racial society.

## II. Patterns of Discrimination

In describing patterns of discrimination, an attempt has been made to subdivide the major differentiating laws and practices into categories which have different kinds of consequences for Black people. Within each category a further distinction can be made between formal and informal patterns, but this will become apparent from the description. There is a very important ambiguity in the overall pattern of discrimination, but this theme will be taken up in the following section.[20]

### *A. The Perpetuation of Material Inequality*

This topic will be dealt with in some detail, since it is the subject of much public debate, both in South Africa and abroad, where the issue of investment in South Africa has received considerable attention. One has to commence this section by considering the most fundamental form of inequality, the effects of which are central to but extend beyond the issue of material inequality; that of voting rights.

Obviously, representation on the central governing bodies of a country secures for a population group generalised access to rewards and privileges of all kinds. Before 1956, limited representation of Africans in the Cape, through three White Members of Parliament, representation of Coloured and Asian men in the Cape who qualified for franchise rights and of Coloured men in Natal existed. After protracted institutional conflict between the Legislature and Parliament, eventually Parliament in 1955 and 1956 passed three separate acts which prevented the courts of law from blocking legislation (The Appellate Division Quorum Act No. 27 of 1955, the Senate Act No. 53 of 1955, and the South Africa Act Amendment Act, No. 9 of 1956). Thus the Separate Representation of Voters Act as amended by Act No. 30 of 1956 and later by Act No. 72 of 1965, Act No. 34 of 1966, Act No. 66 of 1967, and Act No. 50 of 1968, could be passed to deprive all Blacks of representation in the central Parliament. (The alternative provisions will be discussed in due course, but these provisions have not as yet afforded Blacks any effective bargaining power in the central decision-making bodies of the country.)

The "separation" of political representation for members of different race groups extends to formal political party organisation as well. The Prohibition of Political Interference Act, No. 51 of 1968, renders it illegal for anyone to belong to a racially-mixed political party, to assist a political party that has members drawn from a population group other than his own, or to address any meeting to further the interests of a political party or to assist a candidate if the greater majority of those present belong to a population group other than his own.

The effects on political bargaining power of the denial to Black people of the access they possessed to representation in the central Parliament have probably not been very great in concrete practice. Only in a small number of constituencies in the Cape Province was the Coloured vote able to influence the outcome of an election. Given the share of representation of the different political parties and the pattern of non-White voting, the non-White franchise marginally strengthened the opposition party. However, the legislation symbolised a drastic move away from the goal of an eventual unitary, non-racial political democracy and the really significant meaning of the legislation must be seen in these terms.

Turning to more specifically economic matters, the pattern of legislation which has emerged has as its central focus the Industrial Conciliation Act of 1924, as amended in 1937 and 1956 (and later in 1959 and 1966) in terms of which Africans are not regarded as employees, thereby depriving them of certain crucial privileges. These privileges include membership of registered trade unions, and therefore direct access to the industrial relations regulating machinery of the Industrial Councils. Furthermore, it is illegal for employers to collect trade uniod dues from Africans. In the 1956 Act, provision was made for so-callen "Job Reservation"; that is for specified types of work to be reserved for members of a specified race group. This clause has been used firstly to protect White workers and secondly, to protect Indian and Coloured workers from competition with African workers.

The amendments of 1966 introduced further prohibitions on strikes and lock-outs affecting all workers; the right to strike in South Africa is severely constrained and strikes are legal only after protracted processes of negotiation and arbitration; these provisions are open to differing interpretations, but the particular position of Africans will be referred to presently. The Industrial Conciliation Act also made it illegal for any more mixed White, Coloured and Indian Unions to be formed after 1956, and such mixed unions that existed had to form separate branches for different groups, and the central executive of the mixed unions was required to be White. Legislation provides for a system which is officially regarded as a viable alternative to trade union rights. The Bantu Labour Relations Regulation Amendment Act (No. 70 of 1973) refined earlier provisions and provides for:

– all industrial disputes involving Africans to be dealt with under the Act (previously only certain disputes were able to be dealt with);

– the establishment of Liaison Committees or Works Committees within companies (see later for details);

– the establishment of Regional Bantu Labour Committees to deal with disputes arising which cannot be solved by the in-plant committees.

– the attendance, as observers only, by African members of regional and plant committees of meetings of Industrial Councils where matters affecting Africans are being discussed. Any objections to decisions taken by the Industrial Council may be referred to the Minister of Labour by way of appeal, but they have no powers within the Industrial Council;

– where a Liaison Committee or Works Committee has not been able to settle a dispute, the dispute may be referred to the Bantu

Labour Officer in the area concerned (an official of the Government Department of Labour). After 30 days following such a report, if the dispute is not settled by the officer or the Regional Committee, a strike (or lock-out on the side of an employer) may legally occur. Thus, for the first time, Africans may strike legally, although strict prohibitions exist, namely where a wage determination order or regulation is less than one year old, or where an agreement in terms of the Industrial Conciliation Act is current, where Africans are employed in local authorities or essential services, or where a dispute has been referred to the Wage Board (the body regulating wages where no Industrial Council has jurisdiction).

Liaison Committees are bodies on which at least 50% of members are Africans elected by the African labour force, and the employer appoints the remainder and may appoint the Chairman. Where no Liaison Committee exists, African workers may take the initiative and establish a wholly elected Works Committee.

At the time of writing new legislation is being framed to provide for "Industry Committees" to be established for each industry in a region, and for such committees to have increased powers (but apparently no voting rights) at the Industrial Council level. Where no wage determinations or Industrial Councils exist, the new provisions are to provide for direct negotiating rights for the African Industry Committees. The legislation is likely to be extended to the mining sector.[21]

Thus it is seen that provisions regarding the formal industrial representation of African workers are in a process of evolution. To date, 2,276 in-plant Committees exist, representing 608,000 African workers, or 24% of the African labour force in South Africa.[22] (In 1969, under older legislation, only 24 similar committees existed). However, the emerging system has serious weaknesses which the proposed new legislation does not appear to rectify. The kernel of the system – the in-plant Committee – is formed within and restricted to a particular company and comprises only employees of that company. Hence management has considerable power and influence over committee members and their decisions, and even though the law, in theory, protects members from victimisation, there are many indirect strategies an employer can use against employees on a committee (e.g., fire them for alleged laziness, which is extraordinarily difficult to disprove).[23] Since Liaison Committees (as opposed to Works Committees) tend to be overwhelmingly favoured by employers, most committees established are of this type and the Chairman and secretaries are usually White representatives of management. Hence the influence of management on Committee deliberations is very strong. The committees are empowered to "communicate" the "wishes and aspirations" of African workers to management, but are not formally empowered to *negotiate* wages and conditions of employment, since they have no power to sanction management (although this may change in some industries).

Hence, industrial bargaining for the Africans remains inadequate if it is assessed against the benchmark of the powers of a trade union. The South African Institute of Race Relations (a body certainly not unrepresentative of management interests) described the new provisions as merely a "short-term palliative."[24] In this author's view, the committee system contains some very real benefits, particularly in regard to possibilities of effective management-worker *communication* and it has certain potential implications for the emergence of "co-determination" within the factory or company. However, African labour as yet, has no formally sanctioned "power-base" and until trade unions are recognised (not necessarily to replace but to strengthen or "back-up" the committee system) or until the committee system evolves into a "company union" structure *with* formal provisions for inter-company co-operation in regard to labour disputes, African workers will continue to be disadvantaged relative to Whites, Coloureds and Indians.

Unregistered African unions have existed since the First World War. In the 1920s, the Industrial and Commercial Workers Union had a claimed membership of 80,000 but subsequently experienced internal dissension and eventually collapsed as a result of too fast a growth and organizational problems. During and after the Second World War, there was a resurgence of African trade unions, and by 1945 union membership had reached an estimated 145,000. These unions were led or advised by a number of very prominent left-wing unionists and suffered a great deal of State opposition. The Suppression of Communism Act (see later) was used to restrict many officials. By 1961, 60,000 members remained, and in 1969, 13 unions with a combined membership of only roughly 16,000 still existed,[25] and this number became further eroded. Although strikes by African workers were illegal until mid-1973, their occurrence was fairly frequent. During the middle to late 1950s, for example, an average of some 6,000 workers per year went on strike;[26] during the 1960s, the average declined to some 2,000 per annum, but increased slightly towards the end of the decade.[27]

In 1971 and 1972, the incidence of strikes increased, and included a protracted and partly successful strike by some 13,000 Ovambo workers in South West Africa. This was followed by a significant strike of over 2,000 stevedores (dockworkers) in Durban. In early 1973, at least 61,000 African workers went on strike in 160 different strike occurrences, mainly in the greater Durban area. Out of the 160 strikes, wage increases were granted in 118 instances, but these wage increases were relatively small: R2-00 per week or less in 71 instances, and more than R2-00 in 36 instances; the workers initial demands were for much more – R12-00–R15-00 per week.[28]

In the wake of these strikes a resurgence of African trade union activity has occurred, and in January 1975 there existed 20 unregistered African trade unions with a book membership of 55,000 workers. These trade unions are leading a struggling existence, however, since they have no stop order facilities for the collection of dues (the "check-off" system) and dues have to be collected from workers individually.

At the present time the future of African trade unions is uncertain. The Minister of Labour has stated the government's determination to make the Committee system succeed in place of unions[29] and increasingly employers are forming Liaison Committees. While on the one hand, effective communication and negotiations between workers and management (and hence ultimate long-term stability) requires trade union rights for African workers (or a form of organization with equivalent power and legitimacy for workers), on the other hand the pattern of wage differentials and hence the potential effects on industry of African wage demands (see later), if articulated through effective worker representative bodies makes it highly unlikely that a free trade union movement will emerge in the short run. An uneasy situation is likely to continue for some time.

There are a number of other legal provisions which weaken the bargaining power or restrict the rights of African or other Black employees; Horner has listed 57 laws and regulations which in one way or another discriminate or differentiate between the races as regards employment.[30] Prominent among the legal provisions is the so-called "job-reservation" clause in the Industrial Conciliation Act, which as said before, is designed to protect mainly White employees but also Coloured and Indian workers from African competition. In strictly formal terms, the effect of this regulation is usually seriously overestimated. No new job reservation determinations have been promulgated since the beginning of 1972. Job reservation affects only the fringes of the lines of occupational-status demarcation between the races, and for this reason, with a very deeply entrenched pattern of job differentiation according to race, only an estimated 2.6% of the total labour force is potentially affected by job reservation. A majority of applications for exemption from existing job-reservation determinations tend to be granted because of shortages of White and other skilled labour; in 1973, 228 out of 261 applications for exemption were granted by the Minister of Labour, allowing 4,787 Black employees to move into reserved occupations.[31] The presence of the law and widespread ignorance among employers of the exact nature of job-reservation regulations has as a consequence a wider informal effect which significantly restricts the upward occupational mobility of African workers – empirical studies of this effect have been conducted.[32] Furthermore, there is close official surveillance of employment practices by the Department of Labour, in regard to Black job advancement generally, but especially where Blacks may be put in charge of Whites.

The so-called "Pass Laws," or influx control regulations (the Native (Urban Areas) Consolidation Act No. 25 of 1945, as amended several times subsequently, and the Native, later Bantu, Laws Amendment Acts of 1952, 1963, 1964, inter alia) are all based on earlier legislation, some of which dates back to the earlier days of White settlement. For present purposes what is important is that the freedom of Africans to seek work, to seek the highest bidder, and to change employment is severely restricted. An African may only gain permanent residential rights in an urban area outside of the homelands if he or she was born in the area or has worked for one employer for 10 years or for more than one for a period of 15 years continuously, and has not been convicted of a crime carrying a fine of more than R 100. Since 1968 (Bantu Labour Regulations, 1968, Proclamation R74) all non-qualified African urban residents wishing to seek work in an urban area must do so through labour bureaux in the homelands, and their work henceforth is on one-year contracts. They must return to the homeland once per annum and contracts have to be renewed annually. This makes it impossible for such employees to qualify for urban residence, and the contract system has the effect of strengthening official control over the African employee, and of undermining the morale of the Africans themselves.[33]

Given the fact that there is a housing shortage for African families permanently residing in the urban areas, and knowing that there is a vast number of Africans in the rural areas anxious to move into the urban areas, some restrictions on movement to the towns would probably be inevitable, even under an African Government. However, the way in which the laws are administered, and the effects they have on African migrant workers, particularly those living in closely controlled hostel accommodation, inevitably results in a situation of weakened bargaining power for *a majority of African workers*.[34]

There are a number of other laws and practices affecting the equality of employment opportunity. Space does not allow a full discussion. (For further information a publication by Muriel Horrell, *South Africa's Workers*, is relevant.)[35] A brief enumeration of some aspects may be of interest:

- controls exercised by White Trade Unions through Industrial Councils limit the number of Coloured and Indian apprentices in certain skilled trades;
- Africans may not become apprenticed for training in skilled trades in areas outside of the homelands, with the exception of special categories of building and electrical workers employed in African township construction;
- the Group Areas Act (see later) prevents the employment of Blacks in managerial positions in White areas; and
- various regulations have the effect of discouraging Black white-collar employment and some blue-collar employment by making it necessary for employers to go to considerable expense to provide separate facilities, for *each* of the 4 race groups.

A special comment is necessary on Black Education, since access to educational opportunity is central to the whole issue of material inequality and occupational opportunity. In 1972, the "Bantu Education Account" which had pinned African education to a fixed basic amount was abolished, and African education outside of homelands (in which education is separately financed) is funded in the same way as that of other race groups. There is, however, still very considerable inequality in the expenditure on education for different race groups. There are other forms of inequality as well; compared with Whites, the Indian, Coloured and African pupil (in that order) has the disadvantage of larger classes, lower qualified teachers, widespread incidence of schools working on a double-session system, and less adequate free provision of school books. Largely as a consequence of all these factors, the achievements of the different race groups differ markedly – some indication of this is found in the following comparison of the proportions of pupils of different race groups in secondary schools:

| | |
|---|---|
| Whites (1969) | 32% |
| Indians (1971) | 26% |
| Coloureds (1971) | 12% |
| Africans (1971) | 5% |

Although great advances have been made in recent years in providing education for Blacks, factual statistics reveal considerable existing inequality. The same pattern of differentiation can be noted in technical education, although here again, recent advances for Africans have been considerable.

A broad indication of the extent to which occupational differentiation exists between races in South Africa is obtained from comparing the proportions of economically-active people in White-collar versus Blue-collar work; the two categories representing *very rough* indications of differences in *occupational prestige*. Proportions are given for two census years:[36]

| | *Whites* | | *Indians* | | *Coloureds* | | *Africans* | |
|---|---|---|---|---|---|---|---|---|
| | *1946* | *1970* | *1946* | *1970* | *1946* | *1970* | *1946* | *1970* |
| *White-collar* (Professional, Managerial, Clerical, Sales and Higher Technical) | 38% | 57% | 28% | 38% | 5% | 13% | 2% | 5% |
| *Blue-collar* (Artisans, Labourers, Routine Workers) | 57% | 41% | 59% | 54% | 87% | 80% | 95% | 85% |
| *Unspecified or Unemployed* | 5% | 2% | 13% | 8% | 8% | 7% | 3% | 10% |

In these comparisons, the Coloured people particularly appear to be more disadvantaged than they are in practice, since there are many well-remunerated Coloured artisans in the Blue-collar group. However, the dominance of Whites and to a lesser extent Indians, in White-collar occupations is noteworthy. The figures also show, however, that the occupational structure has changed over the years, and that Blacks have made noticeable gains.

Another indication of occupational differentiation and of change is the proportion of unskilled labourers within non-mining industrial occupations:[37]

| | *1936* | *1960* | *1970* |
|---|---|---|---|
| White | 22% | 11% | 4% |
| Indian | 44% | 23% | 16% |
| Coloured | 55% | 49% | 44% |
| African | 90% | 84% | 68% |

Once again, the status differentiation is sharp, but the signs of occupational progress for Blacks are clear; progress which has occurred in inevitable response to shortages of skills in the economy. The government view in regard to occupational mobility for Blacks has been succinctly stated by the South African Prime Minister: "... the government does not stand in the way of changes of traditional work patterns which allow non-Whites to move up into job categories for which they will require higher skills and in which they can earn higher wages than previously, provided these changes come about in an orderly fashion and with the concurrence of the trade unions ..."[38]

The differential distribution of occupations within race groups contributes to the very substantial differences in wages and incomes. The following table, compiled by McGrath, of personal incomes *per head* and *per income earner* in all sections in 1960 and 1970 gives a clear indication of the pattern of differentiation.[39]

The trend suggests that the rates of growth of incomes per earner

| *Date* | | *Personal Annual Income, per head at constant 1963 prices (Rands)* | *Personal Annual Income, per earner at constant 1963 prices (Rands)* |
|---|---|---|---|
| 1960 | Whites | 925 | 2209 |
| | Asians | 153 | 671 |
| | Coloureds | 137 | 407 |
| | Africans | 71 | 202 |
| 1970 | Whites | 1234 | 2644 |
| | Asians | 226 | 768 |
| | Coloureds | 186 | 520 |
| | Africans | 87 | 247 |
| | | *Compound Annual Growth Rates 1960–1970* | |
| | Whites | 2.92% | 1.81% |
| | Asians | 3.98% | 1.35% |
| | Coloureds | 3.10% | 2.48% |
| | Africans | 2.08% | 2.03% |

over the decade favoured the Coloured and African groups slightly, but that for Africans, the effects on *per capita* income were eroded by high population growth.

A major issue to be considered is the relation between racial wage *ratios* and *absolute* wage differentials. Taking manufacturing as an example of trends between 1960 and 1972, we find the following pattern:[40]

*Manufacturing Sector Monthly Wage Differentials*

| | *White/Asian diff.* | | *White/Coloured diff.* | | *White/African diff.* | |
|---|---|---|---|---|---|---|
| | *absolute* | *ratio* | *absolute* | *ratio* | *absolute* | *ratio* |
| 1960/1 | R118 | 3.3/1 | R121 | 3.5/1 | R138 | 5.5/1 |
| 1970 | R236 | 3.9/1 | R242 | 4.2/1 | R263 | 5.8/1 |
| 1972 | R271 | 3.6/1 | R276 | 3.8/1 | R307 | 5.6/1 |

These figures reflect what has been typical in the South African economy generally for many decades; that is for absolute differentials in wages between race groups to increase substantially despite, as is the case in the 1970 to 1972 comparison, the fact that the *ratios* of wages for the different groups reveal a narrowing of the differential.

The wage differentials shown above reflect, to some extent, the racial differences in occupational status and skills. However, according to Etheredge of the Anglo American Corporation,[41] the ratio of skilled to unskilled wages in South Africa is roughly 8.0 to 1 compared with roughly 1.4 to 1 in the U.S.A., for example. This difference is in part a reflection of the highly unequal bargaining power which exists between White (and some skilled Coloured and Indian) workers and Africans in South Africa. Therefore, the problem is not only a matter of differences in skills.

Recent trends indicate that the percentage increases in Black wages are more often than not higher than percentage increases in White wages. Over the 12-month period up to April 1972, salaries and wages of White males in a representative range of occupations increased by 4.6% as against 12.2% for African males.[42] More recently, research by the company Urwick-U.A.L. among a sample of 53,000 salaries in 170 companies, suggested that over the 12 months up to August 1973, African wages rose by 25%, and in the 7 months from August 1973 to March 1974, the rate of African wage increase was 16%; the equivalent rates of increase for Whites were roughly 9% and 9%. The[43] Minister of Statistics in Parliament has given figures which suggested that over the period from 1970 to 1973 (3 years) the average wage of Whites rose by 25.7% and that of all Blacks by 45.8%, compared with a rise in the Consumer Price Index (Cost of Living) of 23.7%.[44]

In the short to medium term, the absolute gap in increases is of greater objective relevance since the difference in buying power of the races tends to increase. Subjectively, however, higher rates of increase in Black wages may be significant in creating a spirit of relative optimism in the Black population. If the higher rates of increase in Black wages continue indefinitely (unfortunately, there is no certainty about this) the *long* term effects will be to reduce material inequality in the society.

The material inequality which exists, as already suggested, is partly a function of differences in skills (possibly to be traced in a very remote sense to initial cultural-technological differences but much more importantly to historic and current inequalities of access to education and training); very much because of the "unfreedom"; legal inequality and lack of bargaining strength of African labour; partly because of the large African "reserve army of labour" in the rural reserves producing an elastic labour supply which keeps wages low; and related to this last factor, the absence of profitable alternative agricultural pursuits for Africans in the overcrowded rural African reserves or homelands.

### *B. Laws and Practices which Separate the Races*

The policies of the National Party Government since 1948 have codified, formalised and made uniform and consistent a pattern of social segregation which, as has been seen in Section I, had its origins in the early history of the country. Basic to social Apartheid are the "race classification" laws, which prior to 1950, were incorporated in a number of different acts passed after 1911, but which did not constitute a rigid system. The Population Registration Act of 1950, as amended successively up to 1973, the Immorality Amendment Act of 1950, the Prohibition of Mixed Marriages Act of 1949 and 1968, as well as a number of other laws, all provide for a formal definition of racial status, and the latter two prevent sexual intercourse and marriage between Whites and non-Whites.

Residential segregation which had emerged informally in many parts of the country prior to 1950, has been formally established by Group

Areas Acts and Community Development Acts promulgated between 1950 and 1972.

The allocation of land for occupation by specified racial groups has generally had the effect of restricting the amount of land relative to population for Africans, Coloureds and Indians.

Furthermore, many hundreds of Indian traders have been denied access to markets within other race groups, and the Indian small-trader class has shrunk noticeably. Areas set aside for non-White occupation are often on less desirable land, further away from centres of work than the land previously occupied.[45] A notable exception to this pattern occurs in some Indian group areas in Durban; one of which (the "Grey Street Area") abuts the central business district of the city; it is also true that an area for Coloureds near the centre of Cape Town has recently been returned to the community after earlier removals.

As would be expected, the degree to which removals in terms of the Group Areas laws have affected the various groups has differed according to racial status; by the end of 1973 the following numbers of *families* had become disqualified to remain in their previous homes:[46]

| | |
|---|---|
| Whites | 1,648 |
| Coloureds | 73,758 |
| Asians | 39,911 * |

* These figures and those on housing shortages which follow, should be read in the light of the population ratios (June 1974): Whites, 4,160,000; Coloureds, 2,306,000; Indians, 709,000; Africans, 17,745,000.

Partly as a result of the allocation of land under Group Areas, partly as a result of differential incomes, and partly as a consequence of differences in local authority policies for the different race groups, wide disparities exist in regard to the current housing shortage; at the end of 1973, the number of dwellings needed by the different race groups was:

| | |
|---|---|
| Whites | 6,100 |
| Coloureds | 62,400 |
| Asians | 16,600[47] |
| Africans | unknown, but much higher than figures for other groups |

Various laws restrict the access of members of non-White races to social and civic amenities available to Whites. It should be noted at the outset that the amenities in White areas are notably superior to those for other races, partly because of the increased spending power of Whites.

The overall effect of these restrictions, however, is to deprive particularly the more affluent and better-educated members of the Black communities of access to a wide range of the most desirable public facilities, and this has led to considerable bitterness among these groups. The laws and proclamations have imbued a great rigidity to a system which would probably otherwise have been maintained by informal practices in a substantially similar overall form – consider, for example, segregation in the United States of America before the Civil Rights Movement.

### *C. Inequalities in Social Services and Welfare*

Here, again, a pattern of inequality according to race exists. State expenditure on Social Services in the form of welfare in 1972 was approximately: R45 per person per annum for Whites, R16 for Coloureds, R12 for Indians and R1 to R2 for Africans.[48] As from the end of 1974, the rates for old age and other state pensions were as follows: Whites R57 p.m.; Coloureds and Indians, R29.50 and Africans R11.25.[49] There are also inequalities in the numbers of pensions received by members of the different race groups, due to a variety of reasons, not all of them discriminatory in a formal sense. Considerable differences exist in the field of health and health services as well.

The position as regards infant nutrition in the rural African homelands is still very serious, as a recent study has shown.[50] Malnutrition and disease are not only the products of poverty – poor dietary habits play a very substantial part – but for the homelands in particular, sheer poverty resulting from irregular or inadequate remittances of money from migrant-worker breadwinners (who often have urban and rural commitments) looms very large in the causation of the problem; hence the organisation of labour in South Africa tends to aggravate problems of poverty and health.

### *D. Separate Development of the Homelands and the Physical Planning Act*

The policy of Separate Development was formulated in response to the need to offer positive alternatives to the denial of rights to Africans in the "White" areas. The policy had its geographic basis in the Land Acts of 1913 and 1936; the latter stipulating that 13.7% of the territory of South Africa would be set aside for African occupation (actually amounting to 25% of the non-desert areas of the country). The political basis of the policy was laid initially with the Bantu Authorities Act No. 68 of 1951 and numerous subsequent acts have been passed to give direction to the policy; (for an analysis of these laws see Muriel Horrell and Nic Rhoodie).[51]

There are 10 different "homelands" for the various African ethno-linguistic (tribal) groups. These homelands consist of 82 blocks of land. The government intends consolidating the land areas when it adds the additional land yet to be purchased for African occupation as guaranteed in the Act of 1936. However, consolidation plans will still leave some of the territories substantially fragmented: KwaZulu, for example, will have 10 separate areas; Bophuthatswana will have 6 areas; Lebowa 5 and Gazankulu 4. The Transkei, on the other hand, will consist of only 2 separate areas, and certain smaller homelands will comprise a single land area.

The average population density of the homelands, excluding absent migrant workers, was 119 per square mile in 1970, compared with a density of 35 persons per square mile outside the homelands. The homelands cannot be said to represent an equitable partition of the land area of the country.

The Bantu Homelands Constitution Act of 1971 empowered the republican government to grant increasing powers of self-government to all the homelands, as had been done for the Transkei in 1963. The Prime Minister in 1972 declared his party to be willing to consider granting full independence to those homelands in which a desire for independence existed. The Transkei is to become an independent state during 1976 and the Bophuthatswana Legislative Assembly has decided to move towards independence as soon as possible. Other homeland leaders are not willing to seek independence; some are not willing to consider independence until additional land is granted (additions exceeding those guaranteed by the 1936 Act), and others, like KwaZulu, are loath to consider independence because it would mean relinquishing rights and claims to privileges and economic resources in the developed ("White") areas of the country.

All Africans in South Africa are legally regarded as citizens of one or other homeland, despite the fact that only 46.4% of Africans were living in their homelands at the time of the 1970 Census. The government view at present is that full citizenship rights and the freedom for unlimited occupational mobility for Africans can only take place within the homelands. It needs to be noted that the homelands do not contain any cities and large towns, and that they are generally poorly served with roads, railway lines and general economic infrastructure. They are "peripheral" areas within the South African political economy and although considerable efforts are being made to develop the homelands, as separate economic entities they are similar to some underdeveloped independent Southern African countries since their major earning capacity is derived, and likely to be derived for a long time yet, from the "export" of migrant labour.[52]

One of the ways in which a shift of African population from White areas to the homelands is being encouraged is through the policy of industrial decentralisation. The Physical Planning and Utilization of Resources Act of 1967 placed controls on the numbers of Africans who could be employed in industry in the established industrial areas. More recently, the provisions have been made more flexible, but African labour-intensive industry is both encouraged by incentives and forced by restrictions on employment to be located or relocated either in the homelands on an "agency" basis (where the land and buildings may not be owned and the tenure of occupation is for a fixed period – say 25 or 50 years) or in "border areas" abutting the homelands, which enables Africans to live in the homeland and commute daily to work. (In practice, however, the distances of commuting are generally longer than distances between township and workplace in the White areas.) Of the two schemes, the border area system has proved to be far more effective and relatively few industries have been attracted into the homelands; the number of industrial jobs created in the homelands by 1973 was a mere 3,828.[53] The finances of the homelands are derived from amounts collected from internal taxation and from grants by the South African Government, which have to be approved by the White parliament.

For Coloureds and Indians no homelands are envisaged, but a policy of "parallel development" is pursued. For Coloureds, a Coloured Persons' Representative Council was established in 1969 with 40 elected and 20 nominated members. This body elects an executive committee whose members take responsibility for various portfolios like finance, education, local government, community development and rural settlements. The budget for this body, however, has to be approved by the White parliament. A similar structure is in the process of development for Indians, but as yet the majority of members of the South African Indian Council are nominated by the White government, and its powers and sphere of operation are more limited as yet than that of the Coloured Persons' Representative Council.

### *E. Security Legislation*

In South Africa the security legislation to protect the established order is extremely strict and pervasive in its effects. The most important laws are the Suppression of Communism Act, the Riotous Assemblies Act, the Unlawful Organizations Act, the Criminal Procedures Act, various General Law Amendment Acts, the Terrorism Act, the Affected Organizations Act, the Criminal Law Amendment Act and various proclamations. These laws make provision for punishment without trial in the form of "banning" of persons (restrictions to particular areas and prohibitions on activities like meeting with more than one person at a time, publishing, addressing meetings, entering factory premises, etc.); house arrest (usually outside of working hours); the "listing" of persons (preventing them from practising certain occupations, joining certain organisations, publishing and communicating with other listed persons); the prohibition of certain gatherings and of political meetings of over 10 people in African areas without special permission, detention without trial for periods of up to 180 days, detention without trial, without disclosure, and without access to legal advice, friends or relatives until the person concerned has replied adequately to all questions; the banning of organisations; preventing certain organisations from receiving funds from outside the country; and the prohibition of various kinds of demonstrations.

While there are undoubtedly countries where the number of political prisoners and restricted persons is higher in relative terms than is the case in South Africa, the laws referred to above have been successful in curbing effective open opposition to the government on the part of Blacks and strongly liberal and radical White groups. The African National Congress, the Pan African National Congress, their related trade union movements, the Communist Party, and a number of other movements have been destroyed or forced underground. At present, the National Union of South African Students and the Christian Institute of Southern Africa have been declared "affected" organisations and may not receive money from outside the country.

## III. Discussion and Evaluation

What has been sketched in broadest outline amounts to a forbidding formal system of differential life-chances, all with deep historical roots. To the extent that phrases such as "institutional violence" and "institutionalised racism" oversimplify conceptions of the situation they can be dangerous, not only as regards an understanding of the situation but, by way of extension, also as a basis for stances in regard to change. One must consider the nature of the interests which the system serves in order to attempt to arrive at a rounded understanding. This consideration must of necessity be brief and synoptic.

Clearly, the material inequalities indicate that class interests of a type are basic in the society. Here one thinks of the White working class which has emerged in a position akin to an "aristocracy of labour" by virtue of the race cleavages in the social and political sphere. In a now well-known essay, Johnstone has argued that "the relations between capitalist development, apartheid policies and the core structure of White supremacy are essentially collaborative, and conflicts which do take place between them are only over the marginal distribution of class benefits and constraints ..."[54] He refers to a range of policy concessions and adjustments in the interests of capital which reflect the pragmatic nature of apartheid as actually applied. He is certainly right in that many exemptions to Job Reservation regulations and Physical Planning Act restrictions on employment, as well as accommodation to the White skills-shortage by allowing some Black occupational mobility or job-fragmentation have occurred, to the benefit of management interests. This point, therefore, cannot be disputed, although, by and large, the more perceptive and policy-minded capitalists would probably disagree that the government has served their needs in a spirit of accommodation. Thus, while Johnstone's argument tends to *equate* White supremacy, Apartheid and capitalist development, the author's view is that the government in recent years has made private enterprise pay a price, as it were, for White unity, the gratification of White voter interests and for White supremacy in the longer term.

The difference between Johnstone's position and this author's position would largely disappear if one conceived of a "class coalition" between capitalists and White workers; if the situation is seen in these terms then the government appears as arbiter in regard to the terms of the "coalition." The notion of class-coalition, however, stretches considerably the definition of class (even if it is seen as a "race-class" system), and raises the important question of the social impulse behind the "coalition."

If, to this difficulty in imposing an exclusively class-based interpretation, consideration of other interests which Apartheid serves is added, then the utility of class as an *exclusive* and *central* analytical tool becomes even more problematic. The nature of Apartheid is such that *status* or *prestige* interests of Whites are also served;[55] the close government surveillance over Black occupational mobility, often to the detriment of capitalist development, attests to this. (Racial status is very definitely "ascribed," and occupational status is closely controlled.) The pattern of race separation in regard to access to residential privileges and all manner of recreational and social amenities quite clearly points to an accommodation of popular (i.e. non-capitalist) White material, social and cultural interests. One can, of course, still attempt to pursue the "centrality of class" theme by subsuming all these additional interests under the rubric of the "social formation" which particular relations of production generate. This, however, seems to be blurring the meaning of class even further, and if one has to encompass the historically-powerful (and currently still potent) element of Afrikaans nationalism, the notion of a class-based social formation as the *essence* of Apartheid becomes so widely extended that it loses much analytical value.

As already argued in Section I, this author concludes that South Africa is rather to be seen as a plural society, with separate Afrikaans and English-speaking corporate or communal groups in an uneasy kind of *basic* political agreement over the need to maintain a White oligarchy in the core areas of the country. This view does not deny the fact that corporate group interests and class interests tend to be superimposed and that class coalition is important in corporate group structure. Nor does it deny that different White groups have different views on how and to what extent White supremacy should be maintained.

The pluralism in South African society is not primarily a pluralism of cultural differences; it is a pluralism in which different communal (ethnic) groups have divergent economic, social, status, political and historico-cultural interests, with race having come to represent an index of most of these differences. Given these corporate group interests, and the salience of the numerical disadvantages of Whites, then many aspects of the rigidity and pervasiveness of Apartheid become explicable, as already suggested.

This particular conceptualisation of pluralism is of some value in a consideration of change. Certain changes in the Apartheid system are taking place and these can be briefly noted. Professor van Zyl Slabbert, an opposition member of parliament, has noted that in very recent times "What the Prime Minister has done is to introduce an element of flexibility in an apparently inflexible situation and for this he deserves credit."[56] Some of the changes have already been referred to in Section II. A few others may be noted. Thirty-year leasehold rights have been re-introduced for Africans in townships in "White" areas with rights to renew, sell, or bequeath (provided they have homeland citizenship cards); restrictions on African businesses in "White" area townships have been lifted; the government is planning to reconsider the laws which prevent wives from living with migrant worker husbands; hotels and restaurants in White areas will be allowed to apply for the right to accommodate and serve Blacks, multi-racial audiences will be allowed under a permit system; Blacks can now attain officer rank in the Defence Force with attendant status vis-à-vis Whites of lower rank; Coloureds, and presumably Indians, are to be appointed to certain statutory boards; magistrates have been instructed to establish multi-racial local committees to investigate and attempt to eliminate race friction, and, as a result of a prolonged confrontation between the Coloured Persons' Representative Council and the White cabinet, a Coloured-White inter-cabinet committee has been mooted by the government to (possibly) offer Coloured people some influence over high-level decision-making as it affects the Coloureds.[57]

One must, however, not be unguarded. These changes, and some others not mentioned, may well be "co-optive" strategies rather than progressive reforms; only time will tell what further advances may or may not be made. What is clear, however, is that policy *adjustments* are taking place. However, government spokesmen have made it quite clear that no deviations from the basic policy of Separate Development will be countenanced, and one must consider this stance in the light of the fact that the present government will rule for the immediate foreseeable future. (It has a comfortable majority support among the White electorate.)

This official orientation would, on the face of it, appear to set a clear limit to reforms and adjustments in policy. Yet, here is where the ambiguity of many aspects of Separate Development is relevant. As far as African homelands are concerned, Separate Development, on the one hand, would consign these areas to the economic and political periphery, on the other, as communal political systems the homelands could allow numerically powerful groups of Africans (Zulus, North Sothos, Tswanas) a freedom to mobilise with relative immunity from the coercive constraints acting upon other Black political movements. The homeland political organisation, within and outside of the homeland areas, could become power-bases from which African leaders might exercise political leverage.[58]

No clear indication for the future exists at this stage. Separate Development for the Coloureds, however, appears to have resulted in a greater degree of popular mobilisation than has ever existed before; the considerably radical majority Labour Party seems to enjoy widespread support in its current confrontation with the government;[59] a confrontation which has led to the widely-discussed probability of the inter-cabinet council referred to earlier.[60] Another factor relevant to change is the evidence of a great sense of bargaining strength and heightened labour action among the African proletariat in the cities (see Section II) which, if it advances, may ultimately create a crucial need for negotiation with "legitimate" Black leaders with support among the African workers.

The possible developments implied in this discussion may not manifest themselves; the government may succeed (for the foreseeable future) in defusing the situation by pursuing a strategy of co-option and consultation on issues not central to power and privilege, thereby winning time. The demonstration effects on Blacks of rapid and radical changes in neighbouring states (Mozambique, Rhodesia) and even the expectations aroused by current adjustments, are, however, likely to create a need for the process of conciliation and policy adjustment to continue.

One must, however, recognise that the corporate interests of White voters set a very definite ceiling on the extent to which any reforms can follow the path of racial assimilation or integration at the level of grassroots political and economic institutions. Basic to peaceful change is how a devolution of power can take place which, initially at any rate, circumvents White voter concerns and interests. The Dutch author Lijphart's concept of "elite co-operation" may be relevant to South Africa; he asserts that in a communally cleaved society, confrontation and reconciliation at a leader level may compensate for the lack of cross-cutting links and loyalties at the mass level.[61] Perhaps the most influential of the homeland leaders (for Blacks), Chief Buthelezi, has spelt out a federal framework in which such an accommodation could take place.[62] The current moves towards a federal or confederal arrangement in South West Africa (albeit currently in danger of producing highly unequal access to resources for different races) is another indication of the currency of this kind of direction for change.[63]

It is not being suggested that a devolution of power, and a progression of reforms of the system of inequality are *certain* to come about along the lines tentatively sketched above. What is suggested, however, is that the plural nature of South African society indicates that corporate group accommodation is probably one of the more feasible ways in which evolutionary (and therefore peaceful) change could occur. Lastly, it needs to be emphasised that this conclusion is in no way intended to suggest that official South African policy is to be condoned or supported as a means of achieving such change (federal or confederal solutions are still officially rejected at this stage). My argument is merely to suggest that there may well be ways of working towards change which do not assume the necessity of violent confrontation or armed struggle, and that these possible processes of change should be taken seriously.

## Notes

1. R. A. Schermerhorn, *Comparative Ethnic Relations*, New York: Random House, 1970, p. 6.
2. C. Orpen, "Authoritarianism Revisited: A Critical Examination of Expressive Theories of Prejudice" in S. J. Morse and C. Orpen (Eds.) *Contemporary South Africa*, Cape Town: Juta, 1975, p. 109; T. F. Pettigrew, "Personality and Sociocultural Factors in Intergroup Attitudes," *Conflict Resolution*, Vol. II, No. I, 1958.
3. Winthrop Jordan, *White over Black: American Attitudes towards the Negro, 1550–1812*, Baltimore: Penguin Books, 1968, Chapter I.
4. I. D. Maccrone, *Race Attitudes in South Africa*, Johannesburg: Witwatersrand University Press, 1957, p. 41.
5. This point is largely based on a re-interpretation of historical material presented by Maccrone (*op. cit.*) in L. Schlemmer, "Racial Attitudes in Southern Africa: The Contributions of Culture, Economic Interests and History," publication forthcoming in a volume being prepared by K. Heard and T. Shaw, Dalhousie University, Canada.
6. For a critical analysis of the Cape 'liberal tradition' see Phyllis Lewsen, "The Cape Liberal Tradition – Myth or Reality," *Collected Seminar Papers on the Societies in Southern Africa in the 19th and 20th Centuries*, Vol. 1, London: Institute of Commonwealth Studies, 1972; T. R. H. Davenport, "The Consolidation of a New Society" in *Collected Seminar Papers on the Societies in Southern Africa in the 19th and 20th Centuries, op. cit.*
7. Adrian Leftwich, "The Constitution and Continuity of South African Inequality: Some Conceptual Questions" in A. Leftwich (Ed.) *South Africa: Economic Growth and Political Change*, London: Allison and Busby, 1974, p. 140.
8. For a discussion of labour legislation in historical perspective, see, inter alia,

Denoon, *Southern Africa Since 1809*, London: William Clowes and Sons, 1972; and P. Randall (Ed.), *Power, Privilege and Property*, (Report of the SPRO-CAS Economics Commission), Johannesburg: SPRO-CAS and Ravan Press, 1972, particularly pp. 51, 52.

9. A policy initiated by the Afrikaans Nationalist-Labour Party *pact* Government which assumed power in 1924.
10. See, for example, M. Legassick, "South Africa: Forced Labour, Industrialisation and Racial Discrimination" in R. Harris (Ed.) *The Political Economy of Africa*, Boston: Schenkman, 1975, (an earlier draft was referred to), and H. Wolpe, "Capitalism and Cheap Labour Power; From Segregation to Apartheid," *Economy and Society*, Vol. 1, No. 4, November 1972. Wolpe makes a distinction between segregation and apartheid; the latter he sees as the ideological and policy mechanism by means of which labour supply was controlled with the emergence of a powerful secondary industrial sector. Segregation was a system appropriate to the earlier phase of accumulation in the agricultural and mining sectors.
11. See, for example, Philip Mason, *Patterns of Dominance*, London: Oxford University Press, 1970, Chapters 11 and 12.
12. For a slightly fuller discussion see Peter Randall (Gen. Ed.), *Towards Social Change*, Report of the Social Commission of SPRO-CAS, Johannesburg: SPRO-CAS and Ravan Press, 1971, pp. 21, 22.
13. Milton Rokeach, *The Open and Closed Mind*, New York: Basic Books, 1960.
14. The account which follows draws heavily on André du Toit, "Ideological Change, Afrikaner Nationalism and Pragmatic Racial Domination in South Africa," in L. Thompson and J. Butler (Eds.), *Change in Contemporary South Africa*, Berkeley and Los Angeles: University of California Press, 1975, pp. 19 to 50; N. J. Rhoodie, *Apartheid and Racial Partnership in Southern Africa*, Pretoria: Academica, 1969; F. A. van Jaarsveld, *Jan Van Riebeeck tot Verwoerd*, Johannesburg: Voortrekkerpers, 1971, F. A. van Jaarsveld, *Die Ontwaking van die Afrikaanse Nasionale Bewussyn, 1868–1881*, Johannesburg: Voortrekkerpers, 1957; T. Dunbar Moodie, *Power, Apartheid and the Afrikaner Civil Religion*, Ph. D. Thesis, Harvard University, 1971 (subsequently published as *The Rise of Afrikaner Nationalism*, Berkeley: University of California Press, 1975; and F. van Zyl Slabbert, "Afrikaner Nationalism, White Politics and Political Change in South Africa," in Thompson and Butler, *op. cit.*, pp. 3–18.
15. Du Toit, *op. cit.*, p. 37.
16. L. Schlemmer, *Privilege, Prejudice and Parties: A Study of Political Motivation among White Voters in Durban*, Johannesburg: South African Institute of Race Relations, 1973, pp. 50–57.
17. Du Toit, *op. cit.*, p. 42.
18. Rhoodie, *op. cit.*, pp. 77, 87–92.
19. De Klerk and Gardner have alluded to this as a factor differentiating the political thinking of some Afrikaners from that of the Anglo-Saxon tradition, see W. A. de Klerk "The Afrikaners" and Colin Gardner, "The English-speaking Whites" in P. Randall (Ed.) *South Africa's Minorities*, Johannesburg: SPRO-CAS (Ravan Press), 1971.
20. For further details on the patterns of discrimination dealt with in Section II, see, for example, Muriel Horrell, *Legislation and Race Relations*, Johannesburg: South African Institute of Race Relations, 1971; Muriel Horrell, *South Africa: Basic Facts and Figures*, Johannesburg, South African Institute of Race Relations, 1973; G. M. E. Leistner and W. T. Breytenbach, *The Black Worker of South Africa*, Pretoria: Africa Institute, 1975; L. Schlemmer, *Employment Opportunity and Race in South Africa*, (Studies in Race and Nations) Denver: Graduate School

of International Studies, University of Denver, 1972/3; United Nations Secretariat Unit on Apartheid, *Apartheid in Practice*, United Nations, 1971.

21. *Daily News*, 28.10.75.
22. The Minister of Labour, quoted in the *Natal Mercury*, 27.11.75.
23. See, for example, report of claims of victimisation in *Rand Daily Mail*, 18.4.74.
24. M. Horrell and D. Horner, *A Survey of Race Relations in South Africa, 1973*, Johannesburg: South African Institute of Race Relations, 1974, p. 280. See also, L. Douwes Dekker, *Are Works Committees Trade Unions?*, Johannesburg: South African Institute of Race Relations, 1973.
25. See Muriel Horrell, *South Africa's Workers*, Johannesburg: South African Institute of Race Relations, 1969.
26. *Ibid*, p. 73.
27. Institute for Industrial Education, *The Durban Strikes, 1973*, Durban: Institute for Industrial Education, 1974, p. 5.
28. Horrell and Horner, *op. cit.*, 1974, pp. 284, 285, and Institute for Industrial Education, *op. cit.*
29. *Natal Mercury*, 27.11.75.
30. Dudley Horner, *United States Corporate Investment and Social Change in South Africa*, Johannesburg: South African Institute of Race Relations (restricted document) 1971, Annexure A.
31. M. Horrell, D. Horner and J. Hudson, *A Survey of Race Relations in South Africa, 1974*, Johannesburg: South African Institute of Race Relations, 1975, p. 248.
32. For an assessment, see L. Schlemmer, *Employment Opportunity and Race in South Africa, op. cit.*, pp. 24, 30, 31.
33. J. J. Durand, *Swartman, Stad en Toekoms*, Cape Town: Tafelberg, 1970, Chapter 4.
34. Paper by Jill Nattrass, Department of Economics, University of Natal, Annual Congress of the Economic Society of South Africa, 1975.
35. M. Horrell, *South Africa's Workers*, Johannesburg: South African Institute of Race Relations, 1969.
36. Department of Statistics, *Bulletin of Statistics* and *Statistical Yearbook*, Pretoria: Government Printer, various dates. The estimates given are not entirely accurate since the "Blue-collar" category contains a small proportion of employees whose status may be equivalent to that of White-collar workers. The comparison is also approximate since the occupational definitions were not exactly comparable in all categories for the two censuses.
37. Quoted by Leistner and Breytenbach, *op. cit.*, p. 23.
38. *Ibid*, p. 29, quoting a speech by Prime Minister Vorster in 1973.
39. M. D. McGrath, "Income and Material Inequality in South Africa," Department of Economics, University of Natal, 1974, p. 9. (Publication forthcoming).
40. Based on information provided from official sources by Leistner and Breytenbach, *op. cit.*, p. 40.
41. See Summary of a paper by Etheredge in *Race Relation News*, Johannesburg: South African Institute of Race Relations, March, 1974.
42. Research by Peromnes Salary Surveys (Pty) Ltd. quoted in *Daily News*, 18.5.1972.
43. Quoted in M. Horrell, *et al.*, *op. cit.*, 1975, p. 236.
44. *Hansard* 1, Cols. 416–417, 1974.
45. See, for example, L. Schlemmer, "The Resettlement of Indians in Durban, and Some Economic, Social and Cultural Effects on the Indian Community," in *The Indian South African*, Durban: South African Institute of Race Relations, 1966.
46. M. Horrell, *et al.*, *op. cit.*, 1975, p. 156.

47. *Ibid.*, p. 156.
48. Calculated from M. Horrell, *op. cit.*, 1973, p. 89.
49. M. Horrell, *et. al.*, *op. cit.*, 1975, p. 389.
50. L. Schlemmer and P. Stopforth, *A Study of Malnutrition in the Nqutu District of KwaZulu*, Durban, Institute for Social Research, University of Natal, 1974.
51. M. Horrell, *Legislation and Race Relations, op. cit.*, 1971, pp. 22–26 and N. J. Rhoodie, *op. cit.*.
52. For further information on Homelands, see M. Horrell, *The African Homelands of South Africa*, Johannesburg: South African Institute of Race Relations, 1973.
53. M. Horrell, *op. cit.*, 1975, p. 214.
54. F. A. Johnstone, "White Prosperity and White Supremacy in South Africa Today," *African Affairs*, Vol. 69, April, 1970, p. 139.
55. See evidence for this in L. Schlemmer, *Employment Opportunity and Race in South Africa, op. cit.*
56. F. van Zyl Slabbert, M.P., "How Much has S.A. Changed?", *Sunday Times*, 5.10.75.
57. See, inter alia, Stanley Uya, "A Balance Sheet for Détente," *Sunday Times*, 21.9.75, and speech by Minister of Bantu Administration and Development, M. C. Botha, *Daily News*, 29.10.75.
58. See my analysis of KwaZulu: L. Schlemmer, "Social and Political Change in the African Areas: A Case Study of KwaZulu" in L. Thompson and J. Butler (Eds.) *Change in Contemporary South Africa, op. cit.*, pp. 107–138.
59. This support is suggested by statements of the Leader of the Coloured Labour Party, Mr. Sonny Leon: see inter alia, *Daily News*, 2.12.75. See also M. Horrell *et al.*, *A Survey of Race Relations in South Africa, 1975*, Johannesburg; South African Institute of Race Relations, forthcoming 1976.
60. See, inter alia, *Daily News*, 24.10.75.
61. Arend Lijphart, *The Politics of Accommodation: Pluralism and Democracy in the Netherlands*, Berkeley: University of California Press, 1968, and P. Randall (Ed.) *South Africa's Political Alternatives, op. cit.*, Ch. 9, 10, 11.
62. Chief M. G. Buthelezi, *White and Black Nationalism, Ethnicity and the Future of the Homelands*, Johannesbuig: South African Institute of Race Relations, 1974.
63. See assessment by Barend van Niekerk, "SWA: A New Spirit of Change," *The Star*, 22.10.75.

# Colour Discrimination and Policy Evolution in South Africa

CAS DE VILLIERS

CAS DE VILLIERS lives in Pretoria, Republic of South Africa. Formerly Editor of the Africa Institute's monthly *Bulletin* and other publications of the Institute, he is at present Director of the Foreign Affairs Association. Author of articles, regular columns, radio talks and a book on the French speaking countries of Africa, co-author of a book on communist strategy and on Africa and the challenges of the seventies. He obtained the degree BA (Hons) in Political Science at the Potchefstroom University and entered journalism in 1966. Was contributing Africa editor of the *Ensiklopedie van die Wêreld.* Travelled extensively in Africa and Europe in the execution of his duties and is a regular commentator on African and international matters.

# Colour Discrimination and Policy Evolution in South Africa

CAS DE VILLIERS

In discussions on discrimination in South Africa, colour or race are usually used as guidelines. Discrimination as such is a phenomenon found throughout the world; indeed, there is no country on earth that can claim to be free of all forms of discrimination. However, it is quite understandable that discrimination based on skin colour or race or ethnic affiliation is particularly indefensible. South Africa, motivated by questions of morality and validity, is herself trying to move away, as far as is practically possible, from this type of discrimination but far more significant content will have to be given to this process in the future.

It would be senseless to deny that discrimination based on colour exists in South African society. Without in any way attempting to endorse such discrimination, but at the same time mindful of the need to warn against too acute a condemnation of South Africa on this question, it would help to outline certain historical circumstances and realities that undoubtedly have a bearing on this important issue. One of these realities is that, although discrimination manifests itself in colour overtones in South Africa, it nevertheless corresponds in large measure with the more general type of discrimination that is found throughout the world and that results from the major differences in levels of civilization that exist between different nations.

In South Africa, in most cases, civilization or educational levels are characterized by skin colour. No one can deny that at this stage the Black or Coloured groups in South Africa have not reached the same living standards or levels of civilization or degree of technical know-how that are to be found amongst the greater percentage of the White group in the country. This inevitably leads to a situation in South Africa where there is a division between that group which provides the majority of entrepreneurs and employers (namely, the White group) and those groups which provide the overwhelming proportion of workers and labourers (the Coloured and Black groups within South Africa).

## I. Status and Skin Colour

Inevitably, skin colour is consequently used to determine status in society; it is indeed unfortunate that the employer/employee pattern with its inherent divisions of authority and status has largely come to be equated with skin colour. Because of this the outside world assumes that colour and nothing else characterizes discrimination in South Africa. Mr. R.F. Botha, South Africa's ambassador at the United Nations, said during debate in the UN on a motion to expel South Africa from the world organization:

> We do have discriminatory practices and we do have discriminatory laws. And it is precisely because of this that the greatest misunderstandings occur and our motives are most misrepresented. But that discrimination must not be equated with racialism. If we have that discrimination it is not because the Whites in South Africa have any "Herrenvolk" complex. We are not better than Black people, we are not cleverer than they are. What we can achieve so can they. Those laws and practices are a part of the historical evolution of our country, they were introduced to avoid friction and to promote and protect the interests and the development of every group and not only those of the Whites. But I want to state here today very clearly and categorically: My Government does not condone discrimination purely on the grounds of race or colour. Discrimination based solely on the colour of a man's skin cannot be defended. And we shall do everything in our power to move away from discrimination based on race or colour.

As a Black middle class emerges in South African society, a development that goes hand in hand with the expansion and improvement of Black educational and training facilities (numerous statistics can be quoted to show the strides being made in this regard), a greater degree of flexibility is discernible. Coupled with this is a steady dimunition of the determining rôle that colour plays in the overall status situation, in which norms of civilization and education play an important rôle. As is to be expected, more and more Blacks are moving into categories of skilled labour and services and this process is increasingly being accepted by Whites without protests being voiced at the principle of equality in labour.

One factor that should never be ignored in assessing the controversial issue of discrimination or racism in South Africa is the fact that deep-seated historical circumstances have resulted in a situation where the White community has for many years seen itself as the guardian, protector and even head of the other, Coloured races in South Africa. These historical processes gave rise to the unfortunate idea of White '*baasskap*' (hegemony) amongst some groups! This, in turn, prompted the use of slick propaganda to present White/Coloured relationships in South Africa as being concerned purely with discrimination based on colour. The fact that this form of discrimination has inbuilt benefits, and has ensured a degree of protection to Coloured groups, who would otherwise simply have been exposed to merciless competition from people living in more sophisticated democratic-capitalist communities, is regarded as totally irrelevant. The evidence provided by peoples such as the Maoris of New Zealand, the Red Indians of America, the Eskimos of Alaska and the Aboriginees of Australia, that less developed groups are always dominated by more sophisticated communities because of their weaker bargaining position is simply ignored when the South African situation is assessed.

## II. Separate Development and Minority Rights

Another factor that should be considered in respect of the severe criticism levelled about discrimination within South African society, is the fact that, as the Prime Minister has stated on several occasions, the South African policy of separate development – its discriminatory connotations and the instances of discrimination notwithstanding – is in no way based on a concept of discrimination; in other words, it is not based on any belief that the human dignity of one particular nation should enjoy a lower priority than that of another. Ambassador Botha in his October 1975 speech to the United Nations declared:

> Our policy is not based on any concepts of superiority or inferiority, but on the historical fact that different peoples differ in their loyalties, cultures, outlook and modes of life and that they wish to retain them.

The principle on which this policy is based is that of differentiation on the basis of what can be described as very real, deep-rooted and far-reaching cultural, religious, social, language and other differences in the heterogeneous community of South Africa. This heterogeneity is reflected in clearly distinguishable and diverse Black and Coloured groups which share the sub-continent of Africa with the White population. These differences are to be seen, inter alia, in the public utterances of Black leaders in South Africa. Chief Mangope of the Bophuthatswana Homeland recently reacted sharply to an appeal by Chief Buthelezi of KwaZulu for Black majority government and pertinently pointed out that he was not in favour of his own Tswana population being ruled by the numerically stronger Zulu nation! Similar sentiments are to be seen in a recent statement by Chief Sebe of the Ciskei. The rejection of the concept of one man, one vote is clearly visible in Africa in the 29 one-party states and 15 military regimes.

South Africa, looking to the background of so many tragedies in Africa and the world in general that can be related directly to the inability of nations and peoples effectively to accommodate group interests in an integrated system, has accepted the concept of separate sovereignty and separate freedoms for her divergent national groups. These separate sovereignties and freedoms are being exercised within the geographical areas which these distinctive nations can rightfully claim to be their national homelands by virtue of their original occupation of these areas. Black nations (which, in spite of the common denominator of a Black skin colour, display deep-rooted differences in cultural and in many other respects) are able to express their national aspirations by virtue of the principle of differentiated development, without being subject to the ethnic tensions that plague the heterogeneous tribal communities of Africa. This policy certainly does not imply that the entrenchment of discrimination is a fundamental motive!

Naturally, one should be honest enough to acknowledge that it is in the interests of White South Africans (who have lived in Africa for more than 300 years, during which period they developed their own language which is indigenous to Africa and during which they, like the Black Africans many years later, were involved in independence and freedom wars aimed at rejecting the Colonial yoke) to safeguard their own political position in this sub-continent. Indeed, it is a matter of survival and a natural and basic desire of all human beings to govern themselves and to have the opportunity to express their own national aspirations without let or hindrance. Were this not the case, an integrated Europe, for example, would not be such a remote ideal as is at present the case and one would not have a history of numerous abortive attempts at creating unity (Ireland, India, the old Federation of Rhodesia and Nyasaland are amongst many examples that can be quoted).

Had group interests not played a significant rôle and reached acute dimensions, 100,000 and more human beings would not have died in the recent Angolan civil war; earlier, the Biafran civil war would not have claimed 1,500,000 human lives; there would have been no war of genocide between the Blacks and Arabs in the Sudan that was to cost more than 500,000 lives; and there would have been no tribal conflict following the separation of Rwanda and Burundi, a conflict that was to claim 200,000 victims; Chad would not have been the scene of a bloody Muslim/Negroid war and there would have been no protracted civil war with its high toll of human life in Ethiopia.

These are but a few examples from Africa; many other Third World countries have succeeded in artificially creating stability through iron-fisted dictatorships in which the most acute forms of discrimination and tribal prejudice are practised!

## III. The Lusaka Manifesto and the Gradual Process

The much discussed Lusaka Manifesto of April 1969, in which Africa demanded recognition of human dignity, itself admits that in many African communities the ideals of equality and human dignity have not been achieved and that these ideals can only be attained by gradual processes. Where Africa, or rather Black Africa, concedes the need for evolutionary development, however, it advocates revolutionary and overnight change in South Africa – even though assumption of power by the Black groups which the OAU endorses could result in a repetition of the Angolan saga with results that would exceed even the dimensions of the horror of Angola. As far as the OAU is concerned, Xhosa, Zulu, Tswana or Sotho control of the whole of South Africa would not be a negation of the principle of majority rule – in the same way that the MPLA Government in Angola was apparently acceptable to the OAU and reconcilable with its ideal of "majority rule" in spite of the fact that there was every indication that this group did not enjoy popular support but achieved control of Angola through violent means.

All this notwithstanding, there are many in Africa and the world who have sympathy and understanding for South Africa and her problems and who are supporters or potential supporters of the South African formula for plural societies.

It is important in order to retain the support of these people, but even more important in the interests of peaceful co-existence in South Africa itself, that there be rapid and meaningful evolution of a policy which allows differentiation to occupy its rightful place but which provides for the total elimination of discrimination based on colour.

Institutionalized discrimination is to be found in various Acts and many of these instances of discrimination have an historical origin. However, they do represent a poison within the South African system that will have to be expunged both in the interests of a peaceful evolution of the country's domestic policy, and also in order to provide a weapon for those who are prepared to defend the country in the international community.

This writer believes that the policy or the framework of self determination is a marketable product within South Africa, and therefore overseas as well, and the proof of this is to be seen, inter alia, in the forthcoming independence of the Transkei. There are simply too many examples around the globe of the essential need to accommodate diverse interests in a plural society to permit the international community to ignore the fact of divergent racial, cultural, ethnic and religious sentiments and their effect on human communities; one need only point to countries such as India (which was compelled to give birth to Pakistan and Bangladesh), not to speak of the far-reaching effects that group interests have had and still have on the system in Ireland, Belgium and Cyprus.

South Africa can demonstrate successfully to the Black peoples within its borders, as well as to the outside world, that integration is not the answer to the problem of elimination of discrimination, because integration produces more acute and damaging forms of discrimination. On the other hand, it is also true that the logical outcome of the policy of self-determination within the South African system, with its divergent socio-economic systems, must be opportunities for all people to determine their own future in their own way within their own territorial areas.

The potential for this is already present in the Homelands principle but far greater content will have to be given to this principle and the pace of Homeland consolidation and Homeland development will have to be expedited. At the same time, and parallel to this development further momentum will have to be given to the moving away from discrimination, or else the relationship between South Africa and sovereign independent Homelands could well lead at an early stage to tension – something which the interdependent communities can ill afford.

## IV. The Third Phase of Separate Development

It is against the background of this factual situation that one must see the statement by the Prime Minister that South Africa's policy of separate development has now entered its third phase, a phase that can be described as the era of greater contact with greater understanding, in contrast with the earlier stages of greater separation aimed at elimination of friction. These concepts would appear prima facie to be paradoxical; but if the historical circumstances of South Africa at specific stages of its development are taken into consideration and if the political realities of the country are taken cognizance of, then these can be seen as a reflection of the logical evolution and development of the policy of separate development and as a further advance towards the ideal of total elimination of colour discrimination. All this implies that certain legislation which was placed on the Statute Book during the period in which emphasis was placed on greater separation will have to be eliminated as concrete expression is given to the new, third phase of separate development.

To those who regard independent Black Homelands as merely another manifestation of discrimination, one can with justification ask whether it really is discrimination to prevent Black nations from seeking their own salvation. Why, it might be asked, was the Federation of Rhodesia and Nyasaland allowed to disintegrate merely because of the national aspirations of the participating partners?; why is it, one might be tempted to ask, that Norway, Finland and Sweden are to-day three countries rather than a single constitutional entity, in spite of their high level of homogeneity in so far as socio-cultural background, language and other aspects are concerned?; and why is it that there is no decisive attempt to unite the peoples of East and West Germany?; why, if one is to pursue this line ad nauseum, is it that the world is quite prepared to-day to accept two Koreas, a Bangladesh, a Pakistan, the separate existence of Northern Ireland and the Irish Republic as well as the withdrawal of Singapore from the Malaysian Federation – but repudiates and rejects the establishment in South Africa of sovereign Black Homelands, several of which have a greater degree of viability measured in terms of capital resources, development potential and even per capita income than many of the current independent Black states of Africa? Why, it could well be asked, must the different nations of South Africa be unwilling victims of the mistakes of British colonialism merely because the outside world would like to see the scale of tragedies that have come from forced integration in so many African countries repeated in the sub-continent of Southern Africa?

The various national communities of Southern Africa will never be able to satisfy those who advocate a process of equality or who regard integration as a *sine qua non* for the elimination of discrimination. In any event, if the one man, one vote concept has any validity, then the whole of Africa is open game for these latter day political missionaries! The fact of the matter, however, is that South Africa and its various communities have been able to demonstrate to those who believe in the inevitability of group interests manifesting themselves in plural societies, that separate freedoms constitute the best guarantee for the recognition of these diverse interests in heterogeneous societies.

This in no way implies that there will not continue to be discrimination within the South African system, for after all discrimination is inherent in human nature and will always manifest itself to a lesser or greater degree in the outlook and actions of human beings. After all, do not the Negro communities of America still protest to-day that there is discrimination practised against them, even though legal impediments against full Negro participation in American society have long since been removed? And do not millions of migrant workers in Europe still in this enlightened age find themselves the victims of racial discrimination to the extent that governments in Germany, France, the Netherlands and elsewhere are unable to protect them effectively against the racial animosity displayed by host populations? No institutionalized or legislative obstacles are placed in the way of these people; yet they are the victims of social discrimination for the simple reason that there is a degree of inherent racial animosity that does not require a student in sociology to unearth and which will for many generations to come play a significant role in the relationships between different human groups.

The Black/White connotation of discrimination in South Africa, however, makes it a more explosive and more exploitable commodity for leftist agents than is the case in other parts of the world. Those whose objective it is to undermine South African society know full well that they must win the hearts and the minds of the people if their revolutionary objectives are to succeed. Communist teaching is that the people are to an army what water is to a fish and in this context South Africa is confronted with a campaign of subversion directed at estranging Black and White. The banner of racial discrimination is raised high in this propaganda campaign.

## V. Moving Away from Discrimination

Quite apart from the element of self-interest which is present amongst all South Africans who desire the consolidation of sound human relationships, the South African policy is, when all is said and done, firmly rooted in morality and justice, as would be expected in a Christian community, and even if no other considerations were relevant it would be essential to seek the progressive removal of discrimination based on colour (as indeed is already the case) in the interests of morality.

The Minister of Information and of the Interior, Dr. Connie Mulder, stated unequivocally in a speech in Middelburg in June 1975 that it was his Government's policy to move away from discrimination. He said that this was no panic-stricken flight but the manifestation of a policy that kept pace with reality. He added that discrimination on the grounds of colour could no longer be accepted. Certain facilities would have to be shared, although separate facilities for all was the ideal of the policy of separate development. Where such separate facilities did not exist, facilities would have to be shared. The Nico Malan Theatre in Cape Town had been opened to all population groups in accordance with this principle. Decisions in this regard would have to be made in accordance with local circumstances.

The Prime Minister, Mr. B. J. Vorster, has repeatedly pledged himself to an improvement in the position of the Black, Coloured and Indian population groups; the elimination of unnecessary discrimination based on colour; the narrowing of the wage gap between the different population groups; the improvement of training facilitites for all population groups and the training of Black diplomats.

The Minister of Bantu Administration and Development, Mr. M. C. Botha, said in a speech in November 1975 that the provision of facilities for Black people in the White areas of South Africa was merely a matter of time. He said that the development of the Black population groups had created new requirements and aspirations over and above basic subsistence needs. He added that he was fully aware of the need to provide a wide range of facilities in order to cushion the effect of modern urban life, and he referred specifically to the provision of facilities such as theatres, cinemas and recreational amenities.

Dialogue between the various national groups represents one of the most important instruments for eliminating friction. The Prime Minister met all the Homeland leaders at a joint meeting in March 1974, and a statement issued afterwards declared that the leaders had discussed various matters of the greatest importance for the Black peoples of South Africa. These included independence for the Homelands, racial discrimination, Homeland consolidation, the wage gap and the disparity in the revenue and expenditure of the Homelands, the position of the urban Black man and Black businessmen in White urban areas, the medium of tuition in Black schools in urban areas and the gradual elimination of influx control. The Prime Minister emphasized that measures which had nothing to do with the elimination of racial friction should be removed from the Statute Book. He also gave a categoric assurance that his door was open at all times for the leaders of the Black and Coloured groups.

### *A. Indians and Coloureds*

Mr. Vorster had a series of discussions in January 1975 with members of the Indian Council, the Coloured Persons' Representative Council and all the Homeland leaders. Ways of moving away from discrimination were frequently raised during the course of these discussions. After the meeting between the Prime Minister and members of the Coloured Persons' Representative Council, a joint statement was issued in which the Premier stated clearly that it was the policy of his Government to eliminate discriminatory measures that no longer served any useful purpose. He said that the Cabinet would discuss the systematic and orderly elimination of unnecessary and irritating measures. One example mentioned in the joint statement was the question of facilities such as hotels for Coloureds, and it was announced that practical ways of removing problems were currently being studied.

It was also proposed that the standard of Coloured education should be raised and that Coloured education should in no way be inferior to that of White education. The Prime Minister emphasized anew that the principle of equal pay for Coloured personnel, especially those in the administration of Coloured Affairs, would be introduced with the minimum of delay. He said that in so far as the position and future of the Coloured population was concerned, he was awaiting the report of the Erika Theron Commission. The Commission was appointed to make a thorough study of the position of the Coloured people in South African society, and to submit recommendations on how the position of Coloureds could be improved.

The *Erika Theron* report was published in June 1976. This report, containing 178 recommendations which could fundamentally change the future of South Africa's Coloured community, inter alia emphatically states:

In the process of constitutional adjustment it will have to be accepted that the existing Westminister founded system of government will have to be changed to adapt it to the specific requirements of the South African plural structure.

The report touches on all issues from race classification and the Immorality Act to labour and consumer problems; from sport, separate amenities and group areas to education, culture and religion; from welfare, medical care, housing, to transport, business and agriculture. The *Erika Theron* report will, regardless of opposition to certain of the recommendations, undoubtedly pave the way towards a new deal for the Coloured people in South Africa and must be regarded as an important document and contribution towards the elimination of racial discrimination within South Africa.

Opposition that one might expect against direct representation for the Coloureds in the South African Parliament and the repealing of the Mixed Marriages Act and Section 16 of Immorality Act, must be seen against the background of the vast contrast within the Coloured community between the more educated and civilised and an underdeveloped section. This naturally also has a bearing on acceptance in the White's community of the larger section of the Coloured community. It would therefore be unrealistic not to realise that some of the recommendations of the *Erika Theron* report will be met by opposition from governmental circles, forced to take cognizance of political realities in a democratic society, but this need not necessarily lead to an altogether stalemate situation, already clear from the fact that by far the majority of the 178 recommendations are acceptable to the government.

It is furthermore quite significant that the government accepts the fundamental declaration of the *Theron* report, touching on the necessity of constitutional adjustments and the weaknesses of the Westminister founded system for the specific needs and requirements of the South African plural structure. South Africans at least realise the necessity of a meaningful accommodation, political and otherwise, of the Coloured community and the *Erika Theron* report with its substantial recommendations can pave the way towards this end. This will, however, also embrace a change of attitudes, but this is a process that has already gained considerable momentum, which is particularly reflected in the new role the Afrikaans press is playing in this respect. Hardly a day passes without comment in news media on matters affecting the position of Coloureds, Indians and urban Blacks. One can rightfully refer to a new consensus developing amongst South Africans on the question of future accommodation patterns in South Africa. The *Erika Theron* report can foster this development.

The *Erika Theron* report may well indicate that the South African policy of self-determination is not a policy moulded into a rigid and inflexible framework. The evolvement of a new accepted deal for Coloureds, Indians and urban Blacks within South Africa, will ultimately be the test stone for this assumption.

As regards the position of the Indian community in South Africa, the Prime Minister has stated in several discussions with delegations of the Indian Council that the Indian population of South Africa had the same prospects as those envisaged for the Coloured peoples. He added that in addition to administering their own affairs, the Indian and Coloured communities of South Africa would also be given a direct say and participation in matters of mutual interest by means of full representation in statutory bodies, councils and commissions.

The Deputy Minister of Information, Mr. Louis le Grange, said in May that the Government had repeatedly stated that it could not endorse discrimination on the basis of race or colour and that the Government would do everything in its power to move away from such practices. He added that this issue would in many respects determine South Africa's future in Africa and accordingly in the outside world at large. He said that the Government's policy in this respect had had beneficial results in numerous areas of South African life. The Department of Coloured Affairs, for example, had taken the initiative in eliminating friction and had asked magistrates throughout South Africa to establish local committees, with equal representation of Whites and Coloureds, which could investigate and remove sources of racial friction.

### *B. Inequality in the Labour Field*

The progress made towards the elimination of indefensible inequality has been most marked in the labour field. The London Institute for the Study of Conflict stated in a report early in 1975, that the urban Black worker in South Africa received one of the highest wages in Africa. The starting salary of Black underground miners on gold and coal mines was increased drastically by 37% in June 1975, as compared with a 14% salary increase for Whites. The National Development and Management Foundation of South Africa reported at about the same time that the wages of Black workers in South Africa had risen by 16% in the preceding 12 months.

Professor P. W. Hoek, writing in *South Africa 1975*, affirms that the wages of Black workers in the White areas of South Africa are amongst the highest on the African continent. According to Professor Hoek, wages for unskilled labourers are roughly twice as high as in most other African states, while the average industrial wage for Black workers in South Africa is 80% higher than in Ghana, which has one of the highest figures in Africa. The purchasing power of the Black population in real terms increased by 69% during the 1960s – a figure substantially higher than the comparable figure for Whites. The Port Elizabeth Municipality has been paying equal salaries for equal work to Coloureds and Whites since July 1, 1975. The Johannesburg City Council has also announced that it is drastically narrowing the wage gap between Whites and Blacks in its employ; since the beginning of 1976, Coloureds have been receiving 85% and Blacks 75% of the salaries earned by Whites in comparable posts.

### *C. Housing*

Housing represents another area of friction in so far as inequality of treatment of different population groups is concerned. Significant progress is, however, being made in eliminating discrimination in this sphere. For instance, a housing project for Coloured workers undertaken by the Cape Chamber of Commerce is nearing completion. This project, undertaken in co-operation with the University of Cape Town and built by a consortium of 58 companies, comprises a complex of 149 houses and has been built in consultation with the future owners.

The Minister of Bantu Administration and Development, Mr. M. C. Botha, announced in Parliament in May 1975 that home ownership for Black citizens in cities outside the Homelands was being re-introduced. He pointed out that about 120,000 of the 440,000 houses in Black residential areas outside the Homelands already belonged to Black owners. He added that trading rights for urban Blacks in their own residential areas were being brought into conformity as far as possible with the conditions pertaining to White trading rights. In all Black residential areas, Black medical practitioners and other professional persons would immediately be given the right to full ownership of their consulting rooms or offices. Ambitious plans for the improvement of housing have been initiated in Lenasia, the big Indian residential suburb outside Johannesburg. Most of the 6,000 houses available to the population of more than 35,000 have been built by the National Housing Commission from funds made available by the Department of Community Development. The other, more luxurious houses, have been built by private contractors for prominent members of the Indian community, and compare with the standard of housing in the most exclusive White residential suburbs.

### *D. Education*

Great strides have been made in the educational sphere in recent years, especially in so far as the provision of educational facilities for non-White groups is concerned. The Minister of Indian Affairs, Mr. S. M. Steyn, revealed in a speech in June 1975 that of the 180,715 Indian children at school in 1974, 11,764 were in the final two years of their school career. About 8,000 Indians above the Junior Secondary level were entering the labour market every year. A total of 2,081 degrees and 910 diplomas had been conferred on Indians at the University of Durban-Westville in the period 1960–1974.

SABRA stated in a report in 1975 that there had been a 295% increase in the number of Indian schoolchildren in the period 1946–1962, in comparison with a population increase of 69% over the same period. Indian pupils have free education and compulsory education is gradually being introduced.

It was also announced in 1975 that an independent university would be established to train Black medical, dental and veterinary personnel. Announcing this, the Minister of Bantu Education, Mr. M. C.

Botha, told Parliament that the university would be established at Garankuwa, north-west of Pretoria. He emphasized that the Government hoped for the co-operation of the three existing Black universities in South Africa so that the new university could be of benefit to all the Black population groups in the country.

### *E. Sport*

The separation of public facilities and recreational and sporting amenities was a principle of separate development that, far from eliminating friction, caused a great deal of friction in its practical application. Not only did it have internal implications but it also was used as an instrument for isolating South Africa in the outside world, as was to be seen in South Africa's exclusion from the Olympic Games, as well as from international rugby, cricket and other areas of sporting endeavour. The question of totally segregated audiences at public concerts also led to many overseas artists, who would otherwise have been prepared to come to South Africa, deciding to boycott the local scene.

A noticeable improvement has been discernible in this area in recent times. Many towns and cities have opened their parks for all races and some libraries have similarly been declared open libraries. Certain hotels and restaurants in White areas have been opened to all races, while in other cities theatres have opened their doors to all population groups.

A welcome evolution has occurred on the sports fields of South Africa in recent years. One of the highlights of the 1973 sporting calendar was the South African Games held in March, which attracted 498 entries from 33 countries and another 993 entries from all race groups in South Africa. Another important milestone in the development of non-White sport was reached in 1973 with the establishment of a special fund for the development of sporting and recreational facilities for non-Whites.

Yet another 1973 sporting highlight was the Derrick Robins cricket tour of the Republic – the tourists becoming the first visiting cricket team to be composed on a multi-racial basis. During its tour, the team played a Black South African cricket team, amongst others. The Italian rugby team that toured South Africa in 1973 also met Black and Coloured sides. The International Wanderers cricket team met a multinational South African XI in an unofficial "mini-test" series in 1976.

Progress towards fuller participation by non-Whites in sport in South Africa began as early as 1970, with the non-White Games. Since then, open tournaments have been held in tennis, golf, athletics, cycling, soccer and many other minor sports, while non-Whites have accompanied tours overseas, either as individuals or as members of mixed teams.

Implicit in the Government's sports policy is the fact that as the various national groups advance in respect of sporting prowess, more and better sporting facilities will be made available to them. They have already been given many opportunities to participate in international competition. Any non-White who can compete on merit in a particular sport is given every opportunity to participate in open and international tournaments at any venue in South Africa. This is in accordance with Government policy that each population group should organize its own activities at club and provincial level, but that full opportunities should be provided for participation in activities at international and multi-national levels.

Dr. P. G. J. Koornhof, Minister of Sport and Recreation, announced in March 1975 that the Government had given its approval to the selection of a multi-national rugby team to play the touring French side, as well as to a multi-national cricket team to meet the Derrick Robins tourists. Dr. Koornhof said in a speech in the Senate in April 1975, that the Government would do everything in its power to help sportsmen and sportswomen of all races to achieve the highest rung in the ladder of their respective sports. He added that considerable progress had already been made in creating facilities and opportunities for the Black and Coloured population groups and that numerous opportunities had been provided for Whites in South Africa to compete against international teams. At that stage, he said, permission had already been granted for 65 multi-national tournaments in South Africa.

## VI. Multi-national Development

The whole question of the desire to move away from discrimination in South Africa remains a delicate one. A Cabinet committee is currently drawing up a report on discriminatory measures that no longer have validity in South Africa. This indicates the high priority placed on this question by the Government. Private organizations, study groups, politicians and others are also concentrating studies on this question.

It is clear that the elimination of measures that are tantamount to the unequal treatment of specific race groups in South Africa is totally reconcilable with the policy of multi-national development.

At the same time, it should be clear that the whole question of discrimination cannot be over-simplified and that there are very real problems and obstacles that defy instant solutions. As the non-White peoples advance towards a higher level of civilization and an improved development pattern and as the Whites show new perspectives in their attitude towards contact with non-Whites within the broad framework of multi-national development, certain statutory strictures and institutions which entrench indefensible and unjust colour discrimination will undoubtedly be removed and eliminated. This, in turn, will help remove obstacles that stand in the way of sound relationships between the various population groups and will lead to the creation of an honourable but more orderly pattern of co-existence.

All this, however, must be achieved within the very specific, and hence restrictive framework of a democratic system, with all the implications this has of dependence on endorsement by the South African electorate. This type of evolution demands political manoeuverability which, in turn, is greatly dependent on a well-informed electorate. It implies the cultivation of sound mutual sentiments and an understanding of electoral limitations and, because of this, even greater demands and challenges will confront South Africa and its leaders. More and more will spontaneous mutual loyalty between the divergent population groups of South Africa depend on the meaningful implementation of a policy totally stripped of its discriminatory elements, a policy which in its implementation will have to take cognizance of Homelands which must indubitably be in a position to accommodate and expand their national aspirations, national pride and human dignity.

South West Africa today is the evidence of political mobility and flexibility in racial attitudes that can also gain further momentum in the Republic of South Africa itself. The process of the elimination of racial discrimination in South West Africa is undoubtedly remarkable, to such an extent that even the country's most outspoken critics have to recognise this fact. If developments in a so-called conservative and rigid White-dominated South West African community, could be that meaningful, then the omens for equally substantial changes in racial attitudes amongst Whites and Blacks in the Republic of South Africa seem to be promising.

South West Africa set a heartening pace and South Africans need not be far behind. The progress of this process in South Africa will be the only real proof for the quality of the adaptibility in the South African community, and for the viability of the policy of self-determination. In this respect I'd like to conclude from an article on the *Lost Tribe* in The Economist on 24 April 1976:

> But the Afrikaner Tribe at the tip of the continent . . . is a very special case indeed. It is built, and organized, around the instinct for survival. It has nowhere else to go. It has been there long enough to have begun to understand the Africa it lives in. It commands a formidable military and security apparatus that can doubtless allow it to survive, bloodily for ten to fifteen years or so. But better than that, its survival instinct, and its loneliness, may lead it to make the adaptations it will have to make if it is to survive for longer than ten to fifteen years.

# Affirmative Action and American Universities

ALLAN C. ORNSTEIN

DR. ORNSTEIN is an American professor, writer, researcher, and Fulbright Hayes Scholar. He is the author of more than 100 articles and 14 books, among them *Race and Politics in School/Community Organizations* (Goodyear, 1974), *Reforming Metropolitan Schools* (Goodyear, 1975), *Teaching in a New Era* (Stipes, 1976), and *Introduction to the Foundations of Education* (Rand McNally, 1977). His consultant work varies and includes work for the Educational Testing Service, American Federation of Teachers, American Educational Research Association, U.S. Congress, and the New York City-Chicago-Evanston-Montreal school boards.

# Affirmative Action and American Universities

ALLAN C. ORNSTEIN

Most Americans agree that the stigma of past discrimination against minorities and women must be overcome, that America is a highly polarized society, and that something must be done to increase equality and depolarization. But the increasing trend toward giving preferential treatment toward people because of their minority or female status is rapidly causing national controversy and uneasiness; there is concern of increasing reverse discrimination against individuals who bear no responsibility for past discrimination. A few middle-ranking bureaucrats who were never elected by the people, and who are not responsible to them, have introduced their own interpretation of the law and have imposed by fiat a quota system based on race and sex.

Guidelines originally set forth in a dispute involving construction companies in Philadelphia – where there were minority hiring problems – have been transferred from this specific situation to all institutions with government contracts of $ 50,000 or more or employing twenty-five or more people or both. Officials in the Department of Health, Education and Welfare have taken a plan devised for an uneducated pool of workers and proclaimed that the same minority percentages must be applied to the work force (since 1972 this has been extended to include females) in other fields such as universities, legal and medical organizations, private industry, labour unions, civil service, and others. And, if qualified persons are not available, standards must then be lowered to meet appropriate body counts. Although this paper will focus on American universities, the data are germane to nearly all sectors of the American economy.

## I. Quotas and Faculty Employment

According to federal guidelines, the goal of equal opportunity has become synonymous with equality of results for certain protest groups, who also claim to be the victims of past discrimination. With this change in the meaning of equality, the U.S. Commission on Civil Rights states that the number of minority persons found in employment at every level must be "equal to their proportions in the population."[1] In other words, the concept of equality has shifted into actual employment of minorities. These minorities include blacks, persons with Spanish surnames, American Indians, Orientals, and women, but not Italians, Poles, Greeks, other white ethnics, poor whites, Catholics, or Jews. Needless to say, those eligible for preferential treatment are not the only ones who have been discriminated against in the past in some way.

Applying the criterion of population proportions to jobs, the Department of Health, Education and Welfare has forced institutions of higher learning to adopt affirmative action plans that will ensure that their staffs reflect the specified balance or else be sued or lose federal funds or both. Already some American universities have had their funds cut off, not because they were found guilty of specific acts of discrimination, but because their attempt to come up with an affirmative action plan did not satisfy a particular bureaucrat. Hundreds of universities have been sued, too. Their cases are pending because faculty or salary ratios were not similar, irrespective of reasons.[2]

By relying on statistical guides for ascertaining the presence of discrimination, and thus ignoring the all important criterion of qualification, the American federal government is undermining the integrity and scholarly functions of universities. Some numerical targets tend to be based on body counts that are proportional to the general population; others tend to be based on the local populace. Both statistical counts are used, generally whichever is more advantageous in a given area to the minorities who are chosen for preferential treatment. But professors are not recruited from the general population (about 12 percent black) or even from the adult population (about 9 percent black) of which the black proportion is less than the total percentages. They come from the pool of college graduates with at least a master's degree and preferably a Ph.D. of which the latter percent of blacks is less than 1 percent. Indeed it is the manpower pool, not the general or adult population, that should be considered in deciding affirmative action policies; this is, in fact, true for all jobs.

In 1972 there were less than 1,500 black Ph.D.'s, not all of them in higher education. It is impossible for institutions of higher learning to have an "adequate" representation of blacks on their faculties without lowering scholastic requirements. Ironically, blacks comprise 5.5 percent of the four-year college faculties.[3] If realistic manpower pools are considered, they are already overrepresented and exceed the racial balance in terms of what their formal education suggests. But the Department of Health, Education and Welfare demands faculty percentages that correspond with population proportions. (The same twisted logic holds true for other sectors of the economy. For example, less than 2 percent of engineers are black; yet in theory Chicago engineering firms are supposed to have a 35 percent black engineering staff to reflect the surrounding population.) But it is difficult to discern whether the differential number of black-to-white academic doctorates reflect so-called racism in society, and nothing else such as cultural and family factors the incidence of higher desertion and illegitimacy, the use of drugs, poor academic performance, and the like. Liberal and minority apologists tend to rely on "racism" to explain away all black-white differences. Any other interpretation is considered threatening, and efforts are made to limit such discussions.

A similar approach can be applied to women.[4] As many as 22 percent of all college and university teaching positions were held by women in 1972, while only 13 percent of all Ph.D.'s have been granted to women. This suggests that there are already more women on American university staffs than would normally be expected. It could be argued that in the past males with the same qualifications as females have had greater opportunities in private industry and government, and thus the options of women have been constricted to university slots. This could account for some of the discrepancies in the Ph.D. pool and in the large number of female faculty members. It would certainly not illustrate university discrimination, but the opposite. Nevertheless, these institutions are being forced to make up for deficiencies that are non-existent (if the manpower pool is considered) in the female-male, as well as the black-white, faculty ratios. Certainly there are no substantial differences in intelligence, academic talent, or scholarly potential between the sexes. It is not easy to determine whether the differential number of female-to-male academic doctorates reflect biases in graduate schools or is merely a consequence of most women devoting their energies to family life rather than careers. Nearly all Ph.D. programmes have admitted candidates on a competitive basis, although some professors have rejected women in the past because of the belief that the degree would be wasted because they would eventually devote their time to marriage and raising children. Studies and statistics suggest that females feel that marriage determines the "success" of many women and that their careers are secondary. Although some feminists might claim that past restricted job opportunities for women hindered their motivation to pursue an advanced degree, and although there may be some validity in this claim, it would be difficult to show this cause-effect relationship.

### A. *Top Positions and High Salaries*

Black and feminist advocates are quick to point out that their groups do not get a fair share of top positions or high salaries. This is also a misleading claim, which nonetheless gets results because of federal pressure and the apprehension of university officials lest they may have to answer the charges of "racism" and "sexism." With institutions of higher learning, the general rule is that the higher positions and salaries tend to go to those who have a doctorate degree and have proven their capability and productivity over the years. The Ph.D. count has already been discussed. As for meritocracy (based on quantity), Richard Lester, in his report for the Carnegie Commission of Higher Education, has summarized several studies that show there are major differences in research and publications between men and women – a difference of about 4:1 in articles and 2:1 in books and monographs – and apparently greater differences between whites and blacks.[5] Several reasons are advanced, with emphasis on the difference in societal and marriage roles between the sexes,[6] the differences in the equality of education and training, and the dual system of admitting and grading white and black college students. Hence, degrees are not equivalent.

In 1973 the male-to-female salary discrepancies were 2.5 percent in favour of men,[7] quite different from today's frequently heard charges of a salary "discrimination gap" between male and female professors. The data for salary discrepancies between races was unobtainable, although current trends suggest reverse racism. No matter how unpopular it seems, the smaller proportion of women and blacks in high paying jobs in the past, and the within-group differences for the same rank, seem to be in part a reflection of the Ph.D. qualification and professional output, and not solely a result of discrimination, as it is often alleged. Thus must be asked the crucial question: Is the institution that seeks to reward merit discriminating? The enforcement procedures of the Department of Health, Education and Welfare, with their witless fervour and bigotry, say yes.

### *B. Arbitrary Goals and Timetables*

In the meantime, arbitrary "goals" and "timetables" are being imposed on American institutions of higher learning by threats of reprisal. The Department compliance officers usually presume the institutions guilty of discrimination against minorities and women until substantial evidence has been produced to the contrary. This reflects the biases of the investigators who are predominantly (85 percent) black or female or both,[8] with blacks occupying most of the top positions. These compliance officers also claim that certain minorities are more eligible than others for preferential treatment. They act as prosecutor, judge, and jury; they review files and records; they sometimes make outrageous demands and threaten to impose, and frequently do, legal and monetary hardships. Not only do the interpretations of the President's Executive Orders (those laws that form the basis of affirmative action) continuously change, whereby institutions are often given ninety days to make "appropriate" adjustments in their numerical targets, but there is also great inconsistency among the Department investigators in making their demands. Zealous threats are also made in violation of the federal guidelines. And many college administrators claim that because they are given insufficient notice of complaints filed against them, they are unable to take remedial action or defend themselves. And the courts seem to be taking the position that the accused must prove their innocence – characteristic of the inquisitorial trials of medieval Europe.[9]

The Department of Health, Education and Welfare has been extremely slow in approving or disapproving affirmative action plans. Delay of up to twelve to eighteen months are common, and the rejection rate is extraordinarily high. For example, between 1972 and 1975 as many as 33 out of approximately 700 plans were approved; it is important to add that most of the plans were approved on the condition that further efforts be undertaken to improve minority hiring and promotions.[10] The remarkably slow action for approving these affirmative action plans does not necessarily connote unreasonable goals and timetables. Rather, it suggests a lack of expertise within the Department to judge the validity of goals for different institutions of higher learning (whose stress on merit and competence vary); the inability of the compliance officers to interpret statistical data; biases (based on sex and race) of screening committee members within the Department; variation in enforcement demands at the regional and national levels (also based on the personal characteristics of the leadership at those levels); changes in regulations and laws; and the small compliance staff and the high turnover within that staff.

During a time of retrenchment and with the threat of legal action or curtailment of federal money hanging over its head, the particular university will rid itself of its potential liabilities when re-negotiating with the Department of Health, Education and Welfare, that is, the practical alternative is to surrender its integrity. And, then, university officials seek to protect their jobs and limit their amount of expended energies; thus, it is common for American university officials to submit to federal pressure.

The following passage from the testimony of former President James Hester of New York University before the Special Subcommittee of the U.S. Congress on Education and Labor in September 1974 illustrates the kind of problem the universities are facing:

> Since 1968, we have been involved in at least 43 complaints before the City of New York Commission on Human Rights, the New York State Division of Human Rights, the U.S. District Court, and the EEOC. Every one of the 34 completed cases has either been dismissed, withdrawn, or results in a decision in favour of the University; nine cases are still pending.[11]

Similarly the University of Maryland, after continuous investigations by local compliance officers, which were construed as both harassment and illegal, turned around and sued the Department of Health, Education and Welfare. The result was that the Department backed down from pursuing its efforts and imposing sanctions. If university officials are willing to confront the bureaucrats, they can curtail some of the mounting abuses. The examples set by New York University and the University of Maryland indicate that the Department can be thwarted. But, for common sense reasons, most institutions of higher learning are reluctant to expend that kind of effort and risk the possible consequences of standing up to the federal bureaucracy. And this suggests that affirmative action may result in a stark remodelling of the criteria of professionalism and merit. In fact, the point may have already been reached, according to President William J. McGill of Columbia University, where "the determination of superior ability and special excellence (is now viewed by) some officials as a mask for continuing discrimination."[12]

Officials of the Department of Health, Education and Welfare contend that absence of proportional representation of minorities and of women in an academic department reflects "exclusion" and "deficiencies." One university department found guilty can result in the entire university having its funds cut off, a twisted and dangerous example of logic. Certainly there could be a department head who discriminated and created an all majority department. However, there could also be a department head who created a predominantly or all-minority department (for example, ethnic studies, home economics, nursing). But the Department of Health, Education and Welfare is only concerned about the absence of minorities and women and usually ignores the latter department. It also fails to consider that the small size of most departments (less than 10 members) would distort the outcome of statistical analysis. Most important, since the late 1960s, the more than 2,500 institutions of higher learning awared Ph.D.'s to only two women in meteorology; six in agronomy (crop agriculture); and less than ten (estimated) in pharmacy, nuclear chemistry, theoretical chemistry, electromagnetism, optical physics, civil engineering, and sanitary engineering. With regard to total fields during this period, American women earned 0.5 percent of the Ph.D.'s in engineering, 2.3 percent in agriculture, 2.9 percent in physics, 3 percent in business administration, 3.5 percent in earth science, 4 percent in ecology, 7 percent in mathematics, and 7.6 percent in chemistry. Although the data are unavailable for blacks, the figures can be expected to be substantially lower since the total supply of Ph.D.'s in all fields for all years through 1972 was 1,500 – with nearly half in the field of education.[13] Even multiplying by 1,000 the degree output each year for the subsequent five years (the period usually provided by the Department of Health, Education and Welfare to make up deficiencies) would not provide a sufficient pool of females and blacks for departments needing such personnel. Over half the departments in colleges and universities had less than fifty female doctorates (and an estimated three black Ph.D.'s available from the nation's manpower pool) from which to recruit during the period 1958–1967,[14] when most hiring was done in American higher education. Therefore, there is no justification for listing hundreds of college and university departments as deficient. In addition, not all women and blacks with Ph.D.'s are available for posts in colleges and universities. Indeed, officials of the Department of Health, Education and Welfare need to understand that the problem is not discrimination, but the dearth of qualified people.

The Department flatly denies that it is promoting a quota system, suggesting that it realizes the courts might rule against a quota system. But the distinction between "goals" and "quotas" is a matter of semantics. It would seem that the pressure tactics used by the federal government turn the goals into quotas. If low percentages of minorities and women are found to hold positions, the figure will be offered as *prima facie* evidence of discrimination. Using this kind of quantitative method alone, a case could be built for almost any group, not just the preferred ones. The Department defends its position on the basis of compensating for past injustices, failing to recognize that it is only perpetuating other injustices.

The Department, however, denies ever inferring the existence of discrimination from purely quantitative disparities between the ratios of those who apply for academic positions and those who are appointed. Nevertheless, since it requires such statistical bookkeeping, it generates pressure to hire along these bases. Moreover, compliance officials have already refused the affirmative action plans of some universities because achievement of acceptable ratios of minorities and women in academic positions was not equivalent to their availability as evidenced by the applications for employment. For example, the affirmative action plan of a large Midwestern university was rejected on the ground that "the achievement of female employment in academic positions [was not] at least equivalent to their availability as evidenced by applications for employment." And when it was pointed out by the President of a large Eastern university in a predominantly white state that the number of minorities who applied for advertised positions were minimal, the compliance officer wrote back that it was the universities' responsibility "to investigate ways of improving transportation between [the closest inner city and the campus] ... as a way of improving the minority applicant flow."

Although the Department repeatedly claims that unqualified persons need not be hired, regional and local officers have instructed university administrators to "consider factors other than mere technical qualifications." What does "other than" suggest when it is necessary to comply with numerical targets? Furthermore, Revised Order No. 4, issued in April 1972, rules that it is discriminatory to require that a new applicant possess qualifications any higher than those required of "the lowest-qualified incumbent." There is no denying that universities have hired their full share of mediocrities. But rather than being permitted to upgrade the work force, universities (and other sectors of the economy) are compelled to lower standards of performance. It opens the door to the hiring of someone who cannot meet current standards or qualifications because some incumbent was hired long ago by some mistake or when standards were lower because of the scarcity of people with advanced degrees or when the institution was struggling for recognition. In effect, the American government has applied Gresham's law to the universities (and elsewhere in the job sector). The result is bound to have a downgrading effect in hiring and promoting personnel. In addition, the Department now insists that an institution "may hold certain vacancies open until such time as qualified minorities are found and considered." This has the same effect of excluding non-minorities and also forces institutions to hire qualifiable (not yet qualified) minority group personnel, since they cannot indefinitely keep a position vacant without loosing the line position. It is easier for an institution to hire a qualifiable person who fills a quota than to explain why someone could not be found and risk federal reprisal.

As a result, American universities have openly indicated to placement bureaus and candidates that they are interested in hiring *only minorities and females*, preferably black females. For example, a large state university on the West Coast told placement bureaus across the country that it was now seeking "an employee balance which is in ethnic and male/female groups, approximate to that of the population of the ... areas from which we recruit. What this means is that we have shifted from the idea of equal opportunity in employment to a deliberate effort to seek out qualified and *qualifiable* (not yet qualified) people among ethnic minority groups and women to fill *all* jobs." And a nearby college has advertised: "We desire to appoint a black or Chicano, preferably female." The department head of a large Southwestern university responded to an inquiry of the placement bureau of another university, stating that although the "four candidates seem qualified for a vacancy they cannot be considered" because every effort must be made "to recruit a minority person." He pointed out that his university recruiting policies had changed and he was "*no longer* [able to] seek *the best-qualified* person available, regardless of race, colour, or creed, as in the past." The president of a Mid-western city college system whose faculty was more than 12 percent black, informed his various administrators that they must hire additional minority faculty members. When the year ends, he said, "many qualified *whites will not be re-hired* and blacks will be sought to fill their jobs." At one of the more than seventy units of the largest state system on the East Coast, a similar directive informs the vice-presidents, deans, and department heads that for the next five years existing vacancies will go to "*qualifiable persons on the basis of race and sex* . . . and temporary preferences [will be given] . . . to members of minority groups." Further, this hiring is to be on a "three-to-one ratio for professors" and a "one-to-one hiring of minorities affecting all of the administrative staff. And the President of a prestigious university on the East Coast sent a directive to his line administrators about a "new and innovative programme to help achieve affirmative action," which includes the "hiring of *unqualified* and marginally qualified *people*."[15]

Thus, the findings of Stuart Gould and Pierre Van Den Berghe, who, with fictitious résumés, each applied for teaching posts in sociology to 176 American universities can be appreciated. Their applications were identical except that one applicant was identified as male and the other as female. Half of all the applicants were described as black; and the other half made no mention of race. Ninety-six institutions replied. Sex did not affect the response rate, suggesting that it is important in only certain fields. But the response rate to the black applicant was 61 percent; to the applicant whose race was not listed, 48 percent. More important, 44 percent expressed follow-up interest in the black applicant, only 9.5 percent in the other applicant (significant at the .001 level). Conclusion: blacks have a decided edge in today's sociology job market.[16]

Considering the university job market as a whole, it is reported that black professors accuse white women of being aggressive and deflecting attention away from correcting racism. There are counter charges by white women that few blacks have the formal credentials for faculty appointments and that those who are qualified or even qualifiable are hired and able to command higher salaries than their white male and female counterparts because of supply and demand.[17] A similar dispute between blacks and white women over the spoils system of "reform" is also evident in private industry and government.[18] And Lester concludes that institutions of higher learning are pirating the limited number of qualified minority and women faculty members from each other, offering higher salaries than those given to comparable and more competent non-minorities and men. Some of the preferred groups lack proper qualifications for the positions, sometimes tenured positions, to which they are appointed. Lester warns that present minority (and in some cases female) hiring trends are hurting standards and undermining faculty quality. He also indicates that salaries between blacks and whites favour the former and run between $ 3,000 to $ 4,000 at the assistant rank and as high as $ 8,000 at the associate and full-professor rank.[19] His statistics are based on pre-1970 data, when affirmative action was in its infancy. The income differences are probably greater today.

Although report after report tell of a Ph.D. glut, there seems to be no problem for a black Ph.D. to find a job. While many whites with the same degree (including females in some academic areas) are underemployed or unable to find jobs in their fields of specialization, blacks (and Chicanos) are receiving several offers with starting salaries that frequently exceed $ 20,000.[20] The average starting salary for a Ph.D. is about $ 12,000; $ 20,000 is comparable to what the average American full professor earns after ten years.[21] These trends may reflect the law of supply and demand. But many would say that the different salary pattern suggests reverse discrimination and is ground for legal action.

Still another interesting twist is that many minorities have discovered a valuable strategy for advancement. In a period of university retrenchment, when few promotions and salary raises are forthcoming, minority and women faculty members have threatened to and actually filed complaints of discrimination. With the aid of government pressure, they receive special salary differentials as well as an extra share of the limited pie.[22] It has become increasingly difficult to discharge a "preferred" person, even if incompetent because most institutions are already under the gun for alleged "deficiencies" that must be "corrected."

What does all this mean? Besides the obvious political ramifications, American colleges and universities (and other sectors of the economy) are no longer hiring or promoting the most qualified candidates. They are instead hiring minorities from a limited and sometimes qualifiable pool, and at unusually high salaries, to fill quotas. To require institutions to commit themselves to achieving a certain proportion of minorities and women on their faculties is to prevent them from choosing the most qualified individuals. It mocks academic standards and it generates hostility and bitterness among more qualified individuals who must be paid less or passed over. Although universities may be required to implement such a policy to reduce racial polarization and to produce equal results, the present affirmative action programme has produced a new kind of social welfare programme that should not be considered performance- nor quality-based. Less competent people cannot compete because they have been situated at a level beyond their capacities. This is bound to create self-doubt and frustration among them. But it also reveals a racism within the liberal community which excuses the incompetence as if it was the best that could be produced by the minority community.

Surely there is need to reduce racial polarization, and some kind of affirmative action plan may be necessary to bridge the existing chasm. But the problem lies with the officials who administer and interpret the present programme. They are an indigenous group of civil servants trained in bureaucratic modes of organization who are promulgating regulations on institutions, aided and abetted by a small group of evangelistic crusaders who are presaging a new kind of racism. This is creating new injustices and new hostilities and elevating the hypocrisy of egalitarian reform, which condemns superior ability and high standards as a mask for continuing discrimination.

## II. Quotas and Student Admissions

Across the country similar quotas are being established for admission into colleges and universities; a dual system of admissions for black and white students, which in turn is producing a dual system of grading. Reformers have come to despair of the ability of black Americans to better themselves educationally, even when special programmes and monies are provided. Compensatory education has been assessed as a failure, and the politics of protest now demands "new standards" for minorities so as to guarantee equality. The concept of equal opportunity has been transformed into the ideology of equal results – at the expense of standards of excellence. In line with this new policy, most colleges and universities are asking student applicants "voluntarily" to respond to a supplementary civil rights questionnaire. The applicant indicates if he belongs to a minority or non-minority group. It can be assumed that a minority applicant gladly fills in the questionnaire, almost guaranteeing himself admission. It is usually taken for granted that the individual who does not volunteer the information is white. Some admission forms now require a photograph, a return of the pre-1954 Brown (U.S. Supreme Court) decision, only in reverse – to limit whites.

The kind of pressure that the universities are faced with is illustrated by a communication to a Western university. It was charged with discrimination against minorities because in one department "out of many applicants only one minority person was enrolled [for the term]." Another illustration is a compliance letter to an Ivy League university which demanded to know why there were no minority students in the Graduate Department of Religious Studies. The department head responded that a reading knowledge of Latin, Greek, or Hebrew was required. The Department of Health, Education and Welfare representative advised: "then end those old fashioned programmes that require irrelevant languages. And start up programmes of relevant things which minority group students can study without learning languages." Clearly, the situation has become irresponsible. Two leading black social scientists, Martin Kilson from Harvard University and Thomas Sowell from University of California, Los Angeles, point out that the Scholastic Aptitude Test and Graduate Record Examination scores for most entering blacks (even at the prestigious universities) are now in the 25th percentile on a national level. Such students are occupying seats that would normally require scores above the 90th percentile.[23] On a nationwide basis, a recent study by the Association of American Law Schools report that all but two of fifty law schools surveyed indicated preferential treatment and the lowering of admission standards toward minorities.[24] Similarly, Jack Shephard indicates that by 1971, 79 out of 100 medical schools reported that admission requirements were being lowered to admit additional minorities. More women were being admitted into medical schools, but their scores were similar to those of white males.[25] The point is, a great many seats are being reserved for minority students whose formal qualifications are questionable. Moreover, seats are being taken away from more qualified students.

For example, Stanford University Law School virtually guaranteed admission in 1972 to any minority student whose grade point average was not below that of the lowest scoring white in the 1971 class and whose Law School Admission Test (LSAT) was within fifty points of that of the weakest student in the previous entering class. In 1973 Northwestern Law School was admitting blacks who scored below the 10th percentile on the LSAT, some of whom were from colleges whose accreditation was under question. The school was, at the same time, refusing admission to white students who scored in the 80th percentile and 90th percentile. The University of Illinois Medical School at Urbana reserved 60 out of 300 places in its incoming classes for minorities as of 1972. In 1974 the University of California Medical School at Davis set aside 10 percent of its seats for minorities. On the campus of the California State University at Fresno, the goals of the 1972 graduate class in social work were to admit "one-third black, one-third Chicano, one-tenth other minorities, and the remainder Caucasian students." These examples are only the tip of the iceberg; they are sentiments that can seriously erode the quality of higher education under the guise of "reform."

The DeFunis case is perhaps the best known example of a student denied admission because of preferential treatment given to minorities. DeFunis, white, with an A average, applied to the Washington University Law School in 1971 and was rejected. He later discovered that thirty-eight other applicants, all minorities, with lower grades and lower LSAT scores were accepted. DeFunis sued the university, charging he was the victim of reverse discrimination. He won his case in the state court and was admitted; the decision was overturned in the federal district court in 1973. The case reached the U.S. Supreme Court in 1974. In a seven-page unsigned opinion, with four justices dissenting, the Court ruled that the issue was moot; any decision reached by the Court would have been made after DeFunis had finished his studies. The dissenting judges argued that DeFunis was still in his last year of law school and still could be subject to a number of unexpected events that might prevent him from graduating. He thus might be faced with another admissions rejection. But most important to the dissenting judges was their belief that the case was not moot for a vast number of other students, and therefore the issue should be resolved for the interests of the public. (Here it can be assumed that a large number of students have had no idea that they were victimized by a quota system and so did not pursue their cases in the courts.) The non-decision of the DeFunis case evoked considerable criticism, and it certainly did not resolve the problem. In 1974 a rejected white medical student at the University of Illinois at Urbana and another at the University of California, Davis filed similar lawsuits.

The question eventually arises: To what extent are we supposed to discriminate against high-achieving students, even those who are from groups that have also known harsh discrimination but have nevertheless done well in school and in various areas of employment? Nathan Glazer touches on this question, reporting on several prominent studies by sociologists, anthropologists, and psychologists; he contends that:

History and social research convince me there are deep and enduring educational differences between various ethnic groups, in their educational achievement and in the broader cultural characteristics in which these differences are, I believe, rooted; that these differences cannot be simply associated with the immediate conditions under which these groups live, whether we define these conditions as being those of levels of poverty and exploitation, or prejudice and discrimination; and if we are to have a decent society, men must learn to live with some measure of group difference in educational achievement, (and) to tolerate them. . . .[26]

Glazer is concerned about society's attitudes towards those differences: Are they solely the consequence of the ill will and "racist" feelings of teachers, administrators, social scientists, and society in general? About the differences he asks, "How elaborate are we to make the efforts to wipe them out, and how successful can we hope to be no matter how elaborate our efforts are? Are our measures to equalize to include the restriction of the opportunities of those groups that seem to find school achievement easy?"[27]

And a related question is: To what extent are we supposed to ignore, even penalize, ordinary students and less-than-average students who are white and come from poor, working, or middle-class backgrounds? No one asks whether a black or Chicano applicant came from a home more advantaged than some white person seeking admission into college or applying for the same job. Thus Paul Seabury cites the frustration of one white person from a poor background:

The ability to think in the abstract is hard for a person with my cultural background and economic background. My parents' . . . income barely exceeded the poverty level. My father is a Southern Baptist with a third-grade education . . . I believe I am a victim. As a non-member of a minority group I feel that I . . . [am] discriminated against constantly. The same admission standards are not applied because a certain percentage of minority students must be admitted in each class regardless of their qualifications. My test scores, undergraduate record, and my family (poor white) deny me admittance to Harvard because I am white.[28]

In reality, both the high-achieving and ordinary white students are going to suffer. They are going to pay the social costs and carry the burden of those of their elders who profited from the old patterns of discrimination. This is, of course, unfair to the present generation of young whites, especially white males. But the greater damage will be that their brotherhood and goodwill will quickly be eroded by the kind of discrimination others have so valiantly fought. Many of these young students must make room for less capable students. Who is going to compensate them for their eventual under-employment and "nouveau poverty"?

### A. *The Meaning of Equality*

Today there is little tolerance for group differences. Yet, all groups are different – some groups are better achievers, some are average achievers, and some are less-than-averages achievers. But the egalitarians prefer to fit everyone into their imaginary bell-shaped curves and mask whatever differences may exist among racial and ethnic groups. One who believes in equality treats a person, not as a member of a group, but as an individual. A belief in equality depends, not on the notion that all groups are equal, but on the idea that all groups be treated equally. The latter philosophy also recognizes that people are are not born equal, that they are unique and possess different abilities and capacities to learn. What equality means is that individuals should be offered the equal protection of the law and equal right to fulfill their unique potentialities, that they should be treated with equal dignity and value as human beings. Paul Kurtz writes, "One who believes in equality need not insist that all individuals, races, or ethnic groups are exactly alike in every way."[29] And Sidney Hook contends, "Our democratic commitment depends on providing equal opportunity for all persons . . . to develop themselves to the fullest." There must be "the recognition and appreciation of the importance of individual differences," which does not depend on the belief that all groups are the same.[30]

Most would agree they want those qualified students to attend colleges, universities, and professional schools who have a reasonable degree of literacy and who can understand their textbooks. Otherwise, there is a regression effect down to the new mean in standards and grades. Moreover, the terminal degree becomes meaningless and especially suspect for minorities who represent a quota, including those who are able students. Thus, under the guise of removing arbitrary barriers that impede the progress of minorities, some students are admitted into college who are functional illiterates.[31] They cannot write a complete sentence nor read above the fifth grade level.[32] Not only do most of them graduate, they also apply considerable pressure on administrators and faculty to expand their enrolment.[33] If the university's mission is to be nothing more than a social action agency, or if the demise of academic standards is fostered in order for society to pay its "reparations" and meet its social responsibilities, then the world of higher education is bankrupt. All the excuses and rhetoric conjured up for abandoning academic quality will not make the new anti-intellectual atmosphere go away, even if the relaxed admissions and grading criteria benefit many non-minority students. But so long as high standards are seen by many blacks as "culturally biased" or manifestations of "white supremacy," black students will continue to be perceived as less than qualified and, in turn, so will those who become professors. Reminders that black entry into the American intellectual mainstream depends on encouraging and holding to high standards of educational excellence continue to be misunderstood by many blacks. So long as it does, the image of black academic identity will continue to suffer.

A double standard already exists in grading blacks and whites in American institutions of higher learning. It predominates at all levels and in all fields of study, including Ph.D. programmes and law and medical schools. By admitting weak students, the system becomes susceptible to accusations of "racism," "discrimination," and legal action if it attempts to maintain standards.[34] Hence there is pressure on many white professors to dilute their grading system for non-white students. It is often not worth the personal costs and potential harassment to grade all students on the same basis, and far too many minority students would fail.[35] But there also is administrative pressure not to fail minority students who represent a quota or open admission policy. A large number of such students drop out on their own accord, and university administrators are often reluctant to maintain standards and thus increase the drop out figures among these academically weak students.[36] Minority students quickly perceive the benefits of the new grading system and also become sophisticated in challenging professors who attempt to maintain standards. The students invent stories or just pressure the professor, which frequently leads to grade changes. In the long run, this procedure is bound to effect the self-esteem of minority students, and not only those who are academically weak. Those of high ability, who excel strictly on merit, will carry the stigma that they, too, were beneficiaries of a double standard, not to mention how it will affect students who graduate without favouritism.

### *B. The Meaning of Qualifications*

One of the best-known examples of such pressure tactics occurred at Wayne State University. Several black students, at the end of their freshman year, were notified by the law school of their dismissal for academic failure. They chained themselves to the doorpost and refused to leave, charging that the university had discriminated against them. The professors denied the charge and responded that test papers were identified by number, not the student's name. A few faculties even said that if they had known which papers were submitted by black students, they would have leaned over backward to help them attain a passing grade. The law school eventually agreed to permit the students to remain. Similar incidents have occurred at various universities, sometimes involving individual students and sometimes, groups of students. In effect, then, graduation will not guarantee equality of academic outcome or professional competence.

But those who have benefited from less rigorous college standards and testing scales often must compete on professional licensing examinations with those who were not favoured. For example, a disproportionately high number of black students who succeed in obtaining their law degrees have difficulty passing state law boards. In Michigan the 1971 results showed that the passing rate was 71 percent for whites and 17 percent for blacks. A law suit has been filed in Michigan, claiming that the test is "culturally biased" against blacks. Between 1970 and 1973, only 22 percent of the whites taking the Illinois law boards failed; among blacks, 55 percent did not pass. A law suit which claims "discrimination" has been filed in Illinois, too. In 1972 Pennsylvania revised its bar examination so that candidates who pass either a multiple choice or essay section (which has been a stumbling block to blacks) were considered to have passed. And one bar association, composed mainly of black lawyers, has called for the abolition of the bar examination in all states because they claim the tests are biased.

The medical profession is experiencing the same kind of pressure. Having changed their entrance standards to increase black enrolments in the medical colleges, at its 1973 annual convention in Philadelphia, the American Medical Association debated the validity of the medical examinations and whether it should be required for students who succeed in obtaining their degrees. There is strong pressure by a consortium of liberal-minority groups to eliminate such exams altogether. The contention is that the person who receives a degree from an accredited medical school should be admitted into practice without further ado. In Chicago prospective teachers who wish to avoid taking or who have failed the relatively simple multiple-choice National Teacher Examination may substitute three years of experience and become permanently certified. The result is that many Chicago teachers "can't spell," and are reading at "the fifth to sixth grade level."[37]

In the meantime, the National Association for the Advancement of Coloured People (and other civil rights organizations) had successfully argued in the courts in such cities as Boston, New York City, Detroit, Chicago, and San Francisco that the written examinations used to select and promote teachers, firemen, and policemen are "biased" and discriminate against minorities, especially blacks. Moreover, the U.S. Supreme Court has ruled in *Griggs v. Duke Power* (1971) that tests can no longer be considered a reasonable job requirement for minorities. All arbitrary barriers to unemployment that demand certain skills or test score results and have the effect of employing minorities in less than their proportion to the population are now considered illegal. If test scores are involved, the employer must now demonstrate that the tests are a valid predictor of job success. That the employer has no discriminatory intention is irrelevant; it is only the effect that matters now. The *Griggs* decision is not aimed at helping white women who fall under affirmative action guidelines or helping poor or ethnic whites who do not speak fluent English. The decision applies only to certain minorities who seem unable to compete on cognitive tests. The Court claimes that tests are biased and that they are not an accurate predictor of job success. But the decision was not related to the technical nature of the tests, for there are many highly reliable and valid predictors of achievement and job performance. As Jerome Dopplet and George Bennett of the Psychological Corporation report, there are some technical limitations to tests. But there are many well-devised (reliable and valid) tests that measure "the individual's present capacity of demonstrating his skills or knowledge for predicting job success."[38] The concept of "cultural bias" entered the picture to mask the politics of the decision – to provide jobs on a quota basis and to eliminate any tool, such as tests to determine appropriate skills and professional competency, that might hinder the quota policy.

The combined implications of the NAACP strategy and the *Griggs* decision make it clear that conventional criteria for judging performance and potential in all jobs are under attack – that is, any job-related skills, such as the candidate's terminal degree or publication record regarding a university position; knowledge of a profession (teaching, law, medicine), as measured by standardized tests; a secretary's ability to read and type; or a bank clerk's ability to do simple mathematical problems, are being attacked.

Tests may be culturally oriented, but the job is embedded in a cultural milieu. Similarly, the ability to write a Ph.D. thesis or conduct research for a professor is not a racially-biased requirement. Nor is it racially biased for a history teacher to have knowledge of history or a lawyer to have knowledge of law or the secretary to understand written instructions, or the bank teller to know how to add and subtract. These are culturally laden factors which are likely to be criteria, or job related. The purpose of a test is to select people who will succeed on the job. Outlawing such tests makes the selection process more subjective and political. It is not possible to claim that all high school or college diplomas are equivalent, or that graduation from a school of law, medicine, or education is sufficient indication of competence. Certifying examinations are necessary. Eliminating them denies that there are dual entrance and grading systems for black and white students, and that within groups there are other large differences. The result is that these differences are perpetuated on the job. Hence, many functional illiterates graduate from high school, and many students with less than average qualifications are now admitted into colleges and professional schools. When these students go out on the job, ironically, they transfer the blame for their failures from schools and teachers to the qualifying tests that reflect the different outcomes in diplomas. Dopplet and Bennett put it this way: "Whenever the number of applicants exceeds the number of job openings, some applicants will be rejected. This is one of the hard facts of life. It is not surprising that those who are rejected sometimes attack the selection procedures on the grounds that these are invalid or unfair."[39]

Society has the responsibility for providing jobs for people with limited skills, but not for replacing qualified personnel with unqualified personnel. Society has the responsibility of providing remedial job instruction for disadvantaged populations, but should also include white disadvantaged populations. The rejection of measurements that register the consequences of educational deprivation or of inadequate knowledge and skills, is merely a political move to kill off the messenger who brings the bad news. It de-emphasizes the harsh reality that quotas will lead to a downward trend in the quality and abilities of people who are and will be employed in a variety of jobs and occupations. New and artificial standards that mock excellence and replace it with mediocrity have little to do with equal opportunity. Using quotas, instead of quality, to select people for college entrance or jobs and promotions rewards the dumb, lazy, and unambitious at the expense of the smart, talented, and ambitious. But the philosophical and moral arguments that are devised are secondary. The political decision to absorb selected groups into society in line with the egalitarian demand for equal results is a larger part of the rationale for the quota decision.

## III. Conclusion

A qualified surgeon is expected when an operation must be performed, yet there are quotas in American medical schools. Seats are reserved for qualifiable students and taken from the more qualified. A skilled lawyer is wanted when a legal matter must be handled, yet there are quotas for candidates applying to American law schools. A skilled pilot and flight mechanic are required to service airplanes, yet the American airlines are coming under pressure to fill quotas. Universities want high standards of scholarship and excellence, yet they are not permitted to hire or promote the most qualified. There may be nothing wrong with producing ordinary doctors, lawyers, pilots, and professors. But there is a point beyond which the definition of "average" can be stretched so that it does serious harm to the viability of society.

Despite the various legal and moral convictions, it takes several years to educate people and turn out qualified professionals for important vocations. No increased pressure is going to increase the supply of doctors and lawyers and such, unless standards are lowered. Instant competency cannot be bestowed. Already, qualified minority group members and women are becoming uneasy about quotas. They are aware that it puts a "less qualified" stamp on them by association. Within a few years it can be expected that people will be asking, "How did that person get the job? Besides filling a quota, does that person have any legitimate qualifications?" If the question of competence is not seriously considered, or if such matters no longer count there will be a decline in public and private services. Although there is less concern about efficiency in some jobs than in others, the placement of less efficient personnel at low levels will raise costs and diminish standards. To what extent each institution can absorb less efficient personnel without disabling itself or without becoming a malfunctioning organization is a difficult question to answer.

The present use of quotas is only part of the issue. It should not be permitted to mask the larger issue – the danger of a *de facto* system of quotas, a rigid system that leaves no room for manoeuvre and that is bound to be a denial of equal opportunity. While special efforts should be made to identify and train individuals of minority status, and other programmes are needed to assist potentially qualified minorities, essential prerequisites and criteria of excellence cannot be dropped for an extended period without social and economic repercussions. The more the importance of merit and ability is diminished, the greater the danger of a decline of society. Abolishing standardized tests, eliminating examinations, bending entrance requirements (for college and employment), downgrading skills or doing away with them, or denying quantitative measures of excellence are wrong and anti-intellectual. Being unable to test for competency, because of so-called cultural biases, is highly political and eliminates any tool to distinguish the qualified from the unqualified, the competent from the incompetent, and all under the guise of affirmative action.

There are those who feel the present affirmative action policy is just, especially those who benefit from it. They, along with their liberal apologists, will disagree with this analysis. But certainly there is need to deal with a greater sense of reality. Who is supposed to share the blame for past injuries? Can we accurately determine who should be penalized? What is the present trade-off between increasing minority employment and decreasing efficiency? How do we assist under-privileged whites? Or, do we continue to ignore them? Are all women included in affirmative action? Or does it mainly apply to selected fields and minority women? Where do the benefits of civil rights begin to fall off and lead to abuses toward the majority population? When do the arbitrary interpretations of a few unelected officials become a matter for the people to check?

The future is now. White males will begin to file reverse discrimination law suits when they compare their formal qualifications with "preferred" candidates, and the recent salaries offered and obtained by minority counterparts with their own salaries. Letters of "no openings" to white candidates will be matched with invitations to minority candidates. White students will learn the advantage of claiming minority status when filling out forms for law, medical, and graduate school. They may eventually file suits against universities for discrimination in the allotment of financial aid (and jobs on campus), showing that many minorities who receive financial assistance come from families with higher incomes than their own.

In the final analysis, ideological imperatives and group interests should not prevail over the norms of the legal order and individual rights. Somehow a balance must be struck between the entitlements from those groups that now claim special privilege and other groups whose rights must not be abridged. Individual merit, measured as accurately as possible, must be a crucial determinant in educational and employment opportunities, rather than proportional representation. A double-standard society will not work for long, and it will breed new racial antagonisms.

## Notes

1. U.S. Commission on Civil Rights, *Federal Civil Rights Enforcement Effort*, U.S. Government Printing office, Washington, D.C., 1970.
2. U.S., Congress, Senate, *Congressional Record* 119 (22, May 1973); Paul Seabury, "HEW and the University," *Commentary* 55, February 1972, pp. 33–44.
3. Alan E. Bayer, *Teaching Faculty in Academy: 1972–73*, American Council on Education Research Report, vol. 8, American Council on Education, Washington, D.C. 1973.
4. There is no attempt to lump together blacks and women here or elsewhere in this paper. The prospects of hiring are different for both groups, as suggested by the pool of talent, terminal degrees, and test scores. There is consistent reference to both groups because affirmative action policies are based on race and sex and seem most concerned about these two groups.
5. Richard A. Lester, *Antibias Regulation of Universities*, McGraw-Hil, New York, 1974.
6. For example, female Ph.D.'s, as a group, spend an average of ten hours a week on child care plus eighteen hours a week on household chores, such as cooking and cleaning, and so on. Data by both male and female researchers conclude that married women subordinate their careers to their marriage commitment. They spend less time and energy (especially research) on professional matters than men. There are other differences, such as lighter teaching loads and the assignment of graduate assistants which favour males. But these differences are light and mainly limited to a few prestigious universities. Moreover, the latter variables may not be a function of sex but reflect differences in research and productivity.
7. *Chronicle of Higher Education*, 5 August 1974, p. 9.
8. Lester, *Antibias Regulation of Universities*.
9. Allan C. Ornstein, *Race and Politics in School/Community Organizations* Goodyear, Pacific Palisades, 1974; *idem*, "Quality, Not Quotas," *Society* 13, January 1976:

10, 14–17; Sheldon E. Steinbach, "Fighting Campus Job Discrimination," *Change* 5, November 1973, pp. 51–52.

10. Lester, *Antibias Regulation of Universities; idem*, "The Fallacies of Numerical Goals," *Educational Record* 57, Winter 1976: 58–64; Robert O'Neil, *Discriminating Against Discrimination*, Indiana University Press, Bloomington, Indiana, 1975. *Chronicle of Higher Education*, 27 January 1975, p. 6; *ibid.*, 19 May 1975, p. 43; and telephone conversation with Miro M. Todorovich, coordinator of the Committee on Academic Nondiscrimination and Integrity, 17 February 1975.
11. James Hester, Statement before the Special Subcommittee on Education and Labor, Congress of the United States, September 20, 1974.
12. *New York Times*, 7 May 1972, p. 12.
13. Commission on Human Resources, National Research Council, *Summary Reports, 1967–1973: Doctorate Recipients from United States Universities*, National Academy of Sciences, Washington, D.C., 1968–1974.
14. Commission on Human Resources, National Research Council, *Doctorate Recipients from United States Universities, 1958–1966* National Academy of Sciences, Washington, D.C.: 1967; Miro M. Todorovich, Statement before the Special Subcommittee on Education and Labor, Congress of the United States, 20 September 1974.
15. U.S., Congress, Senate, *Congressional Record* 119 May 22, 1973; Ornstein, *Race and Politics* (italics added throughout). For additional letters, see these two sources.
16. Stuart H. Gould and Pierre L. Van Den Berghe, "Particularism in Sociology Departments' Hiring Practices," *Race* 15, July 1973, pp. 106–111.
17. *Chronicle of Higher Education*, 23 October 1973, pp. 1–6; *ibid.*, 5 August 1974, pp. 1, 8–9.
18. *Chicago Tribune*, 2 December 1973, sec. 12, p. 34; *ibid.*, 4 March 1974, sec. 2, p. 9; Jules Cohen, "Coping with Affirmative Action against Backlash," *Business and Society Review*, 4, 1973, pp. 32–36; *New York Times*, 30 September 1974, p. 28; Daniel Seligman, "How 'Equal Opportunity' Turned into Employment Quotas," *Fortune*, 87, March 1973, pp. 160–168.
19. Lester, *Antibias Regulation of Universities.*
30. *Chicago Sun-Times*, 4 September 1973, p. 38.
21. *Chronicle of Higher Education*, 29 April 1974, p. 9.
22. For example, one university in Arizona has made available a bonus fund to pay minorities an extra $ 750 a year over their white counterparts. At a south-side Chicago state university more than $ 1,000 was paid across the board to all black and female faculty members, even to those already earning $ 25,000 and $ 30,000, to compensate for past discrimination. At another private university in Illinois, a number of female faculty members filed a class action suit in order to pressure the university to promote them.
23. Martin T. Kilson, "The Black Experience at Harvard," *New York Times Magazine*, 2 September 1973, pp. 13, 31ff.; Thomas A. Sowell, *Black Education: Myths and Tragedies*, McKay, New York, 1974.
24. Committee on Academic Nondiscrimination and Integrity, "Statement for Immediate Release," 9 June 1972.
25. Jack Shephard, "Black Lab Power," *Saturday Review*, 5 August 1972; pp. 32–35ff.
26. Nathan Glazer, "Ethnic Group and Education: Toward the Tolerance of Difference," Journal of Negro Education 38, Summer 1969, p. 187.
27. *Ibid.*, p. 194.
28. Seabury, "HEW and the Universities," p. 44.

29. Paul Kurtz, "The Principle of Equality and Some Dogmas of Environmentalism," *Humanist* 32, March 1972, p. 4.
30. Sidney Hook, "Democracy and Genetic Variation," Humanist 32, March 1971, p. 7.
31. Bernard Bard, "College for All: Dream or Disaster?" *Phi Delta Kappan* 56, May 1972, pp. 55–58; *Chicago Tribune*, 26 March 1976, sec. 4, p. 26.
32. *Chicago Sun-Times*, 15 January 1975, p. 48; *Chicago Tribune*, 29 November 1974, sec. 2, p. 2; Orde Coombs, "The Necessity of Excellence: Howard University," *Change* 6, March 1974, pp. 36–41; Louis G. Heller, *The Death of the American University* Arlington House, New York, 1974.
33. David L. Kirp and Mark G. Yudof, "DeFunis and Beyond," *Change* 6, November 1974, pp. 22–28; Sowell, *Black Education.*
34. Kilson, "Black Experience at Harvard." Also see Martin Kilson, review of "The Education of Black Folk" by Allen B. Ballard, *Change* 5, November 1973, pp. 58–60; Sowell, *Black Education.*
35. Wilson Record, "Can Sociology and Black Studies Find a Common Ground?" Paper presented at the Black Cultural Forum. Portland State University, February 1973; *idem*, "Response of Sociologists to Black Studies," in *Black Sociologists: Historical and Contemporary Perspectives*, ed. James E. Blackwell and Morris Janowitz University of Chicago Press, Chicago: 1974, pp. 368–401; Bayard Ruston, ed., *Black Studies: Myths and Realities*, A. Philip Randolph Educational Fund, New York, 1969. Also see Edward M. White, "Sometimes an A is Really an F," *Chronicle of Higher Education*, 3 February 1974, p. 24.
36. Martin Mayer, "Higher Education for All?", *Commentary* 56, February 1973, pp. 37–47.
37. *Chicago Tribune*, 18 September 1974, pp. 1, 15. It is also reported by the city's black newspaper that about half the number of Chicago's 27,000 teachers, most of whom are black, earn their degrees at one southside university. In 1973 as many as 63 percent of the 826 teacher candidates at this institution failed the National Teacher Examination but were still eligible to teach. See the Chicago *Defender*, 30 March 1974, pp. 1,9ff.
38. Jerome E. Dopplet and George K. Bennett, "Testing Job Applicants from Disadvantaged Groups," *Test Service Bulletin of the Psychological Corporation*, no. 57, 1967, p. 1.
39. *Ibid.*, p. 5.

# Racial Discrimination in Rhodesia

MARSHALL W. MURPHREE AND
DONALD G. BAKER

MARSHALL MURPHREE was born in Rhodesia and educated at a Rhodesian high school. He subsequently studied in the United States at Asbury College (B.A.), Asbury Theological Seminary (B.D.) and at Northwestern University, where he took an M.A. in cultural anthropology under Melville Herskovits and William Bascom. In 1965 he received his Ph.D. degree from the London School of Economics in social anthropology, his studies being directed by Isaac Schapera and Raymond Firth. Since 1970 he has held the Maurice Webb Chair of Race Relations at the University of Rhodesia. He was President of the Association for Sociology in Southern Africa 1975–1976. His publications include: *Christianity and the Shona*, London: Athlone Press, 1969; *Employment Opportunity and Race in Rhodesia*, Denver: University of Denver Press, 1973; "Sociology and the Study of Race: Contemporary Perspectives for Southern Africa," *Social Dynamics*, Vol. 1, No. 2, December 1975; Editor, *Education, Race and Employment in Rhodesia*, Salisbury: Artca Publications, 1975; "Race and Power in Rhodesia" in D. Baker, ed., *Politics of Race*, London: D.C. Heath/Saxon House, 1975; *Education, Development and Change in Africa*, (Hoernlé Memorial Lecture, 1976) Johannesburg: South African Institute of Race Relations, 1976.

DONALD G. BAKER was born and educated in the United States. His undergraduate degree was from Denver University, and his advanced degrees were from Syracuse University, including an M.A. degree in Political Science (1958) and a Ph.D. in Political Science and Psychology (1961). He has taught at Syracuse University, the Graduate School of the State University of New York (Albany), Skidmore College and, since 1964, has been Professor of Political Science at Southampton College of Long Island University, in Southampton, New York. During 1975 and part of 1976 he was a Senior Research Fellow in the Centre for Inter-Racial Studies at the University of Rhodesia. His major research interests focus on the comparative analysis of race relations. His publications include, among others: Editor and Co-Author, *Politics of Race*, London: D.C. Heath/Saxon House, 1975; "Race, Power and White Siege Cultures," *Social Dynamics*, Vol. I, No. 2, December 1975; Editor, with C. Sheldon, *Postwar America: The Search for Identity*, Beverley Hills, Cal.: Glancoe Press, 1969; and numerous other articles on the politics of race especially in English-speaking countries of the world.

# Racial Discrimination in Rhodesia

MARSHALL W. MURPHREE AND
DONALD G. BAKER

## I. The Racial Characteristics of Rhodesian Society

Rhodesia, like many other contemporary national entities, is a society in which various sub-groupings within the population have been differentially incorporated into its social, economic and political structures on the basis of their racial identity. In addition to this however it shares with a small handfull of societies such as South Africa and Fiji[1] the distinction of having this racially-based differential incorporation given ostensible legal and constitutional recognition. The 1969 Constitution under which the Country is currently governed gives explicit attention to the racial structuring of participation in Rhodesia's social and political life, statutory legislation introduced at various periods in Rhodesia's history does likewise, and the historical pedigree of this approach is stated unequivocally in the charge given to the recent Commission of Inquiry into Racial Discrimination by the Rhodesian Government thus: "Having regard to the fact that, from time to time since the settlement of Rhodesia commenced in 1890, it has been deemed desirable and necessary to introduce discriminatory measures in order to protect the special interests of the principal racial communities in Rhodesia ..."[2] Rhodesia therefore stands, with South Africa, as an example of the attempt to achieve political cohesiveness in a plural society by giving explicit legal recognition to racially-defined sectional interests.[3]

Too close a parallel between the South African and Rhodesian approaches should not, however, be drawn. Rhodesia has always been linked socially and politically with South Africa in the journalistic and academic literature, but this analytic association tends to overlook the fact that unlike South Africa's Nationalist Government the Rhodesia

Front Government lacks a clear ideological framework for its policies, nor does it have policies which follow through the implications of racially separate social and political development to their logical conclusion of a regional system of independent nation-states in the South African mode. Much of the Rhodesian legal framework for the system has been modelled on South African precedents and with the same objective, that of maintaining White control over the system. It differs from the South African framework in that, in the economic and social spheres, much of its segregatory impact is oblique and indirect. Its effect here can be characterized as *apartheid* by bye-law and convention, less explicit and more 'liberal'. The effect is nevertheless just as pervasive, and in its lack of provision for an ultimately autonomous arrangement to accommodate black cultural and political aspirations the Rhodesian system is more nakedly one of White political and cultural domination than the South African one. Thus, as Palley puts it, the Rhodesian Front in "mainly applying the negative policies of segregation and European dominance" has denied itself "even the moral justification that Africans will be afforded full opportunity of development in their own areas. For this reason Rhodesian Front policy can be described as well to the right of that of South Africa."[4]

A comparison between the Rhodesian and South African systems of discrimination is not however the major focus here. Rather, the analysis sets out in a relatively direct and empirical manner an overview of the components of contemporary racial discrimination in Rhodesia and the way in which they function corporately for the maintenance of White power. Part II analyzes briefly the historical development of this power system and the interrelated nature of its components, Part III describes the patterns of contemporary discrimination and Part IV briefly examines recent developments, with particular attention to the Government's stated intent of removing "unnecessary" racial discrimination, through the appointment of a commission to investigate the matter and subsequent action based on its findings.

Before turning to this analysis, comment is appropriate with regard to terminological and demographic detail. There are in the Rhodesian population four categories of social race which have socio-economic and political significance: the Blacks, the Whites, the Coloureds and the Asians. Local Rhodesian usage tends to refer to the first of these categories as 'African' and the second as 'European'. In this essay we have used the terms 'Black' and 'White' in accordance with contemporary practice elsewhere except where quoting directly from Rhodesian sources. The Electoral Act defines as 'European' a person who is not an 'African', and as 'African' "any member of the aboriginal tribes or races of Africa and the islands adjacent thereto, including Madagascar and Zanzibar; and any person who has the blood of such tribes or races and who lives as a member of an aboriginal native community."[5] Coloureds not living "as a member" of the 'African' community and Asians are therefore classified for electoral purposes as 'Europeans', but are identified and differentiated in various other social and economic spheres of Rhodesian life.

The latest population estimates for the Country based on an updated projection of the 1969 census yield the following figures for these four racial categories:[6]

| | *Population* | *% Urban* |
|---|---|---|
| Blacks | 6 110 000 | 16.4 |
| Whites | 278 000 | 82.1 |
| Coloureds | 20 900 | 83.7 |
| Asians | 10 000 | 91.0 |
| | 6 418 000 | |

Blacks therefore number slightly over 95% of the population, Whites about 4.3% and Coloureds and Asians together less than 0.5%. The ratio of Blacks to Whites is approximately 22 to 1.

Within these racial categories a number of ethnically defined subcategories also exist.[7] Among the Blacks the most significant division is between the Shona, themselves divided into a number of ethnic subgroups, and the Ndebele. Shona-speaking Blacks are reported in the 1969 Census to number 78.8% of the Black population, while Ndebele-speaking Blacks number 15.8% of the total.[8] Among the Whites by far the largest number are of British extraction, but other ethnic groupings of significant size exist. Among these the Afrikaners are the largest, estimated by Leys to constitute 13.5% of the White population in 1951.[9] Other significant ethnically-visible groups include Jews, Greeks and the Portuguese, whose numbers have been considerably augmented since 1974 by immigration from Mozambique and Angola. System discrimination on the basis of ethnicity can be identified in various periods of Rhodesian history, particularly in regard to certain ethnic categories within the White population.[10] Furthermore, ethnic fragmentation within racially defined groups has from time to time affected their ability to mobilize their resources vis-á-vis other similarly defined groups and thus has significance for the power equation in Rhodesian society. Particularly has this been true in respect to the Black response to White domination. Having noted the importance of ethnicity in the Rhodesian context, it must however be remarked that discrimination in the society has been predominately racial in character and it is the dimensions of this racial stratification, both historical and contemporary, which define the focus of this study.

## II. The Historical Development of Discrimination in Rhodesia

Differentials in group power have shaped the character of Rhodesia's racial stratification system, for the power capabilities of Black and White groups have determined (both historically and more recently) their responses to and interaction with each other.[11] When the power capabilities of groups are vastly unequal, the group with greater resources can utilize its power (especially if it controls major political, economic and social structures) to restrict or destroy the power capabilities of other groups,[12] thus developing and perpetuating its superordinate position. Although it is possible to trace the character of both ethnic and race relations in Rhodesia,[13] what is of most significance are the patterns of racial dominance and discrimination. Those patterns can best be understood through a brief sketch of two closely linked themes: (a) the factors influencing early White-Black contacts and the means by which Whites developed their position of dominance; and (b) the structures and means by which Whites have perpetuated their control. An elaboration of these themes sets the framework for the analysis of contemporary racial discrimination in the subsequent section of this paper.

### *A. Characteristics of Early White-Black Relations*

Among the major factors that must be considered in any assessment of group contact situations are: (a) the belief systems of the interacting groups and how those beliefs influence or determine their perceptions of each other;[14] (b) the motivational factors that precipitate those encounters (e.g., among others, migration, colonization, competition for land and resources, conquest) of the groups;[15] and (c) power capabilities (and differentials) of the groups.[16] Most groups are ethnocentric in terms of their own belief system (i.e., they regard as superior their own norms of behaviour and their cultural, racial, religious and other beliefs), but the intensity or rigidity with which groups hold to their ethnocentric beliefs varies.[17] However under two types of group contact situations the ethnocentrism of groups appears to sharpen and harden: first, where groups find themselves competing with others for scarce or desired resources (land, power, privilege, etc.), or second, where groups fear that the survival of their belief system is threatened.[18] In these situations, then, groups most seriously contest for control of structures or the acquisition of power resources, for their power capabilities (and differentials in power) largely determine the outcomes of their contests.[19]

Early contacts between Whites and Blacks in Rhodesia were of a contractual nature, tribal leaders according missionaries, hunters and traders limited concessions from 1859 onwards. However in 1888 when Lobengula conceded to Cecil Rhodes the right to prospect for minerals, Rhodes went beyond the concession and offered prospective settlers mineral *and* land concessions, and by doing so he induced Whites to settle in Salisbury and elsewhere beginning in 1890. This prompted Black resentment and hostility, but Whites, given their superior weapons and organization, quickly suppressed the 1893 Ndebele opposition. Victorious later in putting down the Ndebele and Shona uprisings of 1896–97, the Whites and Rhodes' British South Africa Company (BSAC), which ruled the colony under a charter, justified their taking of Black lands and cattle as a "legitimate right" of military conquest.[20]

The settlers, mostly English, held cultural (including racial, or somatic) beliefs that assumed the superiority of their own way of life. They viewed themselves as "civilized" and Blacks as "uncivilized". For Whites, their military successes and ability to dominate African society appeared to confirm their notion of European superiority. Moreover, military successes justified in the Whites' mind their taking of the Blacks' cattle and more fertile lands. White confiscations and rule had far-reaching consequences for the Blacks. Dispossessed of their cattle and lands, the rapidly expanding Black population could not sustain itself on its remaining lands, and it was quickly transformed into an economically dependent group. Military defeat and imposed White rule also thwarted the development of Black leadership, demoralized some Black groups, and contributed to the detribalization (and concomitant social disorganization) of many Blacks. When necessary, Whites readily relied upon coercive powers to compel compliance from Blacks.

Southern Rhodesia remained under BSAC rule until the settlers were granted Colony status by the metropole (British) government in 1923.[21] The metropole retained control over "native affairs" during both Company and Colony periods, but "native commissioners", influenced more directly by settlers than by the metropole, exercised almost autonomous rule over tribal groups, dispensing justice, deposing recalcitrant leaders, and utilizing their discretionary coercive powers to restrain Black opposition to White rule. Their coercive powers included the ability to incarcerate and punish, to withhold needed economic goods, and to conscript labour for mining and agriculture. Although in principle the British government retained the right of protecting Blacks (including veto power over legislation affecting indigenous groups), in practice the Company and after 1923 the Colony government manipulated and manoeuvered matters whereby they governed (and used) Blacks as they saw fit.[22] In practice, then, the metropole exercised little real control over Black welfare. The settlers, through their control of political, economic and social structures (as well as their control over tribal structures) were able to restrict the development of Black political and economic resources (and mobilization capabilities), thereby keeping them in a dependent and subordinate position.

Viewed by the White as essentially a "hewer of wood and drawer of water," the Black was usually restricted to menial or unskilled jobs. This, combined with his limited chances to acquire the language, education and skills needed for economic advancement, severely restricted the Black's ability to develop the political and economic resources needed for contesting White rule. Among the Whites there evolved (from their cultural beliefs and the subordinate roles they assigned to Blacks) a loosely articulated ideology that portrayed the Black as an inferior being capable only of menial tasks – an image that was "confirmed" for the White by the tasks that he saw Blacks performing.[23] This White racial ideology has generally taken one of two forms: first, a perception of the Black as *culturally* inferior though potentially the equal of the White if he became "civilized" (i.e., educated and Anglicized), or second, a perception of the Black as *genetically* inferior to the White, either of these conditions precluding his incorporation within White-controlled structures except as unskilled labour. These diverse ideological beliefs are readily evident in any assessment of White policy toward the Black, be it in the past or at present; and at different moments in time either one or the other of these two views has achieved a paramount position in determining policy and practice.

Whichever ideological orientation has held sway, Whites have nevertheless retained control over political, economic and social structures, thereby restricting the Black's access to those structures and precluding his development of power resources.

### *B. Structures of White Dominance*

The outcomes of group encounters are determined by the power capabilities of the involved groups, those capabilities, defined in terms of a group's resources and mobilization capabilities.[24] A group's resources include, among others, its total numbers, physical and financial assets, social organization, belief system, education and skills. More difficult to measure, but certainly a component of a group's resources, are its prestige, authority and prowess, particularly as these are perceived by another group, for such factors, be they actual or simply imagined, clearly influence the other group's behaviour. Mobilization capabilities are of a somewhat different character, for they include a group's morale, motivation, leadership, cohesiveness, adaptiveness and ability (or inability) to cope with or respond to diverse types of situations. Thus one group may possess superior resources to those of another group, but given ineffective leadership, low morale or other deficiencies in its mobilization capabilities, it may find itself unable to mobilize effectively against the other group which has fewer resources but far superior mobilization capabilities. The analysis of White-Black relations in Rhodesia can be viewed as a series of ongoing power contests, Whites, marshalling superior resources and mobilization capabilities, pursuing policies continually aimed at destroying or restricting the resources and mobilization capabilities of Blacks. What has evolved historically have been two major types of White dominance: military/coercive and structural.

(i) *Military/coercive dominance*: Given their superior weapons, equipment and organization, the settlers relatively easily defeated Ndebele and Shona uprisings and opposition to White intrusion and takeover of their lands. By confiscating the cattle and more fertile lands of the Blacks, Whites deprived indigenes of their basic economic resources, forcing Blacks (especially when their increased population could no longer be supported on the remaining lands) into an increasingly economically dependent position. This compelled Blacks to seek work in the White sector, thereby curtailing the Whites' need to rely upon coercive tactics (hut and other taxes, conscripted labour) to force the Black into accepting jobs at what were usually below-subsistence wages.[25]

Within Black areas, Whites imposed a form of direct rule, virtually absolute power vested in "native commissioners" who, supported by military and police forces, could utilize coercive measures for silencing Black critics, potential or present, real or imagined. Moreover, Blacks who sought to leave the reserves to seek economic opportunities (limited as those opportunities were) or who were forced by economic necessity to find work were subject to another type of coercive control: should they disobey or protest against oppressive or exploitive regulations or conditions, they could be fired and expelled from the White areas. Pass laws and regulations closely restricted the rights of Blacks in White areas, and without a job the Black could be expelled from those areas.[26]

Where earlier, general laws for the maintenance of law and order were utilized to control Africans, the postwar emergence of African nationalist and White liberal critics of racial discrimination prompted the enactment of numerous security measures designed to restrict public meetings and gatherings, control the flow of information and permit the detention without trial of persons "in the public interest".[27] Beyond these coercive means, though, Whites have managed to maintain their hegemony and privilege especially through their control of political, economic and social structures. For, by limiting the Black's access to and incorporation within these (and especially economic and political) structures, Whites have, in general, effectively restricted the Black's ability to develop the resources and mobilization capabilities essential for contesting white power.

(ii) *Structural dominance*: Through control of political, economic and social structures, Whites have made allocative decisions that have restricted the Black's acquisition of power resources while strengthening White power resources. Particularly crucial in preserving White hegemony are the *economic structures*. As previously indicated, Whites, by dispossessing the Black of his cattle and more fertile lands, seriously restricted the latter's ability to maintain his economic self-sufficiency. Earlier designations of White and Black lands were finally formalized in the Land Apportionment Act (1930) which clearly demarcated Black from White areas. Hut and other taxes, a rapid increase in the

Black population and the increasing deterioration of Black lands compelled Blacks to seek work in White areas, in agriculture, mining, domestic and the industrial sectors.[28] All of these factors contributed to what has been termed the "pauperization" and "proletarianization of the peasant" Black.[29] Whether intentional or otherwise, White policies have left the Black largely under-trained, unskilled, underpaid and underemployed, and the consequence for him has been "cumulative economic underprivilege."[30]

What Rhodesia has developed historically has been "a web of coercive labour legislation, designed to regulate the mobility of (Black) labour and stabilize employment under contract."[31] This legislation includes pass laws, regulations compelling fulfilment of labour contracts, and measures that tend to restrict the types of jobs open to Blacks. Domestics have remained under control of a Masters and Servants Act that severely restricts their rights; and under the Industrial Conciliation Act (1934), Blacks were excluded from its bargaining stipulations, Whites being given a *de facto* monopoly over skilled jobs. Viewed historically, White society has restricted the development of economic resources and mobilization capabilities of Blacks, in four ways: first, by controlling and limiting the education of Blacks, thereby assuring that Blacks have only limited skills for job opportunities and advancement; second, by restricting the types of jobs available to Blacks; third, by establishing wage scales for industries and other sectors, thereby assuring that various sectors do not compete for (and thereby increase the wages of) Black workers; and fourth by restricting the ability of Blacks to organize their own trade unions. Moreover, by keeping Black labour largely unskilled (and therefore easily replaced by other unskilled workers should the former strike or organize) and by setting rules and pass laws that keep Blacks as basically a form of migrant labour White society has systematically curtailed the economic resources and mobilization capabilities of Blacks. Blacks, as a consequence, occupy an essentially dependent and subordinate position in the society.[32]

Historically, Whites have also utilized *social structures* for maintaining their dominance. As suggested previously, Whites viewed themselves as civilized and Blacks as uncivilized. Many of their efforts as the dominant group, be it as missionaries, educators or administrators of "native affairs," were directed toward destroying tribal cultures and "civilizing" the native groups. This westernization also had a coercive element to it, for the Black who shed his own culture for that of the White was accorded greater access or opportunity for employment within the White sectors. Fundamental, though, was the notion of the superiority of White culture.[33]

Education played a crucial role.[34] Earlier in the century, the government neglected Black education but did allow missionary groups to establish primary and secondary schools. Both government and White society saw little need for educating Blacks except in a vocational sense. Indeed, they criticized missionary schools that provided an academic rather than a vocational education to Blacks, for they argued that (a) Blacks should be trained for servitude and unskilled positions and (b) an academic education had the potential of turning Blacks into critics and opponents of the White dominance system. The consequences of these attitudes toward the Black were far-reaching. The government's refusal to educate Blacks meant that few acquired the educational or technical skills needed to rise above the unskilled worker level. Consequently, Black wages remained low, and few thereby met the financial qualifications for the franchise. Moreover, by limiting the Black's education or awareness of what was going on elsewhere in the world, the White kept the Black man largely ignorant of his subordinate role. Besides, keeping the masses uneducated meant that it was more difficult for potential Black leaders to organize them against White control. The government criticized missionary education because it was often academic rather than vocational, but even that education had a devastating effect on African society. Whatever its intent, one of its consequences was that it inculcated within many Blacks a belief in the inferiority of their own culture and the superiority of European culture.[35] This contributed to detribalization and the destruction of social cohesion within tribal society, thereby further limiting Black abilities of organizing against White rule.

The social system also reflected the dominant-subordinate nature of Rhodesian society, for by both legislation and practice group rights and limitations were and are defined in terms of racial categories.[36] Thus under the Land Apportionment (and, later, Land Tenure) Act, the Urban Areas Act and other measures, agricultural lands, residential and business areas, education, and social amenities (restaurants, bars, hotels, toilets, etc.) are clearly demarcated along racial lines. During the Central African Federation period (1953–63) some of these racial barriers and limitations were removed, but these changes so threatened the White Southern Rhodesian population that it elected to office (1962) a Rhodesian Front party that espoused the return to a racially separated society in which power remained in White hands.[37] Indeed, while social policy historically held *in principle* to the ideological view that "civilized" (i.e., westernized) Blacks should have the same rights and opportunities as Whites, what evolved in practice was a "racial etiquette" that established a hierocratic pattern of relations based on racial factors. Both superordinate and subordinate groups were expected to play specific roles, and infractions of those roles led to coercive measures. When the Federation period attempted to change the character of those roles and relations, Whites felt threatened and supported the Rhodesian Front. Although numerous factors, including the need for Black labour, have prevented the Rhodesian Front from moving entirely in the same direction, its intent has clearly been that of establishing a society closely paralleling that found in South Africa.[38]

It is within *political structures* that society makes those decisions that determine the allocation of power, privilege and resources among groups. Under the 1923 Constitution the Southern Rhodesian Parliament became the legitimate body within which those allocative decisions were made. On the surface it was a "non-racial" document, for it stipulated that any person who met specific educational and financial requirements was eligible to vote. A few Blacks met those qualifications. but, by limiting the educational and employment opportunities of Blacks, Whites effectively disfranchised all but a few Blacks. In later years Whites continued to raise the educational/financial franchise requirements as a means of keeping out increasing numbers of Blacks who otherwise would have qualified for the vote under the old requirements.[39]

Responding to increased Black pressures for the franchise, Whites enacted new constitutions in 1961, 1965 and 1969. Where under the 1923 Constitution there was a common roll of White and Black voters, the proposed 1961 Constitution introduced two separate rolls, an A and B roll which, while assuring continued White rule almost into perpetuity, made many Whites fearful of possible Black rule. The Constitution was approved by the electorate, but shortly thereafter the newly formed Rhodesian Front party campaigned and won the 1962 election on the basis that it would restructure the political system and guarantee continued White rule. Following its election and the subsequent unilateral declaration of independence (UDI) from Great Britain in 1965, the RF promulgated the 1965 and 1969 Constitutions that prevented Blacks from ever achieving a majority position in Parliament.[40]

Thus it has been through the political structures that White Rhodesians have maintained their power: first, by enhancing their own power resources while restricting those of Blacks; second, by modifying franchise requirements or even the political structures when it appeared that Black might threaten White control; and third, by enacting security measures that have severely curtailed the development and mobilization activities of groups (Black and White) that oppose the existing White dominance system. The end result of White dominance has been the emergence of a society based on White power and privilege.

## III. Contemporary Patterns of Discrimination

The contemporary patterns of discrimination in Rhodesia so pervade the warp and woof of the society that it is impossible in an article of this length to give a detailed description of their operations. They can, however, be usefully summarized under five headings: legal and coercive, economic, social, political and ideological, keeping in mind the interrelated nature of discriminatory practice as it spans these categories.

### A. *Legal and Coercive Legislation*

As was mentioned earlier much of Rhodesian legislation which has a discriminatory impact is not ostensibly racial in form. The two principal pieces of legislation which explicitly differentiate between the main racial groups in the society are the 1969 Constitution (especially with regard to the franchise) and the Land Tenure Act of 1969. The discriminatory provisions and effects of these items will be taken up in subsequent sections on political and economic discrimination. Parallel to and in most cases building on these two legal instruments there is however a vast edifice of legislative enactment which is not explicitly directed at any racially distinguished segment of the society but which, given the structure of the society, has the effect of discriminating against the Black population. Particularly is this the case with regard to labour laws and security laws. Labour legislation will be covered in the following section, and we deal here with the legal basis for coercive action which in effect is applied almost exclusively to Blacks.

It must be noted that the 1969 Constitution contains a Declaration of Rights which provides, *inter alia*, for the right to personal property, the protection of the law, protection from search and entry, freedom of expression, assembly and association and protection from "unjust discrimination".[41] However the requirements of system maintenance have necessitated a collection of security legislation permitting the abrogation of these rights when they have, in Black hands, constituted a threat to White control. Although, in Palley's words, they are "couched in non-racial and neutral language,"[42] their operation in practice has been directed almost exclusively against Blacks. A series of legislative enactments providing for this situation can be traced, among the more important being the Subversive Activities Act (1950), which gave government the power to ban meetings, to prohibit or confiscate publications of "subversive" groups, and to establish a security police force; the Public Order Act (1955) whereby individuals could be detained or restricted without charge or trial; the Native Affairs Amendment Act (1959), which prohibited public meetings in the reserves (later, Tribal Trust Lands) unless approved by the district commissioner (thereby curtailing nationalist efforts to recruit members); the Unlawful Organization Acts (1959, 1962) whereby individuals considered a threat to public order could be detained; the Law and Order (Maintenance) Act (1960) and subsequent amendments, which allowed for the banning of meetings, censorship of publications and search and arrest without warrant; and the Emergency Powers Act (1965) which provided for summary arrest and detention without trial. In addition to these measures (with numerous amendments), the 1969 Constitution also approved the right of detention and restriction in the name of public order and safety; and the Emergency Powers (Maintenance of Law and Order) Regulations (1967).[43] Under this last legislation and Section 61 of the Constitution the President may declare a state of emergency rendering inoperative the basic protections of the Declaration of rights to the extent that inconsistent laws are "reasonably justifiable" for the purpose of dealing with any situation which has arisen or may arise during that period.[44] The President may further, in terms of the Emergency Powers Act, "make such regulations as appear to him to be necessary or expedient for the public safety . . ."[45]

Since U.D.I. in 1965 there has been a continuous state of emergency, and thus the sweeping powers indicated above, and the abrogation of the protections of the Declaration of Rights, have been continuous. The discriminatory implementation of these powers can be identified in a number of areas. With regard to the right of assembly and association, Government has used the legislation severely to restrict the convening of political meetings and rallies. Most of this restriction has been applied in the Tribal Trust Lands and Black urban townships, only very rarely to White political groups. Numerous Black nationalist parties have been banned under the Unlawful Organizations Act. The result is that it is extremely difficult for any Black political party to establish any consistent grass-roots infrastructure and organization. With regard to freedom of expression, the legislation permits the Government to prohibit, ban or censor publications. The application of this set of provisions is discriminatory, in that bannings on political grounds have applied almost solely to publications written from the Black nationalist point of view.[46] The legislation also prohibits 'subversive' statements, defined as including, *inter alia*, those which are likely "to excite disaffection against ... the government or Constitution of Rhodesia as by law established or the administration of justice therein," and those which are likely to "... promote feelings of hostility to or expose to contempt, ridicule or disesteem any group, section or class in or of the community of a particular race, religion or colour."[47] Again, the effect of this legislation is discriminatory in that it is Black politicans who, by virtue of their social location, are likely in their activities to be construed as "exciting disaffection" against the Government or the Constitution, and any attack by them on White power as promoting "feelings of hostility" towards Whites.

The legislation also permits detention without warrant by the police, indefinite detention by the Minister of Law and Order and the imposition by the Minister of restriction orders "for the purpose of maintaining law and order." These mechanisms are used largely against Blacks. The few Whites under detention or restriction orders have drawn the attention of the press; what is often not realized is the large number of Blacks under similar orders, stated to be 664 by Rhodesian Christian Care in September 1975.[48]

Writing in 1968, even before some of the legislative measures mentioned here, the former Chief Justice of Southern Rhodesia, Sir Robert Tredgold, had this to say:

> The cumulative effects of the security laws was to turn Rhodesia into a police state. The word has an emotional content and many white Rhodesians become very angry if it is used of their country. Yet, as I understand it, a 'police state' is a state in which the police and the executive are given or assume complete control over all political activity. In this sense it is manifestly true of the Rhodesia of today.[44]

The characteristics of a 'police state' as described in this passage are not, of course, confined to Rhodesia. What is of special note about the

Rhodesian case is that the "cumulative effects" of the security laws there are singularly discriminatory in their application, being utilized almost exclusively to control one segment of the population – the Blacks.

### *B. Economic Discrimination*

The discriminatory mechanisms providing for continued White dominance in the economic sphere of Rhodesian society relate largely to land occupation and usage, labour and education.

Control of land and control of labour are closely integrated in the Rhodesian White dominance system and must therefore be viewed in a single context.

(i) *Land.* As indicated earlier, the Land Apportionment Act of 1930 and its successor, the Land Tenure Act of 1969, effectively legislate a system of racially apportioned land in the country. The country as a whole is divided into two equal parts, ownership, occupation and usage in one half being reserved, with certain exceptions, for Blacks, and likewise for Whites in the other. In terms of the latter and currently effective Act, the White area amounts to 44.95 million acres, the Black area to 44.94 million acres.[50] This arrangement is justified on a "separate-but-equal" type of ideological equasion, the argument being that in Black areas Black interests are to be paramount and in White areas White interests likewise, the effect being to minimize competition and inter-racial strife. The result has been, however, neither separation (since the White area continues to require Black labour) nor equality. Much of the best agricultural land is in the White area.[51] The White area contains most of the land along the railways, every town and significant industrial area and most of the important mine workings. Thus the areas of greatest natural wealth, the areas of greatest industrial and commercial development, are the proprietary right of the Whites, to which Blacks are admitted only on a tenuous basis.

One important effect of the Act is severely to limit the opportunities of Blacks to own land. They cannot, with a few limited exceptions, own land in the White area, and in the Black area most of the land(39.9 million acres) is communally held. Only in the 3,669,379 acres of "Purchase Land" can Blacks obtain freehold title, and this only after fulfilling certain agricultural qualifications.[52]

The situation thus pertains whereby the large bulk of the Black area is reserved for subsistence peasant agriculture on land held communally; Blacks seeking to enter the wage sector of the economy are, in the main, required to enter and reside in the White area, which they do subject to the restrictions imposed thereby. To seek work in this area they must have a permit to do so, and once having found employment they are subject to the residential restrictions attendant on that employment. In the urban areas Black townships are established in which most urban Blacks must reside, the principal exceptions being certain categories of domestic servants, night watchmen, etc. Little of the Black residential accommodation in the townships is available for home ownership, and to move between the townships and places of employment often involves travel over large distances. Black professional and businessmen are precluded by the Act from practice outside the townships or in the more favourable central areas of the towns and cities.[53]

The Act thus serves as a multi-faceted mechanism for maintaining White economic domination. In restricting the amount of viable arable land available to Blacks it helps to ensure a steady flow of cheap labour to White farms, mines and urban and industrial areas. Within the urban areas it severely limits Black occupational stability and capital accumulation and inhibits Black entrepreneurial activity by placing it at a disadvantage in competition with White commerce and industry.

(ii) *Labour.* Labour practice in Rhodesia under contemporary legislation, primarily the Industrial Conciliation Act of 1959, is ostensibly non-racial.[54] Before the enactment of this legislation labour organization had been structured racially, with the result that White trade unionism had gained a dominant formal position in the pre-war period which it has subsequently maintained. Although under the legislation all registered trade unions are non-racial, most of the largest and most influential remain under effective White control since voting strength within these unions is graded according to categories of occupation and most Black workers have minimal voting strength on this basis. Some registered unions are effectively Black in membership, leadership and perspective, but the strength of these unions is vitiated by the fact that their membership is largely unskilled and therefore in a poor bargaining position. Furthermore, Black trade union leadership is severely limited in the scope and vigour of its activities by restrictions placed on its links with international labour organizations and on any connections or pronouncements that are construed by Government as being of a quasi-political nature.[55]

Other discriminatory limitations on the Black labour situation in the wage sector must be noted. Recruitment and placement into middle and higher categories by employment in commerce and industry for Blacks is seriously inadequate and attended by a plethora of discriminatory practices, most of them customary and administrative rather than legislative. This has resulted in a situation whereby even Black aspirants to the positions with good academic qualifications are largely precluded from placement in them. Only 11.6% of the Form IV and Form VI output of the Black secondary school system in 1971 were employed in 1972, and many of these were underemployed in terms of the utilization of their achievements.[56] This situation arises from the combination of a number of factors: White artisan resistance and White employer stereotypes of Black occupational incompetence which inhibit Black apprenticeship registrations and on-the-job training, White customer resistance and legislation requiring separate eating and toilet facilities for Blacks, outmoded job categorizations imported from overseas, poor vocational guidance programmes for Black school-leavers and the pervasive effects of a long occupational tradition which often makes it situationally rational for Blacks in employment to behave in ways confirming White stereotypes of their occupational performance.[57] This situation pertains, in a modified form, not only in the trades but in the professions as well. At the time of writing there was not a single indigenous Black magistrate or public prosecutor in the country, although a number of Blacks with legal qualifications exist. Black doctors are restricted in their practice; only a handful of Black graduates are posted in officer ranks in the Ministries of Agriculture and Internal Affairs. In the Army, Police Force and Prison Service a similar situation pertains. In education, qualified Black teachers may teach only in Black schools, while White teachers may teach in both the Black and the White school systems.[58]

All of these factors create a sustained institutional pattern of occupational disadvantagement for Blacks which, when combined with their position in regard to the occupancy and use of land, result in a self-perpetuating syndrome of economic dependency and underprivilege continually reinforcing their subordinate economic status within the society.

## C. *Educational and Social Discrimination*

(i) *Educational discrimination.* The European and African Education Departments are administered by a single ministry but have developed as distinct and different systems. This is hardly surprising, since different regulations and budgetary provisions exist in regard to education for Whites and education for Blacks. The Government educational system (excluding technical training) is segregated by race, one system serving the Black population and the other serving the White, Coloured and Asian populations. In the second, "European", system there is one administration but Coloured and Asian pupils jointly attend schools segregated from those attended by White scholars.

Differential expenditure on education in the two systems for 1975 is demonstrated in the following table:

*Government Expenditure on Education by Racial Group 1975*[55]

| *Expenditure on* | *European, Asian and Coloured Division* | ± | *African Division* |
|---|---|---|---|
| Primary School Enrolment | 39,613 | | 810,908 |
| Expenditure | $ 11,366,457 | | $ 15,210,862 |
| Expenditure per pupil | $ 286,93 | | $ 18,75 |
| Secondary School Enrolment | 29,448 | | 37,462 |
| Expenditure | $ 14,519,362 | | $ 6,955,746 |
| Expenditure per pupil | $ 493,05 | | $ 185,67 |

The racial disparity in educational expenditure reflected in this table is by no means the complete picture; per capita expenditure in the table related to enrolled students only and when expenditure is contrasted with total population figures the disparity is even greater. Black primary school enrolments represent 133 pupils per 1,000 of the Black population, whereas White student enrolments represent 142 pupils per 1,000 of that population. At the secondary level, Black enrolments represent 6 pupils per 1 000 of the population while White enrolments represent 106 per 1,000.[60]

It should also be noted from the table that there is an extremely high attrition rate in the Black system, producing a broad based educational population pyramid in which pupils in secondary schools represent only 4% of the system, while in the White system the corresponding figures is 43%. Education for Whites is compulsory to the age of 15 and the White pupil automatically goes on to secondary school and if sufficiently bright to Sixth Form where tuition is free. On the other hand the Black child, as Dorsey says, "... enters a system that is voluntary and highly selective. Whether he continues or not at certain levels depends upon his ability to pass examinations and his parents' ability to pay his fees."[61] The attenuated nature of the provision of secondary educational facilities to Blacks is deliberate Government policy for both fiscal and structural reasons.[62] A broadly-based primary system for Blacks providing basic competence in literacy and numeracy serves the dual purpose of providing an effective unskilled work force for commerce and industry as well as contributing to system legitimacy.[63] A restricted secondary system provides for the more limited demands for skilled Black labour while at the same time limiting potential competition with White skilled labour.

Discrimination also exists in the teaching service. In the European Division teachers are public servants; teachers in the African Division are not, being members of the Unified African Teaching Service. Differences in salary scales and emoluments are substantial, teachers in the African Division being disadvantaged.[64]

The dual system of education briefly described here has the important effect of minimizing contact between the young citizens of the Country across racial lines. Even multi-racial sporting events are prohibited on the premises of White schools. The only significant breach in this barrier is to be found in the country's independent (private) schools, a number of which are multi-racial. Even in these schools (which are in terms of the Land Tenure Act in White areas) enrolment of Black students is limited by legislation to 6% of the student body.[65] In 1975 Black students in these schools totalled 561.[66]

(ii) *Social discrimination.* Social segregation in Rhodesia is, to many, a bewildering variant of the South African version, built on a mixture of convention, permissiveness and legislation designed to prevent "forced integration". Insofar as this segregation acts discriminatorily against any racially defined group it is in theory supposed to do so against Blacks in White areas (so defined by the Land Tenure Act) and against Whites in Black areas. In practice however few Whites live or work in Black areas and the discriminatory impact of this social segregation operates almost entirely against Blacks in White areas.

The most important aspect of social discrimination in these areas is that of residential segregation, discussed earlier in the section under Land. Blacks are required to reside in townships set aside for their use and are precluded from purchasing residential property in the White areas. Asians and Coloureds can under general legislation do so, and a few more wealthy Asians do in fact live in some of the White suburbs. However restrictive clauses in title deeds are permitted debarring purchase by members of a given race. How widespread these are in fact is not clear at the moment. A bill to provide for residential segregation between Whites, Coloureds and Asians was introduced in 1967 to prevent "racial friction and the depreciation of property in mainly European areas infiltrated by Coloured or Asian persons"[67] but was not implemented, presumably because purchases of this type have not been numerous and the effect has been achieved by social pressure.

Medical facilities are largely segregated by race. The Municipal Amendment Act of 1967 empowers municipalities to regulate and maintain separate amenities on a racial basis, including parks, sporting facilities, sanitary conveniences and swimming baths. Practice differs therefore from place-to-place; most bus services, parks and offices are not segregated while toilet facilities tend to be so, and swimming baths quite definitely so. Most bars, restaurants and hotels are segregated by social convention, proprietors being enabled to debar customers on the grounds of race by legislation. Some hotels catering to wealthier clientele are integrated, but even these establishments are in terms of the General Laws Amendment Act of 1972 and the actions of the Liquor Board precluded from serving non-resident Blacks after certain hours.[68]

Unlike South Africa, marriage across racial lines is not prohibited by law. Considerable social pressure against such marriages does however exist, and mixed couples are restricted in terms of where they can reside. One township in Salisbury, Westwood, is specifically set aside to house such families, but other than this provision, such couples are generally restricted to residence at such places as missions and the University.[69]

### D. *Political Discrimination*

In 1969, the Rhodesian Front government appealed to the electorate for support of a new Constitution, claiming: "... the present (1965) Constitution is no longer acceptable to the people of Rhodesia because

... it provides for eventual African rule ..."[70] The electorate responded affirmatively, 81% voting approval of a new Constitution that precludes the possibility of Blacks ever achieving a majority. Moreover, its Declaration of Rights states that racially discriminatory legislation is permissable "if such treatment is fair and will promote harmonious relations ..."

The new Constitution made explicit what had previously been implicit: namely, the use of political structures, legislation and administrative practice for restricting the Black's development of political resources while preserving White supremacy. The legitimacy of a society is vested in its political system, and decisions and policy reached and implemented within those political structures are thereby seen as legitimate. Those policy decisions affect life in all spheres: economic, social and political. Consequently, by retaining control of political structures Whites in Rhodesia have been able to make decisions which determine the allocation of resources, power and privilege between themselves and Blacks. Control of the political system is thereby crucial for maintaining power.

Under earlier Constitutions (1923, 1961 and 1965) there existed the *remote* possibility that at some future date (providing Whites did not continue to manipulate franchise requirements) Blacks could become the majority in Parliament.[71] The new Constitution prevents that. At most, Blacks (95% of the population) can achieve parity with Whites (less than 5% of the population). Political power is vested in the lower House of Assembly, composed of 50 Europeans and 16 Blacks (Asians and Coloureds are classified as European for voting purposes). When the Black population pays at least 24% of the total national revenue raised by direct income tax (they presently pay less than 0.5%), the number of Black representatives will gradually be increased until, at some future point, they achieve parity in members in Parliament.[72] However, given discrimination in employment, wages and opportunities for Blacks, the possibility of their ever paying the designated percentage of income tax (or of ultimately achieving parity in Parliament) is remote if not impossible. Even if Blacks did achieve parity, that would mean little, for half or more of their representation in Parliament is through tribal chiefs who remain under control of the Government.[73]

Parliament and the administrative bureaucracy are the legitimate bodies through which policy is enacted and administered. Be it in terms of funds or programmes, Parliament determines the allocation of resources to White and Black groups – and greater resources are (and historically have been) allocated to Whites, be it in terms of supportive services, loans, or assistance to Europeans (in agriculture, commerce or other sectors) or for European education (see the above section on Social Discrimination). It is these differentials in services, opportunities and resources allocated or available to Blacks that severely restricts their ability to compete with Europeans on an equal basis. Discrimination assumes other, and often more subtle forms than that which is evident in legislation. For instance, "non-racial" legislation is enacted that allows political bodies other than the national government to act in a discriminatory manner.[74] Thus, while there is no national legislation segregating public amenities (parks, swimming pools, recreation, etc.), the Municipal Amendment Act (1967) grants local governments the right to set such policies – and local governments do enact discriminatory ordinances. Similarly, in terms of administration, legislation itself may not be discriminatory but the discretionary authority left to public officials in the administration of policy allows them considerable latitude to act – often in a discriminatory fashion – in their dealings with the Black population.[75]

Hence, both directly and indirectly the Government has tried: (a) to restrict the access to or incorporation of Blacks within the political structures where allocative decisions are made; and (b) to differentially allocate those resources (including, among others, education and skills, government supportive services, employment opportunitites, etc.) which Blacks need if they are to compete or contest on an equal basis against the dominant White group. Other tactics and programmes have also been devised by Whites in an effort to curtail the emergence and development of Black nationalist movements and opposition to White control. The three most significant include: the attempt to redevelop traditional tribal authority (the chiefs) as a device for direct rule; the emphasis upon tribalism and tribal differences as a means of splitting or undercutting the development of African nationalism; and the attempt to promote a programme of "provincialization" (somewhat comparable to the South African bantustan or homelands policy) as a means of splintering and keeping powerless African nationalist groups.

Pre-RF Government policy usually followed two strategies aimed at controlling African political involvement: a "middle-class strategy" where the franchise was restricted to "civilized and responsible" Africans and/or a "traditional authority strategy" where government tried to re-establish African tribal chiefs as the "true African spokesmen."[76] In both cases, though, Whites retained power, for they controlled Black access to the franchise and held ultimate power over the chiefs (whose appointment, tenure of office, salary and safety came from the Government). Both strategies "gave the appearance of African involvement without jeopardizing White domination.[77] Where earlier governments tended to emphasize the middle-class strategy, the Rhodesian Front deliberately pursued the second strategy, hopeful that by increasing the power of tribal chiefs it could undermine the growing influence of urban and nationalist leaders. Under the 1969 Constitution half of the Black members of Parliament must be chiefs (selected by the other chiefs), and in recent years the Government has granted broader authority to chiefs in land allocation, consultative matters with government agencies, and in handling local judicial matters. Final power, though, remains with the White-controlled Ministry of Internal Affairs.[78]

A second means for eroding nationalist support has been the policy of tribalism.[79] Indeed, the 1969 Constitution attempts to drive a wedge between the two major African ethnic groups, the Shona and Ndebele, by dividing the 16 Assembly seats evenly between them even though the Shona constitute nearly 70% of the Black population. Moreover, should Blacks obtain additional parliamentary seats, the greater number will go to rural representatives, for it has been the urban Africans who have been more prone to oppose government policy and to join nationalist movements.

The RF's "provincialization" scheme (never fully implemented) constitutes yet another device for preserving White power.[80] Both the Constitution and the Land Tenure Act espouse the policy of separation of groups, the Constitution calling "for the division of Rhodesia into provinces and other regional divisions." This means not only the separation of Black from White areas (as in the Land Tenure Act) but also the further separation of Shona from Ndebele areas or provinces. Although the provinces would be granted a degree of autonomy, ultimate power remains vested in the White-controlled Parliament. By whatever names the policy of provincialization is called (two pyramids, separate development, parallel development), it is highly reminiscent of South Africa's bantustan or homelands policy. There is a difference, however, for where South Africa has now moved toward a policy (though whether or not it is fully implemented remains to be seen) of proposing and granting the homelands their independence (the Transkei received its independence in October 1976), the Rhodesian policy envisages no such recognition of independence to Shona or Ndebele provinces. Rather, Rhodesian policy is aimed simply at preserving White hegemony be it through the curtailing of opportunities and power resources of Blacks or through the pursuit of tactics (vesting power in chiefs, tribalism, provincialization) aimed at emasculating (by a "divide and rule" policy) African nationalist demands for Black majority rule. Race relations in Rhodesia are graphic examples of power relations, and Whites fully utilize their control of structures and resources to preserve White supremacy. Their obsessive desire to retain power is not simply in terms of privilege, for there has emerged a loosely defined ideology that derives from earlier held cultural beliefs about the superiority of Whites and their "way of life." It is this ideology that Whites believe gives them the right (or the legitimacy) to rule over the vast Black population.

### E. *Ideology and Discrimination*

In comparison with South Africa, Rhodesia lacks a clear ideological framework for its racial policies. Since UDI it "has been edging toward more formalized separation of the races," but it "has managed to perfect its system of segregation and control without adopting the ideological baggage that accompanies the apartheid system in South Africa."[81] Nevertheless, it can be argued that Rhodesia's system of "apartheid by bye-law and convention" rests on a cluster of basic beliefs that constitute a loosely-defined racial ideology, one that is based on White cultural beliefs and the cumulative experiences of White-Black contests.

Whether classified as an ideology or belief system, these White racial notions (which hold that Whites are superior to Blacks) serve a number of functions. For example, the beliefs about White and Black capabilities serve a legitimating function, justifying for the Whites their support of racial stratification and discrimination. Whites knowingly use power in some instances to preserve their privileges, but in other cases they employ power for the protection of a culture and way of life (excluding, for the moment, the aspect of privilege) which they believe will be destroyed if Blacks assume power.

Belief systems based on notions of racial/cultural superiority are often dogmatically upheld by a (in this instance, White) group. Thus cases which illustrate that Blacks are as capable as Whites are discounted or simply not recognized (through a process of "selective perception"). Similarly, examples that purportedly show Blacks as less capable or prone to misuses of power are quickly grasped as "confirmation" of the Black's supposed inferiority or threat to White culture. Consequently, ideology serves to legitimatize for Whites their continued control of society. They may justify their power in terms of the "preservation of civilized society or standards," and discriminatory measures against those who do not meet those "standards" are considered legitimate. Efforts to inculcate in individuals these racial beliefs are not directed solely toward Whites, for the power holders use education, the media, and other means for indoctrinating Blacks as well. For, as previously noted, if Blacks can be made to *believe* or accept the notion that they are inferior to or less capable than Whites, it is less likely that they will rebel against their subordinate position. Despite the surface-level emphasis on "civilized standards" and "meritocracy," White Rhodesians have openly used their control of political, economic and social structures to discriminate against Blacks in such a manner that few can acquire those "standards." Moreover, Whites use these racial beliefs to justify repression of Black opposition to discriminatory measures.

Previously two sets of beliefs, overlapping yet distinct, shaped White policy toward Blacks, and the 1976 Quénet Report on racial discrimination has brought into sharp relief these opposing beliefs. Labelled earlier as "cultural" and "genetic", these beliefs rest on different assumptions. The former holds that Blacks, though culturally different at present, are like Whites when educated and westernized. Thus, by becoming "civilized" Blacks can be fully incorporated within European society. The second view holds that Blacks are genetically inferior to or genetically different from Whites, and incorporation in European society (except as subordinate people) is thereby impossible. A more recent version of this genetic view claims that Black and White are fundamentally (whether genetic or not is not said) different culturally, and efforts at westernization or assimilation of Blacks (and their subsequent incorporation into White structures) can only generate hostility and conflict. Hence separation is necessary. It is this assumption, (among others), of fundamental cultural differences that underlies contemporary South African policy aimed at establishing independent homelands. Moreover, there is the fear that Black incorporation within White structures will lead to Black rule (given their larger population), and Blacks will then destroy the separate culture of European (or Afrikaner) society.[82]

Viewed historically, the White Rhodesian settler society (except for liberals and some missionaries) considered Blacks genetically inferior to Whites. However, the metropole (British government) imposed in the 1923 Constitution regulations for Black political participation that were clearly based on the cultural principle: namely, that educated Blacks should be incorporated. However the settlers held political power and Black acquisition of education and financial assets quickly prompted White society to raise franchise requirements and thereby exclude Black participation. Moreover, White policy in both economic and social sectors was discriminatory and clearly aimed at keeping Blacks from fulfilling the "civilized" or "merit" criteria which would have permitted their structural incorporation.

Numerous factors contributed to the gradual incorporation of Blacks within structures, major advances occurring especially during the Federation period (1953–63). However, those Black advances threatened the White community, and even Whites who had earlier upheld "racial partnership" became supporters of a Rhodesian Front party that pledged itself to perpetual White rule. To achieve this, the RF has attempted to evolve a policy that at different times has been referred to as "separate development," "parallel development" or "provincialization," a policy that is somewhat reminiscent of earlier proposals (prior to World War II) for a "two pyramid" policy. At the base of all such proposals, including provincialization, has been the principle of separation of racial groups. Slowly the RF has moved toward the policies of South Africa, but circumstances and events have prevented it from moving as rapidly as many of its members would desire. Consequently, to assure its holding of power the White society and government have pursued discriminatory measures aimed at reducing or restricting the development by Blacks of their power resources. To justify these actions the Whites have relied upon that loosely-defined racial ideology previously noted. Pressures, though, both external and internal, have forced the government to reassess its discriminatory policies, and in 1975 the Prime Minister appointed a commission to investigate and recommend the elimination of "unnecessary" discriminatory measures.

## IV. Current Developments

The Quénet Commission was charged with the responsibility to "advise Government of those cases or aspects of discrimination which are no longer considered desirable and necessary." The Commission published its report in June 1976. Its recommendations were almost immediately rejected by Black nationalists and right-wing individuals and groups joined in opposition, though for opposite reasons. RF parliamentary backbenchers in particular opposed the recommendations (one even referred to the recommendations as a "Frankenstein" monster which, if implemented, would doom White civilization); and at the time of writing (mid-July 1976) the Prime Minister, given the criticism within his party, seems most likely to strike a compromise (by rejecting the major recommendations calling for changes in land tenure and the franchise) rather than face a split within the party. Nevertheless, recognizing the need to make some changes that would (at least from his and the party's perspective) reduce pressures being exerted against the country because of its racial policies, it appears likely that the Prime Minister would gain support from his party for implementing social and economic changes that do not fundamentally threaten the White power structure.

Since the RF 1962 victory and UDI in 1965, pressures against the country have intensified significantly. The external pressures include, among others: (a) the British Government's continued refusal to recognize the Rhodesian Government's legitimacy, resulting in economic and political sanctions against the country; (b) increasing outside African pressures, including the use of other countries as a base for Black Rhodesian guerilla incursions against the Government; and (c) world pressures, including UN economic and political sanctions and, of more recent date, Russian and U.S. interests in African affairs. The major internal pressures include: (a) structural pressures, prompted especially by economic development needs and the increasing shortage of White workers; (b) an intensifying guerilla war that, while being contained at the moment, seriously disrupts the economy and creates political instabilities; (c) Black demands, of nationalists and others, for structural changes, ranging from demands for greater Black incorporation (in present structures) to calls for Black majority rule; and (d) White attitudes and responses, from dogmatic right-wing rejections of any change to the quiet exodus of large numbers of Whites from the country because of fears for the future and/or opposition to Government policy.

The Quénet Commission was established, it appears, in hopes that its recommendations for change might placate criticisms, mute Black opposition, remove some of the external and internal pressures, and possibly lead toward the removal of economic and political sanctions against the Government. However, as indicated, the Report did not have that effect. Indeed, it intensified opposition within the ruling RF party, so much that as of this writing it appears that the Prime Minister may try to prevent a possible split within the party's ranks by jettisoning the major structural recommendations for change (e.g., changes in land tenure and the franchise) while heralding as "major advances" steps taken to remove the more petty types of racial discrimination.

What is significant, though, is that the government has tried by this technique to cope with diverse pressures through the appointment of a commission that would recommend changes in the society. Despite the "gradualist" nature of the Commission's recommendations, the vociferous opposition suggests the tenacity with which racialist beliefs are held in White society. The recommendations are essentially meliorist or gradualist, for they envision the incorporation of Blacks who have acquired the "civilized standards" that Whites see as essential for a society based on "meritocracy." This, as earlier indicated, represents a "middle class strategy," the system incorporating Blacks who will uphold the system by virtue of their incorporation in it. However, as indicated below, even the implementation of most of the proposed recommendations would have only a limited effect in removing racial discrimination or in affording Blacks equal access to or opportunity within political, economic and social structures.

The Quénet Commission exercise, carried out under conditions provoking great cynicism from various quarters, was handicapped by terms of reference which directed it to examine the overt manifestations of racial discrimination rather than its structural foundations. Furthermore, the Commission was infused with a pragmatic, gradualist approach which gave constant consideration to what were considered to be the tolerance levels which Whites would accept (i.e., in terms of their willingness to be dispossessed of privilege produced by discrimination). Thus repeated references to ideal conditions (defined in terms of a meritocratic ideology) are continually juxtaposed with gradualistic assumptions and considerations regarding attitudinal change among Whites.[83]

Given these limitations, the Commission's report is noteworthy for the way in which it identifies and addresses itself to some of the major structural aspects of White dominance which are mentioned earlier in this essay. It pinpoints the Land Tenure Act as "the main cause of friction between the races",[84] and recommends replacement of this Act by a system of land usage with two classifications, "private land" and "state land." "State land" would contain, *inter alia,* areas set aside for occupation by Blacks along traditional communal lines, while "private land" would in effect be thrown open for non-racial occupation by both Blacks and Whites within the limits of gradualism advocated by the Commission. The Report also identifies the racially-based franchise as a further instrument of friction in the society, stating that "the existing European and African rolls emphasized the division between the races"[85] and it recommends a return to a common roll.

The Report also makes an extensive examination of various disabilities suffered by Asians, Blacks and Coloureds in the occupational sphere and makes piece-meal recommendations in respect to a number of them.[86] It also takes up items of social discrimination mentioned earlier in this analysis and makes wide-ranging recommendations for the removal of racial discrimination in sport, public amenities, hotels, bars, restaurants and other public places.

It can therefore be said that a number of major structural components in the system of White dominance are dealt with in the Report: land, labour, the franchise, and social arrangements. The treatment of these issues is incomplete and vitiated by gradualism, but at least they are approached by the Commission and changes recommended. However two major structural factors in the system are left relatively unscathed by the Report's recommendations, education and ideology. The Commission considered in some detail the country's segregated educational system and heard submissions that the provision of educational facilities should be equalized. The Commission noted that the matter was "beset" with the problem of finance and concluded that "Much as one would like to see universal education it is an objective completely beyond the country's resources at present."[87] For the Commission equalization of educational provision implied the raising of standards in the Black system to current levels pertaining in the White system, not a redistribution of currently available resources to the two systems or an integration of the two systems. This is of course an issue of fundamental importance to the current structures of White privilege. For, even if the country's economic and political structures are thrown open to Blacks on a non-racial meritocratic basis, their limited access to or acquisition of the relevant criteria needed for the franchise and employment is severely restricted as long as their educational opportunities are curtailed.

Again, the Commission nowhere significantly addresses itself to the ideological component in the current structures of dominance. Indeed it could hardly be expected to do so, since its whole approach to Rhodesian society is an assimilationist one. It rests on the assumption that removal of racial discrimination equates simply to the removal of all ascriptive racially-defined barriers and that this will lead to the complete absorption of all the country's citizens into a homogeneous society predetermined by White models. Thus the Commission's approach, in this sense, contributes to an ideological reinforcement of the current system however benign its intent may have been. Nowhere in the Report is there the recognition that the removal of racial discrimination in Rhodesia might involve a shift in the cultural perspectives of White Rhodesians themselves, that it would involve the ideological dominance of purely White models and indeed a removal of White dominance itself. In this lies the fundamental superficiality of the Report, for it fails properly to recognize the interrelated nature of the items of racial discrimination it examines or the system maintenance function which they serve.

For the time being, the probability is that those Commission recommendations will be implemented which do not fundamentally alter the structures whereby White power is maintained. Indeed, subsequent palliative measures may be enacted in response to continued pressures (external and internal) – as long as such measures do not significantly alter the present power balance. Fundamental change, however, and particularly that leading toward Black rule appears improbable. System maintenance will continue as long as "existing circumstances" prevail. However, as indicated below, those circumstances are changing – and it is they, not the Commission recommendations, which hold the key to future developments.

Rhodesia has gone "full circle," and it now stands where it did in 1962. At that time, the United Federal Party, hoping to stem Black nationalism by its middle-class strategy of incorporating "civilized" Africans, proposed "the repeal of existing racially discriminatory laws which are either unnecessary or are unfair," calling also for changes in land tenure and franchise.[88] The parallel with the present is indicative. The UFP efforts, though, were seen as threatening the White community's power and privilege, and both then and since it has supported a Rhodesian Front Party dedicated to the preservation of White power. However, persistent pressures have compelled the RF government to pursue steps (as evident in the Quénet Report and the Prime Minister's response) virtually parallel to those of the UFP in 1962, and it is that which has created dissension within the RF Party. It is the right-wing supporters in particular who claim that the Party, if it accepts the Quénet recommendations, has "sold out" on its basic principles. In that, they are historically correct. But pressures, external and internal, have forced the Government to that position, for circumstances have changed.

Given the continuation of existing conditions and circumstances (i.e., a prolonged but "contained" guerilla war, the disorganization of Black nationalist forces, relatively high White morale and support of the Government, no real external threats from outside African military forces, and oblique but consistent South African support), White dominance and racial discrimination could continue for an extended period.

However, circumstances have and are changing, and it is these which will determine future events. Both internal and external factors must be considered here, and particularly those which constitute vulnerabilities for the White system. Internal factors and vulnerabilities cannot be discounted. For example a prolonged guerilla war, even if contained by the Government, could so drain the economy that pressures from business and industry would necessitate concessions from the Government toward Black incorporation. Second, prolonged war and lowered morale could prompt the exodus of Whites from the Country, a move that is already evident. And third, *if* Black groups *could* organize and coalesce, they could exert pressures on the Government for change. For what is evident, even when one takes into consideration the resiliency and determination of White society despite conditions and its pariah status since UDI, is that Whites would not now be in power if Blacks had organized their forces and worked together for the change of the present government.

External factors, though, increasingly appear more significant for change in Rhodesia. To some extent Rhodesia has survived because of its insignificance in the context of international politics. This has changed, however, as a consequence of Russian involvement in African affairs (e.g., Angola, Mozambique), a move that has prompted U.S. concern. Hence the 1976 efforts by the United States and other countries to seek a "solution" to the "Rhodesian problem" before it exacerbates a big power confrontation on the African continent. Consequently, in terms of external factors, intensification of guerilla warfare in Rhodesia, with possible support from other African (or outside) countries could expedite changes within Rhodesia. A second vulnerability for Rhodesia is its reliance on imports and exports, without which it could not survive economically. Despite UN economic sanctions, numerous countries still covertly trade with Rhodesia, and by innumerable surreptitious means Rhodesia breaks these economic sanctions and exports its goods. Without the foreign exchange received from its exports Rhodesia could not survive economically. Should economic sanctions against Rhodesia be stringently imposed it would have difficulty surviving. Hence it is South Africa which constitutes Rhodesia's most vulnerable point. Should South Africa see advantages in the establishment of a Black government in Rhodesia,[89] it most likely would quietly move to bring about that change, for it *controls* the very life-line of Rhodesia: namely, the railroad system through which Rhodesia exports and imports. Without that life-line and South African support, Rhodesia cannot survive. Its continuation rests in the hands of South Africa. Indeed, South Africa exercises over Rhodesia greater power than the British Government ever exerted over its recalcitrant Rhodesian colony, a fact clearly evident in Britain's inability to topple the Rhodesian Front government after it unilaterally declared its independence in 1965.

Thus, if changes are to occur within Rhodesia, they are most likely to occur as a consequence of pressures being exerted on one or more of the major vulnerabilities of the country. These include: (a) its White support, (b) its Black support, (c) export-import factors (i.e., economic sanctions), and (d) South Africa. Were there an exodus of Whites, for example, or should guerilla warfare lead to White disillusionment or the exodus of Whites, it is possible that the Country would be forced to negotiate with Black groups. Second, the Government's support from Black groups should not be discounted. The tribal chiefs and tribal groups are a major factor in bolstering the White group despite their dismissal by analysts or their rejection as a factor by Black nationalists. For, without chief/tribal support, reluctant as it may be, the White Government would be unable to maintain itself in power. However, by criticizing rather than trying to gain support of these chief/tribal elements (who constitute for the present one sector of power), Black nationalists limit their own mobilization of Black support. Should they attempt to induce the chiefs to their side, the vulnerability of Whites would be such that changes would more likely occur. Likewise, were sanctions rigidly imposed and were the techniques by which Rhodesia succeeds in "sanctions-busting" effectively stopped, the country would suffer irreparable economic difficulties. Finally, and perhaps most significantly, if South Africa is persuaded to follow a policy of "shedding" Rhodesia (if only as a means of gaining time for attempting to resolve its own racial problems), then change may come quickly to Rhodesia.

Circumstances, as noted, are changing, for the Rhodesian issue has now been internationalized. The probability is that it will not again "disappear" into the "indifference" or backwaters of international politics until some solution is found. Until that time, despite palliative measures and melioristic actions, White domination and racial discrimination will continue in Rhodesia, preserved by the ability of a White group to restrict the resources and mobilization capabilities of Blacks while it justifies its power on a racial/cultural ideology that is a vestige of an earlier era.

NOTES

1. See especially the following articles on South Africa and Fiji: R. K. Vasil, "Ethnic Discrimination in Fiji: An Indian View," pp. 191–217 and D. Worrall, "Government in the Plural Society: The South African Model," pp. 287–300 in *Case Studies on Human Rights and Fundamental Freedoms, A World Survey, Vol. II*, W. A. Veenhoven, *ed.*, The Hague: Martinus Nijhoff, 1975.
2. *Report of the Commission of Inquiry into Racial Discrimination, 1976.* Salisbury: Rhodesia Government, Cmd. R.R. 6-1976, p. 1. The Commission sat under the chairmanship of Sir Vincent Quénet, Q.C., over the period October1975 – February 1976 and the Report will for reasons of convenience be referred to subsequently as the "Quénet Report."
3. In the manner discussed by Worrall, 1975, pp. 285–300.
4. Claire Palley, "Law and the Unequal Society: Discriminatory Legislation in Rhodesia under the Rhodesian Front from 1963 to 1969," Parts I and II, *Race*, Vol. XII, Nos. 1 and 2, 1970, pp. 15–47 and 139–167, at p. 161. For Rhodesian editorial comment on the differences between South African and Rhodesian policy see M. W. Murphree, "Race and Power in Rhodesia" in *Politics of Race*, D. G. Baker (ed.), London: Saxon House, D.C. Heath Ltd., 1975, p. 275.
5. Section 2(1) of the Electoral Act (Chapter 5). Quoted in the *Quénet Report*, p. 21.
6. *Monthly Digest of Statistics*, June, 1976, Salisbury: Central Statistical Office.
7. We distinghuish between race and ethnicity in the manner adopted by van den Berghe, racial groups being those which are socially defined largely utilizing physical criteria while ethnic groups are those which are similarly defined socially but largely on the basis of cultural criteria. P. van den Berghe, *Race and Racism*, New York: John Wiley and Sons, 1967, pp. 9–10.
8. *Census of Population 1969*, Salisbury: Central Statistical Office, 1976. p. 17.
9. Colin Leys, *European Politics in Southern Rhodesia*, London: Oxford University Press, 1959, p. 95.
10. See B. A. Kosmin, *Ethnic and Commercial Relations in Southern Rhodesia: A Socio-Historical Study of the Asian, Hellene and Jewish Populations, 1898–1943*, University of Rhodesia: D. Phil. thesis, 1974, unpublished.

11. See especially the following studies for a tracing of White-Black relations in Rhodesian society: L. H. Gann, *A History of Southern Rhodesia: Early Days to 1934*, London: Chatto and Windus, 1965; Leys, 1959; Thomas Franck, *Race and Nationalism*, New York: Fordham University Press, 1960; Richard Gray, *The Two Nations: The Development of Race Relations in the Rhodesias and Nyasaland*, London: Oxford University Press, 1960; T. O. Ranger, *Revolt in Southern Rhodesia*, London: Heinemann, 1967, and *The African Voice in Southern Rhodesia*, London: Heinemann, 1970; Cyril Rogers and C. Frantz, *Racial Themes in Southern Rhodesia*, New Haven: Yale University Press, 1962; and Larry Bowman, *Politics in Rhodesia*, Cambridge: Harvard University Press, 1973.
12. William J. Wilson, *Power, Racism and Privilege*, New York: Macmillan, 1973; Ira Katznelson, "Comparative Studies of Race and Ethnicity," *Comparative Politics*, Vol. V, October 1972; Gerhard Lenski, *Power and Privilege*, New York: McGraw-Hill, 1966; Donald G. Baker, "Politics, Power and Race Relations," in Baker, ed., 1975; Joseph Himes, *Racial Conflict in American Society*, Columbus: Charles E. Merrill, 1973.
13. The focus here, as indicated in fn. 7, is on the racial dimension, i.e., Black-White relations.
14. Milton Rokeach, *The Open and Closed Mind*, New York: Basic Books, 1960.
15. E. Franklin Frazier, *Race and Culture Contacts in the Modern World*, Boston: Beacon Press, 1957; Rene Maunier, *The Sociology of Colonies*, London: Routledge and Kegan Paul, 1949; Philip Mason, *Patterns of Dominance*, New York: Oxford University Press, 1970.
16. Lenski, 1966; Hubert M. Blalock, Jr., *Toward a Theory of Minority-Group Relations*, New York: John Wiley, 1967; R. A. Schermerhorn, *Comparative Ethnic Relations*, New York: Random House, 1970.
17. Donald Noel, "A Theory of the Origin of Ethnic Stratification," *Social Problems*, Vol. XVI, Autumn 1968.
18. *Ibid.*, George De Vos, "Social Stratification and Ethnic Pluralism," *Race*, Vol. XIII, April 1972; Katherine West, "Stratification and Ethnicity in 'Plural' New Societies," *Race*, Vol. XIII, April 1972; Donald G. Baker, "Race, Power and White Siege Cultures," *Social Dynamics*, Vol. I, December 1975.
19. Alvin Rabushka and Kenneth Shepsle, *Politics in Plural Societies*, Columbus: Charles E. Merrill, 1972; and fn. 12.
20. See especially Gann, and Ranger, 1967, 1970.
21. For constitutional developments, see especially Claire Palley, *The Constitutional History and Law of Southern Rhodesia*, Oxford: Clarendon Press, 1966, Part I.
22. *Ibid.*, Part I, chaps. 7–9, 14; Bowman, 1973, chap. I; Gray, 1960, chaps. 1–2,5; Franck, 1960, chaps. 1–2.
23. How White images of Blacks serve as part of their cultural beliefs and perceptions is traced especially in: Henri Baudet, *Paradise on Earth: Some Thoughts on European Images of Non-European Man*, New Haven: Yale University Press, 1965; H. Alan Cairns, *Prelude to Imperialism: British Reactions to Central African Society*, London: Routledge and Kegan Paul, 1965; Philip Curtin, *The Image of Africa: British Ideas and Action, 1780–1850*, Madison: University of Wisconsin Press, 1964; Christine Bolt, *Victorian Attitudes to Race*, London: Routledge and Kegon Paul, 1971; Winthrop Jordan, *White Over Black: American Attitudes toward the Negro*, Baltimore: Penguin Books, 1969. Cf., John Rex, *Race Relations in Sociological Perspective*, New York: Schocken, 1970, chap. 6.
24. Blalock, 1967, chap. 4.
25. G. Arrighi, "Labour Supplies in Historical Perspective: A Study of the Proletarianization of the African Peasantry in Rhodesia," *Journal of Development Studies*,

Vol. VI, April 1970; C. van Onselen, *Chibaro: African Mine Labour in Southern Rhodesia 1900–1933*, London: Pluto Press, 1976.

26. Palley, 1966, Part I, chaps. 8–9, 14, and Part II, chaps. 4–5. and also 1970.
27. Bowman, 1973, chaps. 3,7; Palley, 1970. The best survey of these and other facets of race relations in contemporary Rhodesia is Dorothy Davies, *Race Relations in Rhodesia*, London: Rex Collings, 1975.
28. G. Arrighi, *The Political Economy of Rhodesia*, The Hague: Mouton, 1967.
29. Arrighi, 1970.
30. Marshall W. Murphree, 1975, p. 259.
31. Charles Van Onselen, "Worker Consciousness in Black Miners: Southern Rhodesia, 1900–1920," *Journal of African History*, Vol. XIV, 1973, p. 245.
32. On economic developments, see especially: Arrighi, 1967; Marshall W. Murphree, *Employment Opportunity and Race in Rhodesia*, Denver: Studies in Race and Nations, University of Denver, 1973; Peter Harris, *Black Industrial Workers in Rhodesia*, Salisbury: Mambo Press, 1974; Duncan Clarke, *Contract Workers and Underdevelopment in Rhodesia*, Salisbury: Mambo Press, 1974, and *Domestic Workers in Rhodesia*, Salisbury: Mambo Press, 1974; Bowman, 1973, chaps. 6–7.
33. The role of education as a form of "cultural imperialism" is traced by Martin Carnoy, *Education as Cultural Imperialism*. New York: David McKay, 1974.
34. For a brief survey, see Norman Atkinson, *Teaching Rhodesians: A History of Educational Policy in Rhodesia*, London: Longman, 1972.
35. See Frantz Fanon, *Black Skin, White Masks*, London: Granada Publishers, 1970; Albert Memmi, *The Colonizer and the Colonized*, Boston: Beacon Press, 1967; and O. Mannoni, *Prospero and Caliban: The Psychology of Colonization*, New York: Praeger, 1968.
36. See especially Davies, 1975, and the Palley articles and book cited in fn. 21 and 26.
37. Bowman, 1973, chaps. 2–3; James Barber, *Rhodesia: The Road to Rebellion*, London: Oxford University Press, 1967; and Ian Henderson, "White Populism in Southern Rhodesia," *Comparative Studies in Society and History*, Vol. XIV, September 1972.
38. Bowman, 1973, chap. 7.
39. Palley, 1966, Part II, chap. I.
40. Bowman, 1973, chaps, 2, 4, 7.
41. International Commission of Jurists, *Racial Discrimination and Repression in Southern Rhodesia*, London: Catholic Institute for International Relations, 1976, p. 34.
42. Palley, 1970, p. 19.
43. For detailed treatment see Palley, 1970, pp. 38–47 and International Commission of Jurists, 1976, pp. 34–61.
44. Paragraph 11 of the 2nd Schedule of the Constitution, quoted in International Commission of Jurists, 1976, p. 34.
45. Section 4 of the Emergency Powers Act, quoted in International Commission of Jurists, 1976, p. 35.
46. *Ibid.*, pp. 38–40.
47. Section 44(1), Part III, Law and Order (Maintenance) Act, quoted in *ibid.*, p. 41.
48. *Ibid.*, p. 47. The Christian Care enumeration pertained to the organizations' own records only, and pointed out that these did not embody an unknown number of people being held incommunicado.
49. R. Tredgold, *The Rhodesia That Was My Life*, London: Allen and Unwin, 1968, p. 231.

50. Palley, 1970, p. 145. Palley's treatment of land legislation, pp. 139–149, contains valuable detail on this subject. See also International Commission of Jurists, 1976, pp. 11–19; *Quénet Report*, 1976, pp. 5–16.
51. Cf. M. W. Murphree (ed.), *Education, Race and Employment in Rhodesia*, Salisbury: Artca Publications, 1975, pp. 27–30.
52. Palley, 1970, p. 149.
53. *Ibid.*, pp. 143–144.
54. On labour and racial discrimination, detail is to be found in: Murphree, 1973; Palley, 1970, pp. 149–150; International Commission of Jurists, 1976, pp. 25–32; *Quénet Report*, 1976, pp. 34–76.
55. Murphree, 1973, pp. 8–15.
56. See B. J. Dorsey, "The African Secondary School Leaver" in Murphree, ed., 1975, pp. 15–174.
57. See G. Cheater and B. D. Mothobi, "Employment in Commerce and Industry" in *ibid.*, pp. 177–288.
58. *Quénet Report*, 1976, pp. 34–60.
59. Sources: *Annual Report of the Secretary for African Education, 1965*, Salisbury, Government Printer, 1976, pp. 52–53; *Report on Education, 1975*, Salisbury: Government Printer, 1976, pp. 27, 30. Figures for expenditure in the African Division are listed for the year 1974/1975. It should be remarked that the figures given do not reflect total Government expenditure in the categories given, since further amounts for items such as general administration, examinations, etc. are reported separately.
60. Figures for Whites include Asians and Coloureds. Age-specific ratios for the population groups reveal an even greater disparity.
61. Dorsey, in Murphree, ed., 1975, p. 53.
62. *Ibid.*, pp. 46–52.
63. Cf. M. W. Murphree, *Education, Development and Change in Africa*. (Hoernlé Memorial Lecture, 1976). Johannesburg: South African Institute of Race Relations, 1976, pp. 17–21.
64. *Quénet Report*, 1976, p. 28.
65. Dorsey, in Murphree, ed., 1975, p. 53 and International Commission of Jurists, 1976, p. 19.
66. *Report on Education*, 1976, p. 34. It should be noted that the Country's University exists under a Royal Charter which stipulates non-racialism and is fully integrated in its teaching and residential arrangements. Full-time enrolments as of April 1976 were, by race: Blacks 727, Whites 666, Asians 83 and Coloureds 30. See M. W. Murphree, "Universalism, Particularism and Academic Freedom: The Rhodesian Case" in *The Role of Universities in Southern Africa*, D. Welsh, ed. Cape Town and London: Davie Philip and Rex Collins, forthcoming, (title provisional).
67. International Commission of Jurists, 1976, p. 17.
68. Cf. *Quénet Report*, 1976, pp. 17–18, 84–86. Hotels in Black areas are similarly restricted in regard to serving Whites.
69. Cf. *Quénet Report*, 1976, p. 10.
70. *Proposals for a New Constitution for Rhodesia*, Rhodesian Government "White Paper," Salisbury, 1969.
71. Efforts to change franchise qualifications and thereby prevent the incorporation of Blacks are discussed in Palley, 1966, pp. 168–71, 242–46, 309–13, 416–24; cf. Leys, 1959; Gray, 1960; Franck, 1960.
72. Bowman, 1973, pp. 135–38.
73. *Ibid.*, p. 138.
74. See especially Palley, 1966, Part II, chaps. 4–5, and Palley, 1970.

75. *Ibid.*, and Bowman, 1973, pp. 142–44, 151–55.
76. Bowman, 1973, pp. 37–38, and Palley, 1970, pp. 26–29.
77. Bowman, 1973, p. 38.
78. Palley, 1970, p. 27.
79. Bowman, 1973, pp. 137–38, and Palley, 1970, pp. 32–35.
80. Palley, 1970, pp. 35–38.
81. Bowman, 1973, p. 153.
82. See the elaboration of this view especially in N. J. Rhoodie, *Apartheid and Racial Partnership in Southern Africa*, Pretoria: Academica, 1969.
83. Thus the Commission recommends the retention of White (urban) land "as it is" because "we consider there are many Europeans who would not accept a departure from the existing position." The Commission goes on to observe, "... several witnesses ... declared they could see no reason why an African with the necessary qualifications (whether intellectual or material) should not live in a European residential suburb. No doubt that would be an ideal situation but we think the movement should be gradual and unhurried." *Quénet Report*, 1976, p. 15.
84. *Ibid.*, p. 9.
85. *Ibid.*, p. 22.
86. The Report must be severely criticized for both its presentation and the superficiality of its analysis on a number of important issues. The Commission's technique in a number of contentious issues seems to have been to state opposing points of view submitted in evidence and then, in the absence of detailed examination of the issues concerned by the Commission itself, to content itself with the expression of a pious hope that the non-discriminatory situation pertains. See, for example, pp. 64–65 of the *Report*.
87. *Ibid.*, p. 23.
88. UFP 1962 statement as quoted in Bowman, 1973, p. 34.
89. However, it would most likely continue to support the present government if (a) outside military powers intervened or (b) it suspected that what would emerge in Rhodesia would be an unstable rather than a stable Black government.

# The Violation of Human Rights in Uganda

PIERRE NAUDIN

PIERRE NAUDIN is a French journalist by profession. At present he is attached to *Edi-Monde*, a press agency owned by Hachette, and he is responsible for editing a wide range of magazines. He is the author of several novels and essays which have been published by well-known publishing houses, such as Gallimard and Editeurs Français Réunis. He is also the author of an extensive study of the position of black athletes in the United States.

Pierre Naudin is currently engaged in writing a novel around the theme of French and English Knighthood during the Hundred Years War.

# The Violation of Human Rights in Uganda

PIERRE NAUDIN

## I. Amin's Seizure of Power

The regime of Dr. Milton Obote, the former president of Uganda, was overthrown by the army led by Major-General (later General) Idi Amin on 25 January 1971. Obote then fled to Tanzania.

The beginning of Amin's rule was marked by the massacre of troops from Obote's Lango tribe and of the related Acholi. This was followed during May of that year by the announcement that powers of detention aimed at anti-government elements were to be enforced. And in August 1972 Amin declared an "economic war," the first stage of which was the expulsion of non-citizens, mainly Asians. Only a month later, in September 1972, Dr. Obote (with the blessing of Nyerere of Tanzania) made an abortive attempt to regain power in Uganda – he tried to seize Entebbe Airport near Kampala, the capital of Uganda, but failed. Amin then suspended relations with Tanzania. Nevertheless, the attempt failed for various reasons, the most important being listed by Peter Enahoro as follows:[1] Amin's support should not be underestimated; the frustrations of the exiled Obote followers were not shared with equal fervour by the Ugandan people back home; and

> ... the contempt held for Amin's commanders by several of Obote's officers contributed to the failure. In his purge of the army, Amin had directed special attention to the professionally-trained officers. Some of those officers were clearly stooges themselves of the Obote regime. Others were eliminated simply because Amin foresaw that with their superiority of mind and sophisticated training, his own crudeness could not long prevail. Those professionally-trained officers who escaped his scourge formed the heart of Obote's exile force. They knew the junior officers and other ranks with whom Amin had replaced them, and this knowledge only deepened their contempt. That they thought an invading force of 1,500 split in two groups could overrun an army numbering over 12,000 – and perhaps 2,000

of the foreign mercenaries fiendishly loyal to the dictator – was drawn from this disdain.

The army is perhaps the clue to Amin's support and following referred to by Enahoro. And this explains Amin's purge in the army particularly of officers recruited from the ranks of the Lango and Acholi. Those who replaced them were mainly recruited from the ranks of Amin's own ethnic group, the Nubians from the West-Nile area. The Nubian group of tribes includes various tribes such as the Kakwa, Lugbara and Madi. Amin is a Kakwa. Amin also recruited a large group of Nubians from the Southern Sudan who were previously engaged in the Sudanese civil war in the pursuit of secession of that part of the country. This war ended in 1972 after an agreement was reached in Addis Ababa providing for a substantial degree of autonomy for the Southern Region. Yet, a large proportion of Southern rebels who called themselves the "Anyanya" rejected the amnesty offered them by the Sudanese Government and settled in northwestern Uganda from where they were recruited into the Ugandan army by General Amin, in his capacity as head of state and minister of defence, holding all legislative, executive and military powers in the country.

Amin's leadership and power are therefore of the totalitarian and coercive kind and his support and following referred to above must of necessity be viewed with circumspection within the context of the non-recognition of any political aspirations contrary to his own, the passive political role the population ought to play and the purely ceremonial role of government institutions as far as decision-making is concerned. The president's power is furthermore all-inclusive and the principles of the rule of law are virtually non-existent as will be demonstrated later. Suffice to state that manifestations of this situation are the expulsion of Asians without adequate compensation, the banning of all foreign newspaper and magazine journalists in Uganda as well as the constant violations of human rights through the imposition of arbitrary arrests, torture and murder.

These atrocities, inhumanities and violations of human rights earned Idi Amin various fitting labels and descriptions some of which are as follows: *Newsweek* called his regime "... one of the world's more brutal military dictatorships";[2] *Elseviers* wrote: "Oeganda heeft 'n moord-president"[3] (Uganda has a murdering president); Peter Enahoro[4] typified "Big Daddy" as follows:

Amin tramples upon Uganda like a rogue elephant loose on the range. It is not the Asians alone who have suffered from his savage excesses. Even more depressing is the news of the reign of terror which the former heavyweight pugilist has inflicted upon that land;

and *Elseviers* stated emphatically: "Idi Amin: de Hitler van Afrika"[5] (Idi Amin: the Hitler of Africa).

The comparison with Hitler is not totally uncalled for, because Amin himself professed openly his admiration for Hitler's anti-Semitism and persecution of the Jews. Amin's persecution of political opponents and the general violation of human rights caused the International Commission of Jurists (ICJ) to publish a report on 4 June 1974 accusing President Idi Amin's regime of creating a reign of terror in Uganda, killing between 25,000 and 250,000 Ugandans. It has not been possible to determine the precise number of killings.

But who are the Ugandans suffering at the hands of Al-Haj President Idi Amin Dada, V.C., D.S.O., M.C., Honorary Doctorate of the University of Uganda and the man who sends funny telegrams flying around the world?

The population estimation was 10,461,500 in 1972. The major tribes (in numerical order) are the Baganda, Iteso, Soga, Nyankole, Kiga, Lango, Yisa, Acholi, Lugbara, Nyoro, Toro and Karamajong. The Kakwa, Madi and other Nubians constitute only a very small minority group in the country. Idi Amin is as mentioned a Nubian born from commoner parents belonging to the Kakwa tribe of the West-Nile area. The Nubians have risen to a position of favour and privilege since Amin's seizure of power in 1971. Amin is also a devoted Muslim, trying to convert Uganda into an Islamic state. Yet, more than half the population are Christians (31 percent Catholic and 20 percent Anglicans). The remainder consists of 27 percent animists (traditional religions), only 10 percent Muslims and 12 percent smaller groups such as, for instance, Hindus. According to reports, the Nubians who filled the army since Amin's seizure of power, were exclusively recruited from the ranks of Muslim tribe members.

## II. The Purges in the Army

It was reported[6] that when Gen. Idi Amin overthrew Milton Obote's regime in 1971, rapturous crowds danced in the streets of Kampala, and it appeared that "Big Daddy" Amin was just what he said he was: a simple, bluff soldier who had ousted a tyrant and wished to restore civilian government as soon as possible. He released political prisoners, disbanded Obote's secret police and made friendly overtures to the Baganda, the country's most advanced, largest and influential tribe. But soon disquieting stories began to trickle from Uganda.

A small band of Ugandan soldiers fled into Tanzania with reports that Amin was purging the army of north Uganda tribesmen and that thousands of them had already been slaughtered. The refugees named names and supplied grisly details: Brigadier Mohammad Hussein, the Army Chief of Staff, had been killed soon after the coup, his crotch and stomach smashed by rifle butts. Two colonels, five lieutenant colonels and an air force major reportedly had been dispatched in various ways, one disemboweled, some herded into a room that was then blown up with explosives, one suffocated with his own genitals. On the heels of these atrocities, two Americans, a correspondent and a university lecturer, who were trying to investigate reports of a tribal massacre at an army barracks 160 miles from Kampala, disappeared and were never seen again. A court of inquiry concluded that they almost certainly had been murdered by Amin's troops, but the murderers were never brought to trial.

Nevertheless, the purge in the army continued, and the places of the victimized Langos and Acholis were quickly filled by members of Amin's own Kakwa tribe. Lugbaras and Madis were also favoured. It was also reported[7] that corporals and sergeants became captains and colonels, and Amin guaranteed their loyalty by doubling army pay, building comfortable new barracks for the troops and spending an estimated $ 100 million – one-third of Uganda's entire budget – on military arms and equipment.

To win favour from the Baganda, Amin shrewdly arranged to have the body of King Freddie flown home from London for reburial. To make businessmen happy, he halted Obote's nationalization of the country's mines and banks. And to make up for the loss of economic relations with Tanzania, he called on help from Israel, in which he had trained as a paratrooper and which had maintained a military and civilian aid mission in Uganda for years.

But this had not lasted long. Whether it was the word of Allah or the smell of money that caused Amin to switch sides no one can be sure. He paid an unannounced call on Libya's Muammar Gaddafi, whose huge oil revenues have been backing anti-Israel forces all over the Arab world. After a two-day meeting, the two Muslim leaders jointly proclaimed their undying opposition to Zionist "imperialism." Back home, Amin accused the Israeli mission of subversion; shortly after, he expelled all Israeli personnel and broke relations with Israel.

For approximately two years, no further serious purges were conducted. However, Gen. Amin ordered the purge of dissident troops in Malire Mechanized Regiment in 1974. Orders were[8] that Lugbara soldiers and men should be purged because of their opposition to Gen. Amin's fellow Nubians such as the Kakwa and Madi. These were the people who benefitted most from the take-over of businesses left behind by departing Asians after they had been expelled in 1972.

On the crucial night of this purge in the Ugandan Army, General Idi Amin reportedly[9] told his troops: 'If you are not happy with me you should kill me or ask me to resign rather than making the people of Uganda run about during the night.' In fact, General Amin was not about to resign nor was he ready to be given the push. General Amin's impassioned plea was a case of the wolf crying wolf.

Two victims of this purge were, inter alia, Brigadier Charles Arube, one of the Chiefs of Staff, and Lt. Col. Michael Ondoga, a Lugbara whose body was found in the River Nile. Thereafter members of the Lugbara tribe began to press for a full investigation into his death. It was the month in which Amin announced he was giving up his other ministerial responsibilities to concentrate on reorganising the army. Some of that reorganisation apparently involved purging those officers and men who may have liked to see the carpet pulled from under Amin's feet. And Amin, always obsessed with security, simply chose his own time and place for the show-down. At least fifty officers were killed in a night of terror and barrack-room purges. This was not the end of Amin's atrocities, however, because a figure of 500 murdered soldiers and tribesmen was subsequently mentioned.[10]

## III. The Economic War

Shortly after Gen. Amin's seizure of power and the initial purge in the army he announced the economic war which had to be fought in stages: first, expulsion of non-citizens; second, demonetization of old currency; third, allocation of businesses to citizens; fourth, reorganisation of internal and external trade through the establishment of trading corporations and fifth, the reform of the land system and tenure.

The expulsion of non-citizens, especially Asians, will be dealt with more fully in the following section. Some of the implications of the economic revolution will now be discussed.

In an excellent article, Jonathan Rollow describes Amin's economic revolution,[11] and points out that despite the hardships suffered by Africans as a result of the economic programme, the objectives of the revolution still seem to enjoy deep-rooted popular support. He writes that since the Asians left, Ugandans have been plagued with soaring prices and bothersome shortages of essential commodities. The allegedly "exploitive" Asians have been replaced in many cases by far more unscrupulous African traders who are taking advantage of the scarce supply of products by charging two to three times as much as the Asians did. Moreover, the speed with which the Asians were expelled virtually eliminated any chance of a smooth transfer of the businesses, factories and property they left behind. The allocation of businesses was to be handled by ministerial committees composed of military, police, prison and civil service personnel and headed by a cabinet minister. A few days after they had begun intensive interviewing in the capital city of Kampala, Amin suddenly sent the committees up-country to distribute shops there. Allocation of businesses in Kampala was turned over to military committees that in turn handed out many of the firms to friends, relatives and fellow soldiers. A disproportionate number of shops went to members of Amin's own ethnic group, the Nubians and the Kakwa in particular, who come from the West Nile region. Amin is a Muslim, and so the Muslims were also a privileged group when the spoils were divided; the plum was rent-rich Kampala Hill.

Outside Kampala, the average Ugandan did not fare much better. Ministerial committees worked up-country for only a few weeks before military committees took over.

Rollow further writes that to the Ugandan consumer, the expulsion of the Asians and the turnover of businesses to Africans have mainly meant shortages and sharp increases in prices. During the first four months after the Asians were ordered out, imports declined more than 50 percent, and many Africans who were allocated shops found themselves with little or no stock and unpaid bills left by their predecessors. The few Africans who already had businesses were able to charge exorbitant prices since they had virtually no competition until the Asian stores were allocated. But even now that the distribution of businesses is completed, prices remain inflated and intermittent shortages continue.

Mechanical breakdowns and technical inexperience are major

reasons for the continued high prices. Generally, the Asians did not teach their African employees about the mechanics of plant operation, and there are now many factories in Uganda producing less than when the Asians ran them. Some technicians have come in from abroad, notably from Egypt and even from India, but they have not been enough to make any real difference. Meanwhile, many Ugandans trained in one field have found themselves in charge of plants that demand another type of expertise.

Some African businessmen are doing what the Asians were accused of – smuggling foreign currency out of the country by sending more funds abroad with prepaid, pro forma invoices than they receive back in goods. They bank the balance overseas or in Kenya while the consumer is left with fewer products to buy. Orders for imports must be reviewed by the State Trading Corporation but the STC never checks on how many products are actually ordered. Because of the speed and the way in which businesses were allocated, there are also many businessmen, inexperienced and unfamiliar with complicated import procedures, who inadvertently add to the shortages by not knowing how to import merchandise efficiently.

According to Rollow, the biggest question mark in the Ugandan economy, and a major reason for certain shortages, is the allocation of foreign exchange, which is made exclusively by the Bank of Uganda. In the first nine months of 1973, Uganda enjoyed a trade surplus of more than $ 200 million. It was an unusually good year. Unlike most industries, coffee processing had been run by Africans prior to the Asian expulsion. Coffee production almost doubled in the first half of 1973, and the price of coffee rose on the world market.

No statistics have been published on the current balance of payments, but it is doubtful that a probable deficit will cancel the trade surplus. The Bank of Uganda, however, is extremely conservative in granting foreign-exchange allocations to importers.

For the majority of Ugandans, the foreign-exchange mystery doesn't matter very much. High prices and shortages have hit the people in the cities and towns, especially those on salaries who were not allocated a business.

But what about the cause of it all, the expulsion of the Asians?

## IV. The Expulsion of the Asians

The crisis leading to the expulsion of 40,000 Asians from Uganda reached its height during the period 4 August, 1972 to 11 November, 1972.[12] It was preceeded by two Indian Memorandums addressed to Amin and one by Gen. Amin in response to the former. The first Memorandum prepared by Ugandan Indians on their position in that country, was presented to the government on 7 December, 1971. It dealt with education, civil rights, citizenship and immigration, contribution to economic development and also on trade and commerce. In the section on civil rights, the Indians stated that there was a visible lack of equal opportunity to participate in governmental and parastatal bodies, that expatriates were often given preference over local qualified Indians, and that Indians did not have full rights with respect to land acquisition. They added that existing legal provisions could be utilized to combat incitement to hatred as evidenced in the local press, and hoped that the government would consult Indians in any matter which affected them.

Amin's reaction to this document was presented only one day later, on 8 December, 1971. He ignored the first Indian Memorandum largely and presented his own Memorandum instead. Herein he attributed poor Indian-African relations to Indian disloyalty, non-integration, and commercial malpractice.

The Indians then prepared their second Memorandum, dated 4 January, 1972. This Memorandum repeated various statements made in the first Memorandum since Indians felt that Amin had not taken sufficient account of the anxieties, explanations, and proposals which had been put forward in the First Indian Memorandum. Indians also attempted to defend some of the views presented earlier, corrected some of what they regarded as the misinformation which had crept into Amin's attacks, and offered concrete proposals for the future. Amin did not immediately react to this.

But on 4 August, 1972, while travelling south from Karamojong, President Amin addressed the Airborne Regiment in Tororo, a town in eastern Uganda bordering Kenya. In his speech which covered a wide range of topics, Amin announced that Uganda had no place "for the over 80,000 Asians holding British passports who are sabotaging Uganda's economy and encouraging corruption." Amin informed the soldiers that he wanted to see Uganda's economy in the hands of

Ugandans, especially black Ugandans. What appeared a casual insertion in his speech before the troops, finally spelled the end of the Indian presence in Uganda. Amin was immediately attacked for his statement, particularly in the overseas press.

But not being perturbed, he announced the expulsion of Indians on 9 August, 1972 and spoke of expelling non-citizens only. But he changed his mind a few days later when he announced that the 23,000 citizen Indians would also be expelled and that the sale of immovable property was prohibited. Professionals also had to leave and the deadline for departure was 11 November, 1972. But on 22 August, 1972 President Amin announced that Indians holding Ugandan citizenship would under certain provisions be permitted to remain in the country. Nevertheless, a total of more than 40,000 Asians, almost all the Hindus in the country, were subsequently expelled and required to leave. The majority of those who stayed behind, were followers of the Islam faith. Of those who left, some 9,500 were of undetermined nationality. According to the Office of the United Nations High Commissioner for Refugees,[13] about a third of them (some 3,500) went to a number of countries (mostly to India and Pakistan and to countries in Africa) under their own steam. Some 1,600 were resettled directly from Kampala, and went to Canada, Denmark and Switzerland. Some 4,500, however, had nowhere to go and no immediate prospects of resettlement. Speed being of the essence, the High Commissioner, at the request of the Secretary-General of the U.N., contacted a number of countries in Europe and obtained their agreement to accept these 4,500 Uganda Asians on a temporary basis, pending their permanent placement elsewhere. Austria thus accepted 1,534; Belgium 432; Italy 1,942; Malta 369; and Spain 183. These numbers have since been increased by a number of births.

However, ironical as it may be, President Amin was obviously having second thoughts about the Asians. Early in 1974 he went to Pakistan where he attended a meeting of Muslim country leaders in Lahore, there he made trade pacts with Pakistan and others to help pull Uganda out of its economic difficulties.[14] In September he let about 20 Pakistanis into Uganda, including Mohammed Akbar Khan whom he appointed as a Ugandan High Court judge. Now there are some 250 Pakistanis working in Uganda. In fact, the Pakistani expatriates include three judges, four lawyers, three bankers, five university lecturers and five agricultural technicians for equipment repair and water systems. However, reports are that the Pakistanis working in

Uganda are not keen to take up long contracts. They are therefore not prospective settlers, and are like Amin himself, Muslims, while most of the expellees were Hindus.

General Amin has reputedly also asked India for technical experts, but the Indians are more cautious than the Pakistanis. The Indian government said it could not discuss such assistance for Uganda until after there were firm negotiations on compensation for Indian property seized by Amin in 1972 (estimated to be worth at least £ 200 m.).

It is, however, not only a question of compensation, but one of double standards as well. In his article on the Indian exodus from Uganda, H. H. Patel[15] made the following apt remark:

> Africa cannot, even for its own sake, afford one standard for odious actions perpetrated by others and another standard for actions of its own. If a dual standard is accepted then a grave implication follows; namely, that Africa may well come full circle and finally accept – in however twisted a fashion – the old colonial myth that Africa is not quite "ready and civilized" enough to be judged by universal standards of human conduct applicable to all states and men equally. No doubt states and peoples often try to use the double standard to their own advantage, but Africa – for the sake of its own progress and morality – ought to reject such a course.

## V. The Hills Affair

Mr. Denis Hills is a British university lecturer who taught in Western Uganda and who was sentenced to death because of President Amin's dislike of one paragraph in his book on Uganda, entitled *The White Pumpkin* (the manuscript of this book was written in 1973).

The particular paragraph that annoyed the President reads as follows:

> Because of Amin, all prejudices against the black man have arisen again to the surface. He has done harm to his people, and, from his tiny territory, to the cause of Africa as a whole, in that governing like a village tyrant by fear he has reimposed on Ugandans all the habits of submission and servility that one hoped uhuru (independence) was eroding.

The trial of Mr. Hills began on 9 June, 1975 before a Ugandan military tribunal without his counsel or the British Consul in Kampala being permitted to attend. The counsel was told by the head of the tribunal, Major Juma Ali: "Legal representation is not necessary."

After three days of hearings, Mr. Hills was found guilty of treason and sentenced to execution by firing a squad. Major Juma Ali told him he could appeal to the Defence Council, a policy-making body of senior officers, or he could appeal to President Amin for clemency. If the appeals failed, Mr. Hills would be executed in public on June 21st.

After the Kenyan and British Governments, as well as the Parliament of the EEC appealed with no avail for the life of Mr. Hills, President Mobuto of Zaire and King Khalid of Saudi Arabia offered mediation in this matter. Subsequently, President Amin accepted an invitation to fly to Kinshasa for talks with President Mobuto. This he did on June 30th and on July 1st in a statement broadcast over Zaire radio, President Amin announced that he had granted Mr. Hills an apparently unconditional reprieve. He said he had granted clemency because of his "confidence" in President Mobuto and he added that he had decided to leave "everything concerning Great Britain to be discussed by my brother, General Mobuto."

The *Africa Research Bulletin* compiled some press comments on the Hills episode.[16] It reported as follows:

> The African Press, as well as appealing for clemency, was for the most part outspoken in its condemnation of President Amin. A strongly worded editorial in Le Moniteur Africain from Dakar urged the President to stop disgracing the image of Africa by his behaviour. How can Africa hold up its head in the General Assembly of the UN, or criticise the inhuman behaviour of South Africa when it has such beams in its own eye, the paper asked.
>
> In Lusaka, the Government-owned Zambia Daily Mail said that the sentence of death for what appeared to be defamation, rather than treason or sedition, "is harsh, to say the least. The death sentence alone is enough to make the world think that perhaps there is some truth in Mr. Hill's allegations."
>
> Some people may argue that as an ... internal affair it does not merit interference or comment from other countries or even the OAU. The argument is mistaken. The Hills case does not only involve the death of one man. It reflects badly on every independent African state and harms the reputation of those that are proud of the just and humane societies they have built. (ZDM 16/6)

Both the principal Kenya papers, the *Standard* and the *Daily Nation* likened the Uganda military tribunal's verdict to "kangaroo court justice." The *Nation* said that it was unfortunate

> that Gen. Amin is making his country appear unsafe for foreigners only a few weeks before the OAU summit conference in Kampala,

and the *Standard* said that

> any 'blood letting' at this psychological moment would only scare away quite a few potential participants. (DN 15/6, TS 23/6)

Commenting on July 2nd, after President Amin had granted a reprieve, the *Daily Nation* commended the President for his clemency and said that showing clemency to Mr. Hills

is the most rational and humane thing Gen. Amin has done since he assumed power. More than that, though, it is indicative that Gen. Amin has listened to many African heads of state who have asked him to spare Mr. Hills' life.

It is only to be hoped that this reasoning that has sprung from the General's mind and the sense of humanity that suddenly oozed from his heart will continue to do so – for there are still many people in Uganda and outside who need the General's clemency ... (DN 2/7)

Questioned on the Hills affair by a reporter of *Africa Report*, President Amin answered as follows:[17]

This man was most important in the Western part of Uganda. He was lecturing in the teacher training college, not at the university as it was reported. Also he was a spy. Therefore I did not want to tell the British government. 'If you do not do such-an-such I will do this to Dennis Hills.' Rather I wanted to show them that we are capable of administering our people without any assistance – as we did at the O.A.U. Summit. They can see that the people are very happy. I wanted to show that the reports which Dennis Hills was writing against me and against Uganda were false. Therefore I just released him. If Lieutenant General Blair had not been so hot-tempered, I could actually have handed Dennis Hills over to him. He had a hot temper; he had been my Commanding Officer in the time of the King's African Rifles and he thought I was still seeing him as '*bwana mkubwa*'. The time of the *bwana mkubwa* is gone. With this photograph I can show you that the *bwana mkubwa* is now me.

Indeed, Idi Amin is the *bwana mkubwa*. Or is he just a "village tyrant"?

## VI. Concern of the International Opinion

A noted magazine[18] once gave the following description of Amin's regime:

Amin's blatant despotism, his outrageous racist statements, his erratic self-glorifying behaviour, have convinced many people that he is a paranoid with delusions of grandeur. If that were so, his days would probably be numbered, for Ugandans are no more willing than anyone else to be led by a madman. Unfortunately, however, Amin is no pathological accident to be easily swept away. Rather, his power – and his abuse of it – seems to spring from the history and social fabric of Uganda itself, and from the tensions of the Middle East. Like so many new nations, Uganda is the product of colonial happenstance, heir to boundaries drawn by a British administrator who gave little thought to ethnic claims and differences. About 40 tribes call some part of Uganda their homeland ....

To this description one could add the high incidence of mysterious deaths and disappearances of prominent Ugandans. The cases of Brigadier Arube and Lt. Col. Michael Ondoga were already mentioned and will not be repeated here. Not to speak of the purges in the army. Our knowledge of these atrocities is particularly due to the coverage and reporting of Western and some African journalists. No wonder, therefore, that Western journalists were banned in Uganda in 1975 and that journalists desirous of entering Uganda must have the blessing of Amin himself. Most foreign journalists have therefore either left Uganda or were simply expelled by the President. The local press is of course controlled by the government.

Nevertheless, prior to their expulsion, the foreign press had reported many killings, tortures, purges and disappearances, *inter alia* of Godfrey Kigala, Wilson Oryema's son and Benedicto Kiwanuka.

Godfrey Kigala, a foreign ministry official disappeared one evening after a meeting with President Amin himself. He was last seen alive leaving the meeting with two members of the Presidential bodyguard.

The younger son of Wilson Oryema, the Minister of Natural Resources, disappeared mysteriously soon after returning to Uganda from military training in Europe.

Benedicto Kiwanuka was the supreme judge in Uganda but was dragged from the high court by security officers and beaten to death in September 1972. This incident, more than anything else, caused the International Commission of Jurists to investigate conditions in Uganda. Their findings, as well as the concern of Amnesty International will be dealt with shortly. It is interesting, however, to draw the attention to a new trend in Uganda,[19] namely that beatings and murder nowadays do not usually take place on the street. It is normal practice for persons arrested or taken for questioning to be bundled into the boot of soldiers' cars. This is true even where the nature of the offence ostensibly being investigated is quite nominal or technical – not in possession of necessary papers or not being "properly" dressed, for example. Most of the people do re-appear, often after a beating but find it wiser to keep quiet. They feel lucky to have got off lightly.

However, not all people are killed or arrested. Some, or rather only a few, are lucky enough to flee the country, such as finance minister, Mr. Makhweya, who defected to Britain in January, 1975.[20]

In its Annual Report for 1974/75, Amnesty International listed 37 African countries in which people were imprisoned for their beliefs, were denied fair and speedy trials, and/or were tortured or executed during that year. It made special mention of Uganda's records and listed some massacres, disappearences and imprisonment without trial.

The 1974 Report of the International Commission of Jurists (referred to previously) condemned the violations of human rights, arbitrary arrests, torture and murder in Uganda.

It stated that the Uganda constitution had been over-ridden by arbitrary decrees, all political activity suspended and the basic freedoms of association and assembly, freedom of the press, freedom of expression, freedom of education and trade union freedom put into abeyance.

It also stated categorically that there has been a total breakdown in the rule of law and that the armed forces had been put beyond the law and given almost unlimited powers of arrest and search. These powers had been largely used to arrest, detain, torture and kill thousands of civilians from all walks of life who were suspected of opposing the regime.

## VII. Conclusion

Yet, despite international condemnation of Amin's atrocities, some people can still argue that the expulsion of Asians is exceptional and should not be condemned altogether, as manifested in the following paragraph:

> It is suggested, therefore, that Uganda's historical, constitutional, political, social and economic backgrounds coupled with the fact that it is a developing state form a basic criterion for placing Kampala within the exception provided by the human rights instruments, and that the state's action with particular reference to its expulsion of aliens did not constitute a violation of human rights. For where a numerically insignificant alien minority constitutes a dominant economic stratum in a developing state, the concern for human rights, however sincere, need not be stressed to the point of allowing it to impede economic planning and perpetuate alien economic domination and underdevelopment, since to do so would itself constitute a violation of human rights.[21]

## NOTES

1. Enahoro, Peter, "Whither Uganda," *Africa* (London), No. 16, Dec. 1972, p. 14–15.
2. *Newsweek* (Washington), 4 August, 1974, p. 19.
3. *Elseviers* (Amsterdam), Vol. 30, No. 26, 29 June 1974.
4. Enahoro, Peter, "Whither Uganda," *op. cit.*
5. *Elseviers* (Amsterdam), Vol. 31, No. 19, 19 May 1975.
6. Cf. *Newsweek* (Washington), 16 October, 1972.
7. *Ibid.*
8. Cf. *Africa Confidential* (London), Vol. 15, No. 7, April 1974.
9. Cf. *Africa* (London), No. 33, May 1974.
10. Cf. *Africa Confidential, op. cit.*
11. Rollow, Jonathan, "Uganda's Amin's Economic Revolution," *Africa Report* (New York), May–June 1974, p. 36–42.
12. For a full treatment of this subject, see H. H. Patel, "General Amin and the Indian exodus from Uganda," *Issue* (Waltham, Mass.), Vol. II, No. 4, 1972, p. 12–21.
13. Cf. United Nations High Commissioner for Refugees (UNHCR). *Publication of the Information Section,* No. 1, March, 1974, Geneva.
14. Cf. "Pakistanis take Uganda Asian's Jobs," *African Development* (London), February, 1975.
15. Cf. Patel, H. H., "General Amin and the Indian Exodus from Uganda," *op. cit.*, p. 21.
16. Cf. *Africa Research Bulletin* (Exeter, England), June 1–30, 1975, p. 3664.
17. Cf. *Africa Report* (New York), Sept.–Oct. 1975, p. 3.
18. *Newsweek* (Washington), 16 October, 1972, p. 14.
19. Cf. "Uganda: Disappearing Citizens." *Africa* (London), No. 32, April 1974, p. 49.
20. Cf. "Shunned," *The Economist* (London), 1 February, 1975, p. 40.
21. Cf. "Uganda: Expulsion of Aliens, and Human Rights." *African Affairs* (London), Vol. 7, No. 7, 1974, p. 355.

# Dutch Tolerance on Trial: Holland on the Brink of Conflict

A. C. W. VAN DER VET

A. C. W. VAN DER VET (born in The Hague, 1919) made his debut as poet in 1938 and has since published poems, short stories and books of travel. He is a journalist by profession and has been on the editorial staff of *Algemeen Dagblad* since 1948, and was chief editor of this paper from 1958 till 1968. In 1968 he resigned from this post for reasons of health, but he stayed on as general editor. Several times a week he contributes an article for the column titled 'Long-term View', for which he travels much. In the last few years he visited Brazil, China, Surinam, the Dutch Antilles, South Africa and other countries.

# Dutch Tolerance on Trial: Holland on the Brink of Conflict

A. C. W. VAN DER VET

Many generations of Dutch people have been bred and educated to realise that one of the most important of the assumedly abundant excellent qualities of the Dutch is: Tolerance towards people of different races, different faiths, different philosophies of life.

Since the birth of the Dutch State (i.e. since in 1568 the Netherlands provinces started their struggle for religious and political freedom against the Kingdom of Spain, which then ruled over these regions, a struggle which lasted for eighty years and ended with the conclusion of the Peace Treaty of Münster in 1648, when the seven northern provinces of the Low Countries became independent) young people in The Netherlands have been taught that in this country foreigners who suffered religious and racial persecution in their own countries have been hospitably allowed to live here. They were free to settle in the republic on the shores of the North Sea, to profess their faith in freedom; nobody even put a stone in their way, be they black, brown, yellow or red.

Generally speaking, this is true. With Chorus[1] one might say that tolerance is one of the characteristics of the Dutch. But fortunately he has toned down his opinion by adding that

> The average individual Dutchman however is not very tolerant towards his neighbour's views and acts when they differ from his own, but on the whole this nation, led by an enlightened elite, has shown a fair degree of tolerance in the last few centuries towards those who hold different religious and social views. Freedom of faith was recognised in principle and in practice, although the freedom of religious exercise was restricted.

Huizinga[2] says about the Dutch Republic in the seventeenth century:

> Freedom was greater here than elsewhere; so was tolerance, however reluctantly it was given.

He, too, took away some of the strength of his statement. Especially the capital city of Amsterdam, with its cosmopolitan inhabitants, says Chorus, is often praised for its broad views:

Again and again refugees and people who were exiled or went voluntarily into exile have found refuge in this country: Huguenots, English nobles in Cromwellian days, English intelligentsia in the days of the Restoration, French free-thinkers, Spanish and Portuguese Jews, Belgian refugees in the First World War, Austrian, Hungarian and German war victims etc. This tolerance, so it was said, does not spring from indifference as to religious matters. This tolerance, based on principle, is often attended with narrow-mindedness in practice; something strange will soon be regarded as "uncouth," i.e. different from our own way of life.

These two quotations show a certain reserve with regard to the opinion the average Dutchman holds concerning his tolerance as a result of his education. The present author thinks that if Huizinga and Chorus were to write about Dutch tolerance again today, they would be even more reserved. For although it is no doubt true that in the seventeenth century, during the war of independence, the Netherlands knew an extremely high degree of freedom and tolerance and a minimum of discrimination, and although one might say that this situation continued until after World War II, it should also be said that under the influence of a series of events in the years after 1955, some of this tolerance has gone. Religious discrimination in Holland today is, indeed, still rare, but racial discrimination is more common now than it used to be. This may have several causes, of which the following seem to be the most significant:

1. In the past most refugees belonged to elite groupings: intellectuals, writers, rich merchants. In the seventeenth century the Dutch – especially in Amsterdam, a city proudly called the city "on the Aemstel and the Y," which, as our great national poet Joost van den Vondel said "lay gloriously open" and had world-wide power as a trading-centre – regarded the arrival of these foreigners as a favourable contribution to their society. Printers, publishers, cartographers (very important citizens for a young maritime nation), mathematicians, people with advanced ideas about bookkeeping flocked in and their ideas permeated among the citizens of Amsterdam, while the well known shrewdness of the Amsterdam merchants looked upon the newcomers as sources of profit, now and in the future. The "down and out" among refugees have never, in any part of the world, been given a welcome reception – not in Amsterdam either.

2. In the seventeenth century refugees always came in easily controlled and mostly rather small numbers, so that they could hardly make their mark upon a society, neither outwardly nor inwardly.

3. Many refugees were from the start prepared to integrate into Dutch – i.e. mainly Amsterdam – society and their children (and often they themselves after a number of years) considered themselves to be Dutch (Amsterdam) citizens and acted as such. This article will show that these three most important features of those who in the past settled in The Netherlands are no longer found among many "strangers" who have come to live in The Netherlands since 1950. They are looked upon as "strangers" from a religious point of view – although this factor is becoming less important – and as "strangers" especially in racial respects. Therefore those who have grown up in the belief that the Dutch are a tolerant people and that Holland is and was in a position to be one of those rare windows with a worldwide view, will now find with surprise, dismay, compassion and sadness that in the last few years this country has undeniably shown forms of discrimination; publicly, among fairly large numbers of people; and apparently discrimination is on the increase.

The main cause of this difference with the past is probably the disappearance of the three above mentioned characteristics among the foreigners that have settled in this country.

On the other hand some forms of discrimination have always been found in Dutch society, especially religious and social discrimination. Some forms of discrimination are found more or less distinctly in most human societies.

## I. Social Discrimination among Dutchmen Themselves

Although in the Netherlands after 1568 the nobility has never played an important part in society as compared with the German nobility before 1918 and the French nobility until 1789, Holland has always been a typical class society in which it was not so much the nobility as the well-to-do bourgeoisie who played first fiddle, the patriciate.

Until far into the twentieth century Holland used to be a country with an extremely subtle stratified structure of social classes not found to the same degree in any other European country. This appears for instance from the large number of titles of address which especially in letter-writing should not be ignored by someone who wished to function reasonably well socially. Such forms of address are occasionally still used today. The subtle differences between such forms as *Weledele Heer* and *Weledelgeboren Heer*, *Weledelzeergeleerde Heer* and *Weledelgestrenge Heer*, etc. etc. are as far as is known unique in the world.

Of course such differences need not be signs of discrimination. Yet until a short time ago in rural, as well as urban areas, in Holland one of the consequences of the highly stratified bourgeois class society has no doubt been: discrimination by young people who, on the ground of their capacities, wanted and managed to work their way up to higher social classes. In a country where until a few decades ago a careful distinction was made between a "master painter" and an "apprentice," between a working class lad and a middle class boy, it was very difficult to pass from one class to another. Of course Britain also has its "old school ties" and in the United States there are very real differences, especially in provincial towns, between the status of people living on this side of the railroad and those living on the other side – but the possibilities to function in society on the ground of knowledge, ability and diligence are greater there than they are in Holland.

Investigations into the possibilities of vertical mobility in Dutch society have revealed that in Holland class discrimination – of course seldom operating in the open – undoubtedly makes it more difficult for lower-class people to rise on the social ladder than in many other highly developed countries. P. Vinke[3] carried out an investigation among presidents and members of the boards of directors of about 300 public companies established and operating in Holland and the presidents and members of the boards of directors of about the same number of comparable private companies. His conclusion was

> that our country has an economic elite with a largely closed nature, both vertically and horizontally, although it does not completely exclude outsiders from entry. Some intake from the neighbouring social upper layer and, though to a lesser degree, from the two social middle classes (representing more than one third of our professional population) does actually take place. But social rise from the two lower layers to the position of president or member of the board of directors is a great exception.

Forty-five percent of the presidents and 31 percent of the directors of private companies are related to the founders of the companies; for public companies these figures are 16 percent and a good 12 percent.

In a similar study of mobility among the owners of textile factories in the city of Enschede, Van Heek[4] gave even lower figures as far as social mobility was concerned. These factory owners and their relatives formed and still form relatively closed and impenetrable groups, of which there are many in Holland. Kuiper[5] in an investigation into the social origin of members of some liberal academic professions and grammar-school teachers found that these groups contain much lower percentages of people originating from neighbouring social strata. This is caused by many factors, one of which is no doubt the "subtle, mild discrimination" found in the very bourgeois society of The Netherlands, where the social origin of (especially) the father and the mother is of great importance.

## II. Religious Discrimination among Dutchmen

As has already been said the Dutch State came into being during an eighty-year war against Spain which was both a struggle for freedom and a religious struggle. First Luther and later on especially Calvin had many followers in the Dutch Republic, most of all in the northern and western provinces. (The inhabitants of the two southern provinces of Noord-Brabant and Limburg have always been predominantly Roman-Catholic.)

Members of the House of Orange (the ancestors of the present Queen) who witnessed the birth of the Netherlands as a sovereign state and in successive generations served this state as stadtholders no doubt contributed to the fact that, compared with many other countries, Holland has always shown a very high degree of tolerance towards people with other religious views. Especially the founder of the Dutch Republic, Prince William of Orange, surnamed William the Silent, Father of the Fatherland (1533–1584), but also his descendants Prince Maurits, Prince Frederik Hendrik, Prince William II and Prince William III were extremely broad-minded in religious matters.

This is certainly remarkable as the Eighty-Year War was in its early stages clearly a socio-religious conflict. The notorious iconoclastic riots were according to modern views an attack on the rich Roman Catholic Church as an exponent of the Establishment. The hard repressive measures taken by the Spanish Governor Alva in the years 1567–1572 was in the first place a reaction to the iconoclastic riots. Repression leads to resistance. During the rebellion of the so-called Beggars in 1572 churches and convents were their main targets, and especially the Roman Catholic clergy. But already in 1573 the moderate elements, led by Prince William, were in the majority. This was also the result of political wisdom, because in the northern provinces only 5 percent of the population were Calvinists.

After 1576 the war was fought mainly outside the Dutch territory, predominantly with mercenaries, which caused the feelings of hatred to fade away, although some distrust of Catholics – in 1648 still 50 percent of the population – remained. Religious freedom was also kept within certain bounds. Roman Catholic masses were winked at and were held in churches which from the outside were not recognisable as such. One of those secret churches in Amsterdam can still be visited today. It is a most fascinating museum: Our Lord in the Attic, now called Museum Amstelkring. Gebhard and Van der Vet[6] may rightly recall the fact that in the seventeenth century Amsterdam was sometimes called Eleutheropolis, the City of Freedom. It is indeed remarkable that after Amsterdam had become a Reformed city in 1578 secret churches could be founded everywhere in the city while officially the public profession of a religion other than the Reformed was forbidden. In those days, when all over Europe religious persecutions were the order of the day, the Amsterdam authorities, who through their role in world trade had broadened their outlook, were progressive enough to connive at the public profession of other religious beliefs. The result was that religious refugees from all parts of Europe flocked to Amsterdam later followed by political refugees. They built their own churches, secret churches, that is to say warehouses and dwelling-houses the outside of which was left unchanged, but the interior of which was made into a church. There were dozens of them, Roman Catholic, Lutheran, Armenian, Greek Orthodox, Walloon and Presbyterian. Everybody knew of their existence, but nobody minded. But in 1648 Amsterdam was predominantly Roman Catholic. However great tolerance might be, Roman Catholics were excluded from the civil service and from the Dutch East Indian Company. They were bracketed with bankrupts, criminals and other dishonourable persons.[7] This religious discrimination was maintained until the introduction of the first Dutch Constitution in 1798. Clause 5 of the present Constitution of the Kingdom of the Netherlands reads: Every Dutchman is eligible for a government office. Foreigners are eligible for government offices only if they satisfy the conditions mentioned in law.

One of the consequences was that people not belonging to the Dutch Reformed Church, especially Roman Catholics and Dutch baptists went into trade, shipping etc. Also Jews, tens of thousands of whom lived in Amsterdam before the German invasion in 1940 were mainly occupied in trade, but they lived all over the country.

Although the Dutch have shown a high degree of religious tolerance since 1573 it was the Protestant churches that were privileged, divided though they were into various denominations and sects. Catholics and Jews were more discriminated against than the Protestant dissenting groups.

A reaction to this has no doubt been the hard struggle Roman Catholics have always fought until far into this century to strenghten their own identity. The Dutch Roman Catholics – especially those who lived in small communities in the Protestant parts of the country, but those in the southern provinces as well – were known at home and abroad as being "more Roman than the Pope." They certainly professed their faith more intensely, more seriously than Catholics in predominantly Roman Catholic countries.[8]

The gap between Protestants and Roman Catholics was deep and wide and almost created a kind of religious Apartheid. Mixed marriages were out of the question. "Two creeds on one pillow seen makes the devil sleep in between."[9] When King William I (1815–1840) intended to marry the Catholic Belgian countess Henriëtte d'Oultremont it evoked fierce protest in Protestant circles. William decided to abdicate in 1840 and the wedding took place in 1841.[10] In general Catholics and Protestants hardly ever mixed socially. It was only after 1945 that this situation changed.

Since 1798 Catholics had had the same legal status as Protestants; in practice, however, equality did not begin until the liberal revision of the Dutch Constitution in 1848. In their struggle for equal opportunities – the Catholic Emancipation – the Catholics owe much to the Liberal statesman Thorbecke. In 1853 for instance he granted the Catholics the right to appoint bishops in this country. But this caused his fall as Prime Minister.

The extension of suffrage was favourable for the Catholics. From 1878 they had worked in close co-operation with the Calvinists. But this political co-operation did not result in more social contacts, nor in an ecumenical rapprochement. Spiritual differences between Catholics and Protestants remained. So did the differences between Christian Democrats on the one side and Liberals and Socialists on the other side. This was clearly revealed in the textbooks on Dutch national history. The Eighty-year War (1568–1648), the war of independence fought against Spain, became a controversial subject. In the popular rising of

1572 the "Beggars" formed the hard centre of the revolution. In Catholic schools the "Beggars" were described as murderers of priests, in Protestant textbooks as religious heroes, in State schools (attended by children of Liberals and Socialists) as freedom fighters. It is obvious that these circumstances did not make for strong national feelings. It was the Royal House of Orange where the four national currents converged. Dutchmen did not think in national terms but in terms of the reigning dynasty.

All this is history, one might say. But even as late as 1954 the Dutch Roman Catholic bishops, the Episcopate, jointly issued the so-called Mandate, forbidding Dutch Roman Catholics to remain or become members of a large number of socialist organisations or organisations sympathising with communist ideas. It also recommended them not to join a number of organisations in the field of social welfare work.[11] This naturally greatly affected relations between the Dutch Catholic National (political) Party and the socialist Dutch Labour Party; they lost confidence in each other.[12]

After 1965 this controversy weakened, mainly because of the clear trend among Dutch people to denounce their faith. Nevertheless it is still most unusual for a non-Catholic to be appointed burgomaster of a predominantly Catholic place or for someone who is not a member of one of the Protestant political parties to become burgomaster of a municipality with a predominantly Dutch Reformed population. It remains a difficult position for a Catholic policeman to be stationed in a Protestant community, and for a Protestant civil servant to be socially accepted in the Catholic southern part of the country. One might call this a kind of non-legalised apartheid, although at present it has certainly lost its sharp edges.

### A. *The Jews*

Special mention should be made of the position of the Dutch Jews.

Never, as long as the State of The Netherlands has existed, has there been anything like Jewish persecution in this country – of course with the exception of the war years (1940–1945), when Holland lived under Nazi terror. During those years the Jewish community in Holland was decimated; it is not necessary to go into the causes and background reasons here.[13] Mention should be made, however, of the fact that very many Dutchmen voluntarily collaborated with the occupation authorities, betraying Jews in hiding, betraying people hiding Jews, arresting Jews, "looking after" Jewish property and confiscating such property.[14]

But there was hardly any organised form of anti-semitism in The Netherlands. As has been said above the Dutch Republic in the seventeenth century offered sanctuary to Jews from Spain and Portugal, later on from Eastern Europe. And again in the 19th and early 20th centuries, during the pogroms in Eastern European countries, many Jews came to Holland, mainly to Amsterdam, the Jerusalem of the West. The Jewish community in Amsterdam – in the whole of Holland for that matter – has in the course of time become an integral part of Dutch society. The vast majority of Jews in this country consider themselves true Dutchmen. It is likely that partly as a result of this process of assimilation, of their determination to be assimilated, there was little sympathy for Zionism in Dutch Jewish circles before 1940. The innumerable contributions of the Dutch Jews to the country's trade, industry, science and arts are too well known to be mentioned separately. This does not mean, however, that Holland has never seen forms of anti-semitism. For instance in Rotterdam business circles it was – and sometimes still is – quite common to speak deprecatingly of "smouches," "sons of the Old Race" and "dirty Yids," referring to their Jewish colleagues and competitors, and when a middle-class non-Jewish man marries a Jewish girl the couple will be looked at obliquely for the rest of their lives. On the other hand the Jewish community will also find it hard to accept the marriage and the couple. But as has been said before, there has never been any official, strong or general form of anti-semitism in The Netherlands. Not even in the years before World War II, when especially in Germany people were in the grip of collective racial pride. In those pre-war years The Netherlands did have national-socialist movements, the largest being the National Socialist Movement (N.S.B.), founded on 14 December 1931 by a university graduate engineer A. A. Mussert. In his programme issued in 1931 Mussert had left out

all the anti-semitic phrases and proposals of the German example. Membership of the NSB was open to Jews; not many joined the movement, until the summer of 1933 less than 20. (But) the NSB still could not make up their minds as to what their attitude towards anti-semitism should be. More Jews became members (in the summer of 1935 it was said that there were 150 Jews among their 40,000 members), also more, many more anti-semitists.[15]

Gradually this movement grew into a really anti-semitic party, until about 1937 the NSB could be said to have included anti-semitism in its banner; the party's paper, *Volk en Vaderland* (Nation and Fatherland) often contained anti-semitic cartoons. During the German occupation (1940–1945) many NSB members atrociously collaborated with the Germans in their persecutions of the Jews. It should be remembered, however, that (a) the NSB did not start as an anti-semitic movement, (b) among its members many were opposed to anti-semitism.

Quite a different attitude was adopted by other smaller national-socialist movements in The Netherlands. This fact may have caused the NSB in the years 1936–1940 to grow more and more anti-semitic, until during the German occupation, when it had become a political party, the NSB was strongly anti-semitic.

It is beyond the scope of this article to expatiate upon the horrifying Jewish persecutions in this country; they were carried out by the German occupiers, who applied the same sinister methods in occupied territories as they had used in the persecution and extermination of the German Jews. It is with regret that mention has to be made of the hesitance of the Dutch people generally to help their Jewish countrymen during the dark years from 1940 to 1945. Although thousands of Dutchmen risked imprisonment and at a later stage of the war even their lives to hide Jews or help them to escape, thousands of other Dutchmen collaborated with the Germans or continued to do their daily work even when they knew that it would victimise Jews: railway staff running trains packed with Jews to Westerbork concentration camp, policemen (though these were exceptions) who lent the occupiers a helping hand in tracing down their victims and searching houses for Jews.

As to the Dutch police force, it is conceivable that a number of policemen were more or less demoralised by the very vigorous way in which between 1933 and 1940 the Alien Office acted against German Jewish refugees who had entered this country in illegal ways. Although the main facts about that would happen to those Jews who were sent back to Germany were generally known, the Dutch authorities had no scruples in taking these refugees back to the German border as soon as they were discovered. But after 1945 there has not been any sign of public anti-semitism in this country. A Jewish businessman with an internationally high status once (1972) told the present author that of the many countries in which he had lived and worked there were only two where he had never felt any discrimination: Brazil and Holland.

Yet it cannot be denied that there are Dutchmen who sometimes discriminate against Jews. When at the end of 1975 the United Nations General Assembly carried a motion in which Zionism was called a racist movement, the Dutch communication media published discussions and polemics about the matter, some of which gave an attentive reader the impression that anti-semitic feelings were still found among our people. A Jewish girl, Jolanda Vleesdrager, who lives in the village of Oud-Beijerland, wrote a letter to the daily paper Algemeen Dagblad of 9 December;

> A Jew is a stranger in every country except in Holland, the USA and a few other countries. Although anti-semitism is not dead in Holland either. My little brother is sometimes called names at school because he is a Jew.

On being asked about discrimination some Jewish Dutchmen told the present author that they did occasionally meet with – often disguised – discrimination: clubs that prefer not to admit Jews as members, rural communities which make it difficult for a Jew to make social contacts among the inhabitants. All this in spite of the fact that a vast majority of the Dutch Jews have always held the opinion expressed by the young Theodor Herzl, the founder of Zionism as a political movement, that the only right attitude for a Jew was to "assimilate, become part of the nation of which one is a member." J. G. Gaarlandt[16] once more drew attention to the fact that the Jewish people are no separate race, they are a people. However, even in Holland this view is not generally accepted.

## III. Discrimination by Dutchmen against People of a (Partly) Different Race: People of Other Nationalities

This chapter will contain a number of sections which will be dealt with in the following order:

(a) the groups of coloured Dutch people whose Dutch nationality was acquired during the Dutch colonial period. Of these groups some deserve to be discussed separately:

1. the Indo-Dutch or Indo-Europeans
2. the South Moluccans
3. the Surinam people
4. the Antillian people.

b. foreigners who according to the way they are treated by the Dutch can be divided into two groups:

1. foreign guestworkers
2. other foreigners.

### *A. The Indo-Europeans*

Until 1945 the Dutch colonial empire consisted of the Dutch East Indies (now the Republic of Indonesia) and what used to be called "the West." The latter consisted of two entirely different areas: Surinam on the South American mainland, and the Dutch Antilles, comprising six small very different islands.

In the Dutch East Indies since the beginning of the seventeenth century a population group had developed referred to as "Indoes." They are of mixed blood, usually descendants of Dutch fathers and Javanese, Sumatran, Balinese etc. mothers. In the Dutch East Indies before 1940 racial discrimination was negligible; safely sheltered under the loosely held umbrella of Dutch rule the large number of different peoples in that island empire enjoyed a high degree of cultural autonomy (officially, as a colonial empire, Holland did not interfere with the cultures of the peoples of her island empire). Although there was no doubt a great cultural gap between the autochthonous peoples and the Dutch colonisers, Holland was (and still is to the older generations of Indonesians) looked upon as another Mecca; command of the Dutch language was a prerequisite for promotion even in an Indonesian man's own community and those who could afford it often sent their children to Europe to be educated in Holland. But the number of Dutchmen who stayed in the Dutch East Indies after retirement was always small; most of them, civil servants (in the administration, the police force, the legal profession, the army) as well as those employed in trade and industry (on plantations, in banks, commerce, shipping) went out to "the East" on six-year contracts. Such contracts were often renewed but even then there was no intention to stay there permanently. Dutch rule, which in the 19th century often had to be imposed with a hard hand in some parts of the archipelago (especially in north Sumatra) remained undisputed after the beginning of the 20th century, when the wars in Atjeh had been won for Holland by general J. B. van Heutsz (1851–1924). If in general the Dutch in their colonies felt superior to the autochthonous population, there was hardly any racial discrimination and on the whole strong personal ties existed between the Dutch and members of the autochthonous population. If there did exist some form of discrimination it was found among the autochthonous population who discriminated against the Chinese in the country, who were shrewd businessmen, clever negotiators and hard workers and thus often outdid the native population. In the sharply divided class society of the pre-war Dutch East Indies the so-called Indo-Europeans, a mixed-blood group, were not actually discriminated against, yet they clearly formed a class in themselves, ranking between the autochthons and the Dutch. Tens of thousands of them (within their own group someone ranked higher according to the lightness of his skin) were employed in the Dutch administration, as teachers and businessmen, mostly occupying middle posts.

To the Indo-Europeans even more than to the upper classes of the native population Holland was regarded as the Promised Land. Many Indo-Europeans sent their children to Holland to be educated at Dutch secondary schools, grammar schools and universities.

Although before 1940 these Indo-Europeans were often called by nicknames suggesting some degree of discrimination (peanut, blueskin etc.) there was hardly any question of discrimination. It is true, however, that both in Holland and in the Dutch East Indies it was often more difficult for Indo-Europeans to rise on the social ladder than it was for Dutchmen with the same education and experience.

Already before 1940 Indo-Europeans on long vacation in Holland preferred certain towns in which to spend their vacation and in which to leave their children in the care of Dutch families. These towns were first of all The Hague, followed by Haarlem, the Gooi area southeast of Amsterdam, and Apeldoorn. In these towns many of them preferred to live in the same quarter. In The Hague this was the Statenkwartier (Statesmen's quarter) and the Componistenwijk (Composers' quarter). But there was no question of their living in (voluntary) ghettos. The present author knows the situation from experience. He attended a grammar school in the Statenkwartier in The Hague which had a very high percentage of pupils from the East Indies. Clashes between this group and "white" pupils were rare. No discrimination existed in the school clubs and it was rare for a teacher to discriminate against a coloured pupil. But the two groups kept more or less apart; it was a kind of apartheid the existence of which was not realised by most people but which was nonetheless a fact in and out of school hours. Children of the two groups seldom saw each other in their homes, at any rate less than children belonging to the same group. But a factor to be taken into account was that, as a result of the frequent changes of stay in Holland and the East Indies and the changes of school, the East Indian children were on an average two or three years older than their Dutch classmates.

After World War II the Dutch East Indies becames the Republic of Indonesia. In the turbulent years of the transfer of power 330,000 Indo-Europeans expressed the wish to retain Dutch nationality and to settle in Holland. A noteworthy fact – one that is an undeniable credit to Dutch society – is that the whole group of Indo-Europeans was taken up by Dutch society without difficulties of any significance, that they have been completely integrated and assimilated. They have few ties to bind them together; a somewhat sentimental gathering takes place once a year when the Pasar Malam (Evening Market) is held in The Hague, a gay meeting place to nourish nostalgic feelings. That this assimilating process has been achieved so smoothly is the more remarkable because the Indo-Europeans came to Holland at a time when many articles were still scarce and housing was still a serious problem. It is strange that before 1940 little attention was paid in Holland to the, be it modest, cultural expressions of the group. It was not until the Sixties that a few important authors of the group (first of all E. du Perron, but also R. Nieuwenhuys, Tjalie Robinson and others) were recognised in Holland. This resulted in former generations of Indo-European authors, until then unknown in Holland, gaining recognition as well.

If the Dutch as a nation had accepted or would accept other "alien" groups as they have accepted the Indo-Europeans, they would indeed deserve the epithet they like to give themselves, namely that we are a tolerant people without racial prejudices, without a tendency to discriminate against others.

After the arrival and assimilation of the group of Indo-Europeans a long series of events has brought about a change in Dutch society which no longer justifies the Dutch calling themselves a tolerant nation.

### *B. The South Moluccans*

In the Dutch East Indies before 1940 very many inhabitants of the South Moluccan archipelago (with Ambon as the main island) were faithful citizens. Very many served in the Royal Dutch East Indian

Army as professionals, many as non-commissioned officers. They were pious people, devoted to the House of Orange, and had strong family ties.

When in 1949 the sovereignty over the East Indian archipelago was transferred by the Dutch to the Young Republic of Indonesia a treaty was concluded in which the Indonesian government with Sukarno as President undertook to create a federalistic state which was to comprise sixteen federal states (thirteen of which in East Indonesia), in which the majority of the population had expressed the wish for such a state to be formed.

This promise – and with it the agreement for the transfer of sovereignty – was broken by the Sukarno government from the very beginning (not only this condition was broken by them; but that is another story). After the transfer of power the Sukarno government immediately started building a strongly centralised state with all power centralised in the island of Java and the executive power largely in the hands of Javanese people. It has been said before that before 1940 racial controversies and discrimination were relatively rare, but in all parts of the archipelago there has always been some suspicion against the Javanese.

One of the federal states was the R.M.S., the Republik Maluku Selatan, the Republic of the South Moluccas. It was proclaimed in Ambon in April 1950. Sukarno would not hear of it; he regarded the Moluccans, for whom "de Kompenie" (i.e. the Dutch government, at one time symbolised by the United East Indian Company) was their all in all and who used to be the best, and best paid native soldiers in the Royal Dutch East Indian army, as collaborators with the "enemy," the Dutch. The Moluccans, however, called Sukarno a collaborator because during World War II, when the Dutch East Indies were occupied by the Japanese, he had a secret understanding with the occupiers. When in 1947, partly under pressure from the United States of America, an agreement was made between the Dutch and Sukarno for a federalistic state to be formed in Indonesia, both parties to the agreement opposed its enforcement, Holland doing so because it resented the American pressure. In the end Holland tried to force a solution of the dilemma by means of military police actions in 1947 and 1948. The whole world was indignant and finally the transfer of sovereignty took place in December 1949. People in Holland were then beginning to realise that the "federal states," particularly the Republic of the South Moluccas had been betrayed. Although

Holland and the Republic of Indonesia met at a Round Table Conference where the autonomy of, for instance, the South Moluccas was advocated also by Holland, Sukarno proclaimed a state with a central government in February 1950. The federal state of East Indonesia rebelled but in spite of the guarantees given at the Round Table Conference the central government in Java sent an army to East Indonesia where the rebellion was soon quelled. In the meantime the independent republic of the South Moluccas had been proclaimed and up to this day the vast majority of South Moluccans still regard themselves as subjects of this in fact non-existing republic.

For a short time there were fights between Indonesian and South Moluccan soldiers, while in Java there were still about 4,000 men of the Royal Dutch East Indian army and their families. They refused to leave the army and be taken to areas controlled by Indonesians, which was in fact what the Dutch authorities intended to do. The Moluccans sued the Dutch State and won the case in the highest court of appeal on 2 March 1951. The Dutch government was forced by law to permit the Moluccans to migrate to Holland.[17] The above facts in themselves have nothing to do with discrimination of the South Moluccans at the hands of the Dutch government or the Dutch people. Yet they must be mentioned to explain the origin of the problem of the South Molluccans within Dutch society, a problem which in the last twenty-five years has grown into an extraordinary one, probably unique in the world. A problem which has come to adopt features of racial discrimination.

The critical situation in the early Fifties[18] was hardly a suitable time to transport 12,000 South Moluccans to Holland in troop ships. The tragic story of the South Moluccans in Holland is beyond the scope of this article; it would require a whole book to tell it. This much can be said that the group as a whole (in the meantime their number has grown to 33,000 thanks to their large families) has not been integrated into Dutch society. On the contrary, the truth is that especially the young Moluccans, born and bred in Holland, have with increasing aggression turned against the Dutch. The older generations still dream of an autonomous, independent republic of the South Moluccas and have passed this dream on to the younger generation. But whereas the older generations cherish their ideal in a passive way and offered passive resistance against the rare and half-hearted attempts of the Dutch to integrate the South Moluccans into Dutch society, there are sections of younger Moluccans who think that their ideal can be achieved by aggressive action in Holland, not meant in the first place to harm the Dutch, but aimed at Indonesia. In any case these actions aim at persuading the Dutch government to consult with the Indonesian government about the latter's official recognition of the Republic of the South Moluccas. Although it would be rash to say that the South Moluccans in Holland are the victims of racial discrimination it is true to say that racial contrasts have caused the Dutch government as well as the Dutch people to be very hesitant in helping the South Moluccans to feel at home in this country, while the latter did too little to encourage the Dutch to help them. Many South Moluccans have to live in housing estates below the standards one might expect in a welfare affluent society, but even if their accommodation did comply with good housing standards the fact of their being in a more or less isolated position strongly promotes the formation of ghettos.

In areas with many Ambonese families the majority of the Dutch people in the same areas are clearly averse to their presence and for many years there have been frequent disturbances and riots in these areas, sometimes ending in mass fights between Dutch and Moluccan youngsters. This aggressive behaviour on both sides really springs from racial prejudices.

The South Moluccan problem in Holland started to escalate when in 1966 the Suharto government of Indonesia executed the "President of the Republic of the South Moluccas," Mr. Chr. Soumokil. All South Moluccans regarded this as a political murder. Many young Moluccans in Holland then formed militant groupings such as the Free South Moluccan Youth and the South Moluccan Liberation Front; quarrels turned into fights fought first with their fists, then with bicycle chains, finally with real arms. In the late Sixties they formed para-military organisations to preserve law and order; they trained with real military weapons. This took place under the very eyes of the Dutch government and so much in the open that press and television reported on them. These actions were in the first place aimed at Indonesia, but also at the Dutch people because they applied a kind of repressive tolerance and the Dutch government omitted to take action when it became clear that these aggressive actions had long exceeded the stage of ordinary rows in cafés between brown and white boys about a girl. The leaders of the groups within the South Moluccan community, J. A. Manusama, a university graduate engineer and the ex-army officer Tamaela, who are strongly opposed to each other, have since the early Seventies lost their grip on part of the groups of young South Moluccans:

In 1966 a fire was raised in the Indonesian Embassy in The Hague to protest against the death of the President of their Republic, Mr. Soumokil;

In August 1970 thirty South Moluccan youths occupied the residence of the Indonesian Ambassador at Wassenaar, a suburb of The Hague, for the purpose of forcing a talk to be arranged between Mr Manusama and the Indonesian President Suharto, who was at the time expected in Holland for a State visit.

In April 1974 the office of the Indonesian airline company Garuda in Amsterdam was set on fire; the next day an attempt was made to take the Indonesian consul in Amsterdam as a hostage, which attempt failed;

In December 1974 a group of rebellious South Moluccan youths, who had been dispersed by the police after a demonstration, caused Df 1,500,000 damage to the Palace of Peace in The Hague;

On 1 April 1975 the Public Prosecutor in the Arnhem Court of Justice revealed that a plan made by a group of South Moluccans to occupy Soestdijk Palace, the residence of Queen Juliana, had been defeated;

Early December 1975 a number of South Moluccan youths stopped a train between the towns of Zwolle, Groningen and Assen near the the village of Wijster and held a few dozen passengers as hostages for many days; in the meantime the Indonesian consulate in Amsterdam was raided and the people inside the building were also held as hostages for several days. In both cases a number of hostages were killed. The Dutch government did little to prevent this escalation of violence, although they had received several warnings. Early in 1975 Mr Kay Liat Oen, a sociologist,[19] after an investigation he had made, came to the conclusion that

> the radical tendencies among the South Moluccans were bound to take more extreme forms if the Dutch government continued their policy in this matter. (For) the South Moluccans have had enough of the fact that their ideal of an independent republic of the South Moluccas is regarded and approached as a chimera. Therefore their actions are not caused by any dissatisfaction with their living conditions in Holland, nor by feelings of discrimination against them, but should be seen as actions of desperation. Especially the young among them are aware that this is the only way left to them to make people listen to them, and in contrast to their elders they do not shrink from using violence.

One might agree with Mr. Kay Liat Oen that young South Moluccans in general do not think that they are being discriminated against in Holland (about which the present author has strong doubts based on many pronouncements made by South Moluccans), but it cannot be denied that of late years as a result of the escalation of violence, a sense of antipathy against South Moluccans has been rapidly increasing within Dutch society.

Especially the young South Moluccans, according to what Mr. F. J. Aponno a member of the Executive of the *Pemuda Masjarakat* RMS (i.e. Young people from the community of the republic of the South Moluccas) said in December 1975, want to fight on until the Dutch government supports their cause. That is to say until the Dutch government and the Republic of Indonesia discuss the possibility of recognising the RMS. The Dutch government, however, is of the opinion that it would be a lost cause. Another expectation of the aggressive young South Moluccans, who deserve to be called terrorists because of some of their actions, is that their actions will draw the attention of the United Nations Organisation.

One thing is certain: a large section of Dutch opinion is turning against the South Moluccans and this is often manifested in undeniable racial discrimination. Mr. O. Glastra van Loon, a lawyer and a former Under-Secretary of Justice in the Dutch government may be right in saying on television on 6 December 1975 that "this is the result of the kind but vague attitude of the Dutch government for the last 25 years, passing off the South Moluccan cause with a shrug of their shoulders," but the fact is that the escalation of violence as a response to this indifference has frequently drawn attention abroad and caused the Dutch people, even those who were able to show a kind but vague attitude, to turn against them in aversion. More and more old as well as young Moluccans are becoming increasingly aware of the fact that their actions have changed what goodwill they enjoyed among the Dutch into strong feelings of uneasiness, manifesting itself in discrimination. "People are now turning a cold shoulder upon us" is a complaint often heard from older South Moluccans and at the end of 1975 the leaders of South Moluccan organisations in Holland received many threats by telephone, by letter and by word of mouth.

It would be unreasonable to put all the blame on the South Moluccans. Of course, they refused to be integrated and it is at least remarkable from a sociological point of view that the younger generation of South Moluccans, who have never seen the land of their fathers except in pictures, should strongly idealise it and make it a reason for repudiating integration. Of course everyone who refuses to adapt himself and constantly draws attention by his aggressive behaviour is simply begging to be made an outcast. On the other hand little has been done by successive Dutch governments and by the Dutch people as a whole to give the South Moluccans a chance to assimilate. The tragic part of the whole affair is that the South Moluccans strongly contribute to the growth of racial discrimination in Holland at a time when it was already on the increase as a result of events which will be discussed in greater detail later on, whereas in fact it is not their wish to rebel against Holland. In an ocean of misunderstanding and misery 33,000 people who after a 25 years' stay in this country might still be looked upon as displaced persons, are making their position more and more difficult in a country which is becoming more and more averse to them. Both parties are actually to blame for this desperate situation, which at this moment is in full development, so that every conclusion must be a provisional one. But whatever the further developments may be, it is almost certain that the actions of the South Moluccans have released feelings of racial hatred in Holland. In December 1975, after South Moluccans had high-jacked a train and held the passengers as hostages, a church belonging to the South Moluccan community in the village of Elst was badly damaged and set on fire. Many newspapers published letters to their editors in which the writers insisted on the re-introduction of capital punishment for aggressive South Moluccans. In conversations with Dutch people – respectable ones! – taken at random in the last few weeks of 1975 the phrase "All that scum should be shot dead" was commonly heard.

Twenty years ago no ordinary Dutchman would ever have said such a thing. Professor Dr. I. A. Diepenhorst, a level-headed man, wrote on purpose in Elseviers Magazine of 12 December 1975:

> Taking this general background into account it would be wise to use one's common sense and not express foolish ideas. Re-introduction of capital punishment, which was abolished from common criminal law more than a century ago, will bring no solution, neither will hitting out right and left, not to mention the disgraceful suggestion to extradite "all coloured people" from this country.

That this experienced professor thought it necessary to add the last passage to his article shows the depth to which discrimination had fallen in The Netherlands. Are South Moluccans Dutch nationals?

About a quarter of these people in Holland have in the course of time opted for the Dutch nationality instead of the Indonesian. Even as late as 1974 615 of them were naturalised; in 1973 the number was 503. The number of South Moluccans having Indonesian nationality is not known. The others, who on principle refuse to adopt any nationality because they regard themselves as subjects of the republic of the South Moluccas, are stateless, which means that they cannot hold permanent jobs in the Dutch civil service and that they have to apply for a visa whenever they wish to travel outside the Benelux countries. Otherwise the South Moluccans in Holland have the same legal rights as the Dutch, also as far as their political freedom is concerned, for instance they have the right to hold public meetings, etc. For many years people in Holland who had made a study of this problem of the Ambonnese (there were not many who had) saw it as a *social* problem, whereas to the South Moluccans themselves it was a *political* problem. It was not before the beginning of 1974 that a bill of was introduced in the Second Chamber of the Dutch Parliament (up till now Parliament has not dealt with it) to regulate the position of the Moluccans in Holland. The intention is for these people "who as a group were taken to Holland by the Dutch government," if they refuse to become Dutch nationals (75 percent of the group) to be treated in law as if they were Dutch citizens, in common with the South Moluccans born in Holland. But as long as they are not Dutch citizens these South Moluccans, according to this bill of Parliament, will be deprived of the right to vote, nor will they be eligible for election, and they will be excluded from doing military service.

This bill is perhaps a sensible one, but the question remains as to whether it would solve the problem. On 9 December 1975 one of the Ambonnese leaders, Mr. Aponno, said:

> The Korps Pendjaga Keamanan, the police force of Mr. J. A. Manusama, the President of the Republic of the South Moluccas, must be legally armed to enable them to keep the peace in co-operation with the Dutch police, for as a community we now feel the threat of the Dutch people.[20]

Although these words were spoken in the critical period described above they prove the existence in Holland of a certain degree of discrimination among some sections of the Dutch people against the South Moluccans because they are "different from us."

### *C. The Surinam People*

On 15 October 1954 Holland, Surinam and the group of Caribbean islands which are called the Dutch Antilles concluded the *Koninkrijks-statuut* (the Statute of the Kingdom). At that time, when all over the world de-colonisation processes were going on, it was a step which drew great attention abroad.

Because Indonesia had gained independence in a way quite different from what The Netherlands had hoped for and wished, and because it had developed in a spirit and direction different from what had been agreed upon at the transfer of sovereignty, Holland intended to do better with the colonies in the West. According to the *Koninkrijksstatuut* Surinam and the Dutch Antilles became "territories within the Kingdom."

In general outline this meant that Surinam and the Antilles had become autonomous in all respects with the exception of defence and representation abroad, which remained in Dutch hands.

A cabinet of the Kingdom was formed, consisting of ministers from the three parts of the Kingdom, and in the Dutch cabinet a special Office for Surinam and Antillian Affairs was formed and charged with the co-ordination of affairs concerning Surinam and the Dutch Antilles, and the aid to be given to these territories. This Office is presided over by the Dutch Minister of Home Affairs.

The agreement aimed at attaining a form of co-operation and co-existence between an ex-colonial power and some former colonies was of world interest. The Dutch had never bothered much about Surinam and the Dutch Antillles when these were colonies, referred to as "the West," a most incorrect name because it suggested that they formed a close unit, which they do not, neither from a geographical, cultural, ethnical nor from an economic point of view. Nor do they wish to be united.

Before 1940 the Dutch had for a long time been of the opinion that their riches came from The East, the Dutch East Indies, and that Surinam and the Antilles were poor and of no importance for the Dutch economy.[21] Surinam with its 400,000 inhabitants is a thinly populated country and was looked upon as a sleeping part of Latin America where agriculture had once been profitable but had declined a long time ago. It had one major industry, the Bruynzeel Timber company, operating in Surinam's rich woods, while her mineral resources, especially bauxite and to a lesser extent gold, were exploited by American and Canadian companies respectively. The Antillian islands of Caraçao and Aruba were important owing to their refineries for oil, mainly from Venezuela. The island of St. Maarten was a favourite holiday resort for tourists from the eastern part of the United States, but the tourist industry was run mainly by Americans. For the rest Holland had forgotten its Caribbean islands.

The West, however, had not forgotten Holland.

For the people of Surinam and three of the six Antillian islands (Curaçao, Aruba and Bonaire) Holland was the promised land, as it was for Indonesians. The three other islands are different. St. Maarten is half French, this part belonging to the French department of Outremer de Guadeloupe; Saba and St. Eustace are mini-islands, each with no more than about 1,000 inhabitants. Although these three islands are pro-Dutch, the inhabitants prefer to speak English. In the past not many people from Surinam and the Antilles came to Holland for their education, probably fewer than the number of Indonesians (no exact figures are available), which may be due to the low average standard of life in the West. Surinam is inhabited by a wide variety of races; its society is based on racial differences, whereas society in the Antilles is based on colour rather than race.

The original inhabitants of Surinam were Red Indians, mainly of the Trio and Wayana tribes.[22] The first Dutchmen came in 1616 and settled on the Essequibo river. In 1650 the British conquered the area but in 1667 Abraham Crijnssen reconquered it for the Republic of the United Netherlands. The Breda Peace Treaty of 1667, which ended the frequent wars between the English and the Dutch, stipulated that the Netherlands would keep Surinam in exchange for the area now known as Manhattan, i.e. New York.

The Dutch built plantations on the fertile soil along the coast; Indians proved to be unfit for work on these plantations, so a large number of slaves were brought in, mainly from West Africa (the Ghana region), until slavery was abolished on 1 July 1863.

As this caused a scarcity of manpower on the plantations labour was imported on a voluntary basis, contract coolies first from China, then from what is now India and later, even up to 1946, from Java. Thousands of these workers stayed on after their contract had expired, many becoming petty farmers.

This is the origin of a multi-coloured population: seven groups with very few contacts. The Red Indians still living in isolated areas; the forest negroes, descendants of escaped slaves; Creoles, descendants of negro slaves and partly whites; Hindus, Javanese, Chinese, and some whites many of whom are descended from Spanish and Portuguese Jewish refugees.[23]

The Hindus form the largest population group, 37 percent. Economically they are the strongest group because on the whole they are good farmers and hard-working businessmen. There are 31 percent Creoles and 15 percent Javanese. The other groups are small and of little political significance.

One of the strange stipulations of the *Koninkrijksstatuut* was that people from Surinam and the Antilles were free to settle in Holland temporarily and permanently, but Dutch people needed a permit to settle and work in Surinam or the Antilles. Economically Surinam was a weak country; agriculture had much declined after the 19th century; the Creoles, whose ancestors had been slaves on the plantations, regarded work on the land as below their dignity; the capital town of Paramaribo housed more than a quarter of the total population, and after 1950 its population grew steadily; there were few industries and the unemployment figure was high; social benefits were fewer and lower than in the welfare state Holland; racial contrasts were great and the political parties were in fact racial parties.

When the *Koninkrijksstatuut* had been signed many Surinam people migrated to Holland, a slow but steady flow. In the first few years they were students and socially deprived people, who as Dutch subjects according to the *Koninkrijksstatuut* were entitled to receive the same social benefits in Holland as the Dutch. But at the end of the Sixties people in Holland were beginning to get uneasy about this phenomenon. Many Dutch people believed that the majority of the Surinam people had come to Holland only to get social benefits, whereas in fact most of them had a job, labour being scarce in Holland at the time. Another fact was that from the beginning a number of them were social outcasts, engaged in prostitution, or as fancy-men or in the drug trade. So although the rate of criminal offences among Surinam people was not higher than among the Dutch, their crimes drew much attention in Holland. Moreover Surinam people in Holland preferred to live together in the same areas, at first mainly in Amsterdam, much to the annoyance of the Dutch inhabitants of those city quarters.

Surinam people themselves had their misgivings about the situation, especially about the fact that many Surinam graduates of Dutch universities and those who had had a vocational training in Holland did not return to their own country. These misgivings grew. In 1970

Mr. Lion Arons, a Surinam journalist, wrote that 170 physicians practised in Holland while Surinam could do with 70 more doctors, that 200 Surinam high school teachers were employed in Holland, while Surinam was in urgent need of 60, that 10 Surinam university graduate engineers worked in Holland, while Surinam had only one. "As many as 35,000 Surinam people now live in Holland," he wrote, "which is ten percent of our population."

Since then the number has risen to at least 130,000, a good 30 percent of the Surinam population. None of the successive Dutch governments has done anything to check the influx of Surinam people, firstly because they thought that it would be a violation of the *Koninkrijksstatuut*, secondly because having important economic relations with many Third World countries, Holland did not like to appear to be taking discriminatory measures.

Although Surinam is potentially a rich country, fertile, covered with primeval forests, rich in mineral resources,[24] little has been achieved to improve the economy of the country. First because of the lack of interest on the part of foreign investors, secondly by a lack of initiative in Surinam, thirdly by a certain inertness among Surinam people, fourthly by widespread corruption in the administration of the country, fifthly because the Dutch were not interested. According to the notoriously inaccurate Surinam statistics 23 percent of the male labour force in Paramaribo in 1973 were unemployed, while very many were employed in unnecessary jobs created simply because each new government used to reward a number of its adherents with a job.

At the elections of October 1973 a coalition of Creole parties won by a small majority partly owing to controversies among the Hindus.

While racial controversies especially between Creoles and Hindus had increased since the Sixties the Prime Minister, Mr. H. Arron, declared that by the end of 1975 the country would be independent, knowing that this would mean a unilateral termination of the *Koninkrijksstatuut*. In Holland, however, there were strong groups, especially left-wing groups, which had for years insisted on independence for Surinam. "People" in Holland simply wanted to get rid of Surinam. Aversion to the increasing flow of Surinam people into Holland continued to grow and so-called progressive Dutchmen used it as an argument for calling the *Koninkrijksstatuut* in essence a neo-colonial scheme.[25] When Arron had made his declaration thousands of Hindus and Javanese were frightened, for from the start it had been obvious that independence would mean domination by the Creoles. Thousands, mainly Hindus, left the country for Holland.

It is not necessary to deal in this paper with the prolonged and laborious negotiations between the Dutch government and the Arron administration about the "compensation" to be paid by The Netherlands when Surinam became independent or with many other political aspects of the question. It is important, however, to mention one decision made by the negotiating parties. Once Mr. Arron had declared that Surinam would be independent on 25 November 1975 the parties agreed that every Surinam citizen who lived in The Netherlands on that day could opt for Dutch nationality. The result was that at the end of 1974 and until December 1975 tens of thousands of Surinam people, mainly Hindus, sought refuge in The Netherlands. Surinam affairs were conducted by an extremely short-sighted government, so when independence was gained the country had lost all its reasonably well qualified people, most of whom had come to live in Holland. The first independent government of this 144th member of U.N.O. started a campaign to persuade Surinam people to return to their home country, so far with very little success.

Of course the arrival of more than 100,000 Surinam people caused great difficulties in Holland which affected the average Dutchman. Dutch society had undeniably been a tolerant society, but the problems with the South Moluccans and guestworkers (who will be dealt with later on) had caused many hitherto unknown tensions. The influx of Surinam people was simply more than the average Dutchman could cope with. Moreover, they arrived when the Dutch economy was declining; unemployment figures kept rising in 1974 and 1975; the country was facing a recession as it had not seen since 1935. Consequently trade and industry had no jobs to offer to the Surinam refugees. On the other hand it had always been difficult for them to work in trade and industry in Holland even in times of full employment, because many of them found it almost impossible to get accustomed to the Dutch industrial climate and the Dutch way of life in general. In our large cities they lived together in the same areas, making them more or less into Surinam ghettos (the Bijlmermeer, a suburb in east Amsterdam with many new blocks of flats, and the 19th century Kruiskadekwartier in Rotterdam). As tensions between population groups increased in these areas the Dutch government decided that all Dutch municipalities should place 5 percent of the available housing accommodation at the disposal of Surinam people in their district.

This measure had serious consequences especially in rural districts. Some municipal authorities, for instance in the Brabant village of Megen and in the village of Norg in the province of Drenthe, ignored it because they thought that it would upset the population structure of their villages. At Megen 200 Surinam people would have to be accommodated in a parish of 700 inhabitants. Elsewhere protestant clergymen objected to the arrival of so many foreign elements, for instance in the orthodox protestant village of Stavenisse in Zeeland.

With the increase of new arrivals protests grew stronger. How great this increase was shortly before Surinam became independent appears from an investigation made by Elseviers Magazine and the Institute for Public Opinon Polls (NIPO), the results of which were published in Elseviers Magazine on 29 September 1975. To the question: When did you arrive in Holland?, put to a large number of Surinam people 28 percent answered: in 1975, 17 percent: in 1974, 24 percent: in 1971, 1972 and 1973. Of the interviewees 42 percent received some kind of social allowance (in most cases unemployment benefit) and 43 percent were against their country becoming independent. A remarkable thing was that 90 percent answered that they liked being in Holland and that only 46 percent intended to return to Surinam if independence should increase their country's prosperity and employment. Similar investigations have been made by others and their outcome suggests that the presence of Surinam people in Holland might well be permanent.

Although Elseviers Magazine's investigation showed that most Surinam people liked Holland discriminatory tendencies against them are increasing. In many villages and towns committees have been set up to promote the integration of Surinam people into the Dutch community, yet Elseviers Magazine is of the opinion that in the last few years the attitude of the Dutch has clearly turned against people from Surinam. "Employers who refuse to engage Surinam people, villages where the inhabitants are upset at the idea of Surinam people coming to live in their village, be it only temporarily, Surinam children being called '*roetmop*' (soot ball) or '*dropstaaf*' (liquorice stick), or an unemployed workman saying at an Amsterdam employment bureau: "It would be a d—— shame if those niggers were to be taken on while I, a Dutchman, remain unemployed."

Such incidents are gradually giving the impression that our Dutch society is not so tolerant as it was thought to be, it reveals irritations and tensions. The Surinam people do not appear to be aware of the situation or the truth may be as a Surinam welfare officer put it:

Most of them lived under such abominable material conditions in Surinam that Holland with its almost perfect system of social benefits is in any case a real change for the better.

It is becoming more and more questionable whether the perfect system can be maintained now that this country is faced with a grave economic recession.

Elseviers Magazine's conclusion is:

All in all these sad figures present a gloomy view of the future for Surinam people in Holland. As long as the economic recession lasts their chances of employment will remain small. Then there is the problem of growing racial discrimination, which is another threat to their chances of a happy life in this country.

What this weekly paper has said about the problem can be confirmed by everyone who watches the developments in this respect. Taxi-drivers in big cities often refuse to carry Surinam passengers. Cafés and nightclubs in the large cities often refuse to admit them, using irrelevant excuses. The 'man in the street' has an unfavourable idea of Surinam people. In the Summer of 1974 young Dutch boys and girls under eighteen in a youth centre in the province of Gelderland were asked to give their opinion of Surinam people. The almost unanimous answer was: they are workshy, lazy und unreliable. When asked if they had ever had any contact with Surinam people nearly all of them said: No.

Dutch people who regularly meet Surinam people generally hold a more favourable opinion, especially about the Hindus, who are regarded as better than the Creoles. All this does not alter the fact, however, that in a country where until 1940 people had been hardly race conscious, the influx of Surinam people – after the South Moluccans and the foreign guestworkers – has increased racial tensions. In a book titled '*Suriname, gisteren, vandaag, morgen*'[26] (Surinam yesterday, today, to-morrow) the Surinam editor, looking back upon the last stage before independence, says:

But even more alarming was the growing intolerance of Dutch society against Surinam people. The majority of the Dutch population turned more strongly against the Surinam people. This is manifested by the refusal of some Dutch municipal authorities to accommodate them, and by employers shutting their doors in their faces, when Surinam people came to apply for a job.

Recently however a Dutch law was introduced that

anyone who, except for the purpose of giving an objective report, publishes a statement which he knows, or can reasonably suspect to be insulting to a group of people on account of their race, religion or philosophy of life, or stirs up hatred or discrimination against a group of people, or commits an act of violence against others or their property on the ground of race, religion or philosophy of life, will be liable to imprisonment for six months at most or a fine of at most 5,000 guilders.

This has been laid down in section 137E of the Criminal Code, and was introduced when in 1968 The Netherlands had ratified the agreement on racial discrimination passed by the United Nations Organisation. This recently led to a lawsuit commenced by an Indonesian who had been refused admittance into a café in Arnhem. An inhabitant of The Hague, Mr. J. Glimmerveen, founder of the *Nederlandse Volksunie* (Dutch National Union), a small insignificant political party with a clearly racialist programme, was sued when during the elections for the municipal Council of The Hague he distributed a pamphlet saying:

Help us to deliver our city from the pest of Surinam and Antillian people. The Hague must remain white, away with Surinam and Antillian people, who sponge on our energy and prosperity.

At first the man was dismissed from court because the Court in The Hague decided that "Surinam and Antillian people are not one race, they belong to several different races." But the High Court of Appeal decided otherwise and remitted the case to the Amsterdam Court, which on 15 December 1975 sentenced the man to a fine of 1,000 guilders and put him on a month's probation for racial discrimination.

Mr. H. T. A. Knijff, a lawyer, drew attention to the fact[27] that

national laws as well as international agreements are silent about the question as to what is understood by the term "race"; nevertheless any selection based on a person's skin colour should be regarded as an act of racial discrimination, which constitutes an offence against Dutch law.

The presence of so many Surinam people in Holland really presents an extremely difficult problem. It has in the last few years continually upset Dutch society and repeatedly evoked acts of racial discrimination.

## D. *The Antillians*

The Dutch Antilles have a population of 300,000, living in six islands whose populations show marked differences. In the islands of Curaçao, Aruba and Bonaire the Dutch language is used as a medium among educated people, in the smaller islands of St. Maarten, Saba and St. Eustatius it is English.

The people on the whole like the Dutch, and although the Dutch government has more than once expressed their wish for these islands to be given independence (i.e. for them the ties with the *Koninkrijks-statuut*), the Antilles do not want to be independent yet. Their present Prime Minister J. M. C. Evertsz, told the present author in the spring of 1975:

> I have a sovereign state of The Antilles in mind. But some aspects of sovereignty which we, as a small country, will not be able to realise on our own, should be achieved with the help of The Netherlands. Or – if necessary – with the help of another country, though we had rather not do so. (The most important three islands lie only a few dozen miles off the Venezuelan coast) People who claim that the Dutch should leave our islands are taking a short-sighted view.

Mr. M. B. Leiti, Governor of the Antilles, i.e. H.M. representative in that part of the Kingdom, told the present author on the same occasion:

> Of course denying independence to those who want it betrays a colonial attitude. But it is also an act of colonialism to thrust independence upon people who do not wish to be independent, at any rate not in the near future. For it is a colonial way of thinking only to have the interests of the mother country at heart.

The central government of the Dutch Antilles is in Curaçao, in the capital town of Willemstad. The other islands refuse to recognise this central government, and if they were to be given independence Aruba, Bonaire and St Maarten prefer to have closer relations with other countries, Aruba preferring The Netherlands. The number of people from the Antilles who have emigrated to Holland is lower than that of Surinam people; this can partly be accounted for by their slightly better economic situation, partly because there are no racial tensions, partly because, like many islanders, people in the Antilles are strongly attached to their native soil. Antillians who come to Holland mainly do so for educational reasons, and many go back to their country after finishing their studies.

In the last few years Antillian people in Holland have met with the same difficulties as the Surinam people, because Dutch people do not distinguish between the two groups, which is pretty hard on the Antillians, as they do not wish to be treated like Surinam people, whom in general they dislike. This fact may in the last few years have dissuaded many young Antillians from coming to Holland.

## IV. Foreign Guestworkers

Foreign guestworkers are not a typically Dutch phenomenon. They are a worldwide problem. Everywhere in western Europe, in the south of the United States of America, in South Africa, people from less developed or poorer areas migrate to countries with a greater demand for labour, where wages are higher and social security better. In the Sixties millions of guestworkers from Spain and Italy, Yugoslavia and Greece, Portugal and the Cape Verde Islands, from Turkey and Morocco, Malta and Algeria found employment in western Europe. The economic background of this phenomenon in Holland need not be dealt with in detail, as Western Germany, France and Belgium are faced with the same problems. The question of concern is: Are guestworkers in Holland discriminated against?

In the mid-Sixties H. van Emmerik-Levelt and A. W. M. Teulings[28] made an investigation into the attitude of the Dutch towards guestworkers. As far as the present author knows they were the first to make such an investigation. The general picture that emerged was a favourable one. Employers' and employees' magazines as well as daily newspapers had been searched for news items, reports and commentaries on foreign guestworkers. This is what they wrote:

Many articles say that 'foreign guestworkers are diligent and work hard,' 'they have a strong moral sense, but they are primitive people,' 'they are dark and hot-tempered,' 'they are friendly people and do not cause trouble.' On the other hand there were reports of criminal behaviour among foreign guestworkers, and a sore point was considered to be relations between the guestworkers and Dutch girls because these were the source of most emotional conflicts, and did much to promote the growth of prejudice.

When the investigation was made, in 1965, there were indeed often fights, sometimes on a large scale, between guestworkers and young men in the Twente area, where many guestworkers were employed in the textile industry and were evidently more popular with the girls than the local boys. The investigators regretfully said:

The daily press gives the impression that after the provos the foreigners seem to be the most riotous and crime-prone part of the population.

The real situation, however, was different. Wentholt[29] held this opinion:

It is hardly possible for such a situation to arise because the different ethnical groups are too small, too much spread among the autochthonous population, their stay is too short for them to commit wide-spread and serious criminal offences in Dutch society. Of course subtle individual forms of discrimination are possible.

This was the situation in 1965–66; the social pattern has changed since then. Firstly the various ethnical groups have greatly increased in numbers. From 31 May 1960 till 31 December 1973 the total number rose from 117,600 to 296,800. Most of them came from countries which were likely to supply guestworkers. The number of Greeks rose from 400 to 4,000, Italians from 5,000 to 19,400, Portuguese from 100 to 7,400, Spaniards from 200 to 31,800, Turks from 100 to 53,500, Yugoslavs from 900 to 12,000, Moroccans from 0 to 29,600.[30] Secondly the groups were no longer evenly spread among our people, as Wentholt said in 1965. In the large cities (Rotterdam, Amsterdam, Utrecht) they have settled in 19th century working-class quarters in such large numbers that this has resulted in frequent tensions arising between guestworkers and the Dutch people in those areas. Thirdly foreign workers are now staying in this country for longer periods; many have now lived here for many years. Many Spanish wives have joined their husbands with their children. This is permissible when a few years have passed without any complaints about the men having been made. In the wide surroundings of the Koninklijke Nederlandse Hoogovens (Royal Dutch Blast Furnaces) at Ymuiden for instance, large housing estates have been built to house Spanish families, with special schools for their children. Finally Wentholt's statement that there is no question of widespread and serious criminal offences committed by foreign guestworkers has proved to be an illusion in some respects.

It would be stretching matters too far to say that in general guestworkers are being discriminated against in Holland. On the contrary; a large majority of them lead their own lives outside the Dutch community, contacts between them and Dutch people are few and of a superficial nature. The present author agrees with A. J. van der Staay that a good insight into this matter is 'rather difficult to obtain as opinions are often exaggerated'.[31] For it is undeniable that the abnormal makes news. When a few years ago in south Rotterdam rather serious disturbances and fights took place between working-class people in the area and Turkish guestworkers, who had come to live there in pretty large numbers, these incidents were hot news and drew much attention. The fact that in many other places in the country guestworkers live quietly side by side with their Dutch neighbours does not make news.

The successive Dutch governments' policy concerning foreign guestworkers has never been a straightforward one. At first the government did very little; their idea was that employers who needed foreign guestworkers should try and recruit them themselves. There was a great shortage of labour in the Sixties in very many fields, especially for unskilled work, and guestworkers were prepared and able to do this kind of work; moreover Dutch workers were little interested in doing dirty or heavy work, and in working in nightshifts or during weekends, while guestworkers were eager to do these jobs. The government was also of the opinion that employers were responsible for the provision of food and housing, although in this respect the government did keep an eye on what was being done. But as the stream of foreign guestworkers grew the government was forced to take measures. This in fact happened on the instigation of Parliament, for when the budget for 1969 was discussed in Parliament the then Minister of Social Affairs and National Health was requested to write a memorandum on foreign guestworkers in The Netherlands. The Minister, Mr. B. Roolvink, promised to do so,[32] and twelve months later, in January 1970, the memorandum was published, countersigned by the Ministers of Justice, of Economic Affairs, and of Culture, Recreation and Welfare Work. It was widely criticised, mainly because it lacked vision concerning the government's future policy.[33]

It also caused surprise – followed by resentment in later years – that the memorandum should start from the principle that "Holland, a densely populated country, is not fit for mass immigration," while in practice more and more guestworkers were enabled to settle here for years with their families. It may be assumed, however, that so far the increasing numbers of foreign guestworkers have not greatly increased discrimination against them. There was one positive aspect of the problem. After a long period of inactivity with regard to the problem, after long hesitation because many of their members were afraid of competition from guestworkers, the trade unions at last, in the early Seventies, started helping and guiding the foreign workers and giving their members more information about the problems guestworkers had. For many years guestworkers preferred to go to Holland rather than to West Germany, Belgium or France. This can partly be explained by the good social benefits in this country, to which foreign guestworkers are also entitled, provided they have a legal permit to stay. But there are tens of thousands of illegal guestworkers in Holland as they did not enter the country via the official government recruiting channels. This became known during the economic recession, which started in The Netherlands in 1974, when many guestworkers were laid off. All rights and duties under the social laws in Holland are applicable, without any restrictions, to foreign guestworkers, to the same extent as they apply to Dutch employees. In practice the legal position of guestworkers may seem to be weaker, which is often due to their ignorance of their legal rights.

Much has been done to remedy this both by the large industries which employ many foreign workers and by many national, regional and local institutions founded to help foreign guestworkers, for instance by publishing a vademecum in many languages, by establishing offices where foreign workers can talk about their problems with people who speak their language (often difficult to find). This work is done by socially motivated Dutch voluntary workers and is undeniably a meritorious enterprise.

From the study 'Guestworkers in The Netherlands', which has been mentioned before, it appeared that at least in 1972 guestworkers in this country are on the whole more or less satisfied with their jobs, the working conditions and the terms of employment. There have been some complaints about social contacts with Dutch people, colleagues as well as others: there was a sense of being cold-shouldered.

In Holland there has never been a movement such as one finds in Switzerland, conducted by Dr. James Schwarzenbach, which aims at a quick and drastic decrease in the number of foreign workers in their country, the majority of whom are skilled workers. Yet, in Holland there are generally 'mild' forms of discrimination. The average Dutchman is not eager to accept foreign guestworkers into his community, he leaves them alone at work, and has little contact with them out of working hours – although gradually the situation may change when guestworkers have worked for the same employer for many years. The position of the Dutch trade unions remains a delicate one in this respect: on the one hand one of their principles is international solidarity and they do not want guestworkers in a host country to be deprived of their opportunity to find employment or receive higher pay, on the other hand they have to look after the direct interests of their members, their supporters. The large and increasing numbers of guestworkers have worried trade unionists, even during the years when Holland was in need of labour, and especially when in 1975 the Dutch economy declined and the rate of unemployment rose to a level unknown since World War II. On 10 December 1975 the head of the regional Labour Bureau in Rotterdam said that "workers doing general work" (unskilled) had no prospects; the majority of them were people from the West Indies (Surinam and the Dutch Antilles) and foreigners. The lower paid workers feel they are directly threatened by the foreign workers. Anyone who by virtue of his profession is in a position to meet many working-class people must get the impression that since 1973, when employment figures fell, resentment about the number of foreign workers in Holland has grown strongly.

## V. Other Foreigners

Foreign tourists and foreigners in higher paid jobs who stay here temporarily (staffs of embassies etc.) are on the whole of the opinion that the Dutch are a very hospitable people. The Dutch generally do not suffer from xenophobia and the tradition of being an internationally-minded people, which they have built up since the beginning of the seventeenth century as a maritime and trading nation, has resulted in a great openness towards foreigners. Add to this the proverbial phenomenon that "everybody in Holland speaks foreign languages" (which is a rather exaggerated opinion, though it is true that thanks to our schools many generations of Dutch people are more familiar with two or three foreign languages than most other nations) and it is not surprising that on the whole foreigners feel at home in Holland. Therefore Holland has for many years been popular with tourists. For not only do the Dutch not suffer from xenophobia they are on the whole a strongly commercially-minded people. The export trade and the tourist industry are responsible for more than half the gross national income, which may be the reason why the Dutch mix with foreigners more easily than inhabitants of an isolated and inwardly turned country.

But the friendly attitude of the Dutch towards foreigners is part of their national character, which has for many centuries been recognised and appreciated by many foreign observers. On the other hand travellers writing about a tour of The Netherlands have over the centuries complained about the greediness and close-fistedness of the Dutch towards foreigners. In 1743 the Frenchman Montesquieu wrote about Holland in his 'Voyages':

> Lower class people will ask the whole contents of your purse for carrying a suitcase, and inn-keepers, especially small ones, will charge you fifty or a hundred times the price of refreshments, and you have to pay, for the magistrate will not do justice at all.

Chorus[34] mentions many such statements.

But this has nothing to do with discrimination. Discrimination against foreigners has over the centuries been very rare – at the beginning of this paper it was stated that generations of Dutchmen have been taught that tolerance is one of the best qualities of the Dutch.

The conclusion of this paper should be that if in the past there was very little discrimination against coloured people and for historical reasons also against people of different religions, tolerance in our own days has greatly diminished. It is clear that Dutchmen today, confronted as they are with large numbers of Surinam people and even more guestworkers, are now faced with new problems which they have not yet been able to solve satisfactorily. The Dutch in the last quarter of this century are beginning to realise – many with a shock – that it is easier to criticise discriminatory phenomena in other countries than to live in the circumstances of the last twenty years and refuse to discriminate, now that society has outgrown the familiar stability of former generations.

## Notes

1. Prof. Dr. A. Chorus: *A Dutchman Outwardly and Inwardly*, A. W. Sijthoff, Leiden, 1964.
2. Prof. Dr. J. Huizinga: *The Dutch and their Spiritual Qualities*, A. W. Sijthoff, Leiden, 1946.
3. Dr. P. Vinke: *Social Rise and Fall in The Netherlands*, II, H. E. Stenfert Kroese, Leiden, 1961.
4. F. van Heek: *Social Rise and Fall*, Amsterdam, 1946.
5. G. Kuiper: "Vertical Mobility to some Academic Professions," in the anthology

*Social Rise and Fall in The Netherlands.* H. E. Stenfert Kroese, Leiden, 1950.
6. A. C. Gebhard and A. C. W. van der Vet: *The ABC of Amsterdam*, Van Munster, Amsterdam, 1948.
7. Jan and Annie Romein: *Our Cultural Ancestors*, vol. III, Em. Querido, Amsterdam, 1946.
8. Dr. J. A. C. de Mey in the *Tijdschrift voor Geschiedenis* (Historical Magazine).
9. As quoted in M. van der Plas: *From our Rich Roman Catholic World*, Ambo, Utrecht, no date.
10. H. L. Kok: *The History of the Last Honour in The Netherlands*, De Tijdstroom, Lochem, 1970.
11. Dr. W. Drees: *Sixty Years Experience*, Amsterdam.
12. Prof. F. J. M. Duynstee: *Formations of Governments* 1946–1965, Kluwer, Deventer, 1966.
13. B. A. Syes: "Persecution of Jews in The Netherlands," Rijksinstituut voor Oorlogsdocumentatie, Amsterdam, 1960.
14. Dr. L. de Jong: *The Kingdom of The Netherlands in the Second World War*, H.M. Stationery Office, The Hague, 1969 and following years, especially vol. II.
15. *Id.* vol. I.
16. NRC-Handelsblad of 9 December 1975.
17. Dr. W. Drees sr, Prime Minister in a number of governments after 1945, in a broadcast on Dutch television on 8 December 1975.
18. Duynstee, o.c.
19. Kay Liat Oen: "Radical Tendencies among South Moluccans"; doctoral thesis for the Municipal University of Amsterdam.
20. NRC-Handelsblad of 9 December 1975.
21. A. C. W. van der Vet: *Tour of the Kingdom in Disruption*, Nijgh and Van Ditmar, The Hague, 1975.
22. D. G. A. Findlay: *Trio and Wayana Indians in Surinam*, De West, Paramaribo, 1974.
23. Van der Vet: o.c.
24. Dr. F. W. Essed: *A People on the Way to Independence*, Paramaribo, 1973.
25. Prof. Dr. G. J. Krijer: *Surinam, a Neo-colony within the Kingdom*, Boom, Meppel, 1973.
26. S. W. Wolf: Surinam, *Yesterday, Today, To-morrow*, Pressag, The Hague, 1975.
27. *Algemeen Dagblad*, 29 November 1975.
28. H. van Emmerik-Levelt and A. W. M. Teulings: "Foreign workers in the Press," in: *Foreign guestworkers in The Netherlands*, Spruyt, Van Mantgem and De Does, Leiden, 1967.
29. Prof. Dr. R. Wentholt: Social backgrounds and factors, in id.
30. Statistical Memorandum 1975, Central Statistical Bureau, The Hague, 1975.
31. A. J. van der Staay: "Foreign workers and welfare in The Netherlands," in: *Allochtonen in Nederland*, C.R.M., The Hague, 1973.
32. B. Roolvink: Foreign guestworkers, Parliamentary papers, session 1969–1970, no. 10.504, I, II and III, 14 January 1970; H.M. Stationery Office, The Hague.
33. M. van Overeem and A. C. W. van der Vet: "Foreign guestworkers in The Netherlands," *Stichting Maatschappij en Onderneming*, The Hague, 1972.
34. Chorus, o.c.

# The Violation of Human Rights in India

## THE INTERNATIONAL LEAGUE FOR THE RIGHTS OF MAN

The International League for Human Rights, founded in 1942, is an independent, international non-governmental organization affiliated to the United Nations in the human rights field. It works to advance the political, civil, economic, social and cultural rights enumerated in the Universal Declaration of Human Rights and other human rights instruments adopted by the United Nations.

# The Violation of Human Rights in India

## THE INTERNATIONAL LEAGUE FOR THE RIGHTS OF MAN

THE INTERNATIONAL LEAGUE FOR THE RIGHTS OF MAN
777 United Nations Plaza, Suite 6F
New York, N.Y. 10017
Tel. (212)972-9554
Cable Rightsman, N.Y.

May 31, 1976

His Excellency Kurt Waldheim
Secretary-General
United Nations
New York, New York

Your Excellency:

It is with deep regret that the International League for Human Rights must submit a communication to the UN evidencing a consistent pattern of gross violations of human rights and fundamental freedoms engaged in during the last year by the Government of India. Ironically, the conduct of which we complain, directly in contravention of the United Nations Charter, the Universal Declaration of Human Rights, the International Covenant on Civil and Political Rights, and other human rights instruments is being perpetrated by a Government forged of the high and humanistic ideals of Gandhi and Nehru, two of this century's greatest champions of human liberty. So, it is with particular sadness that we transmit this communication to Your Excellency.

The object of our communication is to seek implementation of the principles of the United Nations Charter, Universal Declaration of Human Rights and other applicable human rights instruments for the one sixth of humanity ruled by the Government of India. Accordingly, we respectfully request that this communication be brought before the Working Group of the twenty-ninth session of the Sub-Commission on Prevention of Discrimination and Protection of Minorities. In our view the consistent pattern of gross violations of human rights and fundamental freedoms by the Government of India revealed in this communication and its annexes warrants a United Nations investigation or study in accordance with ECOSOC Resolutions 728F and 1503.

## Introduction

On June 26, 1975, the Government of India on the recommendation of Prime Minister Indira Gandhi issued an Emergency Proclamation which sounded the beginning of the decline of human rights and fundamental freedoms in India. This Proclamation was swiftly followed by anti-libertarian legislation and executive action. The Government argues that its actions were necessitated by a "deep and widespread conspiracy" among Mrs. Gandhi's political opponents and by a need to achieve greater economic progress. We believe that such justifications are legally and morally inadequate to exempt the Government of India from harsh approbation by the conscience of mankind for systematically trampling on the freedom and dignity of tens of thousands of its citizens.

We are convinced that the actions of the Indian Government are incompatible with Article 30 of the Universal Declaration of Human Rights which prohibits the use of any of its provisions, including that which allows the limitation of rights and freedoms under certain circumstances, to "engage in any activity or to perform any act aimed at the destruction of any of the rights and freedoms set forth herein." We believe that the governmental policies and actions described in this communication have this aim and certainly this effect.

The Indian Government's policies and actions are inconsistent with international standards of human rights as enunciated in numerous expressions of international consensus, including the Declaration on the Protection of All Persons from Torture and other Cruel, Inhuman or Degrading Treatment or Punishment, the Standard Minimum Rules for the Treatment of Prisoners, the Commission on Human Rights' Draft Principles on Arbitrary Arrest and Detention, and the International Covenant on Civil and Political Rights, which was unanimously adopted by the General Assembly in 1966 and is now in force having received the required number of ratifications from states in every region of the world.

This fundamental human rights instrument prohibits in Article 4 derogation from obligations except in case of public emergency "which threatens the life of the nation" – and even in such case, only "to the extent strictly required by the exigencies of the situation." Moreover, the measures taken must "not [be] inconsistent with their other obligations under international law ...," and in particular, must not derogate from the Covenant's prohibitions against torture or cruel, inhuman or degrading treatment or punishment (Art. 7), punishment under retroactive criminal laws (Art. 15), and the right to freedom of thought and conscience (Art. 18).

We submit that the Government of India, in proclaiming a national emergency and justifying on that basis the suspension of fundamental freedoms guaranteed in the Covenant, has violated the letter and spirit of Article 4. We cannot accept, on the basis of the information available, that the alleged public emergency, on the basis of which it has imposed measures suspending the freedoms of its people, "threatens the life of the nation." The measures they have taken far exceed in our view, "the extent strictly required by the exigencies of the situation." Nor, according to available information, has the Government of India refrained from violating the Covenant's prohibitions against torture or cruel, inhuman or degrading treatment or punishment, punishing persons under retroactive criminal laws, and respecting the right to freedom of thought and conscience.

In this communication, we shall set forth principles of the Universal Declaration of Human Rights and describe the last year's legislative and executive action of the Government of India which violates these principles. Exhibits are appended consisting of first hand and secondary documentation of the consistent pattern of gross violations which necessitate this communication.

## I. Abrogation of the Right to Life, Liberty, Security of Person and Due Process of Law

*Universal Declaration of Human Rights*

*Article 3.* Everyone has the right to life, liberty and security of person.

*Article 8.* Everyone has the right to an effective remedy by the competent national tribunals for acts violating the fundamental rights granted him by the constitution or by law.

*Article 9.* No one shall be subjected to arbitrary arrest, detention or exile.

*Article 10.* Everyone is entitled in full equality to a fair and public hearing by an independent and impartial tribunal, in the determination of his rights and obligations and of any criminal charge against him.

Since the Emergency Proclamation of June 26, 1975, the regime, under the Government of India Act, and under the Maintenance of Internal Security Act, adopted in 1971 and thereafter strengthened by several amendments ("MISA"), the Government has essentially arrested anyone it has wanted to arrest and has held such persons for as long as it has wished without charges and without the benefit of the ancient writ of habeas corpus which it summarily suspended for all MISA detainees.

The Government's intention to remove judicial obstacles to the course of action indicated by the Emergency Proclamation was revealed by sweeping arrests of political opponents beginning with the Proclamation and continuing to date. It was also revealed by the Presidential order of June 27, 1975, which suspended the rights to petition the courts to enforce fundamental rights under Indian Constitution Articles 14 (equality before the law), 21 (protection against arrest without being informed of the grounds therefore) and 22 (duty to produce arrestee before a magistrate within 24 hours). Two days later, on June 29, 1975, the Government adopted its First Amendment to MISA. That Amendment, made retroactive to June 26th, deprived persons arrested under MISA of the right to be told the grounds for their detention. On July 15, 1975, the Government adopted a Second Amendment to MISA which provided that no MISA detainee had any right to personal liberty by virtue of natural law or common law.

Threatened with the possibility of judicial action to challenge the need for such draconian measures, the Government on August 1, 1975, caused Parliament to approve of an Amendment – the 38th – to the Constitution of India. The Amendment deprived the courts of jurisdiction to review any claim that the emergency powers had been misused.

The effect of the Presidential order of June 27, 1975, and of the 38th Amendment is to deprive citizens of recourse to the courts as to MISA matters. Not only is the writ of habeas corpus unavailable, but as a result of the Fourth MISA amendment, adopted on October 17, 1975, the judiciary is not entitled to disclosure of the grounds of detention and therefore cannot review whether MISA has been properly invoked.

To close the circle and immunize the executive lawlessness from judicial scrutiny, the Government, by Constitutional Amendments 36 and 40 sought to deprive the courts of the power to rule upon disputed elections of persons holding high office and extended to the Prime Minister absolute immunity from criminal or civil process for acts or omissions occurring prior to and during tenure of office.[1]

The targets of these repressive acts have been principally opponents of the Government, ranging in political persuasion from the left to the right. It is reliably reported that among those arrested and detained have been at least three former cabinet ministers, 11 members of the upper house of Parliament, about 20 members of the lower house, the most prominent leaders of almost every opposition party and some dissenters within Mrs. Gandhi's own Congress Party. Reliable estimates of the number of political prisoners now in jail in India range between 30,000 and 75,000.

Through the guise of enacting emergency laws authorizing arbitrary action against and treatment of any person, the Government of India has in one short year created the following conditions in India:

Persons arrested need not be advised of the reasons for their arrest.

Persons detained are not brought before a magistrate promptly, the requirement of arraignment within 24 hours having been repealed.

Detainees are not brought to trial within a reasonable time. Under MISA they can be held for up to one year without bail, without notification of charges, without arraignment or trial.

Since January, 1976, persons released can be re-arrested and detained under the same circumstances.

Many prisoners are deprived of visitors and some are held in solitary confinement and not permitted counsel.

The right of *Habeas Corpus* has been suspended.

The pervasive policy of arresting those who speak or act against the Government continues to dominate the political situation in India. Earlier this year, hundreds of supporters of the state governments of Tamil Nadu and Gujurat were arrested when the Administrations of those states were terminated by Presidential decree.

These facts recited in this portion of our communication are documented in the annexed exhibits. Annexed hereto as Exhibit A is a report by Dr. Homer A. Jack carefully prepared for the *World Conference on Religion and Peace* after an investigation in India. Annexed hereto as Exhibit B is Amnesty International's list of 78 persons who were arrested and are being detained because of their political views.

## II. Torture and Mistreatment of Prisoners

*Universal Declaration of Human Rights*

*Article 5.* No one shall be subjected to torture or to cruel, inhuman or degrading treatment or punishment.

There are many reliable reports that the Government of India has resorted to torture, brutality, starvation, and other mistreatment of prisoners arrested during the last year. Not only is this a clear violation of Article 5 of the Declaration of Human Rights but it is also a human rights violation which is so egregious that the International Covenant on Civil and Political Rights prohibit any infringement of the right even in a time of public emergency.

A case of India's mistreating prisoners was recently reliably reported by Anthony Lukas in the New York Times Magazine of April 4, 1976.

One area scheduled for demolition [by the Government] last fall was a warren of tiny stalls near the Jama Masjid, Delhi's biggest Mosque.

A social worker who had long laboured in the district got wind of the demolition plan and protested to Sanjay about the Government's lack of concern for relocating merchants. Two nights later, there was a knock on the social worker's door at midnight. Eight policemen burst in, arrested him and carted him off to jail, where he spent nine days. He was later released – but only after he had been paraded through the Jama Masjid area in chains, with the police reviling him. So far as I could determine, his only crime had been to dare to differ with the Prime Minister's son.

There is strong evidence that the Government of India has in the last year adopted as official policy more extreme forms of mistreatment and torture as well. In a recent argument before the Bombay High Court, a Government attorney is reported to have contended that the Government could starve prisoners or even shoot them without legal challenge.

Annexed hereto as Exhibit C is a 14 page report supplied by Indians for Democracy, an organization of Indians residing in the U.S.A., who report having received it directly from the Lok Sangharsh Samiti[2] (People's Struggle Committee) in India. This document describes instances of brutal torture of prisoners named therein. Exhibit D, an article by an Indian national and law professor Ved P. Nanda based on a recent visit to India also corroborates the Government of India's inhuman treatment of prisoners. Additional reports of torture are set forth in Dr. Homer A. Jack's report (Exhibit A):

Torture has been reported in the Tihar jail in Delhi and also in Bihar, West Bengal, Uttar Pradesh, and Haryana. Dr. Subramanian Swamy, a member of the Rajya Sabha, claimed in January that 8,000 prisoners had been tortured since the state of Emergency was declared.[3]

Prof. Ved P. Nanda also writes about eyewitness accounts of torture: "The police applied crude means either to extract a confession to a non-existent plot against Indira Gandhi or to seek information concerning the whereabouts and next moves of the organizers of the underground movement. The devices for torture which are being used in police stations and jails in India are as varied as they are inhumane and revolting. The victims who talked with me related incidents where they or other political prisoners were hung upside down; were stripped naked and severely beaten with shoes, steel rods, and gun butts; had burning candles applied to their bare soles, which were then punctured with nails; had chili powder smeared into their noses and other parts of their bodies; were kept awake while icy water was thrown on them on cold winter nights; were starved and even denied water; had rods tied to their necks, creating an intolerable strain on the spinal cord. The doctor I met was not personally tortured. However, while he was in jail as a political prisoner, illegally detained on trumped-up charges, he had treated more than 20 prisoners who, he said, must have been 'mercilessly beaten ...' A member of the Indian Supreme Court Bar Association showed me a resolution adopted by that organization which condemned police atrocities and harassment of attorneys defending Opposition members."[4] These and other instances of torture are being investigated by international human rights organizations.

Article 5 of the Universal Declaration of Human Rights is unequivocal. Nothing in the Universal Declaration permits the use of torture under any circumstances. The International Covenant on Civil and Political Rights explicitly so provides. Accordingly, the barbarous practice of torture by the Government of India, by itself, is ample justification for this communication. The Declaration on the Protection of All Persons From Torture and Other Cruel, Inhuman or Degrading Treatment or Punishment confirms the continuing validity of this principle.

## III. Suppression of Free Expression, Press, Assembly and the Right of Self-Government

*Article 19.* Everyone has the right to freedom of opinion and expression; this right includes freedom to hold opinions without interference and to seek, receive and impart information and ideas through any media and regardless of frontiers.

*Article 20.* (1) Everyone has the right to freedom of peaceful assembly and association.

*Article 21.* (1) Everyone has the right to take part in the government of his country, directly or through freely chosen representatives.
(2) Everyone has the right of equal access to public service in his country.
(3) The will of the people shall be the basis of the authority of government; this will shall be expressed in periodic and genuine elections which shall be by universal and equal suffrage and shall be held by secret vote or by equivalent free voting procedures.

*Article 28.* Everyone is entitled to a social and international order in which the rights and freedoms set forth in this Declaration can be fully realized.

The exercise of the freedoms of expression, press and assembly have been effectively disallowed by the Government of India. Although Article 19 of the Constitution of India grants the right of freedom of speech and expression (among other rights) they have been suspended. Not only have persons been arrested and detained as described above for voicing opposition to Government programmes but strict censorship has been imposed on the Indian press.

In July, 1975, the Government promulgated Censorship Guidelines. These are annexed hereto as Exhibit E. In substance, these Guidelines prohibit the publication, without prior censorship, of opposition speeches in Parliament, reports of details of court matters, names of detainees and their places of detention, demonstrations against the government and matter which may bring the government into hatred or contempt. The Guidelines even are construed as prohibiting quotations from Gandhi, Nehru and Tagore. The censors bar the publication of anything the Government finds objectionable or embarrassing.

In December, 1975, three executive ordinances were promulgated to strengthen the Government's control of expression. The first prohibits publication of matter which would "excite disaffection against the constitutionally established government." The second ordinance repealed the immunity of the press in reporting parliamentary proceedings. The third dissolved the Press Council of India, which had been an independent agency created to preserve journalistic standards and to protect freedom of the press.

In January, 1976, Parliament approved a bill known as The Prevention of Publication of Objectionable Matter Ordinance. This bill provides that the new system of strict censorship will survive the end of the Emergency. Objectionable matter is defined as that which is "likely to bring into hatred or contempt or excite disaffection toward the Government, and thereby cause or tend to cause public disorder . . ." Prohibited also is matter "defamatory to the President of India, the Vice President, the Prime Minister, the Speaker of the House or the Governor of a State." Any violation of the censorship laws is a criminal offence. Journalists have been fined for printing prohibited material and the Government has demanded a deposit of 1,000 rupees as security against the publication of proscribed material.

Members of Parliament are reported intimidated by fear of arrest, thus dampening parliamentary debate. Opposition members have often absented themselves during debates, thus facilitating the passage of repressive legislation proposed by the Government.

Fear of arrest has also curtailed both public debate and private political discussion among students, intellectuals and others traditionally interested in political and social matters.

Pursuant to the Emergency Decree and the suspension of Article 19 of the Constitution, freedom of assembly is also severely curtailed. No more than five persons are permitted to assemble, which means that protest marches, demonstrations and rallies are illegal. This is yet another means of stifling the rights of citizens who differ with the Government. Moreover, whatever illegal demonstrations may occur from time to time cannot be reported in the press under the censorship laws, so that an appeal to conscience in the tradition of Gandhi is rendered impossible.

## Conclusion

It is our view, based on careful study of the evidence that a United Nations investigation is warranted. It is evident that the people of India have no recourse but to appeal to the conscience of the world; all domestic remedies have been effectively severed by Parliamentary or court action. We therefore respectfully request, Your Excellency, that the United Nations undertake an investigation or study of the facts in accordance with ECOSOC Resolutions 728F and 1503. We believe that such an investigation or study will be an important step toward assuring observance of the UN Charter and the fundamental rights and freedoms of the people of India.

With the assurance of our highest respect.

Yours sincerely,

| | | |
|---|---|---|
| Roger N. Baldwin | Jerome J. Shestack | Jack David |
| Honorary President | Chairman | Officer and Director |
| (*signed*) | (*signed*) | (*signed*) |

## IV. Exhibit A: The Erosion of Fundamental Rights in India Today[5]

*by* Dr. Homer A. Jack

### *Introduction*

India is slipping behind what can be called the Khadi(homespun) Curtain. The totalitarianism of India's Emergency is, so far, homespun, full of holes, and not yet of bamboo or iron. Between the strands there is still some freedom, just as between the lines of the censored press there is still some meaning.

India is such a vast country – a subcontinent – and the Emergency has fractured certain communications in India so badly that very few persons outside the central government can perceive the total parameters of the situation there today. Yet this very complexity and inadequacy should surely not serve to inhibit efforts to find out and understand what is happening in this huge slice of the world's population. Indeed, the full implications of what the Emergency has brought and wrought may perhaps begin to be perceived in some respects better by those on the outside. In any case, this Memorandum makes no pretence of being exhaustive; on the other hand, it may contribute to a view of the greater whole.

Despite the Emergency and its continuing aftermath, should India be given the benefit of the doubt? Does India deserve that the observer suspend judgment on the present Emergency in view of her admittedly huge problems? India does merit sympathetic understanding from the world community, but it also merits honest appraisal like any other State. This Memorandum attempts to reflect both sympathy and honesty.

This Memorandum is dedicated to Jayaprakash Narayan (J.P.), whom I have had the honour to know, and with whom I have had the opportunity to work, for a dozen years. To me the enormity, and sadness, of the tragedy of India today is symbolized by the treatment of this single individual. Since the death of Mohandas Gandhi and Jawaharlal Nehru, J.P. has undeniably been one of the greatest persons to walk the Asian stage. May he yet summon the strength to lead his people from bondage.

H.A.J.
*New York*
*March 18, 1976*

### *1. The Years 1975 and 1976*

> June 26, 1975, would join three other dates as landmarks in the nation's search for the good life for all her people.

So stated a large brochure published late in 1975 by the Embassy of India in Washington presumably for the American people.[6] The first date, however, of the history of independent India was 15 August 1947 when India took her freedom, after a long struggle, from the British. Mohandas Gandhi, the "father" of India, was stunned to witness the subcontinent partitioned and engaged in huge communal or religious massacres. He urged the Indian National Congress, founded in 1885 and the principal institutional architect of independence, not to assume political power. However, by then decisions in India were largely in other hands, chiefly those of Jawaharlal Nehru who became the first Prime Minister. At independence, Gandhi continued to attempt to lessen communal violence and himself was assassinated on 30 January 1948.

For more than 15 years Nehru presided over India, which adopted its Constitution on 26 November 1949. Upon Nehru's death in 1964, Lal Bahadur Shastri became Prime Minister, but his tenure was cut short by his unexpected death in 1966. Then Mrs. Indira Gandhi, Nehru's daughter, became Prime Minister. Her Congress Party won a national election in 1967 and soon she presided over the split of the Congress into Congress (R) – for the ruling party – and Congress (O) – for "organization." The later contained many of the defeated ex-leaders. The Congress (R) swept the "mid-term" polls in 1971 yet Mrs. Gandhi almost immediately faced a difficult period in the history of the subcontinent, with massacres in East Pakistan, a wave of a million refugees coming to India, and then the Indo-Pakistan War resulting in the creation of Bangladesh.

While the year 1972 found India depleted by the war, optimism ran high and Mrs. Gandhi had an enviable opportunity to pilot India to new heights of economic and social progress. Instead, stagnation and corruption set in on almost every level. The year 1975 was a crucial one for India and Mrs. Gandhi. A few key events were as follows:

*January 3* – Railway Minister L. N. Mishra died after a bomb explosion.

*March 2* – Minister of State for Housing Mohan Dharia dropped from cabinet, partly for urging dialogue with J. P. (Narayan).

*March 6* – J.P. led a march of 400,000 persons to Parliament in New Delhi demanding the eradication of corruption.

*June 12* – The High Court of Allahabad set aside the 1971 election of Mrs. Gandhi on a petition filed by her opponent, Raj Narain.

*June 26* – A state of Emergency proclaimed by President Fakhruddin Ali Ahmad (on recommendation of Mrs. Gandhi), with the immediate arrest of many opposition leaders and press censorship imposed.

*July 1* – Mrs. Gandhi announced a 20-Point Economic Programme.

*July 4* – The Government banned 26 extremist groups.

*July 23* – The Lok Sabha (lower house of Parliament) approved the proclamation of the Emergency.

*Nov. 7* – The Supreme Court unanimously upheld Mrs. Gandhi's election to the Lok Sabha.

*Nov. 12* – J.P. released from detention – on parole initially – after evidence became available that he was on the verge of death.

*Dec. 28* – Seventy-fifth plenary of Indian National Congress adopted a resolution urging that the national elections (due no later than March 1976) for the Lok Sabha be postponed one year.

The year of 1976 thus began with strong pressures within the Government to continue the Emergency and postpone the national elections. Some of the key events early in 1976 were as follows:

*Jan. 31* – Presidential Rule proclaimed in Tamil Nadu (Madras State), dismissing the legally-constituted state government, which had opposed Mrs. Gandhi.

*Feb. 4* – The Lok Sabha voted to postpone for one year the national elections scheduled for March.

*March 12* – Presidential Rule proclaimed in Gujarat, after the state government fell on a confidence vote, the last State in effect opposed to Mrs. Gandhi.

## 2. *The Emergency Decree*

I trust it will be possible to lift the Emergency soon.

Mrs. Gandhi broadcast these words to the Indian people on 27 June 1975. Two days earlier President Ahmed had proclaimed the Emergency as follows: "In exercise of the powers conferred by clause (1) of Article 352 of the Constitution, I, Fakhruddin Ali Ahmed, President of India, by this proclamation declare that a grave emergency exists whereby the security of India is threatened by internal disturbance."

Article 352 of the Indian Constitution provides for an Emergency as follows: "If the President is satisfied that a grave Emergency exists whereby the security of India or of any part of the territory thereof is threatened, whether by war or external aggression or internal disturbance, he may, by proclamation, make a declaration to that effect." Such an Emergency would cease to be in operation at the expiration of two months unless approved by both houses of Parliament. An Emergency can be continued for six months at a time, but no more than for a total of three years.

Under the Indian form of government, the action of the President was taken on the recommendation of the Prime Minister. It is said that Mrs. Gandhi did not consult with most members of her Cabinet beforehand about declaring an Emergency, but only summoned them at 6:30 a.m., hours after it had been promulgated. In a broadcast on 26 June, Mrs. Gandhi explained the situation. "The President has proclaimed Emergency. This is nothing to panic about. I am sure you are all conscious of the deep and widespread conspiracy which has been brewing ever since I began to introduce certain progressive measures of benefit to the common men and women of India. In the name of democracy it has been sought to negate the very functioning of democracy. Duly elected governments have not been allowed to function and in some cases force has been used to compel members to resign in order to dissolve lawfully elected Assemblies. Agitations have surcharged the atmosphere, leading to violent incidents. The whole country was shocked at the brutal murder of my Cabinet colleague, Shri L. N. Mishra. We also deeply deplore the bastardly attack on the Chief Justice of India."

Concluding the broadcast, Mrs. Gandhi said: "All manner of false allegations have been hurled at us. The Indian people have known me since my childhood. All my life has been in the service of our people. This is not a personal matter. It is not important whether I remain Prime Minister or not. However, the institution of the Prime Minister is important and the deliberate political attempts to denigrate it is not in the interest of democracy or the nation ... I should like to assure you that the new Emergency proclamation will in no way affect the rights of law-abiding citizens ..."

Both houses of Parliament met from 22 July to 7 August 1975 to consider and validate the Emergency. (While the Congress (R) party had a healthy majority, an estimated 30 Members of Parliament were in prison and could not attend.)

Speculation soon arose on how long the Emergency would last. In August, Mrs. Gandhi told *The Saturday Review* that she did not expect "that the present Emergency situation will be unduly prolonged." She scoffed at those who "are saying that the measures we have been taking will never be revoked and that India can look forward to a totalitarian future."[7] However, at the annual meeting of the Indian National Congress in the closing days of 1975, a resolution was adopted urging that the Government continue the Emergency (and also postpone elections for the Lok Sabha). The excuse given was that the Emergency should be continued until "there is the fullest assurance" that the dangers from the forces of destabilization, which led to its proclamation, "have been effectively contained."

The Lok Sabha on 4 February 1976 after a tumultous three-hour debate voted to postpone for one year elections scheduled for no later than 18 March (when its five-year mandate expired). In a sense, this vote made the continuation of the Emergency inevitable, since one reason for not holding the elections was that any campaign would presumably require the release of detained Opposition politicians, including some Members of Parliament.

### *3. Mrs. Gandhi at Court*

Indira is India and India is Indira.

At the 1971 elections for the lower house of Parliament, the Lok Sabha, Mrs. Gandhi was re-elected from the Rai Bareilly constituency in Uttar Pradesh. She beat socialist Raj Narain by 183,309 votes to 71,499. However, Mr. Narain challenged her election in the Allahabad High Court. Several charges of corrupt election practices (under the 1951 Representation of the People Act) were brought against her. There were extensive, prolonged hearings, involving personal testimony by Mrs. Gandhi.

Justice J. L. Sinha ruled on 12 June 1975 that Mrs. Gandhi was guilty, under Section 123 (7), on two charges: 1) she used the services in the election campaign of Yashpal Kapoor, a government civil servant, while he was still in government service, and 2) she obtained the services of officers of the State Government for the construction of the rostrum and loud speakers on several occasions during her election campaign. Justice Sinha further prescribed penalties in the Act and ruled that Mrs. Gandhi should be barred from public office for six years. However, he ordered a stay of 20 days for the implementation of his decision, pending her appeal to the Supreme

Court of India. The Justice also observed that she was an unreliable witness, having made contradictory oral statements to the Court.

The Opposition parties immediately demanded that Mrs. Gandhi resign. Groups outside her residence, on the other hand, chanted, "Indira is India and India is Indira." After several days, Mrs. Gandhi announced that she would remain in office while the conviction was being appealed. (She had earlier advised Party colleagues to quit their positions when similar corrupt practice verdicts were made against them.) On 24 June. Justice V. P. Krishna Iyer – "vacation judge" of the Supreme Court – granted her a conditional stay of the order of the Allahabad Court instead of an absolute one, pending a decision of the full Court. In his judgment, Judge Iyer ruled that Mrs. Gandhi could not vote in the Lok Sabha or draw salary as a member.

Given this Court ruling, the Opposition increased its demands that she resign. This was climaxed by a huge rally in Delhi on 25 June, led by J.P. Also there were Opposition strategy sessions to plan to bring her government down by a wide range of actions. Then on 26 June the Emergency was declared.

The subsequent Parliamentary and judicial action affecting her case can be summarized as follows:

1. The Parliament amended the Election Laws Act of 1951, to take effect retroactively. This changed the election laws so that Mrs. Gandhi could not be guilty for what she did in 1971. This had the effect of preventing the Supreme Court from confirming the verdict of the Allahabad Court.

2. The Parliament adopted the 39th amendment to the Constitution. This did at least three things: (*a*) placed disputes over the election of the President, the Vice-President, the Prime Minister, and the Speaker of the Lok Sabha beyond the purview of the courts; (*b*) rendered invalid all existing laws and court verdicts about the election of the Prime Minister or Speaker of the Lok Sabha, conferred absolute validity on such election, and directed the Supreme Court to dispose of current appeals and cross appeals with regard to such election in the light of the above; and (*c*) banned judicial scrutiny of the election laws and the Maintenance of Internal Security Act (MISA).

3. The Parliament adopted the 40th amendment to the Constitution. This gave the President, Prime Minister, and State Governors immunity from criminal proceedings even after they laid down office and from civil proceedings during their term of office, in respect of acts done by them before and during their term of office. (The Supreme Court nullified the amendment in November.)

4. On 7 November the Supreme Court unanimously upheld Mrs. Gandhi's election and set aside the judgment of the Allahabad High Court. This action was ambiguously reported in the press to make it appear that the Court had overturned Mrs. Gandhi's conviction. The Supreme Court was asked to decide three issues: a) the validity of the amendments to the Constitution which sought to exclude the election of the Prime Minister from the jurisdiction of the courts; b) the validity of the amendments to the People's Representation Act, which made all the corrupt practices for which Mrs. Gandhi was accused retroactively innocent and demanding no penal-

ties; and c) the judgment of the Allahabad High Court. By a unanimous judgment, the Supreme Court upheld the first two issues and, under the circumstances, did not go into the merits of the third – the judgment of the Allahabad High Court.

### *4. The 20-Point Programme*

We are striving to take a country of 600 million people from one age to another not only to provide better physical and material life for them but also to insure full development of their personalities. This cannot happen without some curbs.

Mrs. Gandhi to Parliament, 8 Jan. 1976

A substantial part of the Emergency, but not technically connected with it, is the 20-Point New Programme for Economic Progress. (This was originally a 21-Point Programme, but "strict economy in Government expenditure" found in early versions was later dropped.) This Programme was first enunciated by Mrs. Gandhi in a radio broadcast on 1 July 1975 – less than one week after the proclamation of the Emergency.

Following are brief excerpts from this broadcast:

I am going to speak to you today about some economic programmes which the Government proposes to follow. Some of them are new. Others were set forth earlier but require to be pursued with greater vigour and determination. Please do not expect magic remedies and dramatic results. There is only one magic which can remove poverty, and that is hard work sustained by clear vision, iron will, and the strictest discipline ...

The first and foremost challenge is on the price front. In the last five days, the prices of many articles have shown a downward trend. This trend will have to be maintained. To this end, Government will take a series of steps to stimulate production, speed up procurement and streamline the distribution of essential commodities ...

Our outlook in regard to Foreign Exchange resources is reasonably satisfactory ... State Governments have already been asked to advise dealers to display lists of prices and statements of stocks. Hoarders and those who violate the rules will be severely punished.

This anti-inflation strategy has to be continued ... Government departments and public enterprises have new orders to cut out inessential expenditure.

The vast majority of our people live in the rural areas. We must implement ceiling laws and distribute surplus land among the landless with redoubled zeal ...

The programme of providing housing sites in rural areas will be vastly expanded. Laws will be introduced to confer ownership rights on landless labourers who have been in occupation of house sites of their landlords over a certain period ...

The practice of bonded labour is barbarous and will be abolished ...

We propose to take action by stages to liquidate rural indebtedness ...

Agricultural labour is among the worst exploited sections of our society. A review of the existing legislation on minimum wages for agricultural labour will be undertaken and action will be initiated for suitable enhancement of minimum wages, wherever necessary.

We must go all out to increase production. Water and power hold the key to higher agricultural output ...

The handloom industry is next only to agriculture in the number of people employed ... In the mill sector, the controlled cloth scheme is being improved ...

Fortunes have been made out of urban land at the nation's expense ... Legislation is being initiated to impose ceilings on the ownership and possession of vacant land, to acquire excess land, to restrict the plinth area of new dwelling units and to socialize urban and urbanized land.

Tax evasion is a crime. A great deal of black money so evaded goes into luxury housing ... We are thinking of summary trials.

Our campaign against smugglers will be intensified ...

Licensing procedures have come in the way of new investment, causing delay. These will be simplified ... Licences are being misused ... Penalties for breaking rules will include the confiscation of goods.

Schemes for workers' participation in industries particularly at the shop floor level and production programmes will be introduced.

The movement of food grains, coal, steel, and cement by railways has improved in the last few months. Constraints on the movement of foods by trucks will also be removed ...

People with fixed incomes have suffered severe hardships in the last few years. They need immediate relief. The minimum exemption limit for income tax will be raised from 6,000 rupees to 8,000 rupees.

Students from poor families face special difficulties if they pursue higher studies away from their homes. To help them, essential commodities will be supplied at controlled prices to all hostels and approved lodging houses ... As one of the measures to increase employment opportunities for educated young people, the Apprenticeship Act will be suitably amended.

... What is most urgent is that collectively we should shake off any sense of helplessness. The worst feature of the crisis which was building over the last few months was that it spread cynicism and sapped national self-confidence. There is a chance now to regain the nation's spirit of adventure. Let us get on with the job.

## 5. *The Positive Effects*

The Emergency, and its aftermath, is a complex political phenomena for India and it cannot be regarded in simplistic terms. Some of the effects of the Emergency and the related 20-Point Programme were initially positive. While a comprehensive consideration of the effects of the Programme cannot be made here, some positive results cannot and should not be ignored. Whether these results are worth the price is another question.

### A. Discipline

Punctuality only for railroads?

So asked a bitter critic of the Emergency and one of its chief by-products, discipline. In recent years "indiscipline" in India has been notorious. The Emergency created, overnight, the fear that those who continued along the undisciplined path would be penalized. The supreme penalty in an India of chronic unemployment is, of course, the loss of a job. Thus civil servants of all kinds suddenly came to work on time and appeared to do an honest day's work. Students on all levels came to school with perhaps a new sense of dedication. A new atmosphere of discipline undeniably descended upon India – even at least for awhile in the queues for buses.

This phenomenon was not the result of a national consensus and was not the result of a people determined to change its ways because of inspiration from its leaders. It is not discipline coming from within. The discipline arose largely from fear, supported by an urban public relations campaign. Buses and signboards carry slogans about discipline, from the ubiquitous "davp" – the Directorate of Advertising and Visual Publicity. They remind millions of urban Indians daily that "Discipline Makes a Nation Great," "The Need of the Hour is Discipline," and "Work More, Talk Less."

Some Indians believe that there has been a striking change for the better since the Emergency began in the heightening of the discipline of their fellow Indians. Others suggest that it is fear and not discipline which motivates new work modes. Most expect that the people will soon slip back into their old ways.

## B. Corruption

Now corruption is more expensive.

Corruption most often involves citizens, including businesses, paying for favours or services to individuals on various levels of government or a ruling party. Corruption is not limited to any one country, social system, or period in world history. Yet one wonders if today there may be more temptations for widespread corruption in poorer societies. This may be because there is in such countries a relatively unlimited demand for goods or jobs, but a relatively limited supply. Thus those who want to receive the limited goods or jobs try to ensure success through bribery. Also the lack of social security in many developing countries may explain not only bribery but also the dowery system.

There have been widespread evidences of corruption in independent India. It is a way of life, a custom. It is practiced at all levels. J.P. several years ago asserted: "The galloping political corruption is affecting and degrading, because of the predominant position politics occupies in an undeveloped society, the entire gamut of national life: business, whether it is private or public; administration; the professions; education; even customs, manners, and personal relations."[8]

Attempts to lessen corruption have seldom succeeded. What results have the Emergency so far produced? It is too early to make any overall judgment or conclusion. More persons have been arrested for many kinds of corruption. Many people – both on the giving and receiving ends – are undeniably more wary. As one observer asserted, "Now corruption is more expensive." An outside observer can attest that some of the leaders of the ruling Congress Party, including some of the top officials of the government, do not have a reputation of incorruptibility.

### C. Economic Offences

The modern God of India is corruption and the people must try to recognize it in whatever avatar it manifests itself.

So said J.P.[9] The so-called economic offences: smuggling, foreign exchange violations, and tax evasion make up one such avatar. The Emergency provided a climate, together with existing and new laws, to curb these kinds of corruption.

Through the enforcement of anti-smuggling laws, and the enactment of new ones, there, is a feeling that the bringing of goods into or out of India without duty or authorization has been reduced since the Emergency was declared. The dimensions of these reductions are hard to measure. Yet within six months, 1,700 smugglers were detained and more valuable goods confiscated by the Government than normally.

Immediately after the Emergency began, there were tax raids in various parts of India. The Government introduced the Voluntary Disclosure Scheme (VDS) which offered an opportunity to tax evaders to declare their hidden wealth and bring it into the mainstream of economic activity. They were given the deadline of 31 December 1975 and promised no penalties, including no imprisonment. By the deadline over 13.13 billion of rupees of black money had been declared, which provided 2.5 billion in taxes, with 400 million going to investment in Government securities. Upon the Taxation Law Amendment Act entering into force, the Courts have the discretion of awarding monetary punishment as an alternative to imprisonment.

### D. Inflation and Prices

The socio-economic reality in the village, on close examination, is ugly and distressing in the extreme ... How remote and unreal (are) the brave pronouncements of Delhi or Patna from the actuality at the ground level! High sounding words, grandiose plans, reforms galore. But somehow they all, or most of them, manage to remain suspended somewhere up in mid-air ... What meets the eye is utter poverty, misery, inequality, exploitation, backwardness, stagnation, frustration, and loss of hope.

J. P. Narayan[10]

Have the Emergency and the 20-Point Programme put some of the needed reforms on solid ground? This is not the place to make an evaluation of the economic situation in India today. Inflation had peaked before the Emergency began and certainly the Emergency helped continue this welcome downward trend. However, the Indian economy was also slowing down before 26 June 1975 and this may be continuing. For a number of reasons, including the weather but also factors preceding the Emergency, the 1975 grain crop was a bumper one and this had positive economic effects. It is really too early to make responsible economic conclusions about the Emergency and the 20-Point Programme.

Yet, the huge economic challenge facing India still and also the class structure cannot be ignored. Prof. Kumar Mehta after a visit to India in the summer of 1975 significantly concluded: "Only about 15 percent of the people in India are affected in any significant manner by the national emergency. Only the rich, the middle class, and the industrial employees, which make up the top 15 percent, enjoy some economic prosperity. The benefits from the state of Emergency, namely, that inflation is controlled – crime is down – strikes are banned – discipline in factories and offices is improved – the trains run on time – all these touch primarily the lives of upper classes . . . For the bottom 85 percent, or the overwhelming majority of the Indian people, nothing has really changed by the proclamation of Emergency."[11]

### *6. The Legal Erosion of Fundamental Rights*

> A Government that has to rely on the Criminal Law Amendment Act and similar laws, that suppresses the press and literature, that bans hundreds of organizations, that keeps people in prisons without trial, and that does so many other things that are happening in India today, is a Government that has ceased to have even a shadow of a justification for its existence.
>
> Jawaharlal Nehru, 1936

India is fast going down the slippery slope of totalitarianism. From the latter there is no easy return for any country in any time. This slippage is perceived perhaps more readily outside India than even by many Indian intellectuals on the inside. Yet the signs of descent to totalitarianism are unmistakably present. India is quickly slipping behind a totalitarian Khadi Curtain.

In any summary of these trends, the following negative effects must be discussed: the legal erosion; political prisoners; press censorship; Parliament and elections; surveillance and fear; and workers' rights.

While India was a democratic State before 26 June 1975, there were several laws of the central (federal) government which were hardly democratic. They included:

1. A state of emergency – based on external reasons – decreed for the 1971 Indo-Pakistan War was never lifted and continues.

2. Defence of India Act (DIA). This legislation had at least the relative advantage of requiring that detained individuals formally be brought into court and be charged.

3. Maintenance of Internal Security Act (MISA). This legislation gave the authorities wide powers to detain individuals.

After the declaration of the Emergency, the further legal erosion of democracy continued as follows:

1. The President on 27 June issued an order suspending for the duration of the Emergency the right of any person (including a non-citizen) to petition any court for the enforcement of the fundamental rights conferred under Articles 14, 21, and 22 of the Constitution – and suspending all proceedings pending in any court for the enforcement of these rights.

2. The President on 29 June promulgated an ordinance amending MISA, so that no grounds need be given for detention of a person under

this Act. MISA originally provided that the grounds of detention be supplied to the detainee within a few days after detention. Thus all the authorities must do is make a declaration that the detention of the designated individual is necessary for dealing with the Emergency and give a copy of this declaration to the detainee.

3. The Central Government, on 4 July, in four separate orders banned 26 organizations and parties. Their offices were sealed, documents and property seized, and a large number of their leaders and members arrested.

4. The Central Government, on 15 July, issued an ordinance whereby no persons, including non-citizens, detained under MISA could claim a right to personal liberty by virtue of natural or common law.

5. The 38th amendment to the Constitution was adopted, denying legal redress against misuse by the State of its emergency powers by placing the proclamation of the Emergency outside the jurisdiction of the courts.

6. MISA was further amended to prohibit the release of detainees on bail.

7. MISA on 17 October was amended again to forbid disclosure of the grounds of detention or material or information on which such grounds are framed. This was the government's answer to the court which demanded it to disclose to the judiciary the grounds of detention of individuals under MISA.

8. The Lok Sabha on 22 January 1976 confirmed the earlier Presidential decrees amending MISA. By a vote of 181 to 27, the Lok Sabha tightened MISA so that the Government could re-arrest persons whose detention orders expired (after one year's detention) or were revoked. In addition, the Government could detain political prisoners without having to disclose reasons to anyone, including the Judiciary.

The above decrees and laws do not include other restrictions affecting the press, elections, and trade unions.

Despite this legal erosion of fundamental rights, the Indian Judiciary has so far remained independent and thus remains one of the last safeguards for democracy in India today. The handling of the case against Mrs. Gandhi has been fair on several judicial levels. The handling by the Delhi High Court of the habeas corpus case brought by Mr. Kuldip Nayyar, a journalist who was arrested in July 1975, has been outstanding.[12] Yet if the Judiciary is fair, the environment of the courts raises questions of fairness. The proceedings of the courts are censored before appearing in the press. This puts, in itself, democratic freedoms in jeopardy.

## 7. *Political Prisoners*

Nor do I want to be known as a government leader who lacked the will to act decisively when the legacy of Mahatma Gandhi or Jawaharlal Nehru was blocked or threatened.

Mrs. Indira Gandhi[13]

The arrests under the Emergency began early on the morning of 26 June 1975. It is extremely difficult to estimate the number of political leaders who have been detained. (The persons arrested for economic offences are often mixed in the figures, but an attempt is made to exclude them from the figures used here.) A few estimates, with dates, are as follows:

*15 Aug.* – 17,483 persons, according to figures collected by Amnesty International from data released by state governments.

*23 Aug.* – "less than 10,000," as given by Minister of Information V. C. Shukla.

*December* – "Estimates of those detained under the MISA indicate that the total number may have reached 60,000 to 75,000 . . . Opposition leaders have claimed over 200,000 have been arrested." The *Review* of the International Commission of Jurists.[14]

*January* – "The police obliged (responding to the two-month Satyagraha) and some 80,000 people were taken in: 15.000 in Karnataka, 9,000 in Kerala, 8,000 each in Bihar and Uttar Pradesh, 5,000 in Delhi. Together they brought the total number of political prisoners now held in India to an estimated 140,000." – *The Economist*, London.[15]

*1 Feb.* – Hundreds but "much less than 500" arrested in Tamil Nadu.

*4 Feb.* – Erasmo de Sequeira, M.P., estimated in Parliament that 100,000 political prisoners which the *New York Times* bureau in India said "was more than twice as high as estimates from independent sources" in New Delhi.

*Feb.* – "The most reliable Opposition estimates, however, place the figure (of arrests) at around 100,000, of whom 80,000 are said to remain in custody." *Newsweek*.[16]

*13 March* – Over 100 arrested in Gujarat.

In this period, some persons – the total is unknown – have been released, either on parole or completely. Others are constantly being arrested. The number of persons arrested for political reasons since 26 June 1975 throughout India can conservatively be put as upwards of 50,000. Indeed, one occasionally hears the figure approaching 200,000 individuals.

The persons arrested fall into three or more classes: 1) leaders and members of the several Opposition political parties; 2) leaders of the 26 left- and right-wing extremist groups; and 3) some Gandhian workers. Initially, perhaps the majority of arrests were carried out against members of the Hindu nationalist Jana Sangh Party. Members of other parties involved included the Socialist Party, the Congress (O) Party, the Indian People's Party (Bharatiya Lok Del), and the Communist Party of India (Marxist). While few if any members of the Communist Party of India (CPI) in coalition with the ruling Congress (R) Party were detained, a few of the latter were placed under arrest. Also arrested were a number of leaders of the Opposition parties in the state legislatures, except in Tamil Nadu and Gujarat. After 4 July, 26 organizations were banned and many of their leaders and members arrested: the Rashtriya Sawayan Seva Sangh (RSSS), a paramilitary militant Hindu nationalist group; the Jamaat-e-Islami, a militant Muslim group; Anand Marg, a Hindu group; and 15 factions of the "Naxalities" or members of the Communist Party of India (Marxist-Leninist). Finally, some more militant Gandhians and other constructive workers were arrested, such as Radhakrishna, secretary of the Gandhi Peace Foundation and co-worker with J.P.

Of the personalities arrested, best known were J.P. and Morarji Desai,

M.P., the latter the 79-year-old former Deputy Prime Minister and leader of the Congress (O). Among the 30 Members of Parliament arrested were Chandra Sekhar and Ram Dhan of the Congress (R). Also arrested were Mr. L. K. Advani, President of the Jana Sangh; Charan Singh, Chairman of the Indian People's Party; and Jyotirmoy Bosu, M.P., leader of the Communist Party of India (Marxist).

The legal rights of detaines have been seriously eroded. They are picked up without being shown warrants of arrest. They – and their families – need not be informed of the grounds for their arrest. (Only the authorities themselves have to be satisfied that detention is necessary to safeguard the security of India.) They can be kept in detention for up to 12 months. They cannot be released on bail. If persons who are sought do not surrender, their property can be attached. They cannot appeal to the courts. Indeed, they have difficulty reaching lawyers. A review of preventive detention cases cannot be made by an independent advisory board during the first 12 months of detention.

As for the treatment of detainees, this varies widely. Families as a rule do not initially know where the person arrested is being detained, since under existing censorship rules the names of detainees and the places of detention cannot be published. In some cases families are not permitted normal visits to their relatives in prison even if they know where they are. Some are even kept in solitary confinement, although preventive detention is not legally considered to be punishment for a crime.

Torture has been reported in the Tihar jail in Delhi and also in Bihar, West Bengal, Uttar Pradesh, and Haryana. Dr. Subramanian Swamy, a member of the Rajya Sabha, claimed in January that 8,000 prisoners had been tortured since the state of Emergency was declared.[17] Prof. Ved P. Nanda also writes about eye-witness accounts of torture: "The police applied crude means either to extract a confession to a non-existent plot against Indira Gandhi or to seek information concerning the whereabouts and next moves of the organizers of the underground movement. The devices for torture which are being used in police stations and jails in India are as varied as they are inhumane and revolting. The victims who talked with me related incidents where they or other political prisoners were hung upside down; were stripped naked and severely beaten with shoes, steel rods, and gun butts; had burning candles applied to their bare soles, which were then punctured with nails; had chili powder smeared into their noses and other parts of their bodies; were kept awake while icy water was thrown on them on cold winter nights; were starved and even denied water; had rods tied to their necks, creating an intolerable strain on the spinal cord. The doctor I met was not personally tortured. However, while he was in jail as a political prisoner, illegally detained on trumped-up charges, he had treated more than 20 prisoners who, he said, must have been 'mercilessly beaten ...' A member of the Indian Supreme Court Bar Association showed me a resolution adopted by that organization which condemned police atrocities and harassment of attorneys defending Opposition members."[18] These and other instances of torture are being investigated by international human rights organizations.

### *8. Press Censorship*

Quoting Gandhi on censorship is forbidden.

So one government censor told the editor of one continuing publication in India today. India once had a free press. It may not have been the most responsible press, but it was a lively press reflecting a very wide spectrum of political thought and criticism. There are about 830 daily newspapers with eight million readers, including about 75 English-language papers. On the second day of the Emergency – 27 June – a pervasive censorship began both of the Indian press and of journalists writing for the foreign press (including radio and TV). In a broadcast to the nation, Mrs. Gandhi justified the censorship: "You know that I have always believed in freedom of the press, and I still do, but like all freedoms it has to be exercised with responsibility and restraint. In situations of international disturbance, whether language or communal riots, grave mischief has been done by irresponsible writings. We had to prevent such a situation. For some time, several papers have deliberately distorted news and made malicious and provocative comments. The purpose of censorship is to restore a climate of trust."[19]

On the first day of censorship, the Government simply shut off the electricity supply of many newspapers. After censorship became organized, newspapers were allowed to be printed, but certain topics were completely banned, such as the names of those detained. Other topics could only be reported if referred to the censor. Soon editors were encouraged not to print material if they thought it might be censorable. The resistance to these processes grew. Great spaces in the papers were left blank, but then these were prohibited. Quotations from Gandhi, Nehru, and Tagore ("a land where the mind is without fear") were banned. *The Eastern Economist* printed weekly on its cover page the well-known picture of Gandhi walking with his staff in hand. At first this cover was cleared by the censor, but then he ruled that Gandhi should not be on the cover every week! An advertisement appeared in *The Times of India* in Bombay announcing the death of D. E. Mocracy. Then the Government said advertisements were subject to censorship. Some editorial writers pointed to problems of dictatorship in Spain, Portugal, South Africa, and some Asian countries, making analogies which could pertain also to India.

Soon press guidelines were published. Nothing could be written that caused disaffection, that lowered morale, that affected production. Nothing could appear that denigrated the office of the Prime Minister or the Speaker of the House, that encouraged work stoppages or strained relations between India and any foreign country. No speeches of ordinary Members of Parliament could be reported; this applied to M.P.'s from the ruling party as well as to the Opposition, but quotations from Ministers and the Prime Minister were acceptable. Even certain cartoonists had to have their cartoons censored before appearing. Some papers were told what stories to print, with *The Statesman* on one occasion being told that it was not doing enough to publicize the government's views.

To make censorship effective, various pressure tactics were used. Some presses were locked up. Some journalists were dismissed and one, Kuldip Nayar of the *Express*, was detained. (He was later released by the courts.)[20] Some journalists were fined for printing prohibited material. The government demanded a deposit of 1,000 rupees as security against the publication of prejudiced material.

In this process of censorship, some weeklies have been closed, such as *Everyman's Weekly*, published by the J.P. movement, and the *Motherland* of the Jana Sangh. Others have voluntarily given up, such as the humourous *Shankar's Weekly* and *Freedom First*. The latter resumed publication in January 1976 after its editor, M. R. Masani, received a judgment from the Bombay High Court that the censors did not even act within their own guidelines in banning certain articles before publication.[21] The Minister of Information, V. C. Shulka, frankly prohibited the use of blank columns: "It is a form of protest; it implies you are not accepting the Government rules." Other publications which may still be appearing and carry political comment include *Opinion* from Bombay, *Guardian* from Bangalore, and *Bhoomiputta* from Gujarat.

Mrs. Gandhi's Administration is also manipulating ownership and control of the press, a move started before the Emergency. Efforts were made to induce *The Hindustan Times* to drop its editor, George Verghese, for courageous reporting against corruption. When the Press Council of India was probably about to reveal the political pressures on Verghese, the Press Council was dissolved. In the end, Verghese was dropped.[22] While earlier Mrs. Gandhi pledged to delink newspapers from big business, she reversed herself and pressure evolved so that Mr. K. K. Birla, the owner of *The Hindustan Times*, also joined the Board of the *Indian Express* group. Newspaper boards are being forced to accept government nominees and intimidating owners to remove editors and columnists.[23]

Foreign correspondents have also had to submit to censorship. Foreign dispatches were at first censored, but beginning in July they were exempt from pre-censorship, although correspondents writing for the foreign press were still expected to censor their own dispatches according to the Government guidelines. Those exceeding the guidelines were punished by the periodic severance of communication lines, including telephones, and in some cases expelled. A few foreign correspondents preferred no longer to file dispatches from India under these conditions. Those leaving for one reason or another included Edward Cody of the Associated Press, Lewis M. Simons of *The Washington Post*, Jacques Leslie of *The Los Angeles Times*, Loren Jenkins of *Newsweek*, Peter Hazelhurst of *The Times* (London), Peter Gill of *The Daily Telegraph*, Mark Tully of BBC, and Lawrence S. Lifschultz of *The Far Eastern Economic Review*). Foreign magazines (e.g., *Time* and *The Far Eastern Economic Review*) are not circulated by mail or through newsstands if they contain material critical of the Emergency.

Book publishing has also felt the long hand of the censor, with books published before June 1975 critical of the Gandhi government confiscated or withdrawn. Perceptive commentary on domestic Indian affairs is no longer in the publishing pipeline in India. However, some books published before the Emergency, and for example several praising J.P., are available in some bookstores, often after some persistence on the part of the purchaser.

On 8 December 1975 the Government promulgated three new press ordinances in an effort to fix permanent control of the press even if the Emergency were to be lifted some day. These decrees were made permanent by Parliament in January 1976. The ordinance on the Prevention of Publication of Objectionable Matter defines objectionable matter as any article or picture "likely to bring into hatred or contempt or excite disaffection toward the Government, and thereby cause or tend to cause public disorder." Another category is publishing anything "defamatory to the President of India, the Vice-President, the Prime Minister, the Speaker of the House, or the governor of a state." To be sure, the ordinance includes the following safeguard: "Comments expressing disapprobation or criticism of any law or of any policy or action of the Government with a view to obtain its alteration or redress by lawful means shall not be deemed to be objectionable matter." However, the ordinance gives wide powers to district magistrates and deputy secretaries and, most important, "no proceedings taken under this ordinance shall be called in question by or before any court."

The second ordinance approved by Parliament was the Parliamentary Proceedings Bill. This modified an act of 1956, introduced then by Mrs. Gandhi's late husband, Feroze, which conferred on the press certain immunity in reporting the proceedings of both houses of Parliament.

The third ordinance called for the dissolution of the Press Council. This had been established to evolve a code of conduct for the Press. By decree it went out of existence on 1 January 1976. Not completely unrelated was the combination on 1 February of the four news agencies in India – the Press Trust of India, the United News of India, the Hindustan Samachar, and the Bharati – into Samachar (or News). In explaining this merger to the Lok Sabha, the Minister of Information and Broadcasting, Mr. V. C. Shukla, said that in the past a proper image of India had not been projected to the world media despite dynamic changes taking place in all spheres of activity and this had resulted in "much unfair and motivated criticisms" being "heaped upon India in the world press from time to time," a feeling he insisted was "shared by all responsible sections in the community of journalists."

On 14 February 1976 the Government took another unprecedented action of press control by withdrawing the accreditation of more than 40 Indian reporters (of some 300) to attend official events in New Delhi. Following the tightening of press censorship, the Information Ministry screened all journalists previously given accreditation and eliminated several dozen. These included Indian reporters from both domestic and foreign newspapers. Some of those eliminated for "national security reasons" had been publicly identified with Opposition political leaders. This action did not automatically oust them from their profession, but made them lose such privileges as attending major news conferences or sessions of Parliament.

Mrs. Gandhi in a candid moment in December 1975 told some journalism students: "There are different ways of handling them (newspapers); we have done it crudely because we did not have any experience in this line."

Her father would not have approved either crude or sophisticated action against the press. He once said: "The freedom of the press is not just a slogan from the larger point of view, but it is an essential attribute of the democratic process. I have no doubt that even if the Government dislikes the liberties taken by the press and considers them dangerous, it is wrong to interfere with the freedom of the press. By imposing restriction, you do not change anything; you merely suppress the public manifestation of certain things, thereby causing the idea and thought underlying them to spread further. Therefore, I would rather have a completely free press with all the dangers involved in the wrong use of that freedom than a suppressed or regulated press."

### *9. Parliament and the Elections*

We think that on the whole our parliamentary system is right for India. It may need some small modifications, but on the whole I think this is the right one.

Mrs. Gandhi[24]

The Emergency affected Parliament in several ways. A number of Members, perhaps as many as 30, were placed under detention and could not attend meetings of Parliament. Also for a Parliament in any democracy to function well, the feed-back of public opinion, especially while it is in session, is essential. However, speeches by ordinary members were usually not reported in the press, while those of Ministers were. Thus the full debate was not available to the public prior to parliamentary votes, or even afterwards. There were also charges of intimidation of M.P.'s by the presence of hundreds of security personnel surrounding the Parliament grounds, and even inside.

Given the conditions of the Emergency, the Opposition at times deliberately absented themselves from Parliament and boycotted it during debates. As a result, some acts of Parliament, including amendments to the Constitution, were approved in record time. George Fernandes, Chairman of the Socialist Party of India, made this comment from the underground: "Never in history has an amendment to the Constitution of a country been 'constitutionally,' fed through a parliamentary body, adopted in such unholy haste. This was possible because: the vocal Opposition in Parliament has been silenced; the Presiding Officers were prepared to do her (Mrs. Gandhi's) bidding; the State Assemblies were willing creatures to her will; and, the President (of India), because he is beholden to her, put his signature at her nod. A well-orchestrated military exercise, yes. But certainly not a functioning Parliamentary Democracy."[25]

The Lok Sabha, which confirmed the Emergency in July 1975, was due to expire in March 1976. There were cynical predictions that Mrs. Gandhi, once she called an Emergency, would find excuses to extend the life of the Lok Sabha. (The Rajya Sabha, or Council of States, is not elected directly by the people.) At the 75th plenary of the Congress late in 1975, a resolution was adopted to extend the life of the Lok Sabha. According to Article 83 of the Constitution, the term of the Lok Sabha "may, while a Proclamation of Emergency is in operation, be extended by Parliament by law for a period not exceeding one year at a time and not extending in any case beyond a period of six months after the proclamation has ceased to operate."

Mrs. Gandhi told Parliament on 8 January 1976: "If we held the elections now, we would win. But that is not the point. The point is whether we have greater unity or whether we let loose forces of disruption so that the whole fabric falls apart." The Lok Sabha on 4 February 1976 voted to postpone the March 1976 elections and continue in session for another year after that date. The Minister of Law, Mr. H. R. Gokhale, defended the decision: "The forces which wanted to create instability are still at work. A general election in a vast country like India does create an atmosphere which becomes a disturbance in a situation like this. Although there is considerable improvement in discipline in all spheres of national life, we cannot yet afford to relax our efforts." One overwhelming reason for postponing the elections was that an election campaign would have presumably required the release of detained Opposition politicians, including many others than the 30 detained Members of Parliament.

### 10. *Surveillance and Fear*

Don't quote me, for God's sake.

For several decades India has been one of the freest democracies in the world. All ideologies found anywhere, all political currents, were freely aired in speech or through the printed word. Today the miasma of fear is rapidly spreading. Few citizens have firm evidence that they are being watched or overheard or that their telephones are tapped or that their mail is scrutinized. Few are detained for political remarks. Yet the suspicion of surveillance and the climate of fear persist. Many urban Indians feel that their freedoms are being restricted. There is just enough evidence that their fears are not paranoia. As more than one friend told this author: "Don't quote me, for God's sake."

Friends urge the visitor to adjourn any political talk at a restaurant until "after we leave." One professor observed that "the tearoom at college is dead."

Another level of fear is that of reprisals. Many do not know when someone might try to "settle an old score" by reporting an irregularity to the governmental authorities.

Freedom of assembly is severely curtailed. In theory no more than five persons may freely assemble. This has prevented the holding of political rallies – and any other meetings the Government may fear.

Another type of harassment is the determination to remove squatters, including beggars, from inside some of the big cities. This problem has been a chronic one, some settlers having remained since Partition in 1947. Using the Emergency, authorities have driven squatters out of shacks, often in the centre of the city, and made them go to new land given them on the far outskirts. This may be a desirable goal, but the evictions have been often made too quickly and before sufficient employment and transportation problems could be solved. But with press censorship, new police powers, and a ban on processions, any protests cannot be reflected to a wider public.

How organized is surveillance? There are several levels of police in India today and several levels of intelligence groups. The Border Security Force, established in 1962 after the India-China War, to patrol the frontier, has lately been increased in numbers and used as a para-military force to maintain internal security. The Central Intelligence Bureau has increasingly become a political arm of the Government for surveillance. Also there is RAW (Research and Analysis Wing). This is administered directly by the Prime Minister's Secretariat. Created in 1967, it is headed by Mr. P. N. Kaul. It places people in the highest levels of every ministry. Among its many tasks is to prepare arrest lists and detailed dossiers of potential or actual opponents of the Prime Minister.

## *11. Workers' Rights*

While most Indians work in agriculture, labour unions have arisen in the cities and among railroad and other governmental employees. These are usually related to political parties. The Indian National Trade Union Congress is affiliated with Congress (R) and the All-India Trade Union Congress is affiliated with the CPI. They have been less affected by the Emergency than those related to Opposition parties: the Socialist Hind Mazdoor Sabha, the Marxist Centre for Indian Trade Unions, and the All India Railwaymen's Federation (whose President, George Fernandes, is also chairman of the Socialist Party).

The Emergency has, through certain ordinances and other orders, curtailed the rights of workers. Strikes were banned in such essential fields as civil service, railways, power, and water supply. Some wages were reduced, some working hours raised, some holidays and other leaves curtailed. Profit-sharing bonuses have been slashed and many wage negotiations have been banned.

Some leaders and members of trade unions have not easily complied with these restrictions. Protests have been held and suppressed. In some cases police have fired upon workers, some of the latter being killed. Hundreds of workers have been detained without trial.

The All-India Trade Union Congress, despite being affiliated with the CPI (and thus part of the ruling coalition), called a one-day strike early in January 1976 protesting anti-labour legislation. They agitated against the ordinance cancelling the annual Diwali bonus for workers, which Mrs. Gandhi said would only add to inflation. A number of workers were arrested during this protest in several parts of India, but reportedly most were soon released. However, the Lok Sabha on 22 January debated a law that would cut by one-half the annual mandatory bonus of one month's pay in 1976 and would eliminate it entirely in 1977 in companies that made no profit. When this bill was introduced, the Opposition walked out briefly from the Lok Sabha, joined for the first time by the CPI.

## *12. The Opposition*

### A. J.P. (Jayaprakash)

I have never had any doubt about the ability or integrity of Jayaprakash Narayan whom I value as a friend; and I am sure a time will come when he will play a very important part in shaping India's destiny.

Jawaharlal Nehru

Born in India, educated partly in the U.S.A., Jayaprakash participated in the independence struggle of India. In the post-independence period, instead of participating in party Politics, J.P. spent 20 years with the Sarvodaya (Gandhian constructive) movement, especially with Bhoodan (land distribution) often in close collaboration with Vinoba Bhave. He early opposed the tragedy in East Pakistan and made a world tour to focus world public opinion in favour of an independent Bangladesh. Students in his native Bihar asked him in 1974 to lead a non-party movement against corruption and in 1975 he became an India-wide symbol against Mrs. Gandhi and her party.

When Mrs. Gandhi was convicted of election irregularities in June 1975, J.P. led the Opposition agitation against her retaining her position. Sitting on a chair at the rostrum on 25 June, J.P. was the main speaker at an Opposition rally in New Delhi. Within a few hours after the rally closed, the Emergency was declared, and J.P. was one of the first leaders to be arrested. Taken to a Delhi prison, he was soon transferred to a prison hospital in Chandrigarh because of ill-health. His health degenerated badly, presumably from neglect, and suddenly he was released on parole on 12 November for reasons of health. No government wanted to be responsible for the death of J.P. Removed to a hospital in Delhi, he told the press that the Emergency was "ridiculous," and asked that all political prisoners be freed, that press censorship be ended, and that the parliamentary elections be held on schedule. He was then taken to Bombay for further treatment of his failing kidneys. In the meantime his parole expired and he was unconditionally freed. On 24 December 1975, J.P. was released from the hospital and taken to his brother's apartment in Bombay. He must go to the hospital three times a week for dialysis, a purification of the blood by means of an artificial kidney machine. It now appears that J.P. can give only episodic leadership to the Opposition.

In sickness, as in prison or good health, J.P. appears to Mrs. Gandhi as the chief threat to her regime. Much of its propaganda since 26 June has been devoted to destroying J.P.'s reputation. Mrs. Gandhi and her associates levelled two principal charges against J.P. She told *The Saturday Review*: "The state of Emergency was proclaimed because the threat of disruption was clear and imminent . . . A call is given by a combination of five parties for countrywide civil disobedience, and, over and above all, the armed forces and police are publicly asked to disobey orders – is the situation not grave? These were not the actions of a lunatic fringe to be ignored."

J.P. answered both of these charges, and others, in his "Testament of

Protest." He wrote: "No, dear Prime Minister, there was no plan to paralyse the Government ... The programme was for a selected number of persons to offer 'satyagraha' before or near your residence in support of the demand that you should step down until the Supreme Court's judgment on your appeal. The programme was to continue for seven days in Delhi, after which it was to be taken up in the states ... I do not see what is subversive or dangerous about it. In a democracy the citizen has an inalienable right to civil disobedience when he finds that other channels of redress or reform have dried up. It goes without saying that the 'satyagrahi' willingly invites and accepts his lawful punishment. This is the dimension added to democracy by Gandhi. What an irony that it should be obliterated in Gandhi's own India' ... It was this 'plan' and not any imaginary plan to paralyze the Government that has aroused your ire and cost the people their liberties and dealt a deathblow to their democracy."[26]

J.P. also answered her second charge: "As for the 'one person' who is supposed to have tried to sow dissatisfaction in the armed and police forces, he denies the charge. All that he has done is to make the men and officers of the forces conscious of their duties and responsibilities. Whatever he has said in that connection is within the law, the Constitution, the Army Act, and the Police Act."

An Embassy of India booklet charged that "in 1975, Narayan was inciting open violation of the government's laws. He urged police and the armed forces to refuse to execute their duties." J.P. did indeed call for the disobedience of *illegal* orders. At the public rally on 25 June, J.P. said: "If any Government or party leader intends to use the army as a means to further their own power interests, it is the clear duty of the army not to be so used." The charge against J.P. is an old one, and he wrote in *Everyman's Weekly* in April 1975: "If the rulers do venture to use the army to suppress a peaceful revolution, then the army should not allow itself to be so used. On such occasions the leaders of the revolution may call upon the army to come over to their side, but I have always made it clear that the present was certainly not such an occasion ... I consider it my duty to explain to the police that while I was not asking them to rebel and that they must do their duty, they must not obey orders that are illegal or go against their conscience ... I categorically deny that I have ever asked the armed or the police forces to join the movement or to rebel."[27]

## B. The Opposition Parties

While Gandhi and my father were alive, they were critcized just as much as I am now being criticized.

Mrs. Gandhi[28]

Before the Emergency, early in June 1975, the political Opposition to Mrs. Gandhi and her coalition consisted of a wide range of political parties, except for the Communist Party of India (CPI). Thus the principal parties which formally or informally were in Opposition consisted of the Congress (O), the Socialist Party, the Communist Party of India (Marxist), the Jana

Sangh, and the Bharatiya Lok Del. In addition, by mid-1975 there were obvious political strains within Mrs. Gandhi's Congress (R). Some urged that she begin negotiations with J.P., at least by entering into a dialogue. Some prominent ministers were dismissed for this heresy, including Mohan Dharia and Prof. Sher Singh. After Mrs. Gandhi's conviction by the Allahabad Court, reportedly more than one hundred M.P.'s urged her resignation, if only temporarily.

Immediately after the Emergency, the Opposition seemed to diminish in strength, partly of course because of the arrest of its top leaders, and thousands of its members. A serious demoralization understandably set in.

It took several months for the political opposition to revive itself. Only in two states, Tamil Nadu and Gujarat, was the Opposition in political control of the state legislatures. However, on 31 January Presidential Rule was proclaimed in Tamil Nadu with the central government dismissing the legally-constituted state government headed by the Dravida Munnetra Kazhagam (DMK) Party. Mrs. Gandhi previously accused the state of lagging behind in implementing her economic programme. Then on 12 March Presidential Rule was proclaimed in Gujarat after the state government of the Janata Morcha (People's Front) fell on a confidence vote. Mrs. Gandhi previously accused the state of failing to maintain "law and order."

Leaders of the principal Opposition parties met in Ahmedabad early in 1976 to continue a united effort. This Janata (People's) Front is informally composed of representatives from the Socialist Party, the Congress Party (O), the Communist Party of India (Marxist), Jana Sangh, and Bharatiya Lok Del. They agreed to work together, keeping in touch with J.P. Later, during the session of Parliament in January, Members of Parliament of the Janata Front decided to sit together in the Lok Sabha and try to develop a common strategy.

### C. Satyagraha

The days of Satyagraha are over and an era of discipline is being ushered in to make the nation strong and prosperous.

Mrs. Indira Gandhi, March 1976[29]

After the Emergency, some non-party Sarvodaya workers were imprisoned. It took some weeks for the non-violent forces to regroup, which was slowly done under the leadership of Lok Sangharsh Samithi (People's Struggle Committee). Some Satyagrahis wore black ribbons across their chests and some flew black flags over their houses. While students struck at Jawaharlal University in Delhi late in September because the Administration refused admission to some on political grounds, the mass movement could not begin on a widespread basis even on 2 October, the birthdate of Gandhi. In Delhi, however, a small group of Gandhians held a protest meeting after a traditional celebration at Rajghat attended by Mrs. Gandhi. Those arrested included 87-year-old J. B. Kripalani, Sushila Nayar – Gandhi's physician and former Minister of Health – and two of Mohandas Gandhi's grandsons. The Satyagraha campaign spread beginning on 14 November, the birthday of Jawaharlal Nehru. One thousand persons were arrested in

Tamil Nadu and 1,200 persons were arrested in Karnataka State as part of this campaign.

Here is an eye-witness account by a visitor to Delhi in the third week of December: "Individual demonstrators (Satyagrahis) – ranging from four to 50 in number – shout slogans against Mrs. Gandhi's government and pass out anti-government literature in busy streets. The demonstrators usually wear garlands, people assemble around them, and, since the time and place are announced in advance, the police promptly arrest the demonstrators. Each Satyagraha I saw in Delhi had about 40 active participants who courted arrest and attracted more than 5,000 spectators. The crowds, predominantly Opposition sympathizers, repeatedly shouted slogans demanding an end to the state of Emergency, release of political prisoners, and the restoration of civil liberties. In one case, the police resorted to a mild lathi charge (swinging long wooden poles and clubbing onlookers) before arresting the Satyagrahis. According to Opposition sources (whose information is hard to verify) more than 40,000 persons have courted arrest in cities all over India."[30]

J.P. in a final "testament of protest" to Mrs. Gandhi, written in Bombay from a hospital after release from prison, sharply responded to Mrs. Gandhi's earlier allegation that in June he was planning to "paralyze the Government." It was merely to be selective Satyagraha.[31]

## *13. Outsiders and Outside Pressure*

When no one was in jail, on whose side were they?

So observed Mrs. Gandhi late in December 1975 when she criticized outsiders, including the foreign press, for shedding "crocodile tears" over the loss of democracy, including press freedom, in India.

On the one hand, Mrs. Gandhi appeals to the xenophobic instincts of the Indian people (as of peoples of most nations). On the other hand, she tries to cultivate world public opinion through her interviews appearing in a wide range of publications outside India.

Although one Emergency has been in force since 1971 covering an external threat to India, Mrs. Gandhi has used this external threat as an additional rationale for the Emergency of June 1975. The Indian National Congress meeting in December 1975 asserted that "external forces are promoting discord and instability in this region." It added that "it would be premature to conclude that the dangers of internal and external subversion have been fully surmounted." At a rally in Calcutta, Mrs. Gandhi said: "Let me, as Prime Minister, tell the foreign powers that we will not tolerate interference in our internal affairs. The more they interfere in our internal affairs, the more rigid and determined we will be in dealing with them." While in that speech she mentioned the threat as coming from "both East and West," she constantly implies major CIA interference, without quite using the initials. In another speech she spoke of the "gravest danger of outside interference in India," and that "some powers which tasted success in their destabilization game in Chile nurtured similar designs against India."[32]

Despite efforts of the Gandhi Administration to neutralize "outside" criticism by alleging outside interference, at least the democratic West has not been slow to voice criticisms of her actions. A Free JP Campaign was early established in the U.K., chaired by Hon. Philip Noel-Baker. On 15 August 1975 it inserted a large advertisement signed by several hundred prominent persons in *The Times* (London) with the caption: "Today is India's Independence Day: Don't Let the Light go out on Indian Democracy. Free J.P." The Campaign publishes an Indian news digest, called *Swaraj*. In the U.S., Indians for Democracy emerged, with a fortnightly newsletter, *Indian Opinion*. This organization, composed of Indians, opened chapters in several large American cities and held a weekend seminar. A group of 80 American citizens, predominantly of non-Indian ancestry, on 5 March 1976 issued a statement deploring the loss of fundamental human rights in India.

Not all comments outside India were critical of Mrs. Gandhi. Many persons with continuing business and academic connections with India remained "neutral" or silent, although some became more critical when the elections were postponed in January. One international organization supporting Mrs. Gandhi was the World Peace Council, with its Secretary-General, Romesh Chandra, asserting that Mrs. Gandhi's mass arrests were an "effort to combat a foreign plot to overthrow the Indian Government." According to Reuters, "he named the U.S. Central Intelligence Agency (CIA) and multinational corporations as backers of the moves to unseat Gandhi."[33]

### *14. Summary and Conclusions*

Dear Indiraji, please do not identify yourself with the nation. You are not immortal, India is.

J.P.[34]

1. India continues to face major obstacles in providing even minimum living standards and economic and social justice to her 600 million inhabitants.

2. The Emergency has only postponed real progress toward the economic and social well-being of most of India's people. The programmes of both the ruling Congress (R) Party and the Opposition involve only 10–15 percent of the people of India. Still this is a larger total – 60–90 million people – than the population of most medium-sized States in the world today.

3. The "positive" aspects of the Emergency – some discipline, greater economic productivity and growth – are so far superficial.

4. The negative aspects – an increasing erosion of fundamental rights – are disastrous for the people of India and their future, and for the subcontinent.

5. The organized Opposition to Mrs. Gandhi and her Congress (R) Party (and the Communist Party of India in coalition) appears to be demoralized, but non-violent protests are continuing.

6. The immediate future of India cannot easily be predicted.

a. The erosion of fundamental rights may well continue: a further lessening of legal rights, a further imprisonment of political leaders, further press censorship, further fear and harassment, and further restrictions on trade unions and public assembly.

b. Despite the tradition of non-violence, India is a very violent society and India could experience chaos.

c. An eventual military dictatorship cannot be completely excluded.

7. There are several long-term by-products of the Emergency favouring democracy.

a. Many Indians appreciate democracy today more than when they had it. The Emergency may, in the end, enhance democracy in India.

b. The defects of the democratic process in India's first quarter-century are, in retrospect, more obvious, even though proposals for reform are still hazy. Democracy is not a luxury for India, but the Westminster-cum-Washington democratic institutions may well be modified to deal with Indian conditions and experiences.[35]

8. A first step to reverse the present unfortunate trend would be promptly to lift the Emergency.

9. A second step would be to hold early elections for the Lok Sabha.

10. A real revolution is needed in India in order to give economic and social justice to 90 percent or more of her people. It is hard to know what combination of existing political groups is prepared to work for this goal.

11. India faces continuing problems with her neighbours on the subcontinent, not only with Pakistan, but also with Bangladesh and China.

12. The role of the U.S.A., the U.S.S.R., and China can continue to be helpful or hurtful to India's progress. If India is truly non-aligned toward all three Powers, she might attain the greatest security, within the context of being an active member of the U.N. A semi-permanent membership of India on the U.N. Security Council would be helpful to her self-esteem, although today her "peaceful" atomic programme and her space programme are welcomed by the Indian public.

13. The prognosis for India cannot be entirely negative. No nation which has given the world so much religion and culture for so many centuries and indeed which has produced in one century Tagore, Gandhi, Nehru, and J.P. can be submerged for long.

14. The role of the genuine "friends" of India – non-Indians and Indian nationals and former nationals living outside – can be marginal at most in affecting political changes within India. Perhaps the principal role of outsiders is to maintain links with friends in India and to try to keep the morale of those in India's present Opposition high.

## *Appendix A. Fundamental Rights in the Indian Constitution*

Our first law should be to have our fundamental rights guaranteed in a manner which will not permit their withdrawal under any circumstances.

Motilal Nehru (Mrs. Gandhi's grandfather)

As early as 1918, the Indian National Congress demanded a Declaration of Rights for India. In 1927 the Congress, meeting at Madras, asked its Working Committee to draft a freedom constitution, based on a Declaration of Rights. The Committee was headed by Motilal Nehru – father of Jawaharlal – and prepared a draft, including 19 fundamental rights. In 1931 the Congress meeting at Karachi made a declaration securing for every citizen specific guarantees of fundamental rights. The insistent demands during this colonial period for fundamental rights being enshrined in the constitution of an independent India were due to several factors: 1) the lack of civil liberties under British rule, 2) the discriminatory treatment of untouchables and women, 3) the communal tensions (among religious groups), and 4) the exploitation of the poor, especially farmers.

The Constituent Assembly, after the transfer of power, set up a Constitution Drafting Committee, chaired by Dr. B. R. Ambedkar, a noted lawyer and untouchable. The Constitution they devised tended to follow the U.S. rather than the British legal model.

The Preamble of the Constitution, as approved by the Constituent Assembly in 1949, asserts important rights: "We, the people of India, having solemnly resolved to constitute India into a sovereign democratic republic and to secure to all its citizens: Justice, social, economic and political; Liberty of thought, expression, belief, faith and worship; Equality of status and of opportunity; And to promote among them all Fraternity assuring the dignity of the individual and of the unity of the Nation; In our Constituent Assembly 26 November 1949 hereby adopt, enact, and give to ourselves this Constitution."

Part III of the Constitution is devoted to Fundamental Rights. Among the pertinent articles are 13(2) and 19(1). The former asserts that "the State shall not make any law which takes away or abridges the rights conferred by this Part and any law made in contravention of this clause shall, to the extent of the contravention, be void." Section 19(1) asserts that "all citizens shall have the right (a) to freedom of speech and expression; (b) to assemble peacefully and without arms; (c) to form associations or unions ..." Also Part IV contains "Directive Principles of State Policy," with Article 38 and others dealing with political and social justice.

These Fundamental Rights in the Indian Constitution are not, however, unambiguous. The original Constitution in Part III contained certain exceptions, including preventive detention (Article 22). These were further amplified in the very first Amendment (of more than 40 to date) of 1951 which asserts in part 12(2) that nothing in clause (1)(a) shall "prevent the State from making any law in so far as such law imposes reasonable restrictions on the exercise of rights" based on "the security of the State, friendly relations with foreign States, public order, decency or morality, or in relation to contempt of court, defamation, or encitement to an offence." This clause was further broadened by the 16th amendment to include the interests of "the sovereignty and integrity of India."

The possibility of amending the Constitution in order to whittle away the Fundamental Rights (and other changes) has always been feared. Rajendra Prasad, later the First President of India, prophetically declared:

"I do not know what kind of people will there be in the future Parliament of India. In the heat of extremism or at the altar of some radical ideology they may like to do away with the provisions which we have made in the articles of the Constitution." Mr. J. B. Kripalani in commenting also on the Constitution said that "it was therefore felt necessary to keep the fundamental rights of the citizen outside the possible interference of average men and women who may act under intoxication of power, whether in the legislature or the government." While the Constitution was being drafted, H. V. Kamath warned of the Emergency provisions: "I have studied the major constitutions of the world, but I have not come across any such wide and sweeping provision. I fear that we are seeking to lay the foundations of a totalitarian state. The suspension of fundamental rights is a very grave matter. I will go so far as to say that it is even graver than the gravest emergency with which the state may be confronted."[36]

Already these fundamental rights have been seriously atrophied by amendment. The latter process requires only a two-thirds vote by both houses of Parliament and no referendum (on these parts) by the state legislatures (or directly by the people). In 1967 the Supreme Court ruled that Parliament could not "abridge or take away the fundamental rights guaranteed by the Constitution." But Parliament in 1971 adopted the 24th amendment to Article 13 which gives it power to amend even the fundamental rights. Further Court cases have possibly restricted these fundamental rights still further, including one which asserts that even the Preamble can be amended by the usual process. However, the landmark case of Kesavanand v. Kerala in 1973 raises some hope against the Parliament completely eroding the fundamental rights in the Constitution. Each of the 13 judges wrote a separate verdict, amounting to 1,500 pages in all, and actually upheld the 29th amendment to the Constitution on land reform which was challenged as unconstitutional. However, the essence of the judgment was that parliamentary action could not be immune from judicial scrutiny, especially regarding fundamental rights.

Mrs. Gandhi in addressing the 21st Commonwealth Parliamentary Conference at New Delhi in October 1975 said that democracy is a "generic term" and "forms of democracy vary in each country, in the light of its own history and national character, its size, the diversity or homogeneity of its population, the state of its economic development, and other such conditioning factors." She further quoted her father as saying that "it may be that the Constitution this House may frame may not satisfy that free India." He added that "this House cannot bind down the next generation, or the people who will duly succeed us in this task." She was preparing the Indian people for possible major constitutional changes. Yet the Bar Council of India on 27 December 1975 warned publicly against any "drastic changes" in the Constitution without a national debate. Among the many proposals being circulated is one to create a Superior Council of the Judiciary. This would supercede the authority of the Supreme Court.

Early in March 1976 the Congress (R) Party set up a two level committee to investigate the possibility of changing the Constitution. It will submit its report, including draft amendments, by May 1976. Earlier the Congress at its annual plenary session resolved that "our Constitution be thoroughly re-examined in order to ascertain if the time has not come to make adequate alterations to it so that it may continue as a living document effectively responding to the current needs of the people."

## V. Exhibit B: Amnesty International Report, March 1976

### *Politicians and Parliamentarians Arrested under Emergency Regulations in India following Declaration of Emergency on 26 June 1975*

I. *Members of Parliament* (Members of the Lok Sabha and the Rajya Sabha)

1) *Lal K. Advani.* J.P., Rajya Sabha (Delhi State). President of the Jana Sangh Party. Arrested 26/6/75 in Bangalore. Detained Rohtak Jail, Haryana.

2) *Jyotirmoy Bosu.* M.P. (West Bengal) and Deputy Leader of the Communist Party of India (Marxist) (CPI-M). Arrested 9/7/75 shortly before parliament was reconvened. Now under order to return to Hissar Jail, Haryana, following treatment in hospital. He is reported to have been kept in solitary confinement.

3) *Madhu Dandavate.* M.P. (Maharashtra state) for Socialist Party. Arrested late June 1975; detained in Rohtak Jail, Haryana. His wife is also under detention.

4) *Morarji Desai.* M.P. and leader of the Congress (Opposition) Party. 78 years old. Former Deputy Prime Minister of India and a Finance Minister for seven years. Joined Mahatma Gandhi's civil disobedience campaign against British rule and was a political prisoner for five years. Desai was a close associate to Jawaharlal Nehru. Arrested 26/6/75 in New Delhi. During the first 28 days of his detention, he was allowed only a brief visit by his daughter-in-law and his lawyer. He is detained in Tauru District Jail, Gurggaon, Haryana, reportedly in solitary confinement.

5) *Ram Dhan.* M.P. (Uttar Pradesh). Senior member of the Congress Party. Secretary Congress Parliamentary Party. Known dissident. Arrested 26/6/75. He is detained in Rohtak Jail, Haryana.

6) *Samar Guha.* M.P. (West Bengal) for the Socialist Party. Arrested late June 1975 in New Delhi. He is detained in Rohtak Jail, Haryana.

7) *Noorul Huda.* M.P. for Assam state for Communist Party of India (Marxist).

8) *Jaganathrao Joshi.* M.P. for the Jana Sangh Party. Held in Tihar Jail, New Delhi.

9) *Madhu Limaye.* M.P. for the Socialist Party (Bihar state). Arrested 26/6/75. He is detained in Jaipur Jail, Rajasthan.

10) *S. N. Mishra.* M.P. for the Congress (Opposition) Party (Bihar state). Arrested 27/6/75. He is detained in Rohtak Jail, Haryana.

11) *Piloo Moody.* M.P., Leader of the Swatantra Party and General

Secretary of Bharatiya Lok Dal (Indian People's Party). 48 years old. Arrested 26/6/75. He is detained in Rohtak Jail, Haryana.

12) *Raj Narain*. Member of Rajya Sabha (Uttar Pradesh). Arrested 26/6/75 in New Delhi. Member of the Socialist Party. He is reported to have been transferred from Tihar Jail, New Delhi; his present whereabouts unknown.

13) *K. Chandrasekharan*. M.P. Rajya Sabha (Uttar Pradesh). Member of the Working Committee of the Congress Party. 45 years old. Known dissident in the Congress Party. Arrested 26/6/75; detained in Patiala Jail, Punjab.

14) *Mukhtiar Singh Malik*. M.P. for Jana Sangh Party from Rohtak (Haryana). Detained in Central Jail, Ambala, Haryana.

15) *Narendra Singh*. M.P. for Jana Sangh Party (Madhya Pradesh). Arrested 20/7/75.

16) *Atal Bihari Vajpayee*. M.P. (Madhya Pradesh). Leader of the Jana Sangh Party in Parliament. Arrested in Bangalore 26/6/75. He is reported to have received a one-month conditional release for health reasons.

17) *Sharad Yadav*. M.P. (Madhya Pradesh) from Bangalore. Member of the Socialist Party.

18) *Jeneshwar Misra*. M.P. for the Bharatiya Lok Dal. Arrested 26/6/75. He is detained in Naini Central Jail, Allahabad, Uttar Pradesh.

19) *Hukam Chand Kachwai*. M.P. for the Jana Sangh Party. Arrested 26/6/75. Detained in Central Gwalior, Madhra Pradesh.

20) *Bhagirath Bhanwar*. M.P. for the Bharatiya Lok Dal. Arrested 26/6/75. Detained in District Jail, Indore, Madhya Pradesh.

21) *Mahadeepak Singh Shakya*. M.P. for the Jana Sangh Party. Arrested 2 July 1975. Detained in District Jail Kota, Rajasthan.

22) *Ram Rattan Sharma*. M.P. for the Jana Sangh Party. Arrested 2 July 1975. Detained in District Jail Banda, Uttar Pradesh.

23) *Virendra Kumar Saklecha*. M.P. for the Jana Sangh Party. Arrested 28 June 1975. Detained in Central Jail, Indore, Madhya Pradesh.

24) *Bharion Singh Shaikhawat*. M.P. for the Jana Sangh Party. Arrested 26 June 1975. Detained in Sariska Jail, Alwar, Rajasthan.

25) *Phool Chand Verma*. M.P. (Lok Sabha); arrested after 26 June 1975. Place of detention unknown. Member of the Jana Sangh Party.

26) *Laxminarain Pandeya*. M.P. (Lok Sabha) for the Jana Sangh Party. Arrested after 26/6/75. Place of detention unknown.

27) *Dinesh Joarder*. M.P. (Lok Sabha) for the Communist Party of India (Marxist). Arrested after 26/6/75. Place of detention unknown.

28) *S. C. Angre*. M.P. (Rajya Sabha) from Madhya Pradesh. Arrested after 26/6/75. Place of detention unknown.

29) *Mahadeo Prasad Verma*. M.P. (Rajya Sabha) from Uttar Pradesh. Arrested after 26/6/75. Place of detention unknown.

30) *S. K. Kurdu*. M.P. (Lok Sabha) and member of the Socialist Party. Arrested after 26/6/75. Place of detention unknown.

31) *Rabi Ray*. M.P. (Rajya Sabha) for Orissa and member of the Socialist Party. Arrested June 1975. Detained in Tihar Jail, New Delhi.

32) *G. S. Tohra.* M.P. (Rajya Sabha). Arrested after 26/6/75. Place of detention unknown.

II. *Members of State Legislatures*

1) *V. S. Achuthanandan.* Member of the Legislative Assembly for Alleppy, Member of State Committee of the Communist Party of India (Marxist-Leninist.

2) *Bhagabat Behar.* Member of the Legislative Assembly for Socialist Party.

3) *Sarla Bhadoria.* Member of Legislative Assembly for the Bharatiya Lok Dal.

4) *Jonoswar Bora.* Member of Legislative Assembly of Assam for Socialist Party.

5) *J. P. Bose.* Member of Legislative Assembly of Uttar Pradesh for Socialist Party.

6) *P. K. Chandranandan.* Member of Legislative Assembly for Alleppy. Member of State Committee of the Communist Party of India (Marxist-Leninist).

7) *Gadadhar Giri.* Member of Legislative Assembly for Socialist Party.

8) *Purshottam Kaushik.* Member of Legislative Assembly. Chairman, Madhya Pradesh Unit of the Socialist Party.

9) *Ram Kishan.* Member of Legislative Assembly of Rajasthan.

10) *A. P. Kuryan.* Member of Legislative Assembly for Ernakulam (Kerala) for the Communist Party of India (Marxist).

11) *Hardivari Lal.* Member of Legislative Assembly of Haryana state, Rohtak.

12) *Ram Lal.* Member of Legislative Assembly for Jana Sangh Party, Haryana.

13) *Laxminarayan Muik.* Member of Legislative Assembly for Socialist Party.

14) *Siju Patnaik.* Member of Legislative Assembly (Orissa) for Bharatiya Lok Dal. Held in Rohtak Jail, Haryana. Arrested 26/6/75.

15) *Balbir Singh.* Member of Legislative Assembly (Punjab) for the Socialist Party. Arrested 26/6/75.

16) *Dal Singh.* Member of Legislative Assembly (Haryana) for Bharatiya Lok Dal. Arrested 26/6/75.

17) *K. A. Sivaramabharathy.* Member of Legislative Assembly for Socialist Party. Member of National Committee of the Socialist Party.

18) *B. Talukdar.* Member of Legislative Assembly of Assam for Socialist Party.

19) *Pinari Vijayam.* Member of Legislative Assembly for Coimbatore (Kerala) for Communist Party of India (Marxist).

1) *Mani Ram Bagri.* Leader of Socialist Party in Haryana. Arrested 27/6/75. Detained in Hissar Jail, Haryana.

2) *Sikander Bakht.* President Congress (Opposition) Party for Delhi state. Arrested 26/6/75; detained in Rohtak Jail, Haryana.

3) *Haripada Bharati.* Member of Jana Sangh Party in West Bengal. Arrested in June 1975 and detained in West Bengal.

4) *Chowdhury Chandram.* Chairman of the Bharatiya Lok Dal. Detained in Rohtak Jail, Haryana.

5) *Miralal Jain.* Chairman of the Socialist Party in Rajasthan.

6) *Mulchand Jain.* Former State Finance Minister for Haryana. Arrested 26/6/75; detained in Rohtak Jail, Haryana.

7) *Dharam Singh Kasni.* Communist leader in Haryana. Arrested 26/6/75.

8) *S. Lashkiri.* Chairman, Telugana Socialist Party.

9) *Ashoka Mehta.* Born 1911. Former Congress Minister (Planning and Social Welfare). Former Deputy Chairman Planning Commission. Five times imprisoned under British rule for activities in the Independence Movement. Deputy Chairman of the Congress (Opposition) Party. Arrested 26/6/75; detained in Rohtak Jail, Haryana.

10) *Biman Mitra.* Chairman Bihar Unit of Socialist Party.

11) *Surendra Mohan.* General Secretary for Socialist Party. Arrested 9/10/75; detained in Tihar Jail, New Delhi.

12) *Baldev Parkash.* Leader of the Jana Sangh Party in Punjab. Arrested 26/6/75.

13) *Mohan Punamiya.* Member of the Central Committee of the Communist Party of India (Marxist).

14) *Ugra Sen.* Ex-Member of Legislative Assembly. Chairman Uttar Pradesh Unit of the Socialist Party.

15) *Jagannath Sein.* Former Member of the Legislative Assembly, Haryana. Arrested 26/6/75.

16) *Hangal Sein.* Former Member of the Legislative Assembly, Haryana. Arrested 26/6/75; detained in Rohtak Jail, Haryana.

17) *Charan Singh.* Chairman of the Bharatiya Lok Dal. Held in Tihar Jail, New Delhi. Arrested 26/6/75.

18) *Harbhajan Singh.* Chairman of the Socialist Party in Punjab.

19) *Jaipal Singh.* General Secretary of the Communist Party of India (Marxist) (Delhi state).

20) *Ramanand Tiwari.* Former Home Minister. Chairman of the Bihar Unit of the Socialist Party.

21) *Bhai Vaidya.* Mayor of Poona. Prominent member of Socialist Party. Arrested 26/6/75; detained in Verwada, Maharashtra.

22) *Fateh Singh Vij.* Former Member of Legislative Assembly, Haryana. Arrested 26/6/75; detained in Central Jail, Ambala, Haryana.

23) *H. Bahinipathy.* Former Speaker of the Orissa Legislative Assembly and member of the Socialist Party. Arrested shortly after 26/6/75. Place of detention unknown.

*Gandhi Peace Foundation members and Gandhian workers known to have been arrested under emergency regulations in India following a declaration of emergency on 26 June 1975*

*Arunachalam.* Prominent Gandhian worker, member of Khadi and Village Industries Commission. President of Tamil Nadu Sarvodaya Mandal. Secretary of the Gandhian Museum in Nadurai. Arrested in late June 1975 in

Tamil Nadu (probably in Madurai). Held in preventive detention in Tamil Nadu under the Maintenance of Internal Security Act (MISA). Place of detention unknown.

*Khitish Roy Chowdhury*. Secretary of the Gandhi Peace Foundation in Calcutta. Arrested around 26 June 1975 in Calcutta. Held in Dum Dum Jail, Calcutta, under MISA legislation.

*Manmohan Chowdhury*. Gandhian worker in the Sarvodaya Movement. Former President of the Serva Seva Sangh. Member of Khadi and Village Industries Commission. Son of Nabakrishna Chowdhury, former Chief Minister of Orissa (also adopted by AI). Held in Cuttack Jail, Orissa, under MISA legislation.

*Ravi Sahoo*. Gandhian worker in the Sarvodaya Movement. Arrested around 26 June 1975 in Orissa. Held in preventive detention in Orissa (prison unknown) under MISA legislation.

## VI. Extracts from Exhibit C: Report by Indians for Democracy, "Torture of Political Prisoners in India"[37]

This Report identifies the individuals, the nature of the torture inflicted on them, the date, time, place and the name and rank of the police responsible. It is long and inevitably repetitive. Some instances are covered more than once because corroborative evidence has come from different sources.

The following extracts are selected as typical of the Report as a whole. Editorial linking comment is enclosed in square brackets.

### *Illustrative Cases of Torture and Crimes against Human Rights*

Alarming reports of widespread torture have been received from various States.

The following illustrative cases are excerpted or summarised from the reports sent by the Lok Sangharsha Samiti of the States. The torture inflicted on peaceful satyagrahis appear to have a pattern. The pattern is as follows:

A satyagrahi is taken into custody by the police and no case is registered by satyagrahis. They are kept in illegal confinement for a few days during which they are subjected to physical torture of the following kinds.

(a) Stamping on the bare body with heeled 'ammunition' boots.

(b) Severe beating on the soles of the feet.

(c) Rolling heavy police *lathis* over the bone of the legs, with constable sitting on the *lathi*.

(d) Making the victim crouch for hours in a 'z' position.

(e) Beating on the spine.

(f) Slapping both ears until the victim loses consciousness.

(g) Beating with the butt of a rifle.
(h) Inserting electric live wires in the crevices of the body.
(i) Stripping the body nude and making satyagrahis lie on the slabs of ice.
(j) Burning the skin with cigarettes or wax candles.
(k) Denying food, water and sleep and making the victim drink his own urine.
(l) Stripping the victim, blackening his face and parading him in public.
(m) Suspending him in the air from his wrists tied behind his back.
(n) Putting up on an "aeroplane."

*Andra Pradesh*

Mr. Narsinha Reddy was slapped on the ears severely. Blood oozed from his ear, and he had to be operated upon. On 18.11.75 the satyagraha batch leader, Mr. Ashok of Hyderabad was beaten severely after Satyagraha in the city college of Hyderabad. On 4.12.75, one student Rajawardhan was mercilessly beaten. He vomited blood and fell unconscious. Even then he was not given medical attention. Also beaten severely were the student leaders Mahandra and Bapu Reddy Vidwar Reddy, Supervisor, P.W.D. and Venkateshwara Rao student. On 7.12.75 police arrested 7 persons at Godawari Khani, Karimnagar Distt while they were pasting posters. They were brutally tortured in the police station. Three of them were asked to remove clothes and their bodies were burned with wax candles. Their bodies are full of burns. They were admitted to the Karimnagar Hospital for treatment. The Bar Association condemned the police atrocities and sent memorandum to the Chief Minister, demanding appropriate action against the police officers. Brutal beating of satyagrahis by police is also reported from Karimnagar (14.11.75) Vizag (21.11.75) Kakinada (4.12.75) and Hindupur (2.12.75)

[Comparable incidents are described in Nalgonda, Hyderabad, Warangal, Srikakulam, Visakhapatanam, East Godavari and Kanataka.]

*Kanataka*

Shri Sheikant Betegeri, a youth of Belgaum offered Satyagraha on 14.11.75 along with a batch of Sri Ganpatrao Kulkarni, an industrial well-known social worker. He was severely beaten. Shri Chinnappa Kalled, another satyagrahi from Belgaum and Shri Ashok Mutgekar, a young college student of Belgaum who offered satyagraha on 30.11.75, were put on 'aeroplane', a third degree method whereby the entire body is subjected to excruciating pain. Ashok lost consciousness.

A batch of 8 youths offered Satyagraha at Dharwar on 14.11.75. They were all beaten in police custody. The worst sufferers were Sri Mahindra Shrur, the leader of the batch and Ravindra Desai, a popular youth worker.

Shri Anjaneya Shirur, Head Master, Model Girls' High School, Dharwar was severely beaten.

Shri Shrikant Desai, of Hubli, a final year law student, and State Joint Secretary of the Karnatak unit of Vidyarthi Parishad was inhumanly beaten and put on 'aeroplane' on 27.11.75. Shri Padmanabh, Harihar

(Chitradurga Distt.) and Sri Puttu Swamy were not given food. They were beaten with canes and kicked with boots. They were put on 'aeroplane' and then let off.

Shri Ravi, leader of the student Satyagrahis, was arrested on 2.12.75, at Mysore. After the arrest he was beaten, kicked and finally put on 'aeroplane' in the Devraj Police Station by the Sub-Inspector of Police.

Shri Udaya Shankar, a young student leader of Canara college Mangalore, was taken from his house without warrent by the police on 12.11.75. The police Sub-Inspector, Sri Uttaiah manhandled him, brutally kicked him in the Bunder police station. His body turned red and blue. He was not given water or food. All this was in the presence of the Superintendent of police, Sri Chopra. But obviously this brutality was not considered sufficient. Udaya Shankar was put on 'aeroplane' not once but thrice. He was unable to talk. Shri Anant Hegde, Pandurang Hegde and Garesh Kudwa, three merchants from Mangalore, were taken into custody by the police on 13.11.75. For three days they were kept in the Bunder police station, without proper food or sanitary arrangements. All the three days they were caned and kicked. They could neither bend their knees nor walk. On the 4th day they were handcuffed (against the law) and made to walk the entire distance to the magistrate. When Sri Anant Hedge asked for drinking water the police came near him to pass urine. Shri Shrihari and Narayara Bangera satyagrahis from Kadaba, a village in South Kanara District, were kicked and caned by the drunken police at the station on 20.11.75. They were so brutally beaten that they lost consciousness. They were thrown out of the police station in that very condition. They had to go to their homes after gaining consciousness past midnight. Shri Gopalrao, a B.Sc. student of Bangalore, who offered satyagraha on 24.11.75 was kept in Seshadripuram police station for four days. He was not given food for two days. He was brutally beaten and placed on 'aeroplane'. He remained unconscious all the while he was on the 'aeroplane'.

Shri Raghupati, a M.A. student at Bangalore, was arrested by the police. He was not given food. He was put on 'aeroplane' twice. Shri Shrinat, a student of National college, Bangalore, was arrested on 27.11.75 as he offered satyagraha. He was brutally beaten in the police station and put on 'aeroplane'.

At Udupi on 26.11.75 and at Shimoga on 24.11.75 there were severe lathi charges twice on the college students when they were going in a mammoth procession to protest against the Emergency.

Shri Devendra, Municipal Councillor of Narasinharajpura, Chikmagalur District, offered satyagraha on 20.11.75. Hundreds of citizens joined the procession of the satyagrahis in that small township. The police Sub-Inspector rained blows on his face and felled him down. The police physically dragged him to the police station in the presence of all the on-lookers.

In Kazargod taluka, Kerala State, all the batches of satyagrahis who offered satyagrahas on different days at Kasargod, kumble Manjeshwar and Milleria were severely lathi charged. A number of satyagrahis received severe head injuries and had to be admitted to the local hospital. A number of satyagrahis, after being brutally beaten, were tranferred several miles from their places of arrest and were thrown out of the vans. No food was given to the satyagrahis while they were in police custody.

Smt. Narsamma Garudappa, Bangalore, a woman satyagrahi was arrested on 15.8.75. She was pregnant. She was brought to the hospital for delivery. Her leg was tied with chains to the cot. Shri Sesha, a graduate and full time social worker at Bangalore was rubbed all over the body with poisonous caterpillars. Shri Narasinha Rao, M.A. student at Bangalore, was beaten and put on 'aeroplane' for 20 minutes. "AEROPLANE" The victim's hands are tied behind his back with a rope. The rope is taken over a pulley at the roof and the victim is pulled up a few feet above the ground. The victim dangles in mid-air hanging by his hands tied behind his back.

Other reports of severe beating by the police includes the case of Agondra (student) of Mysore and five other students (3.12.75) Govind Bhatta and four others of Harihar (25.11.75), Pulkeshi student of Bangalore (14.11.75) N. H. Suresh, Suresh Naik, Govindhar, D. T. Srivaram and Someshwar (students) of Bangalore and the satyagrahis at Kananur and Saketeshpura (28.11.75).

The Bangalore Bar Council has unanimously adopted a resolution denouncing the police misbehaviour with Sri Gundaish Shetty, Advocate, President of Bangalore City Bar Association and demanding action against those responsible.

The Advocates' Association, Bangalore (Regd.)

Bangalore
Date: December 9, 1975.

The following resolution was passed unanimously at the Special General Body Meeting of the Advocates' Association, Bangalore, held on the 9th December, 1975, at 2.05 P.M.

The Advocates' Association protests against the handcuffing of Political Prisoners and detainees including the President of the Association and ill-treatment of Political Prisoners by the Police.

General Secretary

Memorandum submitted by a Lawyers Delegation on behalf of the Advocates Association to the Chief Secretary, Karnataka Govt.

To

The Hon'ble Chief Secretary,
State of Karnataka,
Bangalore.

Sir,

Sub: – Reported hand-cuffing of Members of the Bar and ill-treatment of persons arrested either under the provisions of MISA or under the DIR connected with political reasons.

......

We are enclosing herewith a resolution passed unanimously by the Bangalore Bar Association in a Special General Body Meeting held on 9.12.75 for your kind perusal and appropriate action. The General Body was called and a resolution was passed under the following circumstances.

On 5.12.75 the President of Bangalore Bar Association Sri Gundaish Shetty who has been detained under the provision of MISA, was brought to the Munsiff Court where he had to tender evidence as a witness, under hand-cuffs and he was made to walk the distance before the members of the public. We are sure that you will appreciate that this action on the part of the Police is unwarranted and arbitrary. There has been a report that a senior member of the Bar Tumkur viz. Sri Vonkataramaiah who offered satyagraha in connection with the demand for revocation of Emergency, release of arrested persons and removal of Press censorship was also hand-cuffed by the Police at Tumkur. It is also reported that Sri Bagali Shivand Swamy, an Advocate at Davangere was also similarly hand-cuffed.

We invite your kind attention to para 15(ii) of the Model Prison Manual published by the Govt. of India on the question of hand-cuffing for Under-trial Prisoners which is to the following effect:

15 (ii) Undertrial Prisoners should not normally be hand-cuffed except (a) prisoners involved in serious and violent offences (b) the prisoners having notorious or dangerous background (c) violent, aggressive and refractory prisoners and (d) prisoners who have previously escaped.

Apart from hand-cuffing there are reports that persons are subjected to abusive language. Further from the several Habeas Corpus Writ Petitions filed before the High Court, it is disclosed that persons arrested are being retained under the custody of the Police for several days without authority of law and are being subjected to physical torture, and it is only after the writ petitions are filed before the High Court, that persons who were arrested being produced before the Magistrate. The retention of arrested persons beyond 24 hours is not authorised by law, nor are the police authorised to take the law into their own hands and subject the arrested persons to physical torture.

It is on account of the strong resentment among the members of the Bar against these action of the Police that the General Body Meeting was called and the enclosed resolution passed unanimously. We are bringing the above facts to your kind notice so that persons are not hand-cuffed and ill-treated in contravention of the law.

We are sure that you will be pleased to issue the necessary directions in this connection so as to avoid such actions by the Police.

*Kerala*

In the Congress-Communist coalition ruled state Kerala stripping naked and merciless beating was the normal treatment of the satyagrahis.

As a rule as soon as a satyagrahi is arrested and led into the station he is stripped leaving only his ingot or underwear. In a station of Haripad it did not stop with that. Status or no status, doctor or lawyer, all are equal before this Police law. One must consider it his luck if he is produced before the Magistrate within 24 hours. As long as the arrested satyagrahis are in Police custody no tea, coffee or food is given. There have been specific instances of starving them for even four or five days. Sri Gopal Kurip was in police custody for 4 days and no morsel of food was given to him during these days. When he was let free he could not take even a few paces forward. He dropped by the road-side till some good Samaritan helped him.

Some of the methods used to torture prisoners in the lock-ups are:

[The list which follows is almost identical with the one already quoted, but with the addition of j) and k):]

j) When he gasps for breath asking him to jump up and down till he sweats.

k) All the time the dirtiest abuses are hurled at the satyagrahi.

Generally all this is done collectively by a team of 10 to 12 constables encircling the satyagrahis. If the torture has left visible marks on the body or reduced the prisoner to a tell-tale physical condition the police would not produce the prisoner before the Magistrate, for fear that he may reprimand them. If a search warrant, the police would shift the victim from station to station. The MISA has come to their rescue since no immediate relief is available to those arrested under it. For each item mentioned above the harrowing experience of satyagrahis can be given.

*Cannanore* – The lathi charge on 14th November was the worst. 12 satyagrahis were beaten until the lathis broke in pieces. After leaving the beaten on the main road the police inspector carried the leader of the batch to the nearby Maidan and further beat him until he fell unconscious, leaving a constable to prevent people from giving any first aid. The S.I. went away in his jeep. Even that constable suspected the fallen man to be dead and was seen putting his hand in front of his nostrils to see whether the victim was still alive. It was an advocate, Sri Raghavar who rushed to help the unconscious man and take him to the hospital. The Circle Inspector who led this action was Sri Nandan Menon and the S.I. was Pulikod Narayana.

*Idukki* – High Ranges – Udunbanchola Taluka – Pattom Colony Mundiyeruma 16.11.75 3 p.m. custody lock-up beatings by S.I. and constables.

Prabhakaran, Thangappan and Vasu – Nothing except urine to drink. On 16th November a constable came to Prabhakaran, Thangappan and Vasu farmers by profession and said that the S.I. wanted to meet them. They were called to the police station at Mundiyeruma. This was 3 p.m. There was no questioning up to 3.30 p.m. At 8.30 they were given materials to sleep. At 11.00 p.m. when it is biting cold in these high altitude regions (4,000 to 5,000) the S.I. came in fully drunk with a five cell long torch. He shouted who is Thangappan? No sooner had he got up from his deep sleep than the thunder blow with the torch fell on his head. Kicks followed. As earlier planned about six other equally, or perhaps more drunk, walked in. Asking about the details of the bulletin 'Kurukshetra' Prabhakaran was continuously beaten until he became unconscious. Blows were rained on his chest with the butt of the rifle. Vasu was made to lie face upward and heavy blows with elbows were given on his chest. They were given nothing except kicks, blows and abuses in abundance. The next day the victims craved for an ounce of water to quench their thirst. Thangappan wanted it badly at 3 a.m. The constable scolded him and asked him to pass urine and drink it. The thirsty youth had ultimately to pass urine and drank it.

*Calicut* – Farook – 14.11.75 S.I. Gopalkrishnan, Suresh Peter Mannu, etc. Out of 11 satyagrahis only three were produced before the Magistrate. Two others were produced only on 21st after a search warrant had been issued. Meanwhile they had been subjected to the kind of beating that has already been described.

*Quilandy* – 14.11.75 – 10 satyagrahis, only 8 were produced before the Magistrate. Here too drinking water was not given. S.I. 1) Joy 2) Raju.

*Kunnamangalam*: 14.11.75 – 10 satyagrahis – 8 produced before the Magistrate. The other two beaten by D. 1075 and another constable named John.

*Mavoor* – S.I. Thomas, Constable Vallabhadas, D. 1962 D. 2831 lock-up beatings – special feature – chair-sitting pose – Date of satyagraha 22.11.75 – same experience for the earlier batch 19.11.75. On 19th November in the Thoppumpady Junction of Cochin Shri Purshottam Pai offered satyagraha along with ten friends, and again on 2nd December at the Ravipuram Junction of Ernakulam. Their two slogans 'Bharat Mata Ki Jay' and 'Vande Mataram'. As soon as they were asked to enter the van the police party lined up in two rows, and as they entered blows were delivered on their backs. They were taken to Kumbara Police Station of Ernakulam. 10 to 13 constables encircled them, each kept between his knees the head of one satyagrahi, and began to rain blow after blow with right and left elbow on his spine. Sometimes the knees were removed all of a sudden and the victim fell upon his face. The moment he fell down he was pulled up or kicked up, taken by the shoulders and bent back and pounded with the knee on the spine. This was repeated twice or four times. During all this 'treatment' if or when one fell or dropped down he was lifted and on both his ears simultaneously slaps were given. All this continued up to 11.30 a.m. In the afternoon the questioning started. K. Purushottama and Hari of Moovathupusha (he was the leader of the group that came from there) were singled out. Others were again ill-treated. They were asked to sit with their legs stretched and their soles were caned until the canes broke.

Hari was slapped over the ears as described earlier. K. Purushottama was punched again and again on the right eye. It bulged out. The blow on the eye was instantly followed by a torrent of kicks on the back. This was all being closely witnessed by S. I. Sukumaran, and such other instances were repeated at Alleppy on 20.11.75. The satyagrahis were Shri C. Sivadas, Sri Mathu, M. Sc. Chandran and Appu of Pandalam, Mohandas Preman, Raman Namboodiri of Ambalapush, Radhakrishnan Sarasan of Thekkokara, Sahadevan and Mari of Alleppy – total 11.

The officers who conducted torture here were Principal S. I. Srecnivasan South Circle, Inspector – Baly Syrac, the Head Constable – Achari, Crime Branch S. I. Jayaprakash.

*Madhya Pradesh*

Probably the maximum number of political prisoners are in this central Indian State, the second largest in the country. Inhuman treatment and torture are common here. In the capital city of Bhopal a seven year old child suffering from polio was taken into custody to force the mother to come out from underground. When she came out she was imprisoned. The imprisonment of close relatives to get at political leaders gone underground is common here. In Gwalior the district jail is overflowing with political prisoners who are often kept alongside notorious dacoits undergoing a life term. The atrocities perpetrated here are numerous. So much so, an Opposition M.P. has gone on indefinite fast to force jail authorities to treat political detainees properly. The list of cases of torture and ill-treatment are appended herewith:

On 5th December 8 persons took part in a satyagraha at Dewas. They were beaten all the way while they were being taken to the police station, where they were asked to sleep naked. When they refused to take off their clothes even their underwear was torn off by the policemen. The police inserted wooden rulers in their private parts. They were forced to do unnatural acts (Sodomy) with each other under compulsion. They were forced to put genitals in each other's mouths. They were told that they should go out in procession shouting "Atalji murdabad," "Jansangh murdabad" through the city or else they would be forced to sleep with their own daughters. They were threatened that they would be made to eat beef and subjected to sunnat, and under duress they were made to resign from the Jana Sangh. Afterwards they were arrested under I.P.C. 151 and asked to furnish bails. At 11 p.m. when even bails were duly given, all the persons, including those who had given bail were forced to sleep in the police station. At 4 a.m. they were asked to get up under the pretext that they had to meet a senior official. They were then taken to Kannaud forest and left there. The purpose was to ensure that none of them could be present when the cases were taken up in the court next day, so that bail could be forfeited. All this was done in the presence of and under the direction of the Superintendent of Police.

The Madhya Pradesh Lok Sangharsh Samiti has already written to the Prime Minister, the Home Minister, the Chief Minister and others communicating this information and demanding a judicial enquiry.

[Comparable incidents are described in Assam, Bengal and Rajasthan. From Delhi the following is extracted:]

Om Prakash aged 21 who was arrested for offering satyagraha was denied sleep, food and water for two days, and was mercilessly beaten, specially on the neck. He was twice hung upside down, chilli solution poured into his nose with a rod tied to his back. While in this position a rod was poked into his testicles to make the torture more heinous. Later he was made to stand for two days at a stretch. This happened on Nov. 25, 26, 27 while in lock up at the Timarpur police station. Mr. Rasik Agrwal aged 20 (commerce graduate) was similarly tortured at the Timarpur police station on Nov. 28, 29 and 30. Every method of torture stated above was applied on him. He ultimately succumbed and gave out the name of Shri Om Prakash (other than the one mentioned above) as one of his associates. The police went to latters house, but he did not happen to be in. His wife was asked by the policeman to hand over the satyagraha posters which she told him she did not have. She was kicked and abused.

Two young children named Sunil and Majoj were picked up on 17th Nov. at about 10 p.m. from Jogiwara by the Haus Qazi police just to oblige some local Congress (Indira) workers. They were beaten up till they finally broke down to make a planned (by police) confession. They were taken to various residences and were forced to call names. Since the called persons did not appear to be in at one place the father (aged 60) and the wife were taken to the police station. They were made to sit in the cold throughout the night, along with a two months old baby without milk. They were later produced before the Duty Magistrate under DIR.

The ire of the Indian police has been particularly directed against intellectuals. More than 200 teachers of Delhi University were arrested in the pre-dawn swoop of June 26. Even sick and old were not spared. One of them, Prof. O. P. Kohli, President of the Delhi University Teachers Association, who is lame, was made to stand for 24 hours at a stretch in the police lock up while the policeman showered him with abuses, shoe beatings and even pushed him from side to side with sneering remarks. Many a time he fell down at which he was again picked up and made to stand. Teachers had been picked up while lecturing classes. Dr. Prashant, Reader in Hindi, who had his leg fractured and was immobilished for quite a long time, was arrested. Many teachers who were released through some court order were re-arrested at the gates of the jail with fresh charge sheet for the same crime, or no charge at all. Only the united protest of the academic community was able to stop this wave of re-arrests, but many distinguished Delhi teachers, principal O. P. Dogra of the Rajdhani College among them, are still prisoners, and a number of them are being persecuted.

*Haryana*

*Ambala.* A batch of 5 volunteers led by Shri Jai Prakash offered satyagraha on Nov. 23 at Ambala Cantonment with Sarvashri Vijay Kumar, Dinesh Kumar, Sushil Kumar and Dinesh Kumar, all college students. All of them were kept under unlawful confinement till Nov. 28. During this period all of them were beaten with rods and canes. They were also ordered to remove all their clothes except for their underwear on the nights between 24 and 26 Nov, and were made to stand in the open on the roadside. Inspite of the fact that Haryana goes very cold during these days buckets of cold water were poured over their naked bodies. They were not allowed to sleep at all. On 28th Nov. the hands and legs of Shri Jai Prakash were tied with ropes and he was made to sit on a cycle rikshaw. His face was painted black. Afterwards he was taken around the town. At some places the rikshaw was stopped and some persons were forced to spit on Shri Jai Prakash's face. Whenever he raised a slogan he was beaten with a rod by six policemen who were moving the rikshaw. In Dal Bazar he was beaten most mercilessly by the police. At Yamunagagar a batch of three volunteers, viz. Shri Malikchand, Shri Satya Paul and Shri Pawan Kumar courted arrest on Nov. 25. They were brutally beaten at the police station. On Nov. 27 all of them were made to hold their shoes on their heads and were paraded in all the main bazars in the town. A number of policemen were accompanying them on the way. The satyagrahis were being constantly beaten with canes and kicked. Some persons were also made to spit and urinate on their faces. On the evening of Nov. 28 Shri Pawan Kumar fell unconscious and remained in that state for 3 hours.

[Similar incidents were described from Karnal and Rotak in Haryana and a formidable list followed from the Prime Minister's State, Uttar Pradesh. Other reports of similar torture include:]

| *Date* | *Place* | *Victims* |
|---|---|---|
| 1.12.75 | Patlone | Ramprasad, Khubiram, Dalchand |
| 1.12.75 | Bararasipur | Bhoopsingh |
| 2.12.75 | Narhouli | Girji Prasad (student) |
| 5.12.75 | Thana | Deependra Kumar, Arun Chaskar Rameshchandra Agrwal |
| 5.12.75 | Mawana Kalan Thana, Dist. Meerut. | Brahmansinha, Sukhvirsinha and Fatesingh |
| 6.12.75 | Delhi Gate | Rajeshkumar Gupta, Padmakar Datta Sharma, Banwarilal and Radhakrishna |
| 9.12.75 | Kanpur | Mahesh Pr. Gupta, Dinesh Kumar and Kailash Chandra |
| 26.11.75 | Kanpur | Arunkumar Srivastava |
| 29.11.75 | Kanpur | Ramkanta Gupta |
| 1.12.75 | Kanpur | Suresh K. Sinha Arora |
| 6.12.75 | Kanpur | Nandakumar Shukla |
| 9.12.75 | Kanpur | Ashvinikumar and Kahhaialal |
| 9.12.75 | Kanpur | Madan Mohan Davar |

## VII. Exhibit D: "Passage through India, Whip of the New Raj"[38]

*by* Professor Ved P. Nanda

Personal affairs required me to travel to India again last month. As an Indian national and professor of international law at the University of Denver Law School, I had tried to keep myself well informed about affairs in India. I knew from following American press reports that Indira Gandhi's government had imprisoned many political opponents, and I had several times publicly expressed dismay at the trend of events under the declared state of emergency. But little did I understand the extent to which the government was using repressive measures to stifle its opposition.

On arriving at the Delhi airport, I was detained for interrogation, although I carry an Indian passport and did not need a visa to enter the country. "What are you here for? Any political objective?," I was asked. "My mother has been ill. I came to see her."

I then told the interrogating official that as a law professor I had a Christmas holiday, which afforded me the time to travel to India. "Doesn't matter, we've detained professors of law under the emergency powers before." The official shrugged his shoulders and warned me that my activities would be closely watched.

During the next two weeks I had an uneasy feeling that at times I was being followed by intelligence officials. And when I was ready to leave India, I was faced with more bureaucratic hassles. "You don't have the necessary cholera inoculation. Your passport doesn't look authentic," I was told at the airport. I was relieved when I was finally permitted to board the plane.

What I saw and heard during my stay has made me realize that, in sharp contrast with the image which Indira Gandhi's government strives to project abroad, India, a showpiece of democracy for the first twenty-seven years of its independence, is fast becoming a repressive police state. The government has steadily tightened its grip on an already crippled and stifled press, which has buckled under harsh censorship laws. This accounts at least in part for the inadequate coverage of authoritarian measures now being employed by the government to silence both the political opposition and dissident elements within Mrs. Gandhi's ruling Congress Party.

Jagdish P. Mathur, secretary of the All India Jana Sangh, a major opposition political party, related to me several incidents of alleged police brutality in the treatment of political prisoners. I met with Mathur, an opposition leader sought by the police, who had up to that point escaped arrest and was very active in organizing the underground movement, to discuss these oppressive measures and the strategy of the opposition parties. Among the names of the victims Mathur gave me were those of many Delhi residents, some of whom had been released. A doctor, a lawyer, a university instructor, two student leaders and a businessman were those with whom I talked during the next few days to confirm Mathur's allegations.

They all told a similar story. The police applied crude means either to extract a confession to a nonexistent plot against Indira Gandhi or to seek information concerning the whereabouts and next moves of the organizers of the underground movement.

The devices for torture which are being used in police stations and jails in India are as varied as they are inhumane and revolting. The victims who talked with me related incidents where they or other political prisoners were hung upside down; were stripped naked and severely beaten with shoes, steel rods and gun butts; had burning candles applied to their bare soles, which were then punctured with nails; had chili powder smeared into their noses and other parts of their bodies; were kept awake while icy water was thrown on them on cold winter nights; were starved and even denied water; had rods tied to their necks, creating an intolerable strain on the spinal cord.

The doctor I met was not personally tortured. However, while he was in jail as a political prisoner, illegally detained on trumped-up charges, he had treated more than twenty prisoners who, he said, must have been "mercilessly beaten." The sole fault of the lawyer, arrested on the charge of being a "hooligan," was, he said, that he had appeared in court on behalf of a political prisoner. A member of the Indian Supreme Court Bar Association showed me a resolution adopted by that organization which condemned police atrocities and harassment of attorneys defending opposition members. The Bar Association noted that even the families and relatives of such attorneys were not spared police wrath.

From Delhi I took a train to see my mother, who lives in the state of Punjab in northwest India. There I met a recently released leader of the opposition, Madan Gopal, a prominent businessman in the small town of Malerkotla. He was charged with plotting the violent overthrow of Indira Gandhi's government.

"I never met the informant, Vikram Singh; who reportedly overheard the alleged conspiracy," he said. For more than three months Gopal was detained in jail without even a court hearing.

Upon my return to Delhi in the third week of December, I saw two anti-government demonstrations (*Satyagrahas*). These were part of a country-wide movement launched by the united opposition last November 14. In a typical *Satyagraha*, individual demonstrators (Satyagrahis) – ranging from four to fifty in number – shout slogans against Mrs. Gandhi's government and pass out anti-government literature in busy streets. The demonstrators usually wear garlands, people assemble around them and, since the time and place are announced in advance, the police promptly arrest the demonstrators.

Each *Satyagraha* I saw in Delhi had about forty active participants who courted arrest and attracted more than 5,000 spectators. The crowds, predominantly opposition sympathizers, repeatedly shouted slogans demanding an end to the state of emergency, release of political prisoners and the restoration of civil liberties. In one case, the police resorted to a mild *lathi* charge (swinging long wooden poles and clubbing onlookers) before arresting the *Satyagrahis*.

According to opposition sources (whose information is hard to verify), more than 40,000 persons have courted arrest in cities all over India. They claim that the number of political detainees and *Saryagrahis* has exceeded 100,000, certainly not a small number even in a country of 600 million people.

The media in the West have been reporting on the steady erosion of civil liberties in the aftermath of the new six-month-old "emergency." But the press here, dependent upon Indian sources for its news, has suffered from the same censorship which now curbs the Indian press. As a result, it has virtually ignored two important developments in India – the mistreatment and torture of some political prisoners, and the Satyagraha.

These are significant developments because, until recently, political prisoners could be assured of humane treatment. Even the Indian independence leader and the father of the civil disobedience movement, Mohandas Gandhi (no relation of Mrs. Gandhi) and Mrs. Gandhi's own father, Jawaharlal Nehru, were themselves never mistreated in jails under the British rule. The actions of the Indian police toward political prisoners fly in the face of Indira Gandhi's protestations that she is defending and protecting democracy while her opponents are bent on destroying it.

Despite its substantial efforts, I found the opposition disorganized and demoralized. Its leaders were shocked by the suddenness of the declaration of emergency, as well as by the severity of the government's silencing measures. That initial shock is now followed by an equally grim realization that the "emergency" will continue much longer than had earlier been anticipated and that elections scheduled to be held in March 1976 will be postponed for a year, and perhaps for a longer time. (According to *The New*

*York Times* of February 4, they can be postponed a year at a time as long as the emergency is in effect.)

The opposition does not seem to have a definite plan for a follow-up action to the *Satyagraha*, which ended in January. However, those with whom I spoke seem to understand well the need for a united front. "Either we build a united opposition party, resolving our differences, or we sink separately," is how one opposition leader put it.

A blueprint has already been devised to merge several opposition parties. These parties – some of them on the right of the ruling Congress Party, others on the left – do not include Marxist parties which are split among several factions – the Moscow wing, the Peking faction and the Naxalites who stand even further to the left of those vowing allegiance to Peking.

Several opposition leaders are convinced that Mrs. Gandhi chose the totalitarian road at the urging of Russia. They kept reminding me of the large contingents of Soviet technical experts staying at the posh Inter-continental-Oberoi Hotel in New Delhi, who were "in fact counseling and advising her on the appropriate steps to lead India down the primrose path of 'guided democracy.'" This opposition charge, however, is largely unsubstantiated.

Mrs. Gandhi has in the past successfully used a foreign specter to rouse nationalist ire and sentiment. She has skillfully taken advantage of the CIA's involvement in Chile as a warning against possible foreign involvement in India's internal affairs. Similarly, she has occasionally invoked "potential threats" from China and Pakistan to externalize India's internal problems.

It is highly speculative to predict the course of events in India. For the time being, at least, democracy is in full retreat. Were elections to be held today, even the opposition leaders I met acknowledge that the ruling Congress Party would likely be a big winner. Among the many reasons for such an outcome would be: bumper agricultural crops in 1975 and a slowdown of inflation; general apathy of the rural masses, who comprise more than 75 per cent of the country's population; the strong-arm tactics of Mrs. Gandhi's government, which have frightened the electorate, and a general lack of faith in the ability of the opposition parties to work together.

Indira Gandhi still has a charismatic appeal to the illiterate masses (after all she is Nehru's daughter and her name is Gandhi) and a cult of personality has developed around her. Her son, Sanjay Gandhi, known as the *chhoti sarkar* (the mini-ruler) and reportedly being groomed by her to take over, is being merchandised aggressively both in political circles and in the media.

However, India's basic economic and social problems, especially those of land reform and explosive population growth, remain unsolved. And despite the government's propaganda that under the emergency people are more disciplined and productivity has increased, corruption is rampant and the masses are apathetic.

On reflection, the only healthy development for the Indian body politic I saw is the prospect of a unified opposition. Meanwhile, the diplomatic community in New Delhi and India's well-wishers at home and abroad are anxiously watching events, hoping that the current state of emergency is a temporary aberration, the end of which will once again herald the return of democracy in India.

## VIII. "Indira Gandhi and the Village Bosses"[39]

*by* James Manor

In a recent address at Yale, India's Ambassador announced that Indira Gandhi's abandonment of electoral democracy had at last produced real progress toward social and economic equity for the rural poor of his nation. A student then asked why we should believe that the Congress Party, which had apparently made little headway toward this goal in more than a quarter-century of pre-eminence in Indian politics, could suddenly become a force for radical change. It is a question worth exploring.

The most important aspect of this or any political event in India is its impact upon the rural areas, where nearly 80 per cent of the population still lives. The dismay of educated urbanites is very real, very understandable and by now very familiar. But it is from the perspective of the villagers that Mrs. Gandhi's actions must ultimately be judged.

An analogy from the realm of religion will shed light on the relationship between decisions in New Delhi and events in the villages. Anthropologists have found that local practices in rural temples often diverge radically from the "Great Tradition" of Hinduism. For example, villagers in many areas pay only lip service to the high deities of the "Great Tradition," whose roles in Hinduism bear little concrete meaning for their daily lives. Yet these same villagers often lavish attention and alms upon deities known only locally, who are said to have powers to solve everyday problems such as disease or drought, but whose mythical roles stand at odds with higher Hindu teachings. The many localized "Little Traditions" at the village level often stand the India-wide "Great Tradition" of Hinduism on its head.

Something like this occurs in Indian politics as well. Mrs. Gandhi, like her father before her, has for years risen in Parliament to announce bold new laws to promote equality and eradicate caste in the countryside. As in Nehru's day, the Congress Party's majority in Parliament has acclaimed and passed these laws. State legislatures all across the subcontinent, most of which have also been under Congress's control, have generally followed suit. Thus is established the Prime Minister's socialist "Great Tradition." But in politics as in religion, by the time the "Great Tradition" percolates down to the village level, something very often goes awry.

Since the 1930s, the Congress Party has been controlled by the rich peasant castes which provide its power base. These groups rule at the village level in the hierarchical "Little Tradition" of rural India and they would suffer more severely than any other group should Mrs. Gandhi's radicalism be put into action. A redistribution of land and wealth would deprive them of much of their status and power. The eradication of caste would sweep away the governing principle of social relations in rural India.

The dominant castes, whose representatives in Parliament have cheerfully assisted the passage of Mrs. Gandhi's egalitarian laws, quietly sabotage their implementation. By intimidation and enticement, they prevent civil servants from applying these measures. Thus the "Great Tradition" of Indian politics fails to penetrate to the village level. Mrs. Gandhi is less the leader of the Congress Party than its prisoner.

One of the most outrageous examples of this has been the frustration of efforts to stamp out bonded servitude. Under this system, wealthy peasants lend money to their poorer neighbors at usurious rates. They then ensnare the poor or their children as unpaid workers to cover runaway interest which can never be paid off. A 1971 survey of villages in one of India's more advanced states found that although untouchables no longer had to give their daughters over in bond, the system which bore many of their sons away was as deeply entrenched as ever. A government report published in 1973 indicated that this form of servitude was a nationwide phenomenon.

Since the days of British rule, high officials have periodically announced all-out onslaughts on this pernicious institution and in October India's President (an ally of Mrs. Gandhi) decreed yet again that the "bonded labour system stands abolished with immediate effect."

This is even less likely to occur now than before the crackdown of last summer. The main perpetrators and beneficiaries of the bonded labor system are the wealthy peasants who control the Congress Party and prevent the implementation of progressive laws in rural areas. The suppression of the old open politics has strengthened these dominant castes by muzzling opposition to the Congress from whithout and by curtailing competition and renewal within the party.

Well-informed sources with access to the Prime Minister continue to insist that her expressions of concern for the rural poor are genuine. They even claim that she knows that her dependence upon the dominant castes must be broken if she is to translate her concern into action. This may be true and the state of emergency may spring in some obscure way from progressive motives. But after five months, it appears that the dominant castes have tightened their grip over rural India yet again and that the long-suffering villagers have less to look forward to than ever.

## Notes

1. The courts in November, 1975, held Amendment 40 void.
2. The Lok Sangharsh Samiti (People's Struggle Committee) is composed of the four principal opposition parties, Jana Sangh, Congress (o), Socialists, Bharatiya Lok Dal.
3. See Amnesty International, Exhibit B, *Politicians and Parliamentarians arrested under Emergency Regulations in India following a Declaration of Emergency on 26th June 1975*, item (12).
4. *Ibid.*, (13).
5. WCRP Report, World Conference on Religion and Peace, Second Revised Edition.

Dr. Jack has visited India eleven times since 1955, including two visits during 1975. He was active in the India League of America in the 1940's and has edited two anthologies of the writings of Mohandas Gandhi. He has investigated violations of human rights in his own country – the U.S.A. – and in South Africa, South Korea, South Vietnam, the Philippines, East Pakistan, Czechoslovakia, and the Soviet Union. He is Secretary-General of the World Conference on Religion and Peace.

The following recent Memoranda on human rights, written by Dr. Homer A. Jack, and published by the World Conference on Religion and Peace, are also available:

H23. *The Human Rights Commission at Geneva*, by Homer A. Jack. 9 pp. March 1975. 60¢.

H24. *238 Words Toward Religious Freedom*, by Homer A. Jack. 21 pp. June 1975. 60¢.

H25. *Oppression, Suppression, and Repression in South Korea Today*. 28 pp. 1975. $ 1.00.

Write for a full list of Memoranda on human rights. Make checks payable to WCRP and order from WCRP, Room 7B, 777 U.N. Plaza, New York, N.Y. 10017, U.S.A.


6. *India June XXVI*. Washington: The Embassy of India. 1975.
7. "Prime Minister Indira Gandhi Responds to Charges that Democracy in India is Dead." An Interview in *The Saturday Review*. August 9, 1975.
8. *The National Malady: Root Cause*, by Jayaprakash Narayan. Wardha: Sarva Seva Sangh. 28 pp.
9. Cited in *Is JP The Answer?* by Minoo Masani. Delhi: Macmillan. 133 pp. 1975. p. 51
10. Masani, *op. cit.* p. 29.
11. "The Crisis in India," by Kumar Mehta. This is a privately-issued, eight-page memorandum. The author is Professor of Engineering Science at the University of California at Berkeley.
12. "The Great Writ," by S. J. Sorabjee. *Seminar* (New Delhi). December 1975.
13. *The Saturday Review, op. cit.*
14. *The Review*. Geneva: International Commission of Jurists. No. 15. December 1975.
15. *The Economist* (London). January 24, 1976.
16. *Newsweek*. February 16, 1976.
17. *Swaraj* (London). No. 14. (January) 1976.
18. "Whip of the New Raj," by Ved. P. Nanda. *The Nation*. February 21, 1976.
19. *Timely Steps*. New Delhi: Ministry of Information and Broadcasting. August 1975. 77 pp. p. 11.
20. S. J. Sorabjee, *op. cit.*
21. *Freedom First*. Bombay: Democratic Research Service. No. 278. January 1976.
22. "Press Freedom," by R. K. P. Shankardass. *Seminar*. Devember 1975. Also "'Please Kill: Withdrawn by Censor,'" by J. Anthony Lucas. (*More*) (New York). February 1976.
23. "The 'Express' Affair: New Delhi's Story," by Lawrence Lifschultz. *Far Eastern Economic Review*. January 23, 1976. "Indira's Fifth Column," by Denzil Peiris, *Ibid.*, Feb. 20, 1976.
24. *Le Figaro* (Paris). January 23, 1976.
25. *Indira's India: Anatomy of Dictatorship*, by George Fernandes. London: Free JP Campaign Publication. December 1975. 22 pp. p. 18.
26. *Far Eastern Economic Review*. Feb. 20, 1976.
27. *Everyman's Weekly*. April 20, 1975.
28. *Le Figaro. op. cit.*

29. *The Overseas Hindustan Times.* March 4, 1976.
30. Nanda, *op. cit.*
31. The full text is in *The Far Eastern Economic Review.* Feb. 20, 1976.
32. *The New York Times,* Feb. 29, 1976.
33. *Asahi Evening News,* Tokyo. June 27, 1975.
34. *Far Eastern Economic Review.* Feb. 20, 1976. *op. cit.*
35. Suggestions for re-establishing confidence within India and even changes in the polity and Constitution of India are beyond the scope of this pamphlet. Rajni Kothari in "End of an Era" brilliantly describes the breakdown of the consensus in India today and how if Mrs. Gandhi were not convicted in the High Court of Allahabad, some other development would likely have produced a crisis, resulting in the Government's bringing to a virtual halt the constitutional processes. Asserting that "it is not enough to return to the status quo ante as it prevailed before June 26," Kothari urges the launching of a "Second Republic" with a new constitution, but one that is "more democratic, more socially purposive, more institutionalized at the grass-roots and intermediate levels, and one that liberates the Indian people from the clutches of a narrow-based and self-aggrandising elite." *Seminar.* January 1976.
36. "Democracy in a Poor Country," by Ved Mehta. *The New Yorker.* March 22, 1976.
37. "Torture of Political Prisoners in India," March 1976, a 14-page report supplied by Indians for Democracy, an organization of Indians residing in the U.S.A., who received it from the Lok Sangharsh Samiti (People's Struggle Committee) in India. The Committee is composed of the four principal opposition parties, Jana Sangh, Congress (o), Socialists, Bharatiya Lok Dal.
38. "Passage Through India, Whip of the New Raj," by Professor Ved Nanda, *The Nation,* February 21, 1976, upon return from India. He is professor of law and director of the international legal studies programme at the University of Denver College of Law.
39. "Indira Gandi and the Village Bosses" by James Manor, *The Nation,* February 21, 1976. James Manor teaches modern South Asian History at Yale University, USA.

# Women in Bangladesh

ROUNAQ JAHAN

ROUNAQ JAHAN was born in Dacca, Bangladesh, in 1944. She graduated from Dacca University, Bangladesh, in 1963 and received her Ph.D. from Harvard University in 1970. She was a Research Associate at the Southern Asian Institute of Columbia University 1969–1970 and at the Center for International Affairs, Harvard, 1971–1972. At present she is an Associate Professor and Chairman of Political Science Department, Dacca University, Bangladesh. She is the author of *Pakistan: failure in national integration* (New York: Columbia University Press, 1972) and co-author of *Divided nations in a divided world* (New York: McKay, 1974). She has contributed a number of articles in journals. Her major research interests are problems of political development in the Third World countries and status of women.

# Women in Bangladesh*

ROUNAQ JAHAN

It is difficult to write about the women of Bangladesh. Little published material is available on women. Statistical data are outdated because the last census was taken in 1961. The vast majority of Bangladesh's 35 million women live in *purdah*,[1] and little is being said or written about their problems. This lack of data on women is partially explained by the difficulties that researchers (usually male) face in studying women in a *purdah*-dominated society. Additionally, as women are nonvisible and unorganized, their problems are not articulated and hence they fail to draw the attention of researchers.[2] But the fact that nothing is being written about the problems of women in Bangladesh does not mean that the problems do not exist. Indeed the women of Bangladesh are among the most oppressed in the world. This paper attempts to highlight this oppression and to anlyze some of the problems they face today.

The study is divided in three parts. Part 1 describes the lifestyles of women in Bangladesh. A distinction is made between the various categories of women – rural and urban, traditional and modern, working class and middle class. The divergent lifestyles in these categories are analyzed to illustrate the basic inequity – the great distinction between the elite and the mass – that exists in any developing country. The elite women (who are urban and modern) have a very different lifestyle from the mass of the women in Bangladesh (who are

---

* I would like to thank the Ford Foundation, which reproduced and made this report available for discussion in advance of its formal publication. The views expressed are those of the author and do not necessarily represent views of the Ford Foundation.
This article was originally published in *Women Cross-Culturally: Change and Challenge*, edited by Ruby Rohrhich-Leavitt, World Anthropology, The Hague and Paris: Mouton, 1975, pp. 5–30.

rural and traditional). But while their lifestyles are different, both categories of women are oppressed, though the levels and modes of oppression differ. Part 2 of the paper deals with the legal, economic, political, and social status of women in Bangladesh. The dichotomy between the legal and socio-economic status of women is emphasized to indicate their actual status. Part 3 discusses the gradual evolution of the movement for women's emancipation in Bangladesh. The role of the various women's organizations is analyzed. It is hypothesized that because the women's organizations are highly elitist in nature they play only a marginal role in emancipating the women of Bangladesh.

The study is based on some one hundred open-ended interviews that the author conducted with women in Bangladesh in the spring and summer of 1973. The women interviewed included all categories: urban and rural housewives and career women, students, political workers, and persons active in women's movements and organizations. Some parts of the study, especially Part 1, are based on data derived largely from interviews. However, only Muslim women are discussed in this paper. The observations made are not applicable to the Hindu, Christian, and Buddhist women, who constitute roughly 15 percent of Bangladesh's female population.

## I. Women of Bangladesh: Rural and Urban

To describe the lifestyles of women in Bangladesh, one has to distinguish between those of rural and urban women. The overwhelming majority of Bangali[3] women are rural; only about 5 percent of the population is urbanized. While most of the rural women can be broadly classified as traditional, not all urban women can be called modern. If modernity is defined in terms of literacy, urbanization, and adoption of a modern occupation, then only a small fraction of Bangali women can be classified as modern. Of 35 million women in Bangladesh, only 1.75 million are urban; of these urban women a mere 32 percent are literate and only about 1.27 percent adopt a modern occupation. As modern women constitute a miniscule minority of Bangali women, it is useful to describe in some detail the lifestyle of rural women who form the mass of the women in Bangladesh. If generalizations are ever to be made about the women of Bangladesh, it has to be done in terms of the rural women.

*Rural Women*

A brief description of a rural woman's life from birth to death facilitates an understanding of her lifestyle. In the rural areas the birth of a girl is rarely celebrated by parents and relatives, unless she happens to be the first daughter after four or five sons. That usually no *azan* [call for prayer] is given when a girl is born symbolizes the community's disinterest in the girl's arrival.[4] From early childhood on, girls are made fully conscious of the feeling that, unlike their brothers, they are liabilities. Girls are taught the two virtues – patience and sacrifice – of ideal Bangali womenhood.[5] They also learn to accept the essentially inferior status of women in society. As girls grow up they perceive the preferential treatment given to the male members of the family, and they are told that getting less of everything and not complaining about it is the ideal behaviour of good women. In a *milieu* of scarcity, whatever is available – food, clothing, or opportunities for education and health care – is offered first to the men. If the family can afford good food, i.e. meat or milk, the father and sons have the first and major share. If the family has enough resources to send children to school, boys get preference over girls, even if the girls are brighter.

From her childhood a girl is trained to fit into the only socially acceptable role, that of wife and mother. By the time a girl reaches the age of five or six, her mother has produced two or three additional children, and the young girl has to look after them. She also helps her mother in other household chores, i.e. cooking, cleaning, sewing, etc. In rural areas few girls are sent to school. According to the 1961 census, only 21.9 percent of rural females between the ages 5 to 14 (compared to 46.7 percent of males) were enrolled in school. Girls are given some schooling only by economically and socially established families. And that schooling usually consists of learning to read and recite the *Quran* [the Holy Book] and four or five years of formal school attendance. The major purpose of formal schooling is very similar to that of the girl's informal learning at home, i.e. training her to be a good wife and mother. A girl's stock in the marriage market goes up if she has some formal schooling (Ahmad 1966). Educated men prefer wives who can at least read and write letters and keep basic accounts. "Respectable" families[6] in rural areas therefore give their daughters some formal schoolings so that they can be married to educated men employed in urban areas.

Village girls usually drop out of school after the fifth or sixth grade. Only 1.7 percent of rural women above the age of fifteen are enrolled in school, compared to 20.8 percent of men. Girls discontinue schooling at an early age for two main reasons. First, by the time a girl is in the fifth or sixth grade, she has completed basic training in reading, writing, and arithmetic, and any further education is regarded as unnecessary, if not harmful, for a happy married life. Second, after she reaches the age of 12 or 13, a girl has to drop out of school for *purdah* considerations. Few villages have high schools for girls, and the village *samaj*[7] frowns upon girls attending coeducational schools after they have reached puberty. Also, because many villages do not have boys' schools, girls' enrollment becomes even more problematic. A woman's *purdah* observance is more rigidly enforced outside her own village (Ahmed 1966). While it is difficult for a girl to study in a boys' high school in her own village, it is nearly impossible for her to go to a neighbouring village to study.

In rural areas it is customary for girls to go in *purdah* when they reach puberty. But even before that, a girl is made aware of the two separate worlds of men and women. A woman's world is her home, while the man's world is outside the home. Separation of the two worlds is enforced by the pervasive *purdah* system. Women perform tasks at home (cooking, cleaning, nursing children, sewing, etc.), and men negotiate with the outside world (working in the fields, shopping, etc.). Only in very rare cases does a man help his wife in her household tasks, and few women work in the fields, no matter how poor the family is. Here Muslim society in Bangladesh differs from other Muslim countries, e.g. Indonesia, where women work freely in the field and in the market place. However, Bangali rural women do share in tasks that involve earning family income. Women clean and husk rice, prepare fuel, make sugar, and tend the kitchen garden, but their role in earning family income is never acknowledged. Farming is a "two-person" occupation (Papanek 1973)[8] where the wife's role is non-paid and non-recognized. Thus while the two worlds of men and women are interdependent, a woman's world is always regarded as inferior to the man's world.

The rigidity of *purdah* observance, like the extent of schooling, depends very much on the socio-economic status of the family. An easy index of the rising socio-economic status of the family is the increasing rigidity of *purdah* observance. Economic status and *purdah* observance are correlated because only prosperous families can afford to put their women in *purdah*. *Purdah* observance involves two kinds of restrictions on women's movements (Papanek 1971). The first is spatial: women are confined within the walls of their homes, a separate women's wing, separate tank for women's bathing and cleaning facilities, and separate toilet facilities for women. The second type of restriction allows a woman to move out of her home, but only if she is veiled in *burqah* [tent-like veiled clothing for women] or travels in veiled transports (carts, boats, or rickshas with heavy curtains drawn around them). To ensure spatial restriction on women's mobility, the family has to be realtively wealthy, so that it can allocate enough living space and separate tanks and tube wells for its women. The second category of restriction also requires money. Only rich farmers can afford to buy *burqah* for their women; average rural women have only one or two saris.

In poorer rural families, the women have to leave their households and go to the houses of rich farmers to fetch water, to bathe, and to work as part-time household help. When leaving their houses, these women cover their heads with their sari to symbolize their *purdah* observance. And when they visit relatives in the neighbouring villages, they go walking in the evening and use umbrellas as veils. Thus, while the rigidity of *purdah* observance varies among families, at puberty all girls are required to start observing some *purdah*, whether total seclusion at home or imposition of some restrictions on contact with men.[9]

At puberty, not only are girls put in *purdah* but their marriages are also arranged by their families. In rural areas girls are usually married between the ages of 12 and 15. Girls are married early because by 11 or 12 they complete all the informal and formal training necessary for their only socially acceptable roles – those of housewife and mother. Furthermore, after a girl reaches puberty she is regarded as "vulnerable," needing "shelter," and the safest course open to her family is to arrange a marriage for her so that she can move into a permanent shelter (Papanek 1971).[10]

Marriages are always arranged, and the father and other male members of the family have the dominant say in the matter. As the marriage arrangement requires negotiations with the outside world, it is handled by the male guardians of the girl (Ahmed 1966). In Muslim marriage, a girl's consent is mandatory, but the consent is a mere formality.

After her marriage, a girl moves to her husband's household. In the first few years of marriage, her position is very insecure. In her husband's house, a bride has to observe a stricter *purdah*, her mobility is even more curtailed, her work load increases, and the two virtues of Bangali womanhood – patience and sacrifice – instilled in her as a child, are put to a hard test. Her position is inferior to that of the other women of her husband's house, i.e. her mother-in-law and sister-in-law. The only way she can get security in her husband's household is by producing a male heir. The more male children she has, the greater is her security and acceptance.[11]

On the average, a rural woman has eleven or twelve pregnancies. She may have one or two miscarriages, two or three of her children may die young, and six or seven children may survive. She has little control over her body; the decision to have children is totally her husband's. Rarely does a rural woman practice any form of birth control. A survey in Comilla indicated that after six years of widespread publicity about family planning, only about 4 percent of women practiced some measures of birth control (Stoeckel and Chowdhury 1973). Abortion as a means of birth control is sometimes practiced by the poorer section of the rural population but it is considered a sin.

By the time a woman reaches the age of thirty, she is often a grandmother and is regarded as an old woman. Divorce and remarriage are more frequent in rural areas, especially among poor farmers. According to one study of a village in Comilla, approximately 16.5 percent of all marriages ended in divorce (Peter Bertocci, personal communications). In socially established families, divorce is frowned upon. A divorced woman, if she is young, is usually remarried, because an unattached woman, be she single, widowed, or divorced, has no social standing. Additionally she is a financial burden. Young widows are also remarried, sometimes to their brothers-in-law to keep the family property intact. After a certain age, however, it is difficult for widows and divorced women to get married. *The master survey of agriculture*, published in 1961, listed a sharp increase in the number of widowed females after the age of 34, with no such corresponding increase in the number of widowed males, which only indicates that while Bangali men can and do remarry at all ages, women can not (East Pakistan Bureau of Statistics 1961). If a widow or a divorced woman remains unmarried, she has to live under the guardianship of either her father or brother, or father-in-law or brother-in-law. In short, a woman is never regarded as capable of taking care of herself. Before marriage her father is her guardian, after marriage her husband takes that role, and after her husband's death her son becomes her guardian.

*Urban Women*

In Urban areas, there are sharp differences in the lifestyles of various categories of women. Here we would distinguish between two: working-class and middle-class women. There is a third group of westernized women, but they are small in number and play a marginal role in society.

The lifestyle of urban working-class women is not very different from that of rural women, the only difference being the relaxation of *purdah* observance in an urban setting. The majority of urban working-class women are new migrants to cities and they maintain close rural ties.[12] As in rural areas, the birth of a girl is unwelcome and the early socialization process is very similar. Girls from working-class families are also made aware of the separate worlds of men and women, though their housing is conducive to relaxation of *purdah* observance. From childhood, working-class girls are trained to be housewives and mothers. They have to carry the major burden of household chores, including care of baby brothers and sisters, because their mothers go outside to work. The literacy and school enrollment rates among working-class women are low. Most girls leave school after fifth or sixth grade. The drop-out rate is high partly because the family cannot afford to send the children to school and partly because women's education in working-class families is not customary.

Working-class women are married early, ordinarily by the age of 15 or 16. Marriages are usually arranged by parents, but as there is a greater scope for contact between the sexes, some love matches do take place. Divorce and remarriage are frequent. Like rural women, urban working-class women have little say over such a vital matter as the decision to have children. They have nearly as many pregnancies, miscarriages, and surviving children as the rural women.

Working-class women cannot observe strict *purdah*, but they do not repudiate the concept of *purdah*. Indeed, in their minds *purdah* is associated with respectability, and they do observe *purdah* when their economic status becomes more secure. When asked whether they would want their daughters to observe *purdah*, the majority of working-class women answered in the affirmative (personal interview). *Purdah*, in the sense of modesty, restriction on contact between the sexes, and shelter for women, is a universally accepted value in Bangladesh.

Of all the categories of women, only among urban working-class women do we find many women who are their own guardians. Even in cases where there are male guardians, the women are more assertive. This deviant behaviour pattern is explained by their being wage earners.[13] Compared to their rural sisters, working-class women are more politically conscious and organized. Working class women constitute the bulk of all the women's processions brought out by political parties. But while their rate of political participation is high, they are not feminists. This will be elaborated in Part 2 of the paper.

"Modern" Bangali women are urban middle-class women, whose lifestyles are visibly different from that of rural women or working-class women. Ostensibly the modern woman has an easier life and more leisure, but like all modern women in a traditional society, she lives in two worlds. While rural women are more blatantly oppressed and discriminated against, the oppression of and discrimination against urban women is subtle.

The birth of a girl is not a happy event even in an urban middle-class family, though her parents quickly become reconciled to a daughter. She is socialized differently from a rural girl. She grows up in a nuclear family; has greater contact with her brothers, father, and other male members of the family; and her opportunities for education are nearly equal to those of her brothers. The informal learning process at home, where she is taught how to cook, clean, sew, and look after babies, does not start as early for an urban girl. And she is expected to finish school before she is married.

Urban middle-class women do not observe rigid *purdah*, but they do live in a separate world of women. Segregation of sexes starts at puberty. Girls may not wear the veil, but restrictions are put on their mobility and on their contact with males. Between the ages of 11 and 17, boys and girls go to separate schools; and though the university is co-educational, contact between male and female students is restricted. Here again, separate space is allocated for women: there are separate reading rooms and lounges and in classrooms women students occupy separate seats (usually the first two or three rows). A woman may spend four years in a co-educational institution and not exchange four sentences with her male classmates. Indeed, the less contact she has with males, the better her reputation as a good woman.[14]

Marriages are arranged for urban middle-class women. Most women are married between the ages of 19 and 24. Only in rare cases does a woman remain single beyond 24. Single women have no social status even in urban areas, and a good marriage is regarded as the ultimate goal of a woman's life. An overwhelming majority of urban, educated women still accept and prefer arranged marriages because there is little opportunity to meet members of the opposite sex. Girls also have little confidence in their own abilities to find established husbands and they trust their fathers' judgment in arranging suitable matches for them. Nearly all the university students who were interviewed showed an anxiety over security and preferred arranged marriages.

A small percentage of urban middle-class women adopt a career. In a recent survey of a part of the Dacca municipal area, about 10 percent of urban women were found to be working, though nearly 34.4 percent of these women are university graduates.[15] Women's career choices are very much determined by the *purdah* society's imperative of two separate worlds. Papanek (1971) argues that teaching and medicine are regarded as the two most respectable occupations for women because of the presence of a large female clientele. In a *purdah* society women are preferred as doctors for female patients and as teachers for female students, and hence there is a great demand for women in these occupations. Similarly occupations that bring women in contact with men, e.g. nursing and secretarial work, are regarded as non-respectable. In contrast to the pattern in Western countries, many more women go into medicine than into such women's occupations as nursing and secretarial work.

A women's career choice is also determined by her family. Her father usually will decide whether she should study and what she should study. It is again her father or her husband who decides whether she should have a job and what type of a job she should have.

An urban middle-class woman, if she has a job, has some say in the couple's decision to have babies. She often practices some form of birth control. Career women usually have fewer children than a housewife, who tends to have five to six children. The notion of a planned family appears to be acceptable only to the younger generation of urban women. Divorce and remarriage are rare among the urban middle class. Divorce brings disrepute to the whole family and hence is looked down upon.

Thus an urban middle-class woman's life is different from a rural woman's in that she has greater opportunities for education and a career. But she can enter a man's world only by exploiting another class of women – maidservants, mothers, and mothers-in-law – who take over her household tasks and thus provide her with the free time needed for outside work. Even in an urban middle-class family the household tasks are not shared by the husband of a career woman, except for the care of babies, in which the younger generation of men show an interest. Men refuse to share in household work because it is regarded as women's work and hence inferior.

That a woman's status should be inferior to a man's is a thesis universally accepted by Bangali men. In a recent survey of two localities – one rural and one urban – 70 percent of rural men and 80 percent of urban men, compared to 39 percent of urban women, agree with the statement that "It is natural and right for women to have inferior status to men" (author's election survey). Interestingly enough, on the question of whether women should participate in politics, 52 percent of urban women approved of women's participation compared to 55 percent of rural men and 64 percent of urban men. Thus the response of urban men is inconsistent. While 64 percent of urban men support women's participation in politics, only about 20 percent of them regard women as equals. Their deep bias against women is obvious.

An urban middle-class woman is considered as vulnerable as a rural woman, as much in need of male protection and shelter. She is rarely her own guardian; almost always a male relative is the guardian. Thus the basic relationship between men and women remains constant in rural and urban areas. An urban woman has greater mobility, but she can achieve and retain that mobility by not challenging the superior social status of men.

## II. Status of Women: Legal, Economic, Political, and Social

Much is said and written about the legal status of Muslim women, and indeed, compared to the other South Asian religion, Hinduism, Islamic women are treated more equally by the *sharia* (Islamic personal laws). But there is a great difference between the legal status and the socio-economic status of women. Their insecure socio-economic status prevents women from exercising their legal rights.

### *Legal Status*

Three noteworthy legal rights are given to Muslim women by *sharia:* rights regarding marriage, divorce, and inheritance. In Islam marriage is a contract, and the consent of both partners in front of witnesses is required. Because marriage is a contract, divorce is allowed. The marriage contract itself enumerates the conditions under which each partner may initiate divorce proceedings. In the marriage contract provision is made for *Mehr* – a fixed sum of money, part of which is payable to the bride after the wedding ceremony and the rest payable only in case of a divorce. Both the husband and the wife can start divorce proceedings, but it is by far much easier for a husband to divorce his wife. Islamic law allows a man to divorce his wife by simply pronouncing his intention to do so in front of witnesses.[16] A woman is allowed to obtain a divorce by returning the *Mehr*. Such divorces – known as *Khul* – are rarely practiced these days. At the time of divorce, a woman who has minor children can get custody of them, but she can never get their guardianship, which remains with the husband.

Another much publicized legal right of Muslim women is their right to inherit property. After a man's death, his widow inherits one-eighth of his property; and if he dies childless, she inherits one-fourth; daughters inherit one-half of the sons' shares.

But though the law recognizes women's rights in marriage, divorce, and inheritance, in practice women can rarely take full advantage of these rights. As mentioned earlier, a woman's marriage is arranged by her father or other male guardians and she usually consents to such arrangements. Only in rare cases would a woman stand up against the expressed wishes of her guardians.[17]

In cases of divorce, men usually take the initiative. Though the Muslim Family Laws Ordinance, passed in 1961, put a number of restrictions on the male's *sharia* rights regarding polygamy and divorce, in practice prevailing social norms still permit men greater freedom to practice polygamy and initiate divorce.[18] Women initiate divorce only among the poorer sections of population, but here, too, the initiative is taken by the woman's father or other male guardians. Among the poor, *Mehr* is regarded as a bride-price, and the bride's male guardian demands payment of part of the *Mehr* after the wedding ceremony. Often a woman is married several times so that her male guardian can collect more *Mehr*. Among the middle class, the actual payment of *Mehr* is rarely made. Even when a woman is divorced, *Mehr* is renounced because that improves the chances of her remarriage. Men are reluctant to marry divorced women who demand *Mehr* (Ahmed 1966). Few middle-class women initiate divorce, because it involves litigation and is regarded as a disreputable act.

There is a similar gap between a woman's inheritance rights and the actual practice. Widows always demand inheritance, but it is used by their sons. If a widow demands inheritance, she is expected to live in her husband's household and not to return to her parents. It is customary for daughters to renounce inheritance in favour of brothers unless the family is either very rich or very poor. Daughters give up inheritance in exchange for *naior* (Ahmad 1966) – the right to visit the father's house once or twice a year after the father's death. Women give up inheritance for a number of reasons. Partly it is a social custom. The majority of women interviewed argued that they gave up inheritance to be on good terms with their brothers. In case of divorce or widowhood, they would need their brothers' assistance, guardian protection, and sometimes they would come back (especially in case of divorce) to live in their natal homestead. So they did not want to strain relations with their brothers by claiming their inheritance, which was their legal due, and thus risk being rejected by their brothers. Additionally, women who give up inheritance in favour of *naior* indicate their preference for mobility. For a woman, *naior* days are the only days of vacation in a year. In her father's house, a woman has greater mobility, *purdah* observance is less strict, and she is relieved of her household chores. Thus, renouncing inheritance for *naior* appears to be a fair exchange, because inheritance is used by the husband but *naior* is a woman's exclusive vacation. In a social system where a woman always needs a guardian, her legal rights are exercised by the guardian on her behalf.

### *Economic Status*

As discussed in Part 1 of the paper, being a wife and a mother is the only goal of a Bangali woman, and few take up a career. Roughly 10 percent of women are in the civilian labour force and only about 1 percent of these adopt a modern occupation. As Table 1 shows, out of 2,553,212 women in the civilian labour force in 1961, only 214,715 were in the non-agricultural labour force; the rest were in the agricultural labour force. Thus the overwhelming majority of working women live in the rural areas. In urban areas, the largest number of women are employed in factories; Table 1 indicates that nearly half of the female non-agricultural labour force were in manufacturing and mechanical occupations. Urban women are employed in such low-

TABLE 1. *Civilian labour force by main occupational groups and sex (12 years and above)*

| | *1951* | | *1961* | |
|---|---|---|---|---|
| | *Male* | *Female* | *Male* | *Female* |
| Civilian labour force | 11,887,080 | 999,260 | 14,317,776 | 2,553,212 |
| Agricultural labour force | 9,899,006 | 816,461 | 11,997,999 | 2,338,497 |
| Non-agricultural labour force | 1,988,074 | 182,799 | 2,319,777 | 214,715 |
| Professional, technical, and related occupations | 115,713 | 5,231 | 180,686 | 8,195 |
| Managerial, administrative, and clerical occupations | 207,335 | 666 | 201,582 | 944 |
| Transport and communication | 115,744 | 314 | 145,999 | 182 |
| Manufacturing and mechani-caloccupations | 410,081 | 70,137 | 576,706 | 118,516 |
| Sales and related occupations | 477,452 | 24,877 | 504,744 | 18,513 |
| Agricultural, fishing-trapping, and logging occupations | 184,619 | 10,797 | 121,862 | 363 |
| Construction occupations and general labourers | 284,665 | 36,184 | 240,528 | 3,806 |
| Service, sports, entertainments | 191,456 | 34,592 | 230,435 | 58,013 |

Source: Adapted from Government of Pakistan (1961: Table 1A, 96–97).

TABLE 2. *Non-agricultural labour force by occupation and sex, 1961 (ten years and above)*

| *Occupational groups* | *Both* | *Male* | *Female* |
|---|---|---|---|
| Non-agricultural labour force | 2,570,953 | 2,350,044 | 220,909 |
| Professional, technical, and related occupations | 189,021 | 180,800 | 8,221 |
| Architects, surveyors, and engineers | 4,117 | 4,106 | 11 |
| Chemists and physical scientists | 318 | 305 | 13 |
| Physicians, surgeons, dentists, and medical specialists | 7,152 | 6,952 | 200 |
| Nurses and midwives | 3,763 | 783 | 2,986 |
| Professional medical workers and medical technicians | 29,212 | 28,286 | 926 |
| Teachers | 100,883 | 97,342 | 3,541 |
| Lawyers, judges, and magistrates | 4,889 | 4,879 | 11 |
| Administrative and managerial, clerical, and related workers | 202,730 | 201,784 | 946 |
| Proprietors, directors, and managers | 30,812 | 30,627 | 185 |
| Governmental and public service administrators and officers | 2,632 | 2,612 | 20 |
| Sales workers | 528,308 | 509,626 | 18,682 |
| Proprietors and managers and retail traders | 15,774 | 15,707 | 67 |

Source: Adapted from Government of Pakistan (1961: Table 2, 98).

paid jobs as factory labour, street cleaning, and construction work, as well as in professional and technical occupations, e.g. teaching, medicine, and nursing. Middle-class women usually enter teaching, nursing, sales work, research and other related professional "women's" occupations. Table 2 shows that very few women enter traditionally male occupations. In 1961, while there were 3,541 female teachers and 2,986 nurses and midwives, there were only 11 architects and engineers, 13 scientists, 200 physicians, 11 lawyers and judges, and 20 public administrators. In contrast to women in such South East Asian countries as Burma and Thailand and in East and West Africa, few Bangali women go into business. In 1961, only 185 women, as compared to 30,627 men, were classified as proprietors and managers of industrial and business offices. Only 67 women, versus 15,707 men, were in retail trade, and this number might be even smaller – men often register businesses in their wives' or sisters' or mothers' names to publicly cover the real ownership.

Similar to women's occupational patterns in other countries, the majority of women are employed in low and middle-salaried jobs, with very few women in top administrative or decision-making posts. As the top administrative posts are manned by ex-C.S.P. (Civil Service of Pakistan) and ex-E.P.C.S. (East Pakistan Civil Service) members, organizations where women's participation was restricted, women have little input in decision-making processes. Unlike India, where women compete in the foreign service and administrative service examinations, in Bangladesh women were barred from these jobs during the Pakistani days. There is no woman in the Bangladesh foreign service, or in the higher echelons of the various ministeries and the Planning Commission of the Bangladesh government. Administration and planning in Bangladesh are all-male affairs.

The pyramidal structure of the women's employment pattern is also visible in educational institutions. More women are employed as lecturers than as principals of colleges, chairpersons of departments, or deans of various faculties in the universities. In Dacca University during the 1972–1973 session, of a faculty of 566 there were 86 women. There were 166 male Ph.D.s and only 9 women Ph.D.s; 5 women professors and associate professors, and only two women chairpersons of departments. None of the deans were women.

It is, however, interesting to note that few women feel job discrimination. None of the women interviewed, especially those in middle-class occupations, felt that they were discriminated against on the basis of sex in recruitment, in salary distribution, or in promotion. This is an expected response. In other countries, also, women felt little job discrimination before their consciousness about it was raised. Another reason appears to be that since there are only a few women in various jobs, they are usually not in a competitive position with men and hence do not pose a threat. Additionally, even when a woman takes up a career, she keeps to her place. Except for the time she puts in her job, she remains in the women's world and does not question the socially sanctified superior status of men. A career woman is therefore no threat to a man's ego; rather she is a financial asset, as her income helps balance the family budget. Quite frequently an educated, urban man proudly introduces his wife as "my wife who is an M.A. and a professor," or the like. In a society where education is universally valued,[19] having an educated wife enhances a husband's social status.

In sum, very few Bangali women take up an occupation, especially a modern occupation. But once they are in a job, particularly a middle-class job, they face little discrimination. It is difficult for women to break the barriers of tradition, but after they break them, there is greater acceptance.

### *Political Status*

Bangali women won their basic political right, the right to vote, without a fight. It was granted to them by the British colonial government at the same time as it was granted to Bangali men. In all elections from 1937 on, women constituted nearly half of the country's electorate, but their only political role consisted of casting their votes. Bangali women's participation in the movement for Pakistan was marginal. In the hierarchy of the Muslim League there was no woman. There was a separate women's wing of the party, and the major function of women in the Muslim League was to recruit the support of Muslim women for electoral purposes. No attempt was made to organize the women on feminist issues or even to get a pledge of the male leadership on such issues.

In a *purdah* society, the ethos of separate worlds for men and women permeates even politics. Thus separate seats are reserved for women in the parliament and in the political parties women work only in the women's wings. The Bangladesh Constitution provides for 15 reserved seats for women in the Parliament. These women are to be elected, not by the female electorate of the country, but by the three hundred male members of parliament. The constitution does not prohibit women from campaigning for general seats. Indeed, two women contested but failed to win general seats in the March, 1973, election. The reserved seats deter political parties from nominating women for the general seats, as the prominent party women can easily be accommodated in the reserved seats. Similarly, because of the existence of separate women's wings in the parties, the top post a woman can aspire to in any party hierarchy is that of women's secretary. In only one of the existing political parties does a woman hold the post of organizing secretary (Mrs. Motia Chowdhury of National Awami Party, Muzaffer group). There were no women in the first two cabinets, and the two women ministers of state predictably hold the traditionally female portfolios of education and social welfare.

Women are still far from being politically organized. They played a marginal role in the various political movements of the country in the last two decades. Few women took active part in the national liberation movement. While thousands of young men were recruited in the Mukti Bahini (freedom fighters), only a handful of women took arms training, and a few hundred women worked as nurses and teachers in the freedom fighters' hospitals and refugee camps. Only as the victims of the liberation war did the Bangali women receive world-wide publicity. Soon after Liberation, the government of Bangladesh disclosed that thousands of Bangali women who had been raped by the Pakistani soldiers were then made social outcasts. The failure of the various women's organizations to mobilize public support or, for that matter, women's support for the raped women indicates the weak politicization of Bangali women.

### *Social Status*

A woman's social status is separate from, and inferior to, a man's. The religious community takes little notice of the existence of women. Women do not participate in any congregational prayers – e.g. the Friday prayer, the *I'd* prayer (one of the Muslim holidays), or the funeral prayer. Women are deeply religious, but they practice the various forms of prayer individually and in private. Although the idea of *umma* [community] is important to Muslims, women are excluded from any community celebrations. In some of the Muslim countries of the Middle East, women do participate in separate women's congregational prayers, but Bangali Muslim women do not. *Purdah*, the social imperative of sexual segregation, isolates women and confines them to their individual homes.

Papanek (1971) argues persuasively that because *purdah* society regards women as highly vulnerable, there is a need to "shelter" them and to control their impulses. "Impulse control is achieved with the help of restraining social institutions, in ways which are closer to 'shame' mechanisms of social control than those associated with 'guilt'" (1971: 519). The non-acceptance of raped women in Bangladesh is a good illustration of the operation of the "shame" mechanism. If a woman is raped and it can be kept a secret from her social circle, then she is acceptable. It is not raping *per se*, but the *samaj's* knowledge about it that brings disrepute to the family. When a women is violated, the family is more concerned about the loss of face than about her physical and mental health. One organization, which worked with the war-affected women in Bangladesh (the National Board of Bangladesh Women's Rehabilitation programme), informed the author that it maintained strict secrecy about the cases of violated women because their chances of social acceptance depended on it. Where parents were alive, a violated daughter was always accepted back by the parents. Only in rare cases were women who had been in Pakistani army camps taken back by their husbands. These women were not acceptable because the fact of their violation was known by the *samaj*. But many women whose violations were not publicized were accepted back by their husbands after they underwent secret abortions.[20] The National Board of Bangladesh Women's Rehabilitation in Dacca received 22,500 applications from raped women. Of them 19,500 were illiterate and 3,000 were literate; 15,030 were rural and the rest were urban. The majority of cases were not reported because of the family's desire to maintain secrecy.

This anxiety over secrecy is illustrated by the reluctance of Bangali women to talk about the problem of the women who were violated during the war. The majority of women interviewed stated that, while they were agitated by the problem, they rarely discussed it. The father of the nation reflected the same anxiety when he coined the term "war heroines" for women raped by Pakistani soldiers. The term camouflages the state of these women and is less disreputable and shocking than the term "violated" women. The fate of these war-affected women, together with the failure of the non-affected women to mobilize support for the acceptance of these women, reflects the totally vulnerable social status of women.

## III. Women's Movements and Women's Organizations in Bangladesh

The movement for the emancipation of Muslim women in Bengal started in the 1920's. The emancipation of women was closely associated with the modernist movement among the Muslims, and it received sympathy and support from the modernist men. In the twenties and thirties, the movement was primarily concerned with women's literacy, and did not raise questions about employment opportunities or the equal status of women. These questions came up only at the later phase of the movement.

Roughly, the movement for women's emancipation in Bengal can be divided into three periods. The first phase (1910–1947) saw the questioning of rigid *purdah* observance and the demand for women's literacy and school enrollment. The 1920's and 1930's were the periods of *Khilafat* movement and the development of Muslim nationalism in India. The movement for the emancipation of Turkish women and other Middle Eastern women at this time inspired Muslim modernists in Bengal to agitate for women's emancipation at home.

The leadership in the first phase belonged to women from traditional landlord families, many of whom were Calcutta-based and non-vernacular but who later achieved fluency in the vernacular. The movement for women's emancipation was started by a woman from a traditional, landlord family who was married to a "modernist" civil servant. Rokeya Sakhawat Hussain (1880–1932) was not only the pioneer of the women's emancipation movement, she was a true feminist. Indeed, she is the only feminist in the leadership of the women's movement. None of the women who came after her could be called feminists. Rokeya Sakhawat Hussain keenly felt the oppression of the rigid *purdah* system. In her father's and husband's houses she lived in *purdah*, and she had to fight against heavy odds to educate herself. Rokeya felt that the only way a woman could be emancipated was through education, which would enable her to achieve economic independence and to renounce strict *purdah*.

Rokeya was both a publicist and an activist. She wrote a number of short stories, articles, and a novel, all of which depict the stultifying life of women in a *purdah* society. In all her writings, she made scathing attacks on the unequal relationship between men and women and propagated the cause of women's emancipation. In *Sultana's dream* (1905) Rokeya portrays a social system where men are kept in seclusion and women handle all the traditionally male jobs.

In 1911, Rokeya established the first Muslim girls' school in Calcutta, which started with eight students. For twenty years she worked in the school despite bitter criticisms from orthodox Muslims. At the time of her death in 1932, the school had 123 students. In 1916, Rokeya also established a women's organization, Anjuman-e-Khawatein-Islam, which was essentially meant to draw out the Muslim women from traditional families.

After Rokeya's death in 1932, there was not a single women who made the cause of women's emancipation her lifelong interest. In the thirties and forties, there was a small group of Muslim literary women who wrote occasional pieces on women, but these women served more as models for women's emancipation than as active participants in a movement.

The 1947 partition of India and Bengal marked a radical change in women's status and role. The second phase of the women's movement (1947–1970) saw the growth of women's organizations in urban areas. Muslim women took the place of Hindu women in all the women's organizations. In the second phase, though women's organizational activities increased, there was no recognizable movement for the emancipation of women. During this period a large number of women were emancipated, but their emancipation was the result of the general process of modernization and was not due to any feminist movement. There was less of a women's movement in the second phase than there had been in the first.

The most important women's organization that developed during this phase was the All Pakistan Women's Association (APWA). The APWA in Bangladesh was a branch of the central APWA, which had local branches in all the districts and sub-divisions. The APWA had very close ties with the government and the power structure of the country. The leaders were the wives of powerful political and administrative figures. In the districts and sub-divisions, the wives of district and sub-divisional officers were invariably the presidents of the APWA. In Dacca the APWA presidency shifted between the wife of the chief minister and the wife of the governor, depending on the relative power of their husbands in the political system. As the APWA leadership changed with the administration, the organization failed to develop leadership among women. The APWA was very much like a social club of elite women which arranged social and cultural get-togethers. In Dacca APWA women did some voluntary work; they ran schools and managed sewing and handicraft centres. But the APWA's major activities were still confined to the concept of neighbourhood women's clubs. The APWA's major role was to act as a meeting place for middle-class Muslim women who had been in strict *purdah* and were not even used to meeting other women in an organization.

TABLE 3. *Enrollment of male and female students in primary and secondary school and university in Bangladesh 1947–1966*

| Academic year | *Primary school* | | *Secondary school* | | *University* | |
|---|---|---|---|---|---|---|
| | *Male* | *Female* | *Male* | *Female* | *Male* | *Female* |
| 1947–1948 | 1,812,330 | 209,372 | 418,914 | 44,106 | 1,593 | 27 |
| 1948–1949 | 1,900,916 | 630,408 | 504,830 | 43,786 | 1,941 | 44 |
| 1949–1950 | 1,766,040 | 566,629 | 470,549 | 47,253 | 2,237 | 67 |
| 1950–1951 | 1,835,244 | 457,516 | 472,241 | 42,271 | 2,016 | 67 |
| 1951–1952 | 1,868,431 | 606,486 | 434,843 | 45,014 | 2,306 | 85 |
| 1952–1953 | 1,979,744 | 675,021 | 412,893 | 40,548 | 2,209 | 95 |
| 1953–1954 | 1,983,314 | 669,971 | 398,631 | 43,818 | 2,328 | 103 |
| 1954–1955 | 1,938,329 | 666,040 | 410,558 | 46,739 | 2,716 | 142 |
| 1955–1956 | 1,937,730 | 708,526 | 425,299 | 47,821 | 3,130 | 219 |
| 1956–1957 | 1,980,263 | 731,507 | 443,391 | 54,208 | 2,934 | 191 |
| 1957–1958 | 2,039,041 | 755,874 | 431,799 | 59,246 | 3,198 | 252 |
| 1958–1959 | 2,170,915 | 814,343 | 435,435 | 59,600 | 3,680 | 282 |
| 1959–1960 | 2,139,111 | 841,256 | 465,202 | 65,283 | 3,465 | 301 |
| 1960–1961 | 2,405,194 | 925,388 | 466,223 | 66,679 | 3,622 | 348 |
| 1961–1962 | 2,497,333 | 925,899 | 503,617 | 71,250 | 5,432 | 385 |
| 1962–1963 | 2,663,472 | 973,025 | 563,599 | 95,746 | 6,628 | 512 |
| 1963–1964 | 2,709,397 | 1,142,925 | 640,799 | 104,818 | 6,885 | 779 |
| 1964–1965 | 2,830,469 | 1,213,710 | 719,298 | 129,214 | 8,831 | 888 |
| 1965–1966 | 2,951,541 | 1,284,495 | 794,591 | 154,895 | 7,830 | 1000 |

Source: Adapted from Government of Pakistan (1947–1967: 170–173, 186).

The decades of the 1950's and 1960's saw a rapid increase in women's literacy and school enrolment. As Table 3 shows, the rate of increase in female enrolment in schools and universities was much greater than the rate of increase for male students. These rates are of course deceptive, because the base for women was so low at first. The increase in the number of career women was also substantial. As a result, a number of women's organizations developed, especially in the capital, Dacca. In addition to the APWA, nine other women's organizations were established in Dacca at this time. Many were neighbourhood women's clubs, e.g. Gandaria Mahila Samity (formed in 1950), Wari Mahila Samity (formed in 1954), and Purana Paltan Ladies Club. All these associations were formed by the "enlightened" ladies (to quote one woman long associated with women's organizations) of these localities, who wanted to improve the socio-economic condition of lower-middle-class and poor women. Their usual activities included running a neighbourhood primary school and sewing or handicraft centre. It is interesting to note that these associations were formed in the established and affluent neighbourhoods of Dacca in the fifties, e.g. Gandaria, Wari, and Purana Paltan. The motivating force behind these asssociations was the feeling among the "enlightened" women that they should work FOR and not WITH their less enlightened

TABLE 4. *Number of women doctors and registered nurses in Bangladesh, 1964–1969*

*Number of registered medical practitioners in Bangladesh*

| | *Female* | | | |
|---|---|---|---|---|
| *Year* | *F.R.C.S.* | *M.B.B.S.* | *L.M.F.* | *Total practitioners* |
| 1964 | Nil | 42 | 170 | 212 |
| 1965 | Nil | 57 | 182 | 239 |
| 1966 | Nil | 67 | 184 | 251 |
| 1967 | Nil | 203 | 311 | 514 |
| 1968 | Nil | 246 | 319 | 565 |
| 1969 | Nil | 301 | 319 | 620 |

*Number of registered nurses in Bangladesh*

| *Year* | *Senior nurses* | *Junior nurses* | *Senior midwife* | *Junior midwife* | *Lady health visitors* |
|---|---|---|---|---|---|
| 1964 | 36 | 15 | 21 | 24 | 22 |
| 1965 | 38 | 4 | 60 | 22 | 15 |
| 1966 | 25 | 5 | 26 | 16 | 10 |
| 1967 | 25 | 1 | 1 | 25 | 11 |
| 1968 | 38 | — | 31 | 8 | 7 |
| 1969 | 208 | 59 | 38 | 9 | 18 |

Source: Bangladesh Bureau of Statistics (1970–1971: (7), Tables 14.3 and 14.4, 267–268).

TABLE 5. *Number of male and female primary and secondary school teachers in Bangladesh, 1947–1966*

| *Academic year* | *Primary* | | *Secondary* | |
|---|---|---|---|---|
| | *Male* | *Female* | *Male* | *Female* |
| 1947–1948 | 72,703 | 2,921 | 23,418 | 944 |
| 1948–1949 | 67,932 | 2,471 | 23,645 | 952 |
| 1949–1950 | 64,999 | 1,822 | 23,167 | 880 |
| 1950–1951 | 61,942 | 2,873 | 22,452 | 1,238 |
| 1951–1952 | 60,056 | 1,898 | 22,213 | 887 |
| 1952–1953 | 65,175 | 1,913 | 21,017 | 904 |
| 1953–1954 | 69,988 | 1,900 | 20,703 | 935 |
| 1954–1955 | 69,716 | 1,761 | 21,310 | 979 |
| 1955–1956 | 70,111 | 1,863 | 21,848 | 920 |
| 1956–1957 | 69,566 | 1,672 | 22,155 | 1,005 |
| 1957–1958 | 72,882 | 1,843 | 21,820 | 1,089 |
| 1958–1959 | 75,432 | 1,691 | 21,650 | 1,146 |
| 1959–1960 | 76,843 | 1,619 | 22,303 | 1,268 |
| 1960–1961 | 78,803 | 1,721 | 23,097 | 1,357 |
| 1961–1962 | 80,873 | 1,604 | 23,808 | 1,510 |
| 1962–1963 | 84,767 | 1,846 | 25,844 | 1,666 |
| 1963–1964 | 90,487 | 1,960 | 30,782 | 1,797 |
| 1964–1965 | 92,511 | 2,019 | 31,578 | 2,092 |
| 1965–1966 | 94,390 | 2,244 | 33,126 | 2,529 |

Source: Adapted from Government of Pakistan (1947–1967: 174–175).

sisters in the neighbourhood. Apart from these three neighbourhood associations, which were run by vernacular-speaking Bangali women, there were two organizations for non-Bangali and non-vernacular speaking Bangali women, the Anjuman Falah Muslim Khawateen and Baitul Athfab-e-Sabiyya (orphanage for Muslim girls).

In the 1960's the more westernized women formed a number of women's organizations to achieve specific goals. The Business and Career Women's Club was formed in 1960 to look after the interests of career women, i.e. to establish hostels for working women, child-care centres for working mothers, and programmes to encourage and train women from lower-class groups to take up an occupation, etc. The leaders of this organization were mostly non-Bangali women. Bangali women associated with the Career Women's Club were different from the women in the *mahila samity* who were mostly housewives and rarely career women.

In 1960 the House Wives Association was formed for the "meeting of minds and sharing of experiences" by housewives. Here, too, the women were more westernized than were the *samity* women. Two other women's organizations of the 1960's were the Women's Voluntary Association (WVA) and the Zonta club. Foreign women resident in Bangladesh took the initiative establishing the WVA. Wives of the diplomatic community played an active but less publicized role. WVA's major purpose is social work – to raise funds for specific projects. Unlike the APWA, Samity, or Career Women's club, WVA did not have regular social and cultural get-togethers. Instead duties were assigned to individual members and the group met specifically to discuss projects. The Zonta club is the Dacca branch of an international club, very similar to the Lions and the Rotary clubs. Its major purpose is to motivate women from affluent families to donate voluntary service or money for the poorer section of society.

The modes of operation and the leadership patterns of these various women's organizations differed from each other. Roughly speaking, the leaders of the neighbourhood *samities* were Bangali middle-class women, while the APWA and the organizations of the 1960's – the Career Women's club, WVA, and Zonta – were dominated by non-Bangali and upper middle-class women. In many ways the varied women's leadership of the two decades reflected the socio-political reality of the country, which saw a transfer of power from Bangali lawyer-type politicians to non-Bangali bureaucrats. The role of the Bangali women in the organizations of the 1960's was that of intermediaries, the same role the Bangali political-administrative leadership was playing in the country. The organizations of the 1950's and the 1960's did not differ fundamentally. Groups were especially involved with girls' schools, women's sewing and handicraft centres, and women's career-trainings programmes. While the *samity* women raised funds by organizing cultural evenings at the Begum Club, the APWA, WVA, Zonta women raised funds by organizing *meena bazaars* at the Dacca Club or Grand balls at the *Hotel Inter Continental* and the *Purbani*.

The third phase of the women's movement, in the post-liberation period in Bangladesh, is marked by a growing awareness among the women about women's problems, though no concrete programme or organizational leadership has yet come forward. The liberation movement, the fate of the violated and other war-affected women, and the vulnerable position of women in the post-liberation period of lawlessness have led women to raise questions (not publicly) about the stability of the "shelter" provided by men. The women of Bangladesh have found themselves in a state of semi-permanent siege by male aggression – the incidence of abduction and raping of women has increased tremendously since liberation, as have other acts of lawlessness such as robbery and murder, which has severely restricted women's mobility. All this has made feminists of many women of the younger generation, but the women's leadership is lagging far behind. The post-liberation period saw a scramble by Bangali women to move into the positions of organizational leadership left vacant by the departure of non-Bangali women. The APWA was renamed Bangladesh Mahila Samity, and the Awami League women moved into its leadership positions; in the Business and Career Women's club and the WVA, Bangali women are filling the slots left empty by non-Bangali women.

Since 1970, many women have become very active in Mahila Parishad. Its leadership is in the hands of women with leftist (especially pro-Moscow) leanings, and it has branches in various districts outside Dacca. Mahila Parishad leadership partly resembles the old *samity* leadership of middle-class and vernacular Muslim women. In part, it consists of ex-student leaders who were active in student politics or party politics. Of all the women's organizations, Parishad is the most political; it concerns itself with women's problems and it has a systematic programme to recruit the support of the larger masses of women.

Still, there is no women's movement in Bangladesh at present. There are no feminist leaders or feminist journals, or feminist writings. The absence of a movement or leadership has not prevented a growing number of Bangali women from seeking their emancipation. However the process is understandably slow since the rate of social change and modernization is slow. Only an active women's movement with a feminist leadership can expedite the emancipation of Bangali women.

To conclude, Bangali women, both rural and urban, traditional and modern, live in a social system that sanctifies an unequal and inferior status for women. *Sharia* laws grant Muslim women a number of limited rights, but prevailing social norms prevent them from taking full advantage of even these limited rights. So far, the women's emancipation movement has concerned itself with such basic issues as literacy and employment for women. The unequal relationship between men and women is not yet questioned. There has been no serious movement to modify the legal system to give women equal rights of inheritance, guardianship, or marriage and divorce. The small number of women who are educated and seek careers can easily be accommodated by the social system, especially because these women do not challenge the basic rules of the system. The elite women can participate and hence there is no dissatisfied elite group to lead a women's movement. In the absence of a movement, consciousness about the oppression of women is low. In Bangladesh the movement for women's emancipation is part of the process of social change and not a revolutionary movement.

## References


Ahmad, Taherunnessa
1966 *Palli anganader jemon dekhecki* [Rural women as I saw them]. Comilla: PARD.

Bangladesh Bureau of Statistics
1970–1971 *Statistical digest of Bangladesh.*

East Pakistan Bureau of Statistics
1961 *The master survey of agriculture in East Pakistan.* Sixth Round, Table 2.4 (A), page 18.

Government of Pakistan
1947–1967 *Twenty years of Pakistan in statistics.* Ministry of Economic Affairs, Central Statistical Office.
1961 *Census of Pakistan*, volume four. Ministry of Home and Kashmir Affairs (Home Affairs Division).

Hussain, Rokeya Sakhawat
1905 *Sultana's* dream.

Papanek, Hanna
1971 Purdah in Pakistan: seclusion and modern occupations for women. *Journal of Marriage and the Family.* (August): 517–530.
1973 Men, women and work: reflections on the two-person career. *The American Journal of Sociology* 78 (4): 852–872.

Qadir, S. A.
1968 *Modernization of an agrarian society.* Rural sociology research Report 1. Mymensingh: Agricultural University.

Stoeckel, John, Moqbul A. Chowdhury
1973 Fertility, infant mortality, and family planning in rural Bangladesh. Dacca: Oxford.

Zeidenstein, Sondra, Laura Zeidenstein
1973 "Observations on the status of women in Bangladesh." Unpublished paper. Dacca.


## Notes

1. *Purdah*, literally meaning the curtain, refers to the system of seclusion of women prevalent in the Middle East and South Asia. In the strictest sense *purdah* involves keeping women confined within the four walls of the home and veiling

them when they leave the home. In a wider context, *purdah* refers to women's modesty and restrictions on their interactions with males who do not fall within the specified categories of those with whom contact is permitted by the religion.

2. Usually social scientists are attracted to problems that become controversial and debated issues.
3. A Bangladesh national is called a Bangali. It is also spelled Bangalee.
4. After a male child is born, the call for prayer is given welcoming the new addition to the Muslim community. But when a girl is born no *azan* is given. My data show that only in socially established families *azan* is given for girls. One poor woman interviewed in a village in Savar commented, "It is against the *Hadith* to give *azan* when a girl is born."
5. Both the folklore and the religious tradition idolize women who made immense sacrifices for their husbands, e.g. Mahua and Malua (folklore) and Hazera, Sara, Rahima, Khadija, Aisha, and Fatima (religious tradition).
6. By respectable families I mean here the *Bhadrolok* class.
7. *Samaj* connotes the village power structure. It consists of the village notables who make decisions about the various mechanisms of social control.
8. Hanna Papanek describes certain occupations, e.g. foreign service and academic positions, where the wife plays a substantial role in her husband's career though her role is not officially recognized. She hypothesizes that because of the separation of the world of men and women in South Asia, such two-person careers have no future there. However, in farming, weaving, and many other occupations in the rural sector in South Asia women participate actively in their husband's/father's occupations, though their role is taken for granted and hence is unrecognized.
9. After puberty, restrictions are put on a girl's movements, and she can meet members of the opposite sex only with her family's consent. Within the village girls can see and talk to unrelated (non-kin) men, but they address each other in appropriate kin-terms, i.e. "Bhai-bon," "kaka," "mama," etc.
10. A good illustration of this anxiety over a girl's "shelter" was found in 1971 during the Pakistani occupation. As stories spread of Pakistani soldiers' violation of women, parents became anxious to marry off their single daughters so that the responsibility for providing shelter for them could be transferred to another family.
11. Even in cases of women raped by Pakistani soldiers, it was found that women with many children had a greater prospect of acceptance by the husbands as compared to women with one or two children. The typical reaction of husbands who accepted back wives who had borne them several children was "What can I do? She is the MOTHER of so many of my children!"
12. When rural women migrate to cities for jobs, they live in slums where they have friends from their own villages. They visit their rural homes frequently and invest in land in the rural areas.
13. Interview with some social workers who are organizing women's cooperative projects among urban working-class women.
14. Modesty and chastity in women are still highly prized values.
15. Data are taken from the author's election survey of two constituencies where some 2561 interviews were conducted.
16. In most Muslim countries civil law interprets *Sharia* law regarding polygamy and divorce in such a way as to restrict the husband's greater facility in initiating divorce. Thus, in Tunesia, civil law prohibits polygamy on the ground that the Quranic precondition for polygamy (i.e. the husband has to treat all the wives equally) is humanly unattainable.
17. Civil registration of marriages, however, does provide an alternative to ar-

ranged marriages. In this respect Bangali women are better off than women in some other countries, i.e. Indonesia, where religious courts are the only legally recognized authority regarding marriage and divorce.

18. The Muslim Family Laws Ordinance provided regulatory measures and procedures for registration of marriages, polygamy, divorce, maintenance, succession right of children of predeceased father, and child marriage. It empowered the local bodies to deal with these provisions. An evaluation of the workings of the Family Laws Ordinance pointed out that a large number of the marriages in the rural areas were still unregistered, few of the divorces went to the Arbitration Councils, and the councils generally followed the social norms in making decisions regarding polygamy and divorce. The ordinance therefore did not radically change women's status. For details of the evaluation of the ordinance (see Qadir 1968).

19. In Alex Inkeles' survey of peasants, factory workers, and students, which was conducted in the 1960's, an overwhelming majority of women favored education as good and desirable.

20. Two separate women's organizations working with violated women gave the author two different stories on the question of violated women's acceptability. The National Board stated that in 90 percent of cases women were accepted back by their families. Only women who had no families left stayed back in the institute. Another organization mentioned that only where parents were alive could women go back home. Not a single husband accepted back his wife even if she were the mother of five or six children.

# The United Nations and Human Rights: The American Viewpoint

JOHN SCALI

PHILIP HOFFMAN

DANIEL PATRICK MOYNIHAN

LEONARD GARMENT

AMBASSADOR JOHN SCALI, United States Representative to the United Nations. March 1975.

MR. PHILIP HOFFMAN, United States Representative, United Nations Commission on Human Rights. February 1975.

AMBASSADOR DANIEL PATRICK MOYNIHAN, United States Representative to the United Nations, in Committee Three. November 1975.

MR. LEONARD GARMENT, United States Representative, United Nations Commission on Human Rights. March, 1976.

# The United Nations and Human Rights: The American Viewpoint

JOHN SCALI

PHILIP HOFFMAN

DANIEL PATRICK MOYNIHAN

LEONARD GARMENT

## I. Address by Ambassador John Scali, United States Representative to the United Nations, at the Twelfth North American Invitational Model United Nations at the Shoreham-Americana Hotel, Washington D.C. March 6, 1975

### *A New Approach to Human Rights and the United Nations*

Today I wish to speak to you about some of the most important unfinished business confronting the United Nations as it seeks to build the base for a more humane, just and secure world. I have in mind the subject of human rights and the history of its treatment in assorted United Nations forums. In the course of my remarks I will discuss an important new human rights policy which the United States has adopted to strengthen these activities in the United Nations.

I have chosen the subject of human rights not only because of the deep interest it holds for me personally, but because the United Nations' achievements and setbacks in this area highlight the strengths and weaknesses of the organization as a whole. In no other area is the contrast between what nations say and what they do so stark and so vivid. On no other issue is the gap between the ideally desirable and the practically attainable so frustratingly wide. Any review of the history of human rights in the United Nations illustrates the limits of diplomacy in an imperfect world. Yet, such a review also demonstrates, I believe, a central fact: there is often no better alternative to United Nations action to guard human rights, no matter how frustrating and difficult the job.

During its 30 year history, the United Nations perhaps has made less progress in the area of human rights than in any other major field of activity. One can credibly maintain that the world is more peaceful today because of the United Nations. Certainly it is more prosperous than it was three decades ago. It is difficult, however, to demonstrate that the boundaries of genuine human freedom have been significantly extended during this same period. Admittedly the chains of colonialism have almost everywhere been broken and this is a momentous accomplishment. But the hopes of the United Nations founders for a world genuinely free from fear – fear of want, fear of oppression, fear of injustice, such a world remains to be achieved.

Why has progress been so slow? After all, it has been 27 years since the General Assembly adopted without a dissenting vote the Universal Declaration on Human Rights which embodies virtually every freedom protected by our own Bill of Rights and then some. The Human Rights Commission of the United Nations has been meeting since 1946. It has drafted, in addition, to this declaration, a whole series of international treaties strengthening the obligations of states under international law to respect basic human rights. This Commission is now empowered to receive petitions from aggrieved individuals and to investigate the conduct of states which appear to be engaged in serious human rights violations. Surely all this represents progress.

Indeed it does, and against tremendous odds. For the unhappy fact is that the human rights activities of the United Nations were born in contradiction and they live on amidst controversy and confusion. The Charter of the United Nations specifically tasks this organization with promoting human rights, while in the same breath it specifically precludes it from intervening in the internal affairs of any member state. These two provisions reflect the still unresolved conflict over the extent to which a nation's domestic affairs are a legitimate concern of the international community.

However, the contradictions within the United Nations on human rights go deeper than this dispute over the limits of the United Nations' mandate. Not only have the United Nations members remained divided over how far the organization is permitted to go in promoting human rights, but there is also no consensus on the very definition of the term – human rights. Thus, from the earliest days of the United Nations representatives of East and West found themselves using the same words – freedom, justice, rights and dignity – but sharply disagreeing on their meaning.

Of course from the beginning all but the most naive realized that the

Soviet Union was not likely to accept, let alone guarantee, Western style civil liberties. It nevertheless has come as something of a shock to Americans to discover that the environment of liberty which they considered an indispensable foundation of life is thought less important and less necessary by many others.

The concept of human rights which we share with many other Western nations has evolved over the centuries. It has its roots in the Judeo-Christian emphasis on personal salvation. It has been moulded by the historical experience of the British people, from Magna Carta to their present unwritten constitution. This evolving concept of human rights first found logical expression in the works of the 17th and 18th Century philosophers of the Enlightenment. It found practical expression in the events of the American and French Revolutions. Indeed, it is the stirring rhetoric of these two revolutionary periods which continues to best convey our fundamental vision of human rights today.

This Western tradition of human rights centres on the individual and on his need for protection against the society and the state. By freedom we mean personal freedom, the freedom to dissent, to be different, to oppose as well as to agree. Documents such as our Bill of Rights enumerate and protect these individual liberties.

Our forefathers were so imbued with these concepts that they felt them to be, in the words of our Declaration of Independence, self-evident. Today Americans still tend to accept their own view of man's relationship to society unquestioningly and we assume that the rest of the world does too. We sometimes forget that the vast majority of the world's peoples have not been raised in this Western tradition, that they do not automatically share our values and that they, therefore, view human rights issues from a different perspective.

Even our own Western society has produced social thinkers, such as Karl Marx, who have taken a completely different approach to human rights. Marxism almost by definition concentrates on the need of the masses for protection against the individual, the capitalist exploiter. Its collective view of human rights emphasizes the economic as opposed to the political aspects of man's place in society and thus focuses on how material wealth, rather than political power, is shared.

No doubt this view of human rights serves as a rationalization, a shield behind which some governments perpetuate their authoritarian regimes and seek to deprive their citizens of political liberties. We should realize, however, that this view has a strong appeal throughout the Third World. Personal liberties are fine, is the attitude of many, but you can't eat them. You can't wear them, nor will they build a roof over your head. Many Third World leaders feel that the extension of civil liberties must take second place to economic development. Unfortunately, many of these same leaders also have concluded that political freedom and rapid economic growth are incompatible.

Many nations of the Third World also tend to share the Soviet bloc's very restrictive interpretation of the United Nations human rights mandate, at least as it applies to them. Having only recently achieved independence, it is understandable, if regrettable, that these new nations guard their sovereign prerogatives with fierce intensity and that they join together with others as a bloc in resisting international inquiries into what they regard as the domestic affairs of any of their number.

Because the United Nations remains divided about what it is trying to achieve in the field of human rights, its pronouncements on this subject are often so vague and generalized as to be devoid of meaning. Because all nations are reluctant to embarrass their friends, the United Nations tends to confine its critical spotlight to states which for one reason or another find themselves relatively friendless in the international community.

All too often this leads to one-sided investigations of human rights abuses – what United States Ambassador Thomas Melady has called selective outrage.

I urge that those who condemn discriminatory repression in any one country show a similar concern over the repression practised by other nations. For example, I urge all those who are sincerely horrified at the oppression of blacks by whites to express an interest in the oppression of whites by whites, of browns by browns and of blacks by blacks. Unhappily, no race, no country, no continent is immune to the contagion of political repression. The task of the United Nations should be not to adjudge guilt, but to fashion justice.

Politically motivated, partisan criticism, in the guise of objective international study, only weakens the moral authority of the United Nations and thus diminishes its ability to protect human rights everywhere.

Over the years the United States has often played a leading role in stimulating vigorous United Nations efforts on behalf of human rights. We also have played our part in contributing to United Nations failings in this area. We, too, have zealously guarded our sovereign prerogatives, sometimes winding up among the most reluctant to undertake international commitments to uphold basic human rights.

In the early days of the United Nations the United States took a strong lead in drafting the two conventions which would give the force of international law to the freedoms set out in the United Nations Declaration of Human Rights. Then, in 1951, we announced that we would not sign either of these treaties. That same year we did sign an International Convention against the crime of genocide, only to let it languish unratified for the past 24 years.

The picture of human rights in the United Nations which I have painted is not rosy, but it is far from hopeless. Progress, no matter how slow, is better than inertia. The fact that nearly all United Nations members proclaim their belief in freedom and democracy, even if they do not practise these virtues, is at least a beginning. Even though the United Nations' efforts are sporadic and often politically motivated, they do often result in remedial action, leading to a genuine improvement in the conditions of life of those suffering oppression. Frustrated as I am, I have come to the conclusion that even selective outrage is better than complete indifference and that even the most guarded and generalized condemnation of human rights violations is better than their passive acceptance.

I continue to believe that the United Nations can do more to promote human rights and that the United States should play a leading role in stimulating its efforts. Other United Nations members will always remain hesistant to permit international review of their conduct and to bind themselves to higher standards unless we commit ourselves to the same goal. To give visible proof of our commitment, I would urge that the current session of the Senate consider action on the 24-year-old Convention on the Prevention of Genocide, as 77 other nations have done before us. I suggest further that we re-examine the other human rights covenants, such as that protecting civil and political rights and the 1969 international treaty against racial discrimination.

Internationally, I believe the time has come to bury the last vestiges of the dispute between advocates of individual rights and those who support group rights. Thirty years ago there may have been a substantial body of opinion in this country devoted to the preservation of unrestricted *laissez-faire* capitalism. There may have been those who seriously viewed labour unions as conspiracies in restraint of trade and equated Social Security with Socialism. Today, however, there is no major segment of American opinion which disputes the need for positive government action to promote employment, to ensure every citizen an adequate standard of living and to relieve social and economic injustices.

Let us, therefore, stop quibbling over whether the right to a fair trial is more or less important than the right to have one's children fed adequately. I can agree with those who argue that political freedom means little to the human being who lacks food to eat. I would insist, however, that hunger for freedom and hunger for bread go hand in hand. Economic democracy means little without political democracy.

If we are to persuade the Third World of the legitimacy of our concept of individual rights, we must also listen sympathetically to their views. We must help them meet their priorities for economic development if we hope to see them adopt our priorities for individual liberties. I believe the time has come, therefore, to seek a lasting consensus with the many responsible and sincere leaders of developing nations whose problems are very different from our own. Let us concentrate on securing the widest possible agreement in the United Nations on the proposition that both individual and group rights are vitally important, that neither is incompatible with the other and that the promotion of both is a legitimate pursuit for the international community.

I am particularly pleased that in the past few weeks the United States has taken a major step forward to encourage a more impartial approach to studies of possible violations of human rights.

On February 6, Secretary Kissinger instructed the United States Delegation to the Human Rights Commission in Geneva to support thorough studies by the commission of alleged human rights violations anywhere in the world – whenever complaints to the commission indicate a consistent pattern of gross and reliably attested violations. Our only conditions are that allegations be reasonably supported by the evidence available, that the violations appear to be continuing and that the terms of reference of the study do not prejudge its outcome.

This decision by Secretary Kissinger means that the United States will now support international inquiries into alleged human rights violations in nations regarded as friends as well as adversaries. Only a few days ago the United States announced its support for a Human Rights Commission study of the current situation in Chile. Chile has agreed to co-operate with the working group dispatched by the commission. This will, as a result, be the first instance in which the Human Rights Commission will conduct such an on-the-scene study of human rights conditions in a member country.

The Administration has been warmly supported in adopting this more vigorous approach to human rights issues by concerned members of Congress and the public. Last year the International Organization Subcommittee of the House of Foreign Affairs Committee, led by Congressman Donald Fraser, held extensive hearings on the United Nations' role in the field of human rights. Congressman Fraser drew upon these hearings to make a number of very constructive suggestions, several of which the Administration has already implemented, including the new policy which I have just outlined.

I hope that this kind of Congressional and public interest in human rights will continue. I believe that it can contribute directly and meaningfully to the extension of personal freedom around the world and to the strengthening of the United Nations. I realize that progress will continue to be slow and painful. I do not expect other nations to accept as normal an international interest in their domestic affairs when our own Senate is still considering a Human Rights Treaty signed under President Harry Truman. I also realize that it will be difficult to agree in the United Nations on human rights issues as long as many governments believe that individual liberties are inconsistent with their economic and social goals.

Nevertheless, the United States has taken an important step forward in recent weeks by adopting this new approach to human rights issues in the United Nations. With the continued support of the Congress and the American people, much more can be done. I hope, therefore, that human rights will feature prominently in the debates of your Model United Nations and that your discussions will stimulate your interest and understanding of these issues. I believe that you will discover, as I have, how difficult it is to arrive at international agreement in this area and how important it is that we do so.

## II. Statement by Mr. Philip Hoffman, United States Representative, on 14 February 1975, during the 31st Session of the United Nations Commission on Human Rights, when the following item was discussed:

*Question of the violation of human rights and fundamental freedoms, including policies of racial discrimination and segregation and of apartheid, in all countries, with particular reference to colonial and other dependent countries and territories.*

Mr. Hoffman said that his delegation had been among those that had favoured a general discussion of the procedures provided for in resolution 1503 (XLVIII) of the Economic and Social Council. Such a discussion would help the Commission as a whole to obtain a better understanding of the way in which those procedures were to be implemented.

The greatest difficulty under which the Commission laboured was, perhaps, the propensity of sovereign nations to be fully aware of the shortcomings of other countries relating to human rights, but to remain blithely unconscious of their own delinquencies. The procedures laid down in Council resolution 1503 (XLVIII) gave States the opportunity of examining gross and consistent violations of human rights occurring within their own boundaries, and of ascertaining the degree of international concern that they aroused. States which had subcribed to the United Nations Charter were not entitled to claim that the abasement of man, and the acts of cruelty and oppression practised against man, were matters of purely domestic concern. That observation applied as much to unjustified imprisonment, torture and restrictions on freedom of speech, movement or ideas as to *apartheid*. The procedures laid down in Council resolution 1503 (XLVIII) did not set the Commission up as a court to pass judgements on governments. The role of the Commission was to find the best way of helping to promote and protect human rights. It was to be hoped, therefore, that when the Commission came to consider specific cases brought before it, there would be an attitude of co-operative understanding between it and the governments. It was also to be hoped that the Commission and the governments would share a concern for the welfare of the human beings involved and a common desire to remedy the situations in question.

His Government was determined to support the procedures that had been laid down. Whenever the Sub-Commission referred a situation to the Commission as revealing a consistent pattern of gross violations of human rights, his Government would support a thorough study, but without any pre-judgement whatever of the merits of the case.

When, in 1974, the Commission had set out to implement Council resolution 1503 (XLVIII), the method adopted had left it no time to examine any individual cases. It had sought to refine and improve the procedures before implementing them. That, however, could be an endless process, since rules and regulations were never entirely satisfactory. The only way of improving the procedures laid down by the Council resolution was to use them: experience would show how to increase their effectiveness.

His delegation, which wished to pay tribute to the work of the Sub-Commission and the Working Group, hoped that the Commission would be prepared to examine individual cases with detachment and speed, without regard to political or other considerations extraneous to the question.

There were many people all over the world who thought that the principles of the Universal Declaration of Human Rights were not being applied and were thus doomed to wither on the vine. The procedures laid down in Council resolution 1503 (XLVIII) constituted the only device available to the Commission to rectify that situation and to promote the rights and dignity of mankind.

## III. Statement by Ambassador Daniel Patrick Moynihan, United States Representative to the United Nations, in Committee Three, on the U.S. Proposal for a World-Wide Amnesty for Political Prisoners
### November 12, 1975

Mr. Chairman, my delegation rises to address the Third Committee in a matter which may be the most important social, cultural and humanitarian proposal which the United States has made in very many years and which we regard as one of the most important which this Committee will ever have had before it.

In an address on the occasion of the thirtieth anniversary of the United Nations, United States Secretary of State Henry A. Kissinger took note that we are living at one of the rarest moments in the modern history of the world. For at this moment, in all of the world, there is not a single nation-state engaged in war against another nation-state.

It appears to the United States that such a moment invites – calls for – not less extraordinary measures of reconciliation not only between nations, but within them. To this end, the United States desires to propose a world-wide amnesty for political prisoners. It proposes a General Assembly resolution which

> Appeals to all Governments to proclaim an unconditional amnesty by releasing all political prisoners in the sense of persons deprived of their liberty primarily because they have, in accordance with the Universal Declaration of Human Rights, sought peaceful expression of beliefs and opinions at variance with those held by their Governments or have sought to provide legal or other forms of non-violent assistance to such persons.

The United Nations has, in truth, already taken, at this General Assembly, at least two steps in this direction.

A draft resolution in the Special Political Committee, entitled "Solidarity with the South African Political Prisoners," calls on "South Africa to grant an unconditional amnesty to all persons imprisoned or restricted for their opposition to apartheid or acts arising from such opposition . . ."

The United States voted for this resolution.

A draft resolution in the Social, Cultural, and Humanitarian Committee, entitled "Protection of Human Rights in Chile," called for the government there to ensure "The rights of all persons to liberty and security of person, in particular those who have been detained without charge or in prison solely for political reasons."

The United States voted for this resolution.

*If some governments, then all*

Is there, however, any reason to stop there, to limit our concerns to only two members of the United Nations, when there are all together 142 members? The resolution on "Protection of Human Rights in Chile" declares, *inter alia*, that "No one shall be held guilty of any criminal offence on account of any act or omission which did not constitute a criminal offence under national or international law at the time when it was committed . . ." It has to be noted that more and more international pronouncements of this kind declare that there are crimes in international law for which individuals may be held responsible. Similarly, it is more and more held that there are actions against individuals for which governments may be held responsible, at least in the sense that they are expected not to take such actions. The exact state of the law in this area is not one on which there will be universal agreement. Yet, clearly, something akin to common law rights is emerging in international law which protects individuals where "universally condemned" or "abhorrent" actions are involved. It is to these standards that Secretary Kissinger appealed in his address to the General Assembly, earlier in this session, when he raised the issue of torture. Torture, he said, is

> ... a practice which all nations should abhor. It is an absolute debasement of the function of government when its overwhelming power is used, not for people's welfare but as an instrument of their suffering.

Now it follows from these considerations that even as South Africa and Chile are obliged by certain standards concerning prisoners, for example, so equally are all other members of the United Nations. It is implicitly acknowledged, however, that it is for governments themselves to conform to international standards. And if some governments, then all governments.

Hence, at this moment, the singular appeal of amnesty. A moment of peace and of peacemaking, and a mode which allows governments to do what they ought without the appearance of coercion. All governments.

Universality in this matter is of special concern to the United States Government – and we would hope to all governments. There are two grounds for this concern which strike us with special force.

The first is that the selective morality of the United Nations in matters of human rights threatens the integrity not merely of the United Nations, but of human rights themselves. There is no mystery in this matter. Unless standards of human rights are seen to be applied uniformly and neutrally to all nations, regardless of the nature of their regimes or the size of their armaments; unless this is done, it will quickly be seen that it is not human rights at all which are invoked when selective applications are called for, but simply arbitrary political standards dressed up in the guise of human rights. From this perception it is no great distance to the conclusion that in truth there are no human rights recognized by the international community.

A generation ago the British poet Stephen Spender came to this perception in the course of visits to Spain during its long and tragic civil war. He had first come to Spain out of sympathy for one of the sides in that heart-rending conflict. He had returned to England to report what he had seen of atrocities committed by the other side. Thereafter he made several trips to Spain, over the course of which he was forced to realize that atrocities were not a monopoly of one side only; they were indeed all too common on both sides. At which point, to his great and lasting honour, he wrote: "It came to me that unless I cared about every murdered child indiscriminately, I didn't really care about children being murdered at all."

This is what the United States proposal is about. Unless we care about political prisoners everywhere, we don't really care about them anywhere. It is something else altogether that is on our minds, something we conceal with the language of human rights, in the course of which we commence to destroy that language, much as George Orwell, who fought in the Spanish Civil War, saw that it would be destroyed.

*Guilt of the accusers*

Our concern about discriminatory treatment is not eased by scrutiny of the list of co-sponsors of the draft resolutions on South Africa and Chile. These are, to repeat, resolutions calling attention to the plight of political prisoners. The South African draft resolution has 60 co-sponsors. The Chilean draft resolution has 33. The United States has broken down these respective lists according to "The Comparative Survey of Freedom," that great contribution to clear thinking and plain speaking which is the work of Freedom House, an American institution of impeccable credentials, which traces its beginnings to the first efforts in the United States to win support for the nations then engaged in the mortal struggle against Nazism and Fascism in Europe. "The Comparative Survey of Freedom" ranks the levels of political rights and civil rights in individual nations on a scale of 1 to 7, and then gives a general summary ranking "Status of Freedom," by which nations are classified as Free, Partly Free, or Not Free. One of the melancholy attributes of a nation judged Not Free is that, in the opinion of the distinguished political scientists who carry out this survey, the nation is one in which individuals are imprisoned for political beliefs or activities of a non-criminal nature. In other words a nation with political prisoners.

What does "The Comparative Survey of Freedom" tell us about the co-sponsors of these resolutions? It tells us that in its judgment, no fewer than 23 of the co-sponsors of the draft resolution calling for amnesty for South African political prisoners, have political prisoners of their own. In the case of the draft resolution calling attention to the plight of political prisoners in Chile, it would appear that 16 of the co-sponsors fall into the category of nations which have political prisoners of their own.

This leads to a particularly disturbing thought about the processes by which the United Nations has come to be so concerned about human rights in some countries, but not in others. This is that we tend to know about violations of freedom – know at the time and in detail – only in those countries which permit *enough* freedom for internal opposition to make its voice heard when freedoms are violated.

This is the case, is it not, in South Africa, where there are said to be over one hundred political prisoners. For it is not necessary to *go* to South Africa to learn of violations of human rights there. One need only subscribe to the South African press, a press which while no doubt curbed in some ways, or even many ways, is nonetheless capable of frontal assault on the policies of the South African government.

The *Cape Times*, for example, in its lead editorial of November 3 states, referring to an act that has been taking place here in the General Assembly by the United States Government:

> The controversy over detentions and opposition to apartheid between South Africa and the United States is unfortunate for it could harm the Republic's chances of establishing a firmer foothold on world opinion at a critical time. It also illustrates how indefensible the present system of detention is in South Africa. The fact is that unless Mr. Vorster is prepared to reveal reasons for detentions, he will be unable to answer convincingly the United States Government charge that people are detained whose only act is outspoken opposition to apartheid. To term this a "downright lie" as Mr. Vorster has, might sound impressive for domestic consumption, but it is not really satisfactory.

The editorial concludes, and I have the honour to be associated here with my distinguished friend, Mr. Clarence Mitchell, about which this editorial is being written:

> For a start, Mr. Vorster should abolish the iniquitous terrorism act if he wants to deal effectively with the U.S. charge. The act provides for indefinite detention incommunicado and without trial, on the mere say-so of a police officer. There are no effective judicial reviews or guarantees. While the system remains on the statute books, charges such as the recent U.S. delegate's remarks in the U.N. will persist; and they cannot be answered convincingly. South Africa, moreover, will remain in dubious company of countries which bypass the due process of law as part of the ordinary routine.

Is it not also the case that the freedom of the press in South Africa – such as it may be, for we do not assert it to be complete – contrasts sharply with that of its neighbours? In the *Monthly Bulletin* of the International Press Institute of June 1975, Mr. Frank Barton, Africa Director of IPI, is reported as having told the Assembly of that impeccably neutral and scrupulous organization:

The unpalatable fact is – and this is something that sticks in the throat of every self-respecting African who will face it – is that there is more press freedom in South Africa than in the rest of Africa put together.

And what of Chile, that troubled land, where at least one estimate states that there are some five thousand political prisoners, and which is rated Partly Free* by the Freedom House Comparative Survey?

One of the operative paragraphs of the draft resolution on Chile, for which the United States voted,

*Deplores* the refusal of the Chilean authorities to allow the Ad Hoc Working Group of the Commission on Human Rights to visit the country, notwithstanding previous solemn assurances . . .

This is true. But it is only part of the truth. The whole truth would include the fact that Amnesty International and the International Red Cross *were* permitted to visit Chile. Moreover, if the visit of the Working Group had gone through, it would have been the *first time in history* that any government had permitted such a visit.

Are we not forced to acknowledge the point made recently by Mr. Robert Moss, the editor of *The* (London) *Economist's* Foreign Report:

If the military regime in Chile, following the example of all self-respecting Communist revolutionaries, had flatly decided to shut out all foreign reporters, [and] civil rights investigators, for a period of, say, six months after the coup, our diet of horror stories from Chile would have been meagre indeed.

And are we not forced to take note of the report of Milton Friedman, the distinguished American economist who recently visited Chile:

On the atmosphere in Chile, it is perhaps not irrelevant that at two universities, the Catholic University and the University of Chile, I gave talks on "The Fragility of Freedom," in which I explicitly characterized the existing regime as unfree, talked about the difficulty of maintaining a free society,

* The Survey rated Chile as Not Free in 1975. – Ed.

the role of free markets and free enterprise in doing so, and the urgency of establishing those preconditions for freedom. There was no advance or *ex post facto* censorship, the audiences were large and enthusiastic, and I received no subsequent criticism.

It is not the purpose of this statement to be accusatory, or to arouse ill feeling. But is it not the case that this year we have seen any number of regimes completely or almost completely seal off their countries, barring or expelling foreign newsmen, such that at most rumour reaches the outside world as to what is going on inside?

Simple justice requires that the United States, for one, acknowledge that while we have supported at the General Assembly resolutions critical of repressive practices of the governments both of South Africa and Chile at this General Assembly, we have done so in the company of nations whose own internal conditions are as repressive or more so.

And what of Israel, a country rated Free by Freedom House, with high if not perfect scores in Political Rights and Civil Rights? Is it not enough to say that much of the case being made against Israel by other nations today, is made in the first instance by the fully legal opposition parties within Israel, including Arab-based parties, many of which have been quite successful in electing members to public office, and that this opposition is given notable expression in the Arabic language press in Israel which has been described as the freest Arab-language press in the world?

*The undermining of free nations*

Thus we come to the second of the concerns which animate the United States at this point. This is the concern not only that the language of human rights is being distorted and perverted; it is that the language of human rights is increasingly being turned in United Nations forums against precisely those regimes which acknowledge some or all of its validity and they are not, I fear, a majority of the regimes in this United Nations. More and more the United Nations seems only to know of violations of human rights in countries where it is still possible to protest such violations.

Let us be direct. If this language can be turned against one democracy, why not all democracies? Are democracies not singular in the degree to which at all times voices will be heard protesting this injustice or that injustice? If the propensity to protest injustice is taken as equivalent to the probability that injustice does occur, then the democracies will fare poorly indeed.

And it is precisely this standard which more and more appears among us, albeit in various disguises. In 1971, for example, the World Social Report presented to the General Assembly was virtually a totalitarian document – you know of which I speak. I was in this Committee at that time and I said so at that time. The fundamental premise on which the assessment of social conditions in respective countries was made was that the absence of social protest indicated the absence of social wrong. Hence, without exception, the police states of the world were judged most in the right.

Americans, and those who have studied the history of the United States, will perhaps recall the memorable image which Abraham Lincoln once used in a speech given in 1858 which we have come to call his "Framing Timbers Speech." He was protesting what he judged to be the overall purpose being served by many seemingly unrelated legislative measures of the time – the purpose of extending slavery into our Western territories. (For the history of freedom in the United States is hardly without blemish). Lincoln spoke of a "concert" of behaviour:

> We cannot absolutely know that all these exact adaptations are the result of pre-concert. But when we see a lot of framed timbers, different portions of which we know have been gotten out at different times and places and by different workmen ... and when we see these timbers joined together, and see they exactly make the frame of a house or a mill, all the tenons and mortices exactly fitting, and all the lengths and proportions of the different pieces exactly adapted to their respective places, and not a piece too many or too few – not omitting even scaffolding – or, if a single piece be lacking, we can see the place in the frame exactly fitted and prepared to yet bring such piece in – in such a case, we find it impossible to not believe that all understood one another from the beginning, and all worked upon a common plan or draft drawn up before the first lick was struck.

The United States makes no such assertion at this time. But it reserves the right to judge, in the months and years ahead, that there has indeed been a "*plan* or *draft*" involved in all the multifarious activities at the United Nations concerning human rights which with nigh inhuman consistency seem always, somehow, to be directed towards nations at least somewhat more free than most members of the UN, and which now most recently have been directed toward a democratic society that is unquestionably free. We reserve the right to learn that our worst suspicions have been confirmed. But in the hope that we will not be, we here and now declare what our suspicions are. Our suspicions are that there could be a design to use the issue of human rights to undermine the legitimacy of precisely those nations which still observe human rights, imperfect as that observance may be.

To those members of the United Nations who would allay our suspicions we make this simple appeal: Join us in support of our draft resolution calling for amnesty for all political prisoners. The list of known prisoners, a list assembled by organizations such as Amnesty International, is a sufficiently long and harrowing one. But there is far more horror to be felt at the thought of the names we do not know. It is time to free these men and women. The time for this amnesty is past due, and the path is long. Let us take the first step here and now.

## IV. Statement by Mr. Leonard Garment, United States Representative, United Nations Commission on Human Rights, meeting in Geneva, 5th March, 1976, for discussion on:

### *Decade to Eliminate All Forms of Racism and Racial Discrimination*

Under the subject of the Decade to Eliminate All Forms of Racism and Racial Discrimination, the Thirtieth General Assembly engaged in the most destructive act in the history of the United Nations. That act caused severe injury to the already discredited moral authority of the organization. The United States thereupon formally declared that it would not acquiesce or participate in any programme contaminated by language which contradicted the basic assumptions of the effort to promote human rights.

This decision is very precise. It represents the United States position on certain specific work of the United Nations. Our support for human rights, which embodies my country's finest hopes, will not be diminished or diverted by inadmissable actions in the General Assembly or anywhere else in the United Nations.

The general policy of United States support for actions to protect human rights will of course continue despite the corruption and distortion of the language of human rights by United Nations decisions. That policy applies to this Commission with the same force as it does to every other part of the United Nations system, and it applies whenever possible. Or should I say if it is possible?

The United States came to this session hoping to dispel or reduce doubts that the Commission can deal with human rights problems forcefully and impartially. It came here anxious to affirm in some manner the continuing relevance and legitimacy of this Commission.

The United States asked this Commission to recognize the right of conscientious objection to military service; it received the ambiguity of a diplomatic denial.

It called on the Commission, after years of delays and false starts, to complete a Declaration on Religious Intolerance. After five weeks of negotiation one cloudy sentence was added to the draft preamble. What was made transparently clear, however, is that members of this Commission holding the power to block action – the Soviet Union and the Byelorussian Soviet Socialist Republic – are interested in protecting states from private beliefs, not in securing religious freedom. So it is a virtual certainty that there will never be a Declaration, certainly not one that firmly protects individual beliefs.

The United States asked the Commission to welcome the human rights provisions of the Helsinki Declaration. The Commission refused even to pronounce itself on such a straightforward principle. It then adopted the grotesque proposition that human rights are to be recognized only when the state is satisfied in its security.

The United States formally asked the Commission to abandon its obsession with the issue of human rights in only three countries, and to do so by simply initiating investigatory action under the 1503 procedure in two broadly publicized cases. These would have been the first such actions under a procedure which has been in existence since 1970, which was to be the vehicle for acting against serious and systematic violations of human rights, but which has not produced a single action by the Commission in all the years of its existence. But we failed, and we failed after a debate which must remain secret and for reasons which must remain secret because the proceedings are secret. Catch-22 on the international level.

The United States suggested a simple and irreproachable improvement in the 1503 procedures, one that was originally drafted and recommended by a universally respected body of independent experts, the International Commission of Jurists. The Commission declined to take action on this modest procedural simplification of the Rube Goldberg maze of 1503.

The United States raised the issue of political prisoners, and a hearing on the proposal was deferred for a year, ostensibly for lack of time – although there was ample time to spend days wandering over the familiar terrain of ancient and fruitless hatreds.

The incidents I have mentioned are only representative of a much longer list. But they make clear that what has taken place here has a logic and consistency, a logic and consistency that reinforces the position of the United States on the Decade to Eliminate All Forms of Racism and Racial Discrimination. Whenever the United States spoke here of universality, it was answered with parochialism. When it sought consistency, it found radically inconsistent treatment of persons and circumstances. When it attempted to protect human rights by working within the United Nations system, it found the system, and specifically this Commission, incapable of taking action that could command universal respect.

Mr. Chairman, it is a misnomer for this body to be called a Commission on Human Rights. For what the Commission is doing now is a travesty on human rights and a disservice to its history. It is all the more a travesty because the undeniable value of its work in dealing with the historic shame of enslavement of blacks by whites in Africa lends legitimacy to its institutionalized blindness to the enslavement and mistreatment of whites by whites in developed countries of the northern part of the world. And to the extent that the silence of this organization legitimizes these notorious evils it becomes an instrument of evil itself. We are forced to the conclusion at this time that if this group is devoted to anything, it is devoted to political axe-grinding on behalf of narrow partisan interests.

It is in this context, that I repeat the position of the United States on the Decade to Eliminate Racism and Racial Discrimination. The United States will collaborate in efforts throughout the world against racial discrimination. It will continue to work against the effects of past practices. But it does not accept, it cannot support, it will not take part in the United Nations Decade to Eliminate Racism and Racial Discrimination. It has taken this decision and will adhere to it because a majority of United Nations members decided there was more to gain by stimulating hatred and division than by encouraging understanding and collaboration.

So be it. The United States will not participate any further in the debate on this item. And it disassociates itself completely from any action taken by this Commission under this item.

# HUMAN RIGHTS ISSUES: A GLOBAL PERSPECTIVE

## KEY TO NUMBERS ON THE MAP OF THE WORLD

* Correction: The Editors regret that they added a sub-title. Listed above is the Author's original title without this addition.